The Evolution of Rationality

J. Wentzel van Huyssteen

The Evolution of Rationality

Interdisciplinary Essays in Honor of
J. WENTZEL VAN HUYSSTEEN

Edited by

F. LeRon Shults

WILLIAM B. EERDMANS PUBLISHING COMPANY
GRAND RAPIDS, MICHIGAN / CAMBRIDGE, U.K.

© 2006 Wm. B. Eerdmans Publishing Co.
All rights reserved

Published 2006 by
Wm. B. Eerdmans Publishing Co.
2140 Oak Industrial Drive N.E., Grand Rapids, Michigan 49505 /
P.O. Box 163, Cambridge CB3 9PU U.K.

Printed in the United States of America

11 10 09 08 07 06   7 6 5 4 3 2 1

Library of Congress Cataloging-in-Publication Data

The evolution of rationality: interdisciplinary essays in honor of
    J. Wentzel van Huyssteen / edited by F. LeRon Shults.
       p.   cm.
    Includes bibliographical references.
    ISBN 978-0-8028-7134-3 (alk. paper)
    1. Religion and science. 2. Practical reason. 3. Philosophy and religion.
    4. Knowledge, Theory of. 5. Van Huyssteen, Wentzel.
    I. Van Huyssteen, Wentzel. II. Shults, F. LeRon.

BL240.3.E96   2006
201'.65 — dc22

                                        2006026703

www.eerdmans.com

Contents

List of Tables and Figures	viii
Introduction F. LeRon Shults	ix
1. The Evolution of van Huyssteen's Model of Rationality Kenneth A. Reynhout	1

I. PHILOSOPHICAL EXPLORATIONS

2. Traces of Rationality: Acknowledgment, Recognition, and Repetition Calvin O. Schrag	19
3. Rational Theory Building: Beyond Modern Enthusiasm and Postmodern Refusal (A Pragmatist Philosophical Offering) Wesley J. Wildman	30
4. Rationality and Different Conceptions of Science Mikael Stenmark	47
5. Van Huyssteen in Context: A Comparison with Philip Hefner and Karl Peters Jerome A. Stone	73

CONTENTS

6. Religion and the Social Sciences:
   Reflections on the Human Quest for Meaning   87
   Philip Clayton

7. Realism, Religion, and the Public Sphere:
   Challenges to Rationality   107
   Roger Trigg

8. Reason and the Enlightenment   122
   Keith Ward

II. SCIENTIFIC EXPLORATIONS

9. Spirituality and Religion in Paleolithic Times   133
   Jean Clottes

10. Building Bridges to the Deep Human Past:
    Consciousness, Religion, and Art   149
    David Lewis-Williams

11. The Origins of Human Cognition and the
    Evolution of Rationality   167
    Ian Tattersall

12. From the Bison at Niaux to the Kyoto Protocol:
    Science, Religion, and the Challenge of Human Nature   183
    Christopher Southgate

13. Generating Life on Earth: Five Looming Questions   197
    Holmes Rolston III

14. Darwinism: Foe or Friend?   226
    Michael Ruse

15. Rationality and Interpreted Experience:
    The Efficacy of Phenomenal Consciousness   240
    Michael L. Spezio

16. Science and the Self: What Difference Did Darwin Make?   253
    John Hedley Brooke

III. THEOLOGICAL EXPLORATIONS

17. How Music Models Divine Creation and Creativity 277
    Arthur Peacocke

18. Four Gods of Christian Faith 294
    Delwin Brown

19. What Theology Might Learn (and Not Learn) from Evolutionary Psychology: A Postfoundationalist Theologian in Conversation with Pascal Boyer 306
    Niels Henrik Gregersen

20. Toward a Transversal Model of Interdisciplinary Thinking in Practical Theology 327
    Richard Robert Osmer

21. The Psalms and Lyric Verse 346
    F. W. Dobbs-Allsopp

22. Types of Natural Theology 380
    David Fergusson

23. Public Theology in Postfoundational Tradition 394
    George Newlands

    A Complete Bibliography of Works by
    J. Wentzel van Huyssteen 418

    Contributors 423

List of Tables and Figures

Carved stone from Berekhat Ram, Israel	137
Map of the Bruniquel cave, France	141
Statuette of a man with a lion's head, Germany	143
Cave art depicting "sorcerers," France	144
Cave art from the Sanctuary of Les Trois-Frères, France	145
Hand stencil from the Cosquer Cave, France	147
Illustrations of the fortification illusion	157
San rock art based on the fortification illusion	157
San rock painting depicting therianthropes	159
Standing diversity through time for families of marine vertebrates and invertebrates	202
Species diversity changes in vascular plants	202
Changes in the composition of vertebrate orders and numbers of insect genera	203
Number of major families of fossil animals increasing through time	204
Proliferation of number of families on Earth, continuing through major extinctions	204
Four tasks of practical theology	330

Introduction

F. LeRon Shults

The essays in this book have been compiled in celebration of the 65th birthday of J. Wentzel van Huyssteen, James I. McCord Professor of Theology and Science at Princeton Theological Seminary. The breadth of topics explored in this volume is evidence of the impact of Professor van Huyssteen's scholarly efforts not only on a diverse number of disciplines, but also on the shape and texture of the interdisciplinary conversation itself. It is a happy coincidence that this Festschrift is able to be produced so soon after the publication of *Alone in the World?* (Eerdmans, 2006), which is based on his 2004 Gifford Lectures. Each of the essays that follow engages some aspect of his work, whether directly or indirectly, and so provides new avenues for discussion about Professor van Huyssteen's research program. As will soon become clear, however, our contributors also offer significant new methodological and material proposals from a variety of perspectives — philosophical, scientific, and theological.

The title of this book — *The Evolution of Rationality* — points toward a major leitmotif in van Huyssteen's writings. His philosophical contributions to methodological debates about the relation between religion and science have focused on the nature and dynamics of human rationality, which operates across the disciplines. This operation is not "universal," however, but "transversal" — conditioned by the complex concerns and diverse goals that shape diverse forms of inquiry. Professor van Huyssteen has also had a long-standing interest in the sciences of evolutionary biology, and has worked hard to demonstrate ways in which discoveries in these (and related) fields may help us understand the emergence and development of rationality itself. The "evolution of rationality" is a general theme that unites the various chapters of this book, although the contributions come from such a rich variety of disciplinary perspectives.

Readers whose interest is already piqued simply by looking over the table of contents are welcome to skip over the following brief summary of the essays and jump right to the sections they find most intriguing. However, understanding the overall impact of Professor van Huyssteen on the field and the contours of the ongoing discourse will be benefited by exploring each of the three parts. For those who may be unfamiliar with his role in the broader interdisciplinary dialogue, Kenneth A. Reynhout provides an overview of the key themes in Prof. van Huyssteen's work over the last several decades in Chapter 1. As he examines the development of the "postfoundationalist" model of rationality, Reynhout identifies three overlapping "phases" in the evolution of van Huyssteen's own thought.

The remaining chapters are divided into three sections: philosophical, scientific and theological explorations. Because all of the authors are engaged in interdisciplinary dialogue, these sections do not form water-tight compartments. Virtually every essay engages issues that overlap all three of these fields. However, the tripartite organization is intended to respect the way in which the contributors begin with and/or focus on one dimension of the interdisciplinary dialogue. The reader will also notice a diversity of notation styles; although this risks becoming a distraction, the plurality is intended to respect the distinctive styles of the various disciplines represented rather than forcing uniformity.

The essays of Part I are focused primarily on philosophical challenges to our understanding of rationality, challenges raised by evolutionary theory, social science, and developments in postmodern culture. Calvin Schrag explicitly engages and commends van Huyssteen's project, which operates at "the crossroads of the turn from foundationalism to holism." He invites us into a thought experiment on the traces of rationality across the phenomena of acknowledgment, recognition, and repetition, attending to the insights of Hegel, Heidegger, and Kierkegaard. Wesley Wildman outlines the similarities (and dissimilarities) between the projects of van Huyssteen and early pragmatists like Peirce and Dewey, arguing for the value of abstraction and generalization as well as a commitment to empirical fidelity and "correctability." He also offers his own pragmatist philosophical offering in response to the extremes of modern enthusiasm and postmodern refusal in rational theory building. Mikael Stenmark's chapter examines the way in which postmodern philosophy has challenged the very conception of "science" itself. He outlines a variety of ways in which "value" plays (or fails to play) a role in scientific endeavors, and calls for a "responsible" science that is value-directed. Jerome Stone compares and contrasts van Huyssteen's methodological approach to relating science and religion to two other "integrationist" models, those developed by Philip Hefner and Karl Peters. He also explores the substantial or conceptual issues that are at the center of these three proposals for integrating theology and the discoveries of evolutionary biology.

Philip Clayton commends van Huyssteen's willingness to confront the serious challenges that theology faces today in light of debates over rationality. He expands the interdisciplinary discussion by focusing on the way in which reflection on the meaning of the human quest for meaning itself may provide a conceptual arena for dialogue between religion and the social sciences. Roger Trigg also appreciates van Huyssteen's engagement with postmodern philosophy, and presses the conversation further by tackling two major challenges to religious rationality: the assumption that science alone provides real knowledge and the emergence of radical pluralism. He discusses the weaknesses of relativism and defends a robust realism that can carry religious discourse into the public sphere. Keith Ward aims to complement van Huyssteen's model of rationality by offering a philosophical clarification of the varieties of "enlightenments" and their influence on the concept of reason itself. He focuses on Hume, Hegel, and Kant, suggesting that to move "beyond" them will require an integrating or organizing principle that includes aesthetic and moral insights.

The eight chapters of Part II explore the way in which various discoveries and debates within sciences shaped by evolutionary theory may illuminate our understanding of the nature and development of human rationality and its relation to religion. Jean Clottes outlines the connection between spirituality, which he defines in terms of "awakening," and the cave art produced during the Upper Paleolithic. Hinting at the need for a new category — *Homo spiritualis* — he concludes that much of this ancient art emerged within a framework of a shamanic type of religion. In his essay David Lewis-Williams argues that some of this cave art provides evidence not only of the origin of religion, but of an accelerating "social differentiation" that was an integral part of religion. He observes that the complexification of consciousness, religion, politics, and art were all intertwined in the deep human past. Ian Tattersall provides an overview of the emergence of early hominids, and the role of tool-making and other factors in their cognitive development. He argues that the evolution of human rationality was tied to the discovery of symbolic potential and language. Christopher Southgate traces a link between two issues that initially seem an unlikely pair: the Cro-Magnon bison paintings at Niaux and contemporary debates over the Kyoto protocol. The conceptual glue is the ambiguity of the human relation to nature, and Southgate draws on insights from the poet Gerard Manley Hopkins as he addresses the theological and ethical significance of ongoing ecological debates.

Holmes Rolston identifies five important questions that continue to confront scientists as they attempt to understand how life was generated on earth, such as: what is the source of the increase in information and new possibility space, and is biology anthropic (oriented toward human consciousness)? He concludes by observing that such questions lead us to questions about the idea of God as the ultimate ground that generates the possibilities for the emergence of life. Michael Ruse's essay is a defense and commendation of the traditional core of Darwinism — the mechanism of natural selection expounded in *Origin of Species*. Challenging Richard Dawkin's assumption that Darwinism implies atheism, Ruse argues that a "progressive" understanding of evolution actually provides conceptual aid to Christian philosophical theology rather than undermining it. Michael Spezio brings van Huyssteen's emphasis on the concept of "interpreted experience" into dialogue with neuroscientific analysis of "phenomenal consciousness." He argues that both theologians and scientists should become more attentive to the ways in which their sense of first-person agency and their commitments are shaped by a theatre of imagined futures. John Hedley Brooke explores the implications of Darwin's scientific theory on various understandings of the self. He discusses several aspects of the self, such as its dignity, uniqueness, and immortality, which were challenged by some interpretations of Darwinian science.

The chapters of Part III also treat the broad theme of the evolution of rationality, but focus more specifically on religious and theological issues in the interdisciplinary dialogue. The first two essays deal with the way in which we conceptualize the relation between God and the world. Arthur Peacocke argues that music provides us with a model of God's creative interaction with the universe. He depicts God's creation *ex nihilo* as a coming into existence "with time" of "moving patterns," and emphasizes the significance of God's immanent presence in cosmological and biological evolution. Delwin Brown explores four ways of thinking about or "locating" God in Christian faith: God as Source, God as Agent, God as Incarnate, and God as Goal. He observes that these ways of thinking about God's relation to creation give rise to distinct forms of spirituality and practice, suggesting that theological reflection should acknowledge and celebrate this diversity.

The remaining essays explore the implications of new models of rationality for various modes of theological discourse. Niels Henrik Gregersen's chapter is an interdisciplinary thought-experiment in which he imagines a conversation between van Huyssteen and evolutionary psychologist Pascal Boyer. Observing both similarities and differences between their projects, Gregersen identifies challenges and opportunities that could arise from such a dialogue. Richard Osmer explores the implications of discussions of interdisciplinary rationality for the field of practical theology as it engages the social sciences. He surveys a variety of approaches (e.g., correlational, transformational) as well as van Huyssteen's "transversal" approach, and calls for an ongoing discussion of the explicitly theological grounds of these models (such as their relation to the doctrine of the Trinity). From the perspective of biblical scholarship, Chip Dobbs-Allsopp offers some reflections on "lyric rationality," which he illustrates in the Psalms of the Hebrew Bible. With recourse to the ideas of non-narrativity, vocality, utterability, and musicality, he depicts lyricism as a different kind of rationality, a thinking otherwise. David Fergusson addresses the issue of the nature and appropriateness of natural theology, which has come under attack in recent decades. Emphasizing the importance of context, he outlines five distinct functions that natural theology has fulfilled in the church, which allows him to provide a nuanced response to the standard criticisms of this way of engaging other disciplines. Finally, George Newlands explores the relevance of van Huyssteen's work for "public theology." After outlining the basic contours of a postfoundationalist theological engagement with culture, Newlands offers a concrete example by providing a Christomorphic vision of human rights, using as his case study the astonishing transformation and reconciliation that have occurred in Professor van Huyssteen's home country of South Africa.

I conclude this brief Introduction by taking advantage of my editorial privilege in order to add my own expression of appreciation for Wentzel van Huyssteen's life and work. My enthusiasm for and appropriation of his academic methodological insights may be found easily enough in my book on *The Postfoundationalist Task of Theology* (Eerdmans, 1999), so I limit myself here to some personal comments about Wentzel himself. One simply could not ask for a more encouraging dissertation advisor, a more inspiring mentor, or a better friend. During my sojourn at Princeton, my fellow doctoral students and I were welcomed to transgress the boundaries of the disciplines in his seminars but never made to feel like transgressors. I have lost track of the times he and his wife Hester have kindly welcomed me into their home, but I will never forget their overwhelmingly gracious hospitality. All of the contributors to this Festschrift have also experienced this hospitable presence in one way or another and can attest to the way in which Wentzel's transversal personality invites new exploration and opens up new possibilities for dialogue. This book is offered as an expression of gratitude to this consummate interdisciplinary host and aims to honor him by continuing the many conversations he has helped to facilitate.

1 The Evolution of van Huyssteen's Model of Rationality

Kenneth A. Reynhout

Introduction

The purpose of this essay is to trace the chronological development of J. Wentzel van Huyssteen's understanding of rationality as evidenced by his books, articles, and key lectures. Anyone familiar with his work will recognize the *problem of rationality* as a dominant and pervasive theme. What may be less clear to the familiar reader are the subtle, yet important ways in which van Huyssteen's approach and answers to this problem have evolved over the course of his career. By mapping some of these developments, it is my hope that this overview will serve both as a succinct review of van Huyssteen's most important ideas and as a useful reference for engaging the other fine honorary essays included in this volume.

The essay is divided into three sections, each corresponding to a phase in the evolution of van Huyssteen's thought. Each phase exhibits a distinguishing set of goals that drive his strategies for addressing the problem of rationality. The three sections/phases are:

1. *Phase 1: Critical Realism as a Rationality Model for Theology* (1970-1989). This phase is characterized by van Huyssteen's attempts to construct a model that can justify considering certain types of theological reasoning as "rational." This rationality model is a form of *critical realism*, which parallels the growing popularity of scientific realism in post-Kuhnian philosophy of science.
2. *Phase 2: The Interdisciplinary Shaping of Rationality in a Postmodern Context* (1990-1999). In this phase van Huyssteen begins to advocate for a postfoundationalist epistemology as a response to the postmodern, nonfoundationalist challenge in contemporary theology. This postfounda-

tionalist framework becomes the key component of a theory of rationality that can negotiate the complex, interdisciplinary dynamics operating between theology and science in a postmodern context.

3. *Phase 3: The Evolutionary Origins of Rationality and Human Uniqueness* (2000-Present). In this phase van Huyssteen extends the question of the origins of specific theological theories to the ultimate origins of human knowing in evolutionary history (evolutionary epistemology). This focus on human origins is shared with his most recent work on the question of human uniqueness in science and theology, which also serves as a test case for van Huyssteen's interdisciplinary model of rationality.

Notice that the three phases are ordered chronologically, although there is some thematic overlap so the boundary dates are not meant to be firm. A complete bibliography of van Huyssteen's published works is included in the appendix.

Despite the obvious complexities, van Huyssteen's quest to discover the shape of rationality has never been a mere academic exercise. His motivations are, at least in part, a product of his own contextual history. After completing his doctorate in Theology in 1970 at the Free University of Amsterdam, van Huyssteen spent two years working as the minister of a Dutch Reformed church in his native South Africa. It was there that he witnessed most clearly the injustices of the state's apartheid policies, and also how many South African Christians defended these policies by appealing to biblical authority. Van Huyssteen believed that apartheid was wrong, but challenging the official political doctrine meant challenging the traditional, and hence authoritative view of Scripture in the South African church. His appointment as Professor and Chair of Religious Studies at South Africa's University of Port Elizabeth in 1972 gave van Huyssteen the opportunity to publicly confront the specific issue of biblical authority. This, in turn, led him to ask the larger epistemological questions: How do we know *anything* about God or God's will? *Can* we know such things? With his background in philosophy (B.A. and M.A. from the University of Stellenbosch), van Huyssteen knew that the prevailing positivist view of science maintained that we in fact *cannot* have rational religious beliefs. Accepting this position not only immunized apartheid from theological critique, it also robbed theology and the Christian faith of any credible and meaningful witness in the world. Dissatisfied with the unjust political reality, the specious appeals to biblical authority, and the epistemological restrictions of logical positivism, van Huyssteen embarked on his journey to explore the problem of rationality.[1]

---

1. Most of the information in this paragraph came from a personal interview I conducted with Dr. van Huyssteen in April 2005.

Phase 1: Critical Realism as a Rationality Model for Theology

How do we construct theories in theology, and can this kind of theoretical reasoning ever be considered "rational" in any significant sense, particularly when compared with the apparent rigor of the natural sciences? Van Huyssteen finds answers to these driving questions in a rationality model he calls a weak form of "critical realism," which he sees paralleling the growing popularity of scientific realism in post-Kuhnian philosophy of science. It is van Huyssteen's engagement with the philosophy of science, and the critical realist rationality model that emerges from this engagement, that most aptly characterizes this first developmental phase.

The role of the Bible as an "authority" in theological reasoning is another recurrent theme in van Huyssteen's earliest work,[2] but the epistemological problem of rationality, as we've already noted, lurks closely behind by the hermeneutical questions. Furthermore, rationality was clearly an important issue from the start, beginning with van Huyssteen's doctoral dissertation on rationality in Wolfhart Pannenberg's theological method,[3] and following with a number of articles related to methodological issues.[4] Moreover, van Huyssteen's most mature response to the question of biblical authority would eventually materialize as a byproduct of constructing the critical realist model of rationality in conversation with the philosophy of science.[5]

Pannenberg was an especially appropriate choice as a dissertation subject, as he was at that time one of only a handful of systematic theologians explicitly

---

2. "Gesag & Vryheid in Bybelse Perspektief," *Roeping en Riglyne* (1974); "Bybelkunde, Teologie en die Bybel," *Nederduitse Gereformeerde Teologiese Tydskrif* 15 (1975); *Geloof en Skrifgesag* (with B. J. du Toit) (Pretoria: N. G. Kerkboekhandel, 1982).

3. Published as *Teologie van die Rede: Die Funksie van die Rasionele in die Denke van Wolfhart Pannenberg* (Kampen: J. H. Kok, 1970). His was one of the earliest dissertations written about Pannenberg. The essence of this work can be found in "Truth and Commitment in Theology and Science: An Appraisal of Wolfhart Pannenberg's Perspective," *Hervormde Teologiese Studies* 45, no. 1 (March 1989). Reprinted in *Beginning with the End: God, Science and Wolfhart Pannenberg*, ed. Carol Rausch Albright and Joel Haugen (Chicago: Open Court, 1997), and as chapter 3 of *Essays in Postfoundationalist Theology* (Grand Rapids: Eerdmans, 1997).

4. "Hoe waar is ons Teologiese Uitsprake?" *Bulletin van die S.A.V.C.W.* (August 1973); "Teologie en Metode," *Koers* 43, no. 4 (1978); "Opmerkinge oor Geloof en Geloofsuitsprake," *Scriptura* 3 (1981); "Die Sistematiese Teoloog en persoonlike Geloofsbetrokkenheid," *Nederduitse Gereformeerde Teologiese Tydskrif* 22, no. 4 (September 1981); "Thomas S. Kuhn en die Vraag na die herkoms van ons teologiese Denkmodelle," *Nederduitse Gereformeerde Teologiese Tydskrif* 24, no. 3 (June 1983).

5. *The Realism of the Text: A Perspective on Biblical Authority* (Pretoria: UNISA, 1987). An abbreviated version can be found in chapter 7 of *Essays in Postfoundationalist Theology*.

and constructively confronting the challenges posed by contemporary philosophy of science. In an article published in 1981 in both Afrikaans and English, van Huyssteen critically evaluates both Pannenberg's and Gerhard Sauter's attempts to engage the philosophy of science, while beginning to develop his own case for the *necessity* of theological engagement of just this sort.[6] A subsequent article — published first in Afrikaans in 1983 and then again in English in 1986 — continues this argument. If theology is a "critical account rendering of faith" that strives for relevance in the world, then theologians cannot evade the methodological, hermeneutical, and epistemological issues that precede the forming of theological propositions. Furthermore,

> Theologians who in total intellectual honesty are willing to expose their tradition to these questions inevitably find themselves in discourse with the complex course of contemporary philosophy of science. This debate, and its demands, are necessary for a theology addressing itself with awareness and sensitivity to the extremely significant questions surrounding method- and theory-formation in systematic theology.[7]

It is also in this article that van Huyssteen begins his critique of logical positivism, which had created intractable problems for theological rationality. In particular, its narrow test of empirical verification left all metaphysical-theological statements as cognitively meaningless. Van Huyssteen sees three possible responses to this problem: (1) withdraw theology into a ghettoized, autonomous activity, with its own rules of rationality based on either Scripture or creed; (2) capitulate to positivism and admit that religious propositions merely express feelings; or (3) question the rationality model of positivism. Van Huyssteen opts for the latter response, a choice he finds particularly promising given that philosophers of science had themselves been questioning the strict requirements of positivism. Karl Popper's critical rationalism, for starters, emphasized the socio-historical nature of scientific discovery and recognized the critical and progressive nature of science. In addition, Kuhn's paradigm theory further unmasked the ideological character of positivism by

---

6. "Sistematiese Teologie en Wetenskapsteorie, Die Vraag na metodies-teoretiese Helderheid in die Teologie," *Tydskrif vir Christelike Wetenskap* 17, no. 1 (1981); "Systematic Theology and the Philosophy of Science: The Need for Methodological and Theoretical Clarity in Theology," *Journal of Theology for Southern Africa* 34 (March 1981). Reprinted as chapter 6 of *Essays in Postfoundationalist Theology*.

7. "Rasionaliteit en Kreatiwiteit: Ontwerp vir 'n kritiese, konstruktiewe Teologie," *Koers* 48, no. 3 (1983); "Rationality and Creativity: A Design for a Critical, Constructive Theology," Academic Papers Series, Institute for Christian Studies, Toronto, Canada (April 1986), pp. 1-3.

emphasizing the contextual nature of scientific discovery. Both of these theories present their own challenges to theology, but van Huyssteen recognizes that they are pointing toward a post-Kuhnian model of scientific rationality that could ultimately liberate theology from the shackles of positivism.[8] He stops short, however, of identifying this new model as a form of critical realism, although he does begin to develop a set of minimal criteria for a credible model of theological rationality.[9] This task becomes the centerpiece of his most important work in this period.

Theology and the Justification of Faith, published first in Afrikaans in 1986 and then in English in 1989,[10] marks a number of "firsts" in the evolution of van Huyssteen's model of rationality. It is here that he first recognizes the growing popularity of scientific realism in the philosophy of science and its suggestiveness for a parallel theory of rationality in theology. This decision to espouse a critical realist model of theological rationality was not altogether novel; Ernan McMullin, Sallie McFague, and Arthur Peacocke were some of the scholars already advocating for versions of critical realism. But van Huyssteen's critical dialogue with thinkers like Peacocke (155-157) is especially notable because it marks van Huyssteen's first explicit interaction with the interdisciplinary theoreticians of the science and religion dialogue. This interaction will become very important in his later work. Finally, it is also the first time that van Huyssteen explicitly identifies the problem of rationality as an essentially *epistemological* problem, believing that the "epistemological dimension must form the very foundation of all further methodological and thus also of all hermeneutical questions in theology" (xii).

In the preface to this same book van Huyssteen clearly states its main theme as "the search for valid epistemological criteria for a creditable Christian theology" (viii). His strategy for finding these criteria is to focus on the *origins* of theological theories, but from there it is only a small step to the complex issues of *religious experience* and *religious language*. Drawing again on insights from recent developments in the philosophy of science, van Huyssteen deftly notes that experience (manifested as contextual commitments) and the ontological limits of language are also issues for scientists. In the end, he concludes that religious experience and religious lan-

---

8. "Rationality and Creativity," pp. 4-14.
9. "Rationality and Creativity," pp. 25-29.
10. *Teologie as Kritiese Geloofsverantwoording: Teorievorming in die Sistematiese Teologie* (Pretoria: RGN, 1986); *Theology and the Justification of Faith: The Construction of Theories in Systematic Theology* (Grand Rapids: Eerdmans, 1989). Page numbers given parenthetically in the text refer to this English edition.

guage work together in the conceptualizing of theological models. This is not a death knell for theological rationality any more than it is for science, but it does imply that theologians who strive for a critical and reflective theology must remain critically aware of the limits of religious language and how their contextual faith commitments shape their theological reasoning (125-142).

Van Huyssteen identifies three criteria that must be met for theological statements to be considered rational: they (1) depict reality, (2) have critical and problem-solving ability, and (3) are constructive and progressive (147-197). Space limitations will not allow a full summary of these complex criteria, but a few explanatory notes are in order. (1) The metaphorical nature of language liberates its referential use, such that theological models are "not literal pictures, but they are also more than useful fictions" (158). Furthermore, although theological theories cannot escape the various contexts in which they are developed, they can also reach out responsibly across contextual boundaries. It is therefore possible to make valid, yet provisional intersubjective theological statements. (2) Drawing heavily on the work of Larry Laudan, van Huyssteen argues that theologians can construct empirical and conceptual problems and seek appropriate answers to these problems by responsibly engaging the guidelines found in the Bible and in the historical tradition of dogma and creedal formation. But these theologians must also grapple with contemporary scientific thought for their conclusions to qualify as truly rational. (3) As long as "progress" is understood as "convergence to the truth," it will remain an ineluctable barrier to theological rationality. Instead, progress should be understood as a theory's ability to effectively answer the theological problems posed in a particular context and across contextual boundaries.

The rest of the articles from this phase appeared in English during the period between the publication of the Afrikaans and English versions of *Theology and the Justification of Faith* (1986-1989). There is therefore a considerable (and understandable) amount of repetition of material as van Huyssteen introduced his ideas to an English-speaking audience prior to the appearance of his book. Here I will only highlight a few interesting points and the introduction of some new terminology. In an article appearing in 1987 we find van Huyssteen's own estimation of the apologetic importance of clarifying the epistemological status of theological thought:

> the way we deal with this problem will to a great extent determine whether Christian faith today is a curiosity to be tolerated, or whether it is an important dimension of intellectual life which may not only help us to con-

struct adequate models of reality, but also to link that endeavor to our ultimate quest for meaning in life.[11]

In 1988 van Huyssteen first suggested that theology can be a form of "inference to the best explanation," but it is more precisely inference *from* the best explanation. In other words, we infer "*from* the claim that a given theory is the best explanation *to* the conclusion that this explanatory hypothesis is highly likely."[12] In another article from that same year he begins to refer to the goals and criteria of rationality of both science and theology as "epistemic values," the highest of which is "intelligibility."[13] In the next phase we will see this *quest for intelligibility* become an important interdisciplinary resource for van Huyssteen's emerging postfoundationalist model of rationality.

Phase 2: The Interdisciplinary Shaping of Rationality in a Postmodern Context

In van Huyssteen's own words: "my first probing into the problem of rationality in theology and science can be traced back as far as the Fall of 1990, when I was a Visiting Scholar at the Center of Theological Inquiry in Princeton."[14] We have already seen that van Huyssteen's wrestling with the "problem of rationality" can actually be traced back much farther than this, but 1990 does mark the beginning of a new developmental phase in which the problem of rationality becomes the pivotal issue for the *interdisciplinary* problem of theology and science. This interdisciplinary challenge is itself complicated by the oftentimes fractured postmodern pluralism of nonfoundationalist theology. Thus, van Huyssteen's engagement with postmodern relativism and his "postfoundationalist" rebuttal are also important themes in this phase. Throughout, the critical realist model of rationality developed in the previous phase is neither abandoned nor significantly altered. Rather, it is presupposed as his motivation shifts from justifying theological rationality per se to demonstrating how a postfoun-

---

11. "Scientific Realism and Theology: A New Challenge?" *South African Journal of Philosophy* 6, no. 4 (1987): 125.

12. "Experience and Explanation: The Justification of Cognitive Claims in Theology," *Zygon* 23, no. 3 (September 1988): 258.

13. "Beyond Dogmatism: Rationality in Theology and Science," *Hervormde Teologiese Studies* 44, no. 2 (November 1988): 847-848.

14. *The Shaping of Rationality: Toward Interdisciplinarity in Theology and Science* (Grand Rapids: Eerdmans, 1999), p. ix.

dationalist epistemology can negotiate the complex rational demands of the theology and science dialogue.

Two articles from 1988 and 1989 already anticipated this shift in emphasis. In both, van Huyssteen critically evaluates some forms of postmodern, nonfoundationalist theology as being "neo-Wittgensteinian fideism," which he sees as "fatal for the cognitive claims of theological statements." It is notable that at this point he is still referring to his own critical realist position as a form of "non-foundationalism" that is searching for a non-fideist rational basis.[15] These early inclinations began to solidify into a distinctive "postfoundationalist" interdisciplinary theory of rationality in 1990 at a lecture delivered by van Huyssteen at the Center of Theological Inquiry (CTI) in Princeton. From the opening words of this lecture, the shift in emphasis toward the interdisciplinary problem of theology and science is unmistakable:

> It is safe to say that until fairly recently, theological discussions of religious and scientific epistemology have been notoriously vague, imprecise and confused. The intense current focus on the relationship between theology and science — some prefer to talk of the emerging discipline of theology and science — clearly, however, suggest[s] a fall from epistemological innocence regarding this complex and fascinating issue.[16]

It is here that van Huyssteen first questions the standard approaches for relating theology and science (conflict, consonance, etc.), suggesting that we should instead be exploring "the epistemological question of the nature of explanations and explanatory claims" operative in different disciplines.[17]

In addition to this interdisciplinary focus, the distinctive epistemological approach of this developmental phase is introduced in this lecture. In the previous phase, van Huyssteen's most stringent criticisms had been reserved for scientific and theological positivism (biblical or confessional fundamental-

---

15. "Paradigms and Progress: Inference to the Best Explanation? The Shaping of Rationality in Theology," in *Paradigms and Progress in Theology*, ed. J. Mouton, A. G. van Aarde, and W. S. Vorster (Pretoria: HSRC Publishers, 1988), pp. 86-87; "Narrative Theology: An Adequate Paradigm for Theological Reflection?" *Hervormde Teologiese Studies* 45, no. 4 (1989). Reprinted as chapter 9 of *Essays in Postfoundationalist Theology*.

16. "The Explanatory Role of Religious Experience and Beliefs in Theology and Science," draft of an unpublished lecture given at the Center of Theological Inquiry, Princeton, New Jersey (December 1990), p. 1.

17. "The Explanatory Role of Religious Experience and Beliefs in Theology and Science," 5. Phillip Clayton's work on explanation in science and theology was particularly influential for van Huyssteen at this stage.

ism). Here his criticisms are instead raised against all forms of *foundationalism*, undoubtedly referring to the same methodologies but under a different umbrella term. He further extends his criticisms to non- or "antifoundationalism," terms that from now on he uses exclusively to refer to a variety of dead-end postmodern theological methodologies, some of which we've already seen him critique. Van Huyssteen then introduces a new term, "postfoundationalism," to refer to his own attempt to split the difference between foundationalist certainty and non-foundationalist relativism by being contextual yet intersubjective, committed yet fallibilist, provisional yet explanatory.[18]

Two years after delivering this seminal lecture, van Huyssteen was appointed the James I. McCord Professor of Theology and Science at Princeton Theological Seminary. From this new position he entered a prolific period of reflection on the interdisciplinary problem of rationality in theology and science, culminating with the publication of *The Shaping of Rationality* in 1999. In his inaugural lecture at Princeton in 1993, van Huyssteen underscored the apologetic importance of this question:

> The current theology-and-science discussion thus very much presents itself as contemporary apologetics for the Christian faith, and as such it will fundamentally shape our expression of the Christian experience of God. It also shapes our intellectual expression of the Christian faith and cautions us to greater epistemological and methodological sophistication.[19]

It is also in this lecture that we find his first use of the phrase "the shaping of rationality" to describe the complex challenge represented by his research project (125-126).[20]

The Shaping of Rationality would become the title of van Huyssteen's 1999 book — his *magnum opus* on the interdisciplinary problem of rationality — but the nascent contours of this treatment were already emerging in a 1996 article by the same name.[21] Here he both narrows and broadens common understandings of the nature and scope of rationality. In the first place, he sharpens the range of the term "rational" by arguing that it is first and foremost a qual-

---

18. "The Explanatory Role of Religious Experience and Beliefs in Theology and Science," pp. 1-3.

19. Published as "Theology and Science: The Quest for a New Apologetics," *The Princeton Seminary Bulletin* 14, no. 2 (1993): 118-119. Reprinted as chapter 11 of *Essays in Postfoundationalist Theology*.

20. Van Huyssteen would later acknowledge that this phrase was initially inspired by the work of Ernan McMullin: *The Shaping of Rationality*, p. x.

21. "The Shaping of Rationality in Science and Religion," *Hervormde Teologiese Studies* 52, no. 1 (March 1996). Reprinted as chapter 12 of *Essays in Postfoundationalist Theology*.

ity of an individual's decisions, and only derivatively about beliefs, propositions, or communities (116). This is an important modification of van Huyssteen's earlier emphasis on the formation and justification of theological concepts and models. In the second place, he expands the idea of rationality beyond its obvious cognitive interpretation. Rationality (in theology and science) involves a "quest for intelligibility" involving the search for "good reasons for hanging on to certain beliefs, good reasons for making certain moral choices, and good reasons for acting in certain ways" (113). By focusing on how rational agents believe, evaluate, and act in particular situations van Huyssteen is attempting to describe a postfoundationalist rationality that is thoroughly contextual and yet still strives for intersubjective discourse by appealing to the "common resources of rationality" shared across disciplines (125).

In 1997 van Huyssteen proposed that a postfoundationalist model of rationality could respond constructively to the postmodern critique of foundationalism by fully acknowledging (1) contextuality, (2) the epistemic role of interpreted experience, and (3) how our values are shaped by tradition. At the same time, such a rationality model should allow not only for cross-disciplinary conversation, but also cross-contextual and cross-cultural engagement.[22] This connection between interdisciplinary and intercontextual/intercultural concerns illustrates van Huyssteen's growing conviction that his postfoundationalist model of rationality can meet the challenges associated with pluralism in contemporary theology, an argument that gets fleshed out in a number of later works.[23]

The crux of van Huyssteen's argument in this phase is his claim that there are "common resources of rationality" shared across boundaries of discipline, context, and tradition. He had consistently made this assertion throughout this period and had argued for it in a variety of ways, but the most complete treatment of this pivotal claim is found in *The Shaping of Rationality: Toward Interdisciplinarity in Theology and Science*.[24] The three resources of rational-

---

22. "Should We Be Trying So Hard to Be Postmodern? A Response to Drees, Haught, and Yeager," *Zygon* 32, no. 4 (December 1997): 580-581.

23. "Why Do We Make Those Choices? Some Reflections on Faith, Pluralism and Commitment," in *Pragmatism, Neo-Pragmatism and Religion: Conversation with Richard Rorty*, ed. Charley D. Hardwick and Donald A. Crosby (New York: Peter Lang, 1997); "Tradition and the Task of Theology," *Theology Today* 55, no. 2 (July 1998); "Pluralism and Interdisciplinarity: In Search of Theology's Public Voice," *American Journal of Theology and Philosophy* 22, no. 1 (January 2001). For a thorough treatment see *The Shaping of Rationality*, pp. 235-282.

24. *The Shaping of Rationality: Toward Interdisciplinarity in Theology and Science* (Grand Rapids: Eerdmans, 1999), pp. 111-177. Page numbers given parenthetically in the text refer to this work.

ity, or "epistemological overlaps," that van Huyssteen identifies are (1) the quest for intelligibility, (2) responsible judgment skills, and (3) progressive problem-solving.

(1) The quest for intelligibility is "a quest for optimal understanding that as a survival strategy is a most important part of out evolutionary heritage" (174). This pursuit is not unique to science, or even theology and science, but is shared by all the domains within which we form beliefs, make deliberate choices, and act in particular ways. We will see that the evolutionary origins of our rational endeavors become an important focus in van Huyssteen's next developmental phase.

(2) Responsible judgment skills take shape within a back-and-forth process of personal judgment and intersubjective accountability. As such, we exercise rationality in both contextual and cross-contextual movements. On the one hand, the process of rational reflection is embedded within evolving, developing traditions that shape our living contexts and contextual commitments. On the other hand, this very pragmatic movement is incomplete without a self-critical stance in relation to our traditions and commitments. This stance enables an interdisciplinary movement as we reach out beyond the boundaries of a particular context or tradition. It is precisely this back-and-forth postfoundationalist process, van Huyssteen argues, that can be successful in "splitting the difference between modernity and postmodernity" (174-175).

(3) Progressive problem-solving is not to be equated with the "faulty, modernist doctrines of progressive knowledge that too easily conflate rationality with progress" (175). Instead, he advocates for a qualified form of intellectual progress that involves responsible theory choice and theory commitment. In other words, in all disciplines we choose theories, models, and even research traditions that are judged to be the most effective problem-solvers within a concrete context (118). This understanding of progress is recognizably similar to the idea van Huyssteen developed in the previous phase.

Two of the more influential thinkers for van Huyssteen at this stage were Nicholas Rescher and Calvin Schrag. It is from Schrag's work on postmodern rationality that van Huyssteen identifies the metaphor of "transversal rationality" as an essential dynamic in his own postfoundationalist model of rationality (135, 176). Transversal rationality is "a lying across, extending over, and intersecting of various forms of discourse, modes of thought, and action." It emerges "as a place in time and space where our multiple beliefs and practices, our habits of thoughts and attitudes, our prejudices and assessments, converge" (247). Transversal reasoning thus enables us to achieve a "wide reflective equilibrium" (a term he borrows from Schrag and others), a communal space within which deep personal convictions and responsible interdisciplinary judgments can coexist (277-282). In the next phase we will see van Huyssteen test the vigor of this kind of transversal reasoning as he tackles the issue of human uniqueness in both theology and science.

Phase 3: The Evolutionary Origins of Rationality and Human Uniqueness

As we have seen, the question of *origins* has been fundamental in van Huyssteen's approach to the problem of rationality. In this phase van Huyssteen extends the question of origins beyond individual theory formation to the ultimate evolutionary origins of human rationality itself. This extension manifests itself in two related endeavors. The first is van Huyssteen's attempt at developing a comprehensive epistemology that is rooted in the biological origins of human rationality as understood by evolutionary epistemology. The second is his exploration of human uniqueness from both theological and scientific perspectives, in which the evolutionary questions loom large. We will see that this interdisciplinary exercise will also serve as an important test case for van Huyssteen's postfoundationalist model of rationality.

In 1998 van Huyssteen gave the John Albert Hall Lectures at the Centre for Studies in Religion and Society in the University of Victoria, British Columbia, which led to the publication of *Duet or Duel? Theology and Science in a Postmodern World* later that year.[25] This work preceded *The Shaping of Rationality* and was explicitly focused on the interdisciplinary problem of rationality. As such, it would have been both chronologically and thematically justified to include it in our discussion of the previous phase. However, it appears here as a crossover piece that first introduces human evolution as an organizing theme of van Huyssteen's subsequent work.

Van Huyssteen's overall goal in *Duet or Duel?* was to elaborate on the resources for interdisciplinary rationality he saw emerging from contemporary reflection on scientific cosmology and evolutionary biology. Along the way, he begins to grapple with the evolutionary origins of human knowledge. He sees that contemporary evolutionary epistemology points to the "biological roots of all knowledge" and accepts that all knowledge (including scientific and religious knowledge) is "grounded in human evolution" (xiii-xiv). Re-

---

25. *Duet or Duel? Theology and Science in a Postmodern World* (London: SCM Press, 1998; reprint, Harrisburg, PA: Trinity Press International, 1998). Page numbers refer to the reprint edition.

sisting the radical reductionism of thinkers like Richard Dawkins,[26] van Huyssteen recognizes that the common biological origin of all forms of knowledge "reveals a universal intent that links together all our diverse and complex epistemic activities" (148). Such a "comprehensive epistemology" can facilitate a "graceful duet" between theology and science, he contends, by opening up space for constructive interdisciplinary reflection (131-166).

At this stage, van Huyssteen already recognizes the specific theological challenge posed by the process of human evolution for our understanding of *human uniqueness*.

> For most people who study the process of evolution it is very clear that our species, *Homo sapiens*, differs from the two or three million species now living, especially in our ability to reflect critically upon ourselves and our present situation, our past, and our future. . . . Because of this very specific sense in which the human mind appears to be unique in the animal kingdom, on this planet and possibly even in the universe, it is often seen as a direct result of God's special action in the world: a special act of creation by which we humans were created in the "image of God." (137)

Van Huyssteen goes on to suggest that his postfoundationalist approach nullifies the need to choose between this supernaturalistic explanation and a purely naturalistic view of human uniqueness, but he stops short of constructing a specific interdisciplinary proposal. It is the execution of this task that dominates the rest of his work to date.

Inklings of this new research project are outlined in an article appearing in 2000. Much of this proposal seeks to elaborate on earlier material, but he also introduces a new and pivotal consideration of the evolutionary emergence of "cognitive fluidity." Such fluidity is evidenced by the human capacity for imagination, creativity, and symbolic thought, which in turn are prerequisites for the emergence of science, art, and religion.[27] These cultural phenomena, and their connection to human rationality rooted in biological evolution, will become key considerations in his forthcoming interdisciplinary case study. It wasn't until 2001 that the specific issue of human uniqueness came to

---

26. Crucial to van Huyssteen's argument against a Dawkins-like reductionism of religious awareness is the distinction he draws (following Wuketis) between "organic" and "cultural" evolution, the latter being based in the former but not reducible to it.

27. "Postfoundationalism and Interdisciplinarity: A Response to Jerome Stone," *Zygon* 35, no. 2 (June 2000): 432. He later acknowledges that the term "cognitive fluidity" comes from the work of Steven Mithen: "Fallen Angels or Rising Beasts? Theological Perspectives on Human Uniqueness," *Theology and Science* 1, no. 2 (October 2003): 174.

the fore as the explicit driving question behind this new project. In particular, van Huyssteen argues that framing the question of human uniqueness as a conflict between the theological doctrine of the image of God and the scientific understanding of humans as rational animals represents a false dilemma. Instead, he hopes to develop a "scientifically informed, complementary view of the nature of human uniqueness." He anticipates that his interdisciplinary dialogue partners will include evolutionary biologists, paleoanthropologists, archeologists, evolutionary epistemologists, and cognitive psychologists, some of which are introduced here for the first time.[28]

Van Huyssteen's first serious *theological* treatment of the issue of human uniqueness came in 2003. This foray into the multifarious understandings of the Christian doctrine of the *imago Dei* is an important step toward van Huyssteen's own attempt at transversal reasoning, which in turn moves him closer to developing an actual test case for his interdisciplinary model of rationality. For instance, in this article we see van Huyssteen utilizing his theory of traditions, previously developed in conversation with Delwin Brown, in order to map the historical developments of the *imago Dei* in Christian theological reflection. The upshot of this analysis is his call to revise our theological understanding of the image of God so that it "acknowledges our close ties to the animal world and its uniqueness, while at the same time focusing on what our symbolic and cognitively fluid minds might tell us about the emergence of human uniqueness, consciousness, personhood, and the propensity for religious awareness and experience."[29] In more recent articles van Huyssteen has taken steps to answer his own revisionary call,[30] but a full treatment came in the form of the Gifford Lectures at the University of Edinburgh in Scotland in the Spring of 2004. The book that emerged from this prestigious lectureship is titled *Alone in the World? Human Uniqueness in Science and Theology*.[31]

Alone in the World? is impressive, not only for its comprehensive treatment of various scientific and theological perspectives on human uniqueness,

---

28. "What Are Scientists Telling Theologians about Human Uniqueness?" *Research News and Opportunities in Science and Theology* 1, no. 7 (March 2001): 20, 26.

29. "Fallen Angels or Rising Beasts?" p. 177.

30. "Evolution and Human Uniqueness: A Theological Perspective on the Emergence of Human Complexity," in *The Significance of Complexity: Approaching a Complex World Through Science, Theology and the Humanities*, ed. Kees van Kooten Niekerk and Hans Buhl (Aldershot, England: Ashgate, 2004); "Human Origins and Religious Awareness: In Search of Human Uniqueness," *Studia Theologica* 59, no. 2 (2005): 104-128.

31. *Alone in the World? Human Uniqueness in Science and Theology* (Grand Rapids: Eerdmans, 2006).

but also for the way in which van Huyssteen attempts to stay true to his own postfoundationalist, interdisciplinary methodology. After reviewing his postfoundationalist methodology (ch. 1) and the suggestive implications of evolutionary epistemology (ch. 2), he begins his concrete case study by contextually analyzing various approaches to the question of human uniqueness in theology (ch. 3) and in a number of different scientific disciplines (chs. 4-5). Only after giving each rational domain its proper contextual frame does van Huyssteen embark on a specific interdisciplinary proposal (ch. 6).

In the end, van Huyssteen argues that theologians must (1) rethink personhood in terms of imagination, symbolic propensities, and cognitive fluidity that acknowledge humanity's close ties with the animal world, and (2) develop theories of the *imago Dei* that recognize that this quality has emerged by natural evolutionary processes. In contrast to what he sees as a theological propensity for wandering into the "twilight zone of abstraction,"[32] he instead suggests that we reconceive of the *imago Dei* in a highly contextualized, embodied sense. Van Huyssteen not only sees this reconstruction emerging out of his interdisciplinary conversation with the sciences, but also in the working theories of the image of God of some influential contemporary Christian and Jewish theologians.

One of the more fascinating disciplines that van Huyssteen engages in this book is the work of paleoanthropologists and their studies of Paleolithic cave "art," particularly in southwestern France and the Basque Country of Northern Spain (chs. 4-5). He rightly notes that this conversation has been nearly absent in the broader theology and science dialogue, and van Huyssteen's contributions here will undoubtedly be significant. But it is also interesting because of the way in which it illustrates how the problem of rationality continues to pervade van Huyssteen's work. Cave drawings are not merely anthropological curiosities, but are clues to some of the earliest creative, symbolic endeavors of the rational human mind. What's more, the relatively simultaneous emergence of aesthetic sensibility, religious awareness, and "scientific" problem-solving ability in human history reinforces the shared rational heritage of these different disciplines. This observation reinforces the claims that theology can engage in rational discourse across interdisciplinary lines — the claim that in various forms van Huyssteen has spent his career defending.

---

32. *Alone in the World?* p. 153.

Conclusion

Van Huyssteen's multidisciplinary study of human uniqueness concludes with his acknowledging the inescapable limitations of interdisciplinary reflection (ch. 6). The "transversal moment" shared between theology and science can indeed be a fruitful encounter, but the contextual integrity of the disciplinary boundaries must also be respected. For the scientist theorizing about human uniqueness this will mean, among other things, that the propensity for religious behavior and specific religious practices cannot be explained reductively. For the Christian theologian this will mean that he or she "has an obligation to explore other issues that are crucial for understanding human uniqueness, issues that may not be empirically accessible."[33] The fact that disciplines share rational resources is therefore not a license for carelessly transporting ideas and data across disciplinary boundaries.

In a similar fashion, a summative essay of this sort will be challenged by its own set of limitations. Most importantly, it was simply impossible to include all of the ideas, arguments, and people that shaped van Huyssteen's developing model of rationality in significant ways. I was forced to make some difficult decisions about what to include and exclude, and it is unlikely I made every one of these decisions correctly. Nevertheless, my hope is that the final product is both faithful to J. Wentzel van Huyssteen's own ideas and inclusive of the most salient material and contributors related to the evolutionary development of his model of rationality over the course of his career. For the reader who wishes to explore van Huyssteen's work in more detail than this essay could afford, a complete bibliography has been included as an appendix.

---

33. "Human Origins and Religious Awareness: In Search of Human Uniqueness," *Studia Theologica* 59, no. 2 (December 2005): 124.

I. PHILOSOPHICAL EXPLORATIONS

2 Traces of Rationality: Acknowledgment, Recognition, and Repetition

Calvin O. Schrag

The topic of rationality has always occupied center stage in the writings of J. Wentzel van Huyssteen. His books *Essays in Postfoundationalist Theology* (1997) and *The Shaping of Rationality* (1999) immediately come to mind. In these works he deftly wends his way through the thickets of postmodernism, responding to its indictment of rationality within the corridors of philosophical, scientific, and theological inquiries. Recognizing the need to deal with postmodern antifoundationalism in philosophy and the celebration of instability of shifting paradigms and claims for incommensurability in postmodern science, he rises to the challenge of reclaiming a sense of rationality that at once avoids the unredeemable claims for a foundationalist universality among the moderns and the declaration of the bankruptcy of the logos among the postmoderns. He has come to call his refigured notion of rationality *postfoundationalist rationality*. Professor van Huyssteen is of the mind that a postfoundationalist project of the uses of reason will provide a space "where a fusion of epistemological and hermeneutical concerns will enable a focused (though fallibilist) quest for intelligibility through the epistemic skills of responsible, critical judgment and discernment," in the wake of which rationality "will be discovered as alive and well in all our domains of living and also in modes of knowledge as diverse as theology and the sciences."[1]

The development of the project of postfoundationalist rationality begins with a detailing of some of the vagaries that accompany overarching claims for unimpeachable foundational truths in philosophy, science, and theology. It is with these claims that the inflated notions of the reach and range of hu-

---

1. J. Wentzel van Huyssteen, *The Shaping of Rationality: Toward Interdisciplinarity in Theology and Science* (Grand Rapids: Eerdmans, 1999), p. 33.

man reason bequeathed by the Age of Enlightenment are seen to extend beyond their elastic limits. Grand narratives that purport to provide explanations of everything have outworn there usefulness — if, indeed, they ever had explanatory utility! A growing skepticism of universal criteria and norms in philosophical and theological inquiry and in scientific explorations places the telling of tall tales into question and augurs in the direction of local narratives within local contexts of inquiry. Within these contexts one can then readily discern the play of a pluralism of competing perspectives and the ingression of instability and unpredictability.

However, van Huyssteen's sympathetic attitude toward the postmodern posture of skepticism regarding universal knowledge-claims does not blur his vision of certain postmodern misdirections that tend toward an abandonment of rationality itself. To be done with a rationality that seeks metaphysical comfort in a foundationalism that offers to deliver universal criteria of knowledge and value is not to be done with rationality in every sense you please. Indeed in his book *The Shaping of Rationality,* van Huyssteen shows by way of a highly illuminating application of the concept of transversality how one is able to detail the uses of rationality in philosophy, theology, and science by avoiding on the one hand the modernist excesses of claims for unity and universality, and on the other hand the postmodern full-scale rejection of rationality in a celebration of heterogeneity, particularity, and incommensurability.

A key move in van Huyssteen's project of refiguring the resources of rationality across the domains of philosophy, science, and theology, splitting the difference between the metanarratives of universalism and the local narratives of particularism, is what he references as *"the turn from foundationalism to holism."*[2] Rationality, if it is to avoid the dead end of seeking to legitimize metanarratives based on universal epistemic criteria and ahistorical truth conditions somehow laid out in advance, will need to take into account the concrete understanding of self and society that emerges from our contextualized social practices that remain respondent to changing historical scenes. One also, however, will need to address the threats that accompany a debilitating historical relativization of all knowledge and value, simply inverting the *a*historicality of foundationalism to yield a suffocating *anti*-foundationalist historicism. The move to holism is designed to deliver us from this declaration of unacceptable options.

It is at this juncture, at the crossroads of the turn from foundationalism to holism, that I wish to pick up the conversation with van Huyssteen on the

---

2. J. Wentzel van Huyssteen, "Is There a Postmodern Challenge in Theology and Science?" in *Essays in Postfoundationalist Theology* (Grand Rapids: Eerdmans, 1997), p. 267.

issue at hand. I am of the mind that his recommendation for making this turn is eminently sound and sensible, and I take up the task in the limitations of the space allotted to converse with him on a specific aspect involved in the maneuvering of this turn. Proceeding in concert with his request for a fresh approach to the resources of rationality, I propose a thought experiment on the traces of rationality across the spectrum of acknowledgement, recognition, and repetition in the hope of achieving some clarity on how reason plays itself out in our philosophical and theological endeavors.

To begin our collaborative reflections on the shift from foundationalism to holism it might be helpful to sort out what all flies under the flag of "foundationalism." Here the literature is vast and comprehensive. Given unavoidable restrictions of space in our current project we will need to make do with a few sign posts. Foundationalism finds its mission in a quest for certainty. Unimpeachable knowledge-claims is what it is after. Inspired by modern rationalism, it searches for these knowledge-claims either in clear and distinct ideas (Descartes) or in judgments that yield universality and necessity (Kant); or inspired by modern empiricism, it scrounges around for incorrigible sensory impressions (Hume) that provide the building blocks for knowledge about self and world. Foundationalism works hand in glove with a criteriology that sets up the criteria and rules for discovery in advance, designed to govern or regulate the paths of inquiry. Everything is to proceed in a rule-governed manner. Foundationalism makes purchases on a representational theory of knowledge, whereby interior performances of perception and conception are taken to mirror the world of external reality. Foundationalism is elementaristic in its approach, separating the alleged contents of knowledge from the background of ongoing social practices as an amalgam of discourse and action. Foundationalism offers a decontextualized approach to knowledge, quite unconcerned about social sources and evolutionary processes.

Given this brief rehearsal of the principal markers of foundationalism we are already able to discern how holism provides an interesting contrast to the presuppositions and procedures of the foundationalist enterprise. Holism remains profoundly cautious about any claims for certainty in matters of both knowledge and value. Holism is suspicious about criteria laid out in advance, somehow nailed down before our manifold perceptions and wider experiences of the world offer their own testimonies. It is not that criteria are simply ruled out. It is rather they are seen as *postfestum* consolidations instead of apriori rules of epistemological construction, programmed in at the outset. Holism is quick to problematize any foundationalist claims for representation, given the difficulty of reclaiming the "present" that is alleged to be somehow *re*-presented. Holism is "holistic" rather than "elementaristic," insistent on the entwinement of contents of knowledge with the panoply of social practices and changing historical perspectives. Holism resists decontextualization, at least in the first moment of world experience, and emphasizes the bearing of background and foreground in the adventure of knowledge.

We have chosen as the title of our brief essay, "Traces of Rationality: Acknowledgment, Recognition, and Repetition." Our task is to examine how acknowledgment, recognition, and repetition figure in the foundationalism versus holism problematic. We first need to give attention to the distinction and entwinement of acknowledgment and recognition as contributors to the voice of human reason. And here one may well further the cause by picking up a conversation with one of the more notable philosophers in the modern period who had a stake in our topic. In what is surely one of the most frequently quoted passages from his *Phenomenology of Spirit*, Hegel broaches the matter at hand: "Self-consciousness is in and for itself by virtue of its being for another self-consciousness; that is to say, it occurs only as acknowledged *(als en Anerkanntes)*."[3]

Citing Hegel surely ought not be that much of an oddity in dealing with matters of rationality and holism. And beginning with Hegel's reflections on acknowledgment may facilitate matters in getting the conversation going. Yet, to *begin* with Hegel need not commit one to *end* with Hegel! This is not the occasion for an extended discourse on the story of Hegel's philosophical development from his early theological writings to his later system of logic. Discussions of Hegel's alleged "wrong turn" can be found in the works of sundry commentators and critics, and it may well be that Hegel ended up stretching the resources of rationality beyond the boundaries of our terrestrial finitude. All this notwithstanding, Hegel's use of acknowledgment *(Anerkennung)* in his chapter on "Lordship and Bondage" in *Phenomenology of Spirit* provides a promising point of departure for our mini thought experiment.

Hegel's general point in the referenced passage would appear to be quite straightforward and unproblematic. Self-knowledge and self-constitution proceed in concert with the self-knowledge and self-constitution of other selves. To be a self is to be acknowledged in the discourse and action of other selves and to respond to this prior discourse and action. One does not know oneself or become oneself in isolation. One becomes a self only in communication, in dialogue, in agreement and dissent with other selves. This acknowl-

---

3. "Das Selbstbewusstsein ist an und für sich, indem und dadurch, dass es für ein anderes an und für sich ist: d.h. est ist nur als ein Anerkanntes." G. W. F. Hegel, *Phänomenologie des Geistes*, Philosophische Bibliothek (Hamburg: Verlag von Felix Meiner, 1952), p. 141.

edgment by and with the other, however, we need to underscore, is not — at least *not yet* — recognition. And here one does need to proceed with as much semantic clarity as possible. The highlight of the passage is on *acknowledgment*. Unfortunately, the translator of *Phänomenologie des Geistes* not only glossed the German word *Geist* in the title by translating it as "Mind," but he also created semantic mischief by substituting "recognition" *(Wiederkennen)* for "acknowledgment" *(Anerkennung)*.[4] In the massive literature on Hegel's philosophy it is common to find this semantic infelicity in play. That there is a consummate reciprocity in our acknowledging and recognizing is clearly the case, but to blur the distinction between a knowing that is occurrent *(kennen)* and a knowing that is recurring *(wieder-kennen)* is to occlude the play of temporality in the event of self-knowledge. And when this occurring again, a re-cognizing in recognition, facilely slides into "representation" *(Vergegenwärtigung)*, as plainly enough has been the case in the history of the foundationalist epistemological paradigm, then one approaches that disconcerting state of affairs in which the confusion becomes complete.

So this is where our story begins, with what may appear to be a somewhat arcane semantic quibble about the meaning of terms. However, achieving clarity on the grammar of our investigative projects is surely a virtue to be held dear. The acknowledgment that guides self-knowledge and self-constitution is borne by a responsivity to that which is other. As so succinctly phrased by Hegel, self-consciousness exists in and for itself only by being acknowledged by another self-consciousness. The knowledge of acknowledgment, which effects a disclosure of the self to itself, takes its rise within a context of relatedness to a world in which the discourse and the action of other selves have already effected their inscriptions. So from the very start as it were, acknowledgment is always contextualized. Self-consciousness is borne by way of inscriptions by a *Mitwelt*, a world of other selves, which itself illustrates a vibrant intentionality of involvements with a wider surrounding environment of both social and natural history, an *Umwelt*.

As is well known, it was Heidegger who provided a sustained analysis and interpretation of the priority of the *Mitwelt* and the *Umwelt* for the tracking of the self-disclosure of Dasein in its concernful dealings with the world. These world-regions provide the sites for a knowledge of self and world that is pre-theoretical and pre-criteriological, a knowledge which comports its own praxis-oriented understanding and insight *(Umsicht)*. This praxis-oriented understanding, according to Heidegger, is prominently illustrated in

---

4. See *The Phenomenology of Mind*, trans. J. B. Baillie (London: George Allen & Unwin, 1910), p. 229.

our everyday preoccupations that involve the use of tools and utensils. The hammer, before it becomes a decontextualized object having a certain shape, weight, and molecular structure, is understood in terms of its practical bearing on the project at hand. It is, in Heidegger's terminology, "at hand" (*Zuhanden*) rather than simply "on hand" (*Vorhanden*). Also other selves in our "being-with-others" are first acknowledged as other Daseins involved in common social practices before they have conferred upon them a categorial identity. Consolidating the matter at issue, Heidegger expresses it as follows: "Practical behaviour is not 'atheoretical' in the sense of 'sightlessness'. The way it differs from theoretical behaviour does not lie simply in the fact that in theoretical behaviour one observes, while in practical behaviour one *acts* (*gehandelt wird*), and that action must employ theoretical cognition if it is not to remain blind; for the fact that observation is a kind of concern is just as primordial as the fact that action has *its own* kind of sight."[5]

Some may find it odd that we are here using Heidegger's analytic of Dasein to flesh out the dynamics of Hegel's "acknowledgment." But upon reflection it should become apparent that there is nothing odd about doing so. Both Heidegger and Hegel are proponents of a practical holism, and Hegel's take on acknowledgment meshes nicely with Heidegger's notion of a pre-theoretical understanding that has "*its own* kind of sight." The understanding of self and world against the background of a web of social practices — such as the pre-conceptual "seeing" of the hammer as a utensil in the service of a practical project, or the acknowledging and being acknowledged in the face to face encounter with other selves in our daily speaking and acting — antedates the conceptual objectivization of persons and things. Before we construct a system of rules, hypotheses, and beliefs, we are immersed in a practical world of everyday lived experience that offers its own traces of human comprehension. It is this web of practical engagements that makes up the praxis-oriented holism that gives birth to a pre-theoretical understanding.

This pre-theoretical understanding is an understanding that is already coupled with interpretation. In our preoccupations in a concrete lifeworld we surge up as interpreting observers and agents. Tools and utensils come to presence on the crest of a hermeneutical "as-structure." They are *taken as* the appropriate items for fulfilling a task. The as-structure is operative in our encounter with other selves *as* neighbors, *as* friends, *as* disadvantaged or infirm and hence deserving of our care; the world of nature opens up *as* a habitat for our journeying along life's way. Understanding and the as-structure of inter-

---

5. Martin Heidegger, *Being and Time,* trans. John Macquarrie and Edward Robinson (New York: Harper and Row, 1962), p. 99.

pretation are entwined at their very roots. Admittedly, there are different postures of interpretation in the achievement of knowledge of ourselves and our world. Interpretation plays itself out differently in a science of the physical world than it does in a science of human behavior. The world of physical nature is mute. Subatomic particles neither speak nor interpretively understand themselves as mass and motion. Human beings, on the other hand, are self-interpreting agents who understand themselves in their discourse and action in the context of a community of selves.

However, even the world of nature does not initially present itself as theoretically striated with algorithmic quantifiers. The constitution of the disciplinary matrix in which nature becomes an object for scientific explanation is the result of a community of investigators who make use of the "as-structure" in taking phenomena of nature as definable entities subject to explanation. Interpretative understanding goes all the way back even in scientific explanation. There can be no question about Wilhelm Dilthey's contribution to the development of a hermeneutics of the human sciences (*Geisteswissenschaften*), but he simply overstated the case in his celebrated one-liner: "Nature we explain; man we understand." Van Huyssteen does well to caution us about rigid dichotomies that separate the tasks of the human and the natural sciences. Interpretation is called upon both in scientific discovery and humanistic inquiry. It cuts across the culture spheres of science, morality, art, and religion. Admittedly it follows different traces in each of these spheres, but the "as-structure" of interpretive understanding remains in force across the board.[6]

The envelopment of understanding and explanation within what Paul Ricoeur has so felicitously named "the hermeneutical arc" offers certain clues for achieving clarity on how the cognition involved in acknowledgment and recognition might conspire.[7] Although recognition is a complementing form of knowing, a re-cognizing, a kind of "knowing again" something that was set forth in pre-theoretical, praxis-oriented dealings, it does not lose its liaison with the lived time that joins what is with what has been. The moments of acknowledgment and recognition, although distinguishable, intercalate in the dynamic upsurge of a self knowledge occasioned by being acknowledged by other self-consciousnesses. The understanding of self in relation to other

---

6. See particularly van Huyssteen, *The Shaping of Rationality,* pp. 197-221. Also see Calvin O. Schrag, "Explanation and Understanding in the Science of Human Behavior," in *Philosophical Papers: Betwixt and Between* (Albany: State University of New York Press, 1994), pp. 119-134.

7. Paul Ricoeur, *Interpretive Theory: Discourse and the Surplus of Meaning* (Fort Worth: Texas Christian University Press, 1976), p. 87.

selves is an understanding thoroughly temporalized. It does not occur in an abstracted instant. It occurs in the breadth of a now that has fringes that penetrate into the nows of past acknowledgments and the nows of acknowledgments yet to be. We are thus apprized of the extraordinary importance of time in our reflections on rationality.

The distinction and yet intricate connection between acknowledgment and recognition against the backdrop of the insinuation of temporality brings us to the more specific critical moment of our essay, salvaging a holistic rationality from the constructs of foundationalism. One of the principal misdirections of foundationalism is the misconstrual of recognition as representation. Foundationalist knowledge-claims rest on the presupposition that knowledge is made possible by the ability of the mind in an act of representing to accurately map the realities of the external world — whatever these realities might be deemed to be! A theory of representation is believed to undergird all knowledge-claims, the contents of which might consist of incorrigible sense qualia, universal essences, or a matrix of necessary connections. Fueled by an appetite for certainty that has its ground in a selection of alleged unimpeachable givens, foundationalists are particularly enamored with universality and necessity as bedrock criteria for the achievement of genuine knowledge. To have genuine knowledge is to know what is always the case and what is necessarily the case. Representation is called upon to provide such foundational knowledge. Now it is precisely such a slippage into foundationalism that we along with van Huyssteen wish to avoid. To do so, however, requires a jettisoning of the restriction of rationality to the scaffolding of beliefs and the serialization of criteria grounded in a decontextualized theory of judgment. Rationality moves about, and at the very beginning as it were, within a holistic web of pre-theoretical perceptions, feelings, desires, emotions that are meaning-laden and disclose truths about the human condition.

The vagary in the foundationalist edifice of representational knowledge turns mainly on the ambiguity of "presence" and the requirement for its recall in the act of *re*-presenting. At issue is the claim for a primordial presence — a sense impression, a concept, a set of relations — that is then purified through the recall in a rendering present, a *Vergegenwärtigung*. Not only is there an elusiveness in the act of representing, whereby the representational act retrieves a presence that is no longer; there is also the elusiveness of the alleged privileged access to an original presence which the act of representation is designed to call forth. The notion of presence that solidifies the scaffolding in the representational theory of knowledge is very much a fugitive presence, ever escaping determinate location. It is an arrested and mummified present, reified as an elusive abstraction. The sense datum or the conceptual construct, which the foundationalist alleges to be directly present to an attentive mind, takes on the determination of an unmediated given, forcefully impacting the human mind in a discrete presentational immediacy, decontextualized from a continuing past and an ingressing future. The presence in which the presentment of the given occurs is a presence extracted from the duration of the lived temporality in which embodied knowers seek an understanding of themselves and their world.

What is occluded in the theory of knowledge as representation and the accompanying theory of truth as correspondence is precisely the intentionality-laden and transversal dynamics of lived or experienced time, in which past, present, and future conspire in what Heidegger has named the "ecstatic unity" *(ecstasis)* of the three modes of temporality. The qualitative time of lived experience offers traces of a presence that is other than the decontextualized and reified instant of quantitatively measured time, in which time is diagramed as a serial succession of discrete now-points. The present in the lived time that provides the horizon for our engagements and acknowledgments is a *living* present for which the past is still real and the future is already real. This is the ecstatic unity of experiencing presence as a coming from and a moving toward. The self experiences itself as acknowledged by other selves in this having been and going forth.

The notion of lived time is particularly decisive for any critique of the epistemological problem of foundationalism, and it bears specifically on two aspects. The one has to do with the construct of the presence of the object as known, allegedly given to a stable consciousness functioning as a zero-point origin. Such a construct construes the presented object as decontextualized and reified into a fixed point of identity. But our immersion in the duration of lived time precludes any such objectivization and perduring identity. Our signifiers designed to nail down foundational signified contents always appear to come up lame. The embodied referents of our signifying operations suffer the fate of perpetual deferment.

The other aspect in the failure of foundationalism to come to grips with the reality of lived time turns on the inscrutability of self-reference. Within the foundationalist epistemological paradigm, the presence of the knower in the cognitive act remains in limbo — whether this presence be construed as that of a Cartesian ego-cogito, a Kantian transcendental subject, or a Humean sensing self, all of which are called upon to function as the foundational source of knowledge. As the signified content of an alleged presentment remains forever fugitive, escaping hard-knob determination, so is this also the case with the knowing subject. All claims for presence, either on the side of the object or on the side of the subject, appear to be up for grabs.

Noteworthy is Jean-Paul Sartre's critique of foundationalism and its failed effort to locate unblemished givens somewhere at the seat of knowledge. Sartre's target is Husserl's phenomenological foundationalism with its appeal to a timeless transcendental ego as the foundation for the unity of consciousness — a unity which Husserl defines as an apriori and necessary condition *within* consciousness. Sartre does not deny the unity of consciousness, but argues that it is a *product* of consciousness rather than the condition of a founding ego residing in a transcendental basement. He agrees with Husserl that consciousness is always intentional, always directed to its intentional object as a structure of meaning, but he describes the unity at issue as a coefficient of transversality within the dynamics of consciousness itself. Hence, he is able to speak of consciousness in search of its unity as a "consciousness which unifies itself, concretely, by a play of 'transversal' intentionalities which are concrete and real retentions of past consciousness."[8] What we learn from Sartre is that in understanding consciousness as transversal we will stop scrounging around for foundations that take on the mantles of universality and necessity. Transversality enables one to unify without appeals to overarching universals and undergirding necessary conditions, neither of which are receptive to temporal passage and changing conditions, be it the successive moments of consciousness or the changing scenes of social practices.

There is, however, a limitation that travels with Sartre's position on transversal intentionality as the unifying factor of consciousness, and this is a limitation that has a direct bearing on our case for a nonfoundationalist holism. Sartre gives primacy to the retentional span of consciousness and searches for the unifying thread of consciousness in the continuation of the past in the present. Although he jettisons Husserl's transcendental support of a timeless ego, he agrees with Husserl's pictorial layout of internal time-consciousness as a continuing recovery of the past. Thus in both Sartre and Husserl we find an over-determination of the retentional vector of consciousness and an under-determination of the protentional vector. It was left to Heidegger and Merleau-Ponty to give proper due to the workings of the protentional thrust of lived experience, and thus accord the proper due to the future in their existential analyses and descriptions of time.

However, even before Heidegger and Merleau-Ponty there was a Danish philosopher and theologian who set the agendum for all subsequent inquiries into the temporality of human existence with his doctrine of repetition. In his

---

8. Jean-Paul Sartre, *The Transcendence of the Ego: An Existentialist Theory of Consciousness*, trans. Forrest Williams and Robert Kirkpatrick (New York: Noonday Press, 1957), p. 39.

groundbreaking book *Repetition: An Essay in Experimental Psychology*, Søren Kierkegaard frames the issue in a quite straightforward manner: "*Repetition* is a decisive expression for what 'recollection' was for the Greeks. Just as they taught that all knowledge is a recollection, so will modern philosophy teach that the whole of life is a repetition. . . . Repetition and recollection are the same movement, only in opposite directions; for what is recollected has been, is repeated backwards, whereas repetition properly so called is recollected forwards."[9]

This accent on the priority of the future, and the emphasis on knowledge as a repetition in the guise of a recollection forwards, brings us full circle back to our initial reflection on the rationality of acknowledgment and recognition and the attendant problems in the construal of recognition as representation in the designs of foundationalism. We are now able to see the importance of the requirement for a deconstruction of representation so as to retrieve the more vibrant and holistic interplay of acknowledgment, recognition, and repetition that makes up the fabric of our communicative praxis as an amalgam of discourse and action.

Within this postfoundationalist and holistic approach to knowledge there are no reified presences to be re-presented in a curious maneuver of somehow being made present again. In the density of our lived time, in which the openness of the future gives breadth and vitality to a living present and keeps the past from being a collection of reified instants that have simply gone by and have become devoid of meaning, the acknowledgments, recognitions, and repetitions along life's way display their intrinsic transversal intentionalities and insights. The interpretive understanding within our communicative praxis does not need to wait upon a universal principle, either of a metaphysical sort swooping down from on high or of a transcendental sort emerging out of a zero-point origin from below. Rationality, albeit refigured and revalued, is alive and well in the concrete lifeworld of human thought, discourse, and action. And we all stand in debt to Professor van Huyssteen for his instruction that a dismantling of the theoretico-criteriological epistemological paradigm of foundationalism does not require an abandonment of the resources of rationality per se, whether these are to be sought in the domains of science, philosophy, or theology.

---

9. Søren Kierkegaard, *Repetition: An Essay in Experimental Psychology*, trans. Walter Lowrie (Princeton: Princeton University Press, 1946), pp. 3-4.

3 Rational Theory Building: Beyond Modern Enthusiasm and Postmodern Refusal (A Pragmatist Philosophical Offering)

Wesley J. Wildman

The Quest for a Theory of Rationality

J. Wentzel van Huyssteen's most important contribution to the science-religion dialogue may be his relentless insistence that a theory of rationality logically precedes and is implicitly presumed in any proposal for how science and religion relate to one another. This has been a prominent theme in his writings from the time of his first English publications. I have not attempted to read his earlier writings, but, judging from the titles alone, he has been fascinated with the question of rationality since the beginning of his career.

Van Huyssteen is completely correct, of course. There has been an immense amount of premature speculation and hand-waving suggestions about science-religion relations. But the theory of rationality needed to make sense of and evaluate the strategic proposals and methodological suggestions has usually been absent. So he has devoted himself to constructing a theory of rationality against which it is possible to articulate a model of science-religion relations and to evaluate competing proposals.

The first major English work of van Huyssteen in which this interest appears is *Theology and the Justification of Faith: Constructing Theories in Systematic Theology*. This book was written in Afrikaans, published in 1986, and then translated by Henry Snijders into English for publication in 1989.[1] The

---

1. J. Wentzel van Huyssteen, *Theology and the Justification of Faith: Constructing Theories in Systematic Theology* (Grand Rapids: Eerdmans, 1989). English translation by Henry F. Snijders from Afrikaans, *Teologie as Kritiese Geloofsverantwoording: Teorievorming in die Sistematiese Teologie* (Pretoria: Human Sciences Research Council, 1986). Page numbers given parenthetically in the text refer to the English edition.

I am grateful to Kirk Wegter-McNelly for his thoughtful comments on this essay.

aim of the book is to establish the possibility of a critical-realist approach to theory-building in theology. For this purpose, van Huyssteen takes philosophy of science to be an indispensable dialogue partner because it is there, he believes, that the question of human rationality is most sharply and usefully posed in our time: "Accounting critically for their faith presupposes that theologians must be prepared to reflect on their own thought processes, and this places upon them the fundamental task of relating the essence of their faith to the question of the very nature of rationality, as posed in contemporary philosophy of science" (xii).

Closely associated with his commitment to interdisciplinary conversation is a strong aversion to forms of theology that withdraw from such conversation, retreating into an isolated rational ghetto where, "totally ignorant of the process of theory formation," they "lay claim to an indisputable scriptural theology or theology of revelation. The attempts of theologians to describe the nature of theology and theological knowledge without taking into account the problems implicit in this thematics in terms of philosophy of science will therefore have to be exposed as illusory" (xvii). Both convictions — the importance of interdisciplinary engagement and the self-deceptive character of theology that takes refuge in a private world of supernatural authority — run throughout his writings. They are complemented by an intense refusal to reduce the theological task to just what science can recognize as rational. Van Huyssteen does affirm that science is "our best example of the cognitive dimension of rationality at work,"[2] but never to the exclusion of the rational character of theology. In later writings, he appears to affirm a greater parity between the rationality of theology and the rationality of science. His most developed view is that theology shares rational resources with the sciences and every other kind of reflective human activity, while maintaining distinctive subject matter and purposes.

In *Theology and the Justification of Faith,* van Huyssteen lays out his understanding of a critical-realist model of rationality that pertains to systematic theology, understood as a theory-building activity that furnishes a critical account of the Christian faith. He draws the criteria for such a model of rationality especially from what the philosophy of science has taught us about rationality. The three key criteria are the "reality depiction," the "critical and problem-solving ability," and the "constructive and progressive nature" of theological statements (146). Of course, van Huyssteen carefully interprets each criterion against the background of prominent debates in the philosophy

---

2. J. Wentzel van Huyssteen, *Essays in Postfoundationalist Theology* (Grand Rapids: Eerdmans, 1997), pp. 255-256.

of science. For example, his review of critical realism in philosophy of science leads him to stress the elements of theoretical fertility and explanatory success over an extended period of time as the fundamental justification for claiming that theoretical terms refer in science and theology alike. Van Huyssteen also frames each criterion in a way that is sensitive to the special character of the theological task. For example, he argues that reality depiction includes faithful reflection on the many social forms of Christian faith, thereby building contextual sensitivity into his model of theological rationality.

After he settled at Princeton Theological Seminary in 1992, van Huyssteen's sensitivity to theological context took a fascinating turn as he began to engage Postmodernity. His goal was still to articulate a theory of rationality that makes sense of both theological and scientific activity. But now he aimed to split the difference between two disastrous distortions of human rational activity. On the one hand, modernist foundationalism mistakenly supposes that certainty, objectivity, and universality are the marks of rationality, after which theology appears to be a thoroughly irrational activity. On the other hand, extreme forms of postmodern anti-foundationalism are skeptical of every universal claim, including criteria for distinguishing better from worse in any domain of rational activity, after which theology is cast into the outer darkness of utter relativism. Between these two extremes lies a third option, according to van Huyssteen: postfoundationalism. His postfoundationalist account of rationality shares the sensitivity of postmodernism to the terrible way certainty, objectivity, and universality can function as powerful clubs to suppress unwanted and awkward viewpoints, particularly those of socially and economically oppressed portions of humanity that tend to challenge the political and economic status quo. It also shares modernism's interest in taking account of the success of the natural sciences. Yet it does this without supposing rationality is either a matter of epistemic certainty and universality or a self-deceptive struggle against the strangulation of unlimited relativism.

This theme appears prominently in van Huyssteen's *Duet or Duel? Theology and Science in a Postmodern World* (1998), and also in his contributions to *Rethinking Theology and Science: Six Models for the Current Dialogue* (1998).[3] Can there be a theory of rationality that encompasses theological and scientific activity while avoiding the extremes of foundationalism and relativism? Can a theory of rationality have the kind of generality van Huyssteen seeks

---

3. J. Wentzel van Huyssteen, *Duet or Duel? Theology and Science in a Postmodern World*, The 1998 Diocese of British Columbia John Albert Hall Lectures at the Center for Studies in Religion and Society in the University of Victoria (Harrisburg, PA: Trinity Press International, 1998); J. Wentzel van Huyssteen and Niels Henrik Gregersen, eds., *Rethinking Theology and Science: Six Models for the Current Dialogue* (Grand Rapids: Eerdmans, 1998).

for it without falling prey to the postmodernist critique of universality and of the oppressive metanarratives that universal discourses promote? Can van Huyssteen articulate such a theory without venturing into the realm of metaphysics, which is off-limits for post-Kantian foundationalism in both philosophy and theology, as well as taboo for postmodernism's anti-logocentric, anti-ontotheologic, anti-metanarrativistic, skeptical, relativistic microculture?

The clearest and most comprehensive statement to date of van Huyssteen's theory of rationality, as well as its greatest test, is *The Shaping of Rationality: Toward Interdisciplinarity in Theology and Science*.[4] It is this definitive statement that I shall engage in the remainder of this essay. It is extraordinarily rich, however, so I will only be picking up on a few aspects of it: van Huyssteen's positioning of his proposal between or beyond Modernity and Postmodernity, his treatment of generality in theory building, and his metaphysically restrained approach to the themes of truth and reality.

I shall point out that Van Huyssteen's epistemological project is similar to the epistemological project of the early pragmatists Charles Peirce and John Dewey in important respects. This is surprising in view of the fact that van Huyssteen does not deal with these intellectual forebears at all. He discusses the neo-Pragmatist Richard Rorty in *The Shaping of Rationality* but Rorty's project is as different from the early pragmatists' perspective as it is from van Huyssteen's point of view. He mentions Robert Neville's *The Highroad around Modernism*, a work in the Peirce-Dewey tradition, but does not discuss its proposal for understanding rationality, which in many respects harmonizes with van Huyssteen's work. These similarities ramify van Huyssteen's labors, but they also show that his project has neglected roots at least a century old. While van Huyssteen's appreciation for the complexities of science and theology as social phenomena is more sophisticated than these pragmatist forerunners, they may still offer some insights into van Huyssteen's project.

The most important similarity is that van Huyssteen and the early pragmatists all have fully postfoundationalist (in van Huyssteen's terminology) conceptions of human rationality, rooted firmly in the biology and sociality of the human species. The most notable difference is that the early pragmatists offer a clearer answer than van Huyssteen to the question of how personal convictions and local contexts combine with universal features of experience through intersubjective conversation to produce theories of aspects of

---

4. J. Wentzel van Huyssteen, *The Shaping of Rationality: Toward Interdisciplinarity in Theology and Science* (Grand Rapids: Eerdmans, 1999). Page numbers are given parenthetically in the text.

reality that not only work pragmatically but also are true and refer to a reality to some degree independent of human minds. Achieving clear answers to such questions demands, now as always, metaphysical reflection — in the sense of a maximally general form of thinking that is intensely sensitive to the contours of experience. The early pragmatists' hypothetical, fallibilist approach to metaphysics shows that a highly generalized form of thinking is possible within van Huyssteen's understanding of rationality. Their theoretical work shows that metaphysics can help to diagnose the contrast between the universal and local aspects of reason as well as its different ways of working in science, the humanities, and the arts. So van Huyssteen's implicit refusal to offer metaphysical accounts of key features of human rationality is a puzzling interruption of a natural trajectory within his thought, along which he has already traveled a considerable distance.

The early pragmatists, and I with them, would urge van Huyssteen onwards. The apparent need for this urging suggests that van Huyssteen's project may be in thrall to postmodern suspicion of metaphysics, silently refusing metaphysical theory building even when his insights invite and demand it, and when nothing he says prevents it. The early pragmatists offer hypothetical, fallibilist, experientially based, and contextually sensitive forms of metaphysical theorizing that are every bit as hostile to modernist totalizing discourses as van Huyssteen's project is, and assimilate the relativizing force of postmodern critiques of human theorizing every bit as successfully as van Huyssteen's project does.

The Successes and Failures of Foundationalist Epistemology, Revisited

Early Modernity and especially the Enlightenment marked an exciting period in the perennial western philosophical search for an understanding of rationality. It is too easy, however correct, to attack this excitement for naïve hubris. Indeed, many cheap philosophical points have been scored in just this way. But it is important also to notice the reasons modern philosophers believed it had become possible for them to advance beyond medieval philosophy's view of rationality as artful judgment within an overarching theological framework that rooted human reason in the logos structure of divinely created reality.

Certainty is always desirable for creatures prone to worry, with the capacity to imagine alternative scenarios, who constantly confront conflicting opinions on issues that profoundly affect happiness and safety. But certainty was not the overriding goal in the Middle Ages that it was to become in the seventeenth century. In the medieval context, the pervasive assumptions about human rationality were that even its most confident product was dependent on divine creation, which established harmony between human thought and the knowable world, and subject to divine revelation, which established knowledge of the otherwise unknowable world and trumped speculation about this world. Ideally reason harmonizes perfectly with revelation. How was this harmony conceived? Human reason can range broadly across many questions and subject matters, in principle, yet not with equal confidence or competence. When reason is strongest, producing agreement among experts, revealed truth is in perfect harmony. When reason struggles to produce consensus, revelation lights the way with its dispute-resolving power. In theological matters, particularly, the speculative exercise of human rationality was always a kind of incursion into territory where revelation had the final word, through the divinely established authority of the Christian church.

This was a sensible and practical arrangement. It defined basic rules for understanding how human rational activity both connected and failed to connect with the created world. For example, mathematicians could produce proofs in geometry, thus disclosing the basic logos structure of reality that always lay beneath the surface of ordinary reality just waiting for reason to discover it. But theologians could only prove the existence of God; they could not deduce from nature or reason unaided by revelation much of importance about the divine character. This arrangement also provided basic rules for supporting reasonably clear distinctions among social institutions and activities. For example, human rationality could not penetrate politics and economics to any great degree so it needed to defer to, and operate within, the divinely ordained social arrangements of Christendom, with its class hierarchies and significant merging of political and religious authority.

Early modern science and the mathematics that facilitated it appeared to change the rules about the proper domains of operation of human reason. René Descartes famously dreamed of a metaphysics that would extend the apodictic certainty of mathematics to knowledge of natural, human, and divine realities. The new possibility of such certain knowledge may still depend on God, in some remotely ultimate sense, but proximately reason could operate sure-footedly in domains that, until this time, had been subject to the confusions of endless speculation and intractable disagreement. The key was to find in physics, psychology, and metaphysics the correlates of the axioms of mathematics. Descartes called these "clear and distinct ideas" and believed they could be discovered through a kind of disciplined meditative process that attempted to doubt everything. When in this process the corrosive powers of doubt fail, the metaphysician will have discovered an idea that possesses the same shining certainty that Euclid's axioms of geometry inspire in the mathematician. Once the metaphysician assembled enough clear and distinct ideas, they could function as axioms in a deductive system of knowledge that reaches far beyond mathematics to account for human reason itself, for the reality of a world outside the human mind, and even for the existence and goodness of God. Indeed, this was the purpose of Descartes' *Meditations* and, in his judgment and in the judgment of many others, its achievement.

This bathtub-eureka approach to metaphysics was incredibly compelling at the time and only a bloody-minded refusal to appreciate contextual factors in philosophy would harp on its shortcomings. It would turn out that identifying clear and distinct ideas was much more difficult than Descartes suspected, that the logical import of axioms for metaphysical systems was unremittingly vague, and that even the mathematical-axiomatic model for the whole enterprise was fatally flawed. Yet modernity's epistemological infatuation with certainty, with foundationalism, and with the universal relevance of decontextualized philosophical argumentation was born in this grand adventure. Of course, these epistemological virtues (or vices) were not new in themselves. It was the infatuation with them and the optimistic faith in their capacity to bring new knowledge that was new. This infatuation lasted a long time and, in many ways, persists even today, which is to say even after the rediscovery of rationality as an act of judgment that expresses a particular perspective and inherent interests, that has political and economic contexts and effects, and that helps human beings dynamically adjust to a complex natural and social environment. In fact, it was surely in part the political promise of loosening the authoritarian grip of religious institutions that made strong claims for reason's autonomy so compelling, even among profoundly religious philosophers.

The overthrow of medieval assumptions about rationality was a civilization-transforming event, entangled with the birth of nation states and partially managed economies, the birth of new social institutions that brought widespread education and made democracy thinkable, the birth of modern science with its technological fruits, and the birth of modern medicine with its astonishing efficacy. There are several hallowed iconic stories of this change whose repetition serves to legitimate it, such as Galileo's fight with the Catholic Church over the organization of the solar system, Newton's apple and the invention of the theory of gravity, and the key axiom of Descartes' metaphysics: "I think therefore I am." Each symbol is a historical caricature, of course, and this testifies to the importance both of the change and of our struggle to understand it.

The change is impressive. Whatever causes or enables or makes use of this transformation will have the cultural prestige in modern societies that was reserved for the Christian Church in the medieval world. The most prominent recipient of the prestigious mantle of cultural authority is modern science, and especially the natural sciences, which epitomize the rational in Modernity. Science is a cooperative venture that produces theories capable of winning unprecedented cross-cultural agreement, that seeks out its mistakes and corrects its theories as needed, that makes exciting discoveries about the natural and human worlds, that inspires life-changing technological marvels from electricity to blood transfusions, and that effectively resists the arbitrary imposition of political and religious authority. It turns out, of course, that philosophers and scientists alike overreached in their claims for modern science. We have discovered through the philosophy of science and through experience that theory choice in the sciences is a prodigiously complex social feat with uncertain rational standing, that the boundaries between science and other rational enterprises are quite blurred, and that the technological products of science are sometimes pernicious. Yet none of that overturns the significance of Modernity for understanding rationality.

Modernity has delivered on its claims for rationality in science, and in a host of other areas, in a stunning way. We should pay attention to its lessons. Modernity teaches us that medieval philosophy greatly underestimated the power of human reason and seriously misjudged the power of religious authority to trump it through divine revelation. It teaches us that carefully delimited inquiries that win cross-cultural agreement are possible, though only in some domains, and to that extent there is great value in seeking general formulations of our theories about nature and human beings, including cross-cultural and trans-historical formulations. It teaches us that, despite its foundational and universal aspirations, even the best theories — in science as in other forms of inquiry — are always subject to revision and must seek out their own flaws in a ceaseless quest for refinement. It teaches us that we are wise to be suspicious of the arbitrary imposition of religious and political authority and that nothing can extinguish the simple candle of truth no matter how violent the attack. Just as Modernity could not completely overthrow the best insights of the Middle Ages, so must Postmodernity accept these lessons and strive to account for the best insights of Modernity about human rationality.

Beyond Modernity and Postmodernity

I think van Huyssteen would agree with this formulation of the successes and failures of the Modern project in epistemology. Doubtless he would trim here and stretch there. But I intend this quick summary to help diagnose a double bias against Modernity and Postmodernity that I think I notice in van Huyssteen's writings on postfoundationalism. On the one hand, van Huyssteen's exposition of the modern epistemological project emphasizes the postmodern critique of Modernity's grandiose self-assessment while spending less time and energy than is warranted on the real achievements of Modernity in substantiating its claims for universal and trans-cultural aspects of human rationality through scientific and other forms of organized intellectual inquiry. He certainly resists extreme postmodernism's thoughtless plunge into "sheer relativism," but the grounds for this resistance, which I have just sketched, are disproportionately muted relative to the recounting of Modernity's failures of self-understanding, which I have also sketched. On the other hand, van Huyssteen proposes a theory of rationality that is more universal in its implications than he appears ready to admit. It is a courteously presented theory, whose rhetorical framing appears designed to win the hearts of mainstream postmodern thinkers, along with the mainstream of anti-imperialist scientists and culture-engaging theologians. Van Huyssteen reserves his severe criticisms for extreme postmodernists, imperialist scientists, and ghetto-dwelling theologians — easy targets relative to the mainstream of thinking about human rationality. But there is more conflict among his moderate audiences than van Huyssteen allows. Just as he understates the real grounds for supporting universal elements in any theory of human rationality, so he overstates the harmony between his theory, which implies such universal elements, and the postmodern refusal of universality even within its mainstream.

Another way of making this point is to reflect on van Huyssteen's central category for diagnosing the conflict between Modernism and Postmodernism: epistemic foundationalism. He claims Modernism affirms it and Postmodernism rejects it. His postfoundationalism is neither fish nor fowl and thus is a welcome relief from a fruitless fight between impossible alternatives. It is easy to appreciate the overcoming of a futile debate. But van Huyssteen remains silent about the very important fact that postfoundationalism was an early-modern discovery. In fact, foundationalism was quickly recognized as a tempting but impossible dream by a steady stream of thoughtful philosophers almost as soon as it was conceived. The early modern philosopher David Hume was already a postfoundationalist in something like van Huyssteen's sense, rejecting the possibility or value of definite foundations for human knowledge, speaking freely of habits of association and interpretation and judgment, and situating human rationality in a biological, historical, cultural framework. The late-nineteenth-century American Pragmatists Charles

Peirce and John Dewey were explicitly postfoundationalist in their epistemology, expounding a biological, historical, and cultural framework for understanding rationality that incorporated evolutionary theory, affirmed the fallible and hypothetical character of all theorizing, and prized correction of hypotheses in processes of inquiry. This stream of postfoundationalist philosophers was inspired by solid ancient and medieval wisdom about human rationality, in relation to which Modernist enthusiasm for certainty always seemed, well, enthusiastic. In the final analysis, just as van Huyssteen's postfoundationalism is already an old response to Modernist pretensions, so reading the Modern-Postmodern debate in terms of foundationalism does not reach deeply enough into the disagreement.

The disagreement between Modernity and Postmodernity has been the object of a thousand characterizations, most of them fascinating, including van Huyssteen's unusually sensitive offering. In relation to the epistemological corner of the civilizational battle that van Huyssteen's *The Shaping of Rationality* engages, I consider it a multifaceted fight over generality and justice, driven by awareness of cultural and religious pluralism, on the one hand, and the need for security and identity, on the other. To be secure and to know oneself and one's people is, in part, to understand the world around us as far as possible in a particular way, namely, through theoretical interpretations of natural and social reality that take in as much as possible while faithfully accounting for variations and differences. But this is all very complex and something simpler is often more immediately useful. In practice, the quest for security and identity demands a narrative interpretation of reality that minimizes complexities for the sake of maximizing its orienting and action-supporting power. The awareness of cultural and religious pluralism confronts this need with another need, to register details of difference and disagreement faithfully, refusing to ignore complexities. Every time theory building aims for generality, it risks delivering on the need for security and identity at the cost of fidelity to details. And whenever theory building aims to do justice to the details of variation, the chances of a satisfying general interpretation are greatly reduced. The modern epistemological project, whether foundationalist or postfoundationalist, stresses the possibility and value of generality in theory building. The postmodern epistemological project is primarily a watchdog enterprise, pointing out in the name of justice and honesty the failures of the quest for general theories, and especially their disastrous moral and social ramifications.

The disagreement between Modernity and Postmodernity is haunted by shame — over colonialism, over paternalism, over expansionist political and economic ideologies, over the ill effects of consumption and consumerism, over the ecological and social disasters of technology, and over the ongoing failure to transform the world into the disease-free and hunger-free Shangri-La that the modern west pictured. The haunting will end, but not when we get our philosophy of human rationality straight, not when the Western world pays reparations for its colonialist adventures in slavery and exploitation, not when religion either goes away or reclaims its former control over human societies, not when the western world finally imparts its life-transforming wisdom to the rest of the world, and certainly not when the western world humbly withdraws into its own territory and leaves the rest of the world alone. Rather, the haunting will end when we listen to the non-western world closely enough to realize not only that we have a lot to learn from other cultures but also that we actually strongly disagree with an enormous amount of what non-Western people do and believe, from worldviews to religion, from medical treatments to child-rearing practices, from politics to economics. Shame abates in this case when the West notices its particularity, overcomes its embarrassment (as if it must hide the fact that most of its people actually prefer living the way they do), becomes comfortable with being what it is and can be, and articulates that respectfully in relation to real knowledge of the Other with which it remains in dialogue.

Shame is a powerful force in western consciousness at the present time, particularly among the well-informed intelligentsia. Liberalism in politics has lost its way because it is guilt-ridden and does not know how to assert itself without multiplying its sins. Conservatism in politics is dangerous because it is in denial about being guilt-ridden and asserts itself with populist bluster as if there were never much to feel guilty about in the first place. Even philosophical debates in epistemology can be haunted by shame, to the point that we might understate the intellectual weaknesses of a postmodern perspective, lest we find ourselves attacking our own conscience. There is a lot to be ashamed about, to be sure. But we overlook at our peril Postmodernity's double role as the raiser of consciousness about past western sins and also as the conveyor of paralyzing, even if well-earned, guilt and shame.

I appreciate van Huyssteen's courteous entertaining of the postmodern critique of modern understandings of rationality, and I sympathize to a considerable degree. But I think Postmodernity is deeply mistaken, in its own guilt-ridden way, about the possibility and value of generality in theory building. I think that van Huyssteen only truly opposes extreme postmodernists whose universal relativism is already self-defeating, and that he meekly overlooks the deep error of mainstream postmodern thought on rationality. It is every bit as large an error and every bit as morally disastrous as the modern overconfidence in generality that neglects fidelity to details and contexts.

Van Huyssteen should attack Postmodernity at its very guilt-ridden heart, just as he accepts its attack on the ignorant enthusiasm that haunts the house of much modern epistemology.

Generality, Abstraction, and Universality

"Generalizations are empirically flat footed, low energy, center-confirming, periphery delegitimating, abuses of power." I shall call this the "Generality Critique." If the Generality Critique is correct, then it is a victim of its own acuity. The self-referential deconstruction of generalized critiques of generalization is the first reason why intellectuals perpetually suspicious of generalization have to move carefully. I once attended a meeting of the Pacific Coast Theological Society in which a memorable exchange occurred. Someone made a remark about the need for balance between generalizations and details in historical work and noted historian John Dillenberger quietly replied that "Details are everything in history!" — a remark with sufficient weight to close off that phase of the discussion. In context, Dillenberger was pushing back against a perceived rush to generalization, and so the comment was warranted. But, as a matter of fact, while historical scholarship is nothing without attentiveness to details, it is also useless unless it contains generalizations that create understanding of patterns, trends, forces, movements, and styles, and also their failures and exceptions. To rush to pattern recognition is to commit Hegel's error in his *Lectures on the Philosophy of History* all over again, whereby details are coerced into the rational pattern, with the more recalcitrant among them simply neglected or deliberately marginalized. But to stay only with details is to produce a meaningless list of events, a kind of senseless recording of what happened. And even a list requires generally applicable categories for its organization. Evidently, the person to whom Dillenberger responded was formally correct: good historical work does indeed balance generalizations and details.

Some people affirming the Generality Critique unconditionally may be taking an extreme point of view for the sake of some larger social and political purpose. Perhaps van Huyssteen would classify them in his "extreme postmodern" camp. But the danger with this is that rhetoric opposed to generality cannot come clean about its own biases and agendas; generality and systematic analysis are required to diagnose them. Others affirming the Generality Critique do so more moderately because they simultaneously make the "Generality Affirmation," which asserts that "Generalizations are inevitable for human thought and life and thus are valuable when they are formulated artfully." We might appreciate the moral and political agendas of extremists who blindly critique the very generality they rely on for their moral analyses, but most of us prefer the artfulness of the moderates who accept the risk of generalization because of its inevitability and thus seek to generalize skillfully. Van Huyssteen is a moderate in this sense, as are the early pragmatists Peirce, James, and Dewey. Their unapologetic embrace of generality in a characteristically fallibilist form is not present in van Huyssteen, however, and I find this puzzling.

For example, after approving Calvin Schrag's pragmatic and praxis-oriented approach to rationality, van Huyssteen states that the significance of this is (a) "the complete impossibility to think of rationality in abstract, highly theoretical terms" because (b) "rationality is present and operative in and through the dynamics of our words and deeds, and it is alive and well in our discourses and action" (118; my labels). I think this is misleading, if not inconsistent. I am happy to grant (b), as the early pragmatists did, and as van Huyssteen does. But neither this nor Schrag's version of pragmaism entails (a). Whether it is possible to think of rationality in abstract, highly theoretical terms must be an empirical matter, on van Huyssteen's own account. Indeed, whether abstract generalization and highly theoretical constructions are ever possible must be an empirical matter: we have to try and see. A deeply puzzling feature of van Huyssteen's approach to rationality is his simultaneous embrace of fallibilism in inquiry and yet definitive rejection of abstract generality, high theory, comprehensiveness, and universality. I consider this to prejudge a crucial issue about human rationality and the world in which it arises and seek to know van Huyssteen's reasons for preemptively settling on the position he takes. As far as I can see, van Huyssteen's reasons extend only as far as the "(b) entails (a)" reasoning above, which I think is flawed. Van Huyssteen might be correct about (a), and the associated impossibility of abstract generality, high theory, comprehensiveness, and universality. But if he is correct, it is not because it follows from (b) or similar premises. To go further, I would say that van Huyssteen's own theory of rationality challenges the impossibility expressed in (a): it is a coordinated, systematic series of abstract and highly theoretical generalizations, comprehensive in scope and universal in intent. Merely noticing the biological, historical, and cultural embedding of all human rationality does nothing to interfere either with the possibility of such discourse or with its appearance in van Huyssteen's own writings.

A more consistent conjunction of the Generality Critique and the Generality Affirmation does not reject abstract generalization or high theory from the outset, as if somehow we just knew what was possible with human rationality in advance of any experience. Rather, alert to the moral and political and intellectual dangers of generalization but also intrigued by the common features in reality across cultures and eras, we should embrace epistemological fallibilism and also venture both to advance and to correct hypotheses about the rational structures of reality. When we do this, we find that we can generalize in some domains of reality more successfully than in others. For example, generalizing about human nature at the level of emotional dynamics and psychological formation is extremely hazardous while it is more straightforward at the level of the basic glucose-ATP biochemical energy mechanism, which all human beings have in common with most living beings. Generalizing about the right place to put rocks in a garden is not likely to win consensus, no matter how strong the enclosing aesthetic tradition, whereas generalizing about the physical theories that explain why rocks stay put when laid in a garden is an adventure in inquiry that has won massive consensus. Generalizing about moral values across times and eras has been notoriously ineffective, and yet more recent anthropological work has discovered some very basic and widespread moral institutions, and evolutionary psychology has disclosed a partial basis for them.

Abstractions, generalizations, theories, and systems are not ruled out by a postfoundationalist epistemology, whether van Huyssteen's or the early pragmatists'. Postfoundationalism problematizes them and rightly warns their purveyors about lurking moral and political dangers. But it also challenges their detractors to say how they can know what is possible and impossible, in advance, in a theory of rationality or on any other topic. Post-foundationalist empistemology, or in my terminology a pragmatic theory of inquiry,[5] is more than merely a set of warnings. It is a bracing invitation to allow curiosity a full rein, to formulate hypotheses freely and test them as carefully as the realities of social organization and individual ingenuity permit. It overturns the skeptical rule mongering of philosophers from Kant to Comte to Ayer and situates in a proper context the grave concerns of philosophers from Derrida to Foucault to Lyotard. We can no more stop hypotheses about universal features of reality in this new epistemological world than we can ignore warnings about ideological bias lurking in our abstract theoretical constructions. Whether we can produce any useful generalized theories is an empirical question. And I think it is a question we are entitled to answer in the affirmative, even if it means citing as evidence van Huyssteen's abstract, highly theoretical

---

5. See Wesley J. Wildman, "The Resilience of Religion in Secular Social Environments: A Pragmatic Analysis," in *Scientific Explanation and Religious Belief: Science and Religion in Philosophical and Public Discourse*, ed. Thomas M. Schmidt and Michael G. Parker (Frankfurt: Mohr-Siebeck, 2005).

theory of rationality that paradoxically dismisses "abstract, highly theoretical" discourse about human reason as impossible.

Truth, Reality, and Empirical Fidelity

The postfoundationalist epistemology of van Huyssteen, and the pragmatic theories of inquiry of the early pragmatists, promote a freedom of fallibilist, hypothetical investigation that makes foundationalists feel queasy for lack of anything solid to stand on and postmodern skeptics indignant because of the embrace of abstract generality and high theory. But pragmatic theories of inquiry are far from unconstrained. Inquiries produce warranted belief only if their hypotheses can be corrected. Problem recognition, hypothesis formation, and theory correction are enormously complex phenomena and require social settings, traditions that stabilize shared values, and cultural resources to create the leisure and materials for inquiry. But with all of this social and psychological fabric in place, there is still no guarantee that even a single hypothesis in a single inquiry is capable of correction. Just as we cannot rule out in advance the possibility of abstract, generalized theories of anything, so we cannot take for granted that the hypothetical process of theory building will find the traction needed to decide that one hypothesis is better than another.

In some inquiries we never do seem to gain the traction required. Yet in others, strangely enough, we do: hypotheses in such domains produce consensus decisions about their adequacy because they can be corrected relatively quickly. Some inquiries encounter the corrective "feedback mechanism" as a booming voice that exercises a decisive and rapid influence on inquiry whereas others hear only a whisper or nothing at all, after which broad consensus is not possible without arbitrariness or coercion. Any serious test of the hypothesis that I can plunge my head through a metal girder using brute force alone will produce serious injury along with decisive results and probably universal consensus that my hypothesis needs modification. Perhaps I first need to meditate, for instance, or eat something special, or at least pray for special powers before trying again, assuming a successful convalescence. But there is no question that something caused all of the qualified observers to conclude that my hypothesis was false and to modify whatever dangerous process of inquiry led to this incident, accordingly.

The idea of correctability — which I call a feedback mechanism to stress its reflexive operation and to register the possibility of its varying in strength — is amply present in the early pragmatists but seems strangely absent in van Huyssteen. This idea is necessary to make sense of truth and reality in science and theology alike, indeed in all forms of rational inquiry, but it requires metaphysical articulation. This van Huyssteen seems singularly unwilling to provide. This leaves us with an awkward question. We know from van Huyssteen, as he follows Schrag, that "reason is operative in the transversal play of thought and action in the guise of three interrelated moments/phases of communicative praxis, i.e., evaluative critique, engaged articulation, and incursive disclosure" (248).[6] So we know what reason does. But we do not know from van Huyssteen why reason works. His characterizations of reason's function are laced through with normative hints about better and worse evaluative critiques, more and less engaged articulation, stronger and weaker forms of incursive disclosure. He readily invokes ideas such as long-term fruitfulness, responsible judgment, intelligibility, optimal understanding, experiential adequacy, and theoretical adequacy (for example, see 115, but these value phrases are richly present in the book). The basis for these norms remains hidden, however, while the entire collection of such normative ideas seems to function as the rhetorical basis for the usage of any one of them. This leaves the careful reader longing for a direct answer to the question, "why does reason work?"

The early pragmatists centralized the idea of correctability in response to their own version of this difficulty. They had a deficient understanding of the social requirements and implications of inquiry but they recognized that variation in this mysterious feedback mechanism accounts for why some inquiries are more effective than others. Any pragmatic argument for realism turns on the fact that a feedback mechanism sometimes corrects some of our hypotheses with enough force to create consensus among qualified experts in the process of carrying out extended, tradition-borne, socially contextualized inquiries. For the pragmatist, in fact, this is the very meaning of reality: the whence of correctability in rational inquiry. This way of thinking recovers the Pythagorean recognition of happy consonance between the logos of human reason and the Logos of reality but in a decidedly more tentative way. The mystery of correctability may be the pragmatist's basis for speaking of a public, shared reality but the feedback mechanism's variations in strength make reality seem (pragmatically) fuzzy. This is nowhere more true than in religion but there are elements of it even in fundamental physics, or wherever the feedback mechanism is weak or non-existent.

It is this variability in the experienced strength of the feedback mecha-

---

6. Van Huyssteen here refers to Calvin O. Schrag, "Transversal Rationality," in *The Question of Hermeneutics*, ed. T. J. Stapleton (Dordrecht, The Netherlands: Kluwer Academic Publishers, 1994), pp. 69ff.

nism that finally and fundamentally explains different disciplinary styles. In fact, for the pragmatic theory of inquiry, science is defined not in the first instance as the study of particular subject matters using particular methods but by conformation of inquiry to the strongest regions of the feedback mechanism. Science is that correlation of social organization and topics of inquiry that is optimized to produce consensus based on clear and strong correctability. This, in turn, helps to nail down what we think of as physical reality in ontology and functional naturalism in methodology. In other words, the pragmatic theory of inquiry recognizes the dependence of inquiry upon this feedback mechanism and makes it the fundamental metaphysical hypothesis in any theory of rationality. After being centralized in this way, the feedback-mechanism hypothesis serves as the fundamental explanation of disciplinary differences, from different forms of social organization to different ways of producing consensus, and from different topics to different methods. This is a metaphysical hypothesis that connects truth and reality, on the one hand, to the function of norms in human traditions of inquiry, on the other.

It follows that there is an answer, compatible with van Huyssteen's postfoundationalist epistemology, to the question of why rationality works. But it is an answer that cannot be articulated without venturing metaphysical hypotheses that are capable of connecting reality to experience and truth to consensus, hypotheses on the order of the feedback-mechanism hypotheses that I have described. Van Huyssteen seems singularly unwilling to entertain such hypotheses (the absence of "truth" in the index of *The Shaping of Rationality* is a mere symbol of this pervasive unwillingness). The result is a significant gap in his theory of human rationality. I have conjectured that van Huyssteen may be unduly swayed by postmodern detractors of general metaphysical theories, and that this is the cause of his paradoxical pronouncement of the impossibility of abstract, highly theoretical accounts of human rationality. I have argued that he should attack postmodernity's preemptive policing of possibilities as urgently as he attacks the naive epistemological enthusiasm of modernity. In other words, he should more completely move beyond the limitations of both, which is simultaneously to recover the insights of each, always present as shadowy reflections within its opposite. Despite positioning his postfoundationalist epistemology between and beyond modernity and postmodernity, I suspect that the epistemology leans perceptibly, but without due reason, toward the postmodern side.

4 Rationality and Different Conceptions of Science

Mikael Stenmark

One of J. Wentzel van Huyssteen's central claims is that both science and religion have found their identities challenged by a new and pervasive postmodern culture.[1] In this new postmodern world, the modernist ideas of objective truth, universal rationality, and the autonomous individual have been challenged. Van Huyssteen's objective has been to take seriously this postmodern challenge to rationality, while still upholding a credible form of interdisciplinary rationality, and at the same time to show why it is not the case that science finally has claimed rationality at the expense of religious faith and theological reflection. My focus in this article will be on one particular aspect of this postmodern challenge to rationality, namely, the consequences it has for a feasible contemporary conception of science and its implications for the role of religion in scientific practice.

An important question concerns the role which values, ideology, or religion should play in contemporary science. In recent years an influential group of scholars has argued against the received view of science: the idea of an autonomous, value-free, and ideologically neutral science. They have instead maintained that we need a new conception of science in which science and values are explicitly linked. We need a science that is infused with or guided by values, ideology, or religion. Moreover, changes in the political and economic conditions for pursuing science in contemporary society suggest that such a change is already under way.

In this essay I will attempt to explicate and critically compare these dif-

---

1. J. Wentzel van Huyssteen, *The Shaping of Rationality* (Grand Rapids: Eerdmans, 1999).

I gratefully acknowledge the financial support from the Swedish Research Council that made the writing of this essay possible.

ferent conceptions of science. I will define a *view of science* or a *conception of science* as a standpoint about how science should be pursued and related to society. Thus, a view of science tells us who counts as a scientist, how science should be internally organized and related to other institutions in society, what methods should be used, what aims should be achieved, and so on. It specifies how science ought to conduct its internal and external affairs. A view of science is therefore a *normative ideal* that its advocates maintain should regulate (if that is not already the case) actual scientific practice. It states what is to be considered good and bad science.

A very influential view of science has been the conception of a value-free science.[2] In the last decades this view of science has come under severe attack from a very diverse group of people. For instance, among Christians we find people like Alvin Plantinga, who maintains that it is "excessively naïve to think that contemporary science is religiously and theologically neutral, standing serenely above this battle [between theism and naturalism] and wholly irrelevant to it."[3] A number of feminists agree with Helen Longino that from a feminist perspective "the idea of a value-free science is not just empty but pernicious" and what we need therefore is a feminist science.[4] Moreover, the Muslim scientist Medhi Golshani notes that some people "argue that science is an objective and universal enterprise, and it does not depend on any creed or ideology," but maintains that "this is a naïve interpretation of scientific activity."[5] What is interesting with this group of scholars is that they do not merely criticize the value-free view of science but also try to offer an alternative to it.

The aim of this paper is to take a closer look at the criticism of the value-free view and the alternatives proposed. What are the key differences between these views of science? The first thing we need, then, is an account of the value-free view of science. The problem we face is that both its defenders and its critics have given it different interpretations. My strategy will therefore be to offer a fairly reasonable and hopefully representative account of this view of science by identifying some of the key elements such a view could contain. After this has been done, I will suggest some of the major reasons why the

---

2. See Robert N. Proctor, *Value-Free Science?* (Cambridge, MA: Harvard University Press, 1991), for a history of the view.

3. Alvin Plantinga, "When Faith and Reason Clash: Evolution and the Bible," *Christian Scholar's Review* 21 (1991): 16.

4. Helen Longino, *Science as Social Knowledge* (Princeton: Princeton University Press, 1990), p. 191.

5. Mehdi Golshani, "How to Make Sense of 'Islamic Science'?" *American Journal of Islamic Social Sciences* 17 (2000): 1.

value-free view of science has come under severe attack, before identifying and evaluating some of the key elements of this alternative view of science and its rationale. In this way I hope to make a contribution toward finding an answer to the question: to what extent should values, ideology, or religion be a part of contemporary science?

The Value-Free View of Science

A number of terms are used in the debate about a value-free science such as "value-free," "value-neutral," "value-loaded," "biased," and "partisan" — often without much consistency. My strategy will therefore be to choose certain terms, give them a stipulative definition, and use them to identify key elements in these different conceptions of science.

I suggest that we start by simply defining the value-free view of science as the *standpoint that science ought to be free from values in some specific ways.* The alternative to it I shall call the "value-directed view of science," and it could be defined as the *standpoint that science ought to be guided by values in some specific ways.* These are very rough first approximations, but they highlight two important things: (1) that the value-free view does not entail that science ought to be free from values in *all* respects, and (2) that the value-directed view does not entail that science ought to be guided by values in *all* possible ways. So the crucial question is really this: in what ways, more exactly, should or should not science be free from or directed (or infused) by values? By answering this question we identify the key components of these different views of science.

Before I suggest what these key components are, it is important that we understand that it is not merely values that science should be free from. This is often indicated when people talk not merely about a value-free science but also about a "science free from ideology" or a "religiously neutral science." Hence, science ought also to be free from certain metaphysical, religious, or ideological beliefs or claims. The idea seems to be that science should be free from not merely ideological or religious values but also ideological or religious beliefs. I shall therefore often talk not merely about values but also about ideologies and religions.

With these clarifications in mind, I propose that we define the value-free view of science more precisely in this way:

> ▸ The *value-free view of science* is the standpoint that science should be autonomous, neutral, impartial, non-responsible, and non-normative.

Autonomous Science

Science should be autonomous in the sense that the scientists themselves — and not political parties, the government, religious organizations, private corporations, or the like — ought to decide the direction of the research and the kind of questions that ought to be asked (and answered) in scientific research. The greatest benefits and the best theories from science will be obtained by letting scientists follow their own ideas as to what kind of research should be pursued. Science should not be directed by anyone or anything outside the scientific community. Leave science to the scientists, and give them resources to conduct their research with no strings attached! Notice that this does not entail that science should not be guided by values. The idea is rather that the values of or priorities set by scientists and not by non-scientists (politicians, business executives, and so forth) should guide the direction of the research and the sorts of questions that are pursued and answered in scientific research.

Neutral Science

Closely related to the idea of an autonomous science is the idea of a neutral and non-confessional science. Science ought to be a universal enterprise that people could be a part of and benefit from, regardless of which ideology, religion, or conception of the good they cherish. One should not need to make up one's mind about which value system, ideology, or religion one should endorse in order to do science. Therefore, science ought to be neutral in respect to the ideologies and religions that divide us.

Science should also be non-confessional in the sense that a scientist need not, for instance, be a Christian, atheist, feminist, or socialist to qualify as a scientist. The grounds for membership in the scientific community ought to be non-ideological or non-religious. Nor should one receive any special privileges within the scientific community if one adheres to a particular ideology or religion. The key idea, then, is that science should be free from values in the sense that it should not presuppose the acceptance of a particular ideology, religion, or conception of the good. It should not proceed on the basis that one particular ideology, religion, or conception of the good is the correct one.

Impartial Science

Moreover, science ought to be impartial. That is to say, moral judgments, ideological claims, or religious beliefs ought not to be among the grounds for accepting or rejecting theories within scientific inquiry. Science should be impartial in the sense that it should not presuppose the truth of any particular political vision, religion, or ideology in the validation of scientific theories. The choice of scientific theory should instead be determined by criteria such as empirical adequacy, explanatory and predictive power, simplicity, and consistency.

The defenders of this conception of value-free science maintain that it is impartiality that makes intersubjectivity possible in science. First, scientific theories ought to be open to public evaluation; that is to say, the grounds on which a scientist or the scientific community accepts a theory must be accounted for and thus be in principle accessible to other people. Second, because no moral judgments, ideological claims, or religious beliefs are allowed among the grounds for accepting a theory, any other scientist should by using the same methods be able to obtain the same results.

Non-Responsible Science

Science should be non-responsible in the sense that scientists have no special accountability for the applications of science. The ends to which scientific results are to be applied should be determined by society. Within, for instance, the framework of democracy, people are equally allowed to use the teachings and the findings of science to whatever vision of a good human life they endorse, be it a feminist, a Christian, or a Buddhist vision. On the other hand, scientists *qua* scientists should themselves not take side in these debates. To take a stand on questions about the utility of science is not a part of the scientists' task, nor do scientists have any special responsibility that goes beyond those they have as citizens. The only thing scientists should care about in their professional role is finding out the truth, or how nature works.

This does not mean, however, that defenders of the value-free view are compelled to deny that scientific conduct is subject to ethical evaluation or restrictions.[6] Even if scientists are allowed to ask any kind of questions, they are still not permitted to use any kind of methods in obtaining an answer to these questions. The conception of value-free science does not, therefore,

---

6. Michael Root seems to think that the value-free view has this implication. See Michael Root, *Philosophy of Social Science* (Oxford: Blackwell, 1993), p. 130.

necessarily conflict with the need and development of ethical principles for scientific conduct. Hence, on this interpretation, the conception of value-free science does not entail the "ethical autonomy" of science, that is, that scientific practices are not answerable at all to ethical and political values.[7]

Non-Normative Science

Science should be non-normative or merely factual. The mandate of science is to provide us with factual information about the world (justified is-statements), but since one cannot deduce ought-statements (what should be the case) from is-statements (what is the case), one cannot in scientific reasoning obtain normative conclusions from descriptive premises. Therefore, science can provide us with factual information, but it cannot tell us what our ethical obligations are, what policies we should adopt, or which ideology or religion we should endorse. Science ought to be value-free in the sense that it can discover facts (even facts about values, ideology, and religion), but it should not try to provide us with values, that is, try to underwrite a particular conception of the good, ideology, or religion.

I take this to be a fairly plausible account of the conception of a value-free science. But this is not to deny that these key ideas could be expressed in a different way or that other elements could be incorporated in this view of science. Notice also that the value-free view — when it is understood in this way — is compatible with values, ideology, or religion playing *other* roles within scientific inquiry than those discussed here.

The Changing Conditions for Conducting Science

The idea of value-free science has been undermined in at least two different ways. First, studies of actual scientific practice by historians, philosophers, sociologists, and others have revealed many cases in which values, ideology, or religion has in fact influenced scientific inquiry — for instance, cases in which a scientific consensus on a particular theory was based as much on shared ideological values and beliefs as on empirical evidence. The cumulative effect of this kind of study is that the value-free view starts to look like an unrealistic ideal and perhaps not even a desirable ideal, since much of actual scientific practice appears not to be governed by it.

---

7. See John O'Neill, *Ecology, Policy and Politics* (London: Routledge, 1993), p. 157.

Second, a recent change in the conditions under which science is conducted seems also to undermine the value-free view. Today scientific knowledge production or theory construction is generated to a large extent in the context of application. Funds for scientific research are more and more given with an eye to possible applications, for instance, of a military, industrial, or medical kind. There has been an explosion of expectations about science's ability to provide "useful answers" to an ever-increasing range of problems in society. What are understood to be useful answers depends, of course, on the ideology of the funding institution, be it a religious community, company, institution, or government. The separation of science from political or industrial interests has broken down almost completely in research fields such as biotechnology and environmental science. We can, for instance, find clear signals in the European Union's research policy that we need research that can help us develop a sustainable society. This is certainly the case in the Swedish context. We have a movement from environmental research to research *for* sustainable development, a shift from something that seems to be reasonably autonomous to something that is much more politically dependent: research that is conducted on the basis of a particular political vision of what a desirable future human society should look like. Thus, science increasingly serves specific ideological interests and thus by implication fails to serve other kinds of ideological interests. Any attempt to turn science toward the "social good" or any other ideological or religious goal entails a *politicizing* of science, and thus appears to completely undermine the ideal of a value-free science.

If this is what is happening, what alternative conception of science should we adopt instead of the value-free view as a regulative ideal for scientific practice? To what extent should values, ideology, or religion be a part of contemporary science? It is important that we realize that it is one thing to criticize science for not being value-free and stop there, and quite another thing to go on and develop an alternative conception of science that could *replace* the value-free view. My interest is in analyzing those who also take this second, more constructive step.

The Value-Directed View of Science

Let us now take a closer look at the alternative to the value-free view by focusing on each of the five key elements I have identified in the value-free view: autonomy, neutrality, impartiality, non-responsibility, and non-normativity. In the beginning of the essay, I called the alternative view the "value-directed view of science" and defined it roughly as the idea that science should be guided by values in some specific ways. We can now be more precise. As a working hypothesis, I suggest that we simply understand it as the negation of the value-free view in its entirety. That is to say,

> ▸ The *value-directed view of science* is the standpoint that science should be non-autonomous, partisan, non-impartial, responsible, and normative.

Let us take a closer look at each of these key elements of the value-directed view. (Because of space limitations some of these elements will receive more attention than others.)

Non-Autonomous Science

The fact that governments and corporations have become increasingly involved in the funding and direction of research, with the result that science has become more and more politicized and commercialized, means the acceptance of a *non-autonomous science* in the sense that a view of science is accepted in which it is considered appropriate that not merely the scientists themselves but also political parties, governments, private corporations, and the like are allowed to decide the direction of the research and the kind of topics that should be addressed. Today we can see, for instance, in the environmental sciences and biotechnology the growth of a science that is more and more non-autonomous with closer ties between the universities, on the one hand, and industry or governments, on the other.

According to the advocates of these changing conditions for doing science, the greatest benefits from science would be obtained if people other than scientists were also allowed to influence to a significant degree the direction of research. Therefore, we ought to welcome this development of science. Many who argue for a non-autonomous science maintain that not merely people in power but also marginalized people should be allowed to influence to a significant degree the direction of research.

Partisan Science

But even if scientists alone are allowed to choose the direction and topics of research, this would not mean that these choices would be free from values, ideology, or religion since most scientists adhere (consciously or unconsciously) to one ideology or another. Feminists such as Longino and Harding claim that science is disguised androcentric ideology (that is, roughly, a system of ideas that suit men's experiences and minds more than women's and that neglect and misrepresent the latter set of experiences) and that this is the case whether or not science is autonomous.[8] Plantinga and Golshani identify another kind of ideology in science, namely naturalism or atheism.[9] Science claims to be ideologically or religiously neutral, but it secretly favors a particular worldview, naturalism.

This seems to undermine the view of a neutral rather than an autonomous science. But notice that it does this only if it also involves the rejection of the idea that science *ought* to be neutral. The aim of the criticism must not merely be to show how far contemporary science is from approximating the view of science that should be its regulative ideal, namely the value-free view, but to replace it with yet another view of science. The reason is that a defender of the value-free view could respond to this kind of criticism by saying, "Yes, you are right. Please show us how and where in contemporary science we can find these instances of disguised androcentric ideology or naturalism, so we can correct these errors, thus ensuring that science really could become an enterprise of which people regardless of ideology or religion could be a part." This is exactly how Longino characterizes a feminist response to masculine bias in science different from her own:

> Feminists — in and out of science — often condemn masculine bias in the sciences from the vantage point of commitment to a value-free science. Androcentric bias, once identified, can then be seen as a violation of the rules — a "bad" science. Feminist science, by contrast, can eliminate that bias and produce "good," more true or gender-free science. From that perspective the process I've just described [and her own view] is anathema.[10]

Her view includes the rejection of a neutral science and the adoption of a *partisan science,* that is, a science that is aligned with or presupposes the acceptance of a particular ideology, religion, or conception of the good. Science should not stand neutral in respect to the competition between rival ideologies or religions but should choose sides. Longino's conception of a feminist science, Michael Root's perfectionist science, Plantinga's Augustinian science, and Golshani's Islamic science would all be examples of such an alternative

---

8. Longino, *Science as Social Knowledge,* p. 192, and Sandra Harding, *The Science Question in Feminism* (Ithaca, NY: Cornell University Press, 1986), p. 136.

9. Alvin Plantinga, "Science: Augustinian or Duhemian?" *Faith and Philosophy* 13 (1996): 369, and Golshani, "How to Make Sense of 'Islamic Science'?" p. 4.

10. Longino, *Science as Social Knowledge,* p. 191.

view of science. Longino writes, "the neo-Marxists are understood as advocating an alternative vision of nature and natural processes largely on moral and sociopolitical grounds.... In this regard the neo-Marxists stand on the same ground as the feminist scientist. In order to practice science as a feminist, as a radical, or as a Marxist one must deliberately adopt a framework expressive of that political commitment."[11] Root maintains that "the practices of the science should include or be grounded on a view of the kinds of life worth pursuing."[12] Science ought to be designed to push or pull citizens in a direction that reflects and sustains a particular set of values or traditions. Plantinga endorses what he sometimes calls "theistic science," at other times "Augustinian science." He writes that "in doing Augustinian science, you start by assuming the deliverances of the [Christian] faith, employing them along with anything else you know in dealing with a given scientific problem or project."[13] Moreover, Golshani argues for an "Islamic science" by which he means "a science that is framed within an Islamic worldview and whose main characteristics are that it considers Allah as the Creator and Sustainer of the universe; does not limit the universe to the material world; attributes a telos to the universe; and accepts a moral order for the universe."[14]

The advocates of this view of science typically maintain that, although science can be partisan, scientists have an obligation to be *open* about their ideological or religious commitments. They then reject an implicitly partisan science as an illegitimate view of science, arguing that it always should be explicit. Scientists should not appear to be politically or religiously disinterested parties, but should state clearly their own political or religious commitments.

Defenders of partisan science could argue for a science in which all scientists should share the same ideology or religion. This would require, it seems, that we first resolve the conflict between ideologies and religions in society before we can conduct science properly. Rather than accept this kind of monism, advocates of science typically appear to accept pluralism, that is, the idea that we ought to have a plurality of ideologies and religions in science. Within the scientific community and within society, we should accept that some scientists choose to do feminist science, others masculinist science, naturalist science, Augustinian science, Islamic science, left-wing science, or right-wing science. Although it is merely a matter of degree, we should perhaps distinguish between *weakly* and *strongly partisan science*. It seems to me

---

11. Longino, *Science as Social Knowledge*, p. 197.
12. Root, *Philosophy of Social Science*, p. 2.
13. Plantinga, "Science: Augustinian or Duhemian?" p. 377.
14. Golshani, "How to Make Sense of 'Islamic Science'?" p. 4.

that many governments' call for and financial support of research for sustainable development is also an example of partisan science. The idea is that the values that are presupposed in the vision of a sustainable society should guide scientific practice.[15] Science should not be neutral in respect to the vision of society specified in, for instance, *Agenda 21* and the *Rio Declaration* but should actually take as its point of departure this normative-political ideal. This would be an example of weakly partisan science because it is based on a broad, ideological, and religious consensus, something that many people, irrespectively of whether they are socialists or liberals or Christians or atheists, could agree on. Plantinga's Augustinian science and Longino's and Harding's feminist science would instead be versions of strongly partisan science, because they would be accepted neither by many non-Christians and non-feminists nor by many Christians and feminists as well.

However, we should not confuse partisan science with the uses by people in society of scientific theories and results for political or religious purposes. In their criticism against what they call "biological determinism" (that is, sociobiology and the like) and argument for a left-wing science, Leon J. Kamin, R. C. Lewontin, and Steven Rose write:

> biological determinism *(biologism)* has been a powerful mode of explaining the observed inequalities of status, wealth, and power in contemporary industrial capitalist societies, and of defining human "universals" of behavior as natural characteristics of these societies. As such, it has been gratefully seized upon as a political legitimator by the New Right, which finds its social nostrums so neatly mirrored in nature; for if these inequalities are biologically determined, they are therefore inevitable and immutable.[16]

The idea here is that we have a political movement, the New Right, which has a particular ideological agenda. They discover the scientific theories developed by biological determinists and realize their political value, and thus they try to legitimate their political ideology and policies by referring to this set of biological theories. In this way these biologists' scientific work serves the ideological interests of the dominant groups in society. Although Kamin, Lewontin, and Rose classify this as "science as ideology," this would not be an example of partisan science. For biological determinism to classify as partisan

---

15. For an identification and analysis of those values see Mikael Stenmark, *Environmental Ethics and Policy-Making* (Aldershot: Ashgate, 2002).

16. Steven Rose, R. C. Lewontin, and Leon J. Kamin, *Not in Our Genes: Biology, Ideology and Human Nature*, 2nd ed. (London: Penguin Books 1990), p. 7.

science, scientists must have (consciously or unconsciously) aligned with the New Right and its political agenda in developing this research program.

Neither does the fact that certain scientific theories have or might have consequences for ideological or religious convictions make science partisan. There is an important difference between science being *neutral* and its being *relevant* in respect to ideology or religion. Plantinga, for instance, maintains that "in [Herbert] Simon's account of altruism we have an example of a scientific theory that is clearly not neutral with respect to Christian commitment; indeed, it is inconsistent with it."[17] Here Plantinga assumes that science is religiously neutral only if it does not refute or undermine religious beliefs and values. But since that is not the case, science is religiously partisan. This is certainly a possible way to interpret the claim that "science is not religiously neutral." I suggest, however, that we should avoid doing so, simply because science has over the centuries refuted or undermined numerous religious and ideological beliefs. Science has, for instance, discovered that the earth is billions of years old and thus has refuted the religious belief that the earth was created by God around 6,000 years ago. Religious people have held (and advocates of flat earth theory still do) that the Bible teaches that the earth is flat and therefore we ought to believe this. Science has refuted this idea and replaced a geocentric with a heliocentric worldview.

In fact, science has the potential to undermine (or to support, for that matter) any religious or ideological idea that has empirical content or that presupposes the truth of some empirical statements. Here lies also the key to understanding why we cannot expect that science is (or should be) ideologically or religiously neutral in this sense, because investigating empirical claims and developing theories about empirical states of affairs is what science is all about; it is its proper domain. If religious or ideological ideas either contain an empirical element or presuppose its truth, these ideas can be undermined or refuted by scientific theories and data (and they can, of course, also be supported or verified by scientific theories and data). Therefore, we should grant that science can be ideologically relevant in respect to religions or ideologies *x, y,* or *z*, while it can at the same time be ideologically neutral in respect to them. Ideological relevance does not imply ideological partisanship. Science, if ideologically neutral, would (on such an account) belong to neither side in a controversy, say between theism and naturalism or between liberalism and socialism, but could obtain research results relevant for the truth-claims and value judgments involved in such a controversy. Science would, on the other hand, be *ideologically irrelevant* in my terminology if that

---

17. Alvin Plantinga, "Methodological Naturalism?" in *Facets of Faith and Science,* vol. 1, ed. Jitse M. van der Meer (Lanham: University Press of America, 1996), p. 184.

were not possible. If so, all scientific research that might yield results that are ideologically or religiously controversial in any way would need to be abandoned. Thus science is *ideologically relevant* if its results can either support or undermine a particular ideology or religion or set of them.

Non-Impartial Science

A more radical claim than to maintain that science should be partisan is to claim that moral judgments, ideological claims, or religious beliefs ought to be among the grounds for accepting or rejecting theories within scientific inquiry. Not merely should science be influenced by moral visions, ideology, or religion so that, for instance, the direction of research is guided by them, but also theories that conform to moral, ideological, or religious ideals are to be preferred to rival theories that conform less to such ideals.

What is interesting about the defenders of the value-directed view that we have considered so far is that they all also seem to incorporate the idea of *non-impartiality* in their alternative conception of science. Plantinga maintains that Christians as scientists should start from what they think that they know as Christians. In doing science, they should appeal, where appropriate, to what they know about God or God's activity or to what they know by means of the testimony of the Bible.[18] These beliefs ought to be part of the background evidence with respect to which the plausibility and probability of scientific theories are to be evaluated. Hence, science should not be impartial in the sense that it should presuppose the truth of any particular worldview, religion, or ideology such as Christianity, Marxism, feminism, or naturalism in the validation process. Golshani claims that "it is on this basis [revealed knowledge and its effect on scientific knowledge] that we want to elaborate on the relevance of religious science, and in particular Islamic science."[19] Moreover, Longino writes,

> The idea of a value-free science presupposes that the object of inquiry is given in and by nature, whereas the contextual analysis [that is, her own] shows that such objects are constituted in part by social needs and interests that become encoded in the assumptions of research programs. Instead of remaining passive with respect to the data and what the data suggest, we can, therefore, acknowledge our ability to affect the course of knowledge and fashion or favor research programs that are consistent with the values

18. Plantinga, "Science: Augustinian or Duhemian?" p. 380.
19. Golshani, "How to Make Sense of 'Islamic Science'?" p. 4.

and commitments we express in the rest of our lives. From this perspective the idea of a value-free science is not just empty but pernicious.[20]

Scientists should not merely make their ideological commitments explicit when participating in policy making, religious or moral debates, and so forth, but they should also interpret the data in such a way that those theories which guarantee the reinforcement of their own social ideals will be validated. However, "in order to survive and attract participants" this must be done in such a way that "some of the standards/values characterizing the scientific community within which it is proposed" are satisfied.[21] Hence, at least for pragmatic reasons, criteria such as empirical adequacy, explanatory and predictive power, simplicity, and consistency ought to be cultivated if this view of science is adapted, but moral or ideological criteria should be added as well.

One reason Plantinga gives for why we should accept non-impartiality in science is that since Christians know many important things as Christians, it would be unwise or unnatural if they accepted a constraint that did not allow them to use that information in doing science.[22] Why should Christians not use everything they know in doing science? Notice, however, that the issue here is not whether Christians should let their knowledge or at any rate their presumed knowledge influence the kind of research topics they undertake or the hypotheses they propose. If so, they would be engaged in partisan science. The issue about non-impartial science concerns the narrower question whether Christians (or people of other faiths or ideologies) should claim that their Christian (or ideological or religious) convictions ought to be considered a proper part of scientific theory validation. The reason offered by Longino differs from that of Plantinga. She writes, "Background assumptions are the means by which contextual values and ideology are incorporated into scientific inquiry."[23] But since the evidence always underdetermines theories, the acceptance of theories is and should always be affected by something besides the evidence, namely the scientists' ideological commitments functioning as background assumptions. Longino believes that the argument from underdetermination shows the impossibility of an ideologically or a religiously impartial process of theory validation in science. Ideology or religion is always relevant in the justification of scientific theories because it fills the gap between evidence and theory.

It is important for our analysis that we understand that *partisanship does*

---

20. Longino, *Science as Social Knowledge*, p. 191.
21. Longino, *Science as Social Knowledge*, p. 193.
22. Plantinga, "Methodological Naturalism?" p. 192.
23. Longino, *Science as Social Knowledge*, p. 216.

not entail non-impartiality. Whether science is neutral or partisan, it could still generate scientific results that satisfy the demand for impartiality. Perhaps an easy way to see this is to consider an analogous situation. I am one of the coaches of my thirteen-year-old son's soccer team. Imagine that one day his team is playing against another team, but the referee does not show up. We decide to play the game anyway, and the other team agrees that I shall be the referee of the game. My hope is that although I cannot and will not deny that I want my son's soccer team to win the game (being partisan), I nevertheless could avoid unfairly favoring his team over the other (being non-impartial). This may be difficult, but it is not impossible.

So being partisan or not neutral is not equivalent to being non-impartial. To draw that conclusion is actually to commit the fallacy of guilt by association: if you can show that person A is a member of z (for instance, the group of people defending feminist beliefs and values or masculinist beliefs and values), then that somehow is meant to undermine this person's claims, given the assumption of course that it is a bad thing to be a member of z; if it is a good thing, then you are supposed to draw the opposite conclusion. It might nevertheless be more difficult for partisan science than for neutral science to be impartial. The danger with partisan science — seen from the perspective of the value-free view — is that it puts scientists under pressure to find evidence favoring a politically, financially, or religiously desirable conclusion. But if some participants in the value-free science debate are right that neutral science is impossible, then it is important to keep in mind that partisanship does not entail non-impartiality.

Up to this point I have avoided the term "biased" in characterizing these different views of science. Let me now explain how I think we should relate the concept of bias to these other key concepts. I suggest that we restrict the use of impartiality and non-impartiality to the process of evaluating scientific theories. Bias, on the other hand, should be understood as a broader category. "Biased" could be used to characterize elements in the evaluation process, but it could also be used to determine other aspects of scientific practice, for instance, the choice and direction of research and the presentation of scientific results.

But what is to be considered as biased in the evaluation process will in part depend on one's view of science and must therefore be distinguished from non-impartiality. Let us go back to the analogy again. The soccer game between the two teams starts, and I act as referee. After the game (which my son's team won) the coaches of the other team thank me and tell me that I did a great job because in their judgment all my decisions were fair and unbiased. However, they tell me that I made one big mistake. At the end of the game their team should have had a penalty kick that I failed to see. But they still did not think that I was biased. Why? The reason is that they are aware of the fact that the game at that point moved very quickly from one side of the field to the other, and for that reason I was too far away from the ball to be able to really see what happened. So I made an error, a serious error, but I was nevertheless not biased because the most reasonable explanation of my behavior was not that I really wanted (consciously or unconsciously) my team to win and therefore unfairly favored them, but that my lack of speed and my failure to be in the right place at the right time prevented me from seeing the play. Now, suppose instead that I had given my son's team more free kicks than the other team and that I did this, not because the other team violated the rules of the game more than my son's team did, but because I sympathized with his team and wanted them to win. If that was the case, then something besides the evidence of violations of the rules of the game influenced some of the refereeing decisions I made. These decisions were therefore biased.

The point is that the rules of science are set by the accepted view of science, and what counts as biased depends, therefore, on whether one adheres to the value-free view or the value-directed view of science. This is true even if their defenders, generally speaking, could agree that science is "biased" *if something besides the appropriate evidence and standards of evaluation is allowed to influence theory validation in science.* That is to say, the talk of "bias" signifies that something has gone wrong in this scientific process. But whereas any use of evidence or standards that is ideological in character inevitably biases research according to the value-free view, this will not always be the case according to the value-directed view since it is appropriate that scientific theories are evaluated at least partially in terms of their conformity to particular moral, ideological, or religious ideals. Hence what is to be considered as biased in the evaluation process depends on one's view of science.

The concept of bias is often used as a charge against the acceptance of various theories within scientific practice by those who argue for a value-directed view. One strategy is to show that since bias can be found everywhere in science, we need to reject the conception of a value-free science. But if it is used as a charge, then we must be clear about what would count and what would not count as bias according to this new conception of science.

For instance, Longino and some other feminists have argued that male bias can be found in the development and acceptance of the man-the-hunter hypothesis in anthropology.[24] In the 1960s Sherwood Washburn and others developed a hypothesis to explain how quadrupedal apes evolved into bipedal toolmakers with significantly larger brains. According to the man-the-hunter hypothesis, the development of tool-making among intelligent apes was due

24. Longino, *Science as Social Knowledge*, pp. 106-107, 129-130.

to "man-the-hunter," who needed lethal weapons to slay the savage beasts of the African savannah. This theory gives the impression that men evolved by hunting while sedentary women tagged along gathering and giving birth. Men actively and aggressively drove evolution forward. But the plausibility and acceptance of this hypothesis by the scientific community is best explained in terms of its dependence on a particular evaluation of the proper roles of male and female in society.

Grant that it is true that the man-the-hunter hypothesis was at least partially accepted because of male bias in the sense that certain masculinist values and beliefs influenced the validation of this hypothesis, would it be correct to talk about bias here if one accepts the value-directed view or, more narrowly, the idea of non-impartiality? Recall that the talk of "bias" signifies that something has gone wrong in the scientific process. What has gone wrong in this case?

One possibility is that the scientists who accepted this hypothesis did not explicitly state that a particular moral, ideological, or religious ideal, that is, masculinism, was among the grounds for accepting it. The secrecy was the mistake; if they had acknowledged the ideological influence, their theory choice would have been acceptable, even if non-impartial. But suppose they simply were unaware of this ideological influence on their work and therefore could not be blamed for failing to see it. Would we still have an instance of bias? Yes, because this particular theory choice still fails to satisfy the normative ideal, the view of science, which should regulate actual scientific practice.

Another possibility would be to maintain that the validation process was biased because the *wrong kind* of ideology or values directed the theory choice. Scientific hypotheses or theories should be governed by progressive, feminist values and not by conservative, masculinist values. But notice that then the pluralist version of the value-directed view is rejected and a monist value-directed view is presupposed, because the pluralist version allows masculinist values and not merely feminist values to influence the validation process (given, of course, that the other non-ideological criteria are satisfied).

A third possibility would be that the charge of bias amounts to a claim that ideological elements or interests were allowed *too much* of a role in the validation of the hypothesis. Here we face a crucial vagueness in the accounts of a non-impartial science: to what extent should moral values, ideology, or religion be allowed to shape science in the context of justification? Suppose that the advocates of the man-the-hunter hypothesis accept it for purely nonscientific, ideological reasons, without a shred of empirical evidence that could be cited in its favor; then, I think, we have a clear case of bias even according to this new conception of science. Suppose, on the other hand, that there actually is some evidence that supports the man-the-hunter hypothesis, but because of ideological reasons (masculinist values and ideas) these scientists presented it as established truth or at least as the best warranted hypothesis. If this were the case, would we still have an instance of bias?

Longino gives us some guidance here. In her discussion of the man-the-hunter hypothesis and its rival the woman-the-gatherer hypothesis (that is, the theory that tool-making developed among intelligent apes because of "woman-the-gatherer," who needed tools to scrounge and forage for scarce vegetable food), she is anxious to emphasize that the *evidence is indecisive* since the data do not conclusively support any of these theories.[25] Thus, Longino seems to assume that under these circumstances scientists with feminist values and beliefs are justified in maintaining that the woman-the-gatherer hypothesis is to be preferred. This indicates that the influence of ideology in the validation of theories ought to be accepted *only* in a situation in which the theories scientists have to decide among are fairly equally supported by the evidence. In such a situation we ought to let the scientific theories' ideological or political virtues be the determining factor. However, such an interpretation seems to allow that there are also *other* kinds of theory validation situations, situations in which ideological considerations will not be the determining factor because the evidence for a theory — no matter its ideological virtues — is strong or even overwhelming in comparison to any rival theory. But if this is Longino's position, she could not really claim that the idea of a value-free science is not just empty but pernicious, since these other kinds of situations are good examples of ideologically *non*-determined theory choices, that is, of impartial science. In any case, the defenders of a value-directed view that includes the notion of non-impartiality have on this point a lot more work to do in order to develop a plausible alternative to the impartiality element of the value-free view.

Suppose that the evidence available to anthropologists in the 1960s actually pointed in the direction of the man-the-hunter hypothesis, but new data were soon to be discovered that would undermine the hypothesis, would we still have an instance of bias here? The soccer analogy suggests that the answer is no. Recall that in the story I gave I made one big mistake as referee. Near the end of the game the other team should have had a penalty kick that I failed to see. I said that the people who favored the other team still did not think that I was biased. The reason I gave was that they were aware of the fact that the game at that point moved very quickly from one side of the field to the other, and for that reason I was too far away from the ball to be able to see what happened. So I made an error, but nevertheless I was not biased because the most

---

25. Longino, *Science as Social Knowledge*, pp. 109-111.

reasonable explanation of my behavior was not that I really wanted (consciously or unconsciously) my team to win and therefore unfairly favored them, but something else, my lack of speed and my failure to be in the right place at the right time. This suggests that we need to distinguish between scientific validation that is biased, unbiased, and simply mistaken:

> ▸ Scientific validation is *biased* if something besides the appropriate evidence and standards of evaluation is allowed to influence or determine which theory among competing theories scientists consider to be the best warranted one.

If this "something" is moral values, ideology, or religion, according to the value-free view, or too much of moral values, ideology, or religion, according to the value-directed view, we can talk about "ideological bias," and it is this form of bias that has been our main concern here.

> ▸ Scientific validation is *unbiased* if only the appropriate evidence and standards of evaluation are allowed to influence or determine which theory among competing theories scientists consider to be the best warranted one.

> ▸ Scientific validation is *mistaken* or *wrong* if the theory scientists consider to be the best warranted one among competing theories is false or could be shown not to be the best warranted theory.

Given these definitions, at least two things follow. First, a biased theory could still be true. If a theory or a refereeing decision is correctly classified as biased, which entails that something has gone wrong, this does not, however, entail that the theory or the decision is necessarily false or mistaken. At best it gives us a *prima facie* reason to think that it is false or mistaken. For instance, suppose that the only reason why a scientist who is a Christian proposes a theory about human nature is that it is what should be true if Christianity is true. Thus the theory is biased according to both the value-free view and the value-directed view of science. But it is still possible that scientific evidence might in the end be found that shows that the theory is true or the best-supported one. Or let us go back to the referee situation. Suppose that in the game I gave my son's team a free kick, not because I really saw a violation of the rules of the game in a confrontation between two players, but merely because I favored my son's team. However, the truth was that the player of the other team actually committed a foul. Although I did not see it from my an-

65

gle, the player of the other team actually held on to my son's shirt, which is not allowed in soccer. I was biased, but due to happy circumstances I made the right refereeing decision.

Second, scientists could be biased when validating theories only if they adhere (consciously or unconsciously) to a partisan science, because it follows logically that if you are neutral, you could not be biased but only mistaken or in error. If you are not merely in error but also biased in your theory choice, then you are by definition not neutral. Let us go back once again to the soccer analogy to see this. A referee who is neutral — that is to say, not a supporter of either team — could not make biased decisions because bias presupposes partisanship, which is not to deny, of course, that he or she could make wrong or mistaken decisions. As soon as you maintain that the referee is making biased decisions, then you have also said that you do not think that he or she is neutral.

The idea of a non-impartial science is, of course, quite radical, and many scholars who reject the value-free view would probably be reluctant to include it in their alternative, normative conception of science. There might be good reason for this reluctance. Although it is true that studies of actual scientific practice by historians, philosophers, sociologists, and others have revealed many cases in which a scientific consensus on a particular theory was in fact due as much to shared ideological or religious values and beliefs as to empirical evidence, I think Ronald Giere makes an important point when he writes:

> What the history of science (since the Scientific Revolution) does not reveal is many cases in which participants *explicitly* argued for a hypothesis because of its ideological desirability. And those who have, as following publication of Darwin's *Origin*, tended to be outside the scientific community. Evaluation of scientific hypotheses is *supposed* to be strongly based on empirical data, even if in practice this is not always the case. If the data fail to agree more with one hypothesis than another, one is *supposed* simply to withhold judgment, even though there is often in fact a rush to judgment that goes beyond the data. Moreover, discovery of ideological bias in the evaluation of scientific hypotheses is usually taken as a basis for criticism within the scientific community.[26]

---

26. Ronald N. Giere, "A New Program for Philosophy of Science?" *Philosophy of Science* 70 (2003): 20.

Responsible Science

Today, as I have already highlighted, we face a new situation in which the demarcation between traditional knowledge institutions, such as universities, and research institutions has eroded. Scientific knowledge production or theory construction is now generated to a large extent in the context of application. In the new research field of the life sciences, especially in biotechnology, the separation of university and industrial research has broken down almost completely. In light of these changes, it seems difficult to uphold the idea of the non-responsibility of science, in the sense that scientists or the institutions of science have no special accountability for the applications of science. Instead we need, according to defenders of the value-directed view, to develop a *responsible* science in which scientists in their professional role take responsibility for how their results are used in society, by the state, companies, political parties, and religious/antireligious organizations. According to this conception of science, it is part of the scientists' task to consider the question of the possible and proper use of the results of scientific research. Science should in this sense be value-directed and not value-free.

It seems reasonable to assume that good scientists should not begin to carry out a research project without first trying to consider, to the best of their knowledge, certain basic questions about the expected results of the project. How can these results be used? Who will use them? And what is their purpose? Should it be obvious that these applications violate widely accepted ethical principles, then scientists should refuse to carry out the research without adequate modifications. One reason why scientists might have a responsibility as scientists is that they are often in a better position than other people to predict the consequences of scientific research programs. For instance, the physicist Leo Szilard realized as early as 1933 that the enormous energy resulting from a nuclear chain reaction could eventually become a powerful weapon and suggested to other physicists that they should stop publishing their results.[27] Another example would be the self-imposed moratorium on recombinant DNA research, decided upon by prominent molecular biologists at the Asilomar conference in 1975. On this issue we can perhaps today see an emerging consensus.

---

27. See Leslie Stevenson and Henry Byerly, *The Many Faces of Science* (Boulder: Westview Press, 1995), p. 177.

Normative Science

Central to the question of whether science should be value-free is the distinction between facts and values. A cluster of issues in the debate are related to this fundamental and difficult philosophical question, including the following:

- Should values, ideology, or religion have no place at all in science?
- Should values, ideology, or religion be the subject of scientific inquiry?
- Should science strive to tell us which values, ideology, or religion we should cultivate?
- Should the language of science be purely descriptive or factual?
- Should the enterprise of science presuppose the truth or plausibility of certain values (like health, democracy, and justice)?
- Should scientists avoid drawing normative conclusions?

There is space here to focus on merely the first three of these questions. The answer to the first one is No, even if one accepts the value-free view (as I have defined it in this essay). For instance, values, ideology, or religion could be important in the evaluation of the way to carry out research and the methods and means that are acceptable. Nor, in answer to the second question, do I think that the value-free view entails that values, ideology, or religion could not or should not be the subject of scientific inquiry. There is nothing in principle problematic about biologists, for instance, inquiring about the biological basis of morality and religion, and of course the social sciences have a number of important things to say about the place of values, ideologies, and religions in human society.

But if so, should science not go one step further and also try to determine the values, ideology, or religion that we should cultivate (question three)? According to the value-free view, science could and should discover facts (even facts about values, ideology, and religion) but could not and should not provide us with values, an ideology, or a religion. The mandate of science is to provide us with facts about the world. However, since one cannot deduce values from facts (that is to commit the naturalistic fallacy), one cannot in scientific reasoning obtain normative conclusions from descriptive premises. It follows that science can provide us with factual information, but cannot tell us what our ethical obligations are, what policies we should adopt, or what religion or ideology we should commit ourselves to.

This interpretation of the non-normative element of the value-free view should not, however, be confused with another possible interpretation, namely the idea that science is consistent with all value systems, ideologies, or religions. In this view, science could not in any way undermine or support value systems, ideologies, or religions; therefore it is non-normative. Understood in this way we have good reasons, I think, to reject the ideal of the non-normativity of science. To see this, consider what Kamin, Lewontin, and Rose write about certain biological theories of human nature:

> But [biological determinism or biologism] is more than mere explanation: It is politics. For if human social organizations, including the inequalities of status, wealth, and power, are a direct consequence of our biologies, then, except for some gigantic program of genetic engineering, no practice can make a significant alteration of social structure or of the position of individuals or groups within it. What we are is natural and therefore fixed. We may struggle, pass laws, even make revolutions, but we do so in vain. The natural differences between individuals and among groups played out against the background of biological universals of human behavior will, in the end, defeat our uninformed efforts to reconstitute society.[28]

If existing inequalities between the sexes or among social classes or races were biologically unalterable, then this would undercut criticism of these inequalities. So if these theories are true, then it follows that a particular set of ideological ideas are undermined, ideas that we can find, for instance, in socialism and feminism. How could this be, and is this not a successful refutation of the naturalistic fallacy and an argument that shows, as Kamin, Lewontin, and Rose believe, that these biological theories are not merely explanations but politics?

From facts one can infer certain conclusions about what is possible and impossible (or realistic and unrealistic); value systems, ideologies, and religions have presuppositions about what is possible and impossible, and therefore science is not consistent with all value systems, ideologies, and religions. Science is what I have called value relevant or ideologically relevant. But the case of biological determinism does not refute the naturalistic fallacy because the argument presupposes the acceptance of a normative premise and not merely factual premises. The reason why it seems so convincing (*if* the factual premise is true) is that it is a norm most people simply take for granted, namely the norm that *ought implies can*: if a person ought to do a certain action, then it must be possible for that person to perform this action. So if our biology makes it impossible to treat other people in a fair way, then we cannot blame ourselves for this. (In a similar way, I cannot be blamed for not jump-

---

28. Rose, Lewontin, and Kamin, *Not in Our Genes*, pp. 18-19.

ing into the water and trying to save a drowning person if I cannot swim myself.) Thus, if we accept the norm that ought implies can, then scientific results can entail that certain value systems, ideologies, or religions are unacceptable. But this does not mean that biological determinism becomes politics simply because — if true and if the ought-implies-can principle is accepted — it has these political consequences. It becomes politics or, more exactly, normative science, when scholars who are engaged in developing and defending these ideas are driven (consciously or unconsciously) by political motives that aim to show by scientific means that what many of us call "inequalities" are merely natural and therefore ought to be accepted.

Normative science is thus a science that aims to provide us not merely with factual information about the world but also with the appropriate values, ideology, or religion. Science should attempt to offer support or refutation of a particular political vision, ideology, or religion. The attempt to prove or disprove a certain ideology or religion is a proper part of the scientific agenda. It is appropriate that scientists in their professional role maintain that science proves or disproves atheism, Christianity, Islam, feminism, or any other religion or ideology.

Understood in this way, there is a crucial difference between partisan science and normative science, even if that difference might be difficult to uphold in practice. Partisan science is science pursued *on the assumption* that a particular moral vision, ideology, or religion is correct. But I do not think that Plantinga, for instance, believes that part of the mission of science is to prove or demonstrate the truth of Christianity. The truth of Christianity is for him an important question, but one that science is unable to answer. If you think it can, you have completely misunderstood what Christianity is all about. He therefore presumably rejects a normative science in this sense. This is probably also the way we should understand scientific research for sustainable development. Research for sustainable development, in contrast to the environmental sciences in general, should proceed on the basis of this political vision. But the justification of sustainable development is understood to be political and not scientific; it is a product of political argument and negotiation and not of scientific theory validation.

Longino and Harding, on the other hand, seem to understand feminist science as a normative enterprise in some sense. If you are engaged in feminist science, then you try to use science to undermine masculinist values and beliefs and promote feminist values and beliefs. But the idea is not so much that science can directly give us values, but that science should be used to develop theories (1) that undermine the factual claims that the beliefs and values of masculinism or androcentric ideology presuppose and (2) that vindicate the factual claims that the beliefs and values of feminism presuppose.

Edward O. Wilson believes in a normative science in a more direct way. He thinks that biology could and should in the near future justify ethical norms and beliefs and provide us with a new, scientific ethic. Wilson writes, "science may soon be in a position to investigate the very origin and meaning of human values from which all ethical pronouncements and much political practice flow."[29] But not only that, he also tells us that through neurophysiologic and phylogenetic reconstructions of the mind, "a biology of ethics [will be fashioned], which will make possible the selection of a more deeply understood and enduring code of moral values."[30]

Of course, much more work than I have been able to provide in this essay needs to be undertaken to develop and critically evaluate an alternative to the value-free view of science. Although we seem to need such a new view of science, in light of the recent developments of science we must pay attention to the fact that the value-free view contains a number of different ideas, some more plausible than others. The same is true in respect to what I have called the value-directed view. The problem is that it is not clear which of these ideas or elements people reject when they say that they reject the value-free view of science nor exactly what the content is of the new view that should replace the old one.

Moreover, even if the key elements I have identified:

- autonomous or non-autonomous,
- neutral or partisan,
- impartial or non-impartial,
- non-responsible or responsible,
- non-normative or normative,

could be related and to some extent support each other, these elements are not closed under entailment; in other words, it is not the case that if we accept one we have to accept all or if we reject one we have to reject all. It is not the case, for instance, that if we maintain that science should be partisan we also have to maintain that science should be non-impartial and normative. What we need, therefore, is a constructive and conceptually unambiguous discus-

29. Edward O. Wilson, *On Human Nature* (Cambridge, MA: Harvard University Press, 1978), p. 5.
30. Wilson, *On Human Nature*, p. 96. He has more recently developed these ideas further in Edward O. Wilson, "The Biological Basis of Morality," *The Atlantic Monthly* (April 1998). For a criticism of this view, see, for instance, Mikael Stenmark, *Scientism: Science, Ethics and Religion* (Aldershot: Ashgate, 2001), chap. 4.

sion of exactly what elements should be contained in a plausible contemporary view of science (that is, a standpoint about how science should be pursued and related to the surrounding society). The outcome of such discussion will provide an important answer to the question of the role human values should play in the practice of science in a postmodern world.

5 Van Huyssteen in Context: A Comparison with Philip Hefner and Karl Peters

Jerome A. Stone

This essay attempts to give clarity to the work of Professor Van Huyssteen by a comparison of his work with two other writers in the science and religion field who also exemplify the "integrationist" approach of Ian Barbour's fourfold typology and who also focus on evolutionary biology, namely Philip Hefner and Karl Peters. The comparison will involve two parts: first, a discussion of the methods of the encounter of science and theology; and second, the theological content, how science, especially evolutionary biology, enriches theology.

These writers are immensely rich in their use of recent scientific literature. The depiction of major themes in their work in what follows should not be taken as a detailed exposition of their actual practice of dialogue with the sciences.

Methods of the Science-Theology Encounter

Hefner

The central thesis of Hefner's *The Human Factor* is his created co-creator theory: humans are the "created co-creators whose purpose is to be the agency . . . to birth the future that is most wholesome for the nature that has birthed us. . . . Exercising this agency is . . . God's will for humans."[1] My analysis of his

---

1. Philip Hefner, *The Human Factor: Evolution, Culture, and Religion* (Minneapolis: Fortress Press, 1993), p. 27. Part of this material on Hefner is adapted from my article "Philip Hefner and the Modernist/Postmodernist Divide," *Zygon: Journal of Religion and Science* 39, no. 4 (December 2004): 755-772.

method in science and religion has two theses: (1) engagement with the sciences is essential for doing theology, and (2) the pattern for this is the formation of theological statements as fruitful and falsifiable tentative hypotheses, testing them by what he calls a positive and a negative heuristics.

First, theology is not on track nor God rightly obeyed unless we study the processes of nature. Theology must "insist that science and religion are both essential to the whole truth of what is and what ought to be. . . . Encounter with God takes place within the processes of nature."[2] The sciences, especially genetics and evolutionary biology, "open up new vistas for understanding human existence."[3] It is not that "science determines what may or may not be believed religiously."[4] Instead the question is whether a religious symbol or doctrinal formulation renders human experience, including science, adequately.

Second, following the philosopher of science Imre Lakatos, Hefner considers that a good theory, and that includes theological theories, must be *fruitful* for stimulating further reflection and interpreting new data and must also be *falsifiable* in principle. However, "theological statements do not aim at empirical content with the same degree of precision that scientific statements do, nor do they prize prediction in the way that scientific discourse does."[5] Nevertheless, it is "critical that the import of any faith proposal be clear so that its significance can be assessed even if it is not easily tested."[6]

A theory, theological or scientific, cannot be demonstrated conclusively. "It is to be considered to be viable or useful as long as the attempts to falsify it (or test it) are productive for our understanding." We check to see if it has explanatory power, that is, "gives us comprehension of a large body of data that otherwise would be raw and uninterpreted."[7] Further, the falsification need not involve conclusive refutation, but can involve the accumulation of counter-evidence to the point of straining credulity.

Following Lakatos, Hefner's research program involves two types of methodological proposals: a "positive heuristic" which suggests new paths to pursue and a "negative heuristic" which suggests potential falsifiers or paths of inquiry to avoid.[8]

---

2. Philip Hefner, "Is/Ought: A Risky Relationship between Theology and Science," from *The Sciences and Theology in the Twentieth Century*, ed. A. R. Peacocke (Notre Dame, IN: University of Notre Dame Press, 1981), pp. 58-78, 45.

3. Hefner, *The Human Factor*, p. 16.
4. Hefner, *The Human Factor*, p. 141.
5. Hefner, *The Human Factor*, p. 259.
6. Hefner, *The Human Factor*, p. 15.
7. Hefner, *The Human Factor*, p. 18.
8. Hefner, *The Human Factor*, p. 268.

The positive heuristic of the created co-creator theory involves new interpretations of human experience in general and of specific Christian teachings. Some of the new interpretations of human experience include: (1) viewing religion as a transmitting agency for culture analogous to genetic information, religion as promoting altruism beyond the kinship group, and the possibility of cooperation replacing hostility and war, (2) interpreting technological civilization as stretching the evolutionary process, (3) tracing the origins of freedom in evolutionary processes, (4) seeing natural selection as the instrument producing freedom and culture, and (5) exploring the purpose of humans as the evolved co-creators.

The negative heuristic includes: (1) the empirically falsifiable components of Hefner's theories, such as ideas concerning evolution and the theological reformulations which prove to be discontinuous with the tradition, (2) positions forbidden by the co-creator theory, such as separating culture or technology from nature, denying freedom, or deemphasizing either nature or God, and (3) removing the problems of evil and the existence of God from the threat of falsification by showing that they are not susceptible of demonstration.

As I read him, for Hefner testability is not about predictive power, as is often the case in the sciences, but rather the drawing of specific, more concrete, implications subject to public scrutiny. This scrutiny can determine the adequacy of these implications in understanding an area of life. Testing can even be done by reference to a body of relevant scientific literature.[9]

The details of Hefner's practice of falsification involve his Lakatosian distinction between core and auxiliary hypotheses, the auxiliary being subject to falsification because more concrete and specific. The hard core of his position, not subject to falsification, is the concept of humans as God's created co-creators.[10] The protective auxiliary hypotheses include the ideas that: (1) humans are the intersection of two information streams, genetic and cultural, (2) technological civilization is that phase of evolution in which all life is dependent upon human decisions, (3) evolution prior to humans is the instrumentality for fashioning freedom and created co-creators, (4) freedom is nature's way of stretching itself toward newness, and (5) these first four ideas are incorporated within the Christian anthropology of sin and redemption, thus extending the interpretive significance of theology beyond the Christian community.

---

9. Hefner, *The Human Factor*, pp. 41, 42, 45, 48.
10. Hefner, *The Human Factor*, pp. 32, 39, 269-270.

Peters

Generally speaking, for Peters scientific investigations use rigorous, empirically based methods to achieve detailed conclusions open to public criticism, while religious traditions supply wisdom for living.[11] On this view, there is no "warfare between science and religion." Rather, there is a differentiation of function. Scientific inquiry supplies the basic theoretical information about our world and ourselves. The religious traditions, if we sift through them carefully, can supply the wisdom and ritual by which to live — emotional and moral orientation and motivation. This differentiation of function would seem to indicate a real separation between science and religion, a continuation of the fact-value dichotomy. However, since our cultural life is a continual process of innovation and selection, religious practice and theory should be continually winnowed by our scientific understanding. Hence science provides a critical function.

But Peters is yet more subtle. In addition to the differentiation of function in terms of theoretical information and tradition of wisdom, Peters uses the image of two maps to describe the science-religion dialogue. Scientific and religious views are like two maps of the same area, like a street and a subway map. These maps, though different, coincide in certain features, such as subway stations. In particular, two aspects of the scientific map are fluctuation and the selection of some variations for survival. The traditional biblical term for fluctuation is "Spirit," and the term for selection is "Word" or "Logos." Thus the pairs "variation and selection" and "Spirit and Logos" are like different names for the same subway stops which appear on both the scientific and the religious maps.

We need such an image as that of maps with intersecting loci to indicate that the wisdom which the religious traditions supply concerns our orientation to the world which the sciences investigate.

Van Huyssteen

Until his 2004 Gifford lectures, Van Huyssteen's published work in English centered on methodological issues. His first book translated into English, *The*

---

11. Karl E. Peters, *Dancing with the Sacred: Evolution, Ecology, and God* (Harrisburg: Trinity Press International, 2002). Parts of this section are adapted from my article "Power and Goodness of the Object of the Religious Attitude," *American Journal of Theology and Philosophy* 25 (September 2004): 243.

Justification of Faith, developed a critical realism with a metaphorical theory of religious language and an affirmation of theology as provisional and fallible yet with the possibility of rationality, explanatory power, and progress in problem-solving success.[12] Explicit in this view was a rejection of prevailing dichotomies, either a naïve realism or a non-referential theory of language.

Then followed his masterful *The Shaping of Rationality*.[13] Here the notion of overlapping areas of discourse becomes crucial, areas with shared epistemic strategies. This makes even more sophisticated his notion that we can avoid a modernist nostalgia for one form of unified knowledge and the relativism of extreme postmodernism. This view sees rationality as many-sided, rooted in context, tradition, and interpreted experience, and to be judged by both theoretical and experiential adequacy. Rationality involves accountability, the ability to offer reasons for responsible choices. Rationality is not reducible to the rationality of the sciences. This offers both a comfort and a challenge to theology, the comfort that theology can be rational and the challenge that it should be rational by offering the best available reasons.

A key aspect of rationality is assessment. This is often a matter of judgment, not a procedure of following rules, as in the classical notion of rationality. Judgment need not be arbitrary, but can be rational. Epistemic perfection is not the only thing that counts. This is not relativity because our criteria for evaluation, while conditioned, are not completely determined by our contexts. Thus we can critique our communities and traditions even while standing within them. Truth and critique have a place in postfoundationalist rationality. They are not foundationally secured but are based on the interplay of personal judgment and communal feedback. Truth, objectivity, and progress are still viable concepts. We can take conclusions that are rationally acceptable as our best estimates of the truth. Objectivity does not mean being free from preconceptions but that the evidence for a belief is independent from the belief itself. Both theology and the sciences should have experiential accountability, although the nature of this accountability will overlap, again a difference without a cleavage. Explanations in religion and the sciences also are analogous, similar but different. Religious explanations are all-encompassing and personal, often arising from vague questions about the meaning of life. Scientific explanations reach a high degree of interpersonal agreement.

---

12. J. Wentzel van Huyssteen, *Theology and the Justification of Faith: Constructing Theories in Systematic Theology*, trans. H. F. Snijders (Grand Rapids: Eerdmans, 1989).

13. J. Wentzel van Huyssteen, *The Shaping of Rationality: Toward Interdisciplinarity in Theology and Science* (Grand Rapids: Eerdmans, 1997). Some of the material in this paragraph is adapted from my article "J. Wentzel van Huyssteen: Refiguring Rationality in the Postmodern Age," *Zygon: Journal of Religion and Science* 35 (June 2000): 415-426.

In his Gifford lectures, *Alone in the World?*, Van Huyssteen provides a concrete exemplification of this revised notion of rationality by studying the overlap between various theological and scientific attempts to explore a fairly narrow topic, the nature of the uniqueness of the human species.[14] He engages a number of scientists, sometimes spending several pages of exposition, noting areas of agreement and disagreement, and stopping to criticize when he feels they have stepped outside their area of competence in an unwarranted fashion.

The first chapter of *Alone in the World?* explicitly addresses methodological issues. The choice between a universal rationality and relativity is a false dichotomy. We are not prisoners of incommensurable belief systems and isolated disciplines. Our different discourses often intersect. The shared rational space reflects an authentic public realm in which all participants can discuss any claim that is rationally redeemable. Thus we can recover a public voice for theology without succumbing to "epistemological tribalism," scientism, or theological imperialism.

We should not talk about "theology and science" in a generic, abstract sense. There is no blueprint for doing theology and science. We should focus first on the merits of a concrete interdisciplinary problem in terms of a specific science and a specific theology. We need also to be clear as to the difference between these reasoning strategies. There are limits to interdisciplinarity, areas of disagreement in which these disciplines cannot be reduced to or derived from each other. Scientists will wish to back away from overzealous theologians who uncritically transport scientific facts into theology. Likewise theologians can critique reductionist explanations of religion by scientists.

Continuing his revised notion of rationality, van Huyssteen affirms that (1) science and theology are both embedded in traditions, (2) this means that interpreted experience shapes epistemic values, (3) we can discover patterns in our lives consonant with the canons of our religious traditions, and (4) rationality is a skill that binds up our interpreted experiences through rhetoric, articulation, and discernment.

Postmodern transversality replaces modernist universality and the premodern idea of tradition as a repository of truth. Transversality is a mathematical metaphor. A transverse line can cut across two or more geometric figures. It is thought of as in between the universality of an infinite line and the localness of a line segment. Metaphorically it refers to a specific conversa-

---

14. J. Wentzel van Huyssteen, *Alone in the World? Science and Theology on Human Uniqueness* (Grand Rapids: Eerdmans, 2006).

tion between disciplines, in between universal rationality and incommensurability. It is based on overlapping concerns, a reaction against methodological imperialism and isolated language games. This type of conversation proceeds not by universal nor *ad hoc* rules, but by intersubjective agreements reached through persuasive rhetoric and responsible judgments.

Van Huyssteen also develops a theory of tradition. Traditions are dynamic and open to criticism. We are embedded, but not trapped, in traditions. We should acknowledge, criticize, and reshape the traditions in which we stand. A fideist stance renounces the possibility of explaining why we choose our viewpoints. The fact that we lack clear objective criteria for judging the worth of competing traditions does not mean that we have an easy pluralism or radical relativism. We can communicate with those in other traditions and engage in collective assessment, even though we do not agree on everything. Thus theology can become an equal partner in a democratic, interdisciplinary conversation with the sciences. Interdisciplinary dialogue is possible because criteria can be shared across disciplines, even if only for a transversal moment. In these moments, giving reasons for our views is a cross-disciplinary obligation. The goal is a wide reflective equilibrium, a fragile communal understanding, with a toleration for dissensus, not a comfortable consensus. A warning: any convergence between theology and science should not be taken as proof of God's existence or purpose or of the truth of any religion.

The convergence of theological and scientific arguments on human nature is an argument for the plausibility of the comprehensive nature of religious and theological explanations. Furthermore, scientific notions of human uniqueness may ground theological notions in real life and protect theology from abstraction.

Substantive Issues

Hefner

Following his own directive that theology should be scientifically informed, Hefner reinterprets several Christian doctrines. His main point is that the ambience of God's will is extended to include both the evolutionary process and the realm of technology.[15] The concept of original sin points to the discrepancy between what our distant ancestors did on the basis of prepro-

---

15. Hefner, *The Human Factor*, pp. 274-276.

grammed genetic information and what we learn to do through culture. An unrelieved uncertainty characterizes all that issues from culture. The co-creating process becomes demonic all too often. Redemption lies in the fact that the artifacts of our co-creating are acceptable, because nothing is useless or unimportant in the work of God's evolutionary creation. Mutations and adaptations which appear to be failures are necessary for the process. "In the language of the cultus, this is expressed in the thought that our sacrifices are acceptable to the Lord, and they are united mystically with the sacrifice of Jesus Christ."[16] Finally, evil is necessarily a frequent byproduct in an evolutionary process.

Hefner pays particular attention to trans-kin altruism. "Humans face a distinctive evolutionary challenge. . . . [They] must live cooperatively in large communities of persons who are not kin relatives — that is, who are genetic competitors."[17] Hefner's approach is that the myths and rituals of religion carry cultural information packets for trans-kin altruism. Even though these information packages are blatantly underdetermined by the data and they can be subjected to reasonable processes of falsification only with difficulty and even though they appear to be falsified in the light of contemporary science, they continue to serve the survival and flourishing of human communities. We should, in fact, think of a mutual critique and possible reinforcement between the myths and rituals of religious information systems and scientific theories.[18] Part Four of Hefner's *The Human Factor* is an elaboration of this mutual critique.

Peters

One major place where Peters finds an intersection of the scientific and the religious maps is the notion of God as the process of variation and selection. Peters articulates a revisionary evolutionary naturalistic notion in which the creative cosmic mystery is nonpersonal. Specifically, what can be called serendipitous creativity is a two-part process: the occurrence of variations in cosmic, biological, and human history and the selection of some of these variations to continue. In short, God is the creative process that is made up of a set of interactions that create variations plus a set of interactions that preserves some of them. In an inversion of the traditional conflict between evolution

---

16. Hefner, *The Human Factor*, pp. 275-276.
17. Hefner, *The Human Factor*, p. 198.
18. Hefner, *The Human Factor*, p. 195.

and religion, God as the twofold process of variation and selection is, of course, an extrapolation of Darwin's idea of natural selection. For drawing the scientific map of this process Peters uses Ilya Prigone's work in nonequilibrium thermodynamics, which shows how random disturbances of existing systems lead to the formation of new structures. Astrophysicist Eric Chaisson suggests how this dual pattern of chance fluctuation and natural law can be applied to the origin of galaxies.

The cosmic and biological evolutions and social and individual life can be thought of in Daoist fashion as a dance or conversation where no one leads and there is no goal, but each mutually influences the others. The payoff is participation in the dance itself. Thus Peters uses his understanding of the world portrayed by science with a Daoist religious terminology to provide an alternative to the grand teleology that typically goes in scientific or monotheistic dress. Life is meaningful, but its meaning is not to be found in a grand cosmic evolutionary or redemptive process, but rather in local interactions within a cosmic play of interactions.

A second place where Peters finds a point of intersection between the maps of religion and science is human selfhood. Again, the religious map is partially redrawn through insights obtained from the scientific map. He thinks of human selves as webs of phenomenal, cultural, biological, and cosmic strands that stretch out into the past and the future. Our cultural, biological, and physical information streams constitute our "big selves," which stretch out into the future before and after our bodily existence. Here significance can attach to our selves beyond the limits of our bodily selves in terms of the heritage that we receive, modify, and pass on.

Peters sees an evolutionary basis for the conflict of human emotions. He starts with the adaptive advantage of certain emotions and behaviors, ideas from evolutionary psychologists, summarized by Robert Wright. These ideas are placed in the context of primatology by Franz de Waal and by Richard Wrangham and Dale Peterson. The model of the three-part brain developed by Paul MacLean and Victor Johnson is added. The internal dynamics of the model of human personality by the family therapist Richard C. Schwartz brings another perspective. Peters addresses the harmonizing of our emotional conflicts through the idea of "being in self" delineated by Schwartz, the concept of the "core self" developed in the brain research of Antonio Damasio, and the notion of finding our sacred center found in various religious traditions.[19]

Further orientation for living comes from the bioptic vision of science

---

19. Peters, *Dancing with the Sacred*, pp. 93-94, 97-99.

and religion. For example, environmental care will be motivated if we expand the altruism we naturally feel toward family and kin by a picture of evolution that points out the kinship of all living things in their DNA.

Van Huyssteen

If the methodological topic of the Gifford lectures is transversal rationality, the substantive topic is the uniqueness of *Homo sapiens.*

Van Huyssteen has studied, in great depth, a number of paleontologists, paleoanthropologists, evolutionary psychologists, and neuroscientists, focusing on the topic of human uniqueness. He holds up major areas of disagreement and listens carefully to areas of agreement. He is especially concerned to articulate convergences between different disciplines, noting that theories supported by data from multiple disciplines are likely to have greater scope.

He also expounds the views of a number of theologians, including, in addition to the most well known ones, G. C. Berkouwer, Edward Farley, Abraham Heschel, Mary Catherine Hilker, Robert Jenson, and LeRon Shults.

Van Huyssteen starts with a dialogue between paleontology and evolutionary epistemology. In these disciplines there is an increasing awareness of human moral responsibility for defining ourselves. As creatures of culture we determine whom we are going to include as part of "us." Conceptions of humanness have shifted over time, affecting how ancient we conceive ourselves to be and how diverse are the relatives that are to be included. The anti-Nazi reaction after World War II meant that early hominid diversity was accepted slowly, because of fears of excluding them from the Family of Man. However, since the 1970s the trend has been to argue that pre–*Homo sapiens* hominids are not as human as once thought, as well as to appreciate that it is not racist to think non-*sapiens* hominids were radically different from us.

In accordance with his view of tradition, Van Huyssteen treats Darwin's conception of human identity as the canonical core of the ongoing biological treatment of human evolution and the growth of human cognition. He finds five parts to this core: (1) the difference between human and other animals is immense, (2) but this difference is one of degree, not kind, (3) the development of language is crucial, (4) religious sensibility is not innate, although belief in gods may follow from other mental powers, and (5) it is moral sense that best defines our uniqueness, although it also evolved.

He finds that evolutionary epistemology challenges theology to take seriously the implication of the biological origins of human rationality and thus avoid an abstract *imago Dei.* On the other hand, theology challenges any reductionist epistemology. Evolutionary epistemology should treat the phylogenetic memories of our remote ancestors on imagination and religious awareness with respect. Evolutionary epistemology, freed from reductionism, can support the plausibility of religious belief as part of human cognitive capacity, but the theologian cannot go beyond a minimal transversal connection with evolutionary epistemology. It should not use the latter's "hypothetical realism" that the world produces the kind of animals who would want to explain it to argue for the existence of God. On the other hand, the public voice of theology is reinforced by the emergence of religious awareness.

After exploring the canonical core of the Darwinian tradition, he traces the tradition of the *imago Dei*. He studies the key biblical texts — Genesis 1:26-28; 3:22; Psalm 8; Hebrews 2:6-8; and 1 Corinthians 15:45 — in recent exegesis and then explores the history of the *imago Dei* tradition. He finds that the notions in this history have become increasingly abstract and baroque, removed from the biblical texts and engaging in metaphysical pyrotechnics. These abstractions need to be unmasked, aided by a rereading of the biblical texts and a transversal linkage to insights from the sciences.

Van Huyssteen conceives the image of God to be found in men and women who are embodied beings with morally ambivalent natures. He also wishes to revise the idea of "dominion" without exploitative anthropocentrism. In spite of our animal nature, we are designated to bring forward the image of God. Hence our solidarity with the animal world and the responsible care we are to give to nature. This care should be based not on hierarchy, but on the solidarity as embodied beings we have with nature and animals.

Paleoanthropology then adds its voice. First, it agrees with evolutionary epistemology that the first modern humans are distinct in their symbolic, cognitively fluid minds. Second, these minds are physically embodied. Third, some paleoanthropologists, like evolutionary anthropologists, link the emergence of consciousness and symbolic behavior to the emergence of religious awareness. This is an argument for the naturalness of religion, not for the truth of any one religion. This is strengthened, fourthly, by recent arguments for a shamanistic explanation for some prehistoric cave images. Finally, paleoanthropology and evolutionary epistemology agree that such unique characteristics of humans as consciousness, language, and symbolization are essentially related to religion.

The key fact of interest is the rather abrupt transition to the Upper Paleolithic culture about 40,000 to 30,000 years ago. We can conclude that symbolic behavior is the hallmark of this transition and that this behavior implies language. Van Huyssteen is especially concerned with the cave art of southwestern Europe. He grants that interpreting these images is difficult, but the fact of symbolization, unique to humans, is clear. This art is complex, and not all of it is open to religious interpretation. Even if we are not certain what Cro-Magnon artistic images represented, this art reflects a view that they held of their place in the world and a mythology that explained that place. Although we should be cautious, we can argue that Upper Paleolithic images could have functioned as links between the natural and supernatural worlds.

Van Huyssteen focuses on symbolization. For several scientists, human mental life includes biologically unprecedented ways of experiencing the world, from aesthetic to spiritual. The origins of these are intertwined with language, the most distinctive human trait.

When humans became self-aware, they attributed feelings to animals and things, had an urge to tell stories of origins, of good and evil, of how to influence these creatures with feelings, and of how to cope with death. The cave images were not merely expressions of contentment or an artistic sense, but the result of an effort to find meaning in the struggle to survive.

Concerning the shamanistic interpretation of certain cave images, it is worth noting that Van Huyssteen goes from a tentative premise, the plausibility of this interpretation, to a conclusion framed with certainty — the universality and naturalness of religious feeling. This interpretation could also be used just as well to show the illusory character of religion.

The neurotheologians, d'Aquili and Newberg, when the extravagance of their conclusions are muted, can also be used to support the idea of the naturalness of the religious imagination, especially the notions that the quests for causality and holism are essential parts of human cognition.

In opposition to Pascal Boyer, Van Huyssteen asserts that a theory about the emergence of religion does not answer the question of religious validity. Here is a point where the limits of interdisciplinary conversation are reached and where theology can return within its disciplinary boundaries.

Arguments from evolutionary epistemology, paleoanthropology, neuroscience, and evolutionary psychology support the emergence of the symbolic human mind, the naturalness of religious awareness, and the importance of language in these processes. Theologians must recognize that our ability to respond to ultimate questions in worship is embedded in our capacity for symbolic imaginative behavior. Moral awareness, the depths of depravity, and the sense for transcendence all depend on the symbolic ability of humans to code the non-visible through abstract thought.

In conclusion, Van Huyssteen repeats that the search for human uniqueness should not obscure our continuity with animals and should be shaped in terms of our specificity, not our superiority. Our ability to respond to ultimate questions in worship is embodied in the symbolic nature of our species. We can revision the *imago Dei* as emerging from nature, acknowledging our ties with our sister species as we rethink our differences from them.

Conclusion

Methodologically for Hefner, since encounter with God takes place within the processes of nature, theology must study the sciences. The pattern for this is the formation of theological statements as fruitful and falsifiable tentative hypotheses, testing them by what he calls a positive and a negative heuristics. The positive heuristics involves new interpretations of human experience and of specific Christian doctrines. The negative heuristic includes certain ideas which his theory rejects, such as denying human freedom or attempting to demonstrate the existence of God.

The basic methodological stance of Peters is that science and religion have complementary functions. Scientific inquiry supplies basic theoretical information while the religious traditions, if winnowed by scientific understanding, can supply the raw material of wisdom by which to live. In addition, science and religion are like two maps referring to different aspects of the same area yet with discernible points of contact between them.

For Van Huyssteen we need not choose between a premodern tradition as a deposit of truths, a modernist universal rationality, and a postmodern relativity. Instead, there can be points of intersection between different discourses, overlapping areas with shared rational concerns, leading to a transversal rationality. Rather than speaking of science and theology in the abstract, we can isolate concrete interdisciplinary problems in terms of a specific science and a specific theology. At these particular points we can explore areas of agreement and of disagreement. Science and theology are both embedded in changing traditions that should be acknowledged, criticized, and reshaped.

On substantive issues, Hefner uses evolutionary biology to develop his theory of "the created co-creator." Following this he reinterprets several Christian doctrines so as to extend the ambience of God's will to include both the evolutionary process and the realm of technology. In addition, the myths and rituals of religion continue to serve the survival and flourishing of human communities by carrying cultural information packets for trans-kin altruism.

Peters uses the sciences, especially non-equilibrium dynamics, to rethink conceptions of God, selfhood, and the meaning of life. God is an impersonal creative process of variation and selection. The human self is a web of phenomenal, cosmic, biological, and cultural strands, the latter three stretching far into the past and future, forming our "larger selves" and giving significance to our smaller phenomenal selves. Life is seen as a dance or conversation of mutual influence whose meaning is in the dance or conversation itself.

Van Huyssteen finds that the sciences challenge us to rethink the *imago Dei* as involving physical, sexual beings with morally ambivalent natures. Our solidarity with the animal world and the responsible care we are to give to nature cause us to remove the exploitative anthropocentrism from the concept of "dominion." The search for human uniqueness should not obscure our continuity with animals and should be shaped in terms of our specificity, not our superiority. Moral awareness, the depths of depravity, and our ability to respond to ultimate questions in worship are embedded in our capacity for symbolic imaginative behavior. The sciences point to the naturalness of religious awareness, although this does not prove the existence of God or the truth of any one religion.

These writers demonstrate an appreciative yet critical grasp of a large body of scientific literature. They show that it is possible and important to be conversant with the methods, controversies, and areas of consensus in relevant areas of scientific research. All three accept the scientific consensus on the broad outlines of cosmic, biological, and human evolution.

Of the three, Peters is the most thoroughgoing in his revisions of the Western religious tradition and most willing to draw on non-Western traditions. Van Huyssteen is the most focused in his circumscription of a specific area of interest. Hefner is most willing to draw out wide-ranging implications of a scientifically informed Christian theology. If one test of a theory is its fruitfulness for further research and discussion, each of these three thinkers is eminently successful.

6 Religion and the Social Sciences: Reflections on the Human Quest for Meaning

Philip Clayton

J. Wentzel van Huyssteen's rich research program seeks to specify the nature of theology, so that theologians can continue to make significant contributions to contemporary thought and practice. This research program is characterized above all by its focus on moderation and mediation. Van Huyssteen wishes to avoid both an overly objectivized theology and an overly subjectivized theology, theologies that claim too much for themselves and those claiming too little, theologies that insist on their literal truth and those that eschew all truth claims whatsoever. Other scholars have written on the strengths and weaknesses of this research program as a whole, so that task will not be undertaken here.

I concentrate instead on a particular dimension of van Huyssteen's work that I admire: his continuing ability to recognize the areas where theology faces its most serious challenges today. Already in *Theology and the Justification of Faith* van Huyssteen perceived how difficult it is to move from "prescientific language" to the vocabulary of systematic theology: "In some way or other the metaphoric language of our religious experience must be transformed for maximal conceptual clarity." The problem arises because "believers (like professing theologians) draw on the basic commitment of their religious convictions" when they do theology. But "spontaneous religious experience" is radically distinct from abstract, conceptual theological language.[1] Van Huyssteen realized that serious problems have arisen concerning the meaningfulness of religious experiences. Consequently, theologians must somehow provide an account of the ways that meaning arises in and through religious language — if it does at all.

---

1. J. Wentzel van Huyssteen, *Theology and the Justification of Faith: Constructing Theories in Systematic Theology* (Grand Rapids: Eerdmans, 1989), p. 127.

Van Huyssteen's *Theology and the Justification of Faith* made essential reference to the "subjective religious commitment" of believers and theologians. He realized that adding this feature required his program to include "the very specific way people experience their faith" and to make these experiences "meaningful in content too."[2] Van Huyssteen formulated this requirement in the strongest possible terms: "The personal commitment of systematic theologians *ultimately governs their formulation of statements about God.*"[3]

In *Duet or Duel?* van Huyssteen embraced the so-called postmodern shift, thereby increasing the emphasis on the subjective. Theology "in a postmodern world," as he repeatedly insisted, is no longer subject to the dichotomy between scientific rationality and religious faith, which is "a privatized form of subjective experience and opinion."[4] In the same year, and perhaps reflecting the same set of influences, he published an influential essay on postfoundationalism in theology and science, in which he emphasized "the often noncognitive functions of religious models in evoking attitudes and encouraging personal transformation."[5] In the context of discussing the theory on the nature of rational agency that Steven Knapp and I have developed, van Huyssteen emphasized that "the personal voice of the individual rational agent [must] not [be] silenced in this ongoing process of collective assessment."[6]

As a result of the emphases of his research program in theology, van Huyssteen has paid close attention to the major role that the social sciences must play in influencing the theological project. He is keenly aware of the variety of functions that religious beliefs serve in the lives of believers. In *Essays in Postfoundationalist Theology* he notes that religious beliefs "describe the rights and practices of communities," and they "express in the language of faith psychological and sociological needs."[7] He adds that "religious beliefs reflect a general sense of meaningfulness on the part of the believer, a meaningfulness that extends from an existential level to the level of particular theories and dogmas."[8] The ensuing discussion offers an evocative descrip-

---

2. Van Huyssteen, *Theology and the Justification of Faith*, p. 130.

3. Van Huyssteen, *Theology and the Justification of Faith*, p. 132, italics added.

4. Van Huyssteen, *Duet or Duel? Theology and Science in a Postmodern World* (Harrisburg, PA: Trinity Press International, 1998), p. 10; cf. pp. 2, 96, 101, 120.

5. Van Huyssteen, "Postfoundationalism in Theology and Science: Beyond Conflict and Consonance," in *Rethinking Theology and Science: Six Models for the Current Dialogue*, ed. Niels H. Gregersen and J. Wentzel van Huyssteen (Grand Rapids: Eerdmans, 1998), p. 42.

6. Van Huyssteen, "Postfoundationalism in Theology and Science," p. 29; cf. Philip Clayton and Steven Knapp, "Ethics and Rationality," *American Philosophical Quarterly* 30 (1993): 151-161.

7. See van Huyssteen, *Essays in Postfoundationalist Theology* (Grand Rapids: Eerdmans, 1997), p. 231.

8. Van Huyssteen, *Essays in Postfoundationalist Theology*, p. 231, quoting Clayton, *Explana-*

tion of the way in which religious beliefs "often arise from vague and elusive questions concerning the meaning of life" and how they attempt to "provide ultimate meaning in life," offering "a context of security for the believer."[9] Van Huyssteen is certainly right to insist that, on one level, "the explanatory task in the social sciences is closer to explanations in theology than to explanations in the natural sciences."[10]

Indeed, van Huyssteen has worked outward from these crucial insights in the effort to construct a systematic postfoundationalist theory of theology. This theory rests crucially on the relationship between rationality and what he calls "interpreted experience." As he insists in one crucial passage, "we relate to our world epistemically only through the mediation of interpreted experience, and in this sense it may be said that theology and the sciences offer alternative interpretations of our experience."[11] Building from this quest for a meaningful interpretation of individual experience, he has begun to formulate an overarching research program in theology in a detailed and sophisticated manner. He writes:

> For Clayton and Knapp the notion of an individual's self-conception provides the indispensable starting point for an account of ethics. I want to claim the same for our reflection on human rationality: the rational agent's self-conception and self-awareness is not only intrinsically connected to rationality, it is indeed an indispensable starting point for any account of the values that shape human rationality.[12]

For obvious reasons, I endorse and strongly support the starting point that van Huyssteen has selected for his program, as well as many of the conclusions to which it leads him.

Rather than limiting this paper to an exposition of van Huyssteen's own views, however, I would like to explore the implications of this starting point in somewhat more detail. What happens if we look more closely at the ongoing quest of individual persons to interpret their experience in a meaningful manner? In what ways does the quest entail developing broader metaphysical

---

tion from Physics to Theology: An Essay in Rationality and Religion (New Haven: Yale University Press, 1989), pp. 1f.

9. Van Huyssteen, *Essays in Postfoundationalist Theology*, p. 231.

10. Van Huyssteen, *Essays in Postfoundationalist Theology*, p. 232, quoting Clayton, *Explanation from Physics to Theology*, p. 88.

11. Van Huyssteen, *The Shaping of Rationality: Toward Interdisciplinarity in Theology and Science* (Grand Rapids: Eerdmans, 1999), p. 184.

12. Van Huyssteen, *The Shaping of Rationality*, p. 152.

accounts or "theologies" of the sort that van Huyssteen has considered in such detail? What challenges are raised for the standard accounts of theological systems by reflecting in a more explicit (and perhaps more radical) way on the pervasiveness of the human quest for meaning? What threats to theological truth claims arise from this effort to think more deeply about van Huyssteen's own starting point? We will find that the attempt to give a rational assessment of such "meaning constructions" is rather more difficult than he sometimes acknowledges. Although we will come back in the end to a position not distant from van Huyssteen's own, it will be with a greater sense of the difficulty of the task, *and its possible failure*, than many of van Huyssteen's texts have acknowledged to this point.

The Human Sciences and the Construction of Meaning

Some observers of the science-religion debate sense that their interests are not fully captured by the technical concerns of the natural sciences. This lack of fit has led some to reject science (or what they call "Western science") altogether, or to turn to religion *in opposition to* science. Yet, as the last section shows, many of the most important issues for theology arise within the collection of sciences known as the human or social sciences, particularly psychology, sociology, and cultural anthropology.

In contrast to the natural sciences, the human sciences are concerned in the first place with the meaning question, the task of "making sense of one's experience." This question connects inquiry in the human sciences with the religious dimension and leads to theological questions. After all, a person's overall understanding of her experience will deeply affect her actions in the world. As Lindseth and Norberg write in one research article, "When our outlook on phenomena changes, our behaviour will also change."[13] If one moves from here to a metaphysics, it will invariably be a value-laden metaphysics, since in our private and social interactions we are fundamentally valuing beings. Let us therefore look closely at this set of rigorous empirical disciplines that are primarily concerned with a very different set of issues than the natural sciences: questions concerning the meaningfulness of human existence and the study of how meaning is constructed by individuals, societies, cultures, texts, and historical periods.

---

13. Anders Lindseth and Astrid Norberg, "A Phenomenological Hermeneutical Method for Researching Lived Experience," *Scandinavian Journal for Caring Science* 18 (2004): 145-153, quote on p. 151.

Consider the contrasts between the eight different levels in what we might call the hierarchy of meaning:

(8) Making sense of existence as a whole
(7) Integrating these worlds with the world of nature
(6) Integrating multiple social/cultural worlds
(5) A sense of meaningfulness derived from one's social world
(4) A significant group, practice, institution, period of life
(3) A meaningful event or moment
(2) The individual's project of making sense of her experience
(1) Raw data from the world and other humans

Although I will treat the eight "moments" in the construction of meaning as a sort of hierarchy, one might also think of them as a heuristic path, one that can be walked in different directions depending on one's starting point. For example, in a traditional tribal culture the levels of shared social meanings (4 and 5) would probably be primary, and the sense of the self as a separate source of meaning might be secondary.

A few words about each level. (1) I start with the *raw data from the world and other humans*. This represents the input from the world *to an individual subject*. Imagine, for example, an infant confronted with the confusing array of experiences. (2) She must then *make sense of her experience* in order to act in the world, for agency requires an orientation in the world, an ability to act. Peter Berger writes:

> the socially constructed world is . . . an ordering of experience. A meaningful order, or nomos, is imposed upon the discreet experiences and meanings of individuals. . . . Man, biologically denied the ordering mechanisms with which other animals are endowed, is *compelled to impose his own order* on experience. Man's sociality presupposes the collective character of this ordering of reality.[14]

Developmental psychology provides a rich picture of this task. The individual must develop a sense of self, but she must also learn that her environment is predictable and safe, and that she can move from the permanence of objects and individuals to the reliability and trustworthiness of the people around her. Later she will choose role models on whom to model herself. A

---

14. Peter L. Berger, *The Sacred Canopy* (Garden City, NY: Doubleday, 1967), p. 19. Subsequent page references are given parenthetically in the text.

sense of identity emerges only as the individual solves the age-specific tasks demanded at each step. Recall the famous stages of psycho-social development proposed by Erik Ericson: trust vs. mistrust (ages 0-1), autonomy vs. shame and doubt (age 2), initiative vs. guilt (ages 3-5), industry vs. inferiority (ages 6-13), identity and repudiation vs. identity diffusion (adolescence), intimacy and solidarity vs. isolation (early adulthood), generativity vs. self-absorption (young and middle adulthood), integrity vs. despair (later adulthood).

(3) The stress on *individual meaningful events or moments* draws attention to the *particularity* of the task of assigning meaning that humans face. It is always *this* event, *this* moment that the individual must incorporate within the structure of her personality — or, at the very least, these particulars that raise for her the broader philosophical questions of her existence. Again quoting Berger:

> [Without this meaning-imposing structure] the individual loses emotionally satisfying ties . . . [and] he loses his orientation in experience. In extreme cases, he loses his sense of reality and identity. He becomes anomic in the sense of becoming worldless. Just as an individual's nomos is constructed and sustained in conversation with others, so is the individual plunged toward anomy when such conversation is radically disrupted. (p. 21)

Sociologists have labeled the failure of meaningfulness "nomic disruption," recognizing that the disruption could be individual, as in the loss of a friend or spouse, or collective, "such as the loss of status of the entire group." "In both cases," Berger writes, "the fundamental order in terms of which the individual can 'make sense' of his life and recognize his own identity will be in process of disintegration. Not only will the individual then begin to lose his moral bearings, with disastrous psychological consequences, but he will become uncertain about his cognitive bearings as well" (p. 22). The meaning project isn't marginal; it's at the center of our existence.

In the social world, events rarely occur without some significance. Everything we do either has or fails to have an underlying valence of meaning. We do not merely grow older; we pass through a series of rites of passage. In middle-class North America these might include: baptism or circumcision, confirmation, obtaining a driver's license, high school graduation, engagement and marriage, promotions, births, birthdays, retirement, death. Humans do not merely use words and encounter objects; we fashion signs in our language and turn objects into symbols of broad affective judgments of the world. (Think of the affective weight of symbols such as the Star of David, prayer beads, the American flag, the face of Princess Diana, or the insignia of one's alma mater.)

(4) These individual events then form broader *groups, practices, institutions, and periods of life*. One might think of it as a sort of "affective space" in which each person lives. Each group one identifies with provides an important source for one's "sense of significance" — of oneself, one's relationships, and of one's life in general. These may include a church community, a fraternity, or sorority, a sports team, an ethnic group, or a club.

(5) Arising out of this set of connections is *a sense of meaningfulness derived from one's social world*. This phrase for the first time captures the continuing task of the individual agent in the world, namely to create an affective or (as sociologists say) a "semantic" fit among the various components of one's subjective world. This growth task must be repeated at each phase of life, from schooling to the work place, from one's family of origin to one's adult family, from teenage crises through mid-life crises on to the crises of the loss of one's parents and (later) one's own friends, and finally to the events preceding and surrounding one's final illness and death. Each loss, each ambiguity, each unanswered question again raises the urgent task of assigning meaning to a new set of events — for, again, to fail to fit the pieces of life together in a fashion that is meaningful for that individual is for her to lose the ability to act as an agent in that world.

(6) *Integrating multiple social or cultural worlds* is especially important in a pluralistic situation such as ours. Indeed, pluralism is deeply characteristic of the religious situation in which we live, since we today are more aware than ever before of the multiple religious options available to us, and hence of the many ways that our own religious traditions can be interpreted. As Berger writes, "to live in the social world is to live an ordered and meaningful life. Society is the guardian of social order and meaning, not only objectively, in its institutional structures, but subjectively as well, in its structuring of individual consciousness" (p. 21). Society today assigns us multiple personas or roles, many stemming from deeply clashing worlds.

A few years ago I was teaching in Williams College, one of the "little ivies" in Massachusetts. The Admissions Department had the intriguing idea of offering full-ride scholarships to Latino-American students from a high school in East Salinas, California, so that they could attend Williams. As the advisor for some of these young students, I watched the clash of worlds as they were ripped out of their mostly Spanish-speaking society and the context they knew as (mostly) second-generation immigrants in a richly Hispanic California town and suddenly thrown into the world of a competitive, wealthy, overwhelmingly WASP liberal arts college in a small town in the heart of New England. The conflicts that were painfully evidenced in the lives of these students — many of whom survived only a semester or two before escaping back to their own home culture — were dramatic examples of the quest to integrate multiple social or cultural worlds.

(7) Alongside the integration of cultural worlds, we face the task of *integrating these subjective worlds with the objective world around us*. Society is one objective given, as Berger shows:

> The success of socialization depends upon the establishment of symmetry between the objective world of society and the subjective world of the individual. If one imagines a totally socialized individual, each meaning objectively available in the social world would have its analogous meaning given subjectively within his own consciousness. Such total socialization is empirically non-existent and theoretically impossible, if only by reason of the biological variability of individuals. However, there are degrees of success. . . . (p. 15)

One must also find one's sense of self within the natural world. This is no easy task. Nietzsche has most clearly expressed the tension faced by individuals in a dark universe:

> Once upon a time, in a distant corner of this universe with its countless flickering solar systems, there was a planet, and on this planet some intelligent animals discovered knowledge. It was the most noble and most mendacious minute in the history of the universe — but only a minute. After Nature had breathed a few times their star burned out, and the intelligent animals had to die.[15]

(8) The Nietzsche quote shows, finally, the urgency of the highest and broadest task: to *make sense of existence as a whole*. Somehow what we know about the physical universe, with its apparently unbending laws and hostile conditions for life, must be integrated into our sense of who we are and what the world is that we inhabit. At first blush, perhaps this description does not sound radically different from the "religion and the natural sciences" discussion that is already familiar to many. But the individual and social task of

---

15. Friedrich Nietzsche, "Ueber Wahrheit und Lüge im aussermoralischen Sinne," *Nietzsche Werke*, ed. Giorgio Colli and Mazzino Montinari (Berlin: Walter de Gruyter, 1973), Pt. 3, vol. 2, p. 369.

constructing contexts of meaning is actually extremely significant. The impact is perhaps clearer when one adds the premise: *The construction of meaning is ubiquitous; it plays a role in all that humans do and think.*

This conclusion is, however, disturbing for many religious people. We like to think of our religious beliefs as *directly* reflecting rational reflection on the world and/or the self-revelation of God, rather than as the product of social construction. Many become uncomfortable to think of many of their religious beliefs being the result of social factors. In order to understand the real challenge, it is not enough just to be told that sociologists can reconstruct many of the causes of religious belief. One needs to consider the details of some of the data in order to feel their force.

Religious Belief and Practice as Dependent Variables

It seems to bother theologians that religious behaviors often represent a rational choice for men and women in social contexts, quite apart from the question of whether the underlying beliefs are true. "Rational choice theories" in the sociology of religion employ functionalist explanations to explore the social pressures that push individuals to or away from religious commitments.[16]

For example,[17] in an important review article, Richard Lee reviews the findings of a number of sociologists concerning the "Success Proposition" as an explanation of religious behavior.[18] The Success Proposition holds that religion, like many other aspects of culture, is a result of socialization, a consequence of reward and punishment. First, Lee notes that the frequency of religious behavior, such as attending church and participating in church-related activities, increases when there are opportunities for reward or praise of the individual's behavior. The reward can be as simple as the pleasure obtained by agreement with or attention from fellow congregation members. It can include belief in other-worldly rewards or individual recognition within the congregation. As age increases, religious participation generally does as well.

---

16. See, e.g., Christopher Ellison, "Rational Choice Explanations of Individual Religious Behavior: Notes on the Problem of Social Embeddedness," *Journal for the Scientific Study of Religion* 34 (1995): 89-97.

17. I include here only a brief selection from the literature. Readers are encouraged to consult any of the standard textbooks in the sociology of religion (or the psychology or anthropology of religion) for further details.

18. Richard R. Lee, "Religious Practice as Social Exchange: An Explanation of the Empirical Findings," *Sociological Analysis* 53 (1992): 1-35. Page references are given parenthetically in the text.

Other studies examined by Lee show how "the church lifted up the nuclear family as the norm" (p. 10). As a result, another sociologist found that the 40 percent of congregation members who did not fit the family norm (i.e., single mothers, those divorced, older, or married to "unsaved mates") are *least* likely to conform to church norms or actively participate. Interestingly, as educational level increases, so does participation in the church. Further, when changing religious affiliations, persons are more likely to choose denominations that maintain "cultural continuity." Thus, one study found that

> Individuals reared as Episcopalians or Lutherans more often switched to Catholicism than those reared in nonliturgical Protestant traditions, and Catholics disproportionately switched to Lutheranism. Jews, having no traditions similar to their own to which to switch, were more inclined to choose nonaffiliation. (p. 15)

Other studies demonstrate that parental choice is one of the most important, if not the singularly most important determinant in religious life choices and choice of denomination. One study of parents and high school students documented that, if parents claimed no religious affiliation, neither did 85% of their children. Conversely, 90 percent of students who are members of evangelical congregations had parents who were members. If both parents claimed to be either Catholic or Protestant, only 4 percent of their children claimed no religious affiliation.

Leiffer discovered that 40 percent of Methodists joined and/or continued to attend church because of friends or relatives. Schaller found that 60 to 90 percent of new church members were brought in by friends or relatives. The answer most frequently given by those surveyed as to why they attended church regularly was "to keep the family together, to strengthen the family ties" (p. 23).

Finally, Robert Young found that two factors — concern for the fate of others and rejection of the death penalty — were significantly correlated with believers' interpretations of evangelism in the communities he studied. Young hypothesized that this correlation was due to the tendency "to make situational rather than personal attributions, as well as to the relative skepticism with which [his subjects] view the American criminal justice system."[19] He also found a correlation between fundamentalism and a high level of support for the death penalty, as well as between fundamentalism and higher lev-

---

19. Robert L. Young, "Religious Orientation, Race, and Support for the Death Penalty," *Journal for the Scientific Study of Religion* 31 (1992): 76-87, quote on p. 85.

els of authoritarianism, particularly in white fundamentalist churches. He also noted that fundamentalist congregations that were primarily black did not share this authoritarian attitude or support for the death penalty.

Another crucial social scientific perspective in the study of religion is economic analysis. The premise of economic analyses of religious behavior is that religious ideas and institutions function in an open market. Denominations do well when what they supply matches what religious consumers demand. Economists of religion explore "how people choose among religious options and what social forces govern religious taste." The resulting data, they maintain, reveal that "religious choices are akin to other cultural choices."[20]

The Sacred Canopy

What is the significance of such data? Many believers find it disturbing that social factors such as these enable social scientists to reliably predict a range of religious beliefs and behaviors. Let's step back from the social sciences for a moment to attempt to understand the nature of this worry. What is the conception of religion that underlies these predictions? Does it represent a challenge to the truth of religious beliefs? If so, how might religious persons and theologians begin to answer the challenge?

Recall Nietzsche's bleak prediction about the future. In an age dominated by the new Hubble images of deep space, many feel the threat posed by Nietzsche's description of a dark, hostile universe — one that cares nothing about human existence and threatens our future demise through the inexorable force of natural law at some future point in time that we can predict only too well. As a result, many feel the urgency of the task of shielding ourselves from such a universe. One concept clearly functions to stave off the threat and resulting sense of meaninglessness: the concept of God. For if the God of the Abrahamic traditions exists, and if God is good in the way that these traditions have taught, then God will not allow the "heat death" of the universe to be the final demise of intelligent life. God will surely insure that what is best and most valuable about our lives, both individually and as a whole, will be preserved in the end.

I do not here raise the question of *whether* God exists; we return to that question below. For the moment let's concentrate on the *function* of belief in God. A clear function of theism is to establish meaning, and thereby to make

---

20. See Darren E. Sherkat and John Wilson, "Preferences, Constraints, and Choices in Religious Markets: An Examination of Religious Switching and Apostasy," *Social Forces* 73 (1995): 993-1026, quotes on p. 994.

the universe meaningful for believers. The functionalist study of religious belief is most often associated with one important school in the social scientific theory, social constructivism. Only after we have examined its claims and arguments will we be in the position to ask whether theologians should endorse social constructivism and to what extent they should (or can) resist its conclusions.

On the constructivist view, as Berger puts it, "Religion is the . . . attempt to conceive of the entire universe as being humanly significant" (p. 28). Along with its contributions to the individual quest for meaning, religion also makes important contributions to social solidarity, at least within the in-group. Peter Berger writes that religion involves

> the establishment, through human activity, of an all-embracing sacred order, that is, of a sacred cosmos that will be capable of maintaining itself in the ever-present face of chaos. Every human society, however legitimated, must maintain its solidarity in the face of chaos. Religiously legitimated solidarity brings this fundamental sociological fact into sharper focus. The world of sacred order, by virtue of being an ongoing human production, is ongoingly confronted with the disordering forces of human existence in time. . . . Every society is, in the last resort, [persons] banded together in the face of death. The power of religion depends, in the last resort, upon the credibility of the banners it puts in the hands of [men and women] as they stand before death, or more accurately, as they walk, inevitably, toward it. (p. 51)

The sacred is what "stands out" from the "normal" life. It is, in Rudolf Otto's famous words, a mystery that arouses both fear and fascination *(mysterium tremendum et fascinans)*. The sphere of the religious is, as Berger puts it, "something extraordinary and potentially dangerous, though it can be domesticated and its potency harnessed to the needs of everyday life. . . . The cosmos posited by religion thus both transcends and includes [humanity]. The sacred cosmos is confronted by [humanity] as an immensely powerful reality other than [ourselves]. Yet this reality addresses itself to [us] and locates [our] life in an ultimately meaningful order" (p. 26).

The Fear of Functionalism

A very convincing story can be told of how religious belief functions to make sense of our total experience (point [8] in the hierarchy above). I see no point in questioning the power of the functionalist analyses of religion summarized in the last section; the explanatory power of the accounts speaks for itself. Clearly the sociology of religion helps to illumine the myriad ways in which religious belief functions in light of this urgent human need to make sense of our experience.

Indeed, at the functional level religious believers should be no more inclined to doubt these accounts than non-believers. Wouldn't Christians and Muslims, for example,[21] *expect* that belief in God should have the function of providing a center of meaning to one's life and a behavioral orientation that could not be matched by any nonreligious concepts or practices? Rather than being opposed to functionalist analyses of religion, perhaps the religious person should after all be their prime advocate.

Why then the widespread reticence of many believers to embrace functional analyses of religion? Presumably believers and theologians sense that these explanations are just a bit *too* powerful. Don't they account for the details of religious belief and behaviors in a bit too much detail? To put the fear bluntly: is it possible that these explanations, given in terms of the functions of religious belief, explain the existence of such beliefs *better* than the appeal to their truth? If so, the objection continues, aren't believers better advised to suspend their belief in the actual truth of religious claims and to become, at best, agnostic? For if religious believers would continue to hold the same beliefs *even if those beliefs were false* — say, because of the benefits that are to be gained by believing them and acting in certain ways — haven't we stumbled on a reason longer to hold them as true?

What this skeptical argument involves is what is generally called a *theory of error*, that is, a theory that explains why people would hold certain beliefs even if they were false. This argument is well known to students of the sociology of knowledge. If you are a passionate Republican and I then show you that you hold precisely the same political beliefs as your parents do, and that the vast majority of people with an upbringing like yours mirror their parents' political beliefs to a very high degree, then I have explained why you would hold your political beliefs apart from any appeal to their actual truth. In a sense, one might fear, I've *explained them away*. Similarly, if sociological or cultural explanations are able to account for where particular religious beliefs came from, and why a person might tend to think they are true whether or not they really are, then one's reason for believing them to be true has been undercut. Herein lies the deeper worry that functionalist analyses seem to

---

21. Particular issues are raised by the centrality of observance rather than belief in Judaism that distinguishes it from the other two major Abrahamic traditions.

raise for religious believers: *the fact that people hold religious beliefs* — so it is claimed — *is better explained by their function than by their truth.*

Note that this worry is the analog within the social sciences to the threat of naturalism and the apparent impossibility of miracles in the natural sciences. Just as the strict regularities that physics has discovered render the idea of exceptions to physical laws increasingly unlikely, and growing neuroscientific knowledge of how brain processes produce mental phenomena makes it harder to believe that those mental phenomena are caused by a "mind" or "soul," so likewise increasing knowledge of the social and cultural functions of religious belief makes it difficult to ascribe to them a different source.

Anthropology and Theology

How then are believers to answer the functionalist objection? Two forms of the functionalist critique of religion, at any rate, are easily dealt with. One is the response, "Well, that's it for religious belief! Once one accepts the human role in constructing belief, one has proven that religious beliefs are clearly false." Although one sometimes encounters bald claims of this sort, they are unjustified. Functionalist accounts do not demonstrate the falsity of (say) core Christian beliefs. Believing that God exists does not become a mistake merely because that belief functions to make one's life meaningful. Belief in God is sometimes dismissed as mere "wish-fulfillment," as in Freud's famous critique. But is the fulfillment of things we wish for *always* a matter of make-believe? (When two partners believe that they love one another, are they always deceived?) The functionalist critique may support agnosticism, but it provides no evidence for the falseness of religious claims.

Another criticism often raised is that there's no place for revelation after sociology, for we now know that *all* language about God is created only by human beings and only serves particular personal and social functions. But, it turns out, this objection is just as overhasty as the first. Just as religious language could be true, it also could have (at least some of) its source in divine self-revelation.

Nevertheless, recognizing the social construction of meaning does place the believer before one sort of decision: will we embrace or resist the analysis of the social functions of religion outlined in these pages? It seems to me that such analyses offer important insights into the nature of religious belief, and that we should therefore embrace them. Since van Huyssteen's methodology begins with similar starting assumptions, I presume that these implications pertain to his program as well.

On the one hand, one recognizes that the resistance of theologians and believers to functionalist analyses was unjustified. Would it not be a bit silly to try to argue that religious belief does not have psychological, social, and cultural functions? Denying the societal impact of religion, or the impact of society and culture *on* religion, leads to a truncated view of religion. Some of the major debates in science-religion discussions appear to be guilty of this error, for example, when God is introduced only in the role of initiator of the Big Bang or guarantor of the regularity of nature, in total abstraction from the meaning question. Such a God, however helpful philosophically or physically, is far from the God of actual religious belief, religious communities, and religious devotion.

On the other hand, one must be clear on the costs. Accepting the social analysis of religion means thinking harder about the status of our various statements about God. It means admitting that *some portion* of the language of worship and devotion reflects the commitments of our culture and tradition; some kinds of God-talk tell us more about ourselves than about God. Theology and anthropology do not exist in pristine purity, worlds apart, and none of us practices a religion that is completely culture free. (Of course, this will also mean that theology has something to say to anthropology, as we will see.) Is this not the insight to which the sociology of religion leads us? Language about God is not only inherited from above; much of it is also constructed by humans.

What is usually not done in these discussions, however, is to embrace the social analysis, as I think we must do, *and then to give a theological account of what is occurring*. That is, critics act as if the game is over as soon as theologians grant that sociology is right about the dimension of social construction. We must thus explore what kind of a response theologians can give to the functionalist critique. For if one asserts the existence of God, one must be in the position to incorporate and explain the results of the scientific study of religion. Is it possible, then, to give a theological account of the interrelationship between religious belief and social construction? How can we integrate the two? What happens to God after Berger?

Getting to the Metaphysical Questions

Social-scientific accounts of God have less tendency to usurp all place for God if they are integrated with the natural sciences and the theological questions that these sciences raise. For example, first, theological questions in the natural sciences concern the "before" and "after" of physics: what occurred before the Big Bang (e.g., what caused it?) and what may occur after the Big Crunch, if there is one, when the universe collapses back into a singularity? Second, what is the source and significance of the regularity, the extreme law-likeness, that characterizes the observed universe? Finally, what is the significance of the incredible "fine-tuning" that we see in the universe — a large number of variables falling in the incredibly small range that would be required for life to emerge (the so-called Anthropic Principle)?

Of course, physical notions such as the Big Bang or the emergence of complexity do not prove the existence of God or an "intelligent designer" — therein lies the mistake of the "intelligent design" movement. But for those who are theists, notions such as these do suggest a new task: the task of developing a theology of nature, that is, an account of physical world around us given in religious terms. One can of course describe the world in purely physicalist terms — which is, after all, exactly what the physical sciences attempt. But in the natural sciences it is patently clear, even more clear than in the social sciences, that questions arise about the natural world that fall outside the scope of what physicists can test. (David Hume called these the questions of the "before" and "after"; today we might call them meta-physical questions.)

Of course, some critics have tried to argue that meta-physical questions are meaningless. Since they can't be answered in purely scientific terms, it is argued, they can't be rationally discussed at all. Would that humanity could escape its fundamental questions so easily! Although it would take a longer paper to show it, it has turned out to be more difficult than expected to draw sharp conceptual distinctions between the scientific and the meta-scientific. (The epistemic and methodological distinctions are not so difficult to draw.) Conceptually speaking, science shades imperceptibly from its most empirical and testable questions, through progressively more abstract ranges of theoretical reflection, and on to questions that can only be called philosophical and theological.[22] Among leading theoretical physicists one rarely finds the "science has all the answers" attitude that dominates in the popular press (and in some science classrooms). Top scientists are keenly aware of the role of *meta-empirical* questions and assumptions in theoretical physics and are often willing to explore them in great detail (as long as one does not confuse the broader discussions with what we currently know how to test).

The relation between the physical sciences and metaphysics has direct

---

22. See Philip Clayton, "Tracing the Lines: Constraint and Freedom in the Movement from Quantum Physics to Theology," in *Quantum Mechanics: Scientific Perspectives on Divine Action*, ed. Robert Russell, Philip Clayton, John Polkinghorne, and Kirk Wegter-McNelly (Vatican City: Vatican Observatory Press, 2002).

relevance for reconsidering the relation between the social sciences and theology. I suggest that the well-known links between various physical sciences and metaphysical issues provide a corrective to a certain mistaken tendency in social scientific theory. There is nothing absurd about a dialogue between natural science and metaphysics; indeed, as I've argued, one cannot do fundamental physics without raising metaphysical issues. Why then should there be a resistance to recognizing the metaphysical questions that arise out of the social sciences? The reason is surely not that sociologists and psychologists possess more powerful theories than physicists and can thus predict behaviors more precisely, rendering metaphysical questions otiose. Nor is there any reason to think that the human sciences raise *fewer* broader questions than the natural sciences — to the contrary! Could it be that the relative uncertainty of social scientific explanations has caused some in this field to claim a certainty and finality for their theories that is not justified by their methods and data? (Of course, to speak of the motivations of some of the critics of religion is to raise a question that social scientists themselves could study.) If it's natural to wonder about the connections between the Big Bang and a God who might have been its cause — and I have argued that it *is* rational to reflect on this subject — then why wouldn't it be just as rational to look for connections (links, integrations) between the social sciences and metaphysics or theology?

The Social Sciences and Religious Truth Claims

This topic represents, I believe, one of the most urgent questions in the entire religion-science discussion today. One must ask: what is the nature of the universe, and what is the nature of this particular animal *Homo sapiens* who studies it, such that humans would tend to interpret the world, and live in their respective social and cultural worlds, using religious categories in the way that we do? Why would we be the sort of animal that would be fixated on the question of meaning — the meaning of existence, of our own lives, of it all? What is the significance of our raising the question of God for the question of whether a God exists?

The transition from standard social scientific practice to a discourse in which such questions could be thematized is not difficult to sketch. One begins with humans living their lives. Social scientists use standard research methods to establish statistically significant correlations between interesting parameters that describe features of human social existence. One then formulates psychological, sociological, and anthropological theories based on those correlations. The network of these theories becomes the disciplines of social psychology, sociology, or cultural anthropology as we know them today. As in the natural sciences, however, the general study of the social world gives rise to a sort of "grand theory" in the social sciences, as Quentin Skinner has argued.[23] Such broader theories shade over imperceptibly into philosophical anthropology, the philosophical reflection into the nature of humanity.[24] One area of this reflection concerns the religious dimension, the human attempt to view the universe as religiously meaningful. And one response that has been given is the theological response, the belief that human existence is meaningful because God has created the universe and wishes to be in relationship with intelligent life (or all life).

Note that what began as an empirical question in social science gradually expands to the level of philosophical worldviews. Whether one's explanations should reduce down to the biological substratum, up into theological dimensions, or remain emphatically at the level of humanity is a classic philosophical question. Such philosophical and even metaphysical questions arise naturally out of the study of human behavior, although a wealth of social scientific data bear on the debate.

Conclusion

We began by outlining the program of J. Wentzel van Huyssteen, finding it to rely crucially on the way humans make sense of their existence. We then explored the ways in which the functionalist treatment of religious belief in the social sciences appears to challenge or undercut theological truth claims. In the final section I began to sketch a scientific, philosophical, and theological program that could respond to this challenge.

In the natural sciences, it is the metaphysical questions raised by the physical theories themselves that lead to theological discussion. In the human sciences, I suggest, *the meaning question itself* can lead to theological issues. In these fields, where one speaks of metaphysics (i.e., moving beyond the physical world that serves as the backdrop for human social interactions), one must include the values that pertain to agents.

---

23. Quentin Skinner, *The Return of Grand Theory in the Human Sciences* (Cambridge and New York: Cambridge University Press, 1985).

24. One thinks of the "philosophische Anthropologie" of the early twentieth century (Arnold Gehlen, Helmuth Plessner, Max Scheler, et al.); see Louis P. Pojman, *Who Are We? Theories of Human Nature* (New York: Oxford University Press, 2006), and Wolfhart Pannenberg, *Anthropology in Theological Perspective*, trans. Matthew J. O'Connell (Philadelphia: Westminster Press, 1985).

It is interesting to contrast the religious and theological topics that arise out of the natural and social sciences. Typical metaphysical questions arising out of the natural sciences include:

- What occurred before the Big Bang (e.g., what caused it)? What may occur after the Big Crunch, if there is one, when the universe collapses back into a singularity?
- Is Big Bang cosmology compatible with the doctrine of creation?
- What is the source and significance of the extreme regularity and law-likeness that characterizes the observed universe?
- What is the significance of the so-called Anthropic Principle, the large number of variables falling in the incredibly small range that would be required for life to emerge?

By contrast, typical metaphysical questions arising out of the social sciences include:

- What is the nature of the human animal that raises the question of the meaning of its own existence?
- Are there dimensions of human existence that require explanations at "higher" levels than the natural sciences (including sociobiology, primatology, and neuroscience)?
- Are there social scientific reasons to supplement functionalist explanations (or standard causal correlations) with other types of accounts?
- Is there a hierarchy of disciplines that points beyond the positivism typical of the most rigorous work in the social sciences today and that opens the door to philosophical and theological questions?
- Will the parallels with the other higher primates allow scientists to explain human behavior in terms of the more fundamental laws of biology (evolutionary psychology and neurophysiology)?
- Will the human being ultimately be explained using distinctively human terms and predicates?
- Or will explaining the human ultimately require that we go beyond the level of the human to include a trans-human level, for example, humans as made in the image of God and reflecting the divine nature and intentions?

The important thing about this program is that it does not stand in competition with the analyses of the social sciences but is a natural extension of them. We know from social scientific study that we are beings who are always more than, always ahead of, the particular physical environment in which we are located. The satiation of our basic physical desires and needs — food, shelter, work, reproduction — does not put an end to our striving or yearning, but rather gives rise to new projects of self-actualization and other-orientation. The problem of trying to make the pieces fit, of making them meaningful, continues to arise even for those whom the physical world has treated best of all.

What then of the ideas and beliefs that arise out of this process? Are *social communities*, for example, merely fictional constructions of this process, since what really exists are the individuals, the atoms of the whole process? Are the *ideals* that humans strive for — love, justice, compassion — all fictions? Or do we strive to understand some things that are actually *true of the world*? Do the sciences prove that we are alone in a hostile universe, as Nietzsche thought? Or do they provide some signs of another possibility: that humans are pervasively preoccupied with religious symbols and practices because we live in a universe that is open toward transcendence, a universe that is the product of a cosmic order or designer, one who is not *less* intelligent and conscious than we are, one who is also revealed in the physical world, in cosmic history, and in the very character of the being studied by psychologists and sociologists?[25] Could not something of the divine be revealed by studying the animal that struggles with the question of God: ourselves?

---

25. See Berger, "Relativising the Relativisers," in *A Rumor of Angels: Modern Society and the Rediscovery of the Supernatural* (Garden City, NY: Doubleday, 1969).

7 Realism, Religion, and the Public Sphere: Challenges to Rationality

Roger Trigg

J. Wentzel van Huyssteen has quite rightly seen the need for theology to face the onslaught on the possibility of all claims to universal applicability. The reaction to "modernity" has stressed the relevance of context and tradition. It has extolled pluralism, and been suspicious of any claim to superior knowledge and certainty. Such "postmodernism" may dent the pretensions of science to explain everything, but it also removes the possibility of any religion claiming an objective truth, which applies to non-adherents, even though they may not recognize it. The danger is that our former confidence in truth collapses, as it is compartmentalized into different ways of life, and different disciplines. Van Huyssteen has tried to provide an answer to this crumbling of epistemological certainty. We no longer, it seems, have secure foundations, on which impressive edifices of knowledge can be built. We have to proceed more cautiously, while not giving up our grasp of rationality. He points out the contrast between "modernity's universalism" and "postmodernism's radical relativism" and crisply poses the question: "What exactly is it about human rationality that is general or universal, and what about it is relative or changing?"[1] His answer is to fashion a "postfoundationalist notion of rationality," so that "there can be a public place for religious convictions in interdisciplinary conversation."[2]

Van Huyssteen is particularly concerned with the possibility of theology and the sciences being able to communicate with each other. The idea of a postfoundationalist rationality is clearly fashioned from the standpoint of epistemology, and he starts with the importance of our interpreted experience. Epistemology itself, however, can never function in a metaphysical vac-

---

1. J. Wentzel van Huyssteen, *The Shaping of Rationality* (Grand Rapids: Eerdmans, 1999), p. 155.
2. van Huyssteen, *The Shaping of Rationality*, p. 198.

uum. To reason effectively, we must have some conception in principle of what we wish to reason about. Knowledge, in other words, is impossible without an idea of reality. Thus arguments about postmodernism and the slide to relativism, which van Huyssteen properly fears, inevitably push us back to issues about what might be meant by reality, and whether it exists independently of our own shifting understanding.

Van Huyssteen has boldly confronted the question of the role of a public theology in a world molded by the fact of pluralism in belief. In fact, however, the issue is even more challenging than the question of whether theology, as an intellectual discipline, can enter into reasoned intellectual dialogue with other disciplines. The question is whether religion as such can claim any place on the public stage. This is a major political issue in many countries at the present time, not least in the United States. As he has rightly seen, postmodernism forms one of the social currents that has been flowing strongly against the possibility of any public discussion of religious issues. Yet the reason for this is not just epistemological. Some leading postmodernists are, as we shall see, basing their critique of religion not just on its claim to knowledge but also on its reliance that there is anything in any common reality that can be known. In other words, postmodernism certainly does make rational communication problematic between those in radical disagreement with each other. However, it also tends to import assumptions that are explicitly nihilistic. Reason becomes impossible because there is nothing to reason about. Our inability to communicate becomes the inevitable result of this. It is not just a problem in its own right, but a symptom that something even more profound has gone wrong.

Contemporary Challenges to Religion

Religion faces two major philosophical challenges arising from modern society. The first is itself questioned by postmodernism, and consists of an exaggerated respect for science to the point at which it is assumed that science defines truth. Whether this goes under the flag of materialism, physicalism, naturalism, or some other name, the conclusion is the same. It is that the techniques of modern science not only are the sole source of current knowledge. They also somehow limit what can be known. They hence determine the nature of reality. Put like this, it becomes clear that reality is made to depend on human beliefs and capabilities at a given time. It is constituted by what passes for human knowledge, rather than itself providing the possibility and conditions of such knowledge.

Scientific realism links reality explicitly to the procedures of human science. It is thus not strictly realist at all, but highly anthropocentric. Reality is then the product of the abilities of those who are trying to understand "it," whatever "it" is. Science is human science, and, indeed, human science as it is understood at a given time. Since truth is then linked to the self-understanding of scientists in a given era, it does not take much argument to make scientific realism appear nothing more than a species of relativism, rather than of realism. It has certainly lost its grip on the supreme insight of realism, that whatever is to be counted real must be understood as totally independent of human beings, their understanding, their language, and their epistemology. Critics may complain that this opens the possibility of skepticism, but that is an occupational risk for a realist.

The second major challenge arising from contemporary society is the fact of diversity of belief. This is more apparent in the area of religion than anywhere else. It is a cliché that we live in "pluralist" societies, in which there is no settled agreement on such matters. As a sociological fact, this is undeniable, but "pluralism" often comes to mean more than just that there are different beliefs. The suggestion is not just that they are in disagreement but that there can be no principled way of resolving that disagreement. Again we lose any grip on the idea that any religion refers to a reality that confronts everyone. The tendency is to start with the fact of belief, either on an individual or a communal basis, and to consider there is no way of getting beyond that to discuss what the belief is about. Any putative reference drops out, and an epistemological challenge degenerates into a sociological fact. The task of deciding which, if any, religion is true is jettisoned as impossible. It is assumed that we merely have to deal with the political problem of diversity. Since it is assumed that there is no public procedure for settling religious disputes, we have to change our emphasis and ensure that those who have different beliefs can live together. Yet the conclusion results from a major metaphysical assumption that different religions do not attempt to describe the same transcendent reality, and, further, that there is no such reality confronting all humans. If there were, and if there were any possibility of our gaining knowledge of it, it would appear foolhardy in the extreme to ignore it.

The idea that religious truth cannot be a matter for public debate and for public reasoning has to be bound up with the belief that we cannot have any access to an objective reality which exists independently of the believers. It follows that we can understand beliefs only by dealing with believers, if reality is constituted by beliefs about it. If, on the other hand, beliefs are intended to refer to realities which are objective, we face a different situation. In that case, others, besides the believers, can in principle reason about the nature of the realities, since they are not the projection of particular beliefs. They have an independent, self-subsistent reality, which in turn should give them a claim to universal attention. Their presence, or absence, is a matter that is in principle accessible to all. Treating religious beliefs as the private concern of those who hold them would then be to give an inappropriate stress to the believer rather than to what the belief is about. A realist understanding of the nature of religious belief must involve us in consideration of a truth that holds for everyone.

Objective truth concerning a real world is by definition of universal concern. It cannot be put in some private compartment that is of interest only to those with the requisite beliefs and commitments. Realism has to challenge any view of religion that sees it as a quintessentially private matter. Conversely, those who wish to make a principled distinction between the public and the private spheres, with religion placed firmly in the latter, are implicitly, and sometimes explicitly, saying that religion does not deal with matters of public concern that can be publicly discussed. In other words, it makes no reference to any reality accessible to all, because of its objectivity. It does not deal with anything with which "public" standards of rationality can deal. The conclusion must be that because it is a private matter of concern only to particular groups or individuals, it can be explicated only with reference to these people. We are, it seems, faced with a political rather than an epistemological challenge. Since we cannot have access to anything the beliefs purport to be about, we must all work out how to live together, whether we have religious beliefs or no, and whatever kind they may be.

A breakdown of confidence in the truth-claiming properties of religion becomes one of the main forces at work in the contemporary world that results in the view that, while everyone has the right to practice a religion if they wish in a free and democratic society, that is a private and individual choice. It is an expression of personality and not a claim about the world. As such it cannot be rationally questioned, nor is it fit for discussion in the public sphere. Liberal philosophy positively encourages this division between public and private. As John Rawls indicates, a state must be confronted with the fact of pluralism. It must tolerate, and even encourage, the coexistence of many different worldviews, even religions. At the same time, it should not identify itself with any one of them. Thus a philosophical basis is given for the American separation of church and state.

Robert Audi has applied what he terms the "two fundamental commitments" of liberal democracy, namely the freedom of citizens and their basic political equality, to the position of religion in society.[3] He follows the rea-

---

3. Robert Audi, *Religious Commitment and Secular Reason* (Cambridge: Cambridge University Press, 2000), p. 4.

soning of much modern jurisprudence that freedom of religion must entail freedom not to believe as well as freedom to believe. It seems to follow from this that the state should not take sides but be neutral even in the debate between religion and non-religion. Although Audi himself might not follow this line of reasoning, it is clear that it is easier to talk of such neutrality, if it is considered that, actually, there is nothing to adjudicate about. If religious belief has no genuine content and is all a matter of personal preference, there is all the more reason for the state to avoid taking sides.

In fact, pluralism does not mean just the existence of different religions alongside each other. It demands the public recognition of atheism and other forms of rejection of religion. It is ironic, indeed, that the more it is insisted that religion is a private matter, and the more the principle of equality is stressed, the more public acceptance of alternative religions and alternatives to religion is demanded. Audi himself claims that "governmental preference for the religious as such is intrinsically unequal treatment of the religious and non-religious."[4] Following this line of thought, Audi therefore proposes two principles that are intended to prevent any compulsion or coercion of citizens on religious grounds. The so-called "principle of secular rationale" says that "one has a prima facie obligation not to advocate or support a public policy that restricts human conduct, unless one has, and is willing to offer, adequate secular reason for this advocacy or support." By a secular reason he means one that makes no appeal to theological issues. One cannot therefore appeal to religion as a justification for a law. There may indeed be reasons why such appeals could be self-defeating. Using arguments with someone that depend on assumptions the other person is known to reject is not a very effective way of persuading anyone. Appeals to religious authority to someone who is not religious are not very sensible. That concerns the art of persuasion, since it is always more fruitful to use arguments and reasons that are likely to gain acceptance. Audi, however, is saying more than this. He considers that religion has no place on the public stage for reasons connected with the nature of democracy. He goes even further with his "principle of secular motivation."[5] According to that, one should not advocate any public policy restricting human conduct "unless, in advocating or supporting it, one is sufficiently motivated by normatively adequate reason." Thus it is not just a matter of choosing one's arguments carefully in order to convince someone. One must not be primarily motivated by religious reasons at all.

---

4. Audi, *Religious Commitment and Secular Reason*, p. 86.
5. Audi, *Religious Commitment and Secular Reason*, p. 96.

Privatizing Religion

An undercurrent in contemporary thought suggests that somehow "secular" reasons are not just more persuasive, but somehow more rooted in the way things are. If religion is genuinely attempting to connect with reality, the reasons it offers ought to be as grounded in reality as any non-theological form of reasoning. On the other hand, once one gives up on a realist understanding of religion, it becomes totally intelligible that religion cannot play a proper role on the public stage or its arguments be considered of universal application. The privatization of religion makes much more sense if religion is understood as expressing personal ideals or encapsulating a way of life. Unless it is about a reality confronting us all, it cannot claim to be using forms of reasoning that have a universal applicability.

Just how radical this proposed policy can be is seen by the fact that one could no longer, for instance, condemn slavery for religious reasons. Yet from a historical point of view, there is no doubt that the abolition of slavery was motivated by evangelical Christianity. The American civil rights movement in the middle of the twentieth century was also substantially religious in motivation. In both cases, a belief in the equality of all humans in the sight of God played an important role. A liberal might protest that the pursuit of political equality merely aims at the removal of coercion. This, however, only makes it look as if the very grounding of liberal democracy, with its belief in individual freedom, could itself be religious in origin. If that is so, marginalizing religion leaves democracy itself without the ability to offer a basic justification for its own existence.

However that may be, the idea that religion should be regarded as irrelevant in politics and legislation has been a powerful one, although at the same time often itself divisive. It undergirds the French political doctrine of *la laicité*, which, as its name suggests, contains more than a whiff of anticlerical opposition to perceived authoritarianism. Similarly, the venerable American doctrine of the separation of church and state has in recent years become much more about the desirability of separating religion as such from society. The former is private and the latter public. Religion becomes a matter of individuals banding together in voluntary associations, pursuing their separate interests and making rules for themselves, but not legislating for non-members. This suits the idea of a radically pluralist society in which beliefs of a basic sort are not shared by everyone. Instead, what has to be agreed on is a common commitment to a democracy, which respects and encourages diversity and difference. Somehow the society has to be held together, but at what point the very idea of such diversity begins to remove the possibility of one society and any common identity is a question left unanswered.

As we have already seen, another great pressure is keeping religion from the public stage. As well as the respect for diversity, there is also an ongoing commitment to science. The two do not coexist very easily, since science itself wishes to make universal claims and does not want to be seen as just one worldview among many. Nevertheless, despite their different conceptions of truth, relativism and an aggressive scientism, which sees science as the sole custodian of truth, are both opponents of any public role for religion. Exactly what is meant by "science" is always a problem. If it refers not to science as it is presently understood but to a hypothetical science, when all the evidence is in, it begins to look not so different from realism. The scientific millennium is as notional as any other absolute conception of reality. On the other hand, the more what is taken for knowledge in the present day is stressed, the more science's own grip on reality looks shaky. The problem is that we, as humans, are always rooted in a particular time and place, and science, like other forms of human reasoning, wants to push its reach beyond those limitations. There are pressures within science to envisage a reality that cannot wholly be defined by human understanding. Nevertheless, the philosophical temptation has always been to limit reality to what can be currently investigated by science. That alone is susceptible to public checking and can produce settled agreement. Rationality is then restricted to the processes of empirical science. Public reasons become constrained by what is now acceptable to scientists. The difficulty is that, once science confronts the basic claim of realism concerning the independence of reality, it has to acknowledge that no limits in principle should be placed on the nature of the reality being investigated. Science has to be in the business of discovery, not invention.

Nevertheless, many are swayed by the prestige of science to accept even its current findings as exhaustive of reality. As a result, they take science to be the custodian of public standards of knowledge. What cannot be certified as rational by science (and present-day science at that) is not accepted as a public justification for anything. Thus political demands for equality and freedom coalesce with beliefs about the status of science. Both are distrustful of all religion, the former because of its authoritarian tendencies, and the latter because of its metaphysics. They are distrustful of religious claims to truth, and as a result they hold that religion is not a fit subject for public, rational discussion. The willingness of some, even within the religious camp, to make a rigid distinction between faith and reason does not help. Reason is seen as having to make claims that can be checked in the public sphere, while, in contrast, faith is seen as something more subjective, to be chosen and practiced in private. It becomes a personal matter, perhaps concerned with "values."

Yet the idea that science and religion can sit in different compartments because they are concerned with different matters is highly pernicious. The public character of science then means that it has monopoly rights on the concept of truth. Religion is enclosed within the province of personal meaning. It has to concentrate on what matters for individuals. Indeed, since people differ and have different concerns, religion and truth become finally separated. In any sphere, truth has to be about what is of universal concern. In science, discoveries have to be valid equally in Washington and in Beijing. They hold true whether particular people accept them or not. Science depends on the idea of objectivity for its character as a body of knowledge, some tentative and some firmly established. This is not the "objectivity" of a fair-minded scientist at work assessing experimental evidence. It is the strong objectivity of a knowledge that is connected to a reality that exists independently of it. Science gains its authority from its claim to be investigating an ordered world that has its own inherent nature, whether humans find it comprehensible or not. Publicity is in fact a feature of scientific methods for acquiring knowledge. It is not necessarily a characterization of what the knowledge claims to be about. For instance, the other side of the universe is not in a sense publicly accessible.

Many would still hold that the space for reason has to be a public one. If justification is to mean anything, it will be said, it must be public. Religion will still come under suspicion because it cannot appeal to public standards of rationality in the way that science appears to. The conclusion drawn will be that, assuming the right of religious liberty, religion has to be non-public, that is, private. We are back with the contention that religion cannot be allowed into the public sphere. Unlike science, it appears contentious and divisive, precisely because there are no agreed standards with which to settle disputes.

The problem, though, is that this is not the tolerant move we may be led to believe. It is not a matter of "live and let live." The assumption that religious epistemology cannot stand comparison with that of science is bound to carry implications about the nature of religious truth. Consigning religion to the private sphere is not just saying that is not susceptible to normal standards of public justification. It cannot pass muster, it appears, when judged by the best epistemological standards we appear to have for estimating truth. In other words, the privatizing of religion is equivalent to saying that there are no grounds for thinking it true. It cannot be making any claims of universal significance. The conclusion must then be that it does not appear to be about any independently existing reality. The issue of public and private slides into one about truth as opposed to personal preference.

The controversy about the status of science itself takes place against the background of so-called pluralism. Indeed, the tug-of-war between religion and science is actually one between science and many different religions, speaking often with contradictory voices. In one sense, though, this a sociological point about what people happen to believe, and it reminds us that it is a contingent fact about any given society that there is respect for science and its procedures. People can reject science itself as the source of too many modern ills. They can turn to alternative forms of explanation. They can be regarded as irrational for doing so, but if "reason" is connected too closely with what people happen to find acceptable at a given time, a drift away from support for science could undermine its own claim to rationality. Reason has to remain anchored in the inherent characteristics of what is being investigated. The best of all reasons for believing something is that it is true, not that a sufficient number of my fellow citizens agree with me.

Postmodernism and Relativism

Richard Rorty has recently argued that religion has no place in the public sphere. He is writing from within the American tradition of the separation of church and state, but there is more to it than that. He claims: "The epistemic arena is a public space, a space from which religion can and should retreat."[6] Religion may be tolerated, but its reasons cannot be a matter of public concern. Yet, if one cannot give such reasons, there must be a very real question how far one's belief has cognitive content. Without reasons for or against belief, it would seem that it does not matter what I believe, or indeed whether I believe anything. Rorty talks of "the game of giving and asking for reasons," and his conclusion is this:

> To say that religion should be privatized is to say that religious people are entitled, for certain purposes, to opt out of this game. They are entitled to disconnect their assertions from the network of socially acceptable inferences that provide justifications for making these assertions and draw practical consequences from having made them.[7]

---

6. R. Rorty and G. Vattimo, *The Future of Religion*, ed. S. Zabala (New York: Columbia University Press, 2005), p. 36.

7. Rorty and Vattimo, *The Future of Religion*, p. 37.

Rorty is an American pragmatist, and thus places great store on what is "socially acceptable." Nevertheless, there are dangers in concentrating on shifting sociological criteria. When current prejudices and fashions appear to go against religion, that means that religion has to withdraw from public life. That, however, would appear to be a political move, aimed at avoiding embarrassing public criticism. Yet, as Rorty himself makes clear, the withdrawal is an admission that reasoning is inappropriate for religion. If religious people need not be concerned with rationality, the idea that religious assertions have cognitive content is given up. They are not about reality at all.

Rorty's views resonate with the European rejection of modernity, with its ideas of truth and progress. A mark of this rejection is what the Italian philosopher Gianni Vattimo calls "the dissolution of the principle of reality into the manifold of interpretations."[8] The diversity of belief is then seen not as sign of fallibility but as constituting the very possibility of liberty, unconstrained by the demands of a "real" world. Vattimo says that what he terms an "ontology of the weakening of Being" "supplies philosophical reasons for preferring a liberal, tolerant and democratic society rather than an authoritarian and totalitarian one."[9]

Vattimo is explicit in linking a realist understanding, in religion and beyond, with the possibility of conflict and the abuse of authority. He follows a long line who have seen claims to objective truth as leading to the methods of the Inquisition or to the coercion of Leninism. In both cases, critics would say that there is an easy path from claiming truth to a desire to remove error, and from there to the use of all possible means to do so. Vattimo raises the specter of the so-called "clash of civilizations" and says: "It may have been possible to believe in unique truth and morality in traditional closed societies, founded on a single source of authority and a single tradition. Today it has become too dangerous to think like that."[10]

The idea of "danger" in this context would not seem to be an epistemological concept, far less a metaphysical one. It seems to be a matter of political judgment. One might respond by suggesting that perhaps what is even more dangerous is a clash between two sides, one of which believes in objective truth and the other of which does not. One might instance a militant Islam that believes it possesses the sole truth confronting a form of Christianity that does not. There will still be discord, but there will be no opportunity for any

---

8. Gianni Vattimo, *Nihilism and Emancipation* (New York: Columbia University Press, 2004), p. 20.
9. Vattimo, *Nihilism and Emancipation*, p. 19.
10. Vattimo, *Nihilism and Emancipation*, p. 58.

reasoned discussion. There may be intolerance on one side, but, at the same time, the Christian side no longer holds to any idea of universal rationality. The potential for political conflict still remains, without any possibility, however theoretical, of rational resolution. It is all too likely that those committed to a view of universal and objective truth will carry the day against those who have *ex hypothesi* no valid reason for continuing to hold to their beliefs, other than that they are theirs. In fact, a collapse into anti-realism, and from there to an unashamed relativism, leaves people with no way of justifying their beliefs to themselves, let alone to others.

Even a clash between different groups of relativists with different beliefs will still create political difficulties. There is then in principle no common ground on which the parties to, say, a religious dispute can meet. A common relativist hope is that this somehow increases the possibility of tolerance. When, the argument goes, there is no way for one side to think they are right, there is no point in imposing their beliefs on others. Yet why should I be happy that other people have different commitments than my own? Without some principle about the importance of human freedom and autonomy (which cannot be a relativist principle, since it would apply universally), it may be that I, and those who think like me, just want others to conform to our way of doing things. We could appeal to no reason in justification. We may just feel like that. It does, after all, seem a fairly normal human characteristic to prefer the familiar and to despise the alien. Instinct, not reason, would govern our actions, but it is optimistic to think that humans will instinctively prefer toleration to domination, diversity to conformity with their own way of doing things. The urge to compel others may still be strong.

Vattimo, and others such as Richard Rorty, take it for granted that realism somehow is the enemy of toleration and that a belief in any kind of objective truth results in the exercise of power in the imposition on others of what a group sees as true. Truth and authority appear to go together. Indeed, Vattimo puts it very succinctly in a non-philosophical way when he remarks in a dialogue with Rorty that "my basic opinion now is that people hate Christianity because of the priests."[11] Clearly the idea is that, once the notion of truth is allowed, it will not be long before some people or institutions claim to be repositories of it, arrogate authority to themselves, and restrict the freedom of others. Rorty puts it this way: "Cutting oneself off from the metaphysical Logos is pretty much the same thing as ceasing to look for power and instead being content with charity."[12] It may be clever for Rorty to undermine

---

11. Rorty and Vattimo, *The Future of Religion*, p. 68.
12. Rorty and Vattimo, *The Future of Religion*, p. 56.

the idea that Christianity can be true by an appeal to a basic Christian virtue. Yet it merely raises the question why we should pay any regard to anything taught by Christianity. Vattimo for one is on the side of what he terms "postmodern nihilism (the end of metanarratives)." At the same time, it seems that he is unwilling to step outside the Christian tradition. He wants the benefits of Christianity, as he sees them, without its metaphysical baggage, "charity" without "truth." Everything it seems will depend on the contingent fact of a Christian tradition being handed on. Yet once its claim to truth is denied, it is hard to see that it either will be, or should be, transmitted to future generations. Why should it persist in the face of other competing traditions? Even love (or "charity") may be a nice idea, but unless it somehow reflects the basic character of reality it is a pleasing fantasy and nothing more.

Vattimo puts his general position as follows: "A democratic regime needs a non-objective-metaphysical conception of truth; otherwise, it immediately becomes an authoritarian regime."[13] This is in a sense a political argument against realism, but it assumes the importance of democracy, without giving any justification for it. What is wrong with the use of authority and the imposition of power? Where can we stand in order to make such a sweeping claim? The problem with divesting oneself of all meta-narratives is that it leaves nobody with any means of detaching oneself from all practices to make statements with a universal application. The result is that it is very difficult to criticize another practice, even involving the use of arbitrary power, without being accused of using inappropriate criteria for judging it. We can only beg the question by invoking the criteria of whatever practice we are currently participating in. Vattimo betrays his unease by himself referring to charity as "a metarule that obliges and pushes us to accept the different language-games." It is far from clear what such "acceptance" involves. Presumably it involves something more than the toleration of difference, and possibly even the acceptance that each game is as good as any other. Since there is no way of showing otherwise without an appeal to reality, the result must be relativism. As always, it will be far from clear how we can understand alien games from the standpoint of our own. There is no common world in which they are all situated.

It is not surprising that, without a common reality, there can be no way of judging between different practices or "games." The demise of realism can lead very swiftly to the kind of nihilism that Vattimo himself embraces. This, though, can be merely the slinging of slogans. Just as serious is the practical effect of dissolving any idea of an objective reality. It may seem that all basis

---

13. Rorty and Vattimo, *The Future of Religion*, p. 50.

for the use of authority and the abuse of power has been removed. Yet "authority" is itself a complicated notion. Vattimo has seemed to be attacking the political and social authority of the Roman Catholic church in particular. There is no doubt of the resentment this authority has stirred up in many countries over many centuries. Yet authority does not consist merely of the application of political influence and coercion. Authority may be a sociological concept, but it is also an epistemological one. The problem with arguments such as that of Vattimo is that they draw epistemological and metaphysical conclusions from sociological observations. Because the authority of the "priests" is to be challenged, it is thought that any basis for a claim to knowledge must also be undermined. Yet political and other forms of influence can be challenged in the name of individual liberty, itself possibly a notion connected to religious ideas of the freedom of the will. Religion, and Christianity in particular, can produce powerful arguments why this should be so. Yet these arguments will depend on an assumption that Christianity has some valid insight into the human condition. In other words, political arguments about freedom, so far from having to undermine ideas of truth, may need the assumption of religious truth to be effective.

Realism and Reason

One of the greatest problems about an attack on realism is the baleful consequences this brings to the very possibility of human reason. If our beliefs are not about anything, there is obviously nothing in virtue of which they can be mistaken. Whatever set of beliefs and practices we possess is going to be as good as any other. This indeed is the reason why relativism is thought to increase toleration. We cannot tell others they are wrong because we can no longer believe that we are right. We have no reasons ourselves for believing and can give others no reasons for giving up their beliefs. Different language games, or whatever, just exist. A pluralist society must recognize, and even celebrate, difference and diversity. Rationality as a means of establishing communication between different groups, and even sometimes as a way of removing differences, is no longer an option. Indeed, it will be under suspicion as the tool of one particular worldview or way of life. Instead of reason being seen as something to which all can have equal access, reason is seen as itself a way of using power to impose one set of beliefs instead of another. That is in effect what the postmodern attack on modernity amounts to.

Realism, with its insistence on the status of reality as independent of all conceptual schemes and yet the target of human reason, does not give up on the power of reason to show to everyone what is true. Without realist assumptions, science itself becomes pointless. The same has to be the case with religion. Yet if we consider that humans have the power of reason and need the freedom to use it, the mindless imposition of authority is itself opposed to reason. Realism itself, therefore, implies the necessity of freedom to inquire and understand. Put another way, the removal of realist assumptions from the sphere of religion will have major effects. If religion is not about anything from an ontological perspective, it merely embodies the prejudices or personal aspirations of particular individuals and groups. In a free society individuals should not be coerced, but it would seem that they have nothing of importance to communicate with those who do not share their perspective. Theirs is a distinctively private concern, of no relevance to the public stage.

This, not surprisingly, is the view of those such as Rorty who reject the idea that religion could be making any claims about "the world." In particular, the idea of rational justification is no longer seen as having any connections with what is real. It is a matter of what is at the moment socially acceptable. Since science can, at least for now, command intersubjective agreement, it stays within the realm of reason. What is public is what is socially acceptable. Yet what can be socially acceptable has to be restricted to what is in the public sphere. The private, by definition, can never get a foothold in the public arena, since it is excluded from the sphere of what is regarded as rational. The circularity in all this is clear. The rational seems to be defined in terms of what people accept. What is needed is an independent characterization of what it is for something to be a reason, other than that it happens to be accepted as such. We need some account of what is acceptable. The dismissal of realism leaves no possibility of grounding reason. Once we introduce the idea of an independent reality, we gain a target for belief. Without a realist conception of truth, there can be no proper distinction between truth and the fact of belief. Indeed, truth can only be a matter of counting heads. There is no distinction between good and bad reasons.

Realism guarantees everyone access to the same reality. Its stress on objectivity ensures its universal reach. This means that issues of truth, in whatever area, have to become matters of public relevance. The only ground for privatizing religion, and for cutting it off from contributions to public discussion and public life, is if it is thought not to be describing any reality. Despite Rorty's postmodernism, there is no doubt that he gives significant priority to science. Relativism can undermine all claims to truth; and materialism, or naturalism, can also sideline religious claims as unworthy of serious examination. In a curious way, since they contradict each other at times, both can join forces in their attempt to remove religion from a public role. Relativism denies the idea of reality in any context. Naturalism just denies it in the religious context. Religion has to be acknowledged as making claims about a reality that confronts us all if it is to demand rights on the public stage.

Some may still be afraid of the institutional power of some religion. This is, however, a totally different issue from epistemological and metaphysical questions. As has been claimed, authority in the sociological sense must be distinguished from the authority that derives from reason. Institutional power, when exercised for its own sake, can be resisted. We have to be governed instead by the authority of reason, which can enable us to see what is real and can give us justification for belief. Freedom and the ability to reason have always needed each other. We cannot follow reasoning if we are constrained by outside forces. This is true in science, and it also applies to religion. As one recent writer puts it, in advocating that reason and religion come together again: "In a free society truth can find no other way to prevail, and should seek no other way, than simply by the power of persuasion."[14] He is referring to the importance of rational argument. The fact that the writer was Joseph Ratzinger, now Pope Benedict XVI, might suggest that Vattimo's distrust of the priests is not altogether justified. Yet the crucial difference is that Ratzinger is a realist, while Vattimo is a nihilist. Vattimo can allow no scope for reason, and hence can have in the end little conception of human freedom. For him the unguided and arbitrary autonomy of the individual is sufficient. Yet freedom without reason is an illusion, just as rationality without freedom is an impossibility. Both have to be grounded in reality.

---

14. Joseph Ratzinger, *Truth and Tolerance* (San Francisco: Ignatius Press, 2004), p. 144.

8 Reason and the Enlightenment

Keith Ward

I am delighted to be able to record my appreciation of J. Wentzel van Huyssteen's important contributions to theology, and especially to the field of theology and science. His work on the nature of rationality, the possibility of achieving an integrated view of human knowledge in a postmodern world, the necessity of placing theological reflection within a wider model of rationality, and the shaping of interdisciplinary standards of rationality has been of enormous value. In these areas, like many others, I owe him a debt of gratitude for the careful analysis and wealth of insights that he has brought to this important area of scholarship. The following short essay is meant to be a small tribute to his work on rationality in theology and science.

It is sometimes said that modern, or postmodern, culture has moved from an Enlightenment affirmation of the sovereignty of reason over authority and tradition to a world in which reasoning itself is often seen as a defective, culturally bound, and power-motivated human activity. Reason is seen to work within forms of language or life that exist on non-rational foundations, if on any foundations at all. There seem to be no universal standards of rationality, and all people can do is declare their prejudices to one another with varying tones of certitude. My view is that this is a totally incorrect account of the Enlightenment and its aftermath. The search for a notion of rationality that neither claims that reason sets an absolute standard for judging the truth or justification of all beliefs and practices whatsoever, nor sees itself as simply a tool of the drive for power and rhetorical victory, is an important one. What I have to say on this matter should be seen as a small complement to van Huyssteen's own published views.

If we cast a glance back to the eighteenth-century Enlightenment, the first thing we have to do is to distinguish the many differing sorts of "enlightenment" that were on offer. The French, German, Scottish, English, and

American Enlightenments were all notably different, and it can be confusing to lump them all together as "the Enlightenment."

I shall concentrate on the work of David Hume, the great Scottish writer, often seen as a bright scion of the Scottish Enlightenment. He is far from being a defender of the absolute authority of reason, as the arbiter of all beliefs. On the contrary, he combines rather uneasily two very diverse tendencies: a belief in common sense and a confession of skepticism about reason. Hume is completely opposed to rationalism, to any view that there is a faculty of reason that can establish first principles of knowledge with certainty and can derive conclusions from *a priori* principles about the existence of God, of the external world, and even of science (like the principle that every event must have a cause). He held that reason is unable of itself to establish anything: "Reason is the slave of the passions," he wrote (*Treatise on Human Nature*, book 2, part 3, section 3). All knowledge derives from sense-experience, and all moral beliefs are derived from desires. We must limit our beliefs to what that gives us. However, he also had various commonsense beliefs — that other minds exist, that all events have causes, that there are necessary connections in nature, and that physical objects exist unobserved. But we cannot, he thought, justify such beliefs. We have them because they make sense of our experience. It immediately occurred to most other Scottish philosophers that the existence of God is also a commonsense belief that helps to make sense of experience in giving meaning and significance to human life.

Hume, however, thought that religion was distasteful and founded on fear. It makes people slavishly obedient to absurd rules and undermines the pursuit of properly humane and cultivated virtues. Had he conceived of a religion that was humane, that emphasized the social virtues, and that encouraged confidence and hope, his philosophy could have supported it. Common sense is more plastic than Hume supposed, and what seems common sense in one society or to one group of people may seem fantastic to others. Any anthropologist might have made this clear to Hume, but he was an unashamed elitist and assumed that the vast majority of members of the human race were ignorant, superstitious, and bigoted. They could be discounted. So common sense, for Hume, turns out to be the common beliefs of a small subsection of eighteenth-century Scottish urbane society. If Hume represents (one aspect of) the Enlightenment, then the Enlightenment is already "postmodern."

It was not reason, in any grand sense, that supported Hume's opposition to religion. It was almost the opposite. It was a sort of pragmatic evidentialism, a belief that you should have sensory evidence for most of your beliefs, and that other beliefs (like belief in the uniformity of nature, or like the belief in evidentialism itself) should be adopted only if they had a direct role in making experiences more predictable or in making people happier.

Hume's enlightenment, then, was not based on an appeal to the supremacy of reason. It was based on the restriction of reason to sense-experience and desire. Like most Enlightenment thinkers, he opposed tradition and authority, but not in the name of some abstract reason. A large part of his opposition was due to the fact that he thought traditional authorities were too rationalistic, that they gave reason an authority it did not possess. So he had a particular animus against natural theology, which used reason to demonstrate the existence of a creator, and against trying to base morality on a rationally knowable "natural law."

The Enlightenment, at least in Hume's hands, does not make reason superior to faith. It demotes reason from having any power to support faith or any power of its own at all. Reason is not an autonomous legislator. It is a slave. After all, Christian faith is faith in the rationality and intelligibility of the cosmos, created through the *Logos*, the reason of God. If anyone held that reason can decide what is or is not true in religion, it was Anselm of Canterbury, who thought he could even prove that God existed and that he had to become incarnate and die on the cross. Belief in reason has a Christian basis, and when and insofar as Christian faith was rejected, belief in the intelligibility of the world and the trustworthiness of human reason was seriously weakened.

For Hume, Enlightenment was the dethronement of reason and its replacement by sensuality and passion — more neutrally, sense impressions and desires. Even for Immanuel Kant, woken from his dogmatic slumbers by Hume, reason lost its function of disclosing the truth about reality. It became the source of purely formal principles for organizing experiences and desires. The Categories of Understanding and the Categorical Imperative remain absolute for Kant, but they give no information. They organize or regulate the data of sensation and desire. Kant is, after all, famous for his critiques, not his defenses, of reason. For Kant, unlike Hume, there are still universal and necessary principles of reason. But they are revealed as being purely formal, heuristic principles for the regulation of human thought, with no power to show what the real-in-itself is. Reason is not completely dethroned. But it is restricted to the regulation of human sensation and desire and deprived of the power of giving knowledge of objective reality.

The situation, for these Enlightenment thinkers, is not that reason discloses truths about reality, whereas faith must make a rationally unjustifiable leap in the dark. That is the Kierkegaardian misunderstanding of the Enlightenment, a myth that apparently still persists in some quarters. The situation is rather, for Hume and Kant, that reason had in the past made overconfident claims about the intelligibility of the cosmos, as a God-created unity. But now reason must be confined to the realm of human experience and given a purely pragmatic (in Hume) or formal (in Kant) role. In that situation, any statements at all about ultimate reality must transcend reason — and that, of course, must include many basic statements of Humean and Kantian philosophy. It is not that religious faith alone is a leap in the dark. Any statement about ultimate reality is "beyond reason," for reason has a purely pragmatic or formal role, and the content of knowledge must come from elsewhere — and from where, reason cannot tell.

Modern science stands in stark contrast to what Hume thought was obvious. Some modern physicists think that the world is really composed of superstrings in eleven-dimensional space. Some think that it is composed of probability waves in Hilbert space. Some think it is a wholly "veiled" reality, expressible in mathematical terms, but wholly beyond visual imagination. Hardly any physicists think the world is really composed of "impressions and ideas" (though some quantum theorists of a philosophical disposition come near to such a position).

As a matter of fact, the very thing that seemed most obvious to Hume — that we build the world out of conscious data of sense — is itself doubted or denied by most contemporary scientists and philosophers. Conscious sense-data have become oddities, or even illusions, floating as epiphenoma of neurological processes. Reality might be better graspable by reason, doing pure mathematics, than by bare sense-experience, which is content to accept that how things seem is how they really are. And modern physics tells us that how things seem to our senses is more certainly not how they really are.

The Enlightenment, at least in its Humean form, failed not because it made reason too important but because it made human sense-experience and consciousness too important. It rejected the ancient Christian idea that the universe was an intelligible unity, being created through the *Logos* or wisdom and rationality of a divine mind. And it replaced that idea with the supposition that there exist lots of experiences, without any internal connections of intelligibility or any underlying explanations for why they come to exist as they do.

Furthermore, Hume was very selective about what sort of experiences he took seriously as being the basis of reality. In concentrating on the idea of "evidence," he privileged those states of consciousness that were publicly accessible and repeatable. He should never have done so, since (as every first-year philosophy undergraduate knows) on strictly Humean principles one can never be sure that there are any other experiences than the ones we ourselves have. But by concentrating on "experiences" that are discrete, nameable or describable, and atomistic, Hume managed to discount all those deeply personal and very important experiences that cannot easily be separated out as specific "ideas," that are very difficult to describe, and that seem to depend essentially for their character on their place within wider contexts of experience.

An example of what I mean would be the personal experience of perceiving and appreciating a Rembrandt painting. There is certainly such an experience, which many people would claim to have. But whether two people ever have just the same experience of encountering a Rembrandt is not only uncertain but unimportant. What matters is that individuals come to the painting with their own training, preconceptions, and criteria of excellence. Bringing these to the painting, they experience something quite unique to them, something that may reorient their vision and affect the total way they respond to paintings, and to their experience in general, in future. The experience of "seeing the Rembrandt" is explicable only by referring to that past preparation, to the concentration and capacities, and to the total life-experience of the observer.

Hume deals with this sort of experience by simply relegating it to the realm of the purely subjective, without ontological import. The facts are the sense-impressions the painting will produce in any observer. The subjective reactions are the feelings an observer may have, and they tell us nothing about the facts.

In this way, sense-impressions are drained of value and significance. They become purely neutral data to which a number of private responses may be made. All values become subjective, and we have the notion that the real world is without and indifferent to moral import or value. Values are personal desires and aversions, and there are no values in "objective" reality. Such a view makes a religious response to reality irrational — that is to say, untrue to the facts. For a Christian, facts have value or disvalue because the world that God creates is created for the sake of its goodness. In some way it has fallen into corruption or imperfection, and that is a notorious problem for Christian theology. But values of beauty and intelligibility are really there, in things themselves. And God is, of course, the ultimate value, the supreme Good, not just an extra fact.

Among philosophers who have thought of themselves as Christian, G. W. F. Hegel is one thinker at the end of the Age of Enlightenment who tried to rectify the subordination of reason to morally neutral experience by broadening the idea of reason to cover imaginative or intuitive vision. For Hegel, reason was not the slave of passion but a richly creative capacity to integrate experience within a totality that is always in process of development and reappraisal. The dialectic of reason is not a restrictive system of definite concepts. It is a fluid, dynamic synthesis of all available data of knowledge, seeking to integrate all of knowledge into a more or less coherent, but always not quite adequate, whole. In this sense reason does not exclude or determine faith. It may include the disclosures of transcendent reality and value that are the foundation of religious faith as data that must be taken into account in constructing an intelligible and partly provisional synthesis of human knowledge at a particular historical time and place.

For Hegel, reason does have a positive and creative role to play, and part of that role is to integrate scientific and religious claims into an intelligible view of reality. Yet reason is not the arbiter of faith, limiting religion to a more naïve version of what philosophy alone can give — something of which Hegel is regularly and wrongly accused. Religion has experiential data of its own (though neither Hume nor Kant admitted the existence of such data), and rational thought must interpret them justly. For Hegel, rational thought and a broad view of human experience must continually interact to produce new interpretations, which must themselves be checked against the experiences that new historical contexts will generate.

In none of these three influential philosophers of the Enlightenment does reason become the ultimate arbiter of faith. For Hume and Kant, reason has very definite limits. Common sense, sense impressions, and desires form the basis of human knowledge. For Hegel, reason has the task of integrating religious experience and sensibility with other knowledge. Reason seeks to interpret, but it cannot disallow or exclude huge areas of human experience.

Reason does not make ultimate decisions. But there are general criteria of rationality that apply in every discipline. Facts that are relevant to the enquiry in hand must be selected. They must be ranked in accordance with their importance to the matter in hand. We must try to ensure that all relevant facts are taken into account, and we must discern connections between the relevant facts in ways that bring out crucial relationships between them. Above all, we must try to find some principle of integration, some key idea or organizing principle that will enable various sorts of fact to be related to one another in a systematic and coherent way. Rationality is the capacity to hold together a large range of disparate data, to discern significant forms of relationship between them, and to pattern them in a more or less coherent whole.

This sort of rationality requires judgment, discrimination, considered evaluation, and creative imagination. People will vary in the extent to which they possess these qualities, and they will differ in the specific ways in which they exercise them. People can be very rational in one area in which they have a great interest, and yet cavalier and even slipshod in other areas. Yet these are the distinctive capacities of rational persons, and they are what drive quests for greater understanding.

Reason in this sense is not opposed to imagination or intuition. The integrating principle that we find in, or sometimes try to impose on, the data we have is not derived from some simpler set of ideas. It is often generated by a creative leap. The mark of rationality is that we will use the integrating idea to organize the data we have and will not hesitate to confront recalcitrant data when they exist (as they almost always will). Our idea may be modified to a great extent as we come across new data, but it will be rational to maintain it for as long as it promises insight, or what seems to be insight, unless and until it irretrievably collapses. A good example of this is Einstein's insistence that indeterminacy must be an inadequate account of quantum theory. He was reasonable to persist in his views, and even now he may turn out to have been right. The weight of evidence is against him, yet it is not unreasonable to support Einstein, given his stunning ability as a physicist. Differing views can be reasonable, and we must go on testing our hypotheses, not exactly trying to destroy them, but not shrinking from confronting hard cases either.

In a similar sense, God is a hypothesis. Some theologians shy away from that thought, saying that we cannot just adopt belief in God as a matter of probability, or as though theism was a provisional speculation. It must be an absolute commitment. But we can be absolutely committed to a hypothesis that is logically speaking provisional and not certain. I can commit my life to belief in God, but the belief that there is a God is, logically, a hypothesis. It could be wrong, and I must confront cases that suggest it is (like horrendous evil). I am most unlikely to discover it is wrong — what would the overwhelming case be? But the sheer weight of experience could count against it. And I must have sufficient experiences that count for it, if it is to be sustainable.

Human experience often calls for absolute commitments made in theoretical uncertainty. That does not mean such decisions are irrational. It would be irrational to toss a coin or to consult a Haggis. But to be rational allows for diverse decisions or "hunches," based on attitudes that we may be unable to formulate explicitly. I must know all the relevant facts, see as sensitively as possible how they affect those concerned, see what my view might imply for similar cases, and consider how it integrates with my other moral and metaphysical views. Reason will not make my decision for me, but there can be reasonable or irrational decisions.

Rationality is rooted in fundamental human capacities of creativity and sensitivity — creating and articulating new integrating images, being sensitive to wider sets of facts, developing our natural capacities, understanding specific forms of culture in new ways.

The Enlightenment is often presented as the liberation of the human mind from religious tyranny and the triumph of reason over unthinking tradition. On the contrary, it was actually the limitation or even the complete subordination of reason to sense-experience and desire. The message of the Enlightenment lies elsewhere, in a realization that liberty of thought and expression and free critical enquiry promote and do not undermine a genuine search for truth. "*Sapere aude* — have courage to use your own understanding!" said Kant (*What Is Enlightenment?* 1784). That was a genuine advance in human thought. It leaves open the possibility of, and even suggests, a more positive role for reason than Hume, at any rate, allowed. Hegel I have chosen simply as a philosopher who attempted to create a Christian philosophy that was neither rationalistic in the old sense nor contemptuous of reason. For him, reason is the driving force of a creative, imaginative, and dynamic attempt to integrate diverse forms of human experience and knowledge. In this more positive sense, reason does not pose as the arbiter of religious truth. It does not prove the truth of Christianity, nor does it destroy all religious claims. It rather serves as an impetus to rethink religious truth in the light of changing scientific, aesthetic, and moral insights, while also seeking to construe them in the light of general philosophical and religious considerations.

If the Enlightenment is to be challenged, it should not be because it raised reason too high, but because it brought reason too low. In the progress of modern mathematical physics, we have cause to reinstate the mind as able to apprehend an intelligible reality that the senses cannot grasp. We now realize that rational speculation must be tested by careful and precise observation. But if we are to move beyond the Enlightenment, the indications from science are that we should move, not to the babble of innumerable rhetorical discourses without rational foundation, but to a greater confidence in the power of reason, tested by experience, to inform us about how things really are. If we have a reasonably creative interpretation of reason, if we do not have too limited an idea of experience, and if we are willing to consider claimed experiences of transcendent value, this may lead to a reinstatement of the view that reality is the rational creation of a rational God and that it can be comprehended by created reason. The Enlightenment would at last achieve what should have been, but was not, the vindication of reason as the appropriate way of apprehending and appreciating the world as the work of God.

II. SCIENTIFIC EXPLORATIONS

9 Spirituality and Religion in Paleolithic Times

Jean Clottes

When we try to tackle the subjects of spirituality and religion, difficulties abound right from the start. How can archaeologists, who base their research on solid data, remains, and traces, assess a domain that is intangible by its very nature? Should we speak of spirituality and religion in the singular or in the plural when confronted — over tens or even hundreds of millennia — with different forms of humans living in environments that have varied considerably in time and in space? Besides, what do these concepts really mean, even if they appear familiar to us, when applied to cultures and beings that are so remote and alien?

We cannot avoid defining these concepts. Rather than endeavoring to compile the innumerable attempts to do so in the past, it might be preferable to retain their smallest common denominator. We can consider spirituality as an awakening of a consciousness that goes beyond day-to-day life contingencies, beyond "simple" adaptation to material necessities in order to get food, to reproduce, and to survive. Humans then began to question the world around them, and in it they tried to find a reality different from the one perceived through their senses, the one to which — like other animals — they always reacted instinctively.

With religion a major step is taken. One could say that, at its most elementary level, it is the organizing of spirituality. The world, interpreted through the human mind and thus transcended, now acquired a precise meaning. As a consequence, humans could evolve complex rules of behavior in order to avoid catastrophes, to facilitate everyday life, to obtain the help of the mysterious supernatural powers or to help them maintain the world's indispensable harmony — never assured, always threatened. Humans were now conscious of being able to influence their own destiny — or so they believed — in a different manner than when facing the material dangers of their environment but with the same purposes, that is, solving the problems linked to their survival.

Thus considered, spirituality and religion are closely linked, since the awakening of a form of consciousness that goes beyond material contingencies and the attempts — however tentative — to organize and to take advantage of those new perceptions cannot long be separate.

Awakenings of Spirituality

What were the initial causes of the awakening of spirituality? The literature on the subject is abundant without dispelling uncertainties. One can hardly deny that the development of the brain played a major part. Wherever one chooses to put the threshold and the first stammers of spirituality, it is no less certain that, for millions of years, the creatures that preceded that crucial evolutionary step were adapted to their biotope and could survive, that they had a relatively sophisticated social organization (as is also the case with some primates), that they had invented and perfected tools and were on the way to becoming fully human.

The criteria of what being human means have changed considerably over the past half century, and *Homo faber* is a memory of only historical interest. One might be tempted to substitute for him *Homo spiritualis*, a creature who starts to perceive the world as far more complex than he could tell at first sight and who endeavors to adapt as best as possible to the new complexity by appealing to powers beyond the material universe.

How could we not surmise that dreams played a crucial role in the process? Many other mammals dream, as all cat and dog owners know. Humans, however, possess the unique ability to remember their dreams and to refer to them when awake. It seems logical to assume — as was done many times in the past — that this gave rise to the idea that another world existed where people traveled in their dreams. This apparently simple idea entails three main consequences. The first one is the acknowledgement or belief that the mind is distinct from the body, because the latter does not move around when a person is dreaming. The second consequence stems from the instinct of survival, which is why it is particularly strong: how can one profit by the existence of the other world(s) and its (or their) peculiarities? The third consequence is linked to the preceding one: since that world of the dreams exists, with such strange characteristics, could it not influence or even determine everyday events in our own world? Those ideas in turn entail a series of other consequences that will inextricably intermingle in a variety of ways. They directly spring from a full consciousness of dreams and could lie at the root of spirituality and religions.

The question then for archaeologists is not so much that of chronology (how can one date the event?) as that of the available means that would enable them to perceive its consequences in the behavior of early humans in their relation to the universe. From that point of view, the evolution of hunting strategies and techniques or that of tools is not much help: the fact that hunting for small and then for bigger animals succeeded foraging and carrion-eating or that bifaces followed choppers throws no light on possible changes concerning spirituality.

The mastery of fire by *Homo erectus* may truly have given a considerable impetus to exchanges and conviviality among humans (Otte 2001), but basically this is just a new tool, even if a tremendous one. As to the natural curios that very ancient humans brought back to their habitation sites, like the Acheulian crystals at Singi Talat in India, their importance has been somewhat played down nowadays, as more and more examples have come to light of animals that display such curiosity, apparently without any utilitarian purposes. For the same reasons, the formal harmony and symmetry of some bifaces, which look *to us* like works of art, cannot be taken as an undisputable testimony of artistic creation and as a proof of the existence of spirituality in any form. At least, they are not sufficient in themselves for us to draw such a conclusion, particularly when we consider some "natural" examples like the complexity and inner beauty of certain bird nests.

The clues that are generally looked for in order to determine the existence of spirituality belong to three different domains: burials, art, and — admittedly more controversially — complex actions not immediately attributable to practical concerns.

Animals can in some cases evince sorrow in face of the death of one of their own, but they do not bury the dead and — more importantly still — they do not deposit grave goods with their bodies. With the help of ethnological comparisons, the hypothesis was made that the humans who deliberately buried their dead believed in the existence of another world and that the offerings accompanying the dead were meant to facilitate their passage and sojourn in the world of the beyond. In addition, these offerings could also testify to the deceased's social status and to the esteem and love that were theirs in life.

As to art, its definition is fully as tricky as that of spirituality and religion (Anati 1989). It could have as its basis a sort of distance from the real world. Its forms and modes will no doubt be many, but the same fundamental process will underlie them: the projection upon the world around the artist of a strong mental image that will infuse reality before transfiguring it and recreating it into a different form (Clottes 1993). From this point of view, art does testify to the existence of spirituality. As André Leroi-Gourhan put it: "If the perception by Paleoanthropians of the unusual is a necessary step, symbolic figuration is the decisive sign of an accession to abstract values" (Leroi-Gourhan 1980:132).

Finally, the traces and remains from certain actions can in no way be explained away either by natural causes or by practical ones. In such cases one must be extremely cautious; before ascribing to them a "ritual" or "symbolic" meaning, it is necessary to contemplate all other possible causes and discard those causes only when they entail gross impossibilities. We shall see a few such examples. This kind of clue is all the more valuable when associated with one of the other two.

Ancient Humanities

None of the above-mentioned clues, which might reveal the existence of a form of spirituality, exists for the most ancient humans, *Homo habilis* and others. An unworked pebble that vaguely suggests a human head when held in a certain position was found at Makapansgat in South Africa, in a layer dated to about three million years ago. It can be assimilated to the other natural curiosities referred to above: its color or unusual form might have caught the attention of one of those ancient humans who picked it up.

On the other hand, with *Homo erectus* (or *Homo ergaster*) under his diverse guises (particularly *Homo heidelbergensis* in Europe) and with his main culture called Acheulian, we are beginning to get a multitude of testimonies that support and reinforce one another as more come to light.

One of the earliest described is the presence of iron oxides (in particular, hematite and limonite), which can be used for their coloring properties. Many such minerals were discovered in archaeological contexts that can date back to hundreds of thousands of years, in Africa, India, and Europe (Lorblanchet 1999). We naturally do not know the precise use to which they may have been put: body decoration? hide curing? various rites evidenced in so many cultures all over the world? The fact that the coloring properties of these iron oxides is obvious cannot be taken as proof that they were indeed used to materialize symbols or a form of spirituality.

Attention has been attracted, too, to lines engraved on bones excavated from Acheulian contexts. As is always the case, there has been fierce controversy as to their intentional versus fortuitous nature. All the same, it does

Spirituality and Religion in Paleolithic Times

Fig. 1. This small stone, dated to more than 250,000 years at Berekhat Ram (Israel), may evoke a human figurine. The circular groove is manmade.
Photo F. d'Errico.

seem that some engraved sequences, like those at Bilzingsleben (Germany), could indeed be deliberate (Bednarik 1995).

The most curious object ever found in an Acheulian layer is a small volcanic stone dated to between 250,000 and 280,000 at Berekhat Ram in Israel (Fig. 1). It was interpreted as a figurine representing a woman. But this interpretation is not obvious enough to entail immediate agreement. We must never forget that, if we automatically project our mental images on the material world around us and interpret it in function of these images, the action is a consequence of a very long process of education and evolution that we are no longer aware of. We cannot surmise that archaic humans had the same thought processes and ways of looking at things. Recently, however, an in-depth microscopic work (d'Errico and Nowell 2000) has shown that the Berekhat Ram stone had indeed been summarily worked.

Cupules, that is, small round cavities superficially dug into the rock, have also been found under Acheulian layers in central India (Madhya Pradesh) on two sites (Auditorium Work and Daraki-Chattan). Being particularly resistant, they are better preserved than any other form of art, which has logically led some archaeologists to surmise that they only represented the tip of the iceberg and that they could well be the only symbolic expression to have survived to this day while all the others had been destroyed (Bednarik 2003). Whether or not cupules represent a symbolic expression is, however, a moot point.

Finally, more than thirty human skeletons, dated to about 300,000 years ago, were found in the same place, called Sima de los Huesos, at Atapuerca, near Burgos in Spain, at the bottom of a natural shaft. Their accumulation is reminiscent of collective burials. In addition, a spectacular quartzite biface, exceptionally well made, could be a funerary deposit or offering.

It is likely, then, that as early as the Acheulian the humans who preceded *Homo sapiens* had already crossed some sort of threshold. Even if we cannot be entirely certain about the existence of art, at least as defined above, the necessary conditions are met for a form of symbolic thought and mental distance from mere material reality.

The Neanderthals

With the Neanderthals, we stand on more solid ground. As usual, specialists fight over details — even if admittedly important ones — while sharing a number of concepts that are less talked about. We could roughly distinguish two broad schools among them: one school would "rehabilitate" Neanderthals. Essentially uninfluenced by modern humans *(Homo sapiens sapiens)* and sometimes ahead of them, *Homo sapiens neandertalensis* would have invented everything by themselves (art, body ornaments, burials, grave goods, etc.). For the other school of thought, the relatively late "inventions" attributed to Neanderthals, like body ornaments, would in fact be due to the influence and perhaps in part the acculturation from the more modern Cro-Magnons. The latter proposal sounds more logical since the novelties appeared with Neanderthals only when the two species of humans became contemporary and not during the scores of millennia that had preceded the arrival of the strange newcomers.

Be that as it may, this is not of prime importance for our purpose, as most specialists agree about the mental abilities of Neanderthals. They were most certainly different from those of modern humans, but they included spirituality and possibly religion (about a debate on the subject, however, see Lewis-Williams 2002).

Neanderthals buried their dead and occasionally deposited offerings with them. Nearly thirty voluntary burials are attributed to them in Europe and the Middle East. One of the most famous is that of a three-year-old discovered at La Ferrassie in the Dordogne (France). A limestone block bearing eighteen small cupules on its lower side was on top of the grave. In this case, evidence of complex thoughts exist at three levels: the will to protect the body by burying it; the deposit of a worked stone; and the nature of the work on the stone itself, as the cupules are organized in four or five small groups, which might have had a symbolic meaning. This would be enough to establish the existence and conditions of these people's spirituality, but we have other clues too.

The cave of Régourdou, in the Dordogne (France), provided another example, this time of a complete Neanderthal human burial, with a stone wall separating it from a brown bear partially buried in a pit. Two bear leg bones prolonged the human body that had been deposited on bear hides. Grave goods (bear bones and stone implements) were left on top of a slab covering the body. A number of big stones protected the whole. Then, the Neanderthals put a deer antler on top of the mound and covered it with another layer of stones before making a small fire. Other man-made structures with brown bear remains were discovered nearby, some predating, others postdating the human burial (Bonifay 2002, Bonifay and Vandermeersch 1962). These examples show the spiritual importance attached to bears in Neanderthal beliefs.

Neanderthals made extensive use of color. Scores of examples of pigment remains were found on Mousterian sites, like Pech de l'Azé I in the Dordogne. Their use was probably not restricted only to material tasks, like hide curing. Archaeologists also discovered bones bearing regular rhythmic striations in France (La Ferrassie, Montgaudier, Arcy-sur-Cure) and in Bulgaria (Bacho Kiro). It is important to point out that these intentional engravings are not naturalistic. It is quite possible that they may have had a symbolic function, but one can argue whether they really are art in the strict sense of the word (the same could be said for cupules).

Fairly recently, a limestone block with a long sliver of bone inside two communicating natural holes was found in a Mousterian level at Roche Cotard, in Indre-et-Loire. It was improperly dubbed a "mask" because, when holding it in a particular *ad hoc* position, one could see a face in it — with some imagination (Lorblanchet 1999:133). It is more than a *lusus naturae*, as it seems to have been roughly worked and the bone was deliberately stuck into the holes. It is reminiscent, however, of the natural curiosities already mentioned, and it is not possible to assert that a naturalistic representation was meant.

Lastly, another example, though not well known yet, is quite intriguing. The entrance into the deep Bruniquel cave (Tarn-et-Garonne, France) was long ago blocked by a scree. Spelunkers managed to get into the cave and discovered two stone structures side by side (Fig. 2), hundreds of yards from the entrance. The structures consisted of broken stalactites and stalagmites piled on top of each other. One is an oval (5 meters by 3.5 meters) and the other is a circle (1.5 meters in diameter). In the bigger one, a small fire included a fragment of bear bone that had been burnt not long after the death of the bear, as the bone was still fresh at the time of burning. A radiocarbon analysis by the Centre des Faibles Radioactivités at Gif-sur-Yvette (France) dated it to more than 47,600 years ago (Rouzaud, Soulier, Lignereux 1995). The stone structures were not the remains of huts — a hypothesis made at the time of discovery — because the cave had not been inhabited. In any case, it would not have made any sense to build a real hut in such a naturally protected place deep underground. All we can say is that the structures delineate a particular space and that their very old date attributes them to Neanderthals and not to modern humans. Venturing into the depths of a cave long inhabited by bears was not a commonplace activity. It required practical (torches) and mental preparation to face the real and imaginary perils of the strange place. The most plausible hypothesis, considering the circumstances that exclude any immediately practical activity, is that of a ritual type of behavior.

Modern Humans

With our direct ancestors Cro-Magnons *(Homo sapiens sapiens)*, the problem becomes quite different. Our task is no longer to question the existence of their spirituality and religion(s), which are admitted by all, but to study their nature, modalities, chronology, and evolution.

The earliest voluntary burials we know are dated back to around 100,000 years ago in the Middle East (Qafzeh in Israel). Those at Sungir in Russia, hardly more than 20,000 years ago, provide one of the best examples of beliefs in a life beyond death and of the importance attached to it: thousands of worked beads and other rich burial goods were deposited to accompany the dead. In a number of cases the bodies were covered with red ochre.

The oldest symbolic object so far attributed to modern humans was discovered at Blombos Cave, near The Cape (South Africa). It is a polished and worked piece of hematite engraved with a complex geometric motif consisting of three parallel lines and a series of crosses (Henshilwood et al. 2002), found in a layer dated to between 70,000 and 80,000 years ago.

When modern humans reached Europe, about forty millennia ago, the testimonies to their spiritual and magical/religious activities became more and more numerous. In addition to burials, which strangely enough are not

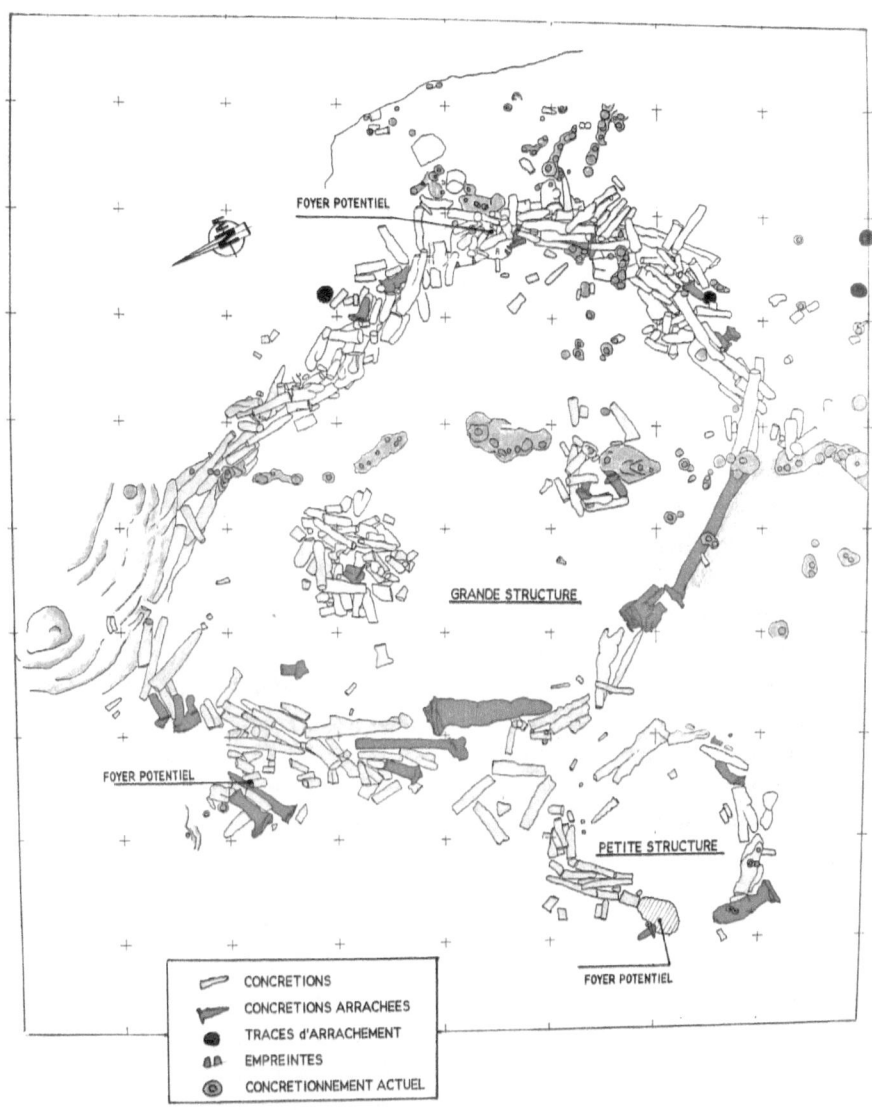

Fig. 2. In the deep Bruniquel Cave (Tarn-et-Garonne, France), the structures made by heaping broken stalactites and stalagmites in an oval were dated to more than 47,600 BP. Mapped by Rouzaud et al., in Spelunca n°60, 1995.

very numerous, these activities mostly belong to three domains: portable art, wall art, and traces of particular actions preserved inside caves.

Among the themes represented in both forms of art, one of the most fascinating is that of the composite creature, part human and part animal. It would persist from the Aurignacian (ca. 30,000 BP) at the Hohlenstein-Stadel and Hohle Fels (Germany), with humans sporting a lion head (Conard 2003) (Fig. 3), until the Middle Magdalenian (ca. 14,000 BP) with the so-called "Sorcerers" in Les Trois-Frères in the French Pyrenees (Fig. 4, left). Similar images belong to intermediate periods. We can cite the man with the head and wings of a bird at Pech-Merle (Cabrerets, Lot), the man with a seal's head at Cosquer (Marseille), the man with a bird's head at Lascaux in the famous Shaft Scene, and the Gabillou Sorcerer with a bison head (Fig. 4, right).

To venture deep underground into the complete dark in order to make paintings and engravings is an exceptional occurrence in human history. Those actions cannot be ascribed to any recognizable practical necessity. If such a tradition persisted for so long (more than 20,000 years), it must have entailed the powerful constraints of beliefs passed on from one generation to the next. In fact, when they were in the caves either 32,000 or 12,000 years ago, the Palaeolithic visitors behaved in exactly the same way: they went everywhere, to the very ends of the deep caverns (Niaux, Réseau Clastres, Rouffignac), slithering into tiny recesses, exploring side galleries, climbing avens (Bernifal), or going down shafts (Fontanet) — in all of these places we find their traces.

From their actions and behavior in the caves, two different forms of logic are apparent, at all periods. Sometimes, Palaeolithic people left their drawings on the walls of huge chambers or on extensive panels. There, the paintings are organized in spectacular compositions (Chamber of the Bulls at Lascaux, Salon Noir at Niaux, Panel of the Lions at Chauvet, Panel of the Horse at Labastide). Sometimes, the engravings may be inextricably superimposed on one another (Sanctuary at Trois-Frères [Fig. 5], Apse at Lascaux). This implies participants in collective ceremonies, which may have occurred frequently or infrequently. The highly visible, carefully drawn images could play a part in the perpetuation of the beliefs about the natural and spiritual world(s) and of the rites to command the help of the supernatural powers. Paintings and engravings are also found in minuscule recesses or passages where only or two persons could fit at any given time (Portel, Tuc d'Audoubert, Candamo, Diverticule des Félins at Lascaux, Cosquer, etc.). Parallel to a logic of the spectacular, this is a logic of the secret retired place and of drawing for its own sake.

The walls themselves always played a vital role. If many researchers have

Fig. 3. Mammoth ivory statuette of a man with a lion's head, dated to about 32,000 BP at Hohlenstein-Stadel (Germany). Photo by Thomas Stephan, Ulmer Museum.

Fig. 4. The composite creatures often called "Sorcerers" in the French caves of Les Trois-Frères in the Ariège (left) (tracing by H. Breuil) and Gabillou in the Dordogne (right) (tracing by J. Gaussen) are part human and part animal.

long remarked the use of natural contours, they paid less attention to fissures, holes, and the openings of passages or shafts, despite the fact that such locations attracted a considerable number of figures.

In addition, numerous bits of animal bones stuck into the cracks of the walls were found in nearly a score of Upper Paleolithic caves. One of them, at Gargas (Hautes-Pyrénées), was dated to 26,860 ±460 BP. Others pertain to the Middle Magdalenian in the Volp Caves (Montesquieu-Avantès, Ariège). Repeated in different places throughout the millennia, these apparently non-utilitarian gestures confirm the use and the value attached to caves and to cave walls for uncounted generations. This longevity cannot have been a co-incidence. It materializes beliefs that spanned the whole duration of the Upper Paleolithic.

Spirituality and Religion in Paleolithic Times

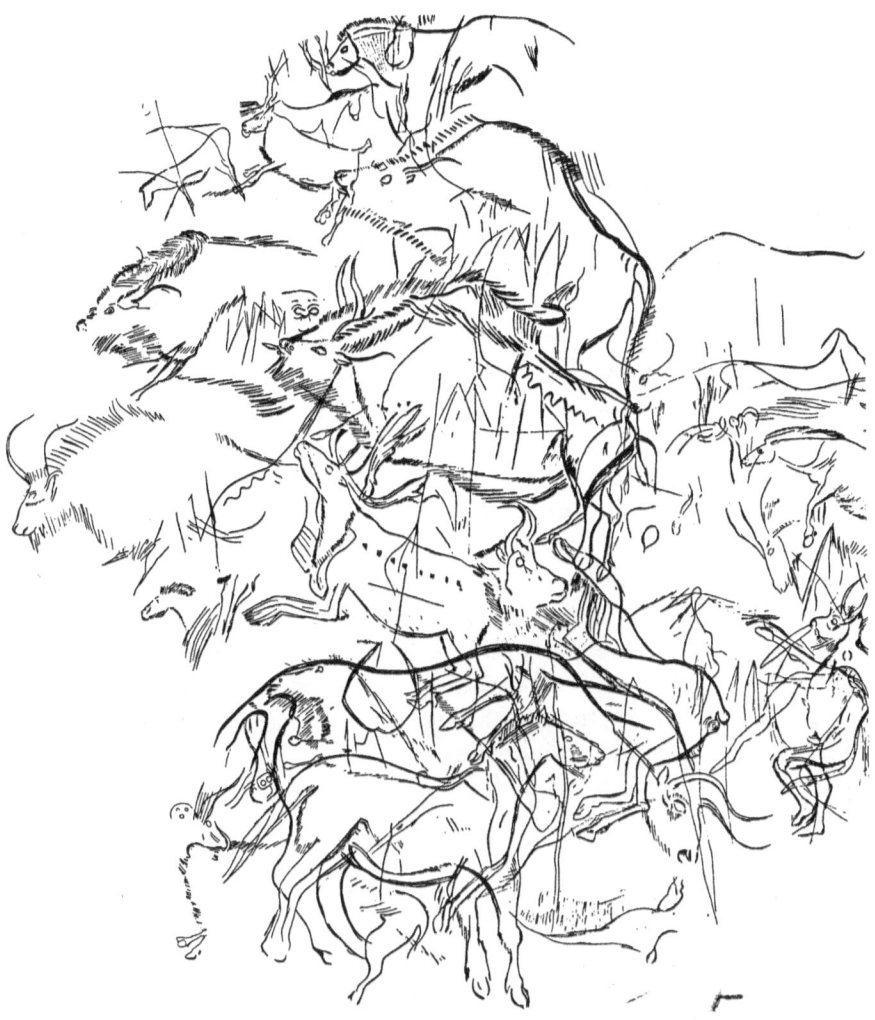

Fig. 5. In the Sanctuary of Les Trois-Frères (France), many engraved figures were superimposed upon one another during the Middle Magdalenian, at about 14,000 BP. They testify to a succession of ceremonies in the deepest part of the cavern. Tracing by H. Breuil.

Venturing underground meant facing ancestral fears, deliberately entering the realm of the spirits in order to meet and contact them. The analogy with the mind journey of the shaman is obvious, but the subterranean adventure went far beyond a metaphorical equivalent of the shaman's travel in trance. It was indeed a concrete journey in an environment where one could

145

physically move and where spirits were literally at hand. The Aurignacians and their successors must have been conscious of trespassing into the world of the supernatural spirits and fully expected to find them there.

We have all sorts of evidence of the ways in which they looked for the spirits they believed to live inside the caves, on the other side of or inside the walls. Thus, the walls were a sort of thin permeable veil between the world of the supernatural powers and the world of humans. The constant use of natural reliefs depicting the contours of animal bodies is best explained by the conviction that animal spirits were there in the rock, half out of it already: by drawing them the painters established the contact they had been hoping for. Fissures, hollows, and ends of galleries and shafts probably played a similar role, providing passages toward the innermost world of the rock where the spirits, the dead, or the gods resided.

A desire to capture part of the power of the underground world can explain not only why they drew animals and geometric signs but also why they stuck those bits of bones into the cracks of the walls. This kind of gesture has been described many times and in all sorts of cultural contexts (for example, the Wailing Wall in Jerusalem, where the faithful put their prayers on pieces of paper that they deposit between the stones). Its elementary symbolism is clear: it is a will to go beyond the ordinary limits of our lay environment and to approach the supernatural or the sacred. In the caves, these actions could have been due to uninitiated individuals, perhaps sick people or children who participated in their own way in the ritual activities, thus partaking of the beneficent cave power. Hand stencils and handprints might have played a similar role. When applying one's hand on the wall and projecting sacred paint onto it, the hand became part of the rock, taking up the same red or black color (Fig. 6). A concrete relationship was then established with the world of the spirits (Clottes and Lewis-Williams 1996).

As to composite creatures and fantastic animals displaying attributes of different species — like a bison with a horse's head, for instance — it is well known that such creatures are an integral part of shamanic visions.

All these observations lead to the conclusion that a great part of the art in the caves was done within the *framework* of a shamanic type of religion (Clottes and Lewis-Williams 1996, 2001; Lewis-Williams 2002). This does not explain everything, far from it. In particular, we remain mostly ignorant of the nature and details of their myths and sacred stories, which probably evolved over time and space into considerable complexity, as all religions do. We have gone a very long way, though, from the beginnings of spirituality. The clues left by those Cro-Magnons of the Upper Paleolithic enable us to make comparisons with historically known cultures of hunter-gatherers.

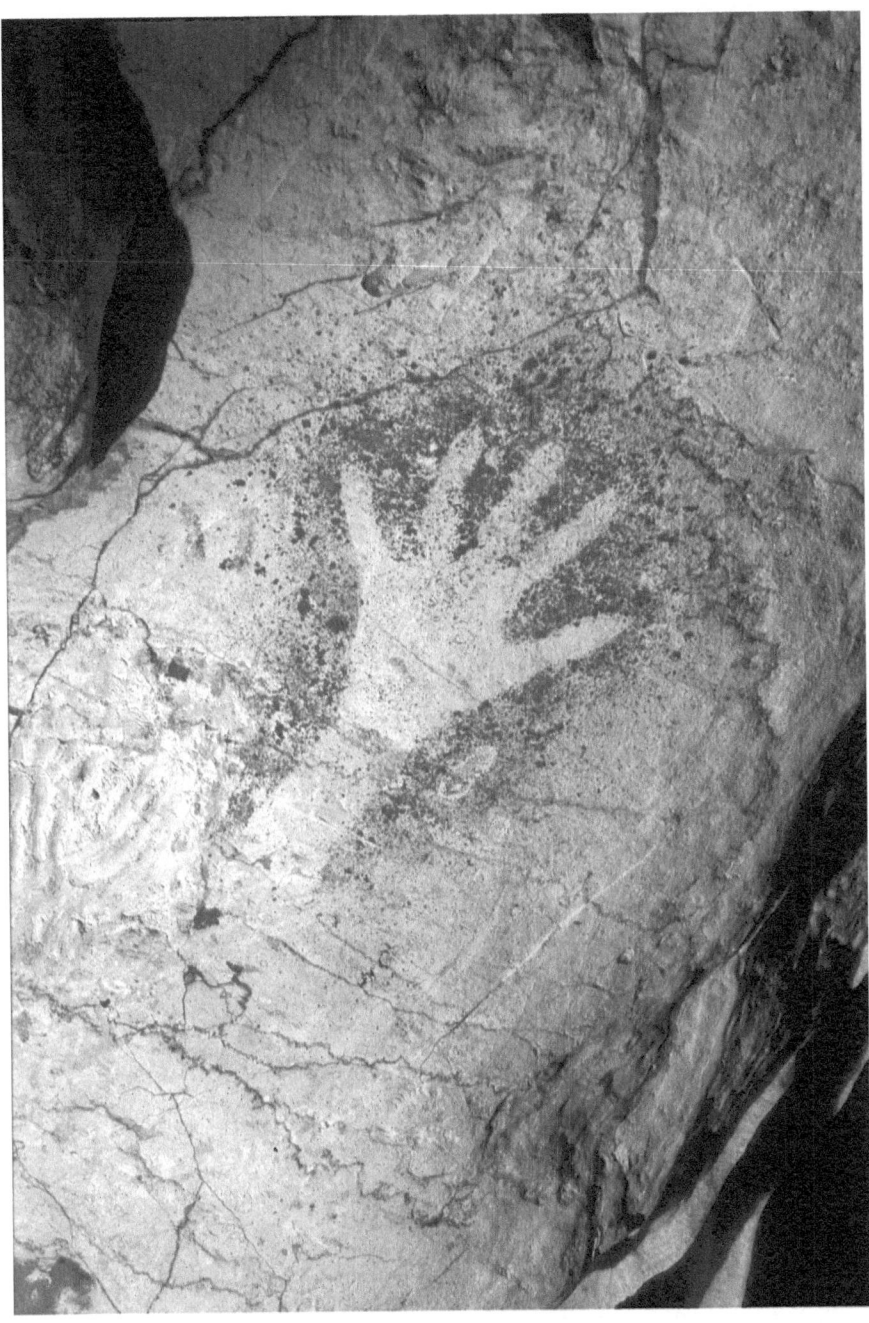

Fig. 6. A spectacular hand stencil, dating to about 27,000 BP in the Cosquer Cave (Marseille, France). Photo J. Clottes.

Though we only perceive "Palaeolithic religion in a faint penumbra" (Leroi-Gourhan 1964:151), its practitioners are finally very close to us.

References

Anati, E. 1989. *Les Origines de l'art et la formation de l'esprit humain.* Paris: Albin Michel.

Anati, E. 1999. *La Religion des Origines.* Paris: Bayard Editions.

Bednarik, R. 1995. "Concept-Mediated Marking in the Lower Palaeolithic." *Current Anthropology* 36/4: 605-634.

Bednarik, R. 2003. "The Earliest Evidence of Palaeoart." *Rock Art Research* 20/2: 89-135.

Bonifay, E. 2002. "L'Homme de Néandertal et l'Ours *(Ursus arctos)* dans la grotte du Régourdou (Montignac-sur-Vézère, Dordogne, France)." In Th. Tillet and L. Binford (eds.), *L'Ours et l'Homme*, pp. 247-254. Symposium Auberives-en-Royans, Isère, France, 1997. ERAUL 100.

Bonifay, E., and B. Vandermeersch. 1962. "Dépôts rituels d'ossements d'ours dans le gisement moustérien du Régourdou (Montignac, Dordogne)." *Comptes-rendus Académie des Sciences de Paris* 225: 1035-1036.

Clottes, J. 1993. "La Naissance du sens artistique." *Revue des Sciences Morales et Politiques*, pp. 173-184.

Clottes J., and D. Lewis-Williams. 1996. *The Shamans of Prehistory: Trance and Magic in the Painted Caves.* New York: Harry Abrams Inc.

Clottes J., and D. Lewis-Williams. 2001. *Les Chamanes de la Préhistoire. Texte intégral, polémique et réponses.* Paris: La maison des roches.

Conard N. 2003. "Paleolithic Ivory Sculptures from Southwestern Germany and the Origins of Figurative Art." *Nature* 426: 380-382.

Errico, F. d', and A. Nowell. 2000. "A New Look at the Berekhat Ram Figurine: Implications for the Origins of Symbolism." *Cambridge Archaeological Journal* 10/1: 123-167.

Henshilwood, C. S., et al. 2002. "Emergence of Modern Human Behavior: Middle Stone Age Engravings from South Africa." *Science* 295: 1278-1280.

Leroi-Gourhan, A. 1964. *Les Religions de la Préhistoire.* Paris: P.U.F.

Leroi-Gourhan, A. 1980. "Les Débuts de l'Art." Colloques internationaux du C.N.R.S. 599. *Les Processus de l'Hominisation*, pp. 131-132.

Lewis-Williams, J.-D. 2002. *The Mind in the Cave.* London: Thames & Hudson.

Lorblanchet, M. 1999. *La Naissance de l'art: Genèse de l'art préhistorique dans le monde.* Paris: Editions Errance.

Otte, M. 2001. *Les Origines de la Pensée: Archéologie de la Conscience.* Sprimont: Pierre Mardaga éd.

Rouzaud F., M. Soulier, and Y. Lignereux. 1995. "La Grotte de Bruniquel." *Spelunca* 60: 27-34.

10 Building Bridges to the Deep Human Past: Consciousness, Religion, and Art

David Lewis-Williams

Can we ever know how the earliest fully human beings thought and how they conceived of the world around them? A first reaction is to say that immaterial things like the thoughts and beliefs of 40,000 years ago (the time when *Homo sapiens* groups on their journey from Africa reached western Europe) are lost forever. Wander through the Louvre and the 32,000-year-old Chauvet Cave in France and we see pictures on walls. But we are so overwhelmed by the many obvious differences between the two locations that we conclude that the chasm of time cannot be bridged. This response is, of course, in many ways entirely justified. Yet there is a method by which we can build a bridge to at least some aspects of the deep human past. The Louvre is not the best place to start such a quest. A better starting point is rock art made by people who, at least until recently, lived hunter-gatherer lives comparable to, though certainly not identical with, those of Upper Paleolithic people and about whose lives we do know something — though, even then, lethal traps await the unwary.

Indeed, reference to any sort of "bridge" between an ethnographically known rock art and the images made in the French and Spanish caves between 35,000 and 10,000 years ago will raise the hackles of many researchers and invite charges of ahistoricism — reducing the past to the present, albeit a non-Western present. This visceral (rather than cerebral) reaction, one that has come into fashion fairly recently, is founded on a fundamental misconception: the method that builds the bridge is not a simple analogy between,

---

I thank colleagues who kindly commented on drafts of this paper: Geoff Blundel, Jeremy Hollmann, David Pearce, and Ben Smith. The illustrations come from the archive of the Rock Art Research Institute, University of the Witwatersrand. I thank the National Research Foundation for financial support (grant number: 2053693).

on the one hand, a recent hunter-gatherer rock art and, on the other, Upper Paleolithic images.

We therefore need to ask: Are there any grounds for a *soupçon* of ahistoricism *in certain clearly defined contexts?* This is another way of asking if there are any foundations — any commonalities — on which we can build a bridge to the deep past. To clarify some of the problems created by the misunderstandings that surround the notion of ahistoricism and to sketch a blueprint for a bridge, I begin with a widely recognized and apparently uncontentious categorization of the world's rock art — yet one that unfortunately conceals from unwitting researchers the route to that bridge.

Researchers commonly distinguish between, on the one hand, rock arts for which they have some relevant ethnography, some record of the makers' beliefs, and, on the other, arts for which there is no relevant ethnographic record whatsoever (Chippindale and Taçon 1998:6-8). Taken at face value, this categorization suggests that the San (Bushman) rock art of southern Africa falls into the first category and Upper Paleolithic cave art into the second. The distinction implies three tacitly accepted corollaries:

- first, that the mere existence of an ethnographic record renders explanation of rock art images easy;
- second, that in the absence of ethnography researchers must depend solely on formal methods (e.g., the shapes and other features of images, information "which is immanent in the images themselves" [Chippindale and Taçon 1998:7]);
- third, that the appropriate methods used for the study of the two categories of rock arts are necessarily different.

To mitigate the naiveté of these corollaries we need to examine exactly *how* ethnography "explains" rock arts. Then, having clarified what is in fact a complex and far-from-easy process, we can move on to the second, supposedly "uninformed," category of rock arts — those that are a tantalizingly misted window opening onto the deep human past. To say that in these cases we are reduced to formal methods is incorrect.

San Ethnography and Rock Art

One of the curious points about the history of San rock art research is researchers' use, or rather ignoring, of San ethnography (Lewis-Williams 1995c). Some of the most illuminating and directly relevant ethnography was published as long ago as the 1870s (Orpen 1874; Bleek 1875; see also Bleek and Lloyd 1911; Lewis-Williams 2000; Hollmann 2004), yet it is only in recent decades that researchers have thought it worthwhile to explore this early record and then to move on to the much more voluminous twentieth-century ethnography on the San of the Kalahari Desert in Namibia and Botswana (e.g., Marshall 1976, 1999; Lee 1979; Katz 1982; Biesele 1993; Guenther 1999). The difficulty that held up research was confusion over the method to be employed in linking ethnography to rock art images. To many researchers, San ethnography was opaque, a rigmarole of childish tales that they could not convincingly relate to specific images. In the end, no evidence could be found to support the idea that the images illustrated folktales. Then, in the 1970s, the situation changed.

First, researchers of that time realized that the ethnography does not "explain" the art in any direct way, as their predecessors hoped it would. Both the ethnography and the art need to be understood in terms of tropes, metaphors, cosmology, and mystical experiences that were (and still are) characteristic of the San (Lewis-Williams 1972, 1981; Lewis-Williams and Pearce 2004). When San people were asked to provide direct explanations of their rock art (as did indeed happen), they couched their observations in the same obscure categories of San thought as the images themselves, not those of Western anthropological discourse. It is these San thought patterns that afford understanding of the ethnography and the images.

Second, and as a result of seeking metaphors and tropes common to both ethnography and rock art, researchers of the 1970s began to recognize that the San were a shamanistic people, though there is still some debate as to whether this word is appropriate (e.g., Hamayon 1998; Lewis-Williams 1986, 2004). Certainly, the San have ritual specialists who enter a state of trance to perform the sorts of tasks that shamanistic people the world over perform (e.g., Katz 1982; Biesele 1993; Marshall 1999; Guenther 1999). That much is indisputable; the word that we use to denote such people in San communities is a secondary question. I feel that "shaman" does denote such ritual specialists and, moreover, it links the San to a worldwide pattern of religious behavior that has many geographic and temporal variations.

One brief and incomplete example of how both ethnography and images have to be simultaneously explained and how both point, each in its own way, to a shamanistic context will have to suffice. In 1873, a young San man, Qing, took Joseph Millerd Orpen to rock art sites in what is today southern Lesotho (Orpen 1874; Lewis-Williams 1980, 2003). When Orpen questioned his guide about the images that depict men with antelope heads and hoofs (therianthropes), he did not reply that they were hunters wearing masks or people dressed up as animals, as numerous twentieth-century researchers later concluded. Instead, he said that "[t]hey were men who had died and now lived in rivers, and were *spoilt at the same time as the elands* and by the dances of which you have seen paintings" (Orpen 1874:2; his italics).

Each of the phrases in this now well-known statement needs to be explained, to be translated into Western thought (Lewis-Williams 1980, 2003). But here I deal with only a couple of points that are most relevant to, and illustrative of, my overall argument concerning bridging the gap between the present and the distant past. I note that Qing linked the therianthropic images to

- eland,
- "spoiling," and
- "the dances of which you have seen paintings."

This conceptual triad — an antelope, "spoiling," and paintings — lies at the heart of San religious thought. We need to consider each element.

The eland *(Taurotragus oryx)* is the largest and fattest African antelope. It is also the animal that San image-makers in many parts of southern Africa most frequently depicted. Significantly, they believed it to be the favorite creature of the trickster-deity /Kaggen. It also features in three rites of passage: boys' first-kill, the Eland Bull Dance of girls' puberty rituals, and marriage observances (Lewis-Williams 1981). The species has a further key significance. For the San, the quantity of fat that an eland, especially a male, carries is an indication of its great potency. This potency (*n/om* in the !Kung language and *!gi:* in the now-extinct southern /Xam language) was an invisible (at least to ordinary people) "electricity" that can be controlled for the good of humankind and that facilitates contact between people and the supernatural realm. Sometimes, images of eland were made with eland blood mixed into the paint; thereby, they became "reservoirs of potency" (How 1962; Lewis-Williams 1986; Lewis-Williams and Dowson 1990; for the presence of blood of unknown species in pigment see Williamson 2000; Blundell 2004:159-163).

The dances to which Qing referred — and which the San painted in considerable and unmistakable detail — are shamanistic trance dances during which shamans activate supernatural potency so that it "boils" and causes them to fall into deep trance. Two of the idioms that the San use to denote deep, sometimes cataleptic, trances are "to die" and "to be spoiled." When Qing said that the antelope-headed men in the paintings had been "spoilt ... by the dances," he meant that they had entered trance. The San believe that, in this "spoilt" condition, shamans travel to the spirit realm, where they plead for the sick, fight off malevolent spirits of the dead, make rain, and guide antelope into the hunters' ambush. They also believe that, having activated potency and traveled to the spirit realm, shamans assume animal characteristics, sometimes related to the species that they "own" and from which they derive their power (Lewis-Williams 1981; Blundell 2004). These species are clearly comparable to the "animal helpers" of shamanistic societies in other parts of the world, though researchers seldom, if ever, use the term in southern Africa.

Qing's rather convoluted comments show that there is no clear, direct explanatory link between the ethnography and the rock art images. For instance, if we do not know what "spoilt . . . by the dances" means, we shall have little chance of understanding what Qing was saying. He explained the images in terms of his own thought patterns, and his remarks consequently remained buried in the literature for nearly a century. San verbal accounts *parallel* their pictorial images. One has therefore to "decode" both the ethnography and the images. Once this methodological key is recognized, a pattern begins to emerge that embraces not only ritual and images but also mythology and cosmology: the painted images are but a part of a complex web of beliefs, cosmology, and experiences (Lewis-Williams and Pearce 2004).

This process of emergence warrants further attention because it is related to the bridge that can be constructed, as I explain in a later section, between ethnographic rock arts, such as that of the San, and "non-ethnographic" rock arts, such as that found in the Upper Paleolithic caves of France and Spain. The nature of this bridge and its components became clear in two stages.

First, researchers realized that there needs to be a constant to-ing and fro-ing between San ethnography and the images (Lewis-Williams 1981:131). The ethnography alerts us to features that we had not noticed in the art; at the same time, specific images direct us back to the ethnography. There is thus a process of mutual illumination that, even after four decades of research, shows no sign of abating: there can therefore be no "final explanation," though this lack of finality does not mean that we cannot be confident about the correctness of what we already know. The old notion that the San were simple people who lived a simple life and made simple images depicting that life is now demonstrably false.

Second, another source of evidence entered the explanatory equation and is enjoying increasing prominence. Once it became clear that San rock art can be termed shamanistic, it was necessary to explore laboratory research done on altered states of consciousness — but without any reference to, or knowledge of, San rock art (Lewis-Williams 2001). Immediately, a new vista opened up (Lewis-Williams 2002b).

Neuropsychology

Arguments concerning the meaning of rock art that include neuropsychological research into altered states of consciousness accept as indisputable the proposition that the human brain and its associated nervous system are universals. Further, they accept that fully human consciousness is not a simple, unitary state, but rather a complex, mercurial "package deal" from which no one is exempt.

Consciousness can be usefully thought of as a spectrum (Lewis-Williams and Dowson 1988; Clottes and Lewis-Williams 1998; Lewis-Williams 2002a). At one extreme is what we may loosely call "alert consciousness," in which state subjects are aware of their surroundings and are able to respond to them in rational, thought-out ways. As we move toward the other end of the spectrum we pass through states that are more introverted and meditative, such as reverie and day-dreaming, and then on to sleep and dreaming, and, finally, to deeply altered states in which all the senses hallucinate. Everyday life necessarily entails shifts, some quite subtle, along this spectrum that extends from alert states to sleep. In more unusual conditions, subjects experience deep, hallucinatory trance. These conditions include not only certain pathologies (e.g., temporal lobe epilepsy, migraine, and schizophrenia) and the ingestion of psychotropic substances, but also pain, audio- and rhythmic driving, hyperventilation, and sensory deprivation. (Interestingly, it is easier to define altered consciousness than alert, or what is considered "normal," human consciousness. One cannot study one without the other.)

The transition to deep hallucinatory states may be thought of as passing through three stages — what has been termed the "neuropsychological model" (Lewis-Williams and Dowson 1988; Lewis-Williams 2002a). This model deals principally with visual hallucinations, though all the senses hallucinate and need to be considered. It is possible for subjects to pass so swiftly into the final stage that the first two pass unnoticed.

In the first stage, subjects experience the visual percepts known as "phosphenes," "form constants," and "entoptic phenomena." They comprise a range of luminous, pulsating geometric forms, and include zigzags, dots, nested catenary curves, grids, sets of parallel lines, and brilliant meandering lines. In the second stage, subjects try to make sense of these forms: according to their emotional state, they construe them as familiar objects that may range from, say, a cup of water, if the subject is thirsty, to a bomb, if the subject is fearful. The third stage is approached via a swirling vortex. Subjects feel drawn into this vortex and construe it as a tunnel, a long passage, a whirlpool, or something similar. On the "far" side of the vortex lie a hallucinatory realm of monsters, vivid experiences that may be terrifying or ecstatic, transformations into animals, and laws of causality different from those that obtain in the material world. In this extreme state, entoptic phenomena may be experienced peripherally or integrated with iconic hallucinations. Subjects participate in, rather than simply observe, this realm.

Now, if the human nervous system is universal, as we believe it to be, we can say that shamans all over the world, at all times, and regardless of their cultural background had, and still have, the potential to experience all three stages, as well as the transitional vortex. This much is universal. By contrast, the content of stages two and three (but not of stage one) is culturally informed. People "see" what they expect to see. Inuit shamans may see and interact with polar bears; San shamans see and consort with "spirit" eland and the spiritual forms of other African animals.

The researcher who first made all this abundantly plain was Gerardo Reichel-Dolmatoff (1978). He worked with the Tukano and other shamanistic people of the Amazon basin. They told him that the geometric forms that they painted on the walls of their houses were what they saw after ingesting the hallucinogen *yajé* (*Banisteriopsis* sp.). Reichel-Dolmatoff recognized that the forms were universal. How the Tukano understood their entoptic phenomena was cultural. For instance, they said that a set of undulating lines represented "the thought of the Sun-Father," while horizontal crenelated lines represented the Snake-Canoe of their Creation Myth.

Armed with the results of neuropsychological research on altered states of consciousness and the brilliant use that Reichel-Dolmatoff made of those results, it was possible to revisit many San images that had hitherto been entirely enigmatic and that were not explained by the ethnography.

San Visionary Experiences

Megan Biesele has for many years studied the importance of !Kung shamans' experiences in considerable detail. She works through the medium of the !Kung language, which she speaks fluently. She found that subsequent versions of what happened during a specific religious revelation (such as the "gift" of a new medicine song imbued with potency) may vary as people remember and talk about the occasion. But what does not vary is the understanding that those believed to have received the revelation were

> experiencing some sort of altered state of consciousness at the time. . . .
> These states, whether dreams, trances, or day-time confrontation with the

spirits, are regarded as reliable channels for the transfer of new meaning from the other world into this one.... Though dreams may happen at any time, the central religious experiences of Ju/'hoan [!Kung] life are consciously and, as a matter of course, approached through the avenue of trance. (Biesele 1993:70)

Researchers who question "the supposed centrality of hallucinatory experience in visualization and the production of rock art" and simplistically argue that San myth should be seen as "determining, rather than determined by" trance experience (Solomon 1997:3) should note Biesele's insistence that "religious experiences of Ju/'hoan life" are principally, "and as a matter of course, approached through the avenue of trance." The centrality of religious revelations during altered states of consciousness, together with their associated metaphors and transformations, explains more images in greater detail than any other view of San rock art. Researchers should therefore examine San rock art with the findings of neuropsychology in mind.

In the rock engravings (petroglyphs) of the central southern African plateau, many geometric images, formally comparable to entoptic phenomena, are interspersed amongst iconic images of animals and, less frequently, human beings (Dowson 1992; Lewis-Williams 1988; Lewis-Williams and Blundell 1997). As in other parts of the world, researchers at first believed that these two different kinds of images constituted two distinct but parallel arts, the one purely "symbolic," the other iconic, or representational. Now, in the light of neuropsychological research, we know that the geometric images are no different in origin from the apparently representational ones: both kinds of image are seen in altered states of consciousness, where, moreover, they are sometimes combined. Both are characteristic of the spirit world, though we do not know what the San believed about the geometric images; the ethnography is silent on this point (an exception is the "threads of light" that lead San shamans to the spirit realm; this vision probably derives from entoptic meandering lines).

Despite this general limitation, there are some geometric images that we are beginning to understand, not through "formal" methods but by means of an interweaving of neuropsychological research and ethnography. An example is a semi-circular line from which numerous antelope legs protrude (Fig. 1; for another example see Lewis-Williams 1986). I have argued that such images derive from the entoptic phenomenon sometimes known as the migraine scotoma, or fortification illusion (Lewis-Williams 1995a). It is a scintillating arc, the outside edge of which is serrated, or crenelated. In the interior of the curve there is a blind spot that appears to the subject as a "black hole":

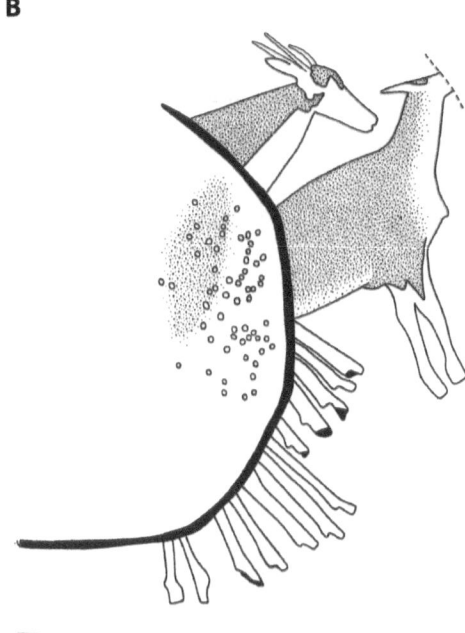

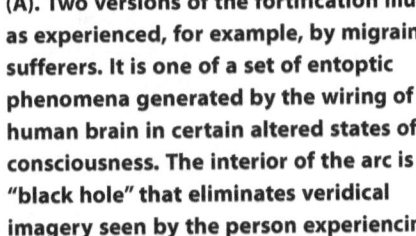

Fig. 1
(A). Two versions of the fortification illusion as experienced, for example, by migraine sufferers. It is one of a set of entoptic phenomena generated by the wiring of the human brain in certain altered states of consciousness. The interior of the arc is a "black hole" that eliminates veridical imagery seen by the person experiencing the mental percept.
(B). A San rock painting based on the fortification illusion. Two eland antelope and numerous antelope legs seem to emerge from the "black hole" within the arc, which was probably believed to afford access to the spirit realm. Scale in centimeters.
(C) Three San rock paintings that appear to be derived from the fortification illusion. In the past, they were mistaken for depictions of boats.

it causes veridical percepts that it covers to "disappear." It seems that the San construed the pulsating periphery of the curve as the flashing of antelope legs as seen by a hunter concealed behind a low bush. The "black hole" within the arc seems to have been apprehended as an entrance into the spirit world that lay behind the surface of the rock wall (Lewis-Williams and Dowson 1990). Sometimes animals or anthropomorphic images are shown "disappearing" into the "black hole."

The motif, together with throbbing aural hallucinations, thus suggests passage to the spirit world via the drumming of antelope hoofs. Indeed, a !Kung San woman has explicitly associated the sound of pounding hoofs with the revelation of a potency-filled, shamanistic "medicine" song:

> She saw a herd of giraffes running before an approaching thunderstorm. The rolling beat of their hooves grew louder and mingled in her head with the sound of sudden rain. Suddenly, a song she had never heard before came to her, and she began to sing. G//aoan (the great god) told her it was a medicine song. (Biesele 1993:67)

The conclusion that the San construed the fortification illusion as an animal-pervaded, animal-facilitated entrance to the spirit world is corroborated by other images that are painted to give the impression that they are emerging from, or entering into, the rock face, often via steps, cracks, or other inequalities (Fig. 2). The rock was, I argue, a "veil" suspended between this world and the spirit world (Lewis-Williams and Dowson 1990). It was the task of San shamans to pass through the rock (via the mental vortex), to experience what was happening in the spirit world, to see all God's wondrous animals that lived there, and then to return to the material world and to re-create (rather than merely depict) their visions on the "veil." Thus many of the images of San rock art were not simply "pictures" of animals that had been seen walking in the countryside. Rather, they were "things-in-themselves," re-created or "fixed" apprehensions of spiritual things. The images were sources of potency and persuasive evidence for the existence of a realm that ordinary people were unable to visit.

A brief caveat needs to be entered at this point. Image-makers are not insensate photocopiers. They do not automatically reproduce their mental imagery exactly as they experience it. Rather, they process their imagery in culturally informed ways. That is why shamanistic arts around the world evince different styles, while they have fundamental commonalities of content.

The conceptual context of San shamanistic trans-cosmological journeys and the "processed" re-creations of their experiences were a three-tiered uni-

Building Bridges to the Deep Human Past

Fig. 2. A San rock painting showing therianthropes emerging from a deep crack in the face of the wall of a rock shelter. One of the heads bleeds from the nose, as do shamans in trance. The fish, eels, and turtles indicate that the adjacent figures are "underwater" in their trance experience. The bunch of flywhisks is another reference to the trance, or healing, dance. The painting depicts a vision of the spirit realm emerging from behind the "veil" of the rock face.

verse (Lewis-Williams 1996, 1997c; Lewis-Williams and Pearce 2004). As is common in shamanistic societies, the San believed in a tiered cosmos: above the level on which people lived was a spirit realm, and below the level of daily life was another. (In some shamanistic societies these realms are subdivided.) I argue that the remarkable universality of these beliefs (they recur in many religions) derive from experiences "wired into" the human nervous system. One of those experiences is a sensation of weightlessness and flight that, together with a subject's participation in stage-three hallucinations, gives rise to notions of a spirit realm in or above the sky. The other experience is passing through the constricting vortex; this gives rise to feelings of passing underground or underwater to another realm. Today, the tunnel experience is closely associated with near-death experiences (Siegel 1977:132; Horowitz 1975:178; Willis 1994; Siegel and Jarvik 1975:127, 143; Grof and Grof 1980; Drab 1981; Fox 2003).

These "wired" experiences of altered consciousness are the only viable explanation that I know for the universal, though hardly likely, belief that there are spirit worlds above and below us, that these worlds are populated by supernatural beings and creatures, that transformations take place in them, and that it is possible for people who have mastered the techniques of altered consciousness to visit the spirit realms. It is this understanding that enables us to construct a bridge to the Upper Paleolithic.

West European Upper Paleolithic Cave Art

As I have pointed out, some researchers have unfortunately assumed that this bridge is a simple, comparative analogy between San rock art (or some other ethnographically known instance) and Upper Paleolithic art. What I have already said shows that this is not the case (Lewis-Williams 1991). A *simple* analogy assumes that the more commonalities that exist between the source of an analogy and its object, the more likelihood that trait X in the source will also be present in the object (e.g., Chippindale and Taçon 1998:8). It is this simplistic understanding of analogy that has misled some archaeologists and others to believe that all analogies necessarily lead to false conclusions.

A more sophisticated kind of analogy is founded on strong relations of relevance (Wylie 1988). The phrase "strong relations of relevance" means that some causal or otherwise ineluctable, universal link exists between A and B. Consequently, if A is found in the archaeological record, B must also have been present. Of course, it is extremely difficult to find strong relations of relevance that are not trivial.

Nevertheless, an analogical bridge that is founded on non-trivial relations of relevance can be constructed to the Upper Paleolithic (Lewis-Williams 1991, 1997, 2002a). This bridge is, at least in the first instance, neurological: the people of the Upper Paleolithic had fully modern nervous systems and therefore had the potential to experience all parts of the spectrum of consciousness and all stages of the neuropsychological model, though, as I have pointed out, the contents of their hallucinations would have differed from those of present-day people. If we find persuasive evidence in the archaeological record for those stages and experiences (A), we can posit the involvement of altered states of consciousness (B) in the making of the images.

The evidence in Upper Paleolithic caves has been adequately discussed and need not be rehearsed here. Briefly, it concerns imagery attributable to all three stages of altered consciousness, blends of images (e.g., therianthropes), "floating" imagery, and images emerging from the rock face (Lewis-Williams and Dowson 1988; Lewis-Williams 2002a).

The inference that Upper Paleolithic image-making was in some way associated with altered states of consciousness is only a first step in the elucidation of Upper Paleolithic cave art. Having made it, we should move on to a wide range of other characteristics of the content and context of the art that are also compatible with, and explained by, what we know about altered states of consciousness (Lewis-Williams 1997a, 2002a).

Further, and most importantly, all people, no matter what their cultural context, have to make sense of the full spectrum of altered consciousness; if they are to live sane, viable lives they have no alternative but to develop shared explanations for altered consciousness of various kinds. They have to divide the spectrum into segments and to place differential value on those segments. For instance, some societies place great value on dreams as divine communication. Others, such as sections of modern Western society, accept that dreams are caused by random firing of synapses in REM sleep: for these societies, dreams do not bestow any moral, religious, or political advantage. Upper Paleolithic people must have had their own communally accepted ways of understanding and placing values on the full spectrum of human consciousness. They had no other option.

Seen in this light, the subterranean images of Franco-Cantabria can be accepted as the products of a specific and historically situated — probably unique — form of shamanism, *not as a replica of any ethnographically known shamanistic community*. What are some of the implications of this proposition? How much evidence does it explain? Does it explain more evidence than other, competing, explanations?

It seems likely that physical entrance into the underground passages and chambers was seen as equivalent to psychic entry into the vortex and thus a supernatural realm: the caves were the entrails of a nether world (Lewis-Williams 2004; Clottes and Lewis-Williams 1998, 2001). In that realm, shamans sought spirit animals by touch, sight, the play of light and shadow, the visual image-projection of altered states that has been likened to a slide or film show, and sound; shamans often construe aural hallucinations as the utterances of animals. Altered states, whether induced by sensory deprivation in the dark, silent passages, or by the ingestion of psychotropic substances, or by other means, enabled Upper Paleolithic ritual specialists to pass through the membrane of the entrails into the very depths of the spirit realm that lay beyond. They then "fixed" their visions on the surface of the membrane in order to control them and to derive power from them. Once "fixed" (by engraving or painting), *some* of these images may never have been revisited. They were not "art" made for "viewing" (Conkey 1987, 1991). On the contrary, they were the detritus of a concatenation of rituals that began with the gathering of the raw materials from which paint (in itself often a powerful substance) was made and (perhaps) ended when the image-maker abandoned the image in the dark underworld (Lewis-Williams 1995b). But people knew that the images were there, and, even if largely unseen, they continued to influence belief and behavior.

Other images, generally larger, more elaborate, and requiring the labor of more than one person (e.g., those in the Hall of the Bulls and the Axial Gallery in Lascaux), were probably socially constructed to act as participants in (not merely a backdrop to) communal rituals. These rituals may have been preparatory to novices' explorations of the depths of the caves and vision quests that would bestow power on them (Lewis-Williams 2002a).

Each Upper Paleolithic cave needs to be studied in terms of its images, its spaces, and other evidence of human activity (for instance, the tiny pieces of bone thrust into cracks in Enlène, or the teeth and larger pieces of bone placed in niches in Les Trois Frères). In this way, we shall be able to start to discern temporal and regional variations in Upper Paleolithic shamanistic practices; I do not argue that Upper Paleolithic shamanism was static and geographically uniform (Lewis-Williams 1997a).

Mention of communal — but dynamic rather than static — shamanistic activity brings me to a final point. When human beings make sense of the spectrum of consciousness, they do so socially, not individually. But shared beliefs are always open to contestation. The raw material of altered states of consciousness (visions and other experiences) is a site of social struggle (Lewis-Williams 1997; cf. Lewis-Williams and Dowson 1993; Lewis-Williams and Pearce 2005 on Neolithic social discrimination). People do not merely accept the received explanations of the spirit world; sometimes they challenge and try to subvert them. The caves thus became contested templates for social differentiation. Movement into and through the constructed (by the making of images and other ritual activities) underground spaces had social implications. Who had access to various parts of the caves, what they were permitted to do in those parts, and who remained at the entrance of the cave or went well beyond it were social issues that were negotiated through time. Altered states of consciousness and movement through caves thus combined to become instruments of social discrimination.

Consciousness, Religion and Art

All in all, I argue that the caves of Western Europe provide one geographically and historically specific set of evidence for an origin not only of religion, as has indeed often been claimed, but also for accelerating social differentiation as an integral part of religion. At the heart of all these complex processes lies the inescapable need to make sense of the spectrum of altered consciousness. Almost inevitably, people everywhere interpret some mental experiences as contact with supernatural realms above and below the surface of the earth and go on to ascribe special status to those who are able to access those realms. This necessity is the bridge that gives us some insight into the mental and social activities of Upper Paleolithic people.

The structure and electro-chemical workings of the human brain produce a complex nexus of experiences. In making sense of those experiences, a community develops notions of a supernatural realm, the defining feature of religion, and, necessarily, differential access to it. The principal and continuing historical features of human society as we have come to know them are intertwined religion and politics. Religion, through its foundation in supernatural revelations and injunctions, can lend politics a destructive fanaticism, as history amply exemplifies. If those revelations originate in the functioning of the human brain as it has been formed by millennia of evolution, we need to ask if it is possible to envisage religion without a supernatural component. Is belief in supernatural realms and influences today an anachronism?

References

Biesele, M. 1978. "Sapience and Scarce Resources: Communication Systems of the !Kung and Other Foragers." *Social Science Information* 17:921-947.

Biesele, M. 1993. *"Women Like Meat": The Folklore and Foraging Ideology of the Kalahari Ju/'oan*. Johannesburg: Witwatersrand University Press.

Bleek, W. H. I. 1875. "A Brief Account of Bushman Folklore and Other Texts." Cape Town: Government Printers.

Bleek, W. H. I., and L. C. Lloyd. 1911. *Specimens of Bushman Folklore*. London: George Allen.

Blundell, G. 2004. *Nqabayo's Nomansland: San Rock Art and the Somatic Past*. Uppsala: University of Uppsala.

Chippindale, C., and P. S. C. Taçon. 1998. "An Archaeology of Rock-Art Through Informed Methods and Formal Methods." In C. Chippindale and P. S. C. Taçon (eds.), *The Archaeology of Rock-Art*, pp. 1-10. Cambridge: Cambridge University Press.

Clottes, J., and J. D. Lewis-Williams. 1998. *The Shamans of Prehistory: Trance and Magic in the Painted Caves.* New York: Harry Abrams.

Clottes, J., and J. D. Lewis-Williams. 2001. *Les chamanes de la préhistoire: texte integral, polémique et réponses.* Paris: La Maison des Roches.

Conkey, M. 1987. "New Approaches in the Search for Meaning: A Review of Research in 'Palaeolithic Art.'" *Journal of Field Archaeology* 14:413-430.

Conkey, M. 1991. "Contexts of Action, Contexts for Power: Material Culture and Gender in the Magdalenian." In J. M. Gero and M. Conkey (eds.), *Engendering Archaeology: Women and Prehistory,* pp. 57-92. Oxford: Basil Blackwell.

Dowson, T. A. 1992. *Rock Engravings of Southern Africa.* Johannesburg: Witwatersrand University Press.

Drab, K. J. 1981. "The Tunnel Experience: Reality or Hallucination?" *Anabiosis* 1:126-152.

Fox, M. 2003. *Religion, Spirituality and the Near-Death Experience.* London: Routledge.

Grof, S., and C. Grof. 1980. *Beyond Death: The Gates of Consciousness.* London and New York: Thames and Hudson.

Guenther, M. 1999. *Tricksters and Trancers: Bushman Religion and Society.* Bloomington: Indiana University Press.

Hamayon, R. N. 1998. "'Ecstasy' or the West-Dreamt Asiberian Shaman." In H. Wautischer (ed.), *Tribal Epistemologies: Essays in the Philosophy of Anthropology,* pp. 163-174, 188-190. Aldershot: Ashgate.

Hollmann, J. C. (ed.). 2004. *Customs and Beliefs of the /Xam Bushmen.* Johannesburg: Witwatersrand University Press.

Horowitz, M. 1975. "Hallucinations: An Information Processing Approach." In R. K. Siegel and L. J. West (eds.), *Hallucinations: Behaviour, Experience and Theory,* pp. 163-195. New York: Wiley.

How, M. W. 1962. *The Mountain Bushmen of Basutoland.* Pretoria: Van Schaik.

Katz, R. 1982. *Boiling Energy: Community Healing among the Kalahari !Kung.* Cambridge: Cambridge University Press.

Lee, R. B. 1979. *The !Kung San: Men, Women and Work in a Foraging Society.* Cambridge: Cambridge University Press.

Lewis-Williams, J. D. 1972. "The Syntax and Function of the Giant's Castle Rock Paintings." *South African Archaeological Bulletin* 27:49-65.

Lewis-Williams, J. D. 1980. "Ethnography and Iconography: Aspects of Southern San Thought and Art." *Man* 15:467-482.

Lewis-Williams, J. D. 1981. *Believing and Seeing: Symbolic Meanings in Southern San Rock Paintings.* London: Academic Press.

Lewis-Williams, J. D. 1986a. "The Last Testament of the Southern San." *South African Archaeological Bulletin* 41:10-11.

Lewis-Williams, J. D. 1986b. "Cognitive and Optical Illusions in San Rock Art Research." *Current Anthropology* 27:171-178.

Lewis-Williams, J. D. 1988. *Reality and Non-Reality in San Rock Art.* Twenty-Fifth Raymond Dart Lecture. Johannesburg: Institute for the Study of Man in Africa, Witwatersrand University Press.

Lewis-Williams, J. D. 1991. "Wrestling with Analogy: A Problem in Upper Palaeolithic Art Research." *Proceedings of the Prehistoric Society* 57/1:149-162.

Lewis-Williams, J. D. 1992. "Ethnographic Evidence Relating to 'Trance' and 'Shamans' among Northern and Southern Bushmen." *South African Archaeological Bulletin* 47:56-60.

Lewis-Williams, J. D. 1995a. "Seeing and Construing: The Making and 'Meaning' of a Southern African Rock Art Motif." *Cambridge Archaeological Journal* 5/1:3-23.

Lewis-Williams, J. D. 1995b. "Modelling the Production and Consumption of Rock Art." *South African Archaeological Bulletin* 50:143-154.

Lewis-Williams, J. D. 1995c. "Perspectives and Traditions in Southern African Rock Art Research." In K. Helskog and B. Olsen (eds.), *Perceiving Rock Art: Social and Political Perspectives*, pp. 65-86. Oslo: Novus forlag.

Lewis-Williams, J. D. 1996. "'A Visit to the Lion's House': Structure, Metaphors and Sociopolitical Significance of a Nineteenth-Century Bushman Myth." In J. Deacon and T. A. Dowson (eds.), *Voices from the Past: /Xam Bushmen and the Bleek and Lloyd Collection*, pp. 122-141. Johannesburg: Witwatersrand University Press.

Lewis-Williams, J. D. 1997a. "Art, Agency and Altered Consciousness: A Motif in Upper Palaeolithic (Quercy) Art." *Antiquity* 71:810-830.

Lewis-Williams, J. D. 1997b. "Harnessing the Brain: Vision and Shamanism in Upper Palaeolithic Western Europe." In M. W. Conkey, O. Soffer, D. Stratmann, and N. G. Jablonski (eds.), *Beyond Art: Pleistocene Image and Symbol*. Memoirs of the California Academy of Science, No. 23, pp. 321-342. San Francisco.

Lewis-Williams, J. D. 1997c. "The Mantis, the Eland and the Meerkats: Conflict and Mediation in a Nineteenth-Century San Myth." In P. McAllister (ed.), *Culture and the Commonplace: Anthropological Essays in Honour of David Hammond-Tooke*, pp. 195-216. Special issue of *African Studies* 56/2.

Lewis-Williams, J. D. 2000. *Stories That Float from Afar: Ancestral Folklore of the San of Southern Africa*. College Station: Texas A&M University Press; Cape Town: David Philip Publishers.

Lewis-Williams, J. D. 2001. "Brainstorming Images: Neuropsychology and Rock Art Research." In D. S. Whitley (ed.), *Handbook of Rock Art Research*, pp. 332-357. Walnut Creek, CA: Altamira Press.

Lewis-Williams, J. D. 2002a. *The Mind in the Cave: Consciousness and the Origins of Art*. London and New York: Thames & Hudson.

Lewis-Williams, J. D. 2002b. *A Cosmos in Stone: Interpreting Religion and Society through Rock Art*. Walnut Creek, CA: Altamira Press.

Lewis-Williams, J. D. 2003. *Images of Mystery: Rock Art of the Drakensberg*. Cape Town: Double Storey. (*L'art rupestre en Afrique du Sud: Mystérieuses images du Drakensberg*. Paris: Le Seuil.)

Lewis-Williams, J. D. 2004. "On Sharpness and Scholarship in the Debate on 'Shamanism.'" *Current Anthropology* 45:404-406.

Lewis-Williams, J. D., and G. Blundell. 1997. "New Light on Finger-Dots in Southern Africa Rock Art: Synesthesia, Transformation and Technique." *South African Journal of Science* 93:51-54.

Lewis-Williams, J. D., and J. Clottes. 1998. *Shamans of Prehistory: Trance and Magic in the Painted Caves*. New York: Harry Abrams.

Lewis-Williams, J. D., and T. A. Dowson. 1988. "The Signs of All Times: Entoptic Phenomena in Upper Palaeolithic Art. *Current Anthropology* 29:201-245.

Lewis-Williams, J. D., and T. A. Dowson. 1990. "Through the Veil: San Rock Paintings and the Rock Face." *South African Archaeological Bulletin* 45:5-16.

Lewis-Williams, J. D., and T. A. Dowson. 1993. "On Vision and Power in the Neolithic: Evidence from the Decorated Monuments." *Current Anthropology* 34:55-65.

Lewis-Williams, J. D., and T. A. Dowson. 1999 (1989). *Images of Power: Understanding Southern African Rock Art*. Johannesburg: Southern Book Publishers.

Lewis-Williams, J. D., and D. G. Pearce. 2004. *San Spirituality: Roots, Expressions and Social Consequences*. Walnut Creek, CA: Altamira Press. Cape Town: Double Storey.

Lewis-Williams, J. D., and D. G. Pearce. 2005. *Inside the Neolithic Mind: Consciousness, Cosmos and the Realm of the Gods*. London: Thames and Hudson.

Marshall, L. 1976. *The !Kung of Nyae Nyae*. Cambridge, MA: Harvard University Press.

Marshall, L. 1999. *Nyae Nyae !Kung: Beliefs and Rites*. Cambridge, MA: Peabody Museum, Harvard University.

Orpen, J. M. 1874. "A Glimpse into the Mythology of the Maluti Bushmen." *Cape Monthly Magazine* NS 9/49: 1-13.

Reichel-Dolmatoff, G. 1978. *Beyond the Milky Way: Hallucinatory Imagery of the Tukano Indians*. Los Angeles: UCA Latin America Center.

Siegel, R. K. 1977. "Hallucinations." *Scientific American* 237:132-140.

Siegel, R. K., and M. E. Jarvik. 1975. "Drug-Induced Hallucinations in Animals and Man." In R. K. Siegel and L. J. West (eds.), *Hallucinations: Behaviour, Experience and Theory*, pp. 81-161. New York: Wiley.

Solomon, A. 1997. "The Myth of Ritual Origins? Ethnography, Mythology and Interpretation of San Rock Art." *South African Archaeological Bulletin* 52:3-13.

Williamson, B. S. 2000. "Prehistoric Stone Tool Residue Analysis from Rose Cottage Cave and Other Southern African Sites." Unpublished Ph.D. diss., University of the Witwatersrand, Johannesburg.

Willis, R. 1994. "New Shamanism." *Anthropology Today* 10/6: 16-18.

Wylie, A. 1988. "'Simple' Analogy and the Role of Relevance Assumptions: Implications of Archaeological Practice." *International Studies in the Philosophy of Science* 2:134-150.

11 The Origins of Human Cognition and the Evolution of Rationality

Ian Tattersall

Introduction

Human beings pride themselves on their capacity for rational thought, and it is certainly true that human ratiocinative abilities are among the most striking of the qualities that distinguish *Homo sapiens* from even its closest living relatives in nature. Nonetheless, it is equally true that human beings do not act rationally all — or even much — of the time. Neither are most complex human actions either completely rational or completely irrational. Apparently, the specialized and uniquely human capacity for rational cognition has been grafted on to an underlying, and preexisting, cognitive substrate of a very different kind. This strongly suggests that, at some point in its evolutionary history, one hominid lineage (hominids being members of the zoological family to which *Homo sapiens* and its non-ape relatives belong) acquired a neurobiological innovation, probably a relatively minor one in terms of overall brain organization, that made possible the unprecedented human cognition that is familiar today. Exactly what that innovation might have been is beyond the scope of this contribution. Rather, I want to look here at the evolutionary context within which this fateful acquisition was made, to examine some of its correlates, and to suggest the timing and the pattern of the events that led up to it.

The fact that *Homo sapiens* is the lone hominid on Earth today tends to reinforce the reductionistically attractive view that our species is the outcome of a long-term process of refinement within a single evolving lineage, and

---

I am most grateful to F. LeRon Shults for his invitation to participate in this well-deserved tribute to our esteemed friend and colleague J. Wentzel van Huyssteen.

that our vaunted mental capacities are the result of a slow, generation-by-generation process of fine-tuning by natural selection over the eons, as smarter individuals out-reproduced dumber ones. Almost certainly, though, this received notion that *Homo sapiens* with all its uniquenesses is the result of a long and single-minded slog from primitiveness to perfection is altogether wrong (Tattersall 1995). Examination of our rapidly expanding fossil and archaeological records indicates that over the course of hominid evolution significant change has been not only episodic but relatively rare, and that modern symbolic cognition probably emerged in a rather recent, short-term, and emergent event, as the result of a chance combination of new elements with preexisting ones, some of them extremely ancient indeed.

Early Hominids

The story of the hominid family begins some six to seven million years ago, with the emergence in Africa of early bipedal hominoids. (Hominoidea is the zoological superfamily that includes humans, apes, and their fossil relatives.) A combination of geological and climatic events ushered in a gradual trend toward drying and greater seasonality of rainfall following about 7 million years (7 myr) ago or a bit earlier, and as a consequence the formerly fairly monolithic dense humid forests of Africa began to fragment and to yield to more open woodland formations. This shrinking of their ancestral habitat forced hominoid populations in various parts of the continent to spend more time on the ground (Kingdon 2003). Some of these ancient apes, already in the habit of holding their trunks upright while moving and foraging in the trees, found it easier to move upright on their hind-limbs while on the ground than to move quadrupedally in the manner of the living apes; and presumably it was an early hominoid of this kind that gave rise to the ancestral hominid, the earliest member of the "human" family Hominidae.

Several fossil forms dating from the 7-4 myr period have been classified in Hominidae, though together they make a fairly motley assemblage, unified principally by the claims made for them of upright bipedality (see Schwartz and Tattersall, 2005). The extinct creatures concerned include the recently described 7-6 myr-old *Sahelanthropus tchadensis* cranium from the Central-West African country of Chad; the 6.0 myr-old fragments of *Orrorin tugenensis* from Kenya; the equally fragmentary 5.8–4.4 myr-old *Ardipithecus ramidus/kadabba* fossils from Ethiopia; and the 4.2 myr-old remains of *Australopithecus anamensis* from northern Kenya. Of these, only the last can be interpreted definitively as bipedal on the basis of preserved parts; but if all of these rather heterogeneous fossils are properly classified as hominid, they very powerfully make the point that, from the very start, the history of Hominidae has been one of evolutionary experimentation, rather than one of linear development (Tattersall 2002). From the beginning, it seems, the hominid family has had an (evolutionarily routine) tendency to toss new entrants (species) on to the evolutionary stage, to sink or to swim in competition with their own relatives or other components of the biota.

The earliest well-known representative of this radiation of early bipeds is *Australopithecus afarensis,* the species that embraces the famous 3.2 myr-old partial skeleton from Hadar, in Ethiopia, popularly known as "Lucy" (Johanson and Edey 1981). This species is by now known from literally hundreds of specimens from Ethiopian sites that date in the 3.8–3.0 myr range. And it was creatures of similar kind that probably also made the famous trackways discovered at Laetoli, in Tanzania (Leakey and Harris 1987). These provided astonishing behavioral confirmation that hominids were up and moving on their hind feet 3.5 myr ago. Still, these short-statured early hominids, though upright bipeds on the ground, were not bipedal in the way we are. In contrast to the narrow pelvises of the quadrupedal apes that do not have to support guts lying above them, those of the early bipeds were broad like ours, indeed even more laterally flaring. But their overall body proportions remained archaic, with relatively short legs and long arms, narrow shoulders and long, somewhat curved extremities (Johanson and Edgar 1996). These qualities would have served the early hominids well when sheltering and foraging in their ancestral habitat of the trees, even as they clearly moved on two legs while on the ground. These creatures thus showed what was in a sense a compromise between ancestral and modern body forms, but it would be wrong to regard it as "transitional." Instead, it was a successful adaptation that seems to have stayed essentially stable over several million years, even as new species of archaic hominid continually came and went (Tattersall 2004). Still, it was successful within a fairly closely defined range of environments, which included the forest itself, the thinner forest edges, and the adjacent woodlands, in which grassy patches were dotted with trees.

Yet radical as their body structure was, these early hominids are nowadays widely viewed by palaeoanthropologists as "bipedal apes" (e.g., Aiello and Dean 1990). This is because, for all the novelties seen in their locomotor skeletons, their skulls remained remarkably ape-like. Modern humans have tiny faces tucked *beneath* the front of huge balloon-like braincases; the early hominids showed the opposite, ape-like conformation, with ape-sized brains housed within small cranial vaults that lay *behind* large, aggressively jutting faces. What is more, there is nothing in the record to suggest that the early hominids had moved beyond the level of cognition typical of the modern apes. And as intuitively gifted as the apes are, there is little in their behavior to suggest that it is underwritten by elements of the ratiocinative process that underpins modern human thought (Byrne 1995).

The First Stone Tool Makers

At around 2.5 myr ago, the first stone tools appear (Schick and Toth 1993; Klein 1999). These are fairly rudimentary utensils, consisting principally of sharp flakes detached with a single blow from a fist-sized cobble; but they represented an enormous extension of hominid economic capability, especially in permitting access to a resource — animal protein — that would previously have been largely off-limits to small-bodied foragers. The cobbles themselves were also used as hammers in breaking the bones of mammal carcasses to provide access to the fat-rich marrow within. The introduction of stone-flaking also implies a significant advance on the cognitive front, not only because this activity involves a degree of insight into the mechanical properties of stone that is apparently denied to living apes (Toth et al. 1993), but also because the earliest stone toolmakers also showed a remarkable degree of foresight, carrying cobbles of the right kind around with them for considerable distances before making them into tools as needed. With the inauguration of the archaeological record we have the earliest confirmation that hominids had indeed moved cognitively beyond the ape league. Beyond this, however, it is unclear what the implications of the new behavioral expressions are for the ways in which these hominids subjectively experienced and interacted with the wider world around them.

Still, it is increasingly evident that the first stone tool makers were physically not significantly different from their non-toolmaking predecessors. In 1964 Louis Leakey and colleagues created the new and unexpectedly ancient species *Homo habilis* ("handy man") to contain various fragmentary hominid fossils from Olduvai Gorge, apparently largely because their search for the remains of the maker of the crude stone tools found in the 1.8 myr-old lowest sedimentary layers of the Gorge was guided by the seductive and then widely accepted notion of "Man the Toolmaker" (e.g., Oakley 1963). But there is in fact little that is morphologically "advanced" in the odd assortment of specimens available by the end of 1964, or indeed in the entire miscellany of 2.5–1.8 myr-old fossils that have subsequently been pigeonholed in the category of "early *Homo*" (Tattersall 1995; Schwartz and Tattersall 2005). And this disconnect between episodes of morphological and behavioral "advancement" points up a theme that we find consistently repeated throughout hominid evolutionary history: the appearance of new kinds of hominid is *not* associated with the appearance of new kinds of behavior — and vice versa. On the face of it this might seem a little counterintuitive, for innovations on these two levels do appear self-reinforcing, and certainly it would be convenient if each of them could be taken as "explaining" the other. However, a moment's reflection reveals that any behavioral innovation must inevitably find its first expression *within* a species. For there is no other place it can do so: any such novelty has to originate with an individual who can hardly differ much from his or her own parents or offspring. Under linear constructs of the evolutionary process behavior and morphology drive each other onward in an endless virtuous circle; but seductive though this notion is, it is vehemently belied by the nature of the preserved record.

The First Hominids of Modern Body Plan

At just under 2 myr ago, we witness the appearance of hominids with rather larger braincases and smaller faces than any known from earlier in time. Usually grouped together into the species *Homo ergaster* (when not unwisely allocated to the eastern Asian species *Homo erectus*), these new hominids are most spectacularly represented by the amazingly complete 1.6 myr-old "Turkana Boy" specimen from northern Kenya (Walker and Leakey 1993). This miraculously preserved skeleton is the remains of an individual who had died at the chronological age of eight years, but who had reached the developmental stage of a modern child four to six years older (the highly prolonged developmental process of modern humans appears increasingly to have been a very late acquisition). Despite his tender years he was already five feet three inches tall, and it is calculated that, in striking contrast to his very short-statured predecessors, he would have surpassed six feet had he survived to maturity. He was slenderly built, with long legs; and indeed, despite many differences in detail, he possessed the basic body proportions of those who live in tropical climes today. Here at last, more or less out of the blue, was a hominid who was built to stride across the open tropical savanna, far from the shelter of the trees to which his ancestors had been confined.

Yet for all of its morphological novelty *Homo ergaster*, both on its appearance and for several hundred thousand years thereafter, wielded a stone-working technology that was effectively identical to that which had already been used by its archaically proportioned and physically distinctive predecessors for half a million years and more. Just as the first stone toolmakers were apparently unsignaled by any physical modification, this radically new kind of human arrived unaccompanied by any technological advance. For it was not until about 1.5 myr ago that a truly new kind of stone tool appeared on the scene. This innovation was the "Acheulean" hand axe, a large stone tool (usually from about six to nine inches long) made by fashioning a large stone core (or, later, flake) symmetrically on both sides to a set and regular pattern, usually a flattened teardrop shape (Klein 1999). For the first time, it seems, hominid toolmakers were manufacturing stone implements to a "mental template" that was held in their heads before toolmaking started. Instead of just going after a physical *attribute*, namely a sharp cutting edge, the toolmakers were aiming at a precise and predetermined *shape*. Sometimes such tools were made in "workshops," places on the landscape at which they were produced in astonishingly large numbers. Here again, in the increased subtlety of mental process that this new technological style hints at, we can surely infer a cognitive advance of some kind. But once more, we have little way of relating this technological innovation to any change in the toolmakers' subjective experience of the world, or to any capacity for symbolic abstraction.

It was in the period just following 2.0 myr ago that we have the first evidence for hominid movement beyond the African continent. For many years just what it was that permitted hominids to leave their natal continent has been vigorously debated. Was the crucial ingredient larger brains, with the implication of greater intelligence? Was it improved technology, allowing hominids to penetrate a wider variety of climes? Or was it simply the new striding body form, which emancipated hominids from their former dependence on at least some degree of tree cover, allowing them to cover large linear distances? In the light of discoveries over the last decade at the 1.75 myr-old site of Dmanisi, in the Caucasus (Republic of Georgia), today's front-runner is the third possibility. Four hominid crania from Dmanisi are quite variable (and archaic) in morphology, but have in common that none of them is strikingly large in brain size. Stone tools recovered at the site are no more advanced in technology than those being produced at the same time at classic African localities such as Olduvai. So, while postcranial bones recovered at Dmanisi have yet to be described, the fact that by Dmanisi times essentially modern hominid body form had presumptively emerged in Africa strongly suggests that it was modern "walking machine" proportions alone that account for the unprecedented mobility.

Whatever the case, once hominids had emerged from Africa they diversified throughout the Old World, just as would have been predicted for any successful mammalian family. Possibly as long ago as 1.6–1.8 myr, hominids had penetrated to the far eastern bounds of Asia, and by about a million years ago they had at least made incursions into the less hospitable climes of Europe (Bermudez de Castro et al. 1997). Again, the stone tools associated with these early émigrés, in regions as far apart as Spain and China, remained relentlessly primitive; we have no clear reason to believe that any significant cognitive advance facilitated the spread of hominids throughout the Old World.

Shelters and Spears

By about 600 thousand years (600 kyr) ago, a species usually known as *Homo heidelbergensis* had appeared in Africa, and not long thereafter it also showed up in Europe and subsequently in eastern Asia, too (Tattersall and Schwartz 2000). In its cranial anatomy this new hominid species was substantially more similar to modern humans than its predecessors had been, but its brain size was still substantially below the modern average and its face was still relatively large and somewhat forwardly thrust. Interestingly, the earliest Eurasian representatives of *Homo heidelbergensis*, at least, still made and used remarkably crude stone tools, emphasizing once again the disconnect between biological and technological innovation in human prehistory.

It was not until about 300 kyr ago, in both Europe and Africa, that a new type of stone tool making appeared (Klein 1999). This involved the fabrication of "prepared-core" tools, whereby a stone nucleus was carefully shaped with multiple strikes, in such a way that a single final blow would detach a large flake that was in essence a finished implement. This development was facilitated by the introduction of hammers made not of stone, but of softer materials such as bone and antler that permitted finer modulation of the applied force. Once again, we can see in this development some increase in cognitive sophistication, although of course the full degree of that increase is very hard to surmise. Parenthetically, it is worth remarking here that human beings have great difficulty in imagining *any* forms of complex consciousness other than their own. It is impossible for us to grasp exactly what is going on in the mind of a living ape, which we can at least observe, let alone to read the minds of our extinct "so near but yet so far" relatives with only highly indirect evidence to hand.

Still, at around this time it is clear that something was stirring cognitively among our predecessors. At the site of Terra Amata, on the Mediterranean coast of France, indications have been found of the first deliberately constructed shelters known. These were large oval structures formed by implanting the trunks of saplings in the ground, reinforcing the periphery with stones, and bringing the tops of the saplings together in the middle. Just inside a break in the ring of stones that marks the entrance to one of these huts is a shallow, scooped-out depression containing blackened animal bones and heat-fractured stones. This is a hearth where a controlled fire had burned, and at between 350 and 400 kyr old it is probably the earliest such feature known. Constructed hearths and shelters are also known at the 350 kyr-old site of Bilzingsleben, in Germany, and from this point on fireplaces gradually become a more regular feature of the archaeological record.

From the same early period, too, come some miraculously preserved wooden spears from the 400 kyr-old site of Schoeningen, in Germany (Thieme 1997). Wood is a highly perishable material and rarely preserves for long, but swampy anaerobic conditions at Schoeningen assured the natural conservation over the ages of several large and beautifully shaped javelins, six to seven feet long, which are effectively identical in their physical properties to their Olympic equivalents today. Most importantly, their weight is concentrated toward the front. Before this discovery, with only stone tools to go on, many archaeologists had guessed that hominid hunting techniques in this period had been fairly unsophisticated, and that if wooden spears had been used they would have been of the thrusting rather than of the throwing kind. The remarkable discovery at Schoeningen of weapons that would have been used most effectively in ambush-hunting has forced a rethinking of such assumptions and has also served as a sharp reminder that the stone tool record that preferential preservation normally forces us to rely on in fact gives us only a very partial glimpse of the technologies, let alone the larger lifestyles, of our ancient predecessors.

The Neanderthals

Of all extinct hominid species it is *Homo neanderthalensis* that provides the most instructive contrast with our modern species *Homo sapiens*. This is for several reasons. First, the Neanderthals are by far the best-known of all extinct hominid species, with many dozens of sites and fossil individuals known (Tattersall and Schwartz 2000). Second, they occupied the same landscapes concurrently with *Homo sapiens*. And third, they were more complex behaviorally than any other well-known kind of extinct hominid. For example, despite arguments to the contrary (Gargett 1989), most authorities concur that they independently invented the practice of interring the dead, a factor that may at least partially account for the large number of Neanderthal fossils that have been recovered. And there is also evidence that at least in some times and places Neanderthal groups afforded long-term care and protection to handicapped members (Trinkaus and Shipman 1992).

The Neanderthals are the best-known and the latest-surviving species of an endemic group of European hominids that had its origins around a half-million years ago or possibly a bit more (Tattersall and Schwartz 2000). First known at around 200 kyr ago, *Homo neanderthalensis* ultimately spread to occupy nearly all of Europe and a wide swath of western Asia by the time of the last glacial episode, which began a bit more than 100 kyr ago. The Neanderthals disappeared at a little less than 30 kyr ago, some 10 kyr after *Homo sapiens* first entered their European redoubt from a place of origin that ultimately lay in Africa. The Neanderthals had brains as large as our own, but skulls and bodies that were quite distinctive. In contrast to the tall, high cranial vaults and small, tucked-under faces of *Homo sapiens*, *Homo neanderthalensis* housed its big brain in a long, low cranial vault, and Neanderthal faces protruded forward below heavy arching brow ridges and were curiously swept-back at the sides. The bones of the Neanderthal skeleton were generally heavier than ours, and the pelvis flared beneath a conical thorax that contrasts dramatically with our own barrel-shaped ribcage. Although they have been seen by some paleoanthropologists merely as a bizarre variety of *Homo sapiens* (Trinkaus and Shipman 1992), these hominids in fact betrayed a long independent evolutionary history in the form of almost every bone of their skeleton.

The Neanderthals were expert craftsmen in stone (Klein 1999) and indeed carried the prepared-core technique of stoneworking to a high level of perfection. But there was nonetheless a kind of monotony to their craftsmanship, in the sense that Neanderthal tools were essentially similar over the entire vast expanse of time and space that these hominids inhabited. This contrasts dramatically with the productions of the Cro-Magnons, the *Homo sapiens* who entered Europe at about 40 kyr ago. The Cro-Magnons made stone tools using rather different techniques; but, more importantly, they used softer materials such as bone and antler to make tools, and they did so with an exquisite sensitivity to the mechanical properties of these materials, something never shown by Neanderthals on the rare occasions when they employed soft substances. Most importantly of all, however, the material record bequeathed us by the pre-contact Neanderthals contains virtually nothing that can convincingly be interpreted as a symbolic object (White 1989). Everything they made was strictly utilitarian.

The material production of the Cro-Magnons, in contrast, was drenched in symbol (White 1989, 2003). Well over 30 kyr ago the Cro-Magnons were painting powerful animal and abstract images on the walls of caves. Soon they were making bas-reliefs on the walls of shelters. They carved statuettes and made engravings on plaques of bone and other soft materials. They made notations on such plaques, too, some of which may even have represented lunar calendars. They made music on bone flutes with multiple holes and complex sound capabilities, and they may even have played xylophones made with cleverly struck long strips of flint. And if they did this, they doubtless sang and danced as well. They buried their dead with grave goods and in sumptuously decorated tunics that were sewn with delicate-eyed bone needles. They even baked ceramic statuettes in rudimentary but remarkably effective kilns.

The Cro-Magnons, in other words, were *us*, *Homo sapiens* in the fullest sense of the term. And the contrast between the Cro-Magnon and Neanderthal material records gives us the most direct glimpse yet possible of the extraordinary ways in which our species differs from all of its predecessors. Nobody can doubt that the Cro-Magnons possessed the full panoply of modern human linguistic and reasoning abilities. In contrast, although it is clear that the Neanderthals had many other achievements to their credit, it is entirely reasonable to suppose that these now-extinct hominids did not.

The Origin of Modern Cognition

The Cro-Magnons entered Europe as behaviorally fully fledged *Homo sapiens* some 40 kyr ago, and in the space of not much more than ten millennia the Neanderthals were gone for ever. But Europe was not the only region in which Neanderthals and anatomically modern *Homo sapiens* coincided. Neanderthals were already present in the Levant, specifically Israel, well over 100 kyr ago, and persisted there until about 45 kyr ago or less (Johanson and Edgar 1996). At the same time, anatomically modern *Homo sapiens* is recorded in the same region at well over 90 kyr. It is not known exactly how the Neanderthals and the anatomical moderns managed to coexist; one (probably imperfect) guess is that the "cold-adapted" Neanderthals moved in when the climate became cooler and moved back north when it warmed up, while the "tropically adapted" (because ultimately African-derived) *Homo sapiens* did the reverse. But whatever the case, what does seem significant is that during this entire period of "co-existence" the two hominid species are associated with virtually identical stone tool kits (Klein 1999). There is very little to suggest that they exploited the environment in significantly different ways, and there is little compelling evidence that early Levantine *Homo sapiens* was routinely indulging in symbolic behaviors. It is only once Cro-Magnon–equivalent stoneworking techniques appear in the Levant (at about 45 kyr ago) that evidence for Neanderthal inhabitation of the area finally ceases, as it does not very long after in Europe, following the arrival of the Cro-Magnons.

The evidence from the Levant thus points us yet again to a phenomenon that we have been able to track virtually throughout the hominid prehistoric record: behavioral and physical innovation do not proceed hand-in-hand. Clearly, modern symbolic cognition was not possessed (or at least was not expressed) by the earliest anatomically modern *Homo sapiens*. Instead, what seems to have been acquired with the biological reorganization that gave rise to the anatomically distinctive *Homo sapiens* was a *potential* — a potential that had to be discovered by its possessor before it could be exploited. This points in its turn to a routine evolutionary phenomenon known as *exaptation*. Although the notions of structure and function would on the face of it seem to be inextricably intertwined, in biology structure has to *precede* function, if only because without structure there can be no function.

In evolutionary history there are many examples of structures arising before they are recruited in a new way. Perhaps the most famous of these examples is provided by the feathers of birds, which make flight possible. But birds had possessed feathers for insulation for many millions of years before ever coopting them for purposes of flight. Something similar seems to have happened in the case of *Homo sapiens*. The behavioral innovation that most obviously distinguished the Cro-Magnons from their predecessors was the production of symbolic objects, and these in turn point to symbolic processes in the minds that produced them. Clearly, there must be a biological basis for modern symbolic reasoning. But the record shows that this biological potential was not exploited until well after its presumed time of acquisition. We must thus conclude that this fateful innovation was a byproduct of a change that was initially advantageous — and therefore evolutionarily successful — in some other respect. Exactly what that other respect may have been is (fortunately) unimportant in the present context.

Symbolic reasoning is expressed behaviorally, so it seems reasonable to conclude that whatever it was that stimulated the discovery of this fallow new potential was itself behavioral. And the most convincing — perhaps the only plausible — releasing mechanism appears to have been the invention of language, something that it appears is irresistible to the human mind, as is shown by its spontaneous invention (in signed form) by deaf Nicaraguan school children (see Corballis 2002). Language is, indeed, the ultimate symbolic activity. It involves forming intangible mental symbols, and combining and recombining them in our brains to permit us not only to communicate, but to pose the "what if?" questions that allow us to interpret and relate to each other and to the world around us in new ways. Once language had been invented, it opened the way to the discovery of all of the other aspects of the human potential — a process that is still continuing today, each time a new technological miracle is announced.

Where was the symbolic potential discovered? Almost certainly, this was initially in Africa, for it is in that continent (in which both molecular and fossil evidence suggest that anatomically modern *Homo sapiens* emerged some 150 kyr ago [Paäbo 1999; White et al. 2003]) that we detect the first glimmerings of symbolic behaviors. Near the southern tip of Africa, archaeological strata almost 80 kyr old at Blombos Cave (Henshilwood et al. 2003) have yielded the world's earliest overtly symbolic object, an ochre plaque bearing a geometrical engraving, as well as gastropod shells pierced almost certainly for personal adornment (Henshilwood et al. 2004). Not far away, remains from the Klasies River Mouth living site have been interpreted as showing both ritual activity and a symbolic arrangement of space at over 100 kyr ago (Deacon and Deacon 1999). Similar early expressions have been reported from other parts of Africa. Still, the history of the spread of symbolic behaviors was probably not a simple one, with a single point of origin giving rise to a spread along all available routes. Instead, as with most innovations in hominid prehistory, it was probably affected by a host of adventitious influences. Thus the human symbolic potential may have been rediscovered at different times and in different places: southern Africa, for example, dried out and became more or less deserted by humans for several tens of thousands of years following Blombos times, and it is quite plausible that local extinction consigned the local Blombos symbolic tradition to oblivion.

The unfortunate reality is that the record we have at present of very early symbolic production is not only quite sparse but also doubtless biased by the fact that, while all fully human societies are symbolic, not all produce symbolic materials of the kind that might be expected to preserve in the archaeological record. Nonetheless, even though the uniquely abundant and well preserved record of Cro-Magnon creativity is relatively late, it does provide an astonishing contrast with the penecontemporaneous Neanderthal record, and in doing so it presents us with a unique mirror in which to see reflected the entirely unprecedented cognitive uniqueness of behaviorally modern *Homo sapiens*.

Symbolic Cognition and Rationality

Interestingly, it was the matter of *how* modern human consciousness could have evolved that caused the deepest disagreement ever to fissure the relationship between Charles Darwin and Alfred Russel Wallace, the co-inventors of the notion of evolution by natural selection. Darwin was entirely content to see the workings of natural selection as the unambiguous explanation for the ultimate achievement by the human lineage of symbolic consciousness. Wallace, on the other hand, impressed by the narrow but apparently bottomless gulf that this quality forms between human beings and even their closest living relatives, simply could not see how this could be so. For after all, natural selection is not a creative force; it can favor only what is already there, which makes it very difficult to account for the truly new. And if anything in nature is totally new and unprecedented, it is symbolic consciousness.

Ultimately, it seems to me that both men were right, at least in the sense that, while natural selection cannot conjure novelty into existence (Wallace), the modern human brain that gives us our unique capacity is certainly the product of a very long and accretionary evolutionary history (Darwin). All evolutionary change has to be based on what was there before, and the human symbolic capacity is clearly the emergent result of some new wiring element that, added to what already existed, produced something that would have been entirely unpredictable had anybody been around to predict it. We still do not know how what we experience as consciousness is produced in our brains, but we do know that those brains, like those of our apparently non-symbolic precursors, are the end product of some four hundred million years of vertebrate evolution during which new structures were gradually added while the functions of old ones were maintained (Allman 1999). The result is that newer structures in the brain communicate via some very ancient ones indeed, and the sum total of what we experience as our consciousness is produced at least as much by the old, "emotional" centers of the brain as by the higher association areas that permit symbolic thought. In our daily lives we experience this duality all too often, in our frequently conflicted responses to situations of every kind. Our capacity for rational symbolic reasoning is overlain upon more ancient, intuitive capacities that are still powerfully able to express themselves; and it is the combination and interaction of the two that make each of us what we are. And thank God for that. For without intuition and emotion we would be calculating automatons, bereft of love, charity, and hope; and without our capacity for symbolic reasoning we would be unable, among other things, to thank God.

Although it may ultimately prove that the one mystery the human intellect is unable to penetrate is that of its own biological underpinnings, one thing seems evident. The modern human rational mind, both made possible and limited by the superimposition of a symbolic capacity upon a preexisting intuitive base, is a recent development and an *emergent* one. And it is important to remember that, even now, human minds are never *purely* rational. What is more, despite the reductionist appeal of sociobiological explanation of human behavior that is daily so evident in the latest press revelation that this behavior or that is due to "mental adaptation" to some supposed "ancestral environment," it is clear that the human mind is *not* fine-tuned for anything. It is the outcome of a whole host of historical accidents; and indeed, there is a plausible argument to be made that an engineer could never have designed the remarkable mechanism that resides in our skulls, precisely *because* engineers are supposed (at work, at least) to be supremely rational! Human beings are simultaneously both more and less than optimized problem-solvers.

It is, of course, useless to deny that as individuals we are to a certain extent the prisoners of our genes; we mostly emerge into the world with the basic dispositions we will always exhibit (often very different from those of our parents or children). But as a whole, our species *Homo sapiens* appears, aside from being linguistic, to have no specifiable moral or behavioral condition at all (Tattersall 1998). After all, with very little difficulty you can find a fellow human being to illustrate both components of any pair of descriptive antitheses you might care to come up with. Not much support for the notion of essential rationality there. Clearly, our species has not been finely honed by natural selection to be a creature of any specific, or even usefully describable, kind (notions such as "featherless biped" don't get us far). Yet while it may at some level feel frustrating that our species appears to lie beyond its own imperative to categorize everything in sight, this is in fact no bad thing. Because from a biological point of view it is precisely the lack of genetic determinism in our evolutionary past that makes possible our own exercise of free will.

Bibliography

Aiello, Leslie, and Christopher Dean. 1990. *An Introduction to Human Evolutionary Anatomy.* London: Academic Press.

Allman, John Morgan. 1999. *Evolving Brains.* New York: Scientific American Library.

Bermudez de Castro, Jose Maria, Juan Luis Arsuaga, Eudald Carbonell, Antonio Rosas, Ignacio Martinez, and Marina Mosquera. 1997. "A Hominid from the Lower Pleistocene of Atapuerca, Spain: Possible Ancestor to Neandertals and Modern Humans." *Science* 276:1392-1395.

Byrne, Richard. 1995. *The Thinking Ape: Evolutionary Origins of Intelligence.* Oxford: Oxford University Press.

Corballis, Michael. 2002. *From Hand to Mouth: The Origins of Language.* Princeton: Princeton University Press.

Deacon, Hilary, and Janette Deacon. 1999. *Human Beginnings in South Africa: Uncovering the Secrets of the Stone Age.* Cape Town: David Philip.

Gargett, Robert H. 1989. "Grave Shortcomings: The Evidence for Neanderthal Burial." *Current Anthropology* 30:157-190.

Henshilwood, Christopher, Francesco d'Errico, Royden Yates, Zenobia Jacobs, Chantal Tribolo, G. A. Duller, Nicolas Mercier, J. C. Sealy, Hélène Valladas, I. Watts, and A. G. Wintle. 2003. "Emergence of Modern Human Behavior: Middle Stone Age Engravings from South Africa." *Science* 295:1278-1280.

Henshilwood, Christopher, Francesco d'Errico, Marian Vanhaeren, Karen van Niekerk, and Zenobia Jacobs. 2004. "Middle Stone Age Shell Beads from South Africa." *Science* 304:404.

Johanson, Donald, and Maitland Edey. 1981. *Lucy: The Beginnings of Humankind.* New York: Simon and Schuster.

Johanson, Donald, and Blake Edgar. 1996. *From Lucy to Language.* New York: Simon and Schuster.

Kingdon, Jonathan. 2003. *Lowly Origin: Where, When and Why Our Ancestors First Stood Up.* Princeton: Princeton University Press.

Klein, Richard. 1999. *The Human Career.* 2nd ed. Chicago: Chicago University Press.

Krings, Matthias, Anne Stone, R. W. Schmitz, H. Krainitzki, Mark Stoneking, and Svante Paäbo. "Neandertal DNA Sequences and the Origin of Modern Humans." 1997. *Cell* 90:19-30.

Leakey, Mary D., and John M. Harris. 1987. *Laetoli: A Pliocene Site in Northern Tanzania.* Oxford: Clarendon Press.

Oakley, Kenneth. 1963. *Man the Tool-Maker.* 5th ed. London: British Museum (Natural History).

Paäbo, Svante. 1999. "Human Evolution." *Trends in Cell Biology* 9:M13-16.

Schick, Kathy D., and Nicholas Toth. 1993. *Making Silent Stones Speak: Human Evolution and the Dawn of Technology.* New York: Simon & Schuster.

Schwartz, Jeffrey H., and Ian Tattersall. 2005. *The Human Fossil Record,* vol 4. New York: John Wiley and Sons.

Tattersall, Ian. 1995. *The Fossil Trail: How We Know What We Think We Know about Human Evolution.* New York: Oxford University Press.

Tattersall, Ian. 1998. *Becoming Human: Evolution and Human Uniqueness.* New York: Harcourt Brace.

Tattersall, Ian. 2002. *The Monkey in the Mirror: Essays on the Science of What Makes Us Human.* New York: Harcourt.

Tattersall, Ian. 2004. "What Happened in the Origin of Human Consciousness?" *Anat. Rec. (New Anat.)* 276B:19-26.

Tattersall, Ian, and Jeffrey H. Schwartz. 2000. *Extinct Humans.* Boulder: Westview Press.

Thieme, Hartmut. 1997. "Lower Palaeolithic Hunting Spears from Germany." *Nature* 385:807-810.

Toth, Nicholas, Kathy Schick, Sue Savage-Rumbaugh, R. A. Sevcik, and D. M. Rumbaugh. 1993. "*Pan* the Toolmaker: Investigations into the Stone Tool Making Capability of a Bonobo *(Pan paniscus)*." *Jour. Archaol. Sci.* 20:81-97.

Trinkaus, Erik, and Pat Shipman. 1992. *The Neandertals: Changing the Image of Mankind.* New York: Alfred A. Knopf.

Walker, Alan, and Richard E. Leakey. 1993. *The Nariokotome* Homo erectus *Skeleton.* Cambridge, MA: Harvard University Press.

White, Randall. 1989. "Visual Thinking in the Ice Age." *Scientific American* 260/7:92-99.

White, Randall. 2003. *Prehistoric Art: The Symbolic Journey of Mankind.* New York: Harry N. Abrams.

White, Timothy D., Berhane Asfaw, David DeGusta, Henry Gilbert, Gary D. Richards, Gen Suwa, and F. Clark Howell. 2003. "Pleistocene *Homo sapiens* from Middle Awash, Ethiopia." *Nature* 423:742-747.

12 From the Bison at Niaux to the Kyoto Protocol: Science, Religion, and the Challenge of Human Nature

Christopher Southgate

It is a privilege to be asked to write in celebration of the work of J. Wentzel van Huyssteen, and I begin by recording my appreciation not only of his contribution to the science-religion debate but also of his friendship and encouragement of my own work over the last ten years.

In view of van Huyssteen's interest in the cave-paintings of our Cro-Magnon ancestors, and his use of that phase of human development as a basis for his consideration of the nature and distinctiveness of human beings, the Grottes de Niaux seem a very plausible starting point for this essay. These caves in the foothills of the French Pyrenees show some of the finest "art" of the Upper Paleolithic period, now dated in Europe from 45,000 to 10,000 years ago.[1]

What follows can be no more than a brief allusive sketch, a marking of some territory for exploration of the nature and calling of human beings. I want to come to Niaux by way of the Jesuit house at St. Beuno's in North Wales, and the other places that stirred the poetic and metaphysical imagination of the nineteenth-century Catholic poet Gerard Manley Hopkins (1844-1889). Hopkins's intense contemplation of nature and his wrestling with the human calling will be the key motif in the first half of the essay. In the second half I move to some thoughts as to how the human animal confronts, or does not confront, the crises it currently faces — exemplified by the difficulties experienced in implementing the Kyoto Protocol on climate change.

Hopkins developed a metaphysics of "inscape" as a way of describing the realities of creatures. This is a much-discussed term,[2] but for our purposes

---

1. David Lewis-Williams, *The Mind in the Cave* (London: Thames and Hudson, 2002), p. 39.
2. For two very different construals of inscape see Walter Ong, S.J., *Hopkins, the Self, and*

here the inscape of an entity may be considered to contain what sort of thing it is scientifically — what patterns and regularities govern its existence — but also its particularity, its "thisness."[3] (The scholastic term is *haecceitas*, coined by Duns Scotus, who greatly influenced Hopkins.) As we noted above, every creature has both its pattern of life and membership of its species, and also its particularity as an individual creature. The scientific account of an organism is based on trends, regularities, patterns, over a range of individuals — the perception of the particularity of a specific creature, its "thisness," is more the preserve of the poet and contemplative.

Hopkins has another, related term, "instress," which is still more difficult to pin down than "inscape." The poet seems to use "instress" for: (1) the cohesive energy that binds individual entities into the Whole, (2) the impact the inscape of entities makes on the observer, and (3) the observer's will to receive that impact. Theologically, one might associate all three of these aspects of the relation of humans to other creatures with the work of the Holy Spirit, the "go-between God."[4] We shall see below that it is also possible for creatures to "instress" inappropriately, not discerning the work of God.

The value of this odd terminology is that it gives full value to descriptions of entities in scientific terms, as being examples of whatever class of entities they belong to, but also acknowledges their particularity and createdness. It is important to admit that my use of "inscape" and "instress" in what follows is an inference from Hopkins's thought, rather than an effort to follow his not-always-clear system exactly. (Hopkins himself did not follow exactly the thought of his chosen mentor Duns Scotus.) I seek here to pick up on hints in Hopkins's work that may be generative in the contemporary theological conversation with the sciences, especially ecology.

Human beings, then, may be said to have a capacity to "instress" the reality of creatures, a capacity that for Hopkins both depends on God and also responds to the fact of creatures being created by God. Armed with this insight, we now consider the Grottes de Niaux, and the cave-art culture of which they

---

God (Toronto: University of Toronto Press, 1986); and Bernadette Ward, *World as Word: Philosophical Theology in Gerard Manley Hopkins* (Washington, DC: The Catholic University of America, 2002).

3. It would be interesting for someone expert in Buddhist-Christian dialogue to explore the relation of this concept to the Buddhist idea of "suchness." For a Christian appropriation of "suchness" see Jay McDaniel, *Of God and Pelicans: A Theology of Reverence for Life* (Louisville: Westminster John Knox Press, 1989), pp. 97-99.

4. This phrase is John V. Taylor's in his *The Go-Between God: The Holy Spirit and the Christian Mission* (London: SCM Press, 1972). See also Denis Edwards, *Breath of Life: A Theology of the Creator Spirit* (Maryknoll, NY: Orbis Books, 2004).

are an example. The paintings in those caves, in some cases deep underground, such that the painters must have brought lights and materials a very considerable distance in order to begin their work, are stunning in their vividness. As Picasso said of the work at Altamira, "None of us could paint like that."[5] I myself have never seen the European bison, but in the Grottes de Niaux I felt I understood bisonness, *felt* bison, as I had never dreamed of doing. In Hopkins's terms, I had received from the painter the full charge of instress of bison.

To claim this is not to dissent from David Lewis-Williams's fascinating assessment of the significance of cave art in terms of the shamanic systems that may have operated in Magdalenian society.[6] However, what Lewis-Williams does not point out — perhaps takes for granted — is that in order to paint bison as these shaman-influenced artists did, these humans must have *known* the characteristics of bison very thoroughly. By dint of generations of observing, tracking, and hunting, and, presumably, talking of bison and teaching children about them, the Magdalenians knew their wild animals with an intensity and accuracy that is very rare in contemporary humans (other than hunter-gatherers). They possessed the sort of contemplative appreciation — of the elements of nature that particularly interested them — for which Hopkins himself worked so hard (as evidenced by his journals,[7] and his fascinating series of letters to *Nature* about sunsets[8]).

Lewis-Williams's point, however, is that the paintings are not art in the sense that we would understand it, but part of a mystical shamanic encounter with the spirit world, for which the interior of caves was both symbol and catalyst. That accords with my sense that the painters "instressed" bison (ibex and horse are also particular noteworthy at Niaux) in a heightened, spiritual sense that went beyond mere depiction. As van Huyssteen says, "What . . . should be of primary interest to theologians working on anthropology, is that human mental life [from the Upper Paleolithic onwards] includes biologically unprecedented ways of experiencing and understanding the world, from

---

5. Lewis-Williams, *The Mind in the Cave*, p. 31.

6. Lewis-Williams also makes the important point that too much discussion in this area is excessively Eurocentric and presupposes that the rapid transition *Homo sapiens* made in Europe was the pattern elsewhere. Discoveries in South Africa, for instance, suggest a much earlier dating for the first symbolic artifacts and a much more gradual transition to fully modern behavior. *The Mind in the Cave*, pp. 96-99.

7. Gerard Manley Hopkins, S.J., *The Journals and Papers of Gerard Manley Hopkins*, ed. Humphry House and Graham Storey (London: Oxford University Press, 1959).

8. In *Nature*, 27 (681) p. 53 (1882); 29 (733) p. 55 (1883); 29 (740) pp. 222-223 (1884); 30 (783) p. 633 (1884).

aesthetic experiences to spiritual contemplation."[9] Gerard Manley Hopkins was keenly interested in the sort of description of the world we now call science (as witness his letters to *Nature*). But W. H. Gardner says of him that he would have parted company with the (scientific) rationalists in saying that "the human spirit must be nourished by the spurting fountains of suprarational instress, by that 'deep poetry' which is nothing less than intuitive ontology — the knowledge of the essence and being of all things."[10] It is my contention that this is a helpful way to consider what the Magdalenians were attempting. They strove to be deep poets of their environment as well as hunter-gatherers within it, both to see "their" animals and to "see through" them to a deeper reality.

All this may be thought untestable, and therefore unimportant. Sadly, though paleoanthropologists may learn many things about the Cro-Magnon in the future, we shall never know much about what Hopkins would have called their "pitch," their inner sense of individuality, of being themselves, and how it caused them to view the world. This is of particular importance, both for van Huyssteen's work and for my argument here, in terms of how humans have evolved — culturally and biologically — since then.

The biggest single cultural development has of course been agriculture. Though it is noteworthy the extent to which trade, and sophisticated social distinctions, already existed within prehistoric hunter-gatherer societies, agriculture gave human communities unprecedented power to alter the biodiversity of ecosystems and to establish societies containing groups with the leisure to plan such transformations. Significantly, however, this has not been accompanied by prudent conservation of the resources that allowed those communities to thrive. Human beings have evolved that blend of "embodied imagination, symbolic propensities and cognitive fluidity" that van Huyssteen regards as the basis of personhood,[11] but they have not, typically, evolved a long-range ecological wisdom in relation to their environment. As van Huyssteen continues, "*Homo Sapiens* is not only distinguished by its remarkable embodied brain, by a stunning mental cognitive fluidity expressed in imagination, creativity, linguistic abilities, and symbolic propensities. As real-life, embodied persons of flesh and blood we humans are

---

9. J. Wentzel van Huyssteen, "Interdisciplinary Perspectives on Human Origins and Religious Awareness," unpublished paper to a symposium at Les Eyzies, 2004.

10. W. H. Gardner, *Gerard Manley Hopkins: A Study of Poetic Idiosyncrasy in Relation to Poetic Tradition*, vol. 2 (London: Oxford University Press, 1958; reissue, first published by Secker and Warburg, 1949), p. 350.

11. Van Huyssteen, "Interdisciplinary Perspectives."

also affected by hostility, arrogance, ruthlessness and cunning"[12] — and, he might have added, a thoroughly shortsighted view of our own self-interest. As far as we can judge, it has always been so. Just as human hunter-gatherers were instrumental in many prey species going extinct, so there is evidence from 3,600 years ago of human over-farming leading to "the land bellowing like a bull."[13]

To go back to the terminology we have been using, humans have frequently failed to "instress" their environment in a way that enabled them to understand the need to preserve its ability to sustain them. A particularly dramatic case of unsustainability is that of the Polynesian culture of Easter Island,[14] but the pattern has repeated itself time and again. Humans have transformed many environments, but often in ways that profoundly damaged ecological richness, and moreover that contributed ultimately to the unusability of that land for that purpose. The vast prairie-lands, now grainlands, of the American Midwest are in the middle of this process. Their extraordinary fecundity derived from the last Ice Age. They are still incredibly productive, but suffering appreciable and continuing erosion. They will not recover until the next glaciation.[15]

I offer here first an ecological and then a theological description of the sort of creatures agricultural humans have been. Ecologically, one could claim as Reg Morrison does that, with the advent of agriculture, humans altered their ecological profile and by doing so became a "plague mammal."[16]

What is remarkable, particularly in the light of the accuracy and "deep poetry" with which our ancestors "instressed" the nonhuman world even 30,000 years ago, is that humans still find it so hard to operate to their long-term self-interest. The evolutionary epistemology that is taken by van

---

12. Van Huyssteen, "Human Origins and Religious Awareness: In Search of Human Uniqueness," *Studia Theologica* 59, 2 (2005): 1-25, at 22.

13. Reg Morrison, *The Spirit in the Gene: Humanity's Proud Illusion and the Laws of Nature* (Ithaca, NY: Cornell University Press, 1999), p. 99.

14. Morrison, *The Spirit in the Gene*, pp. 139-141. Morrison's own thesis seems to be that humans' spiritual bent acts as the biosphere's insurance policy, ensuring that we do *not* look wisely to our own ecological self-interest, and therefore are certain to die back at the end of each plague cycle. That is the reverse of the case van Huyssteen and I would want to make — that spirituality is intrinsic to the growth of human rationality. But the events of Easter Island, where the building of vast statues continued even though the means to move them, and the means to ensure food supplies and to continue to communicate with the outside world, had been destroyed by deforestation, surely constitute Morrison's most telling example.

15. William F. Ruddiman, *Plows, Plagues and Petroleum: How Humans Took Control of Climate* (Princeton: Princeton University Press, 2005).

16. Morrison, *The Spirit in the Gene*, pp. 96-98.

Huyssteen and others[17] to inform our understanding of the world seems to fail us when it comes to sustainability of agricultural and technological practice. The current crisis over climate change can be seen as just the latest example of our inability to look to our long-term self-interest as a species. It is my contention that there is a profound unwillingness on the part of most contemporary human societies to understand the nonhuman world at a deep imaginative level, to "instress" it. As a result, wherever humans interact with the nonhuman creation it tends to become impoverished, a travesty of itself.

I give a small but revealing instance from my own recent observations. On a brief visit to Japan in 2005 I went not to Kyoto but to the earlier capital of ancient imperial Japan, Nara. On the edge of Nara is a fine park where some of the major shrines are to be found, and within which is a herd of protected deer. On my first day I walked in the outer reaches of the park, and came upon a group of these deer browsing in a meadow. They were as I have always experienced (instressed) deer, cautious herbivores to be found in elaborate social groupings, usually with the males and females separate, keeping a wary eye on the human observer. The beauty of their inscape rests not only on their grace of movement but on their social relationships, and their wariness of predators, all the product of millions of years of evolution. On my second day, near the temples of Nara, deer biscuits were on sale for the tourists to buy and amuse themselves by feeding the creatures. The behavior of the deer was a revelation: they pushed and jostled one another, and humans, around the biscuit stall, males mixed up with females as they shoved and snatched. Here were two completely different animal behaviors within a mile of one another. One of my abiding memories of Nara (in many other ways a fascinating and delightful place) is of a small Japanese child howling and hiding behind her parent's leg because the aggressiveness of the deer had frightened her. Perhaps that will be her impression of what deer are like for many years to come. But she had not seen, or felt, deer as they truly are, only the travesty of their behavior caused by humans using them as a source of amusement.

Clearly there are far more enlightened examples of sustainable practice, and informed and low-impact relationships with wild nature, in all sorts of places across the world. But that we are a species that routinely destroys habitats for our own purposes, and compromises evolved patterns of animal behavior, cannot be denied. Ecological descriptions, of course, offer no prescription. They merely note that human beings are a particular sort of species, a plague mammal — if that term be accepted — with a long track rec-

---

17. See J. Wentzel van Huyssteen, *Duet or Duel? Theology and Science in a Postmodern World* (London: SCM Press, 1998), especially pp. 141-154.

ord for transforming and impoverishing a range of ecosystems. Our adapted mechanisms of behavior, our evolved epistemology, do not enable us to grasp the complexity of the relation between our local and our global, our short- and our long-term interest.

Which brings us to theological description. One way to formulate human unwisdom and unsustainability of practice would be to say that humans have failed to have "that mind that was in Christ Jesus" (Philippians 2:5); they have made their advantage and glory a "snatching-matter."[18] Hopkins said of Lucifer that he had "instressed his own inscape," adoring his own image rather than that of God in the servanthood of God's Christ. That constituted his "fall." While I do not wish to pursue the language of a historical "fall," still less one from an Edenic paradisal state,[19] it is possible to regard this snatching at resources, and humans' admiring of their own image and ingenuity at the expense of truly working to understand the nonhuman world, as an index of human "fallenness." To talk of servanthood, of refusing to snatch at status or advantage, is commonplace in the discussion of right relationships between Christians but has been sadly lacking in addressing relationships with the nonhuman world.

Humans, then, can be thought of as "fallen," not only in interpersonal relationships, but in relation to other creatures and our environment as a whole. A more positive way to look at our place in the world is that our true environment includes God; we can never and shall never "find our place" on this planet unless we find our home with and in the love of God, the one in whom we live and move and have our being (Acts 17:28).[20] Finding our home would mean recognizing (instressing) God's creative activity in all other species as well as our own. In a recent article[21] I discussed the range of possible understandings of humans' relationship to the nonhuman creation — from a biocentric approach through various understandings of human stewardship of creation to the "cre-

---

18. Hopkins's own translation of *harpagmon* in Philippians 2:6. See Christopher Devlin's introduction to *The Sermons and Devotional Writings of Gerard Manley Hopkins*, ed. Christopher Devlin (London: Oxford University Press, 1959), p. 108.

19. For vehement rejections of the traditional form of the doctrine of the Fall see Arthur Peacocke, *Theology for a Scientific Age*, enlarged ed. (London: SCM Press, 1993), pp. 222-223; and John Polkinghorne, *Reason and Reality* (London: SPCK, 1991), pp. 99-101.

20. This has been an important motif in the work of Arthur Peacocke, who summarizes his approach in his *Paths from Science towards God: The End of All Our Exploring* (Boulder: Westview Press, 2001). The implications of the text from Acts are explored in a variety of ways in *In Whom We Live and Move and Have Our Being: Panentheistic Reflections on God's Place in a Scientific World*, ed. Philip Clayton and Arthur Peacocke (Grand Rapids: Eerdmans, 2004).

21. Christopher Southgate, "Stewardship and Its Competitors," in *Environmental Stewardship*, ed. R. J. Berry (Edinburgh: T&T Clark International, 2006), pp. 185-195.

ated co-creator" model offered by Philip Hefner.[22] All have their merits in particular contexts. To recognize the specialness of our role — as the creature capable of consciously instressing God's creative activity — takes us away from a biocentric conception of humans toward an understanding of humans as priests of creation, the species that offers up creation's praise to God, the species that combines "the fruit of the earth and the work of human hands" in sacramental action. This is a way of thinking that would reject any hint of exploitativeness or arrogance as to our position, and it attracts a number of authors. It has been usefully set in the context of the science-religion debate by Peacocke.[23] Human priesthood of creation is an idea strong in Eastern Orthodox theology, as in this sentence from Vladimir Lossky: "In his way to union with God, man in no way leaves creatures aside, but gathers together in his love the whole cosmos disordered by sin, that it may at last be transfigured by grace."[24] The idea is beautifully expressed in this passage from Wendell Berry:

> To live we must daily break the body and shed the blood of creation. When we do this knowingly, lovingly, skilfully and reverently it is a sacrament. When we do it ignorantly, greedily and destructively it is a desecration. In such a desecration, we condemn ourselves to spiritual and moral loneliness and others to want.[25]

The language of priesthood will be more helpful to some readers than to others, but I hope it might be widely conceded that learning to instress truly the character of the nonhuman creation, and to offer it up in praise to God, would be a sign that we had at last begun to find our home in God, to become, in Irenaeus of Lyons' famous phrase, "fully alive."

All of this is not to deny the sheer extent of the challenge posed by living as a population of over six billion, a population within which exist huge and seemingly intractable poverty, and also huge and seemingly insatiable material aspiration. It is to say that we shall need all our rationality, our poetry, and our ingenuity to engage with the challenges that now confront us. One of van Huyssteen's great contributions has been to help the community looking at the relationship between science and religions to see that the science-religion relationship is not the hackneyed old caricature of a necessary con-

---

22. Philip Hefner, *The Human Factor* (Minneapolis: Fortress Press, 1993).

23. Arthur Peacocke, *Creation and the World of Science: The Bampton Lectures 1978* (Oxford: Clarendon Press, 1979), pp. 295-297.

24. Vladimir Lossky, *The Mystical Theology of the Eastern Church*, trans. Members of the Fellowship of St. Alban and St. Sergius (London: J. Clarke, 1957), p. 111.

25. Wendell Berry, *The Gift of Good Land* (San Francisco: North Point Press, 1981), p. 281.

flict; rather, it may be seen, within a post-foundationalist understanding, as the paradigm example of human rationality.[26] And it is in engaging with these great global challenges of justice and ecological concern, which are also challenges to what human nature is and what it is called by God to be, that we need to see this paradigm example at work.

One way in which this may happen is through the use of science as a meeting place for understanding from the different world faiths.[27] Another will be for theologians and ethicists to help societies see why sometimes new science has led to international cooperation — perhaps the best recent example is the 1987 Montreal Protocol (on the restriction of ozone-layer depleting chemicals) — and why, on the other hand, the funding of science and technology often remains skewed toward unsustainable practice.

One of the remarkable features of science is that, although funded largely from within the Western capitalist system, it is capable of giving that system very unpalatable news. Climate change is a very striking example. No proponent of global capitalism or funder of big science could have wanted to discover this about the planet. The response of U.S. administrations and legislators has been all too predictable.[28] World markets as they are currently geared favor U.S. society as it currently lives. Part of the Kyoto Protocol to the United Nations Framework Convention on Climate Change (1997) was an ambitious and innovative attempt to generate a new market in carbon-trading that would at least restrict release of greenhouse gasses. Such a market would mean a different sort of economy. Given the political will, the U.S. could dominate the new system as it dominates the current one, but the will is currently lacking. Science, then, has a huge role in telling us where our long-term self-interest will truly lie. Its voice should not be listened to uncritically — even the least suspicious expressions of postmodernism recognize that — but it has a remarkable ability to characterize the world in ways that do not simply accord with the wishes of its paymasters.

---

26. This is helpfully summarized in J. Wentzel van Huyssteen, "Foreword," in *God, Humanity and the Cosmos: A Textbook in Science and Religion*, ed. Christopher Southgate (Edinburgh: T&T Clark, 1999), pp. xix-xxv.

27. For introductions to this area, see Ted Peters and Gaymon Bennett, eds., *Bridging Science and Religion* (London: SCM Press, 2002); and W. Mark Richardson and Gordy Slack, eds., *Faith in Science: Scientists Search for Truth* (New York and London: Routledge, 2001).

28. Slow as George W. Bush has been to address this issue, it should not be forgotten that the U.S. Senate had already inflicted a massive defeat on Kyoto-type proposals before Bush took office. The obstacle to change in U.S. energy policy has not only been in the executive branch. For an overview of human impact on climate and its likely future results, see Ruddiman, *Plows, Plagues and Petroleum*.

It is often supposed that religion had a place in establishing social cohesion within early human societies and in enabling individuals and families to look beyond their narrow (genetic) self-interest. This is an argument advanced many times over the years, with varying motives.[29] In the twenty-first century, religion has a place (among many other considerations) in teaching the rich nations of the world to "desire what we cannot desire"[30] (however much we know we should), namely the long-term interests of the many across the globe and of future generations, beyond our own narrow socioeconomic interests.

But the shared importance of science and religion goes far beyond that. It has to do with a shared concern for the real. Our self-interest cannot reside, ultimately, in self-delusion. In the search to say more about, and respond to, the-way-things-really-are (a search that we know to be philosophically fraught with danger but nonetheless necessary) the sciences and the world faiths offer us a range of understandings of the present and the future. Each religious picture will be in conversation with the scientific, but will say more, because it will say something of how the future *should be*, how it will be as a result of contact with a deeper reality than science can characterize. In the case of the Christian vision, religion will say something about humans' "specific task and purpose to set forth the presence of God in this world."[31] But both types of rationality are deeply committed to opposing self-delusion, mere "amusing ourselves to death,"[32] the mere instressing of our own inscape at the expense of an openness to a more profound and more surprising reality.

Which brings me back, finally, to Hopkins and the particular contribution Christian theology can make to this issue. I discussed earlier how Hopkins's intense contemplation of the world enabled him to see into its sacramental quality, its deep affinity to its Creator. He was correspondingly saddened by the attitudes and activities of human beings he saw ignoring "inscape," cutting down his favorite trees, "Strokes of havoc unselve/The sweet especial scene" ("Binsey Poplars"), marring the world with the impact of in-

---

29. For summaries see John Bowker, *Is God a Virus? Genes, Culture and Religion* (London: SPCK, 1995); and Christopher Southgate, Michael Robert Negus, and Andrew Robinson, "Theology and Evolutionary Biology," in *God, Humanity and the Cosmos*, 2nd ed., ed. Christopher Southgate (Edinburgh: T&T Clark International, 2005), ch. 6.

30. Devlin, "Introduction," *The Sermons and Devotional Writings of Gerard Manley Hopkins*, p. 117, writing of the thought of Ignatius of Loyola.

31. Van Huyssteen, "Human Origins and Religious Awareness," p. 17, citing also Philip Hefner, "Bio-cultural Evolution and the Created Co-Creator," in *Science and Theology: The New Consonance*, ed. Ted Peters (Boulder: Westview Press, 1998), pp. 174-188.

32. The title of a book by Neil Postman.

dustries so that "all is seared with trade; bleared, smeared with toil/And wears man's smudge and shares man's smell" ("God's Grandeur"). At the same time the sense of human distinctiveness and value is also very marked in his work; he refers to human beings as nature's "bonniest . . . clearest-selvèd spark" ("That Nature Is a Heraclitean Fire and of the Comfort of the Resurrection"). In his poem "Ribblesdale" Hopkins is very aware of the present tension and future possibilities of humans' relationship with the nonhuman creation, and he associates this (in his epigraph) with Romans 8:19-20 — verses from that strange but fascinating passage in which St. Paul turns his attention from the salvation of those in Christ to the condition and future salvation of the nonhuman world, writing:

> For if all creation is full of eager expectancy, that is because it is waiting for the sons of God to be manifested. Creation was subjected to futility (not by its own choice but by the will of him who so subjected it); yet with a hope to look forward to, namely, that creation itself would be set free from the thralldom of decay, and obtain that liberty which is bound up with the glory which belongs to the children of God. The whole creation, as we know, has been groaning in a common travail until this very hour.[33]

The creation, then, is depicted as awaiting the glorious liberty of the children of God. It has a "travail," a painful birthing process to which God has subjected it. While not supposing for a moment that St. Paul had any such understanding, it is hard to avoid some identification between this travail and the evolutionary process, which has been (presumably) part of God's will for the creation and has given rise to human beings and to so many other beautiful and intricate natural forms, yet has done so by means of a process full of struggle, suffering, and extinction.[34] There are just hints of this perception in Hopkins's sadness in "Heraclitean Fire" that "nature's bonfire burns on" but sweeps away the "mark" of the individual creature, even the human being.

Of itself, Hopkins's contemplative method is interesting and sometimes inspiring. But technically innovative though his verse is, his engagement with the impact of humans on the natural world is essentially premodern. He shows little awareness of the ambiguities of the evolutionary world. He wrote

---

33. Romans 8:19-22 in the translation by Heinz W. Cassirer, *God's New Covenant: A New Testament Translation* (Grand Rapids: Eerdmans, 1989).

34. For an analysis of the implications of this for theodicy, see Christopher Southgate, "God and Evolutionary Evil: Theodicy in the Light of Darwinism," *Zygon* 37, 4 (2002): 803-824.

of the world as "charged with the grandeur of God" ("God's Grandeur"). Darwin too used the word "grandeur" in describing his "view of things,"[35] but he was acutely conscious of the ugliness of much of nature, and that its beauty emerges only in a process involving much suffering. Hopkins could celebrate "all trades, their gear and tackle and trim" ("Pied Beauty"), but nowhere did he explore the tension between this and the polluting effect of trades at large. So the poet offers us a model for a scientifically, poetically, and theologically informed contemplation, but little that can help us with environmental ethics in the complexities of our current world. The same might be said of Martin Buber, the Jewish contemplative philosopher with whose method Hopkins has something in common. Hopkins's comment that "when you look hard at a thing it seems to look hard at you"[36] is very close to this passage from Buber, contemplating a tree:

> That living wholeness and unity of the tree, which denies itself to the sharpest glance of the mere investigator and discloses itself to the glance of one who says *Thou*, is there when he, the sayer of *Thou*, is there: it is he who vouchsafes to the tree that it manifest this unity and wholeness; and now the tree which is in being manifests them. Our habits of thought make it difficult for us to see that here, awakened by our attitude, something lights up and approaches us from the course of being.[37]

Behind both methods of engaging with the nonhuman world lurks a very strong sense of God as the one whose interest in all relationships cannot be ignored. Part of the strength of Buber's insight was that he saw that relationships never remain in that ideal realm of true interpersonal (or interentity) meeting — they are constantly slipping back into the "I-It." That is the relation which allows the entity to whom the "I" relates to be used as a commodity, a means to an end, a resource to be exploited. This thinking of Buber's is a very important corrective within human interaction, but it is hard to apply in any developed way to the nonhuman world, since we continually need to use and to trade (though not to "exploit") elements of the nonhuman world in order to survive. More ethically productive is H. Paul Santmire's recent adaptation of Buber. Santmire notes Buber's own struggle to say how there can be true mutuality between a human and a non-sentient

---

35. In the coda of *On the Origin of Species by Means of Natural Selection, or the Preservation of Favoured Races in the Struggle for Life* (London: John Murray, 1859).
36. Hopkins, *Journals and Papers*, p. 140.
37. Martin Buber, *I and Thou*, trans. Ronald Gregor Smith (London: Continuum, 1958 [first edition 1937; German original 1923]), p. 95.

creature such as a tree.[38] He proposes instead a third type of relation beyond "I-It" and "I-Thou" that he calls "I-Ens."[39] This can be between a human and a nonhuman creature, or even between a human and a part of fabricated nature such as a building or a city. An Ens, for Santmire, "does not fit into a utilitarian description of the world . . . it confronts me directly with an exclusive claim, a claim that will not allow me to pass beyond it, in order to set it in a larger schema of means and ends."[40] It is a relationship that involves recognition of beauty and wonder and of the need for humility and gratitude. Santmire quotes a Hasidic saying used by Buber: "there is no rung of being on which we cannot find the Holiness of God everywhere and at all times."[41]

There are hints here of something very generative for our relation to the nonhuman world. Santmire's formulation speaks of respect, but also of something much more than respect, something more like priesthood. The implication of the Romans passage — as implied in Hopkins's invocation of it in the epigraph to "Ribblesdale" — is that the consummation of nature must await humans' recognition of their true calling in respect to the creation.

Humans, then, are in Hopkins's terms the distinctive creatures with the capacity to instress creation, and the future of that creation depends not only on our working out of that capacity *but also* on our ability to accept spiritual transformation and come to find our freedom in its true form, in the Christ-minded service of God. These are, of course, profoundly theological imperatives, but they must also involve a thorough engagement with the concerns of science. As van Huyssteen says, writing of the doctrine that humans are created in the image of God,

> it is precisely the porousness of the boundaries between theology and the sciences that will allow for a creative rethinking of the notion of the *imago Dei* in Christian theology. The convergence of theological and scientific arguments on the issue of human uniqueness may give us an argument for the plausibility and comprehensive nature of religious and theological explanations for a phenomenon as complex as *Homo Sapiens*. At the same time, it may also protect theological reflection from exotically baroque abstractions when trying to revision the notion of the *imago Dei*.[42]

---

38. H. Paul Santmire, *Nature Reborn: The Ecological and Cosmic Promise of Christian Theology* (Minneapolis: Fortress Press, 2000), p. 68.
39. This term is the participle of the Latin verb *esse*, to be.
40. Santmire, *Nature Reborn*, p. 69.
41. Quoted in Santmire, *Nature Reborn*, p. 72.
42. J. Wentzel van Huyssteen, Synopsis of the Gifford Lectures, April/May 2004.

Our contemplation of and engagement with the nonhuman world must be based on scientifically informed understanding, not merely a romanticization of wilderness, but a Darwinian appreciation of its processes.[43] Again, we must also take with all seriousness the way in which our attributes and perceptions are shaped by being evolved animals.[44] But science can take us only so far. It is from theology, again, that we derive the ethical imperative to make of our lives a pattern of healing servanthood, from which the snatching that has been such a strong instinct of ours has been banished forever.

Ethical prescriptions can come from pragmatism, that is, consideration of our own future self-interest, or from principle, from a further look at what our species is called to be. In the end our global self-interest as evolved beings and our theological imperatives must cohere. That is what it means to investigate, and seek to live by, the ultimately real.

---

43. This point is trenchantly made by Lisa H. Sideris in her *Environmental Ethics, Ecological Theology, and Natural Selection* (New York: Columbia University Press, 2003).

44. Southgate, "Stewardship and Its Competitors."

13 Generating Life on Earth: Five Looming Questions

Holmes Rolston III

Events on Earth stand in marked contrast with events on other planets, such as the gases that swirl around Jupiter, or the winds that blow on Venus. On Earth, climatological and geomorphological processes continue in the Pleistocene period more or less as they did in the Precambrian. But Earth history is quite different because in biology — unlike physics, chemistry, geomorphology, or astronomy — something can be learned. Once upon a time, signals appeared! Where once there were matter and energy, where these remain, there is information, symbolically encoding life. There is a new state of matter, neither liquid nor gaseous nor solid, but vital. With the passing of cold and warm fronts or the uplifting and eroding of mountains, there is no natural selection. Nothing is competing, nothing is surviving, reproducing, nothing has adapted fit. To come into being, to survive, an organism needs to gain, to use, to transmit relevant information.

If we ourselves are to gain the information we wish about this generating of vital information, we need to figure out five big unknowns.

Creating Information

In nature, in the Newtonian view there were two metaphysical fundamentals: matter and energy. Einstein reduced these two to one: matter-energy. In matter in motion, there is conservation of matter, also of energy; neither can be created nor destroyed, although each can take diverse forms, and one can be transformed into the other. In the biological sciences, the novelty is that matter-energy enters into rich information states. The biologists still claim two metaphysical fundamentals: matter-energy and information. They can do so listening to a founder of cybernetics. Norbert Weiner insists: "Information is information, not matter or energy" (1948:155).

In physics and chemistry, throughout natural history, matter has been structurally transformed by energy, sometimes with impressive results, as with the construction of the higher elements in the stars or the composition of crystals, rocks, mountains, rivers, canyons on Earth. There are mathematical kinds of information (bitmaps). There is also a sense in which historical information is present, passively, on the surface of the moon. A geologist can read off from the way that craters are overlaid on each other which of the impacts came first. But the really spectacular constructions that are manifest in biological diversity and complexity do not appear without the simultaneous genesis of active information about how to compose, maintain, and communicate these vital structures and processes. This advanced, proactive information is recorded in the genes, and such information, unlike matter and energy, can be created and destroyed.

In living things, concludes Manfred Eigen, this is "the key-word that represents the phenomenon of complexity: information. Our task is to find an algorithm, a natural law that leads to the origin of information. . . . Life is a dynamic state of matter organized by information" (1992:12, 15). Bernd-Olaf Küppers agrees: "The problem of the origin of life is clearly basically equivalent to the problem of the origin of biological information" (1990:170). George C. Williams is explicit:

> Evolutionary biologists have failed to realize that they work with two more or less incommensurable domains: that of information and that of matter. . . . Matter and information [are] two separate domains of existence, which have to be discussed separately in their own terms. The gene is a package of information, not an object. . . . Maintaining this distinction between the medium and the message is absolutely indispensable to clarity of thought about evolution. (In Brockman 1995:43)

John Maynard Smith says: "Heredity is about the transmission, not of matter or energy, but of information. . . . The concept of information is central both to genetics and evolution theory" (1995:28). Together with his colleague, Eörs Szathmáry, he analyzes "the major transitions in evolution" with the resulting complexity, asking "how and why this complexity has increased in the course of evolution." "Our thesis is that the increase has depended on a small number of major transitions in the way in which genetic information is transmitted between generations." Critical innovations have included the origin of the genetic code itself, the origin of eukaryotes from prokaryotes, meiotic sex, multicellular life, animal societies, and language, especially human language (Maynard Smith and Szathmary 1995:3).

The most spectacular thing about planet Earth, says Richard Dawkins, is this "information explosion," even more remarkable than a supernova among the stars (1995:145). And, adds Klaus Dose:

> More than 30 years of experimentation on the origin of life in the fields of chemical and molecular evolution have led to a better perception of the immensity of the problem of the origin of life on Earth rather than its solution.... We do not actually know where the genetic information of all living cells originates. (1988:348)

When sodium and chlorine are brought together under suitable circumstances, anywhere in the universe, the result will be salt. This capacity is inlaid into the atomic properties; the reaction occurs spontaneously. Energy inputs may be required for some of these results, but no information input is needed. When nitrogen, carbon, and hydrogen are brought together under suitable circumstances anywhere in the universe, with energy input, the spontaneous result may be amino acids, but it is not hemoglobin molecules or lemurs — not spontaneously. The know-how, so to speak, to make salt is already in the sodium and chlorine, but the know-how to make hemoglobin molecules and lemurs is not secretly coded in the carbon, hydrogen, and nitrogen. The essential characteristic of a biological molecule, contrasted with a merely physicochemical molecule, is that it contains vital information. Its conformation is functional. With the typical protein, enzyme, lipid, or carbohydrate this is structural, keyed by the coding in DNA, and interlocked with an information producer-processor (the organism) that can transcribe, incarnate, metabolize, and reproduce it.

In the course of evolutionary history, one would be disturbed to find matter or energy spontaneously created, but ought we not be equally disturbed to find information appearing *ex nihilo*? Nature has spontaneously assembled itself as an open cybernetic system several billion years long and gaining spectacular diversity and complexity. Life is a river that runs uphill, and even if it nowhere runs uphill very steeply (if we look at its incremental assembly bit by bit), the river as a whole runs far uphill. Each living creature in the stream is quite highly ordered. Some forces are present that build order in superseding steps out of disorder. Organisms must be constructed along a long negentropic pathway. This requires the continual introduction of information not previously present. Though no new matter or energy is needed, if there are to be generated these on-going evolutionary constructions, making niche-step by niche-step these dramatic structural/functional climbs, new information is needed in enormous amounts. The usual turn here is to conclude that nature is self-organizing (autopoiesis), though, since no "self" is present, this is better termed spontaneously organizing. Nature is spontaneously auto-cybernetic. An autopoietic, autocybernetic process can be just a name, like "soporific" tendencies, used to label this mysterious genesis of more out of less, a seemingly scientific name that is really a sort of mystic chant over a miraculously fertile universe. Any metaphysically adequate account needs a ground of this information.

Contingent versus Inevitable Creativity

Contemporary biologists are divided across a spectrum whether this creative cybernetic evolutionary history is entirely contingent or quite probable, even inevitable. If life on Earth is a one-off event, sheer contingency, we need not expect it elsewhere. If life is intrinsic to the physics and chemistry, we should expect it elsewhere. If we find some trends, some mixture of the inevitable and the contingent, we will not only wonder what to expect elsewhere but what to make of discovering ourselves here on Earth. Such trends, which are a *sine qua non* of historical interpretation, are neither absolute laws nor mere contingencies; they are never directly observable and may be difficult to detect in a limited span of time or range of observation. They show up statistically, but statistics deals poorly with cybernetically developing trends, with sometimes critical initiating discoveries, such as when photosynthesis, or neurons, or endoskeletons appeared.

There are eminent biologists — though they tend to be molecular biologists rather than paleontologists — who find Earth's evolutionary history to be inevitable, at least in outline, and therefore predictable. Christian de Duve, a Nobel prizewinner, concludes: "Life was bound to arise under the prevailing conditions, and it will arise similarly wherever and whenever the same conditions obtain. There is hardly any room for 'lucky accidents' in the gradual, multistep process whereby life originated." After life arises there is contingency as to its directions and species, but this is "constrained contingency" so that the general trends in the development of life — cellular organisms, multicellular organisms, solar energized organisms, increasingly diverse and complex organisms, and intelligent organisms — are likewise inevitable. "Life and mind emerge not as the results of freakish accidents, but as natural manifestations of matter, written into the fabric of the universe. I view this universe [as] . . . made in such a way as to generate life and mind, bound to give birth to thinking beings" (1995:xv-xvi, xviii).

"This universe breeds life inevitably," concludes George Wald, another Nobel laureate (1974:9). Life is an accident waiting to happen, because it is blueprinted into the chemicals, rather as sodium and chlorine are preset to form salt, only much more startlingly so because of the rich implications for life and because of the openness and information transfer also present in the historical life process. Whatever place dice-throwing plays in its appearance and maturation, life is something arranged for in the nature of things. The dice are loaded.

When the predecessors of DNA and RNA appear, enormously complex molecules bearing the possibility of genetic coding and information, these are conserved, writes Melvin Calvin, yet another Nobel laureate, "not by accident but because of the peculiar chemistries of the various bases and amino acids.... There is a kind of selectivity intrinsic in the structures." The evolution of life, so far from being random, is "a logical consequence" of natural chemistries (1975:176, 169). To continue with Nobel prizewinners, Manfred Eigen concludes "that the evolution of life ... must be considered an *inevitable* process despite its indeterminate course" (1971:519; 1992). Life is destined to come as part of the narrative story, although the exact routes it will take are open and subject to historical vicissitudes. Stuart Kauffman agrees: "I believe that the origin of life was not an enormously improbable event, but law-like and governed by new principles of self-organization in complex webs of catalysts" (1993:xvi; 1995).

Life originated at start-up events and then kept on further generating. Perhaps we can gain some clue about the nature of the evolutionary start-up from what happened afterward over the subsequent millennia. David Raup and John Sepkoski graph marine invertebrates and vertebrates, an overall rise, with climbs and drops, especially at times of catastrophic extinctions, from zero to perhaps 750 families (Fig. 1 on p. 200) (Raup and Sepkoski 1982). During the relatively flat part of the marine curve, life moves onto the land and greatly diversifies there, from the Silurian Period onward, not shown in this graph. That requires also considerable evolution of complexity, since the terrestrial environment is more demanding.

Plants develop steadily on the land masses, graphed by Karl Niklas (Fig. 2 on p. 200). For animals, it is in the vertebrates, most of all, that advance is difficult to deny (Fig. 3 on p. 201) (Niklas 1986). Norman D. Newell graphed the numbers of all families, terrestrial and marine, vertebrate and invertebrate, increasing through evolutionary time (Fig. 4 on p. 202) (Newell 1963). Rather interestingly, Sean Nee and Robert M. May find that the catastrophic extinctions do not much suppress these trends. Even in the most extreme cases, "approximately 80 percent of the tree of life can survive even when approximately 95

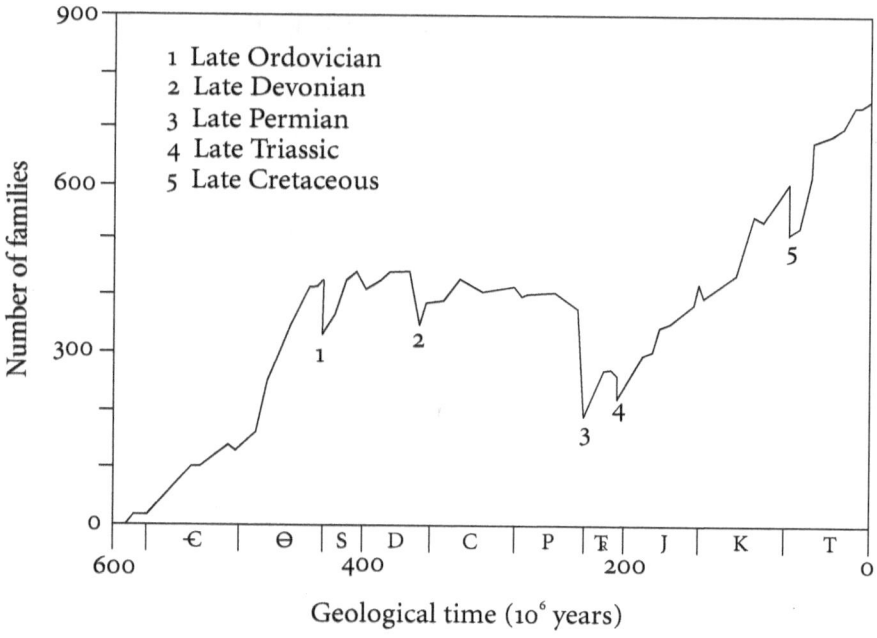

Fig. 1. Standing diversity through time for families of marine vertebrates and invertebrates, with catastrophic extinctions numbered (Raup and Sepkoski, 1982)

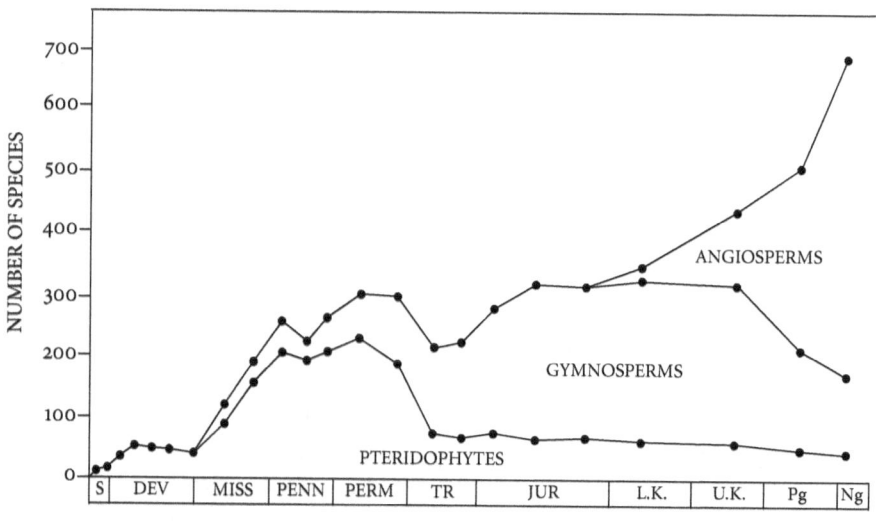

Fig. 2. Species diversity changes in vascular plants (Niklas, 1986)

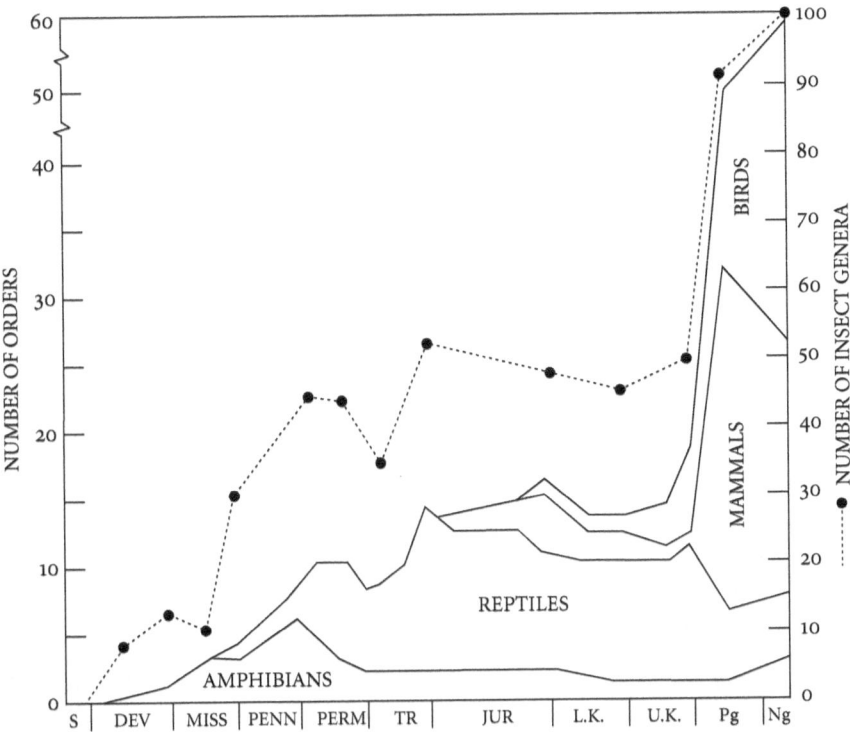

Fig. 3. Changes in the composition of vertebrate orders and numbers of insect genera (Niklas, 1986)

percent of species are lost." To use their metaphor, mass extinction cuts off the twigs of the tree of life (the species) but the main branches (the families, orders, classes) persist in species that do survive. "Much of the tree of life may survive even vigorous pruning" (Fig. 5 on p. 202) (Nee and May 1997; Myers 1997).

A graph of increasing complexity is more difficult to produce. Nevertheless increases in capacities for sentience (ears, eyes, noses, antennae), increases in capacities for locomotion (muscles, fins, legs, wings), increases in capacities for manipulation (arms, hands, opposable thumbs), increases in neural networks with control centers, brains, surpassing mere genetic and enzymatic control, increases in capacities for acquired learning (feedback loops, synapses, memory banks), increases in capacities for communication and language acquisition) — all these take increased complexity. Nothing seems more evident over the long ranges than that complexity has increased; in the Precambrian there were microbes; in the Cambrian Period trilobites were the highest life form; the Pleistocene Period produced persons.

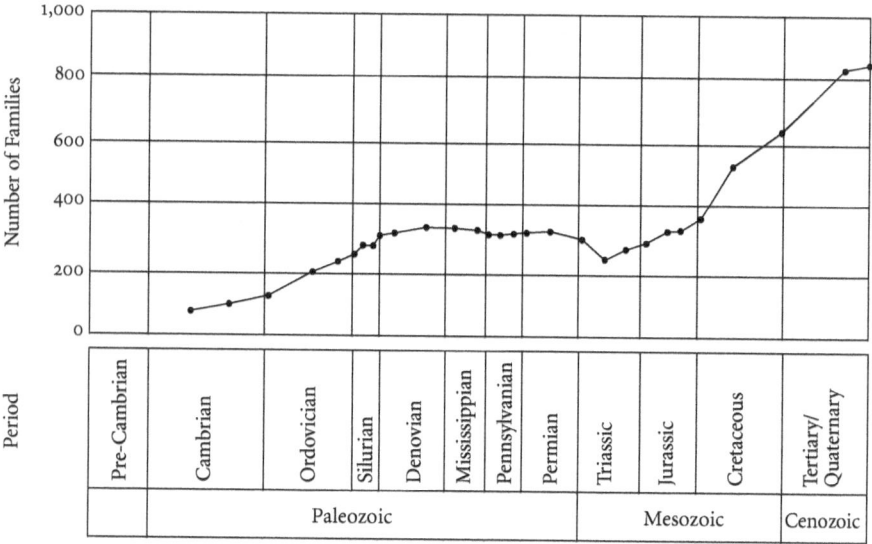

Fig. 4. Number of major families of fossil animals increasing through time (Newell, 1963)

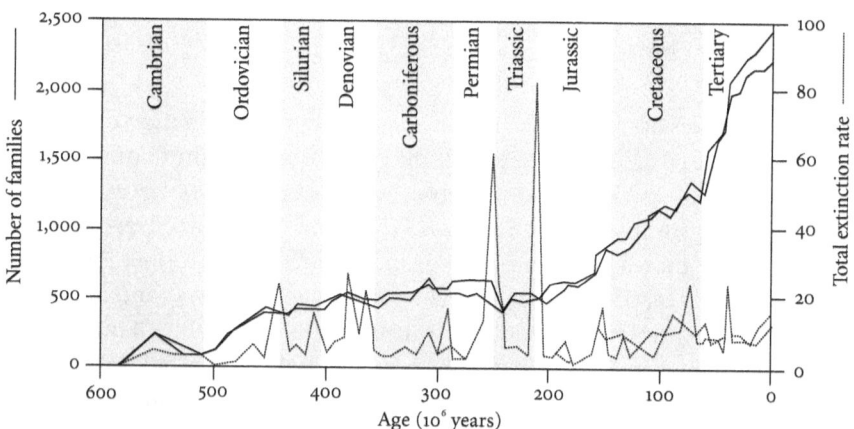

Fig. 5. Proliferation of number of families on Earth, continuing through major extinctions (Myers, 1997; Nee and May, 1997)

Ernst Mayr asks:

> Who can deny that overall there is an advance from the procaryotes that dominated the living world more than three billion years ago to the eucaryotes with their well organized nucleus and chromosomes as well as cytoplasmic organelles; from the single-celled eucaryotes to metaphytes and metazoans with a strict division of labor among their highly specialized organ systems; within the metazoans from ectotherms that are at the mercy of climate to the warm-blooded endotherms, and within the endotherms from types with a small brain and low social organization to those with a very large central nervous system, highly developed parental care, and the capacity to transmit information from generation to generation? (Mayr 1988:251-252).

The lower forms remain too; there must be trophic pyramids, food chains. There cannot be higher forms, all by themselves. These must be superposed on lower forms, embedded in communities. So there can seem only change, not progress, if one looks at the monocots and dicots, the crustaceans and flatworms. But if we are to have the whole story of what is going on, we must look at the uppermost forms. These do seem to get built up over time.

Simon Conway Morris, a prominent Cambridge paleontologist, has been quite outspoken about how "life . . . is full of inherencies." "Life shows a kind of homing instinct" (2003:8, 20). Looking back across Earth's natural history and wondering if things might have been otherwise, searching the possibilities for "evolutionary counterfactuals," "possibly . . . we shall discover in the end that there are none. And, despite the almost crass simplicity of life's building blocks, perhaps we can discern inherent within this framework the inevitable and pre-ordained trajectories of evolution?" (2003:24).

True, much in evolutionary history can seem contingent, if one considers only the fortunes of this or that lineage, which is typically the focus of analysis. The history begins to look different when one considers the evolution of skills, irrespective of what lineage they happen to be in. Assuming more or less the same earthbound environments, if evolutionary history were to occur all over again, things would be different. Still, there would again be plants and animals; photosynthesis or something like it; primary producers and secondary consumers; predators and prey; parasites and hosts; autotrophs and heterotrophs; ecosystemic communities; cells and membranes; birth or hatching; seeds reproducing; coding and coping; natural selection; sight; mobility with fins, limbs, or wings; smell; hearing; convergence; and parallelism. Life would evolve in the sea, spread to the land and the air.

Play the tape of history again. If played just once more, the differences would strike us first. Leigh Van Valen continues: "Play the tape a few more times, though. We see similar melodic elements appearing in each, and the overall structure may be quite similar. . . . When we take a broader view, the role of contingency diminishes. Look at the tape as a whole. It resembles in some ways a symphony, although its orchestration is internal and caused largely by the interactions of many melodic strands" (Van Valen 1991:48).

Maynard Smith agrees that complexity has increased, but, to the contrary, finds no cause to think it would happen again. "There is nothing in neo-Darwinism which enables us to predict a long-term increase in complexity." But he goes on to suspect that this is not because there is no such long-term increase, but that Darwinism is inadequate to explain it. We need "to put an arrow on evolutionary time" but get no help from evolutionary theory.

> It is in some sense true that evolution has led from the simple to the complex: prokaryotes precede eukaryotes, singled-celled precede many-celled organisms, taxes and kineses precede complex instinctive or learnt acts. I do not think that biology has at present anything very profound to say about this. . . . We can say little about the evolution of increasing complexity. (1972:89, 98-99).

Contrary to de Duve, Eigen, Calvin, Conway Morris, or Kauffman, Maynard Smith and Eörs Szathmáry find "no reason to regard the unique transitions as the inevitable result of some general law"; to the contrary, these events might not have happened at all (1995:3).

Evolutionary history wanders in the first place because of atomic and molecular chance, unrelated to the needs of the organism. Selection is operating over this chance, but that selection does not introduce any ordered direction, because it is not selection for advancement, only selection for survival. The biggest events (the coming of mammals and humans) not less than the smallest events (the microscopic mutations) are accidental or random with respect to anything the theory can predict or retrospectively explain. It might first seem that in one part of the theory, the supply side, internal to the organism, one finds randomness, but that in another part of the theory, the retention side, external to the organism, one might find progress, because the "better" are selected. From among the myriad trials that come momentarily into existence, the fittest are selected to stay. The new events occur at random with respect to their direction, but are preserved for the direction they take.

But when we look more closely at even the retention side — so this claim runs — randomness is equally present there. There is no direction in the microevolution (random variants), and no direction in the macroevolution either (selection headed nowhere), a twice-compounded randomness. Selection is for survival, yes; but there is only changing genetics that records changing morphology and behavior that tracks drifting environments. This does give local trends (hair growing whiter as environments grow colder). But there is no covering law, or trend, enabling one to say that microbes, or mammals, or humans could statistically be expected. They just occur as historical events, and the theory is surprised by them, although in retrospect they are consistent with the theory. Among the equally fit, some are more complex, some less so, and while survival might have been possible without advancing complexity, there is nevertheless advancing complexity in some few forms, consistent with, but not required by, the principle of natural selection.

Stephen Jay Gould spent his career "denying that progress characterizes the history of life as a whole, or even represents an orienting force in evolution at all" (1996:3). "We are the accidental result of an unplanned process ... the fragile result of an enormous concatenation of improbabilities, not the predictable product of any definite process" (1983:101-102). "Natural selection is a theory of *local* adaptation to changing environments. It proposes no perfecting principles, no guarantee of general improvement" (1977:45). Natural selection provides no reason to believe in "innate progress in nature"; none of the local adaptations are "progressive in any cosmic sense" (1977:45). "Almost every interesting event of life's history falls into the realm of contingency" (1989:290).

Michael Ruse surveys the conclusions of evolutionary biologists at great length. "A major conclusion of this study is that some of the most significant of today's evolutionists are Progressionists, and ... we find (absolute) progressivism alive and well in their work" (1996:536). Nevertheless, they are all wrong, because, biased, they are reading progress into the evolutionary record. They have slipped into "pseudo-science." "For nigh two centuries, evolution functioned as an ideology, as a secular religion, that of Progress" (1996:526). The fashionable account at the moment is that the British read progress into nature from their cultural gestalt. Scientists continue to do this because we humans have an innate disposition to long for order. That biases us to read progress into a Darwinian nature, when the truth of the matter is that Darwinian nature is disorderly, not progress. Today, argues Ruse, the more "mature" scientists, unbiased, have "expelled progress" from evolutionary history (1996:534). "Evolution is going nowhere — and rather slowly at that" (1986:203).

But then one has also to conclude that all those Nobel laureates are immature scientists! Perhaps a better conclusion to draw at this point (despite

Ruse, and puzzling about the Nobel laureates) is that there isn't any conclusion. Maybe we do not even know whether we humans are competent to make such a judgment. We do not know where the information that is generating life is coming from; we do not know whether its arrival was contingent, necessary, improbable, or probable.

Possibility Space: Omnipresent versus Emerging

We do not know how or when generating such information became possible. We do know, of course, that it did become possible, since here we are. For scientists, the question is about the generating the actual out of the possible. Metaphysicians also need to generate those possibilities. Once again, metaphysicians and scientists are located along a spectrum. On one end of this spectrum, all the possibilities are always there, front-loaded (as it were) into the system. From the Big Bang on there is a world of infinite possibilities. On another account, along the spectrum, new possibilities appear during the circumstances of evolutionary history. That certainly seems the case in human history. We regularly say that new possibilities open up; we mean that opportunities once not there came into being.

Perhaps there are degrees of possibility. Possibilities are of various kinds. With originating life, the developing possibility route is not so much logical, or empirical, or even physical; it is historical. Science does not handle historical explanations very competently, especially where there are emergent novelties; science prefers law-like explanations in which there are no surprises. One predicts, and the prediction comes true. If such precision is impossible, science prefers statistical predictions, probabilities. One predicts, and, probably, the prediction comes true. Biology, meanwhile, though prediction is often possible, is also full of unpredictable surprises — like calcium endoskeletons in vertebrates after millennia of diatomaceous silica and chitinous arthropod exoskeletons. As life becomes more complex, it becomes more historical.

There is no induction (expecting the future to be like the past) by which one can expect, even probably, trilobites later from prokaryotes earlier, or dinosaurs still later by extrapolating along a regression line (a progression line!) drawn from prokaryotes to trilobites. There are no humans invisibly present (as an acorn secretly contains an oak) in the primitive eukaryotes, to unfold in a law-like or programmatic way. The ancient ancestral forms are not proto-vertebrates, or pre-terrestrials, nor are gymnosperms about-to-be angiosperms, as though the descendant forms were latent among the functions of the predecessors. Originating events often become what they become only retrospectively: Vertebrates began (possibly) with the notochords of primitive chordates.

Nevertheless, there is the epic story: eukaryotes, trilobites, dinosaurs, primates, swarms of wild creatures in seas and on land, followed by humans who come late in the story. What makes the critical difference in evolutionary history is increase in the information possibility space, which is not something inherent in the precursor materials, nor even in the evolutionary system.

The accounts by Calvin, Wald, Eigen, Conway Morris, and Kauffman suggest that the possibilities are always there, latent in the physics and chemistry. De Duve puts it this way: "The universe has given life and mind. Consequently, it must have had them, potentially, ever since the Big Bang" (2002:298). But of course all such possibilities are seen only retrospectively. If, *per impossibile*, some scientist had under observation the elementary particles forming after the first three minutes, nothing much in them suggests anything specific about the coding for life that would take place, fifteen billion years later, on Earth. After Earth forms, the lifeless planet is irradiated by solar energy, as are other planets as well. In orogeny and erosion, or the shifting of the tectonic plates, the possibilities of building geological structures seem always to be there.

At the microscopic levels, quantum physics depicts an open system and nested sets of possibilities; but, at first, all the atoms and molecules take nonliving tracks. There really isn't much in the physics and chemistry of atoms and molecules, prior to their biological assembling, that suggests that they possess, pushed down inside them, any tendencies to order themselves up to life. The order does not seem to be arising "bottom up." Only later, do some atoms and molecules begin to take living tracks, called forth as interaction phenomena when cybernetic organisms appear.

From a more comprehensive view, if there is some "inside order" to matter that makes it prolife, perhaps it is distributed over the whole system and not just in capacities in the particles. Such order would be "top down." But, despite the anthropic principle, such order is not generally evident in the systemic astronomy, since far the vastest parts of the universe are lifeless. Nor, on Earth, are the meteorological or geomorphological systems all that suggestive of inevitable life. They mostly seem kaleidoscopic variations on geophysical and geochemical processes. Even after things have developed as far as the building blocks of life, there is nothing in a "thin hot soup" of disconnected amino acids to predict that they will arrange for DNA molecules in which to record the various discoveries of structures and metabolisms specific to the diverse forms of life, dinosaurs or lemurs.

When in biology there open up entirely unprecedented levels of achievement and power, we do not conclude that such possibilities are possessed inside the atoms and molecules apart from their systemic location, since atoms and molecules would not even be collected into a hot soup except for the Earth-world in which this is possible, nor can this or that sequence of DNA code for anything unless there is an environment in which to behave this way or that, with a niche to fill. All these events may come naturally, but they are still quite a surprise. Recent microbiology has been revealing their enormous complexity. We do not know that life, if it occurs on some other planet, being there also built of the same atoms, must select these same biochemistries, although the amino acids found on meteorites and the prebiotic molecules guessed to be present in interstellar dust clouds can suggest that the potential for life is omnipresent in matter.

Making this survey, can one insist that the probabilities must always have been there, or at least the possibilities? Can one claim that what did actually manage to happen must always have been probable, or, minimally, improbably possible all along the way? Push this to extremes, as one must do, if one claims that all the possibilities are always there, latent in the dust, latent in the quarks. Such a claim becomes pretty much an act of speculative faith, not in present actualities, since one knows that these events have taken place, but faith in past probabilities always being omnipresent. Is the claim some kind of induction or deduction, or most-plausible-case conclusion from present actualities? Speculation about such possibilities always being there is easy, provided one does not have to specify any of the details. But this perennial and vast library of possibilities is mostly imaginary.

For in fact, on Earth, there really isn't anything in rocks that suggests the possibility of *Homo sapiens,* much less the American Civil War, or the World Wide Web, and to say that all these possibilities are lurking there is simply to let possibilities float in from nowhere. Unbounded possibilities that one posits ad hoc to whatever one finds has in fact taken place — possibilities of any kind and amount desired in one's metaphysical enthusiasm — can hardly be said to be a scientific hypothesis. Alfred North Whitehead cautions against this as a metaphysical mistake (1978:46). This is hardly even a faith claim with sufficient warrant. It is certainly equally credible, and more plausible, and no less scientific, or metaphysical, to hold that new possibility spaces open up en route. But one will need an explanation adequate to this effect.

Karl Popper concludes that science discovers "a world of propensities," open to historical innovation, the possibility space ever enlarging.

> In our real changing world, the situation and, with it, the possibilities, and thus the propensities, change all the time. . . . This view of propensities al-

lows us to see in a new light the processes that constitute our world: the world process. The world is no longer a causal machine — it can now be seen as a world of propensities, as an unfolding process of realizing possibilities and of unfolding new possibilities. . . . New possibilities are created, possibilities that previously simply did not exist. . . . Especially in the evolution of biochemistry, it is widely appreciated that every new compound creates new possibilities for further new compounds to synthesize: possibilities which previously did not exist. The possibility space . . . is growing. . . . Our world of propensities is inherently creative. (1990:17-20)

The result is the evolutionary drama. "The variety of those [organisms] that have realized themselves is staggering." "In the end, we ourselves become possible" (1990:26, 19).

But — the reply comes — since all those things did come in subsequent evolutionary and cultural history, their possibilities must have been there all along. You were not listening when we discovered that matter is self-organizing, autopoietic. That posits enormous capacities, there from the start; and nothing in the historical drama ought to take by all that much surprise one who believes in self-organizing nature. Thomas R. Cech, a molecular biologist and Nobel laureate, reviews the origin of life:

> If intrinsic to these small organic molecules is their propensity to self-assemble, leading to a series of events that cause life forms to originate, that is perhaps the highest form of creation that one could imagine. . . . At least from the perspective of a biologist, I have given an account of how possibilities did, in times past, become actual. When this happened, life originated with impressive creativity, and it does not seem to me that possibilities floated in from nowhere; they were already present, intrinsic to the chemical materials. (1995:33)

Suppose that a meteorite lands on Earth, releasing some iron atoms as the incandescent meteor crashes into the ground. Suppose some of those iron atoms make their way into my diet, and into my blood. Would not such meteoric iron, from outer space, work just as well as any terrestrial iron atom carrying oxygen to my brain? Does that not mean that such iron atoms have had from time immemorial the capacity for entering into cognitive processes? Passively perhaps, if overtaken by mind, but actively there is no such self-contained potential. A single atom of iron has no such possibilities within itself at all. To claim that it does is like saying that ink and paper have all the possibilities of the Library of Congress latent within the bottle and secretly coded in the paper pulp fibers. Entering into thinking processes becomes a possibility for such an extraterrestrial iron atom only with its encounter with (only relative to) the systemic company of enormous amounts of information.

One can insist that it must always have been possible to put carbon atoms into organic cells and silicon atoms into computers, since we humans do that now somatically and technologically — and the atoms are no different from what they have been for billions of years. But it may have always been possible to do this *with* these atoms, providing that one had the know-how to do such things, but not possible lacking such information. Such information has to become possible. That is a different claim from claim that it has always been possible *for* carbon and silicon to self-organize into organism and computers.

We know that water, as a polar molecule, has various features that have turned out to be fortunate for supporting life. But you can know all about the polarity of water, and nothing known there leads you to predict lipid bilayers later on, built with their hydrophobic heads and hydrophilic tails and used to make membranes that enclose the life structures. In the forest, a scientist encounters a tree, the wood functioning to hold the leaves up to the sun. But what new can we do with wood? We can build a violin and play music. This gives us no cause to claim that a violin is lurking in the possibility space of the tree with its wood.

Seeds sprout plants. Earth sprouts biodiversity. Michael Polanyi says: "From a seed of submicroscopic living particles — and from inanimate beginnings lying beyond these — we see emerging a race of sentient, responsible and creative beings. The spontaneous rise of such incomparably higher forms of being testifies directly to the operations of an orderly innovating principle" (1964:386-387). But the problem with the metaphor of a "seed" is that we now know what is in a seed: DNA coding the species of life. Neither in carbon and oxygen atoms nor in the geomorphology of planet Earth is there any such information seeded in, neither for making trilobites and dinosaurs, or for *Homo sapiens* sprouting myriad cultures, sprouting ethics, science, and religion.

Enthusiastic metaphysicians will reply that all actual events materialize in a global possibility space. The possibility space is always there. There is no such thing as the creation of possibilities that were not there. New doors may open but only into rooms that previously existed, albeit unoccupied and with no furniture. One does not need to get possibilities from nowhere because there are infinite possibilities everlastingly, or at least since the Big Bang. The proof of this lies in what has subsequently happened. But surely the possibility space of serious alternatives does enlarge and shrink. There are times of opportunity, in which taking one direction opens up new possibilities, and taking another shuts them out. Along the way, new possibility space for genetic engineering is brought into the picture, and this is linked with the appearance of new information.

Co-option Generating Novel Possibilities

Something seems to be introducing layer by layer new possibilities of order, not just unfolding some latent order already there in the startup set-up. The biological constructions are historical, but they are not simply linear combinatorial processes. True, in the DNA molecules the coding is linear, and the changes are incremental in the linear sequences. But these changes also involve reassorting blocks that reshuffle to produce surprises. A few changes in the linear sequence produce quite different folding patterns at tertiary and quaternary levels in the finished protein. Novel possibilities open up whole new regions of search space; old molecules recombine to learn new tricks in unprecedented circumstances. Evolution improvises.

Such composition is not linear because it requires co-option: "An existing gene (and its product) is recruited to a new function" (Conway Morris 2000:3). For example, lens crystallins used in eyes first evolved in an altogether different role, as heat stress proteins. Surprisingly, they get used to make eye lenses (Wistow 1993). Darwin had already noted this: "The swimbladder in fishes . . . shows us clearly the highly important fact that an organ originally constructed for one purpose, namely flotation, may be converted into one for a wholly different purpose, namely, respiration" (Darwin 1968:220-221).

Hearing evolved from cells in the side of an aquatic vertebrate's body that were sensitive to pressure, helpful to a swimming animal, an original use that has been lost from the reptiles onward. These cells were co-opted to become the hair cells in mammalian ears. That required constructing the external, middle, and inner ears, with small bones co-opted and modified to amplify sound, vibrating an oval area on the cochlea of the inner ear. This jiggles the microscopic hairs (stereocilia) on the ends of the hair cells. These cells synapse with neurons. The hairs are sensitive to movements as small as 0.3 nanometers (about the diameter of a large atom). Mechanical movement of the cilia opens and closes ion channels letting sodium ions into the cell, and this constitutes an electric current, which triggers the synapsizing, producing perceptible noise, over a volume differential of a trillion times from softest to loudest.

Animals need to know frequencies as well as volume, and here the firing frequencies of the usual synaptic transmissions can track frequencies at the lower ranges, but the higher frequencies are too fast for this method. So ears improvise something else. There has further evolved a basilar membrane packed with hair cells and rolled up in the cochlea (about the size of a pea) that, using different widths and stiffness of the membrane, can differentiate how far along it a traveling wave will go, and so the auditory system responds to different frequencies ending up at different places on the membrane. There is a tonotopic map on the basilar membrane of the frequencies being heard. Further, on the basilar membrane, there is a system of outer hair cells that amplify the inner hair cells. With this the ear can detect frequencies up to 20,000 hertz. A trained musician can distinguish between a tone of 1,000 Hz and another of 1,001 Hz, which requires that the musician detect a difference of only 1 microsecond in the sound wavelengths.

But where is the sound coming from? That too is useful information. Animals have two ears, and the differential travel time of sound from the source to the slightly separated ears, can be used to locate the sound. But again, this only works in the range 20-2,000 hertz, above which frequency the wavelength is too short to figure location out this way. There is not enough interaural time. So another way is improvised. One ear is in the shadow of the sound, compared to the other. Now the auditory system sends the signals to the superior olive nucleus in the mid-brain, and there the sound from one ear is compared to the sound from the other for the intensity differential resulting from the sound shadow, and the location of higher frequency sounds is computed. Persons can locate a sound source in the horizontal plane with a precision of 2 degrees (Bear et al. 2001: ch. 11). Meanwhile, a spin-off from this auditory system is the vestibular system, co-opted to maintain bodily balance.

One could say that such complex ears were latent in the possibility space of pressure cells, which were latent in the possibility space of carbon, oxygen, nitrogen atoms. But an equally plausible account is that co-options opened up new possibility space, and the new genetic information achieved proves of value in an evolutionary search for better environmental information (heard in the ears). With continuing co-option, these vertebrate ears open up the possibility of animal communication — and, in due course and much later, of human language, which makes culture possible, with its cumulative transmission of ideas orally communicated from mind to mind.

Spoken language requires simultaneously the evolution of genes for speech, and such genes, differentiating humans from other primates, arose at a highly critical period in our evolution. The FOXP2 gene, called a speech gene, arose less than 200,000 years ago and became the subject of strong selection, making language and culture possible. Acetylcholine, an ancient molecule was around for millennia doing other things in plants and bacteria; when nerves appear it gets co-opted for use in synaptic transmission, which makes mental life possible. Ideas pass from mind to mind, and for this hearing is more important than sight — at least until the invention of writing. Millennia later, written language (needing those eyes and their crystallins) transforms cultures by making possible the transmission of thoughts non-orally, across centuries and peoples. Printing makes possible massive public communication, followed by radio, television, electronic communication, the internet. Escalating co-option drives the information explosion.

Often, though not always, there is gene duplication, and one copy serves the former function; the new copy can be modified in exploratory directions. There are remarkable forks off the preexisting pathways, which served some other function (and may continue to do this). Things get recruited for new roles. Previously disconnected parts working along unrelated pathways are co-opted off and put together to start serving a novel function, perhaps only slightly well at the first. Radically different selection pressures begin to work in new directions that are completely unanticipated when they occur. Once launched, the novel functions may improve steadily and completely transform the course of natural and human history.

Perhaps it all takes place by slight modifications of a precursor system. These incremental changes keep "bootstrapping" on themselves and hence the self-organization. But these slight modifications are sometimes made in new, unprecedented directions. The co-opting modification is not improving the initial function but angles off in a new direction. The change is not iterative; it is metamorphic. Co-option breaks up channelized and entrenched developmental lines (more and better pressure cells) and opens up new directions (hearing at a distance, meaningful sounds). Restriction enzymes, one of the most important features of genetic innovation, and a principal tool in genetic engineering, were first invented by bacteria to cut their parasites into pieces. They turned out to be useful for organisms to cut their own genomes into pieces and reshuffle them in the search for co-options.

Complex operating systems in both nature and culture cannot be designed from scratch at the start, but they have to evolve by additions to previous versions and, with co-option, these previous constructions come eventually to fulfill functions that had nothing to do with their initial construction. One can say, well, it just happens this way. But a metaphysician needs an explanation for the arriving possibilities.

Evolutionists can make *ex post facto* explanations. After the events have taken place, the paleontologist can say, well this is what happened, and this is what resulted. But prior to the events, if asked what would be the result, if such and such happened, one could never, from the knowledge of the constituent parts, say in advance what the results would be. Much less could one predict that such results had to happen. Perhaps one will say, since it has so often happened in evolutionary history, that there must be some tendency in biological nature to co-opt, a disposition to improvise, to be opportunistic. But where is such tendency located? Hardly from "bottom up" in the precursor materials. Hardly either from "top down" in the planetary system.

Maybe the possibilities lie somewhere in the mid-scale genetics. Simon Conway Morris builds much of his case for inevitable evolution on repeated convergences, such as the evolution of marsupials in Australia parallel to the evolution of placentals worldwide. (He has an index of five pages of convergences, 2003:457-461.) "Convergence occurs because of 'islands' of stability, analogous to 'attractors' in chaos theory" (2003:127). "The details of convergence actually reveal many of the twists and turns of evolutionary change as different starting points are transformed towards common solutions via a variety of well-trodden paths" (2003:144). Within the cell Conway Morris notices "some of the proteins being recruited in quite surprising ways from some other function elsewhere in the cell" (2003:111). "Evolution is a past master at co-option and jury-rigging: redeploying existing structures and cobbling them together in sometimes quite surprising ways. Indeed, in many ways that *is* evolution" (2003:238).

But does this add up to making the whole life story more or less inevitable? Some events are "quite surprising" indeed. About 2.7 billion years ago eucaryotes developed from the ongoing procaryote line. Much later, but before plants and animals had diverged, by endosymbiosis what were once-independent organisms fused into other, larger and quite different organisms to become mitochondria transferred into the pre-plant/animal line, and became the powerhouse organelles for all subsequent life. There emerges a new kind of system where the organism has highly efficient and specialized power modules (the mitochondria), something not possible to either of the precedents before they interacted, criss-crossed, synthesized, and transformed each other. The "information" about how to do this was not present before in the preceding organisms, but now there has appeared new "information" (coded in the revised DNA in the nucleus and the residual DNA in the mitochondrion) that makes this new, high-powered form of life possible.

About 1.6 billion years ago the plant and animal lines diverged; and later still, by another remarkable endosymbiosis, plastids, once free-living, made the lateral transfer into the plant line to become the chloroplasts critical for the capture of solar energy. Again, new, higher-powered forms of life are possible, both in the plants and in the animals that feed on plants (Dyall et al.

2004). Perhaps one can say that endosymbiosis is likely to occur; there are frequently "mobile elements" that transpose and reshape evolution (Kazazian 2004). But is there any "inherency" in the earliest microbial life making inevitable or even probable these two especially vital endosymbioses, both thought to initiate as singularities, and both dramatically changing the history of life on Earth? One can say that evolution is disposed to exciting serendipity. In such cases of co-opted emergence, repeatedly compounding, something that is genuinely new pops out, pops up. The novelty is, of course, based on the precedents, but there is genuine novelty not present in any of the precedents. What emerged required the precedents, but the presence of the prior organisms did not determine or make inevitable these results. There are critical turning points in the history of life that hinge on events more idiographic (unique, one-off events) than nomothetic (law-like, inevitable, repeatable trends). Things get recruited for new roles. Novel possibilities open up whole new regions of search space; old molecules recombine to learn new tricks.

Sometimes the explanatory account is by laws applied to initial conditions, and the same laws again reapplied to the resulting outcomes, now treated as further initial conditions. But sometimes, with co-options, endosymbioses, lateral genetic transfers, mutations, the outcomes are not just further sets of initial conditions. The novel outcomes revise the previous laws; the rules of the game change, and the future is like no previous past. One can say that all this surprising serendipity is somehow "inherent" from the start; but the explanatory power of such a claim is rather vague. The main idea in co-option is the unpredictable and unexpected; co-option is as revolutionary as it is evolutionary.

Environmental and structural constraints remain, but the constraints are not what they were before, now that the organism is equipped with these new potential capacities. The amount of information in an organism is transforming into its capacity for self-reformation, though the self-reformation is also provoked, evoked by environmental challenge and stress. The self-organizing becomes self-transcending.

Was all that resulted all along present in the possibility spaces of all the predecessor organisms? Maybe some of the possibility was within one organism, some within the other. Isn't it equally plausible to believe that new possibility space appeared with the co-option of the mitochondria and chloroplast predecessor organisms to novel functions? Some achievements that are genuinely new pop up. These are based on the precedents, but there is novelty not present in either of the precedents. What emerged required the precedents, but the presence of the prior organisms, which became precedents, did not require or determine these results. Biologists, a century back, used to call such events "saltations." Physicists, pressed for words from their discipline, might call it a "quantum leap." Maybe we need a new term: "cybernetic leap." Biologists inclined toward chance may call this "tinkering" (Jacob 1977). Biologists impressed with the results will call it evolutionary "exploring." One needs a metaphysics for such co-option because there appear new ontological levels, both actual and possible (sight where before was only heat stress protection; language where before was only skin pressure sensibility; sight and language opening up the possibility of writing/reading). Co-option is the key to historical creativity.

Retrospectively, of course, after these novelties happen, the historian can trace the steps by which events happened. One can claim that the possibilities were always there; one can with equal plausibility claim that new possibility space has opened up en route in the course of natural history. Prospectively, if one could stand at each present moment, at each "now" over the course of evolution, there is always the great unknown. There is the generation of new possibility space in which information breakthroughs become possible. The pivotal element in a metaphysics of such evolutionary biology is the future, not the past, not even the present. Past and present are necessary but never sufficient for the future. In that sense our accounts will always be insufficient, incomplete, before this capacity for future innovation.

Anthropic Biology?

A number of physicists and astronomers have argued that the universe has been "fine-tuned" from the start and in its fundamental character for the subsequent construction of stars, planets, life, and mind. These results have been summarized as the "anthropic principle" (an unfortunately anthropocentric term; "biophilic principle" would have been better) (Barrow and Tipler, 1986; Leslie, 1990). Startling interrelationships are required for the cosmological processes to work; astronomical phenomena depend critically on the microphysical phenomena. In turn, the mid-range scales, where the known complexity mostly lies, in Earth's biodiversity or in human brains, depend on the interacting microscopic and astronomical ranges.

Biology has seemed a stark contrast — at first at least. Biology has also developed at ranges of the very small and of big-scale history. Molecular biology, discovering DNA, has decoded life; and evolutionary history has located the unfolding of life in natural selection operating over incremental genetic variations across enormous time spans, with the fittest selected to survive. The process is prolific, but biology is more "pushy" about life than is it "fine-tuned." Indeed, as we have seen, biologists are quite mixed about how to mix inevitability and contingency in the overall events of natural history. This "pushy" evolution is also "bushy," incessantly generating species, diversity — new branches and twigs on a bush. Incidentally, perhaps evolution will generate complexity, but — so many claim — there is no tendency toward progress. At this point, one would be radical indeed to suppose that biology is anthropic, headed for the generation of human beings. Recalling, and redoubling, Michael Ruse's phrase, that would be super-pseudo-science: humans arrogantly supposing themselves to be the destiny of all earlier, all other life on Earth.

Still, despite their evolutionary origins, humans are a radically new kind of species on Earth, and somehow we got here. What is quite surprising in humans is not so much that they have intelligence generically, for many other animals have specific forms of a generic intelligence. Nor is it that humans have intelligence with subjectivity, for there are precursors of this too in the primates. The surprise is that this intelligence becomes reflectively self-conscious and builds cumulative transmissible cultures. An information explosion gets pinpointed in humans. Humans alone have "a theory of mind"; they know that there are ideas in other minds, making linguistic cultures possible. The final looming question is: What kind of explanations does science offer for this appearance and emergence of humans? Is biology anthropic?

Animal brains are already impressive. In a cubic millimeter (about a pinhead) of mouse cortex there are 450 meters of dendrites and one to two kilometers of axons. Human brains multiply the cortex in mice three thousand times. This cognitive development has come to a striking expression point in the hominid lines leading to *Homo sapiens,* going from about 300 cubic centimeters of cranial capacity in chimpanzees to 1,400 in humans. The connecting fibers in a human brain, extended, would wrap around the Earth forty times. In body structures generally, such as blood or liver, humans and chimpanzees are 95 percent to 98 percent identical in their genomic DNA sequences and the resulting proteins.

But this is not true in their brains. "Changes in protein and gene expression have been particularly pronounced in the human brain. Striking differences exist in morphology and cognitive abilities between humans and their closest evolutionary relatives, the chimpanzees." So concludes a team of molecular biologists and evolutionary anthropologists from the Max-Planck Institutes in Germany (Enard et al. 2002). The puzzle is how so little genetic difference can make such an enormous brain-power difference. "This is one of the major questions that those of us interested in our own biology would like to ask — what does that 1.5% difference look like?" asks Francis Collins, Director of the National Human Genome Research Institute (in Gibbons 1998).

Some trans-genetic threshold seems to have been crossed. The human brain is of such complexity that descriptive numbers are astronomical and difficult to fathom. A typical estimate is 10^{12} neurons, each with several thousand synapses (possibly tens of thousands). Each neuron can "talk" to many others. This network, formed and re-formed, makes possible virtually endless mental activity. The result of such combinatorial explosion is that the human brain is capable of forming more possible thoughts than there are atoms in the universe. On a cosmic scale, humans are minuscule atoms, but on a complexity scale, humans are the most sophisticated of known natural products. In our hundred and fifty pounds of protoplasm, in our three-pound brain is more operational organization than in the whole of the Andromeda galaxy.

Genes make the kind of human brains possible that facilitate an open mind. But when that happens, these processes can also work the other way around. Minds employ and reshape their brains to facilitate their chosen ideologies and lifestyles. Our ideas and our practices configure and reconfigure our own sponsoring brain structures. Michael Merzenich, a neuroscientist, reports his increasing appreciation of "what is the most remarkable quality of our brain: its capacity to develop and to specialize its own processing machinery, to shape its own abilities, and to enable, through hard brainwork, its own achievements" (Merzenich 2001:418).

In the vocabulary of neuroscience, we have "mutable maps" in our cortical representations, formed and re-formed by our deliberated changes in thinking and resulting behaviors. For example, with the decision to play a violin well and with resolute practice, string musicians alter the synaptic connections and thereby the structural configuration of their brains to facilitate fingering the strings with one hand and drawing the bow with the other (Elbert et al. 1995). The human brain is as open as it is wired up. Our minds shape our brains.

Does this fit into the evolutionary picture? Maybe, but not without a looming question. Conway Morris asks whether "intelligence is some quirky end point of the evolutionary process or whether in reality it is more-or-less inevitable, an emergent property that is wired into the biosphere," whether "given time, evolution will inevitably lead . . . to the emergence of such properties as intelligence" (2003:148, 196). His answer: "We may be unique, but paradoxically those properties that define our uniqueness can still be inherent in the evolutionary process. In other words, if we humans had not evolved then something more-or-less identical would have emerged sooner or later" (2003:196). "The science of evolution does not belittle us. . . . Something like ourselves is an evolutionary inevitability, and our existence also reaffirms our one-ness with the rest of Creation" (2003:xv-xvi).

Conway Morris simultaneously finds, however, that "what evolution cannot do is see into the future diversification as far as the envelope of possibilities is concerned, although it can be equally sure that a great deal of what does one day evolve will have emerged in parallel circumstances in other times and places" (2003:307). In evolutionary biology "we can only retrodict and not predict" (2003:12). At this point Conway Morris seems to want it both ways: both inevitability and openness in natural history. The account seems to be that, despite these inherencies and inevitabilities, they can only be known *ex post facto*. If some extra-terrestrial biologists had had Earth under observation back in the pre-Cambrian, the headings of natural history were not then predictable. They would not have known what the future was to be. But after these inherencies home in, converge on intelligent life, after these surprises do happen, biologists, terrestrial or extra-terrestrial, can see that they had to happen, more or less as they did.

Humans evolved *out of* origins in natural history, but they seem to have done just that: to have made exodus from determination by genetics and natural selection and to have passed into a mental and social realm with new freedoms. Richard Lewontin puts it this way:

> Our DNA is a powerful influence on our anatomies and physiologies. In particular, it makes possible the complex brain that characterizes human beings. But having made that brain possible, the genes have made possible human nature, a social nature whose limitations and possible shapes we do not know except insofar as we know what human consciousness has already made possible.... History far transcends any narrow limitations that are claimed for either the power of the genes or the power of the environment to circumscribe us.... The genes, in making possible the development of human consciousness, have surrendered their power both to determine the individual and its environment. They have been replaced by an entirely new level of causation, that of social interaction with its own laws and its own nature. (1991:123)

The genes outdo themselves; this is unexpected co-option taken at a pitch. Despite finding other kinds of progress undeniable in the evolutionary record, Ernst Mayr reflects on the evolution of intelligence: "An evolutionist is impressed by the incredible improbability of intelligent life ever to have evolved" (1988:69). Mind of the human kind seems to require incredible opening up of new possibility space.

J. Craig Venter and over two hundred coauthors, reporting on the completion of the Celera Genomics version of the human genome project, caution in their concluding paragraph:

> In organisms with complex nervous systems, neither gene number, neuron number, nor number of cell types correlates in any meaningful manner with even simplistic measures of structural or behavioral complexity. . . . Between humans and chimpanzees, the gene number, gene structural function, chromosomal and genomic organization, and cell types and neuroanatomies are almost indistinguishable, yet the development modifications that predisposed human lineages to cortical expansion and development of the larynx, giving rise to language culminated in a massive singularity that by even the simplest of criteria made humans more complex in a behavioral sense. . . . The real challenge of human biology, beyond the task of finding out how genes orchestrate the construction and maintenance of the miraculous mechanism of our bodies, will lie ahead as we seek to explain how our minds have come to organize thoughts sufficiently well to investigate our own existence. (Venter et al. 2001:1347-1348)

Stuart Kauffman ponders this ongoing co-option of what he calls "pre-adaptations," adaptations previously used for some other function:

> Consider the concept of Darwinian pre-adaptation, the idea that a feature that was selected for one purpose turns out to be useful for a second purpose. . . . Do you think you could ever say ahead of time what all possible Darwinian pre-adaptations are? . . . We can never say ahead of time what the relevant variables are in the evolution of the biosphere. This means the biosphere keeps inventing new functionalities and we can't say ahead of time what they are. That's a radical new kind of failure to predict. It's not quantum uncertainty, and it's not chaos theory. Still, it's the kind of uncertainty that seems central. Life keeps inventing things. (Kauffman 2002)

He calls this "the mystery of the emergence of novel functionalities in evolution where none existed before: hearing, sight, flight, language. Whence this novelty? . . . I was led to doubt that we can prestate the 'configuration space' of a biosphere. . . . Life is doing something far richer than we may have dreamed, literally, something incalculable" (2000:5, 7).

Does anthropic physics indicate that biology too must somehow be anthropic — only we cannot yet see how? Or does biology, finding a "massive singularity" (Venter) with the coming of humans, remain open to configuration spaces that can never be prestated, to a future in which new possibility space will be generated? We do know with absolute certainty that we are here, and with virtual certainty that elaborated biodiversity and biocomplexity has managed to happen on Earth. So there isn't any doubt about these results. Nor is there serious doubt that these results are wonderful. But biology still stutters how nature generates such a wonderland. More plainly put, the five looming questions are still unanswered.

*   *   *

At the end of our searching, there rises on the horizon a final looming question, a sixth suggested by wondering about these five. Does such an evolutionary generation of life on Earth leave possibility space for faith in God? Almost anything can happen in a world in which what we see around us has actually managed to happen. The universe has never yet proved as simple as we previously thought. Or less mysterious. The story is incredible, and true, progressively more so at every emergent level: a universe fifteen billion years old, exploding from a vacuum, fine-tuned from the start, immense in size, coming to a unique and most complex expression point in Earth, generating a natural history with rich biodiversity, at the apex of which we humans stand, finding out who and where we are, discovering that we humans ourselves confront an open future and have staggering, escalating possibilities for good and evil.

There does seem to be demanded a ground generating these possibilities that so surprisingly, if regularly, break previous records of attainment and power. We live on a wonderland Earth, and we ourselves are the apex of these wonders. Nothing now known in any of these sciences prevents our finding this Ground holy, praising Spirit in, with, and under nature.

References

Barrow, John D., and Frank J. Tipler. 1986. *The Anthropic Cosmological Principle*. New York: Oxford University Press.

Bear, Mark F., Barry W. Conners, and Michael A. Paradiso. 2001. *Neuroscience*. 2nd ed. Baltimore: Lippincott Williams and Wilkins.

Brockman, John. 1995. *The Third Culture: Beyond the Scientific Revolution*. New York: Simon and Schuster.

Calvin, Melvin. 1975. "Chemical Evolution." *American Scientist* 63:169-177.

Cech, Thomas R. 1995. "The Origin of Life and the Value of Life." In Holmes Rolston III (ed.), *Biology, Ethics, and the Origins of Life*, 15-37. Boston: Jones and Bartlett.

Conway Morris, Simon. 2000. "Evolution: Bringing Molecules into the Fold." *Cell* 100:1-11.

Conway Morris, Simon. 2003. *Life's Solution: Inevitable Humans in a Lonely Universe.* Cambridge: Cambridge University Press.

Darwin, Charles. 1968. [1859.] *The Origin of Species.* Baltimore: Pelican Books.

Dawkins, Richard. 1995. *River out of Eden: A Darwinian View of Life.* New York: Basic Books, HarperCollins.

de Duve, Christian. 1995. *Vital Dust: Life as a Cosmic Imperative.* New York: Basic Books.

de Duve, Christian. 2002. *Life Evolving: Molecules, Mind, and Meaning.* Oxford: Oxford University Press.

Dose, Klaus. 1988. "The Origin of Life: More Questions than Answers." *Interdisciplinary Science Reviews* 13:348-356.

Dyall, Sabrina D., Mark T. Brown, and Patricia J. Johnson. 2004. "Ancient Invasions: From Endosymbionts to Organelles." *Science* 304:253-257.

Eigen, Manfred. 1971. "Self-organization of Matter and the Evolution of Biological Macromolecules." *Die Naturwissenschaften* 58:465-523.

Eigen, Manfred, with Ruthild Winkler-Oswatitsch. 1992. *Steps Towards Life: A Perspective on Evolution.* New York: Oxford University Press.

Elbert, Thomas, et al. 1995. "Increased Cortical Representation of the Fingers of the Left Hand in String Players." *Science* 270 (13 October): 305-307.

Enard, Wolfgang, et al. 2002. "Intra-and Interspecific Variation in Primate Gene Expression Patterns." *Science* 296 (12 April):340-343.

Gibbons, Ann. 1998. "Which of Our Genes Make Us Human?" *Science* 281 (4 September):1432-1434.

Gould, Stephen Jay. 1977. *Ever Since Darwin.* New York: W. W. Norton and Co.

Gould, Stephen Jay. 1983. "Extemporaneous Comments on Evolutionary Hope and Realities." In Charles L. Hamrum (ed.), *Darwin's Legacy, Nobel Conference XVIII,* 95-103. San Francisco: Harper and Row.

Gould, Stephen Jay. 1989. *Wonderful Life: The Burgess Shale and the Nature of History.* New York: W. W. Norton.

Gould, Stephen Jay. 1996. *Full House: The Spread of Excellence from Plato to Darwin.* New York: Harmony Books.

Jacob, François. 1977. "Evolution and Tinkering." *Science* 196:1161-1166.

Kauffman, Stuart A. 1993. *The Origins of Order: Self-Organization and Selection in Evolution.* New York: Oxford University Press.

Kauffman, Stuart A. 1995. *At Home in the Universe: The Search for Laws of Self-Organization and Complexity.* New York: Oxford University Press.

Kauffman, Stuart A., 2000. "Prolegomenon to a General Biology." In *Investigations,* 1-22. Oxford: Oxford University Press.

Kauffman, Stuart A. 2002. "Consciousness: It Blows My Mind." Metanexus Interview by Jill Neimark. Online at: http://www.metanexus.net/metanexus_online/show_article.asp?5605

Kazazian, Haig H., Jr. 2004. "Mobile Elements: Drivers of Genome Evolution." *Science* 303:1626-1632.

Küppers, Bernd-Olaf. 1990. *Information and the Origin of Life*. Cambridge, MA: MIT Press.

Leslie, John, ed., 1990. *Physical Cosmology and Philosophy*. New York: Macmillan.

Lewontin, Richard C. 1991. *Biology as Ideology: The Doctrine of DNA*. New York: HarperCollins Publishers.

Maynard Smith, John. 1972. *On Evolution*. Edinburgh: University of Edinburgh Press.

Maynard Smith, John. 1995. "Life at the Edge of Chaos?" *New York Review of Books* 52, no. 4 (March 2, 1995): 28-30.

Maynard Smith, John, and Eörs Szathmáry. 1995. *The Major Transitions in Evolution*. New York: W. H. Freeman.

Mayr, Ernst. 1988. *Toward a New Philosophy of Biology*. Cambridge, MA: Harvard University Press.

Merzenich, Michael. 2001. "The Power of Mutable Maps." In Bear et al., *Neuroscience*, 418. 2nd ed. Baltimore: Lippincott Williams and Wilkins.

Myers, Norman. 1997. "Mass Extinction and Evolution." *Science* 278:597-598.

Nee, Sean, and Robert M. May. 1997. "Extinction and the Loss of Evolutionary History." *Science* 278:692-694.

Newell, Norman D. 1963. "Crises in the History of Life." *Scientific American* 208/2 (February):76-92.

Niklas, Karl J. 1986. "Large-Scale Changes in Animal and Plant Terrestrial Communities." In D. M. Raup and D. Jablonski (eds.), *Patterns and Processes in the History of Life*, 383-403. New York: Springer-Verlag.

Polanyi, Michael. 1964. *Personal Knowledge*. New York: Harper and Row.

Popper, Karl R. 1990. *A World of Propensities*. Bristol, UK: Thoemmes.

Raup, David M., and J. John Sepkoski Jr. 1982. "Mass Extinctions in the Marine Fossil Record." *Science* 215:1501-1503.

Ruse, Michael, 1986. *Taking Darwin Seriously*. Oxford: Basil Blackwell.

Ruse, Michael. 1996. *Monad to Man: The Concept of Progress in Evolutionary Biology*. Cambridge, MA: Harvard University Press.

Van Valen, Leigh M. 1991. "How Far Does Contingency Rule?" *Evolutionary Theory* 10:47-52.

Venter, J. Craig, et al. 2001. "The Sequence of the Human Genome." *Science* 291 (16 February):1304-1351.

Wald, George. 1974. "Fitness in the Universe: Choices and Necessities." In J. Oró et al. (eds.), *Cosmochemical Evolution and the Origins of Life*, 7-27. Dordrecht: D. Reidel.

Weiner, Norbert. 1948. *Cybernetics*. New York: John Wiley.

Whitehead, Alfred North. 1978. [1929.] *Process and Reality*, corrected edition. New York: Free Press.

Wistow, Graeme. 1993. "Lens Crystallins: Gene Recruitment and Evolutionary Dynamism," *Trends in Biochemical Sciences* 18:301-306.

14 Darwinism: Foe or Friend?

Michael Ruse

It gives me great pleasure to offer this tribute to Professor J. Wentzel van Huyssteen. In their sheer joy in living and their love of God's creation, he and his beautiful wife Hester seem to me to represent the epitome of the Christian life. To be in their presence is to be reminded forcefully of the very worth of existence. As one who has gone before him (I was 65 in June 2005), it is now my delight to offer some advice from an older man to a younger one.

My topic is evolutionary theory, a subject that fascinates both Professor van Huyssteen and me. Far be it from me to suggest that a man who comes from such a warrior race as the Dutch of South Africa would ever flee from a fight, but there are indeed times when I fear that he — like too many other Christians interested in the relationship between science and religion — quails if not quakes before the onslaughts of the non-believers, particularly those who argue that the dominant paradigm in evolutionary studies, Darwinism, implies atheism. In reply to this charge, the Christian thinkers (for let me no longer be personal) agree with the central thesis. Darwinism does imply atheism.[1] Hence, if we are to remain evolutionists, we must find some other theory. And hence the hunt is on — mutation pressure, non-equilibrium thermodynamics, order for free. If such people are really desperate, then they go beyond science. Just as Darwin's great American friend, the botanist Asa Gray, supposed that the raw building blocks of evolution —

---

1. Professor Van Huyssteen discusses Darwinism at length in his book *Duet or Duel? Theology and Science in a Postmodern World* (Harrisburg, PA: Trinity Press International, 1998). I take him there to be agreeing with Keith Ward against Richard Dawkins that "natural selection cannot even account for all the known facts" (p. 123). The real point of difference seems to be that Darwinism fails to give an account of the purpose that Ward and Van Huyssteen see in the course of evolution.

what today we call mutations — have to be guided by someone (or Someone) above, so now we have suggestions that God does his work down at the quantum level or some such thing.

I say, nonsense! Would Augustine give way at this point? Would Aquinas agree with his critics and slope off into the night? What of Luther and Calvin in the sixteenth century, or Jonathan Edwards in the seventeenth, or John Henry Newman in the nineteenth? They would — they did — stand and fight, confident that truth cannot be opposed to truth, and that if Darwinism is indeed the true evolutionary theory, then this must be the starting point for theology, not the end. Somehow Darwinism must be made a point of strength rather than of weakness.

Darwinism

I have elsewhere argued this position at the general level (Ruse 2001). Let me now focus a little more intensely. The subject is Darwinism, and by this I mean (in an absolutely straightforward manner) that theory first expounded by Charles Darwin in his *Origin of Species* in 1859. And this means the mechanism of natural selection.

> A struggle for existence inevitably follows from the high rate at which all organic beings tend to increase. Every being, which during its natural lifetime produces several eggs or seeds, must suffer destruction during some period of its life, and during some season or occasional year, otherwise, on the principle of geometrical increase, its numbers would quickly become so inordinately great that no country could support the product. Hence, as more individuals are produced than can possibly survive, there must in every case be a struggle for existence, either one individual with another of the same species, or with the individuals of distinct species, or with the physical conditions of life. It is the doctrine of Malthus applied with manifold force to the whole animal and vegetable kingdoms; for in this case there can be no artificial increase of food, and no prudential restraint from marriage. (Darwin 1859:63)

Note that, even more than a struggle for existence, Darwin needed a struggle for reproduction. It is no good having the physique of a theologian if you have the sexual desires of a philosopher. But with the struggle understood in this sort of way, given naturally occurring variation, natural selection follows at once.

> Let it be borne in mind in what an endless number of strange peculiarities our domestic productions, and, in a lesser degree, those under nature, vary; and how strong the hereditary tendency is. Under domestication, it may be truly said that the whole organization becomes in some degree plastic. Let it be borne in mind how infinitely complex and close-fitting are the mutual relations of all organic beings to each other and to their physical conditions of life. Can it, then, be thought improbable, seeing that variations useful to man have undoubtedly occurred, that other variations useful in some way to each being in the great and complex battle of life, should sometimes occur in the course of thousands of generations? If such do occur, can we doubt (remembering that many more individuals are born than can possibly survive) that individuals having any advantage, however slight, over others, would have the best chance of surviving and of procreating their kind? On the other hand we may feel sure that any variation in the least degree injurious would be rigidly destroyed. This preservation of favourable variations and the rejection of injurious variations, I call Natural Selection. (Darwin 1859:80-81)

This is the key to Darwinism. Note however that natural selection is not just a mechanism that brings on change. It brings on change of a particular kind. It moves organisms in the direction of adaptation, or as Darwin himself often said, contrivance. Natural theologians from Plato on had pointed to the features that organisms have that allow them to survive and reproduce — hands, teeth, ears, and so forth — and it is these to which natural selection speaks. These features were not created miraculously by God, but were the end result of a long, lawbound process. Those organisms that had adaptations — those organisms that had better adaptations — won in the struggle for life, and those that did not, lost (Ruse 2003).

Of course, there has been much change and advance since Darwin, notably the development of a theory of heredity. First this was so-called Mendelian genetics, and then, building on this since the 1950s and the Watson-Crick discovery of the double helix, molecular genetics. But this only reinforces the centrality of natural selection. Most importantly, the only way in which you are going to get any directional change whatsoever is through selection. The new building blocks of evolutions — mutations in today's language — are random. This does not mean that they are uncaused or even unquantifiable. It does mean that they do not occur based on need. Suppose that a predator works by sight and that its prey is adaptively camouflaged because it has white skin against a white sandy shore. Suppose now that a hurricane changes the sand to a dark volcanic grit. It does not follow that the prey will now get mutations to black. It might as easily get mutations to red, blue, or pink with yellow polka dots.

Talking of the ubiquity of natural selection does not mean that organisms are always optimally adapted. The lag time from environmental changes, as just illustrated in the last paragraph, might mean a bad failure in adaptive excellence. There are other factors too. For instance, one made much of by evolutionists is the possible conflict between adaptations for survival (natural selection) and adaptations for reproduction (where one has the selective process usually sub-labeled sexual selection). Perhaps the peacock's tail falls into this category. From the viewpoint of escape, it is hopeless. From the viewpoint of turning on peahens, it is fantastic.

There are lots of controversies amongst Darwinians, but do not take most of these as truly threatening the Darwinian paradigm. For instance, to refer to Richard Dawkins himself, there is much debate about what is the central focus of selection. Is it the gene, the DNA molecule found in the heart of the cell? Many think that it is. Others want to promote the significance of the whole organism, and yet others argue that some kind of group perspective is needed. Natural selection impacts not so much on the individual but on the species perhaps, and adaptations reflect this. But do not be misled by these controversies. "Man bites dog" is bigger news than "Dog bites man." Likewise an attack on selection is going to garner more public attention than praise of selection. The fact is that well over 90 percent of active evolutionists use natural selection, first, second, and third. But do not take my word for it. Look at the contributions to the journals *Evolution* or *American Naturalist.* Or look at the leading textbook in the field, *Evolutionary Analysis* by S. Freeman and J. C. Herron. Even someone like Stephen Jay Gould, whom I shall have cause to mention shortly, thought in terms of selection most of the time, even though admittedly he thought it was overemployed and wanted to give more role to things like chance (Gould 2002).

Richard Dawkins

Why is evolutionary theory — Darwinian evolutionary theory, that is — taken to be such a threat to Christianity? To give the discussion some real content, let me look briefly at some of the thinking of the atheists' atheist — the man before whom too many good Christians turn white and shake. I refer of course to Richard Dawkins, the author recently of the polemical anti-Christian collection *A Devil's Chaplain,* and of other more scientifically oriented works, including his great exposition of modern thinking about natural selection, *The Selfish Gene*. He is insistent that if you are a Darwinian, there is no God, no meaning, and no nothing.

> In a universe of blind physical forces and genetic replication, some people are going to get hurt, other people are going to get lucky, and you won't find any rhyme or reason in it, nor any justice. The universe we observe has precisely the properties we should expect if there is, at bottom, no design, no purpose, no evil and no good, nothing but blind, pitiless indifference. As that unhappy poet A. E. Houseman put it:
>
> > For Nature, heartless, witless Nature
> > Will neither know nor care.
>
> DNA neither knows nor cares. DNA just is. And we dance to its music. (Dawkins 1995:133)

Let me say, as I begin, that I share completely Dawkins's convictions about the truth of Darwinism, that I probably have no more religious convictions than he, and that I think he is an absolutely terrific writer. The point as I see it is to dig beneath his brilliant polemics and to see if in fact his (and my) Darwinism implies his (and my) non-belief. I shall argue that far from doing so, if I were a Christian Dawkins would be my favorite bedtime reading — except it would probably make me too excited to sleep.

How on earth can one even start to make the kind of case I am proposing? Let me begin by pouring water on the altar. Dawkins is gloriously and unambiguously opposed to any kind of religious belief or practice. "Only the willfully blind could fail to implicate the divisive force in religion in most, if not all, of the violent enmities of the world today. Those of us who have for years politely concealed our contempt for the dangerous collective illusion of religion need to stand up and speak out" (Dawkins 2003:160-161). It was not often that I felt much sympathy for the late John Paul II, but even I had a twinge of feeling for a fellow sufferer when, the late prelate having endorsed Darwinism, Dawkins responded: "Given a choice between honest to goodness fundamentalism on the one hand, and the obscurantist, disingenuous doublethink of the Roman Catholic Church on the other, I know which I prefer" (Dawkins 1997b:399). There is little wonder that Dawkins has referred to his own move from Christianity to atheism as a "road to Damascus experience."

To be honest, Dawkins is somewhat lightweight on his precise reasons for thinking that Darwinism implies atheism. Obviously at one level he thinks that Darwinism implies the falsity of the early chapters of Genesis, subscription to the truth of which he takes to be essential to Christian faith. At another level, however, as the passage just quoted makes clear, he thinks it is more a question of Darwinism simply brushing Christianity aside. A religion — any religion — appeals to the supernatural, and science — Darwinism especially — makes such appeal otiose. Hence, no religion — and a very good thing too.

There is a bit more to Dawkins's thinking than this, and some of it will come out in a minute or two. For a moment, let me say that if I were a Christian, thus far I would be supremely unworried. No modern Christian takes Genesis literally; most would argue that it is heretical, in the light of what we know about the ancient Jews and so forth, to pretend to a literal interpretation. Genesis is surely true — God is creator of heaven and earth, we are made in his image, we are deeply sinful — but the details in the text must be understood metaphorically. I suspect that no modern Christian is going to be worried by A. E. Houseman either. Just because Darwinism gives us a naturalistic account of origins, it does not mean that God does not exist. There is a difference between saying that you *can* think of the world without God and saying that you *must* think of the world without God. In fact, of course, many modern Christians agree with Kierkegaard that unless one can think of the world without God, faith is never genuine. It requires a leap into the absurd.

To be candid, I think we are already deep into the heart of the arguments of people like Dawkins when they go after Christianity. And if you say to me that we have not dug very deeply, I would agree with you. I think that the arguments of anti-Christian Darwinians tend to be very shallow. It is just that they tend also to be so very nasty, and when you combine this with the authority that science has in our society, many (including those who should know better) think that real arguments have been put forward. But rather than end here, let us extend to Dawkins a courtesy that he does not give his opponents, and look again to see if there is substance to his critique of Christianity.

I think in fact that Dawkins does have another argument. Not a new one, but clearly one that he thinks reinforced by Darwinism. It is the problem of evil. This argument is expressed most clearly in one of Dawkins's books: *River Out of Eden: A Darwinian View of Life*. In a chapter entitled "God's Utility Function," he starts by writing:

> "I cannot persuade myself," Darwin wrote: "that a beneficent and omnipotent God would have designedly created the Ichneumonidae with the express intention of their feeding within the living bodies of Caterpillars." Actually Darwin's gradual loss of faith, which he downplayed for fear of upsetting his devout wife Emma, had more complex causes. His reference to the Ichneumonidae was aphoristic. The macabre habits to which he re-

ferred are shared by their cousins the digger wasps. . . . A female digger wasp not only lays her egg in a caterpillar (or grasshopper or bee) so that her larva can feed on it but, according to Fabre and others, she carefully guides her sting into each ganglion of the prey's central nervous system, so as to paralyze it *but not kill it*. This way, the meat keeps fresh. It is not known whether the paralysis acts as a general anesthetic, or if it is like curare in just freezing the victim's ability to move. If the latter, the prey might be aware of being eaten alive from inside but unable to move a muscle to do anything about it. This sounds savagely cruel but as we shall see, nature is not cruel, only pitilessly indifferent. This is one of the hardest lessons for humans to learn. We cannot admit that things might be neither good nor evil, neither cruel nor kind but simply callous — indifferent to all suffering, lacking all purpose. (Dawkins 1995:95-96)

Then, later in the chapter, Dawkins talks about organisms being excellent examples of design-like engineering. If we tried to unpack the engineering principles involved in organisms, the problems of pain and evil come to the fore. Meaning by the notion "utility function" the purpose for which an entity is apparently designed, Dawkins writes as follows:

Let us return to living bodies and try to extract their utility function. There could be many but, revealingly, it will eventually turn out that they all reduce to one. A good way to dramatize our task is to imagine that living creatures were made by a Divine Engineer and try to work it out, by reverse engineering, what the Engineer was trying to maximize: What was God's Utility Function?

Cheetahs give every indication of being superbly designed for something, and it should be easy enough to reverse-engineer them and work out their utility function. They appear to be well designed to kill antelopes. The teeth, claws, eyes, nose, leg muscles, backbone and brain of a cheetah are all precisely what we should expect if God's purpose in designing cheetahs was to maximize deaths among antelopes. Conversely, if we reverse-engineer an antelope we find equally impressive evidence of design for precisely the opposite end; the survival of antelopes and starvation among cheetahs. It is as though cheetahs had been designed by one deity and antelopes by a rival deity. Alternatively, if there is only one Creator who made the tiger and lamb, the cheetah and the gazelle, what is He playing at? Is He a sadist who enjoys spectator blood sports? Is He trying to avoid overpopulation in the mammals of Africa? Is He maneuvering to maximize David Attenborough's television ratings? (Dawkins 1995:104-105)

The point seems to be that if there be a God, then he is one who certainly is nothing like the Christian God: he is unkind, unfair, and totally indifferent. And indeed, this is the point at which Dawkins ends the discussion of this chapter.

> If Nature were kind, she would at least make the minor concession of anesthetizing caterpillars before they are eaten alive from within. But Nature is neither kind nor unkind. She is neither against suffering nor for it. Nature is not interested one way or the other in suffering, unless it affects the survival of DNA. It is easy to imagine a gene that, say, tranquilizes gazelles when they are about to suffer a killing bite. Would such a gene be favored by natural selection? Not unless the act of tranquilizing a gazelle improved that gene's chances of being propagated into future generations. It is hard to see why this should be so, and we may therefore guess that gazelles suffer horrible pain and fear when they are pursued to the death — as most of them eventually are. The total amount of suffering per year in the natural world is beyond all decent contemplation. During the minute it takes me to compose this sentence, thousands of animals are being eaten alive; others are running for their lives, whimpering with fear; others are being slowly devoured from within by rasping parasites; thousands of all kinds are dying of starvation, thirst and disease. It must be so. If there is ever a time of plenty, this very fact will automatically lead to an increase in population until the natural state of starvation and misery is restored.
>
> Theologians worry away at the "problem of evil" and a related "problem of suffering." On the day I originally wrote this paragraph, the British newspapers all carried a terrible story about a bus full of children from a Roman Catholic school that crashed for no obvious reason, with wholesale loss of life. Not for the first time, clerics were in paroxysms over the theological question that a writer on a London newspaper *(The Sunday Telegraph)* framed this way: "How can you believe in a loving, all-powerful God who allows such a tragedy?" The article went on to quote one priest's reply: "The simple answer is that we do not know why there should be a God who lets these awful things happen. But the horror of the crash, to a Christian, confirms the fact that we live in a world of real values: positive and negative. If the universe was just electrons, there would be no problem of evil or suffering."
>
> On the contrary, if the universe were just electrons and selfish genes, meaningless tragedies like the crashing of this bus are exactly what we should expect, along with equally meaningless *good* fortune. Such a universe would be neither evil nor good in intention. It would manifest no in-

tentions of any kind. In a universe of blind physical forces and genetic replication, some people are going to get hurt, other people are going to get lucky, and you won't find any rhyme or reason in it, nor any justice.

Dawkins then plunges into his quotation from Houseman, arguing that that is the end of theology. Christianity is just plain wrong — and a dangerous illusion for that matter.

Natural Selection: Contingent or Necessary?

What do we say about this? I would argue that, paradoxically, Dawkins himself of all people gives us a way out of this problem — a way out that significantly strengthens the Christian's hands rather than otherwise. In saying this, let me not be misunderstood. As it happens, I agree with Dawkins that the problem of evil may be insurmountable for the Christian. On this, I am with Dostoevsky in *The Brothers Karamazov*. I just don't think the unhappiness of a child justifies any ends. If Auschwitz was the cost of everlasting happiness, I just don't think that God should have got into the creation business in the first place. But that is not quite my point here. My point is whether Dawkins's Darwinism as such makes things worse. I do not think that it does.

Christians feel that they do have arguments about evil that make possible consistent Christian belief — specifically that moral evil is due to human sinfulness and that that is the cost of free will, and that physical evil is simply the consequence of a law-bound universe. To say that God is all powerful is not to say that God could do the impossible, only to say that he is going to do the best. This is the argument of the great German philosopher Leibniz. It is physical evil — at least not moral evil — that is at the heart of Dawkins's repudiation of Christianity, so let us concentrate on this here. And to do so, let us focus on the matter of natural selection and of its scope. Dawkins (1986) jocularly refers to himself as being somewhere to the right of Archdeacon Paley on design, meaning that for him, like all good Darwinians, natural selection rules *über alles*. But there is more than this. Dawkins pushes his selectionism to the extreme. Dawkins (1983) has argued that if you eschew supernatural explanations, then the only conclusion for a scientist is that natural selection was responsible for the nature of the organic world. The world is design-like. It is full of adaptation — to repeat and extend the list given earlier: hands, teeth, noses, eyes, hearts, brains, penises, vaginas, leaves, flowers, fins, scales, wings, feathers. And faced with this list, the only possible explanation is natural selection. Lamarckism is false, and other options like mutationism do not address the problem. Where there is life, there must be natural selection.

But consider what this means in the light of Leibniz's argument, that God — having created a law-bound universe (and there are theological arguments for this) — could not then avoid some natural evil. God cannot do the impossible, and if pain from a fire was to have a good side — namely that you learn to avoid fire — then necessarily pain from a fire had a bad side — namely that it hurts. It seems to me that if you agree that God did create a law-bound universe, and that the mark of the living is its design-like nature, its adaptedness, Dawkins is offering you a piece of candy. The only way in which God could get things working is through natural selection, and since natural selection involves a struggle for existence, then so be it. Natural evil is a necessary consequence of having living beings.

As I have said, I myself would question whether the creation was worth all of the pain and suffering, but that is another matter and not something that you can lay at the feet of Richard Dawkins. He is the Christian's friend on these issues — organic creation equals natural selection equals pain and suffering. You can't have one without the other. Here, incidentally, Dawkins is of much more comfort to the Christian than is Stephen Jay Gould. As noted above, the latter spent years trying to show that the living world is not that adapted, and then concluded that natural selection is not that needed, let alone necessary.

Progress

I want now to push things a little further. I raise the issue of progress. However you define it, the Christian has to believe in progress — a rise from the simple to the complex, from the organism with little worth to the organism with maximum worth, from the monad to the man, from the blob to the Briton. The Christian might perhaps think that there are higher forms than humans (angels?), the Christian might think that there are important beings elsewhere in the universe, and perhaps the Christian might think that we humans could have had green skin or six fingers; but the Christian cannot think that we humans are here by chance. We are made in the image of God, we are a major (even if not the sole) reason why God created heaven and earth, and so beings with intelligence and a moral sense had to appear at some point. The existence of *Homo sapiens* cannot be a chance phenomenon. That is a bottom-line demand by the Christian.

Many Darwinians think that this is another good reason why Christianity and Darwinism are opposed. Gould, to take one example, was adamant that we humans came by chance. "Since dinosaurs were not moving toward markedly larger brains, and since such a prospect may lie outside the capabilities of reptilian design . . . , we must assume that consciousness would not have evolved on our planet if a cosmic catastrophe had not claimed the dinosaurs as victims. In an entirely literal sense, we owe our existence, as large and reasoning mammals, to our lucky stars" (Gould 1989:318).

I have to say that, if you believe this, you cannot believe the Christian position on the special status of humankind. But again, Richard Dawkins comes to the rescue! He has always been an ardent progressionist.

> Notwithstanding Gould's just scepticism over the tendency to label each era by its newest arrivals, there really is a good possibility that major innovations in embryological technique open up new vistas of evolutionary possibility and that these constitute genuinely progressive improvements. The origin of the chromosome, of the bounded cell, of organized meiosis, diploidy and sex, of the eucaryotic cell, of multicellularity, of gastrulation, of molluscan torsion, of segmentation — each of these may have constituted a watershed event in the history of life. Not just in the normal Darwinian sense of boosting evolution itself in ways that seem entitled to the label progressive. It may well be that after, say, the invention of multicellularity, or the invention of segmentation, evolution was never the same again. In this sense there may be a one-way ratchet of progressive innovation in evolution. (Dawkins 1997a:216-217)

Dawkins (1989) speaks of all of this as the "evolution of evolvability." He does not simply pull the idea out of a hat but argues for it on the basis of what evolutionists call "arms races" (Dawkins and Krebs 1979). This idea, which goes back to Darwin himself, was developed and championed in the twentieth century by Julian Huxley. As in human arms races, two lines compete against each other, getting more efficient and complex and sophisticated in reaction to the other. Writing at the beginning of the last century, when Germany and Britain were competing on the sea, Huxley wrote: "The leaden plum-puddings were not unfairly matched against the wooden walls of Nelson's day." He then added that today "though our guns can hurl a third of a ton of sharp-nosed steel with dynamite entrails for a dozen miles, yet they are confronted with twelve-inch armor of backed and hardened steel, water-tight compartments, and targets moving thirty miles an hour. Each advance in attack has brought forth, as if by magic, a corresponding advance in defence." Explicitly, Huxley likened this to the organic world, for "if one species happens to vary in the direction of greater independence, the interrelated equilibrium is upset, and cannot be restored until a number of competing species have either given way to the increased pressure and become extinct, or else have answered pressure with pressure, and kept the first species in its place by themselves too discovering means of adding to their independence." And so finally: "it comes to pass that the continuous change which is passing through the organic world appears as a succession of phases of equilibrium, each one on a higher average plane of independence than the one before, and each inevitably calling up and giving place to one still higher" (Huxley 1912:115-116).

Dawkins buys right into this kind of thinking, using modern examples — drawing especially on electronic advances in weaponry — and suggesting that humans with their consciousness are basically the winners in the arms race, because they have the biggest on-board computers. Referring to a notion by the brain scientist Harry Jerison, the Encephalization Quotient (EQ), which is a kind of measure of absolute IQs across species — done by taking actual brain size and then subtracting the portion of the brain needed to keep the brute going (whales need more than shrews) — Dawkins triumphantly crowns the winner. "The fact that humans have an EQ of 7 and hippos an EQ of 0.3 may not literally mean that humans are 23 times as clever as hippos! But the EQ as measured is probably telling us *something* about how much 'computing power' an animal probably has in its head, over and above the irreducible amount of computing power needed for the routine running of its large or small body" (Dawkins 1986:189).

Again, note the force of the point I am making. I am not arguing that Dawkins's argument is well taken. In fact, apart from the empirical objections that have been leveled against arms races, I do not at all see that they will necessarily lead to consciousness or that consciousness is such a good thing. For a tetrapod, there is often much to be said for being stupid and for racing along in the middle of the herd. It always seems to me that, at best, arms races lead to a kind of relative progress — better bombs, better legs — than any kind of absolute progress the Christian really needs — the kingdom of heaven, a superior kind of being.

Nor am I arguing that this all means that Dawkins is really slipping religious content into his thinking. I think some Darwinians do. Edward O. Wilson (1992), a fervent believer in evolutionary progress, uses this idea of upward advance as a support for a kind of Herbert Spencer–type world picture, where we humans have the moral obligation to promote the well-being of life's winners, namely humans. Although Dawkins clearly thinks that we should promote the well-being of humans, he does not want to do this in the name of progress. In fact, he takes to task Britain's fuzzy-minded king-in-waiting, who mistakes inherited position for intelligence, and who argues that genetically modified foods are morally wrong because they interfere with the course of nature. Dawkins (2002) argues (correctly I think) that you cannot extract morality from the ways of evolution.

The point I am making is simply that, well-taken argument or not, Dawkins is an evolutionary progressionist who thinks that humans emerged naturally and predictably from the way of evolution — at least, predictably in the sense that the processes of evolution keep pushing organisms up the scale and consciousness is at the top of the scale (at least as we know it). And that, I take it, is just what the Christian needs. Once again, the Christian should welcome the writings of Dawkins, not fear them.

Conclusion

Over a hundred years ago, the high-church Anglican priest Aubrey Moore wrote about the relationship of biological evolution to Christianity: "Darwinism appeared, and, under the guise of a foe, did the work of a friend" (Moore 1890:268). If I have persuaded Professor van Huyssteen to look again at Darwinism, and to look now at how it can strengthen his theological commitment to Christianity, I shall be delighted. If I have spurred him or others to take me to task, arguing that, with friends like me, Christianity needs no enemies, I shall have good reason to take up pen again. Either way, for me it is a win-win situation. One more reason why I thank Professor van Huyssteen, whom we celebrate in this volume.

Reference List

Darwin, C. 1859. *On the Origin of Species*. London: John Murray.
Dawkins, R. 1976. *The Selfish Gene*. Oxford: Oxford University Press.
———. 1983. "Universal Darwinism." In D. S. Bendall (ed.), *Molecules to Men*. Cambridge: University of Cambridge Press.
———. 1986. *The Blind Watchmaker*. New York: Norton.
———. 1989. "The Evolution of Evolvability." In C. G. Langton (ed.), *Artificial Life*, 201-220. Redwood City, CA: Addison-Wesley.
———. 1995. *A River Out of Eden: A Darwinian View of Life*. New York: Basic Books.
———. 1997a. "Human Chauvinism: Review of *Full House* by Stephen Jay Gould." *Evolution* 51/3:1015-1020.

———. 1997b. "Obscurantism to the Rescue." *Quarterly Review of Biology* 72:397-99.
———. 2002. "An Open Letter to Prince Charles." In M. Ruse and D. Castle (eds.), *Genetically Modified Foods*, 16-19. Buffalo: Prometheus.
———. 2003. *A Devil's Chaplain: Reflections on Hope, Lies, Science and Love*. Boston and New York: Houghton Mifflin.
Dawkins, R., and J. R. Krebs. 1979. "Arms Races between and within Species." *Proceedings of the Royal Society of London* B 205:489-511.
Freeman, S., and J. C. Herron. 2004. *Evolutionary Analysis*. 3rd edition. Englewood-Cliffs: Prentice-Hall.
Gould, S. J. 1989. *Wonderful Life: The Burgess Shale and the Nature of History*. New York: W. W. Norton Co.
———. 2002. *The Structure of Evolutionary Theory*. Cambridge, MA: Harvard University Press.
Huxley, J. S. 1912. *The Individual in the Animal Kingdom*. Cambridge: Cambridge University Press.
Moore, A. 1890. "The Christian Doctrine of God." In C. Gore (ed.), *Lux Mundi*. London: John Murray.
Ruse, M. 2001. *Can a Darwinian Be a Christian? The Relationship between Science and Religion*. Cambridge: Cambridge University Press.
———. 2003. *Darwin and Design: Does Evolution Have a Purpose?* Cambridge, MA: Harvard University Press.
Wilson, E. O. 1992. *The Diversity of Life*. Cambridge, MA: Harvard University Press.

15 Rationality and Interpreted Experience: The Efficacy of Phenomenal Consciousness

Michael L. Spezio

> *A grim specter has crept upon us almost unnoticed, and this imagined tragedy may easily become a stark reality we all shall know.*
>
> Rachel Carson, *Silent Spring*

Introduction

Robert Audi provides the following story as a non-controversial illustration of irrational decision-making:

> Consider Tom, who is (irrationally) afraid of heights. Suppose that as a result of his fear he impulsively takes an ugly route to visit a friend, thereby avoiding a safe but mountainous road. Assume further that whereas on the mountain route he would not *see* the land below in a way that frightens him, on the ugly route he will have to negotiate many dangerous curves. If he knows this, yet, fearing just being high up, takes the ugly route against his better judgment, his doing so would be irrational. For the motivating fear is irrational, and in addition he chooses, against his better judgment, the route he knows is significantly dangerous. (1990)

The author is a postdoctoral scholar in psychology and neuroscience at the California Institute of Technology and an ordained minister in the Presbyterian Church (U.S.A.). I am grateful for the support and mentorship of Ralph Adolphs in allowing me time to think about and work on the problems addressed in this essay, and for fostering such a dynamic, interdisciplinary intellectual environment in the social cognition and emotion lab at Caltech. I am grateful to Greg Peterson, Bob Russell, LeRon Shults, and Teresa Sabol Spezio for helpful conversations.

Of course, it is relatively non-controversial to hold that freely doing or believing something against one's better judgment, if said judgment is truly better, is irrational. Audi presents Tom in the story taking the ugly route against his better judgment, motivated by only his irrational fear of heights, and gives this as the reason to conclude that Tom's decision is irrational. Yet a problem arises when one asks how Tom, a person with acrophobia, would conclude that taking the mountainous road is the better judgment. Audi does not say how this happens, though he does say that Tom knows (1) that the mountainous road does not offer any views that might elicit the extreme fear that comes with his phobia, and (2) that the ugly road has numerous dangerous curves. Knowing both of these facts, as Audi and we now know them, Tom should (and in Audi's story, does) conclude that taking the mountainous route is the better judgment.

The crux of the problem here is hinted at by the first fact Audi says Tom knows. Audi deliberately italicizes the word "see" to make it clear that Tom will have no visual experiences eliciting Tom's type of extreme fear. Presumably, Audi thinks that if Tom would actually *see* views that reinforced his phobia and elicited extreme panic, this might affect Tom's ability to safely drive the car. What if Tom only *imagines* such views? Say that Tom is driving along on the mountain road and mentally images himself in his car high up on a mountain road, without being able to actually see how high he is. Might such imagery in itself elicit a panic attack? Now, if during Tom's decision-making process, he engages in what is known as mental time travel and imagines himself in the future, high up on the mountainous road, and then imagines himself imagining how high up he is and imagines himself reacting in panic, he might well conclude that he will not be able to safely drive the route. Indeed, just imagining this future scene may be enough to elicit physiological responses associated with panic. So Tom's phenomenal experience via mental imagery gives him a prediction of how unsafe his driving will be on the mountain road. Perhaps Tom has no phobia of dangerous curves on a road, and perhaps he is a relatively good driver. So he decides that it is safer to take the ugly route, and it is his phenomenal experience via mental imagery that has provided the reason for why this is the better judgment. His decision is perfectly rational, *contra* Audi's claim.

The project in this chapter is to argue for the insight that falls out of this analysis of Audi's story: namely, that phenomenal consciousness plays an important role in human rationality. J. Wentzel van Huyssteen points to this possibility in his book *The Shaping of Rationality*, where he argues that rationality is impossible in the absence of *interpreted experience*.[1] To be sure, van

---

1. I owe van Huyssteen a debt for helping me recognize the possibility that theories of ra-

Huyssteen rejects views of rationality that base reason in "isolate, epistemic consciousness," but he nevertheless argues against "jettisoning of the vocabulary of subjectivity per se" (1999).

I will argue that in fact it is impossible to jettison phenomenal consciousness (p-consciousness) as a factor in rational decision making involving personal choices by typical human agents. These include choices that answer the questions What will I do? and What will I believe? I will show evidence that p-consciousness is crucial for the rationality of those personal decisions that are viewed to have the greatest effect on one's future. This efficacy of p-consciousness in rational choice is widely overlooked in theories of rationality, perhaps due to widely held epiphenomenalist views of p-consciousness. Part of my purpose will therefore be to explore the implications of my argument for theories of rationality, including the postfoundationalist rationality so admirably described and defended in van Huyssteen's work. To do this, I will first review van Huyssteen's postfoundationalist approach to rationality, including the importance of first-person experience for rational belief and choice. I will then draw on the work of Ned Block to argue that p-consciousness cannot be subsumed into another category of conscious experience, such as representation. This will lead to an argument for the role of p-consciousness in agent rationality, drawing from work on mental time travel and on a few well-accepted historical accounts of life-changing decisions. To the degree that p-consciousness is active in rational choice, it will need to be accounted for in evolutionary theories of rationality, an area I will briefly address. Finally, I will point to some implications of the argument for theological and scientific constructions.

Postfoundationalist Rationality

The kind of rationality under investigation here stresses the parallels rather than the differences between theoretical and practical reason. As alluded to above, such rationality will provide justification for answers to the theoretical question, What will I believe? and the practical question, What will I do? Both have to do with shaping personal attitudes toward either propositions or intentions, and both emanate from first-person perspectives rather than striv-

---

tionality, including evolutionary theories thereof, have generally overlooked a crucial aspect of rationality in the form of phenomenal consciousness. Van Huyssteen's eloquent elucidation of interpreted experience as a necessary component of human rationality led to the development of the views in this chapter. Needless to say, however, all failures of rationality within it are my own.

ing for some sort of ideal third-person account of justification. One way to put this is that both result in new constructions of the agent, the agent's community, and their relation. Postfoundationalist rationality explicitly rejects any attempt to divorce rational belief and choice from personal perspective and situational context. Thus, widely held conditions for rational beliefs and choices are not endorsed by postfoundationalist rationality. Such widely held conditions include the requirements that rational beliefs and choices be "universally evident in terms of empirical facts and the rules of logic, and must necessarily flow from the information given" (Van Huyssteen 1999). These requirements are part of a foundationalist program that seeks propositions whose rational justification is self-evident and that can be used to provide a foundation for the justification of all other rational beliefs and choices. Taking seriously the argument from postmodernism that such a God's-eye view is not possible within human experience, postfoundationalist rationality looks to perspective and context within an account of rational justification.

It is important to note, however, that postfoundationalist rationality rejects the radical view that there are "many rationalities," and thus "does not make rationality itself relative" (Van Huyssteen 1999), such that every community and agent are not rational simply because they have practices they name as defining rationality and they follow those practices. Rather, "all domains or levels of rationality are held together in the common or shared quest of finding the best available reasons to attain the highest form of intelligibility" (1999). The notion of intelligibility here is not divorced from the notion of action, for intelligibility is cashed out as effective and "progressive problem-solving" (1999).

Another way in which postfoundationalist rationality reaches across contexts while at the same time emphasizing perspective and contextuality is by emphasizing the centrality of human experience: "This postfoundationalist model of rationality . . . very specifically implies an *accountability to human experience*" (Van Huyssteen 1999). So human experience is granted a privileged place, as a serious and mature response to foundationalism's failure to demonstrate objectivity. By experience, however, what is meant is not some "isolate, epistemic consciousness," but rather, an interpretive perspective that aims toward communal discourse recognizing a shared project of intelligibility:

> In the absence of the availability of modernist rules, metanarratives, or transcendental standards for rationality, each of us is left with only one viable option: in assessing what rationality is, I must assess it as I see it, from where I stand. As a human being with a distinct self-awareness, and a very

specific quest for intelligibility, I can step into the reality of communicative praxis/praxial critique only from where I stand, and begin any intersubjective conversation only by appealing to *my* rationality. (Van Huyssteen 1999)

Narrativity of experiences stemming from sensation, perception, memory, and imagery thus becomes a core aspect of rationality on a postfoundationalist view.

One of the open questions motivated by this account of rationality is whether the rationally efficacious conscious experience that is entailed by concepts of self-awareness includes a role for phenomenal consciousness. An answer to this question is important in order to gain a better understanding of the evolution of rationality in general. More importantly, the degree to which phenomenal consciousness is efficacious in decision making will clarify just how personal a stance is required for a complete description of postfoundationalist rationality.

Interpreted Experience and Phenomenal Consciousness

Not surprisingly, first-person experiences of agents in relation do not appear in most traditional accounts of human rationality. It is one of the benefits of the postfoundationalist account that it elicits a renewed effort to examine first-person experience, and consciousness in particular, in relation to rationality. The lack of such an effort in classical accounts is most likely due to the influential notion that phenomenal consciousness (p-consciousness) is an epiphenomenon, lacking any influence on subsequent belief formation or decision making for action. It may be wondered, then, whether taking p-consciousness seriously as an aspect of rationality is precluded by a physicalist view of human nature, which may, on some views, create obstacles to an approach that seeks serious discourse with scientific views of the human. This is a commonly held misconception regarding epiphenomenalism, and it deserves some attention before moving to a direct consideration of p-consciousness in rationality.

The central issue is whether according p-consciousness a role in human decision making commits one to some type of substance or property dualism. The answer is no, according to at least two influential physicalist treatments of consciousness. On one such view, Owen Flanagan points out what might be termed the evolutionary question weighing against the epiphenomenalist view of p-consciousness:

The biggest problem the epiphenomenalist faces is explaining how, given the massive connectivity of the brain, *any* feature as common, well-structured, and multimodal as phenomenal consciousness could supervene on certain neural processes without having interesting and important causal effects in other parts of the neural network. . . . The epiphenomenalist will need to show that there is a cul de sac in each of the relevant areas where phenomenal consciousness is stopped dead in its tracks so that it makes no causal contribution to other neural events. This, I suggest, is a research program destined to fail. The brain doesn't work that way. (1997)

On the second view, Ned Block (1997; 2004) takes a more philosophical approach in arguing that p-consciousness cannot be conceptually reduced to or identified with functional or representational accounts of experience. Functionalism holds that mental events are just the causal relations between them and any inputs and outputs, independent of any one structural implementation. Representationalism holds that mental events in perception are just data that represent external objects. To counter arguments that attempt to subsume p-consciousness under functionalist or representationalist accounts of experience, Block introduces a physicalist example of experience using a set of twins. One twin undergoes a manipulation at birth of the neural network for color perception so as to fully invert all color perception. For example, Twin A sees red and green normally, but Twin B sees red when looking at the color green and sees green when looking at the color red. Suppose they learn the same color words for objects, such that when they look at an object they both call red, Twin A sees red but Twin B sees green. But this cannot happen according to the functionalist and representationalist accounts of p-consciousness. The twins are both representing the same thing but are having separate p-conscious experiences. Further, because they are looking at the same thing (e.g., a stop sign) and interpreting it in the same way, they are intending the same object, resulting — except for the difference in p-consciousness — in the same functional processes evoked by and the same role played by the object. Yet the twins have separate p-conscious experiences of the object, so p-consciousness cannot be conceptually accounted for by functionalism. It must be noted that the arguments Block makes are controversial and, not surprisingly, are countered by proponents of functionalism and representationalism.

Nevertheless, taken together, Flanagan's pointed denial of epiphenomenalism and Block's denial that p-consciousness can be conceptually subsumed under other accounts of experience provide an important argument from dedicated and influential physicalists for the reality and efficacy of p-consciousness. One must recognize, though, that the perspectives put forward by Flanagan and Block ultimately hold that p-consciousness *as the first-person experience of an agent* will be identified eventually with some neural account of p-consciousness, much like the concept of heat is identified with molecular motion in thermodynamics. This contention, of course, rests on just the kind of foundationalist, perspective-free assumptions we already rejected as untenable on a postfoundationalist view. Perhaps, then, there are better ways to frame p-consciousness within an understanding of human experience.

One such way is to interpret p-consciousness in an emergentist sense, drawing on the important work of Philip Clayton (2004). Alternatively, one can take a decidedly pragmatist approach, in the sense of William James, and take seriously the contextuality that accompanies every human inquiry and provisional answer, something that is so keenly evident on a postfoundationalist view. Some may erroneously conclude that this move away from physicalism also moves away from an affirmation of human embodiment in the world and a moving toward some kind of substance dualism. Nothing could be farther from what is intended here. It is thus important to see that human embodiment does not in fact entail that the body is simply a physical object wholly describable by a scientific physicalism. Instead, embodiment holds up notions of human sensuality, emotionality, movement, desire and feeling. It must not be restricted to the idea of the body as an animate machine or piece of meat, for example. One can reject a view of human bodies that would make them, and therefore humans, wholly accessible to scientific inquiry while at the same time affirming that human persons have no possibility apart from or except for human bodies.

Postfoundationalism already tells us that experiences of human nature are always contextually and perspectivally embedded. One may identify overarching, conditioning perspectives: the p-conscious I, the relational You, and the distanced She/He. To allow experience to inform our conceptual systems — and to avoid shutting out or cutting away compelling experiences — we do well to focus on a humanity in three persons. Of course, this tripartite conceptualization of human experience is just an abstraction, and of course which perspective is accorded primacy will depend upon the permeating context and the interests of the inquiring agent(s). Yet the tripartite schema can help frame inquiry into compelling experiences so that they are given the serious consideration they deserve. Most mainstream neuroscience and much cognitive science recognize first- and third-person experience of human nature, give ultimacy to third-person accounts, and leave out the key second-person perspective altogether.

It bears saying that third-person (i.e., scientific) accounts of human nature are absolutely desired and required within certain contexts and in view of specific interests of inquiry. Within these contexts and in view of these interests, cognitive science must have primacy, and of course it generally does without much question. Third-person scientific accounts of human nature are legitimate in these situations, since they are defined in such a way as to bracket, or temporarily suspend inquiry into, first- and second-person experiences. The experimenters bracket their first- and second-person experiences, and the experiments generally do not inquire after the first- and second-person experiences of experimental subjects. This method is responsible for the tremendous progress in cognitive science to date, and there is nothing in the tripartite view of human experience to challenge its validity. Indeed, cognitive science should be encouraged to develop to the fullest extent possible a third-person account of human nature. The one caution is that science should not then turn around and dismiss compelling first- and second-person experiences not included in its conceptual schema. A theology that views humanity in three persons can thus seriously engage cognitive science on questions of human nature.

Having seen, both on physicalist and pragmatist views, that p-consciousness cannot be explained away by other theories of human experience, we are now ready to explore the contribution of p-consciousness to agent rationality.

P-Consciousness and Agent Rationality

Rational agents, especially in decisions likely to significantly affect them and their relations to the world, must necessarily engage in imagining what the effects of the decision *will be like*. That is, when deciding whether she will believe or do something, a rational agent making a rational decision must imagine (1) what the future effects of that decision *will be like* for her; (2) what the future effects of that decision *will be like* for others affected by her decision; and (3) memories of past personal experiences that can inform the decision in any way. Of course, this does not exhaust all activities a rational agent must undertake in making a personal decision, but without these creative imaginings it is difficult to imagine that a personal decision could be rational. For example, regarding the effects of a choice on others in part entails understanding the preferences of those others. I have called this process "minding the other" to emphasize the imaginative aspect of shaping another's mind and the necessity of turning one's attention (e.g., "mind your elders") toward another. Of course, minding of this sort cannot rationally occur in the absence of communal engagement and shared understanding with those likely to be affected by the agent's choice, something we already saw was crucial to a postfoundationalist rationality.

An even more compelling argument for the centrality of p-consciousness to rational decision-making is that rational choice requires mental time travel, and mental time travel of the human kind appears to require p-consciousness, or the sense of what future consequences (e.g., intelligibility, problem solving) will be like. At least, it is not clear how a rational agent would proceed to rationally evaluate, articulate, and disclose her choices without a narrative of her imagined future and the imagined futures of others as a result of those choices, and without a capacity to receive the same back from others. Or, as described by Suddendorf and Corballis,

> Mental time travel comprises the mental reconstruction of personal events from the past (episodic memory) and the mental construction of possible events in the future. It is not an isolated module, but depends on the sophistication of other cognitive capacities, including self-awareness, meta-representation, mental attribution, understanding the perception-knowledge relationship, and dissociation of imagined mental states from one's present mental state. These capacities are also important aspects of so-called "theory of mind," and they appear to mature in children at around age four. Furthermore, mental time travel is generative, involving the combination and recombination of familiar elements, and in this respect may have been a precursor to language. (1997)

While some evidence suggests that nonhuman animals exhibit a form of mental time travel, it is not obvious how rational choices made by humans would proceed without mental time travel that is p-conscious, at least for choices involving significant long-term personal and communal stakes.

A final note on mental time travel and p-consciousness, which I will add in support of the position here, draws on one of the seminal events of the twentieth century: the publication of Rachel Carson's *Silent Spring* and the irruption of environmentalism in the United States. It is a commonly held position in environmental history that Carson's work helped spark the U.S. environmental movement, and the way in which the book opens deserves our careful attention. Carson's first chapter is entitled "A Fable for Tomorrow," and it is literally a story about the future of an imagined "town in the heart of America." Carson writes:

> Then a strange blight crept over the area and everything began to change. . . . There was a strange stillness. The birds, for example — where

had they gone? Many people spoke of them, puzzled and disturbed. The feeding stations in the backyards were deserted.... It was a spring without voices... only silence lay over the fields and woods and marsh.... A grim specter has crept upon us almost unnoticed, and this imagined tragedy may easily become a stark reality we all shall know. (1962)

Carson emphasizes the phenomenal quality of silence and uses it to evoke a stricken landscape. She consciously invents an "imagined tragedy" to her purpose of rational persuasion for a new American environmental future. Historical reflection leads one to conclude that it worked.

Evolutionary Selection for P-Consciousness?

I will only touch briefly on the implications of the foregoing discussion for the place of p-consciousness in the evolution of human rationality. A central issue is whether, on the new view of the efficacy of p-consciousness in human rationality, there can be any adaptationist account of p-consciousness. Perhaps, following most current accounts of human evolution, the system for p-consciousness is something akin to what Stephen Jay Gould and Richard Lewontin (1979) would call an evolutionary spandrel, a system that arose in evolution as a "necessary byproduct" of other systems under direct selective pressure.

The first thing to note is that most treatments of cognitive evolution, including the evolution of rationality, view p-consciousness as an epiphenomenon or explain it away in terms of representationalist or functionalist accounts. Nevertheless, at least one author, a developmental psychologist, has speculated that the ability to use autonoetic awareness, or p-consciousness of the self and personal experiences, "to generate self-centered mental models of potential future situations and potential behaviors in these situations" results from ecological and social selective pressures in evolutionary history. On this view, p-consciousness for mental time travel may have been an advantageous capacity that allowed humans to more effectively choose futures in situations than did the heuristics afforded by bounded rationality.

There is great difficulty in establishing a highly probable account of selection on p-consciousness, however, due in large part to the dearth of suitable methods to test its function in third-person contexts. Scientific experiments into the neural correlates of consciousness, for example, often rely on first-person verbal accounts and always rely on the first-person p-conscious intuitions of the scientists themselves. Establishing effective studies of p-consciousness in nonhuman animals, then, is highly challenging and fraught with implicit assumptions, though it can be done. Presently, however, it is enough to argue, based on the foregoing discussion, that p-consciousness may be viewed as a possible site phenotype in an adaptationist program and need not be relegated to spandrel status absent further study.

Implications for Theological and Scientific Constructions

A postfoundationalist account of rationality holds that human experience is central to reasoned choice regarding belief and action. The account of p-consciousness here lends weight to this claim and suggests ways in which agents rely on their phenomenally conscious experience to more fully imagine possible futures and to more effectively share visions of these futures within and across communal contexts. One surprising outcome of this analysis is that both theologians and scientists should become increasingly aware that, when discussing their commitments in the theater of rational exchange, imagined tragedies and envisioned triumphs will have large roles to play in how those commitments are received. Some choices for this belief or that action may be literally nightmare scenarios for some people, and care will be needed to express future visions in ways that take in and are sensitive to these imaginings.

At the same time, more work is needed on the part of scientists and theologians to craft ways of recognizing when phenomenal, future images contribute to rational discourse and when they detract from it. As this work continues, and even as we mentally travel in time to a future in which consensus is *not* the goal of rational discourse between theology and science, both theologians and scientists have good reasons to explore the neglected perspective of the second person of human experience. This is the ethical standpoint, one in which the other is met as the You, in the sense of limiting the I, with the goal of creating the space to allow new discourses to emerge that will be unlike any we can presently imagine.

Bibliography

Audi, R. 1990. "Rationality and Valuation." In P. K. Moser (ed.), *Rationality in Action*, 416-446. New York: Cambridge.

Block, N. 1997. [1990.] "Inverted Earth." In N. Block, O. Flanagan, and G. Güzeldere (eds.), *The Nature of Consciousness: Philosophical Debates*, 677-693. Cambridge, MA: MIT.

Block, N. 2004. "Qualia." In R. L. Gregory (ed.), *Oxford Companion to the Mind*. 2nd edition. Oxford: Oxford University Press.

Calvin, W. H. 2004. *A Brief History of the Mind*. New York: Oxford University Press.

Carson, R. 1962. *Silent Spring*. New York: Houghton Mifflin.

Clayton, N. S., T. J. Bussey, and A. Dickinson. 2003. "Can Animals Recall the Past and Plan for the Future?" *Nat Rev Neurosci* 4/8:685-691.

Clayton, P. 2004. *Mind and Emergence: From Quantum to Consciousness*. New York: Oxford University Press.

Debiec, J., and J. E. LeDoux. 2003. "Conclusions: From Self-Knowledge to a Science of the Self." In J. E. LeDoux, J. Debiec, and H. Moss (eds.), *The Self: From Soul to Brain*, 305-315. New York: New York Academy of Sciences.

Emery, N. J., and N. S. Clayton. 2004. "The Mentality of Crows: Convergent Evolution of Intelligence in Corvids and Apes." *Science* 306/5703:1903-1907.

Evans, D. 2004. "The Search Hypothesis of Emotion." In D. Evans and P. Cruse (eds.), *Emotion, Evolution, and Rationality*, 179-191. New York: Oxford University Press.

Flanagan, O. 1997. [1992.] "Conscious Inessentialism and the Epiphenomenalist Suspicion." In N. Block, O. Flanagan, and G. Güzeldere (eds.), *The Nature of Consciousness: Philosophical Debates*, 357-373. Cambridge, MA: MIT.

Geary, D. C. 2005. *The Origin of Mind: Evolution of the Brain, Cognition, and General Intelligence*. Washington, DC: American Psychological Association.

Gigerenzer, G., and R. Selten, eds. 2002. *Bounded Rationality: The Adaptive Toolbox*. Cambridge, MA: MIT.

Gould, S. J., and R. Lewontin. 1979. "The Spandrels of San Marco and the Panglossian Paradigm: A Critique of the Adaptationist Programme." *Proceedings of the Royal Society of London B*, 205/1161:581-598.

Harman, G. 1997. [1990.] "The Intrinsic Quality of Experience." In N. Block, O. Flanagan, and G. Güzeldere (eds.), *The Nature of Consciousness: Philosophical Debates*, 663-675. Cambridge, MA: MIT.

La Cerra, P., and R. Bingham. 2002. *The Origin of Minds: Evolution, Uniqueness, and the New Science of the Self*. New York: Harmony Publishers.

Lear, L. 1997. *Rachel Carson: Witness for Nature*. New York: Henry Holt & Co.

McNeil, D. W., S. R. Vrana, B. G. Melamed, B. N. Cuthbert, and P. J. Lang. 1993. "Emotional Imagery in Simple and Social Phobia: Fear versus Anxiety." *J Abnorm Psychol* 102/2:212-225.

Mele, A. R., and P. Rawling, eds. 2004. *The Oxford Handbook of Rationality*. New York: Oxford University Press.

Papineau, D. 2003. *The Roots of Reason: Philosophical Essays on Rationality*. New York: Oxford University Press.

Pinker, S. 1997. *How the Mind Really Works*. New York: W. W. Norton & Co.

Rothman, H. K. 1998. *The Greening of a Nation? Environmentalism in the United States since 1945*. Fort Worth, TX: Harcourt Brace & Co.

Spezio, M. L. 2004. "Freedom in the Body: The Physical, the Causal, and the Possibility of Choice." *Zygon* 39:577-590.

Spezio, M. L. In press, a. "Brain and Machine: Minding the Transhuman Future." *Dialog*.
Spezio, M. L. In press, b. "Narrative in Holistic Healing: Empathy, Sympathy, and Simulation Theory." In J. D. Koss and P. Hefner (eds.), *Spiritual Transformation and Healing*. Lanham, MD: Altamira.
Stanovich, K. E. 1999. *Who Is Rational? Studies of Individual Differences in Reasoning*. Mahwah, NJ: Lawrence Erlbaum Associates.
Suddendorf, T., and J. Busby. 2003. "Mental Time Travel in Animals?" *Trends in Cognitive Sciences* 7/9:391-396.
Suddendorf, T., and M. C. Corballis. 1997. "Mental Time Travel and the Evolution of the Human Mind." *Genet Soc Gen Psychol Monogr* 123/2:133-167.
Tuliving, E. 2002. "Episodic Memory: From Mind to Brain." *Annual Review of Psychology* 53:1-25.
Van Huyssteen, J. W. 1999. *The Shaping of Rationality: Toward Interdisciplinarity in Theology and Science*. Grand Rapids: Eerdmans.
Velleman, J. D. 2000. *The Possibilities of Practical Reason*. Oxford: Clarendon.

16 Science and the Self: What Difference Did Darwin Make?

John Hedley Brooke

In April 2002, the journal *Science* published a fascinating section on new models of the self suggested by the latest scientific research.[1] There were references to the self as understood in immunology, to the recognition and rejection of self in plant reproduction, to self-representation in nervous systems, and to the many selves of social insects. Christian theologians might not worry too much about the social insects: there is nothing shocking in the idea that their colonies are so tightly integrated that they seem to function as a single organism. And it is perhaps not too disconcerting to learn that individual insects, through genomic imprinting, may have a fractured self — in which maternal and paternal subsets of genes acquire their own identities and work at cross-purposes with each other.[2] But it might be more disconcerting to read of new ways of interpreting *our* selves. This same issue of *Science* contained the suggestion by Patricia Churchland that our problems in speaking of the self should be recast in terms of the self-representational capacities of the brain. This recasting offers leverage to the brain sciences and other advantages as well. It deflates what Churchland sees as the "temptation to think of the self as a singular entity and encourages the idea that self-representing involves a plurality of functions, each having a range of shades, levels and degrees."[3] Another advantage, she contends, is that it broadens enquiry beyond humans to other species. Hence her suggesting that "varying levels of coherence operate in all nervous systems of any significant complexity."

It would be right to detect a challenge here to certain religious under-

---

1. "Reflections on Self: Immunity and Beyond," *Science* 296, no. 5566 (2002): 297-316.
2. David C. Queller and Joan E. Strassmann, "The Many Selves of Social Insects," *Science* 296, no. 5566 (2002): 311-313.
3. Patricia Churchland, "Self-Representation in Nervous Systems," *Science* 296, no. 5566 (2002): 308-310.

standings of the self. Churchland disparagingly refers to a "mysticism" in which "traditionalists prefer to hive off the fundamental questions about the self or consciousness as philosophical in the 'armchair only' or 'forever-beyond-science' senses of the term."[4] When she speaks of extending enquiry to embrace the self-representing capacities of other species, we are reminded that the dissolution of the divide between humans and animals has a long history — back to Charles Darwin and earlier. In the introduction to one of his less familiar books, *The Expression of the Emotions in Man and Animals*, Darwin took on the physiologist and natural theologian Charles Bell, who had insisted on the divide. But, Darwin protested, "man himself cannot express love and humility by external signs, so plainly as does a dog, when with drooping ears, hanging lips, flexuous body, and wagging tail, he meets his beloved master."[5] Such protestations remind us that what excited Darwin was the continuity between humans and animals more than their differences.

Recognizing the distinguished work on human uniqueness that informed Wentzel van Huyssteen's Gifford Lectures, I take up that theme in this chapter and do so primarily as a historian of science. It is widely recognized that the natural sciences, and evolutionary theory in particular, have challenged the biblical idea of our being created in the image of God. Van Huyssteen himself notes that "it is no longer possible to claim some past 'paradise' or period in which humans possessed moral perfection, a state from which our species has somehow 'fallen' onto perpetual decline."[6] How else might we characterize Darwin's challenge to human self-perception? In this brief essay, I shall try to show that the task of evaluating the impact of Darwin's theory in its original context is not straightforward. I shall follow a relatively simple structure, identifying points that might be made in any standard textbook, but in each case raising strategic questions that add nuance and qualification. As Michael Ruse has shrewdly observed, "everyone wants something special for humans, spiritual if not physical,"[7] and this can blur distinctions between the sacred and the secular.

Three preliminary points deserve special emphasis. One answer to the question, What difference did Darwin make? is that it depends on where you were. If one were living in Paris in the early 1860s, the chances are he made no difference at all. Students of the life sciences in France would have been famil-

---

4. Churchland, "Self-Representation," p. 309.

5. Charles Darwin, *The Expression of the Emotions in Man and Animals* (Chicago: University of Chicago Press, 1965), p. 10.

6. J. Wentzel van Huyssteen, "Fallen Angels or Rising Beasts? Theological Perspectives on Human Uniqueness," *Theology and Science* 1 (2003): 161-178, at 170-171.

7. Michael Ruse, *The Evolution-Creation Struggle* (Cambridge, MA: Harvard University Press, 2005), p. 259.

iar with theories of organic transformation that had already been around for fifty years or more and that had the additional merit of having been proposed by Frenchmen, notably Jean-Baptiste Lamarck and Etienne Geoffroy St. Hilaire.[8] On my last visit to the Paris Natural History Museum in the Jardin des Plantes, Darwin's name was still eclipsed. It mattered where you were. How one reacted as a Calvinist Christian could depend on location, as David Livingstone has shown.[9] In Belfast there were local reasons for intransigence. It was there in 1874 that the physicist John Tyndall gave his presidential address to the British Association for the Advancement of Science. This was a high-profile public event in which he deplored the low value placed on scientific education in Ireland. Epitomizing the process that Frank Turner has described as "contesting cultural authority,"[10] Tyndall went on the offensive, announcing that the entire domain of cosmological theory would be wrested from theology. Tyndall's aggression was deeply alienating, especially to clergy who had been denied a platform for their harmonizing positions. A local event, in other words, could have the effect of associating Darwinism with those other "isms" unwelcome in Presbyterian circles: monism, materialism, and atheism. By contrast, Presbyterians in Princeton, with notable exceptions, proved more receptive. In Scotland the situation was different again. Livingstone has found that Darwinian ideas began to infiltrate Scottish Calvinism just as the Irish became more hostile. The reason? He suggests that the Darwinian challenge was pretty tame compared with that emanating from higher biblical criticism, for which William Robertson Smith was chastised by his Scottish brethren.[11]

A second preliminary observation relates to time rather than to place. Theories of evolution had been around long before Darwin. His grandfather, Erasmus Darwin, had been a proponent. We also know that when the grandson began his abortive medical training in Edinburgh he was introduced by Robert Grant to the ideas of Lamarck.[12] Mid-Victorian theories of social evolution generally owed as much to the Lamarckian Herbert Spencer as to Darwin.[13] Fif-

---

8. John H. Brooke, *Science and Religion: Some Historical Perspectives* (Cambridge: Cambridge University Press, 1991), pp. 296-303.

9. David N. Livingstone, *Putting Science in Its Place* (Chicago: University of Chicago Press, 2003), pp. 116-123.

10. Frank M. Turner, *Contesting Cultural Authority: Essays in Victorian Intellectual Life* (Cambridge: Cambridge University Press, 1993).

11. Livingstone, *Putting Science in Its Place*, pp. 117-119.

12. Janet Browne, *Charles Darwin Voyaging: Volume 1 of a Biography* (London: Pimlico, 1996), p. 83.

13. John C. Greene, "Biology and Social Theory in the Nineteenth Century: Auguste Comte and Herbert Spencer," in *Science, Ideology and Worldview: Essays in the History of Evolutionary*

teen years before the *Origin of Species* appeared, evolutionary ideas had already caused rage in the colleges of Oxford and Cambridge and yet were all the rage in less cerebral milieux. This, as James Secord has reminded us in his fine book *Victorian Sensation*, was because of the notorious *Vestiges of the Natural History of Creation*, published anonymously in 1844 and, worryingly for a clerical elite, a best seller.[14] Reading the outburst from one of Darwin's mentors, the Cambridge geologist Adam Sedgwick, it would be difficult to deny that new perceptions of the self were already in the offing. If animal instincts had developed into human reason, religion was a "lie," morality was "moonshine," humanity had lost its special status, and all distinction between moral and physical was "annulled."[15]

A third preliminary observation concerns the meaning we give to the phrase "Darwin's theory of evolution." We correctly credit Darwin with the evolutionary mechanism of natural selection, but in doing so we sometimes forget its controversial status during a long process of assimilation. We may also forget that he himself developed doubts about its sufficiency, conceding in his *Descent of Man* (1871) that he had probably given too much weight to natural selection in the first edition of his *Origin of Species* (1859).[16] Not only that, but there were so many different facets of Darwinism that to speak of Darwin's "theory" can be facile. Darwinism could mean many things: natural selection; sexual selection; the accumulation of gradual changes rather than sudden mutations; a process governed by laws not divine intervention; a process governed by chance as much as, or even rather than, design; a liberal laissez-faire polity, and so on. Indeed one analyst has identified at least fourteen different meanings of "Darwinian evolutionism," according to the scope of the theory and the different metaphysical constructions placed upon it.[17] To compound the problem, Darwin's own language was often am-

---

Ideas, ed. John C. Greene (Berkeley: University of California Press, 1981), pp. 60-94; James R. Moore, "Herbert Spencer's Henchmen: The Evolution of Protestant Liberals in Late Nineteenth-Century America," in *Darwinism and Divinity*, ed. John Durant (Oxford: Blackwell, 1985), pp. 76-100; Diane B. Paul, "Darwin, Social Darwinism and Eugenics," in *The Cambridge Companion to Darwin*, ed. Jonathan Hodge and Gregory Radick (Cambridge: Cambridge University Press, 2003), pp. 214-239, esp. 226-229.

14. James A. Secord, *Victorian Sensation: The Extraordinary Publication, Reception, and Secret Authorship of "Vestiges of the Natural History of Creation"* (Chicago: University of Chicago Press, 2000).

15. Secord, *Victorian Sensation*, p. 245.

16. Charles Darwin, *The Descent of Man and Selection in Relation to Sex* (London: Murray, 1906), p. 93.

17. David Ray Griffin, *Religion and Scientific Naturalism: Overcoming the Conflicts* (New York: State University of New York Press, 2000), pp. 244-265.

biguous in that his metaphors could be read in different ways according to one's preference. For example, his image of a repeatedly branching tree for the evolutionary process could be read as denying any sense of direction. And yet branching trees still grow upwards, the image, in that sense, permitting references to greater complexity and even progress.

Do such nuances matter? They surely matter very much if we are to give an informed answer to questions about the Darwinian impact. They matter because, during a long period when it was appropriate to speak of the *eclipse of Darwinism*, there was still scope for models of theistic evolution in which divine providence was seen in processes of complexification.[18] The Darwin we think we know, and the impact we may think he had, are to a significant degree artifacts of the 1930s and later, as the new neo-Darwinian synthesis began its triumphal march. We are so used today to finding "Darwin's dangerous idea" permeating every aspect of our culture,[19] from Lee Smolin's "cosmological natural selection"[20] to the "competition among ensembles of neurons," which according to Antonio Damasio "represent varied choice options,"[21] that it can be difficult to discern what difference Darwin made in his own day.

It would be perverse to suggest that no significant threats arose to religious understandings of the self. I have tried to summarize them in another recent essay.[22] At the same time, the obvious points conceal important qualifications. For example, Richard Dawkins will say that Darwin made a colossal difference because, after 1859 but not before, it was possible to be an intellectually fulfilled atheist. But if we focus on that consequence alone, we may miss the fact that Darwin was also appropriated for theistic purposes. It is well known that one of Darwin's earliest converts was the clergyman, Christian socialist, and novelist Charles Kingsley, who argued that the God of old who had made all things had now been surpassed in wisdom by the God who could make all things make themselves.[23]

---

18. Peter J. Bowler, *The Eclipse of Darwinism* (Baltimore: Johns Hopkins University Press, 1983), and *Reconciling Science and Religion* (Chicago: University of Chicago Press, 2001), pp. 122-159.

19. Daniel Dennett, *Darwin's Dangerous Idea: Evolution and the Meanings of Life* (New York: Simon and Schuster, 1995).

20. Lee Smolin, *The Life of the Cosmos* (London: Phoenix, 1998), pp. 374-399.

21. Antonio Damasio, "Brain Trust," *Nature* 435 (2 June 2005): 571-572.

22. John H. Brooke, "Darwin and Victorian Christianity," in Hodge and Radick, eds., *Cambridge Companion to Darwin*, pp. 192-213.

23. John H. Brooke and Geoffrey N. Cantor, *Reconstructing Nature: The Engagement of Science and Religion* (Edinburgh: T&T Clark, 1998), pp. 162-163.

To examine those aspects of the self that were threatened by the Darwinian synthesis I shall consider in turn the *dignified,* the *unique,* the *immortal,* the *moral,* the *knowing,* the *aesthetic,* and the *suffering* self.

A Dignified Self?

As Janet Browne has shown, Darwin became a household name in part because of press cartoons depicting him as ape-like.[24] Since the relevance of his theory to human identity was often tempered by humor and satire, it is not always easy to gauge how grievously it was felt. To assert continuity between humans and ape-like ancestors could be deeply shocking; and yet it remained the case that, in many of their attributes, humans were distinctive and not *merely* advanced forms of their primate relatives. Even today the caution has to be issued that "extrapolation between ape and human species must keep in mind that apes are highly evolved and are not primitive humans."[25] Nevertheless, for those who wished to uphold a traditional Christian understanding of human uniqueness, Darwin's conclusions were no laughing matter. The Bishop of Oxford, Samuel Wilberforce, is often caricatured in this context;[26] but it is true that he was affronted by the threat to a dignity that derived from his being made in the image of God:

> Man's derived supremacy over the earth; man's power of absolute speech; man's gift of reason; man's free will and responsibility; man's fall and . . . redemption; the incarnation of the Eternal Son; the indwelling of the Eternal Spirit, — all are equally and utterly irreconcilable with the degrading notion of the brute origin of him who was created in the image of God and redeemed by the Eternal Son.[27]

---

24. Janet Browne, "Commemorating Darwin," *British Journal for the History of Science* 38 (2005): 251-274, esp. 253-254.

25. Nancy R. Howell, "The Importance of Being Chimpanzees," *Theology and Science* 1 (2003): 179-191, at 180.

26. John H. Brooke, "The Wilberforce-Huxley Debate: Why Did It Happen?" *Science and Christian Belief* 13 (2001): 127-141; Frank A. J. L. James, "An 'Open Clash between Science and the Church'? Wilberforce, Huxley and Hooker on Darwin at the British Association, Oxford, 1860," in *Science and Beliefs: From Natural Philosophy to Natural Science, 1700-1900,* ed. David M. Knight and Matthew D. Eddy (Aldershot: Ashgate, 2005), pp. 171-193.

27. Samuel Wilberforce, "Darwin's Origin of Species," in Samuel Wilberforce, *Essays Contributed to the Quarterly Review,* 2 vols. (London: Murray, 1974), vol. 1, pp. 52-103, at 94.

When Wilberforce reviewed Darwin's *Origin of Species*, he tried hard not to launch a theological diatribe. Only in the concluding section of an extensive review did he allow religious considerations to intrude into what, until that point, had been a largely philosophical critique. We must also ask whether the threat Wilberforce felt to human dignity was at all new. Was this a uniquely Darwinian challenge? Surely not. The evolutionary hypothesis of Lamarck had worried Darwin's mentor Charles Lyell in the late 1820s and early 1830s for a similar reason. Indeed, it has been argued that one of the main reasons why Lyell had turned his face against an increasingly popular interpretation of fossil-bearing strata as a record of progressive *creation* was that he discerned just how easily such a model could lend itself to a reinterpretation in which the progression was achieved through entirely natural causes.[28] A Lamarckian threat to human dignity had already left its mark on paleontology, and Lyell devoted volume two of his famous *Principles of Geology* (1830-33) to a refutation of the French biologist. Lyell's anxiety and discernment turned out to be justified when Robert Chambers's *Vestiges* appeared in 1844. We have already had occasion to note Sedgwick's splenetic reaction to a book that in some respects destroyed human dignity more effectively than Darwin's *Origin*. This is because Chambers openly embraced human development from lower forms of life whereas in Darwin's *Origin* man was conspicuous, but by his absence. In *Vestiges* we find an account of the workings of the human mind that stressed the operation of natural law, giving rise to Sedgwick's charge of "base materialism" and "rank infidelity." As Secord has insisted, it was not so much with Darwin as with *Vestiges* that evolution had "quite literally moved off the streets and into the home."[29]

There nevertheless remains the deeper issue intimated above. If humans, with their high degree of self-consciousness, were different only in degree from the ape-like creatures from whom they were derived, the implied degradation could indeed be serious. Humans, however, had surely emerged from their progenitors with capacities that transcended those of their forebears? Surely there was space in that transcendence for a more sophisticated riposte than that of Wilberforce to a Darwinian reductionism? In fact Darwin would iterate it himself:

---

28. Michael J. Bartholomew, "Lyell and Evolution: An Account of Lyell's Response to the Prospect of an Evolutionary Ancestry for Man," *British Journal for the History of Science* 6 (1973): 261-303.

29. James A. Secord, "Behind the Veil: Robert Chambers and *Vestiges*," in *History, Humanity and Evolution*, ed. James R. Moore (Cambridge: Cambridge University Press, 1989), pp. 165-194, at 186.

> The feeling of religious devotion is a highly complex one, consisting of love, complete submission to an exalted and mysterious superior, a strong sense of dependence, fear, reverence, gratitude, hope for the future, and perhaps other elements. No being could experience so complex an emotion until advanced in his intellectual and moral faculties to at least a moderately high level.[30]

With that in mind we might ask, How typical was Wilberforce? Did he really speak for the entire English Church? Not at all, as we know from the more liberal response of Frederick Temple, a future Archbishop of Canterbury.[31] It has even been suggested that he "spoke only for a minority."[32] Henry Acland, the moving spirit behind Oxford's Natural History Museum, wrote to Richard Owen: "Whatever views Mr Huxley, or you, or Mr Darwin, or the Bishop of Oxford may have as to the essential Nature of Man, you all agree that however he so became, he is in some manner made in the image of God, by the ordinance of God."[33] To many observers what ultimately mattered was the attributes humans demonstrably have, irrespective of the mechanism by which they had come to possess them. When modern theologians, such as Robert Jenson, describe human beings as praying animals they encapsulate the point.[34] The continuity that Darwin affirmed between humans and their animal progenitors certainly dispensed with separate creative acts for each species, but it did not preclude the emergence of attributes, such as a sense of moral responsibility, that seemed to make less sense when predicated of other primates. And from another perspective, the impact of Darwin's theory of human evolution can hardly be said to have been decisive. The fact that students of animal behavior still have to protest that we do not take seriously enough that chimpanzees, for example, have a sense of self-identity and may lay claim to personhood[35] suggests a continuing reluctance in their audience to relinquish a distinctively human self.

---

30. Darwin, *Descent of Man*, p. 146.
31. John Durant, "Darwinism and Divinity: A Century of Debate," in Durant, ed., *Darwinism and Divinity*, pp. 9-39, esp. 19-20; Timothy M. Gouldstone, *The Rise and Decline of Anglican Idealism in the Nineteenth Century* (Basingstoke: Palgrave Macmillan, 2005), pp. 98-104.
32. Secord, *Victorian Sensation*, p. 514.
33. Cited by Secord, *Victorian Sensation*, p. 514.
34. Van Huyssteen, "Fallen Angels," p. 168.
35. Howell, "Importance of Being Chimpanzees," p. 187.

A Unique Self?

To the question, What differentiates humans from the rest of creation? Darwin's contemporaries sometimes gave an answer in explicitly religious terms. His cousin Hensleigh Wedgwood had once proposed that in humans alone is there an innate sense of God. Darwin's encounter with native Australians and Fuegians on the *Beagle* voyage called this into question. It was a theme to which he would return when writing about religion in his *Descent of Man*. "There is ample evidence," he wrote, "derived not from hasty travellers, but from men who have long resided with savages, that numerous races have existed, and still exist, who have no idea of one or more gods, and who have no words in their languages to express such an idea."[36]

Without trivializing the problem, there is nevertheless a countervailing question. Darwin himself referred to it as a "higher" one. It was whether there *exists* a Creator and Ruler of the universe. This question he freely, if a little ambiguously, admitted "has been answered in the affirmative by some of the highest intellects that have ever existed."[37] It is not therefore clear that the Darwinian threat extended to the existence of the most unique self of all — a Creator with the power to determine the laws of nature, including what Darwin was happy to describe as the *law* of natural selection.

A related question is whether the idea of evolution might not itself provide the very resource necessary to deal with the problem posed by the aboriginal Australians and Fuegians. If one could speak of the *evolution* of religious sensibility, of the development of an understanding of God, there was a way of responding to the twin challenges of Darwin and the higher criticism. As one commentator on the work of Robertson Smith has noted:

> Evolution makes sense if one believes, as Smith did, in a chosen people for whom truths were slowly revealed over a long period of time. Thus Smith saw Jews as gradually evolving from a period of ignorance about God's plan for them through ever higher forms of moral awareness, with Christian revelation representing the evolutionary peak. . . . [N]ot only was Christianity an improvement on Judaism, but, for Smith, Presbyterianism was a higher form of Christianity than Roman Catholicism.[38]

---

36. Darwin, *Descent of Man*, p. 143.
37. Darwin, *Descent of Man*, p. 143.
38. T. O. Beidelmann, *W. Robertson Smith and the Sociological Study of Religion* (Chicago: University of Chicago Press, 1974), pp. 38-39.

That reference to "ever higher forms of moral awareness" might serve as a pointer to the fact that even among today's Darwinians there are those who reaffirm human uniqueness. For Richard Dawkins we are not only unique in having conscious foresight. It is also the case that "we, alone on earth, can rebel against the tyranny of the selfish replicators," and should do so.[39] There is an imperative to *teach* altruism because we are born selfish. Critics have observed that it is not entirely clear from where Dawkins could derive his higher moral sensibilities if the universe is as pitiless as he describes.[40] Christian theology has less of a problem in this respect because the concept of human uniqueness embraces what both Philip Hefner and J. Wentzel van Huyssteen describe as a distinctively human task: "to set forth the presence of God in this world."[41] This is, of course, to give a theological rather than a naturalistic explication of *imago dei* and one that belongs to the domain of functional rather than substantive interpretation. Because of that, it might be objected that such an articulation is insufficient to meet another of the Darwinian challenges — the threat to the immortal self. It may be the Christian's privilege and responsibility to proclaim the presence of God in *this* world; but is there not a sense in which Darwin, by animalizing humanity, closed the door to the next?

An Immortal Self?

On the subject of immortality Darwin became both agnostic and evasive. In private correspondence he would counsel that "as for a future life, every man must judge for himself between conflicting vague probabilities."[42] But there was more to his challenge than that. Darwin belonged to a group of thinkers who forged a new vocabulary for the discussion of what had so often been called the soul. As Thomas Dixon has shown, it was during the nineteenth century that a secularization of language occurred in which references to human emotions replaced reference to the passions and affections of the soul.[43] No one, Dixon writes, ever wrote a work called *The Psychology of the Passions*

---

39. Richard Dawkins, *The Selfish Gene* (Oxford: Oxford University Press, 1989), p. 332.

40. Holmes Rolston, *Genes, Genesis and God* (Cambridge: Cambridge University Press, 1999), p. 265.

41. Van Huyssteen, "Fallen Angels," pp. 170 and 177.

42. Charles Darwin, in *The Life and Letters of Charles Darwin*, 3 vols., ed. Francis Darwin (London: Murray, 1887), vol. 1, p. 307.

43. Thomas Dixon, *From Passions to Emotions: The Creation of a Secular Psychological Category* (Cambridge: Cambridge University Press, 2003).

nor one called *The Emotions of the Soul*. His point is that the words "passions" and "affections" belonged to a network of words such as "of the soul," "conscience," "Fall," "sin," "grace," "Spirit," "Satan," "will," "lower appetite," and "self-love." By contrast, the word "emotion" was embedded in a different network of terms such as "psychology," "law," "observation," "evolution," "organism," "brain," "nerves," "expression," "behavior," and "viscera."[44]

Darwin's contribution to the secularization of the soul was a curious one, in that he was more Lamarckian than Darwinian when explaining how the expression of emotions had evolved. He did not argue that most emotional expressions had been inherited because they were useful. His model was the inheritance of acquired characteristics. But the challenge was still a potent one because Darwin proposed that a good mode of explanation was one that could be applied, with satisfactory results, both to humans and to the lower animals.[45] This was a principle reflected in Darwin's account of affectionate cats, humble dogs, impatient horses, irritated bulls, and grieving, jealous, or depressed monkeys.

What questions might introduce nuance and perspective here? One might be whether there was not a degree of circularity in the anthropomorphic language Darwin used when describing animal behavior. He was not unaware of this problem but clearly considered anthropomorphic projections less vicious than the arrogance he so deplored when humans presumed to think themselves worthy of the attention of the deity.[46] Another question might be whether it *was* Darwin who made all the difference. The idea that mental powers were not the consequence of a nonmaterial soul but should be correlated with the states of a material brain had already been advanced by the Scottish philosopher and psychologist Alexander Bain. Bain's materialism was perhaps the real bane to religious thinkers because it appeared to belong to a deliberately anti-Christian program.[47] Such a direct assault on the Christian religion was not Darwin's style; nor did he consider it particularly effective.

One might even ask whether the challenge of monistic to dualistic accounts of the human self has not had a far longer history. In the eighteenth century Joseph Priestley had rejected the dualism of matter and spirit, without compromising the doctrine of the resurrection of the dead, which he re-

---

44. Thomas Dixon, "The Psychology of the Emotions in Britain and America in the Nineteenth Century: The Role of Religious and Antireligious Commitments," *Osiris* 16 (2001): 288-320, esp. 289-290.

45. Dixon, "Psychology of the Emotions," p. 308.

46. John H. Brooke, "The Relations between Darwin's Science and His Religion," in Durant, ed., *Darwinism and Divinity*, pp. 40-75, esp. 66.

47. Dixon, "Psychology of the Emotions," p. 303.

garded as fundamental to his rational Christianity.⁴⁸ It is a position that radical Protestants had sometimes favored long before Darwin. To be resurrected at God's behest was to leave the initiative with the divine sovereign in a way that the automatic survival of an immortal soul did not. A non-reductive monism finds favor today in some Protestant circles,⁴⁹ but how would Roman Catholic thinkers respond to this kind of challenge?

From recent research in the Vatican archives, it is clear that during the later years of the nineteenth century texts sympathetic to biological evolution written by Catholic thinkers encountered objections behind the scenes.⁵⁰ And the objections did revolve around human uniqueness and the account of Adam's creation in Genesis. A complex machinery of consultation and censorship could lead to an author's retraction without an official public denunciation. But there was a way forward that eventually found recognition in the twentieth century. This was to follow the lead of the Catholic evolutionist St. George Mivart in allowing the evolution of the human body, but keeping every soul a distinct creation.⁵¹ This may be a problematic move, aesthetically repugnant to an uncompromising naturalism, but it has proved enduring in communities where a dualistic ontology of matter and spirit, body and soul, has been upheld. The theological defense of an afterlife, that a loving deity would not discard its morally perfectible creatures, underlines the need to return to the moral self and to another Darwinian challenge.

A Moral Self?

In his review of the literature on *imago dei,* Van Huyssteen writes that "the human person has . . . emerged biologically as a center of self-awareness, identity and moral responsibility."⁵² Was there no challenge in early Darwinism to the existence of moral imperatives? There are fascinating issues here because belief in moral absolutes could be one of the ways in which Victorian

---

48. John H. Brooke, "'A Sower Went Forth': Joseph Priestley and the Ministry of Reform," in *Motion toward Perfection: The Achievement of Joseph Priestley,* ed. John G. McEvoy and A. Truman Schwartz (Boston: Skinner House, 1990), pp. 21-56, esp. 39.

49. Warren S. Brown, Nancey Murphy, and H. Newton Malony, eds., *Whatever Happened to the Soul?* (Minneapolis: Fortress, 1998).

50. Mariano Artigas and Rafael Martinez, "New Light on Catholic Responses to Evolution," paper presented to European Science Foundation Workshop on "Science and Human Values," Vatican Observatory, Castelgandolfo, July 3-7, 2002.

51. Brooke and Cantor, *Reconstructing Nature,* pp. 255-262.

52. Van Huyssteen, "Fallen Angels," p. 169.

thinkers, overcome with religious doubts, could find a way back to faith. Did Darwin's theory block that kind of recovery? From within Darwin's own family we catch a glimpse of the pain. There was a sentence in Darwin's autobiography that his wife Emma wished to delete. It referred to the constant inculcation of a belief in God in the minds of children. Darwin had asked whether this might not produce such a strong and inherited effect on their brains that it would be "as difficult for them to throw off their belief in God, as for a monkey to throw off its instinctive fear and hatred of a snake." A worried Emma wrote to her son Francis in 1885: "There is one sentence in the Autobiography which I very much wish to omit, no doubt partly because your father's opinion that *all* morality has grown up by evolution is painful to me; but also because where this sentence comes in, it gives one a sort of shock."[53]

All morality has grown up by evolution. That was painful. And if that is how Emma read him, is it surprising that others would see in Darwin's theory a recipe for the relativity of moral values? It would create new openings, one of which Emma herself specified: it would "give an opening to say, however unjustly, that he considered all spiritual beliefs no higher than hereditary aversions or likings."[54] Darwin did make a difference in facilitating (though surely not originating) secular accounts of morality.

Yet even here there are questions that invite deeper reflection. Emma was wanting to imply that it would be unjust to characterize her husband's position so crudely. And we might ask whether Darwin really was a relativist on ethical matters. The answer may be surprising; but he made it clear that he was not seeking to undermine the golden rule that we should treat others as we would have them treat us. This, in his view, was the highest form of ethical principle. His goal was not to erase it but to explain how it might have developed. And if we also ask how Darwin accounted for the moral sense, it transpires that he gives to religion a role in its refinement. He observes that the foundation of morality *used* to be seen in a form of selfishness. His preference was to speak of a "deeply planted social instinct."[55] In contrast to the utilitarians, he wanted to speak not of the greatest happiness principle nor of a calculus of pleasure and pain. His own prescription was that the standard of morality should be the "general good or welfare of the community," not the general happiness.[56] The moral sense had originated in the social instincts "largely guided by the approbation of our fellow-men, ruled by reason, self-interest, and in later times by

---

53. Nora Barlow, ed., *The Autobiography of Charles Darwin* (London: Collins, 1958), p. 93.
54. Barlow, ed., *Autobiography of Darwin*, p. 93.
55. Darwin, *Descent of Man*, pp. 183-184.
56. Darwin, *Descent of Man*, p. 185.

deep religious feelings."[57] One could believe in natural selection without succumbing to a selfish individualism. As Darwin saw it: "A tribe including many members who, from possessing in a high degree the spirit of patriotism, fidelity, obedience, courage, and sympathy, were always ready to sacrifice themselves for the common good, would be victorious over most other tribes; and this would be natural selection."[58] Sacrifice of the self was not outlawed in Darwin's universe. Not surprisingly, this passage from the Darwin corpus has been excavated by those who, like David Sloan Wilson, have wished to reassert the efficacy of "group selection" in evolutionary processes.[59]

A rather different question, which comes to the fore at this point, is whether moral principles can in fact be derived from evolutionary theory at all. In his Romanes Lecture of 1893 on "Evolution and Ethics," T. H. Huxley famously set human ethical imperatives in opposition to those that might be deduced from the workings of nature: "Social progress means a checking of the cosmic process at every step and the substitution for it of another, which may be called the ethical process; the end of which is not the survival of those who happen to be the fittest, in respect of the whole of the conditions which obtain, but of those who are ethically the best."[60] As we have seen, Richard Dawkins has sometimes sounded like an echo: "Let us try to teach generosity and altruism because we are born selfish."[61] On this view, it looks as if we have to escape the biological legacy. Indeed, Dawkins has described himself as a passionate anti-Darwinian when it comes to politics and how we should conduct our human affairs, in which case the question from where we derive our moral precepts may still have an urgency that Darwin has done little to diminish or disturb.[62] There was a moral issue of great moment to Darwin himself: the practice of slavery, which he found abhorrent. As Adrian Desmond and James Moore have observed in their introduction to a new edition of the *Descent of Man*, there was a "political intensity behind [Darwin's] evolutionary crusade."[63] His assault on polygenist accounts of human origins was reinforced by a theory of common descent that unified rather than sepa-

---

57. Darwin, *Descent of Man*, p. 203.
58. Darwin, *Descent of Man*, p. 203.
59. David Sloan Wilson, *Darwin's Cathedral: Evolution, Religion, and the Nature of Society* (Chicago: University of Chicago Press, 2002), p. 5.
60. T. H. Huxley, "Evolution and Ethics: The Romanes Lecture, 1893," in T. H. Huxley and Julian Huxley, *Evolution and Ethics, 1893-1943* (London: Pilot Press, 1947), p. 81.
61. Dawkins, *Selfish Gene*, p. 3.
62. Rolston, *Genes, Genesis and God*, p. 265.
63. James Moore and Adrian Desmond, "Introduction" to Charles Darwin, *The Descent of Man* (London: Penguin, 2004), p. xxix.

rated the races. But whence the moral imperative? If, as Moore has suggested, there was a residue of Christian values in Darwin's attitude, there was in Darwin himself further evidence of the fact that moral precepts need not be changed by science. There was a real sense in which his evolutionary science served a moral purpose, as it did also for Alfred Russel Wallace, co-founder with Darwin of the theory of natural selection.

Like Darwin, Wallace was averse to polygenism; unlike Darwin he was willing to reconstruct the relations between the sexes, giving women a more proactive role in the selection of mates.[64] Generally, however, women did not fare better in the value-systems of the Darwinians. Some, like the American feminist leader Elizabeth Cady Stanton, looked to the Darwinian theory as a vehicle of emancipation. In *The Woman's Bible,* she surmised that "if . . . we accept the Darwinian theory, that the race has been a gradual growth from the lower to a higher form of life, and the story of the fall is a myth, we can exonerate the snake, emancipate the woman, and reconstruct a more rational religion for the nineteenth century."[65] Yet, in one of the most subtle interpretations of the Darwinian revolution, Robert Young argued that evolutionary theory was used largely to naturalize the same values that were already embedded in early Victorian society.[66] On the specific issue of the gendered self, it is notable that Darwin's most fervent apostle, T. H. Huxley, had to be reproached for excluding women from the meetings of the Ethnological Society. A Darwinian herself, Eliza Lynn Linton complained:

> [W]hat are the facts of woman's personal condition? We are thrown into an active hand to hand struggle for existence all the same as men. . . . The battle of life is a very serious matter to some of us, and we are frequently hindered and heavily weighted. . . . [I]t is not fair to exclude us from the means of knowledge & of active thought, of extended views — such as we get from attending learned discussions — on the simple plea of our womanhood.[67]

Darwinian liberalism had its limits.

---

64. John Durant, "Scientific Naturalism and Social Reform in the Thought of Alfred Russel Wallace," *British Journal for the History of Science* 6 (1972): 31-58.

65. Cited by Edward J. Larson, "Evolutionary Dissent," *Science and Spirit,* March/April 2005, p. 52.

66. Robert M. Young, "The Impact of Darwin on Conventional Thought," in *The Victorian Crisis of Faith,* ed. A. Symondson (London: SPCK, 1970), pp. 13-35.

67. Cited by Evelleen Richards, "Huxley and Woman's Place in Science: The 'Woman Question' and the Control of Victorian Anthropology," in Moore, ed., *History, Humanity and Evolution,* pp. 253-284, at 274.

A Rational Knowing Self?

In much of classical Christian theology, the faculty of reason served to differentiate humans from other creatures. In current discussion the ability to understand abstract concepts remains a criterion for discrimination. Van Huyssteen has written that "the imperative to *understand*, therefore, is something altogether basic for us as humans."[68] In one respect, therefore, Darwin changed little: the twenty years during which he labored on his theory were in a quest for understanding that, in its impetus and success, underlined rather than diminished distinctive human powers. The homology with current understandings is nicely shown in Dawkins's line that "there is true solace in the blessed gift of understanding."[69] But there were, of course, consequences. For Dawkins that very understanding requires that we digest the "unwelcome message of the Devil's Chaplain" that we are products of an undersigned natural process that is horribly cruel and wasteful.[70] There had been consequences for Darwin himself. I am thinking of his agnosticism on religious matters and one of its many roots. It was an intriguing kind of agnosticism because it did not prevent Darwin from having convictions, one of which was that the universe could not be the product of chance alone. But then the twist: should one trust one's own convictions? If the human mind has developed from that of less well-endowed species, perhaps it was never designed to answer theological and metaphysical questions.

Darwin here preferred humility to what he saw as the arrogance of theologians, who think they can reason about God or that the universe revolves around humankind alone. He definitely regarded the enterprise of natural theology as incurably anthropocentric. But two questions lead, once again, to nuance and qualification. When we read critiques of natural theologies, even science-based natural theologies, is it Darwin's argument that makes all the difference? The critiques already supplied by David Hume and Immanuel Kant were more foundational, as Darwin himself recognized when alluding to the infinite regress that plagues the cosmological argument. "I am aware," Darwin wrote, "that if we admit a first cause, the mind still craves to know whence it came, and how it arose."[71] The respect in which Darwin subverted the design argument of William Paley is, of course, a commonplace; but an ontology in which the *laws* of nature themselves could be said to be designed was far less

---

68. Van Huyssteen, "Fallen Angels," p. 171.
69. Richard Dawkins, *A Devil's Chaplain: Reflections on Hope, Lies, Science and Love* (London: Weidenfeld and Nicolson, 2003), p. 11.
70. Dawkins, *Devil's Chaplain,* p. 11.
71. Darwin in F. Darwin, ed., *Life and Letters,* vol. 1, pp. 306-307.

vulnerable.⁷² Moreover, as Bernard Lightman has shown, in works of science popularization, a natural theology continued largely unscathed by natural selection:⁷³ "we can trace an unbroken line of descent in the natural theology tradition from the mid-nineteenth century to the present."⁷⁴

Another question is this: if we cannot trust our convictions on metaphysical matters because of our evolutionary development, can we be sure that we can trust our convictions on physical matters, if our minds are similarly constrained? How rational is our rationality, even within the practice of the sciences? To my knowledge Darwin did not face that question head-on. The fact that he did not has led at least one Darwin scholar to wonder whether Darwin's belief in the rationality of his science still owed something to his residual theism.⁷⁵ The fact is that theism and agnosticism were far from mutually exclusive. As Lightman has emphasized, agnosticism in the Victorian period very often meant an *affirmation* of theism combined with uncertainty on specific matters of religious doctrine.⁷⁶ It would be foolish to pretend that Darwin did not offend many religious sensibilities, and still does in some quarters. But he continued to say that he had never been an atheist, in the sense of denying the existence of a God.⁷⁷ What difference then should Darwin make to the credibility of theism? Very little, if we accept the judgment of his main protagonist, T. H. Huxley. In his well-known account of the reception of the *Origin of Species*, Huxley insisted that Darwin's theory was perfectly compatible with belief in the prescient designer of an initial state of the universe from which all life had evolved. Darwinism had no more to do with theism than had the first book of Euclid.⁷⁸

72. John H. Brooke, "Revisiting Darwin on Order and Design," in *Design and Disorder: Perspectives from Science and Theology*, ed. Niels Henrik Gregersen and Ulf Gorman (London and New York: Continuum, 2002), pp. 31-52, esp. 36-38.

73. Bernard Lightman, "Victorian Sciences and Religions: Discordant Harmonies," *Osiris* 16 (2001): 343-366, esp. 355-362.

74. Lightman, "Victorian Sciences," p. 362.

75. Neal C. Gillespie, *Charles Darwin and the Problem of Creation* (Chicago: University of Chicago Press, 1979), pp. 144-145: "The theology of the *Origin* suggests that at one time, [for Darwin,] the rationality and moral probity of God underlay the rationality and meaningfulness of science."

76. Bernard Lightman, "Ideology, Evolution and Late-Victorian Agnostic Popularizers," in Moore, ed., *History, Humanity and Evolution*, pp. 285-309.

77. Darwin in F. Darwin, ed., *Life and Letters*, vol. 1, p. 304.

78. T. H. Huxley, "The Reception of the 'Origin of Species,'" in F. Darwin, ed., *Life and Letters*, vol. 2, pp. 179-204.

An Aesthetic Self?

The specification of aesthetic virtues has been closely linked to the development of science. In the universes of Copernicus, Kepler, and Newton, unity, symmetry, and harmony were prized epistemic virtues. Historically, reference to the aesthetic self has even allowed a theological justification of scientific activity. According to the eighteenth-century taxonomist Linnaeus, humans alone could appreciate the beauty of the Creator's works, from which it followed that science, as a privileged vehicle for revealing that beauty, was nothing less than a religious duty.[79] It would not normally be seen as a religious duty today; and yet it is striking how the writings of the secular Darwinians resonate with that earlier faith. Dawkins again:

> All the great religions have a place for awe, for ecstatic transport at the wonder and beauty of creation. And it's exactly this feeling of spine-shivering, breath-catching awe — almost worship — this flooding of the chest with ecstatic wonder, that modern science can provide. And it does so beyond the wildest dreams of saints and mystics.[80]

In a pre-Darwinian universe, appreciation of beauty in nature (for example, the song and plumage of birds) was often accompanied by the belief that it was a beauty designed, at least in part, for human delectation. Surely Darwin's theory of sexual selection made a difference? An elderly Mary Somerville certainly thought so. In Darwin's universe had not beauty been reduced to utility? As she put it, the beauty of nature is "irrelative to man's admiration or appreciation." It is not clear, however, that the blow was so decisive. If we ask whether the beauty we still perceive in the world should be conserved, we would usually answer yes, even if the birds sing for birds rather than for us. On this point of conservation, Mary Somerville herself was something of an activist, berating not the theories of males but the actions of members of her own sex. "Many women," she wrote, "without remorse allow the life of a pretty bird to be extinguished in order that they may deck themselves with its corpse." What might be seen as a female sensibility toward the preservation of beauty in the world could increase her sensitivity to a female foible.[81]

Again with reference to the aesthetic self, we might ask whether Darwin's

---

79. Brooke and Cantor, *Reconstructing Nature*, pp. 207-243, esp. 224.

80. Richard Dawkins, "Is Science a Religion?" *The Humanist* 57, no. 1 (1997), cited by Ruse, *Evolution-Creation Struggle*, p. 208.

81. John H. Brooke, "Does the History of Science Have a Future?" *British Journal for the History of Science* 32 (1999): 1-20, at 16-17.

theory of natural selection could explain how human minds had become so responsive to beauty. This is not an idle question because several of Darwin's scientific allies argued that there were features of the mind that natural selection was powerless to explain. Even Alfred Russel Wallace considered that mathematical prowess, musical ability, and our aesthetic sense eluded reductionist explanation. Because they were not universally distributed, it was not clear that they could have had survival value.[82] Even Darwin's beloved continuity between humans and animals almost lapsed as he reflected on the appreciation of beauty. Among the concluding remarks to his book on the emotions was the following assertion:

> It can hardly be doubted that many animals are capable of appreciating beautiful colours and even forms, as is shown by the pains which the individuals of one sex take in displaying their beauty before those of the opposite sex. But it does not seem possible that any animal, until its mental powers had been developed to an equal or near equal degree with those of man, would have closely considered and been sensitive about its own personal appearance.[83]

Blushing was strictly for humans.

A Suffering Self?

Darwin was no stranger to suffering. Incapacitated for days at a time, his wretched symptoms have been ascribed to both physical and psychosomatic causes — the latter because of his nurturing of a theory he knew would be disruptive of cherished beliefs.[84] When his daughter Annie died early in 1851, a deeper existential suffering took hold. The cost to Darwin's residual faith has been brilliantly analyzed by James Moore.[85] Why would a beneficent God permit such an innocent child to suffer and die? In his desperate correspondence with his wife Emma during Annie's demise, Darwin tacitly referred to a trust in God.[86] But behind his cruel loss was a philosophical issue that, in less

---

82. M. J. Kottler, "Alfred Russel Wallace, the Origin of Man, and Spiritualism," *Isis* 65 (1974): 145-192.
83. Darwin, *Expression of the Emotions*, p. 363.
84. Adrian Desmond and James Moore, *Darwin* (London: Michael Joseph, 1991), p. 233.
85. Moore, ed., *History, Humanity and Evolution*, pp. 195-229.
86. Charles Darwin to Emma Darwin, April 21, 1851, in *The Correspondence of Charles Darwin*, ed. Frederick Burkhardt, vol. 5 (Cambridge: Cambridge University Press, 1989), p. 20.

emotional moments, he would articulate with stark clarity. The existence of so much pain and suffering in the world was one of the strongest arguments against belief in a beneficent deity; and yet it was what one would expect on the theory of natural selection.[87] This latter consistency was the new challenge in the context of an age-old theological problem. In a sense the theologians' problem had become Darwin's solution — a solution to a different problem: how new species may derive from old.

What difference did this make? Is it even possible that Darwin's solution might mitigate the theodicy problem? Modern theologians have sometimes been tempted to say so, and it is interesting to see how quickly the idea was seized by Darwin's contemporaries. His American correspondent Asa Gray adopted it in his attempts to reconcile natural selection with natural theology: without the competition, the pain, the suffering, there would have been no motor to drive an evolutionary process that had led to the creation of human beings. The Darwinian struggle for existence had been a *sine qua non* of the possibility of human beings emerging.[88] Cruelty and wastage in nature had to be subsumed under a broader economy. Whether this would have given Darwin consolation on the death of Annie is a moot point; but, in the early drafts of his theory, he had toyed with a new theodicy. On a separate creation view, the Creator had to be directly responsible for even the most repulsive of creatures — a whole train, Darwin noted, of "vile molluscous animals"[89] — including the wretched ichneumon, which laid its eggs in the bodies of caterpillars. But suppose species evolved through an interplay of secondary causes, a creative interplay between random and determinate processes? One might then argue that a world in which it had been possible for humans to evolve was a world in which less congenial forms could also emerge. Perhaps this might to some degree exonerate the deity, just as Descartes had once argued that his mechanistic embryology absolved God of direct responsibility for monstrous births? To those interested in developing such a theodicy Darwin did make a difference but, potentially at least, in ways favorable to religious reflection. It has also proved possible to see in the Darwinian focus on suffering a gift to theology in an additional respect — in the opportunity it affords to reemphasize the compassion of the suffering Christ, identifying with a world groaning in travail.[90] To other religious thinkers Darwin made virtually no difference at all. His critique of

---

87. Barlow, ed., *Autobiography of Darwin*, p. 90.

88. Asa Gray, *Darwiniana*, ed. A. Hunter Dupree (Cambridge, MA: Harvard University Press, 1963), pp. 310-311.

89. Brooke, "Relations between Darwin's Science and Religion," pp. 46-47.

90. John F. Haught, *God after Darwin: A Theology of Evolution* (Boulder: Westview Press, 2000), pp. 45-56.

Paley's physico-theological argument from contrivance to Contriver held no terrors for John Henry Newman, who, in his *Idea of a University*, had already rejected the physico-theologies of the scientists on the ground that they had nothing to say about the fundamentals of Christian doctrine.[91]

Conclusion

What is the point of tracking all these nuances? Surely we know only too well that Darwin's science has been the inspiration for secular constructs explicitly hostile to religious sensibility and discourse. Returning to where I began, we know only too well that latter-day Darwinians invoke his name to underpin the greatest challenge of all — the challenge to an *integrated* self, as competing mental states are conceived to vie with each other to be the one that momentarily irrupts into consciousness. But there is a rationale for the strategy I have adopted in this essay. It is to show how the invocation of incommensurable worldviews and a supposed irresolvable conflict between them can itself be simplistic. There were ways of interpreting Darwin's theory, some proposed by Darwin himself, that simply do not fit a simple dualism between the sacred and the profane. Those who habitually invoke a clash of worldview often have polemical reasons for so doing. Here is Daniel Dennett in *Darwin's Dangerous Idea*, referring to Teilhard de Chardin's *Phenomenon of Man*: "The problem with Teilhard's vision is simple. He emphatically denied the fundamental idea: that evolution is a mindless, purposeless, algorithmic process."[92] I am not myself a devotee of Teilhard; but we should note how Dennett squeezes him out of the picture by having him condemned by orthodox Darwinism as well as by orthodox Catholicism. It is in Dennett's interest to exclude all mediating positions, just as it tends to be for young-earth creationists. But there is a tacit admission by Dennett himself that the strategy does not quite work. In a revealing footnote he has to concede that "Teilhard's book had an unlikely champion in England, Sir Julian Huxley, one of the contributors to — indeed, the baptizer of — the modern synthesis." Dennett even admits that some of the doctrine he is supporting can be found in Teilhard. Consequently "some of Teilhard's views can certainly be applauded by some orthodox Darwinians."[93] Though this footnote ends less propitiously, there are perhaps spaces for dialogue after all.

---

91. Nicolaas A. Rupke, *The Great Chain of History: William Buckland and the English School of Geology, 1814-1849* (Oxford: Oxford University Press, 1983), p. 271.
92. Dennett, *Darwin's Dangerous Idea*, p. 320.
93. Dennett, *Darwin's Dangerous Idea*, p. 321.

III. THEOLOGICAL EXPLORATIONS

17 How Music Models Divine Creation and Creativity

Arthur Peacocke

Whosoever is harmonically composed, delights in harmony; which makes me much distrust the symmetry of those heads which declaim against all Church-Musick. For my self, not only from my obedience, but my particular Genius, I do embrace it: for even that vulgar and Tavern-Musick, which makes one man merry, another mad, strikes in me a deep fit of devotion, and a profound contemplation of the first Composer. There is something in it of Divinity more than the ear discovers: it is an Hieroglyphical and shadowed lesson of the whole World, and creatures of God; such a melody to the ear, as the whole World well understood, would afford the understanding. In brief, it is a sensible fit of that harmony, which intellectually sounds in the ears of God.

Sir Thomas Browne, Religio Medici, 1642

Creation with Time

Most of us can recall, I think, how — as we grew through childhood — we began to acquire a sense of our self-identity and to ask, Who am I? and, perhaps later, What am I here for? This growth in our sense of self is paralleled by a growing awareness of the world as distinct from this newly discovered self, and we wonder at the sheer givenness of the world in which we are set. Before and behind the desolation and tragedies that we experience, there does in-

---

This essay is a condensed and modified version of the first and second "movements," written by Arthur Peacocke, of *The Music of Creation* by Arthur Peacocke and Ann Pederson (Minneapolis: Augsburg-Fortress Press, in press).

deed lie the sheer givenness and wonder of the world. We are all impelled to ask that mystery-of-existence question which haunted the Ionian Greeks when science was born: Why is there anything at all?

The profound prose-poem of the first chapter of Genesis that opens the Hebrew Bible is a response to this perennial question posed by humanity. In it, "God" acts directly by "letting be" the different kinds of existence. "And God said, Let there be . . . ; and there was . . ." (Gen. 1:3, AV) is how God is depicted as creating "the heavens and the earth" (1:1, AV). The relationships between what is thereby given existence are established, in that seminal work, simply by a commanding word of the Creator: "And God made the firmament and divided the waters. . . . *And God said,* Let the waters under the heavens be gathered together. . . . *And God said,* Let the earth bring forth . . ." (1:7, 9, 11, AV), etc. This manner of creating is echoed much later in the Bible in the Prologue to the Gospel of John: "In the beginning was the Word, and the Word was with God, and the Word was God. The same was in the beginning with God. All things were made by him; and without him was not anything made that was made" (John 1:1-3, AV). Here the "Word" (*Logos* in the Greek) is God in God's mode as Creator, and scholarship has shown that, in the milieu which the author was addressing, this *Logos* was a conflation of the active, creative self-expression of the "word of the Lord" of the God of the Hebrews and the inbuilt principle of rationality of the world that the Greeks saw as especially reflected in human rationality, which was thereby empowered to discern that basis of universal, cosmic order.

However, these traditional considerations, potentially richly significant as they indeed are, still leave most of us with a lacuna in our imaginative resources for explicating what meaning could, or might, be attributed to speaking of God, the Ultimate Reality, as "giving existence to" something other than God, that is, to everything that is. There is an enigma concerning this emergence of reality from the non-real, this birth of the temporal from the non-temporal. Can a more "local habitation and a name" be given to this "coming into existence" that might be grasped more intuitively?

I suggest that the experience of *music*[1] can afford the very imaginative and metaphorical resources we need for this and other purposes to enrich our apprehension of creation — and one cannot but think immediately of the mystery and wonder of the opening of Joseph Haydn's *Creation,* which splendidly tracks the Genesis text. Pertinently, "Ring out, ye crystal spheres" recalls

---

1. Note that this essay does not concern the very proper, long-hallowed use of music to express by its content Christian devotion and aspirations, but rather the form and nature of music *in itself* to model divine creation and creativity.

Milton in his *Ode on the Morning of Christ's Nativity* and thereby reminds us of the ancient notion that the rotation of the planets made a harmonious sound, humming the joy of God in creation. The idea goes back to Pythagoras, who identified the numerical relation between the harmonics of a string with that between the orbits of the planets. And the ancient Hebrews, too, as we hear from the book of Job, thought of "the morning stars" singing together in a chorus of joy at creation: "Whereupon are the foundations [of the earth] fastened? or who laid the cornerstone thereof; When the morning stars sang together, and all the sons of God shouted for joy?" (Job 38:6-7, AV).

However, today we are much more likely to ask: Why does the world manifest the implicit rationality and beauty that the scientist and artist discern? or, perhaps, influenced by science itself, How did there come to be matter, energy, space, and time, all so closely related in Einstein's famous equation? Indeed, we might well think it hopeful to turn to science to answer such fundamental questions about our very existence. Science is, in fact, concerned with *origins*, that is, in tracing the existence of everything as far back *in* time as it can go. The sciences can indeed extrapolate back to some 13 billion years ago to that singularity popularly called the Hot Big Bang when all matter and energy were concentrated in a minute space of unimaginably high density and temperature. From this point in our clock time the universe expanded, forming the space our radio-telescopes scan today.

But what happened at or "before" the Hot Big Bang? Theoretical physicists — recognizing the intimate interlocking of space, time, matter, and energy — strain to penetrate this most difficult of all the questions that nature poses by attempting to combine in one theory the well-established theories of fundamental physics.[2] Although they have had some successes with postulating that there was an "inflationary" period of extremely rapid expansion that preceded in time that expansion the course of which astrophysicists have been able to track, this does not settle the basic problem about the emergence of matter-energy in space-time. Currently there is intense investigation and speculation[3] about some Grand Unified Theory (G.U.T.) unifying the funda-

---

2. Quantum mechanics, relativity, and gravitational theory.

3. Proposals include: quantum fluctuations in a quantum field (which is certainly not "nothing" even if not a "thing") giving rise to matter-energy; superstring and M-theories that postulate filaments whose vibrations give rise to what were previously thought of as "elementary" particles and that require, respectively, ten or eleven dimensions that *include* the usual four, three of space and one of time (see Brian Greene, *The Fabric of the Cosmos* [New York: A. A. Knopf, 2004]); and the distinction between time and space breaking down in or around the singularity (see S. Hawking, *A Brief History of Time* [London: Bantam and Transworld, 1988]).

mental four natural forces and even about a "Theory of Everything" (T.o.E). But would they explain why there is anything at all, that mystery-of-existence question already posed? Scarcely, for in principle they cannot say *why* the relationships and laws are actually what they are and *why* they should operate at all, for they are not logically necessary. Beautiful and intellectually exhilarating though the G.U.T. and/or T.o.E. would be if and when discovered, it would still not explain its own existence and efficacy.

We are not here asking what happened "before" the Hot Big Bang since our clock time itself is so inherently related to the emergence of matter-energy; instead we are asking why there should be relationships of this kind at all that might begin to explain the origin of the universe with time. It transpires that there can be no scientific account of the very existence of a universe of this kind, for all-that-is is contingent, since all could have been otherwise.

It is in response to such questions that theists affirm that the world does not just happen to be — that it owes its origin to an ultimate Being. The doctrine of creation, as it is more formally called, is *not* about what happened at a point *in* time and space, for both of these are aspects of the created order. To affirm that the world is a creation means that it is all the time and everywhere given existence and has been endowed with being and becoming by an ultimate self-existent Reality other than itself — that Reality we name, in English, as "God" who transcends all that is created.[4] Although the sciences cannot account for the actual existence of the world, their success, which is based on the application of human rationality and experiment, does confirm the underlying unity and oneness of all-that-is. They point to the world being one and intricately interconnected in space and time by regular relationships often expressible in terms of mathematics. Moreover, the world is richly diverse in its manifestations, both in living and non-living systems. So the source of its existence, "God," must be of unfathomable richness — a diversity in a profound unity. Here I seek to show how features of music and the experience of it can enrich, inform, and stimulate our imagination and intuition of the nature of divine creation of the world — a world now revealed to us by the sciences as affording an even richer and more profound context for the image of God as the supreme Creator-Composer, the incomparable Improviser, than we have ever had before.

---

4. See Arthur Peacocke, *Paths from Science towards God* (Oxford: Oneworld, 2001), chs. 3-7.

Creation as a Coming into Existence

A Coming into Existence with Time of Patterns

Consider first how music, and the experience of it, might illuminate the notion, fundamental to many religious traditions, that the real is created out of the non-real, that creation by God is *creatio ex nihilo*, that all-that-is and all-that-has-been and, indeed, that all-that-will-be is "given existence" by an Ultimate Reality — God — who/which is other than what is created. For the principal stress, for example, in the Judeo-Christian doctrine of creation is on the dependence on God of all entities and events: it is about a perennial relationship of all-that-is to God, and not about the beginning of the Earth or of the whole universe at a point in time. It is an affirmation that any particular event or entity would not happen or would not be at all were it not for the sustaining creative will and activity of God.

In accord with ancient insights, time along with space, matter, and energy, has had to be conceived, since Einstein, as inherent in and intrinsic to the very nature of the created world and closely interlocked, as the equations of relativistic physics that relate them continue to be corroborated. God, as the self-existent Ultimate Reality, is thus to be conceived as giving existence to each segment of time, "all the time," as it were — that is, if God ceased to will the existence of each successive moment with all its events and their interrelations, they simply would not *be* at all. So time is in itself a positive (and not evil, as some have alleged) intrinsic feature of a world declared as created "very good" (Gen. 1:31, AV) in the Judeo-Christian tradition.

Many have been accustomed to think of "creation" as an event *in* time — at, say, 4004 BCE, if we follow Archbishop Ussher in the eighteenth century, or even 13 billion years ago if, like many astrophysicists today, we confuse the Hot Big Bang "origin" with that "creation" — so the notion of creation *with* time does not come at all easily. It is at this point that music can be an imaginative resource.

But *from* what may God be said to be creating? The "nothing," the *nihil* referred to in the classical assertion that God creates *ex nihilo*, is indeed non-existence and can be depicted only by what it lacks: it is without time, timeless, and without order, a chaos where no forms have duration warranting their being described as existent, as entities capable of being named, the "formless void" of the opening of Genesis (Gen. 1:2, NRSV). It is such a *nihil*, such a timeless state, that Haydn depicts musically, and remarkably, in "The Representation of Chaos," the slow orchestral introduction to his oratorio, *The Creation*. With outstanding originality he used what might at first sight appear the recalcitrant, and to us formal, resources of late-eighteenth-century Classical music (aleatoric music being then unheard of) to create an impression of formlessness and so of ambiguity and a sense of mystery.

Because Haydn was steeped in, indeed was himself one of the originators of, the Classical style of the 1790s, the work is not, on critical analysis, entirely formless. Indeed, just before the narrating angel, Raphael, starts the oratorio by announcing "In the beginning God created the heavens and the earth," the music superbly evokes the sense of fragments of order appearing kaleidoscopically with a hint of a sense of succession and so of the emergence of segments of time. Patches of ordered patterns in the form of short arpeggios are, almost randomly, dispersed throughout this "Representation of Chaos."

It is tantalizingly significant that a rising arpeggio also dominates the supreme musical instantiation of the coming into existence with time of patterned order — the musically unique opening bars of the Prelude to *Rheingold,* the beginning of Wagner's *Ring* cycle. At first, there is the nothingness of the pregnant silence of the audience — usually, and certainly in Bayreuth's Festspielhaus, almost palpable in its intensity of anticipation; then, coming not so much from the abysmal depths of earth and sea as from before the dawn of time, an E flat from eight double basses and then bassoons, so quiet and low that it is felt through the skin rather than heard through the ears, followed by an almost painfully long pause. Then a succession of very low, faint notes of the rising major chord of E flat; persistently, imperturbably, relentlessly the horn notes ascend, building up the chord, calm but swelling in sound and gathering momentum with strings and woodwind until they merge into a reiterated stream of undulating sound (arpeggios) to become the music of the surging, swirling waters of the Rhine. We have been witnessing the beginning of the world, the emergence of the beginning of the state of nature, for that chord based on E flat (in both its major and minor forms) is the basis of all the subsequent motives in the *Ring* that represent the idea of nature in its various manifestations.

The curtain rises and we find ourselves submerged *in* the Rhine's water — water, the symbol of the primordial chaos at the world's beginning in the ancient Babylonian and biblical myths. In the myths, order is created from and out of the mythical waste of waters, and in the *Ring* cycle primal form arrives with the native progeny of the Rhine, the Rhinemaidens, whose voices float above its lower pulse. Wagner has conducted us, subtly but surely, from nothingness into primal form with time.

A Coming into Existence with Time of Moving Patterns

The musical examples exemplify, and give precision and meaning to, another aspect of the mysterious creation of time: how the potential becomes actual. We perceive through them that time is sensed only through what is experienced as movement, the movement of shifting patterns — the same *becomes* different. The existence of time is established with the emerging *movement* out of nothing, and to be movement is to be movement of something, so that entities come into existence with process. In both of our musical examples so far, the arpeggios — at first fragmentary in Haydn, explicit in Wagner — are gradually woven into and give way to larger units that are transformed into even richer complexes.

There is an ebb and flow between these new patterns of sound at their various stages of elaboration, a kind of polarity, differentiation, and articulation that is rather like the rhythm of breathing. So, in both this music and in Creation itself, there is first the undifferentiated, the inchoate, then a gradual transformation into identifiable and perceivable forms possessing duration, followed by patterns of periodic exchange in the succession of these forms, which begin to be articulated as distinct entities. These latter constitute the discrete organizing beats of *rhythm*, the birth of which itself characterizes created time with its content of created entities. Rhythm unfolds the possibilities of polarization and differentiation that time possesses; and, just as the rhythm of breathing is essential to life, so is rhythm essential to creation. Thus it is significant that images of breath/spirit/wind appear in the opening of the Genesis account of divine creation and some thousand years even earlier in the Hindu "Creation Hymn" of the *Rig-Veda:*

> There was not non-existent nor existent; there was
>   no realm of air, no sky beyond it.
> What covered in, and where? And what gave shelter?
> Was water there, unfathomed depth of water?
> Death was not then, nor was there aught immortal: no
> Sign was there, the day's and night's divider.
> *That One Thing, breathless, breathed by its own nature:*
> Apart from it was nothing whatsoever.[5]

The emphasized line implies some kind of rhythmic process symbolized as breathing, a moving between two poles. Going from nothing to something

---

5. "Creation Hymn" of the *Rig-Veda,* ed. R. O. Ballou, The Pocket World Bible (London: Routledge and Kegan Paul, 1948), p. 30.

is as if a point (one, timeless) becomes a line with an added dimension ("time") capable of curving into a variety of shapes ("creation" of entities) singled out by intervals and peaks. All of which is the secret of rhythm in music, which thereby illuminates divine creation *with* time that involves permanence as a pattern of change, change *in* permanence.

Furthermore, physical reality, especially as revealed by quantum mechanics and relativity theory, has several characteristics: its incompleteness of becoming and its pulsational character; the compatibility of the emergence of novelty with past causal influences; the individuality of events within the continuity of flux; the impossibility of instantaneous space and of simultaneous time and their replacement by that of "co-becoming." These are not readily visualized. Hence, in the light of the themes already developed here, it is not surprising that a number of authors have proposed that a source of models of, or analogies for, such imageless, dynamic patterns that might model conceptually the scientifically discovered dynamic nature of physical reality is to be found in the musical experience. For example, A. N. Whitehead long ago noted in his organic theory of the nature of the physical world that

> a pattern need not endure in undifferentiated sameness through time. The pattern may be essentially one of aesthetic [that is, qualitative] contrasts requiring a lapse of time for its unfolding. *A tune is an example of such a pattern.* Thus the endurance of the pattern now means the reiteration of its successions of contrasts.[6]

In ordinary experience, "movement" refers to progression through *space* at succeeding times, yet time has been the focus of our discussion so far, for when one thinks of *moving* in music, the involvement of time is instinctively discerned — but what corresponds to "space" in music? It has been claimed that, just as visual icons are "multidimensional" for Orthodox Christians, so "music attempting to be an icon may well be pan-dimensional."[7] Although rhythm clearly contributes to the sense of movement in music by adding, as it were, an extra dimension to characterize particular points, or succession of points, in time, equally determining roles are attributed by musicologists to other factors: melody, often thought of as the *horizontal* dimension of music (even though it depends on "pitch"); harmony and counterpoint, similarly thought of as the *vertical* dimension; and timbre and texture (com-

---

6. A. N. Whitehead, *Science and the Modern World* (New York: Macmillan, 1926), p. 193; emphasis added.

7. Ivan Moody, "Icons in Music? Two Works by Taverner," *Sobornost* 1 (1988): 37.

binations of different timbres), almost another dimension. Music can thereby contribute to our apprehension of that sense of the balance of becoming and passing which is also manifest in the evolving complexes of the natural world, and so it enriches our understanding of the natural world as "the creation."

The subtleties and complex possibilities in music are paralleled by those of the created order in another respect, reference to which has already occurred *en passant* — namely, that the moving patterns that come into existence with time have potentialities that are actualized only *in* time.

Creation in Time

From what has been said so far, it is increasingly apparent that music can be a very rich resource for unraveling the subtle relation between divine creation and time, for music releases us from our mechanistic perception of physical time, the time marked by the clocks that dominate modern life. One has only to look at the accelerating processes of cosmic and biological evolution to realize that equal intervals of clock time do not have equal significance. Expositors of the world of science have frequently found that one needs, for example, a logarithmic scale to denote clearly the succession of various distinct stages in natural processes. Clock time does not provide an adequate metric. The same can be said also of the psychological experience of time, the rate of whose passage varies widely according to the content of what is being experienced. For all of us, time can "amble, trot, gallop and stand still," in "divers paces with divers persons."[8]

Because time is its medium, music can show time as a basic aspect of reality in a way relevant to the processes both of creation, which science unveils, and of our individual psychology, for "music is temporal art in the special sense that in it time reveals itself to experience."[9] Listening to music can reveal to us what time really is, for musical time brings to expression experiential aspects of reality that physical (clock) time is unable to do. Zuckerkandl[10] has been especially percipient in making this contrast in the following way:

---

8. Rosalind in Shakespeare's *As You Like It*, Act 3, scene 2, ll. 301-4, in William Shakespeare, *Complete Works* (Oxford: Clarendon Press, 1988).

9. V. Zuckerkandl, *Sound and Symbol* (London: Routledge and Kegan Paul, 1956), p. 200.

10. Zuckerkandl, *Sound and Symbol*, p. 202.

Physical Time Concept	Musical Time Concept
Time is order, form of experience	Time is content of experience
Time measures events	Time produces events
Time is divisible into equal parts	Time knows no equality of parts
Time is perpetual transience	Time knows nothing of transience

The "musical time concept," as he calls it, clearly corresponds closely to the characteristics of "creation" time, that is, to what has happened in the processes of cosmological and biological creation. Here we shall look more closely at the way in which musical time can illuminate our perception of these processes, for music is fundamentally involved with ordered changes of structure, with a flux that is not chaotic. It unfolds a temporal sequence and simultaneously reveals total patterns — both of which the scientist characteristically seeks in interpreting natural processes, seeing time as "the carrier or locus of innovative change."[11] Hence, as Jeremy Begbie urges, "music can be most theologically [and we would add, scientifically] fruitful precisely in and through its ability to interact positively with time, and this is closely bound up with its thoroughly physical character."[12]

What features of musical time might be significant for our perception of creation?

The Relation of Past, Present, and Future

In music there is an unfolding in time of the composer's intentions, and the significance of any given moment is constituted both by what precedes it and by the way it forms a growth point for what follows. Past, present, and future interpenetrate each other: just as the scientist amalgamates natural sequences into one theoretical structure, so too the time sequence of musical experiences can often be apprehended in the memory as an organic complex. Yet particular notes, rhythms, harmonies, and dissonances — all that constitutes the music — have a different impact on the listener according to what has gone before. Each instantaneously experienced effect itself is the initiating point of and gives a distinctive meaning to its sequel. This is analogous to the way in which any meaning and significance we might wish to attribute to any

---

11. Harold K. Schilling, *The New Consciousness in Science and Religion* (London: SCM Press, 1973), p. 126.

12. J. Begbie, "Theology and Music in the Arts," in *The Modern Theologians*, ed. David F. Ford, 2nd ed. (Oxford: Blackwell, 1997), p. 688.

given stage of the world's natural history are dependent both on what precedes and on what follows the point in question. At any instant, then, music leans, as it were, toward the future, the basis of which is that, in a series of tones, each tone has a dynamic quality that signals incompleteness and a pointing toward the next expected tone. "Listening to music, then, we are not first in one tone, then in the next, and so forth. We are, rather, always *between* the tones, *on the way* from tone to tone; our hearing does not remain with the tone, it reaches through it and beyond it."[13]

Music and Creation as Process

This inbuilt anticipatory character of music raises an interesting question. Is a piece of music — say, a Beethoven sonata — therefore played *toward* its closing cadences as if that were its goal? Surely not. What matters, what is intrinsically valuable, is the experience of playing, and listening to, it. Although a given human work of musical composition attains a kind of finality in its closing cadence, it would be nonsense to suggest that the "meaning" of a musical work was to be found only there. Each instant, with its concurrent stored memory of the past as the ambience of the present and its ability to be forming the reaction to the music yet to be heard, has a significance that is *sui generis* and takes its meaning from its relation to the whole that is being gradually unfolded. The significance is in the *process*, as such.

This provides an important clue to how we should apprehend the presence of God in creation. For, since coming into existence with time is of the essence of and intrinsic to creation, music helps us to understand creation through understanding time and its potentialities. Hence it is appropriate that a model of the world as the music of the divine Creator-Composer also illuminates God's relation to the human listener to that music of creation as it unfolds in time. The model also properly includes the listener to a musical work — say, to that Beethoven piano sonata — and recognizes that there are times when one can be so deeply absorbed in it that for a moment one is actually thinking the music *with* the composer. In such moments we experience

> music heard so deeply
> That it is not heard at all, but you are the music
> While the music lasts.[14]

---

13. Zuckerkandl, *Sound and Symbol*, pp. 136-137, and passim.
14. T. S. Eliot, "The Dry Salvages," *The Four Quartets*, ll. 210-212.

Yet if anyone were to ask at that moment, Where is Beethoven now? one would have to reply that Beethoven-as-composer was to be found only in the music itself. The music would in some sense be Beethoven's inner musical thought kindled in us, and we would genuinely be encountering Beethoven-as-composer. The whole experience is one of profound communication from composer to listener. This very closely models God's immanence in creation and God's self-communication in and through what God is creating. The processes revealed by the sciences are in themselves God acting as Creator, and God is not to be found as some kind of additional factor added on to the processes of the world. God, to use language usually applied in sacramental theology, is "in, with, and under" all-that-is and all-that-goes-on. In reflecting profoundly on the world, and worlds, unveiled by the sciences, we can indeed also experience in those moments the immanence of the transcendence of God as Creator of all-that-is. As scientific "listeners" to the music of creation, we encounter its Creator.

"Ends" in Music and Creation

Although the conclusion of a well-constructed musical composition is not its *goal*, nevertheless when it does arrive the listener experiences a sense of completion and, in that sense, a consummation, a rounding-off, of the whole organic, complex growth of the work. Such endings usually, in the Western tonal music with which we are here concerned, consist in well-recognized cadences in which a harmonic chord is followed by one based on the tonic key of that piece of music. Jeremy Begbie has shrewdly pointed out[15] that in some works the end is anticipated by the earlier occurrence of the concluding cadence. He argues convincingly that this expresses the capacity of historical time to mirror anticipatorily consummatory events of spiritual significance, and he develops this in relation to Jesus' resurrection and the consummation of history in traditional Christian eschatology. Might this not also be applied to the processes of divine creation, especially to biological evolution in which crucial transitions occur whose significance is fully realized only in relation to wider wholes? One could instance the movement of amphibia onto land, when oxygen was breathed directly, and also the development of elementary brains and nervous systems. Each stage might have the appearance of closure and might seem to be the culmination of a long, preceding process act, whereas in a longer perspective it can be seen indeed as the prefiguring of a

---

15. J. S. Begbie, *Theology, Music and Time* (Cambridge: Cambridge University Press, 2000), pp. 111ff.

later consummation in a more complex organism and environment. Again, it is the *process* that is significant.

Resolution of Tension and Repetition

One of the widely agreed characteristics of Western tonal music is that it involves a basic tonal structure that has been described[16] as that of equilibrium-tension-resolution, where "tension" refers to a wide range of musical situations that arouse a sense of anticipation and incompleteness, a sense that something else must follow. The means whereby this pattern is basically effected are, broadly speaking, rhythm and melody. Meter bears a complex relation to rhythm, which "refers to the variegated pattern of durations given in a succession of tones."[17] Melody is a series of tones possessing a dynamic quality through the relation of the notes to the context of a "key," which is a series of notes proceeding upward from a "tonic" note to form a scale (major or minor in most Western music, but not confined to these). Different combinations of the notes of such scales, because of their various kinds of interrelatedness, produce different kinds of harmonies, and some sequences of these harmonies, "cadences," engender to varying degrees a sense of anticipation succeeded by closure and completion.

Begbie has illuminatingly related this basic feature of music as equilibrium-tension-resolution to the narrative of creation-fall-redemption in the Christian tradition, with its future-directedness and concomitant need for patience in the face of delay and the incompleteness of the present.[18] In this perspective, the processes of divine redemption are slow and often hardly discernible; and, in the context of this volume, one sees a parallel in the slow, patient operation of divine creativity through the eons of cosmic and biological evolution that have led to the emergence of sentient self-conscious persons capable of a dynamic, personal, and fulfilling relation to their Creator. "A thousand years in thy sight are but as yesterday when it is past, and as a watch in the night" (Ps. 90:4, AV).

Musical processes, like natural ones, frequently involve repetition, sometimes exact but more often with subtle changes. Repetition within a piece of music, whether immediate or remote, does not lead to boredom, for it always

---

16. See Begbie, *Theology, Music and Time*, p. 30, for the musicological literature relevant to this statement.
17. Begbie, *Theology, Music and Time*, p. 41; the comments here depend on the exposition in his chapter 2, "Music's Time."
18. Begbie, *Theology, Music and Time*, chapter 4, "Resolution and Salvation."

expresses a difference in sameness. However, "What is striking about music is that relations of sameness would appear to play a more crucial role than relations of difference."[19] Clearly, with no explicit external reality being denoted in music, repetition is essential for imprinting the shape of any section of music so that it can be recognized again and produce a sense of coherence and of intelligible form.

The processes of natural creation likewise establish over very long periods what at first appear to be but a mere repetition of the form, say, of a biological organism. But its context of other organisms, both predatory and symbiotic, and of climate and geology can change, so that its role in the ecosystem in which it is embedded is subtly modified, and the possibilities of its own future evolution are thereby modified over a longer period of time than is obvious in that shorter term over which its stability is so first noted by the biologist.

Time as "Very Good"

The first chapter of Genesis famously concludes (v. 31) with the judgment that "God saw everything and, indeed, it was very good." However, it has sometimes been deemed that time — because of its ability to dissolve all humanly created physical and social structures — is contrary to all order and undermines all that is good and reestablishes chaos. However, the musicologist Zuckerkandl strongly opposes "the dogma that order is possible only in the enduring, the immutably fixed, the substantial" and that music is "irreconcilable with order." For, he continues, "Hearing music, we experience a time whose being is no longer a swift flare-up in the passage from one nonexistence to another nonexistence, which reveals itself rather as a self-storing and self-renewal than as a transience. . . . Order, liberated from all relation to things, pure order, bodiless, detached, and free, not as a mere concept, not as a dream, but as a vision beheld — it is to music that we owe our awareness that such a thing can exist."[20] In music we experience ordered change that is *not* futile or inferior because it is transient, a dynamic process that can attain its perfection only through and by the passage of time. In music, time is therefore experienced as "very good" and assures us that, in spite of much to the contrary in our immediate experience, even short times can be fulfilling and creative. Music can reinforce the theological intuition that our limited span can be highly significant and life-enhancing,

---

19. Begbie, *Theology, Music and Time*, p. 156, and chapter 6, "Repetition and Eucharist," whose exposition we again gladly follow here.
20. Zuckerkandl, *Sound and Symbol*, p. 241.

for it can continuously bring forth new birth out of the death of dying notes, cadences, and sequences. Temporality is to be seen as a *good* gift of God, as expressed in Haydn's great choruses of *The Creation* — the familiar "The heavens are telling" and "Achieved is the glorious work" — which depict the continuing divinely created transformation of that primeval chaos that can still threaten our tranquility and peace of mind. Time is intrinsic to the order created by God: our time and God's eternity are not irrevocably incommensurate. Both are held in existence within God's own Being.

Time as the Locus of Innovative Change: Moving Patterns with Potential

For a century or so now, the scientific accounts of geology, biological evolution, and, more recently, cosmology have vindicated that description of time by the physicist Harold Schilling as "the carrier or locus of innovative change."[21] In and with time, atoms have emerged from quarks, molecules and macromolecules from atoms, living cells from self-copying macromolecules, organisms from cells, ecosystems from organisms. As we saw with music, out of notes there is similarly engendered melody, harmony, and timbre, which with time through meter and rhythm create musical forms. In a flight of fancy, Ursula Goodenough, cell biologist, can even write: "Patterns of gene expression are to organisms as melodies and harmonies are to sonatas. It's all about which sets of proteins appear in a cell at the same time (the chords) and which sets come before or after other sets (the themes) and at what rate they appear (the tempos) and how they modulate one another (the developments and transitions). When these patterns go awry we may see malignancy. When they change by mutation we can get new kinds of organisms. When they work, we get a creature."[22]

Theme and variations. Time in the created world unfolds the new, bringing out potentialities. Schilling's description of time can be pertinently applied to musical time, for music can be a kind of metaphor both for the processes of the world and for our individual, qualified experiences, which are never uniform or constant, but rather often patterned variations. In music, new melodies and developments emerge intelligibly, yet inventively, out of earlier themes and fragments; and similarly, in the processes of the world, new forms

---

21. Schilling, *New Consciousness in Science and Religion*, p. 126.
22. Ursula Goodenough, *The Sacred Depths of Nature* (New York: Oxford University Press, 1998), pp. 58-59.

develop from what precedes them — often surprisingly, though *post hoc* intelligibly in the light of the sciences. Composers often resort to creating variations on a theme. The *Goldberg Variations* — an essentially private work that J. S. Bach created for a harpsichordist to cheer the sleepless nights of his aristocratic employer — are based on the constancy of the fundamental, lower harmony of a sarabande (a form of dance) that Bach had earlier included in the notebook he made for his young wife, Anna Magdalena. One has to listen carefully to the *bass* in the deceptively simple opening aria (the sarabande), for it is this, rather than the delightful upper tune itself, that provides him in its simple, songlike symmetry with the opportunity to develop a wonderfully rich and diverse set of variations before finally returning to the aria, now invested with a rich significance that could not have been anticipated at the outset. Is there not here a parallel with the instances in biological evolution when some less obvious characteristic of a living organism is the locus controlled by a mutation that becomes, as it were, the launching pad for crucial developments that help the organism to survive in new circumstances?

Fugues and chance. It is also now clear from biological evolution and work on certain complex systems that, in the ongoing processes of the world, new forms of both inorganic and living matter emerge by a combination of what may be designated as "chance" and "law." To their mutual interplay is to be attributed the inherent creativity of the natural processes of the world. This has raised a question for any theistic doctrine of creation: how is the assertion of God as Creator to be interpreted, indeed rendered intelligible, in the light of this interplay between random chance at various levels and "necessity"? This necessity arises from the stuff of the world having its particular "given" properties and law-like behaviors, which can be regarded as possessing potentialities that are, as it were, written into creation by the Creator's intention and purpose and are gradually actualized by the wide-ranging exploration that the operation of what we call "chance" makes possible.

It is here that the nature of musical creativity in composing a fugue appears to be especially helpful as a model of God's creative activity. A fugue (from Latin *fuga*, "flight") is a musical form in which "three or more voices enter imitatively one after the other, each giving chase to the previous voice which 'flies' before it."[23] In a fugue there is an elaboration of simpler units according to (often conventional) rules — intermingled with much spontaneity, and even episodic surprise.

God as Creator "begins" with, as it were, the fundamental divinely created properties of space-time-matter-energy, which through their inherent

---

23. *The New Oxford Companion to Music* (Oxford: Oxford University Press, 1983), p. 731.

potentialities in time have become the diverse, complex, richly articulated world we observe today. As Creator, God might therefore now be seen as like a composer who, beginning with an arrangement of notes in an apparently simple subject, elaborates and expands them into new shapes by a variety of devices. Time does indeed "fly" as in a fugue. Thus J. S. Bach creates a complex and interlocking harmonious fusion of his seminal material, both through time and at any particular instant, which, while beautiful in its elaboration, reaches its consummation only when all the threads have been drawn into the return to the home key of the last few bars — the key of the initial melody whose potential elaboration was conceived from the moment it was first expounded. So God may be conceived of as aware of the potentialities of the order initially created in time, which become actualized through those interlocking, to us random, circumstances we call "chance."

The listener to such "flying" music experiences, with the luxuriant and profuse growth that emanates from the original simple structure, whole new worlds of emotional experience that are the result of the interplay between an expectation based on past experience ("law") and an openness to the new ("chance," in the sense that the listener cannot predict or control it). Thus might the Creator be imagined to give existence to the unfolding of the God-given potentialities of the universe, nurturing by divine redemptive and providential actions those that are to come to fruition in the community of free beings — an Improviser of unsurpassed ingenuity. God appears to do so by a process in which the creative possibilities, inherent (by divine intention) within the fundamental entities of that universe and their interrelations, become actualized within a temporal development shaped and determined by those self-same potentialities.

> There is no marvel greater or more sublime than the rules of singing in harmony together in several parts, unknown to the ancients but at last discovered by man, the ape of his Creator, so that, through the skilful symphony of many voices, he should actually conjure up in a short part of an hour the vision of the world's total perpetuity in time; and that, in the sweetest sense of bliss enjoyed through Music, the echo of God, he should almost reach the contentment which God the Maker has in His Own works.[24]

24. Johannes Kepler, in the translation of Karl Popper, *The Unended Quest* (Glasgow: Fontana/Collins, 1976), p. 59, based on the Latin text of D. Perrkin Walker, "Kepler's Celestial Music," *J. Warburg and Courtauld Institute* 30 (1967): 249ff., taken from J. Kepler, *Gesammelte Werke*, ed. Max Caspar (Munich, 1940), vol. 6, p. 328.

18 Four Gods of Christian Faith

Delwin Brown

Introduction

What is the location of God, as God is understood in Christianity? Or, as a child might put it, where is God? This may be an odd way to discuss Christian concepts of God, but I do not think it naïve, nor, as I hope to show, is it without important practical as well as theoretical implications. Thinking about Christian views of God in this way is important because whatever else the term "God" is or does for Christians, it denotes that which the believer thinks to be *most* important, that which is of ultimate concern. Thus, wherever it is that God is located, that is the domain or dimension of perceived reality which is ultimately important to the believer. On this dimension all other things of importance depend and from it their relative significance is derived. For this reason, the various ways of locating God tend to give rise to different forms of Christian existence, more specifically, to different types of Christian theology and different forms of disciplined Christian practice.

This essay examines four ways of locating God — God as source, God as agent, God as incarnate, and as God as goal. Further, it offers suggestions about the different forms of disciplined Christian life — forms of "spirituality" — toward which these views incline the believer. We should acknowledge at the outset that these different ways of locating God may and often do exhibit similarities, for example with respect to God's personality, power, and revelatory efficacy. In addition, we should recognize that in most of their formulations each position affirms elements of the others, at least as subordinate themes. Those who speak of God as agent (whether strongly as lord, or more reservedly as guide) will also insist that God is in some sense the source of creation and, further, is incarnate in it. Likewise, those who emphasize God as goal will also affirm that this eschatological reality is incarnate and is somehow an agent in the cosmos and human life. The differences between the positions are, indeed, matters of degree or emphasis.

These differences are important, however, because contained within each of these perspectives on God are particular vectors, inclinations toward distinctive ways of thinking, acting, and being as a Christian. Each perspective has certain strengths and deficiencies. In my judgment, moreover, each might be formulated as a conceptually defensible and pragmatically justifiable religious standpoint. But for our purposes in this discussion the important point is that they are distinctive perspectives on God and thus also distinctive perspectives on religious life and thought within Christianity. In other words, each view of God is, or can be made, a reasonable belief and a socially valuable belief — pragmatically speaking, a "true" belief. But it is interesting that they are not easily and, one might argue, not helpfully assimilated to one another. They may be, in certain formulations, plausible conceptions of compatible Gods, but they are not so obviously conceptions of the same God. All could conceivably be true beliefs, in one form or another, but they are not readily reducible to one another or combinable with each other — not without stretching the canons of theoretical plausibility to the breaking point, and, even more important for our present considerations, not without diminishing the practical genius of each perspective, its elucidation of a religious mode of life.

Four Views of God

God the Source

We begin with the point of view that locates God at the "beginning," as the grounding of all that is. In a sense this is simply to speak of God as "creator," but in a very special sense. Here God is creator, not as the one who starts things off, not as the cosmic first cause. Rather, God is claimed to be the immediate basis of everything in every moment. God is always anew the creator, ground, or source of all.

What this means can perhaps be clarified if we were to imagine that there has always been a world of some sort. In this case, God as the source or ground of things would not be its chronological beginning, because if the world is infinite then it would have had no beginning. Instead, God would be the source in the sense of being the underlying reality out of which this world continuously lives, the grounding of all things and each thing anew in every moment.

The philosophical way of stating this perspective is to ask, why is there something rather than nothing? Why is there anything at all? Those who ask the question say that the question is valid even if the "anything" that is had no beginning. Even if the world in its most comprehensive sense ("reality") is eternal one can still ask, why is there an eternal world, and not no world at all?

Critics respond that this is a foolish question. We cannot even imagine "nothing" or "no world at all," they say, so the question is simply a succession of words without meaning. The question makes no sense. Defenders reply that, on the contrary, it makes the most basic kind of sense because, finally, it is a way of naming the ultimate wonder of things. God, on this view, is the Mystery in whom we live and move and have our being. In speaking of God, we are speaking about the mysterious givenness of things.

If talk about God is indeed talk about what is ultimately important, then viewing God as source or ground, in the special sense described, would appear to have certain implications for Christian self-understanding. First, of course, is an encompassing sense of wonder. The paradoxical truth about things, ultimately, is that there are no ultimate answers. To be is to be filled with wonder. Yet, if the testimony of this tradition can be taken seriously, what often follows, secondly, is a sense of gratitude for the gift of participating in this mystery. In this sense, life itself is taken to be of value, a value that transcends considerations of how life is best lived, how things ought to be, or where things are going. These latter issues are not eliminated, but they are subordinated to a more important claim, namely, that life is a mysterious given of intrinsic value. Hence, to be is also to be grateful.

Wonder and gratitude do not eliminate other questions, such as how we ought to live, but they make these questions somewhat secondary. Further, the mysteriousness from which the gift of life comes makes answers to such questions always more than a bit tentative. After all, who can be dogmatic about the "will of God" if God is Mystery? We may hope to have the best indication possible in our human, fallible state about what is right and true, but in the final analysis the ways of God are not our ways, nor are the truths of God like ours. Not surprisingly, then, Christian piety based on this view of God emphasizes experience, not intellection, and typically the experience is said to be mystical in character.

This understanding of God has a long Christian heritage. In theology it is called the "apophatic" tradition, a term derived from a Greek word meaning "negation" or "denial." The positive point of the apophatic impulse is to recognize the mystery of God. Though usually not the dominant view in Christianity, this approach has almost always been present in its history. Pseudo-Dionysius, Meister Eckhart, Nicolus Cusanus, Julian of Norwich, Gregory of

Nyssa, Gregory Palamas, and Symeon the New Theologian express it in various ways. Apophaticism has been especially important in Eastern Christianity. And there are modern Western exemplars of this viewpoint to one degree or another, even in the twentieth century. Paul Tillich's "God above Gods" has sometimes been interpreted in this way,[1] as has H. Richard Niebuhr's "radical monotheism."[2] A more recent example can be found in the works of Robert C. Neville.[3] Neville's view is built on the assumption of God as Creator, the creator of all "determinate" things (i.e., things, we might say, that are this and not that). But if God is the source of all that is determinate, then God must be indeterminate. And whatever is indeterminate cannot be known in human categories because all of our thinking is predicated upon determinate distinctions.

Neville proceeds (questionably, one might argue) to say some quite specific things about God, but more commonly the apophatic tradition expresses its "knowledge" of God in mystical terms. It has usually been a quiet and generous mysticism, one that makes few claims to knowledge in any conventional sense. Christ, on this view, is usually said to mediate awareness of the Mystery and, conceptually, to teach us the vast difference between our ways and God's. The revelation in Christ underscores, rather than overcomes, our blessed ignorance. The Holy Spirit is the presence of the Mystery to us. What is sufficient for salvation is not a set of conceptual claims; it is a sense of immediate immersion in the Mystery that grounds all things.

God the Agent

A second way of locating deity is to think of God not as ground of the world, but as an agent within the world. That God is also creator, in some sense, is not denied, but the emphasis here is on God's agency, as lord or guide, in relation to the processes of nature and history. This is no doubt the most common way of locating God in Western Christianity and it takes many forms. Usually God is viewed as personal agent, a person who acts, but this view, too, has variations. For example, there is the historic debate about the efficacy of

---

1. Paul Tillich, *The Courage to Be* (New Haven: Yale University Press, 1952), pp. 186-190. These notes refer to the most representative, or in some cases the most popular, twentieth-century presentation of each point of view discussed.

2. H. Richard Niebuhr, *Radical Monotheism and Western Culture* (Lincoln: University of Nebraska Press, 1960).

3. Robert C. Neville, *Recovery of the Measure* (Albany: State University of New York Press, 1989); *A Theology Primer* (Albany: State University of New York Press, 1991), pp. 30-35.

the divine will. Does God will everything that transpires in nature and history or, instead, are some things permitted but not willed by God? In the modern period differences about the relationship of divine agency and the natural process became prominent. Is the natural system of causes and effects the way in which God's agency is manifest, or is God's agency to be found alongside, and sometimes in contradiction to, the natural process?

Most recently the discussion of God's agency has focused on divine power. Can God do anything God wants to do anytime God wants to do it, or are there limits on God's power? And if there are limits, are they voluntarily self-imposed by God, or are they for some reason necessary and unavoidable, even for God? "Free-will theists" contend that God freely chooses to limit God's power in order that humans, too, may have free choice.[4] Hartshornian process theologians, on the other hand, argue that there are, in addition to divine self-limitations, some limits to God's power about which even God has no choice.[5] Those who believe God's power is to some degree limited tend to speak of God as guide. Those who believe God's power to be absolute speak of God as lord.

While there are indeed differences within this view of God as agent, there are also commonalities. All agree that God is the fundamental agency that makes for right in the cosmic process. Here the intuitive focus is on divine action. God is efficacious by willing, not simply by being, and the divine volition issues forth in specific worldly activities that make a difference. These activities, moreover, are interactive; what happens in the world is thought somehow to affect God's activity. So the focus, too, is on history, including the history of the cosmos, of nature — not on inscrutable beginnings or endings, not on creation or eschatology. How is God acting in the world, and what does this tell us about God's will?

In this way of locating God, therefore, God is experienced as direction. That the nature of divinity is ultimately mysterious is not denied, but it is assumed that we do know enough about God and God's will to know what we should be doing to support the divine purposes. Divine actions are guides for human action. Views vary on the clarity of these guides. For example, if the

---

4. See, e.g., Clark H. Pinnock, *Most Moved Mover: A Theology of God's Openness* (Grand Rapids: Baker Book House, 2001); Clark H. Pinnock, Richard Rice, John Sanders, William Hasker, and David Basinger, *The Openness of God: A Biblical Challenge to the Traditional Understanding of God* (Downers Grove, IL: InterVarsity Press, 1994).

5. Charles Hartshorne, *The Divine Relativity: A Social Conception of God* (New Haven: Yale University Press, 1948); *Omnipotence and Other Theological Mistakes* (Albany: State University of New York Press, 1984); David Ray Griffin, *God, Power, and Evil: A Process Theodicy* (Philadelphia: Westminster Press, 1976; Lanham, MD: University Press of America, 1991).

words of Scripture are held to be God's direct "speech," then the guidance is as clear as the words themselves. If, instead, Scripture is taken to be the key, or a key, to finding divine guidance in personal experience, current events, and so forth, then the clarity of the divine direction will correlate with the specificity of these. But whether the focus is on the words of the Bible, the Word proclaimed through the Bible, the wisdom of the church, or the divine lure in nature, history, or personal experience, God is doing something in the broad here and now, and what God is doing gives direction to our lives.

Knowing God's will, however, is not passive; it is active, and in fact quite analytical. Indeed, locating God as the agent at work in the present generally leads to an emphasis on the importance of the intellect in the Christian life. Even for the serious biblical literalist, knowing God's will requires careful thought, a consideration of hermeneutical alternatives, a weighing of the textual evidence. Likewise, those who discern God's will through consensus in the Christian community depend in part on discussion, analysis, and mutual criticism within the church. Christians who look for guidance in broader "signs of the times" often place their theological readings in the context of secular systems of thought — sociological, philosophical, or scientific — in order to critique, transform, and support their judgments about God's will.

It should not be surprising, then, that this approach promotes a considerable degree of confidence about our knowledge of the will of God. And why not? In the Christian vision of things the human mind is one of the many gifts of God. It may be limited and fallible, even "fallen," but so is every other human capability. If these other "all too human" capabilities — emotion, experience, intuition, volition, discernment — may be relied upon despite their imperfections, then we are no less entitled to rely on our intellect, confident that it can and will lead us to an adequate, even if fallible, understanding of truth.

This way of locating God, therefore, is commonly associated with extensive theological systems or "systematic theologies." God is an active agent, a force in the cosmos — in nature, history and individual experience. That action is important because it is a reasonably specific guide to how we ought to live our lives. And it is discernable. The process of discernment, however, is an arduous endeavor, involving careful, self-critical, disciplined reflection. The theological systems of the Thomists, the Calvinists, the fundamentalists, the Barthians, the Hartshornian process theologians, the liberation theologians, and now the "post-conservative evangelicals" (or "openness theologians") — as different as they are in other ways — all illustrate this perspective.

God the Incarnate

Every form of distinctively Christian reflection about God assumes that God is to some degree incarnate. After all, Christians regularly speak of God's revelation in Jesus Christ, and this certainly is to claim that God is incarnate in some sense. But sending a message — even a quite extensive and vital message — is not the same as "being there." In the early church there arose the conviction not only that God speaks to us in Christ, but also that Christ means "God is with us," God is present. Even that claim, however, is not quite sufficient to capture the radical character of the "incarnationism" that developed in the first few centuries of Christian history. Certainly, God speaks and God is present, but there is more: The meaning of Christ is that God, in some very real sense, "is" us. The patristic theologians, such as Athanasius and Irenaeus, made this extraordinary claim for soteriological reasons. "What has not been assumed," they said, "cannot be healed." In this most radical sense, to speak of God the Incarnate is to say that in some way "God the savior" is "God the creature."

In the twentieth century this idea was articulated in ways that depart from anything remotely envisioned by theologians of the ancient church. The most radical version of Christian incarnationism was expressed by the so-called "God Is Dead" theologies.[6] Of course, even its critics recognized that this claim was not to be taken at face value. The God who died, according to this view, is the transcendent deity of the classical tradition. God is incarnate — fully incarnate, not only in the classical sense of being fully with us, but in the still more radical sense of being only with us, with us only. Thomas J. J. Altizer spoke of God as the Divine Word who is one with human flesh. William Hamilton focused more on the particularity of Jesus as the model of the divine in this world. In either case, the Christian doctrine of the incarnation was taken to mean more than that God "came down" at a particular point in history; it was the claim that God is always at one, fully at one, with humanity and with the creation.

A more moderate, and perhaps ambiguous, expression of this view is that of Dietrich Bonhoeffer who said that God is teaching us to live as people who can get along very well without the transcendent God of tradition.[7] Whatever Bonhoeffer meant precisely, his words helped to inspire a celebration of secularity and the rise of secular theologies, such as that of Harvey Cox, just

---

6. Thomas J. J. Altizer, *The Gospel of Christian Atheism* (Philadelphia: Westminster Press, 1966); William Hamilton, *The New Essence of Christianity* (New York: Association Press, 1961).

7. Dietrich Bonhoeffer, *Letters and Papers from Prison* (New York: Macmillan, 1953).

after the mid-twentieth century.[8] Together these varied voices formed a singular witness to the view that God is present in and with the world, not above and beyond it.

The focus on the worldly presence of the divine in these so-called "liberal" theologies parallels, ironically, more pietistic forms of popular Christianity. In the latter we often find the practical equation of God with Christ, and an understanding of Christ as present to and with the believer in ways that effectively jettison divine transcendence. This is illustrated by the role of the icon in Orthodoxy, if Vladimir Lossky is correct; the icon *is* the presence of deity, not merely a vehicle for making deity present.[9] It is also more than merely suggested in some classical interpretations of the Eucharist, such as Nicholas Cabasilas's fourteenth-century *Commentary on the Divine Liturgy*. Artistic depictions central to popular American piety in the first half of the twentieth century illustrate this, too. Although sentimental and aesthetically dull, paintings such as Warner Sallman's *Head of Christ* or *Christ at Heart's Door* can hardly be construed as anything other than radical incarnationalism.

As different as they might be in other ways, these views share an emphasis on divine presence rather than divine power. The incarnate God has power, but it is what happens when the oneness of the divine and the human, or the divine and the natural, or the divine and the concrete, are felt and reflected upon. Wherever God is present, there is divinity. This presence is above all an affirmation of the value of the mundane, of some aspect of the world here and now. But it is also a comfort. The incarnate God not only elevates life; God also assumes our suffering. The God who is empty of transcendence is fully exposed to the pain of the world. If God is with us in our humanness, then God is with us in our suffering. To be incarnate in one is to be incarnate in the other. Theologians of the ancient church struggled with the paradoxical idea that the transcendent, omnipotent God could truly suffer and die. They resolved the paradox by saying that God does not truly suffer. Radical incarnationism resolves the paradox the other way: the God who does not suffer is not truly God.

Human agony also emerges as the pain of not knowing, of not having good solutions, clear answers, entirely suitable alternatives. According to radical incarnationalism, God is with us, too, in these struggles, not as the provider

---

8. Harvey Cox, *The Secular City* (New York: Macmillan, 1965); *God's Revolution and Man's Responsibility* (Valley Forge, PA: Judson Press, 1965).

9. Vladimir Lossky, *The Mystical Theology of the Eastern Church* (Crestwood, NY: St. Vladimir's Seminary Press, 1976), p. 189: "An icon . . . is a material centre in which there reposes a divine energy, a divine force, which unites itself to the human art." Cf., too, Leonid Ouspensky and Vladimir Lossky, *The Meaning of Icons* (Boston: Boston Book and Art Shop, 1952).

of ready-made solutions but as the companion who validates our uncertainties and empowers our search. Jesus does not offer answers, prescriptions, blueprints; Jesus models an adventurous searching that enters life in its concreteness, accepts its ambiguities, and trusts its potential for good. Theologies growing out of this way of locating God are not comprehensive systems; they are fragments — tentative, limited, modest explorations into the nature of a worldly God.

God the Goal

Early in the twentieth century Albert Schweitzer contended that Jesus was an itinerant preacher whose apocalyptic message was fixed on the end or consummation of history.[10] Schweitzer's claim was an offense to the theological establishment of the day. As the century progressed, however, his general contention was increasingly accepted, not only as a portrayal of Jesus but even, by some, as a way of locating God. If Jesus is the agent of the eschaton, then Christianity is an eschatological religion, and God is an eschatological reality.

This viewpoint has had advocates throughout Christian history — Joachim of Fiore is an oft-cited example — but generally it has been an eccentric, sectarian position in relation to establishment Christianity. In the twentieth century, however, it became one of the alternatives at the center of Christian thinking, thanks in large part to the emergence of secular, especially Marxist, forms of utopianism.[11] Wolfhart Pannenberg[12] and Jürgen Moltmann[13] represent this recent development. In different ways, Pannenberg and Moltmann locate God in the future. For Moltmann, God will become who God is with the realization of the kingdom of God. For Pannenberg, there is an important sense in which, as he says, God does not yet exist. In neither case is the point to deny God's reality, but rather to insist on the fundamental and determinative character of the future — the power of the future over the present. American theologians Carl Braaten[14] and Ted Peters[15] have also developed this theme.

---

10. Albert Schweitzer, *The Quest of the Historical Jesus* (London: A. & C. Black, 1910; 3rd ed., 1954).

11. E.g., Ernst Bloch, *Man on His Own* (New York: Herder and Herder, 1970); *Atheism in Christianity* (New York: Herder and Herder, 1972).

12. Wolfhart Pannenberg, *Theology and the Kingdom of God* (Philadelphia: Westminster Press, 1969).

13. Jürgen Moltmann, *The Theology of Hope* (New York: Harper & Row, 1967).

14. Carl Braaten, *The Future of God* (New York: Harper & Row, 1969).

15. Ted Peters, *Futures, Human and Divine* (Atlanta: John Knox Press, 1978).

The biblical basis for this way of understanding God is the centrality of the message of the kingdom or reign of God in the New Testament, at least as the implications of this message are worked out in terms that are credible today. The kingdom is the point at which God will be "all in all," and that alone is the true being of God. The resurrection of Jesus is the key, the proleptic disclosure, of the reality of this coming kingdom. The revelation in Christ is not the realization of the kingdom, but the promise of its coming. Christian life now is lived in anticipation of the fulfillment of this promise.

Pannenberg supplements his explication of the biblical message with philosophical considerations. He points out, for example, that human experience is always driven by an anticipation of the future. In fact, he says, the behavior of every living organism is oriented toward what it might become in the future. The future, thus, is a power that draws all things toward and eventually into itself. The eschatological future, we might say, is the realization of the value inherent in all particular things. Since God is the realization of all value, God is — comes to be — eschatologically.

While the exegetical and philosophical arguments undergirding this view might be complex, the practical perspective to which it gives rise is quite obvious: life is lived in active hope. That hope is rooted in an anticipation of movement toward the kingdom of God and its ultimate realization beyond or at the end of history. This means, first, that the historical status quo is never satisfactory, never sufficient unto itself. From the future God calls all things forward into the fullness of the divine reality. We can appreciate the goodness of the present, modest though it is, but we can never ratify it as being adequate to the redemptive completeness toward which we are being called. Living in anticipation means, second, that the past and present are never binding and never fixed. The power of the future in the present frees us from enslavement to present conditions, and opens us to the newness of the future. The binding power of the past is never final. The ultimate power is the emancipating power that comes from the God of the future, freeing us for the future. But, third, the anticipation of this way of life is this-worldly. The kingdom of God, according to the New Testament, is the fulfillment of this world, not its abrogation. So living in expectation of the future is living in expectation of the future of this world.

The life of anticipation is never simply an attitude; it is an active way of life. Anticipation is a working toward God's future. But precisely because that future is the future of this empirical world, anticipation produces an analytical theology, one that pays careful attention to the current state of the world in order to know better how to serve its coming future. Theological reflection is more than biblical interpretation and philosophical reflection; in order to serve the world's future we must be aware of the concrete state of things. This means that theology must also be informed by political, economic, social, and historical data. Given such an anticipatory, activist, analytical framework, it is not surprising that this way of locating God has sometimes been expressed as a political theology, a theology of hope, and a theology of liberation. Even if the coming of the kingdom is in the final analysis God's doing, humans live in the expectation of that future and work to serve God's transforming aims for the world.

Summary and a Question

The discussion to this point has identified four ways of locating God. It is apparent that these are really four ways of understanding God's relationship to the creation. It is also clear that these are not simply abstract ideas; they tend to give rise to distinctive forms of Christian life. If by "spirituality" we mean a disciplined form of life embracing the whole person, individual and social, we may say that these ways of locating God tend to produce distinctive types of spirituality with their own styles of theological reflection.

Views of God that focus on God as source move the Christian toward a spirituality of wonder and gratitude, a mode of life rooted in joyous celebration of the inscrutability of things. Theology undertaken within this perspective will be mystically inclined. Its most important task will be to witness to the mystery of God.

Views of God that emphasize God as agent lend themselves to a spirituality of guidance. God's will as guide, and obedience to that will, are primary. Theology is an explication of God's will as it pertains to all of life, and thus theology is likely to be systematic and comprehensive in character.

Where primacy is given to God as incarnation, the form of Christian life that follows might be called a spirituality of presence. The believer is "at home" in that presence, be it the secular world, the natural world, or the world of iconographic concreteness. And since that with which God is at one is the world in all of its complexity, the theology that accompanies this way of life is likely to be a fragmentary one. Theology will be a tentative exploration of the presence of a deity who is somehow at one with the manifold creation.

Locating God as goal of all things provides a different way of orienting life. It gives rise to a spirituality of hope. The disciplined life is focused on the future and serves its coming, so theology will try to be attentive to every discernible movement toward that future. Theology, in other words, will be empirical, an analysis of the dynamics and structures of social and historical life.

The actual connections between ways of locating God in relation to the creation, on the one hand, and styles of religious or Christian life and thought, on the other, are not rigid and mechanical ones. An unfathomable number of variables undermines any simplistic analysis of these relationships. Nevertheless, it is difficult to deny that these four concepts of God press rather forcefully in four different directions, toward four distinct forms of Christian thought and practice. To the degree that this is the case, it would also follow that the assimilation or amalgamation of their foundational notions of God will diminish their capacity to generate distinctive modes of religiousness.

This gives rise to a question: If it is desirable to preserve these distinct modes of "Christianness" as enriching ingredients of our diverse religious heritage, should the theologian's desire for rational neatness (clarity, coherence) be allowed to press them into some one unitary conceptuality? Doing so would not preserve these different perspectives; it would only weaken and dissipate them. The power of each mode of life, each form of religiousness, depends on the view of God that founds it. Collapsing the views or combining them would degenerate them. If these forms of spirituality should be sustained because individually they are of value, then preserving their distinct views of God is of some considerable religious importance, it would seem, whatever the cost to our desire for rationality.

19 What Theology Might Learn (and Not Learn) from Evolutionary Psychology: A Postfoundationalist Theologian in Conversation with Pascal Boyer

Niels Henrik Gregersen

Evolutionary psychology is a relatively new discipline that undertakes to discover and understand the structure and function of the human mind as a product of evolution. More specifically, the approach of evolutionary psychology presupposes (1) that the human mind is a functionally specialized system that works on the basis of physiologically specialized brain modules, and (2) that all faculties of the human mind have developed as a result of natural selection for specific adaptive purposes. Since the human species lived in hunter-gatherer societies for more than 99 percent of its existence, evolutionary psychologists furthermore assume (3) that also modern human beings live and breathe in the mental schemata developed in hunter-gatherer societies. These mental schemata are taken to influence not only everyday life mentalities but also concepts of rationality and religion far beneath the threshold of our consciousness.

In what follows, I wish to entertain a conversation between the postfoundationalist philosopher and theologian, J. Wentzel van Huyssteen, and a proponent of evolutionary psychology, Pascal Boyer. I do this because van Huyssteen and Pascal Boyer both assume that human rationality has biological roots and is informed by natural selection. Now, since van Huyssteen has mostly worked on sociobiology, evolutionary epistemology, and paleoanthropology, the conversation will be undertaken in the form of a thought experiment: how could a postfoundationalist theologian, who broadly shares Wentzel van Huyssteen's view of human rationality and religion, respond to the challenges and possibilities in evolutionary psychology? What can be learned, and what should not be learned?

Van Huyssteen's Postfoundationalist Concept of Rationality

Let me begin by reflecting on the development of van Huyssteen's concept of rationality. For decades, van Huyssteen has been arguing for a concept of rationality that is intrinsically humane and able to host a rich variety of rational practices, from scientific to religious discourse and practice. In his *Theology and the Justification of Faith* (1989; published in Afrikaans in 1986), van Huyssteen set out to clarify the role of theory in systematic theology. He did so in critical conversation with Karl Popper's critical rationalism, Thomas Kuhn's theory of paradigm shifts within science, and Larry Laudan's argument for a relative progress in science, due to its problem-solving efficiency. Taken at face value, *Theology and the Justification of Faith* defends theology as a theorizing project within a broadly critical-realist framework. Theological statements are thus presented as "reality depicting" and are presumed to form a coherent unity of assumptions.[1]

At a closer reading, however, the book entails quite a few caveats, which, read with hindsight, anticipate later developments of van Huyssteen's work. "I think that anyone considering the possibilities of scientific realism for theology should be extremely wary of uncritical, superficial transferring of the realism of science to the domain of religious belief, and to theology as the reflection on the claims of this belief," says the author, and he goes on to argue that the reality depiction of second-order theological statements presupposes the claims of first-order religious commitments: "At the basis of the reasons for using this term [of critical realism] is the *conviction* that what we are provisionally conceptualizing in theology really exists."[2] In a similar way, theological statements are seen as resting upon a fluid network of religious metaphors and models, which are not fully translatable into theoretical and explanatory statements: "[W]e are not simply describing realities that are equally accessible by other means. Language does not merely represent or re-

---

1. J. Wentzel van Huyssteen, *Theology and the Justification of Faith: Constructing Theories in Systematic Theology*, trans. H. F. Snijders (Grand Rapids: Eerdmans, 1989), pp. 133-147.

2. Van Huyssteen, *Theology and the Justification of Faith*, p. 155; emphasis added. Van Huyssteen's early position is presented in condensed form in "Experience and Explanation: The Justification of Cognitive Claims in Theology," *Zygon: Journal of Religion and Science* 45, no. 4 (1988): 247-262, reprinted in van Huyssteen, *Essays in Postfoundationalist Theology* (Grand Rapids: Eerdmans, 1997), pp. 162-179. Here the author points out that he is only willing to argue "for a qualified and weak form of critical realism" (p. 167), insofar as the referential claims are derived from "[a] basic assumption and good reasons," without the reasons being conclusive, and without the claim of a progressively convergent realism. Cf. my article "Critical Realism and Other Realisms," in *Fifty Years in Science and Theology: Ian G. Barbour and His Legacy*, ed. Robert J. Russell (Aldershot: Ashgate, 2004).

flect reality; it also constitutes reality. In this sense metaphoric language opens up to us, both creatively and exploratively, the reality of which we speak, since what we see as reality is to a large extent creatively and exploratively determined by the metaphoric potential of the language in which reality is depicted."[3]

One way of characterizing van Huyssteen's argument is to say that his basic philosophical framework in *Theology and the Justification of Faith* is hermeneutical in nature. Language only refers to reality in the context of linguistic networks that open up possibilities of human engagement while redescribing reality in linguistic form. This hermeneutical orientation may also explain why van Huyssteen has never followed attempts to apply, say, a Lakatosian model of rationality to the justification of religious truth-claims.[4] Apart from pointing out differences between scientific theories and theological language (differences that are also acknowledged by proponents of a Lakatosian program for theology), van Huyssteen does not seem interested in keeping apart the *explanans* and the *explanandum*, the explanatory theory and the subject-area to be explained. There is (if my hermeneutical interpretation of van Huyssteen's work is correct) no principled divide between the first-order level of religious experience and language, and the second-order level of theological theorizing. Accordingly, theology has the role of redescribing (in second-order theological terms based on first-order religious language) the world of nature (and culture) as already described and partially explained by the sciences.[5]

Van Huyssteen's later work, epitomized in *The Shaping of Rationality* (1999), has both emphasized and transformed this hermeneutical orientation. The hermeneutical orientation has been emphasized in so far as he continues to underline the pre-theoretical character of rationality and point to the formative role of traditions as "boundaries of our habitations."[6] However, the

---

3. Van Huyssteen, *Theology and the Justification of Faith*, pp. 137-138.

4. See van Huyssteen's criticism of Nancey Murphy's bold thesis, *Theology in an Age of Scientific Reasoning* (Ithaca: Cornell University Press, 1990), in "Is the Postmodernist Always a Postfoundationalist? Nancey Murphy's Lakatosian Model for Theology," *Theology Today* 50, no. 3 (1993): 373-386, reprinted in *Essays in Postfoundationalist Theology*, pp. 73-90.

5. The concept of "redescription" comes up only occasionally in *Theology and the Justification of Faith* (e.g. p. 157), but attains a central role in J. Wentzel van Huyssteen, *Duet or Duel? Theology and Science in a Postmodern World* (London: SCM, 1998), pp. 125-128 and 160-164. As kindly acknowledged by van Huyssteen, I have used this term since the early 1990s in order not to conflate the task of offering causal explanations and the task of giving semantic explanation or interpretation. This term itself, however, has its provenance in Donald Davidson's concept of "radical interpretation," where no formal translation schemes exist.

6. See J. Wentzel van Huyssteen, *The Shaping of Rationality: Toward Interdisciplinarity in*

hermeneutical orientation has also been transformed by a stronger pragmaticist orientation. Rationality no longer resides first and foremost in the capacity to form statements and open up horizons, but in the capacity of rational agents to form responsible judgments and seek optimal understandings, given the specific context and the specific problems to be solved. Human rationality is indeed humane.

There are several philosophical inspirations behind this shift of orientation in van Huyssteen's work.[7] The first name to be mentioned is probably Nicholas Rescher, from whom van Huyssteen learned to speak of the many dimensions of rationality. Alongside the cognitive dimension, we have the evaluative and the pragmatic contexts that correspond to the human pursuit of values and appropriate actions. With Rescher, van Huyssteen regards science as the prime case for the cognitive pursuit of truth, but he insists that scientific rationality is just one subset of rationality at work.[8] Another source of inspiration is Harold Brown's theory of rationality, which led van Huyssteen to see the concept of rational beliefs to be derivative to the reasoning of agents, who are making the rational estimates about truth, values, and adequate behavior.[9] Finally, Calvin Schrag devised the term "transversal rationality" to describe the fact that rationality is not domain-specific but emerges in the intersection, crossover, or interweaving of forms of rational discernment in different areas of life, from the sciences to religion and everyday practices.[10] This comprehensive view of rationality accentuates that rational agents are always embedded in communicative contexts, in which agents have to account for their views, have to take issues with the "best bets" on the market of ratio-

---

Theology and Science (Grand Rapids: Eerdmans, 1999), pp. 252-259, where he (following Delwin Brown, *Boundaries of Our Habitations: Tradition and Theological Construction* [New York: SUNY Press, 1994]) discusses how rational self-reflection is shaped by traditions, without being tied up with nonnegotiable truth claims.

7. Again, this pragmatic orientation is anticipated in van Huyssteen's reception of Larry Laudan's work, in *Theology and the Justification of Faith*, pp. 172-190.

8. Van Huyssteen, *Essays in Postfoundationalist Theology*, pp. 246-247; *The Shaping of Rationality*, pp. 128-129. "[T]he selection of science as our clearest example of the *cognitive/theoretical dimension* of rationality at work is indeed justified. What is not justified, however, is any claim for the superiority of scientific rationality, and any attempt to extend uncritically the nature of a strictly scientific rationality to the rationality of religious or any other reflection" (*The Shaping of Rationality*, p. 162). Cf. Nicholas Rescher, *Rationality* (Oxford: Clarendon Press, 1988).

9. Van Huyssteen, *Essays in Postfoundationalist Theology*, pp. 247-254; *The Shaping of Rationality*, pp. 142-150. Cf. Harold Brown, *Rationality* (London: Routledge, 1990).

10. Van Huyssteen, *The Shaping of Rationality*, pp. 132-139. Cf. Calvin O. Schrag, *The Resources of Rationality: A Response to the Postmodern Challenge* (Bloomington: Indiana University Press, 1992), and esp. "Transversal Rationality," in *The Question of Hermeneutics*, ed. T. J. Stapleton (Amsterdam: Kluwer, 1994).

nal ideas, and have to persuade others by rational performances. On the one hand, there exists no solitary epistemological subject à la Kant (but only contextually situated individuals). On the other hand, van Huyssteen points to the rational procedures that serve to guide our behavior, even where there are no foundational starting points and where the steps forward cannot be controlled by following rules set up prior to our walking. We should avoid conformist appeals to a homogenized ideal of rationality, yet also escape the danger of a fideistic retreat to an allegedly safe position of non-foundationalism. The interweaving of arguments from one domain of experience and self-reflection to another demands a capacity for transcommunal learning processes.

The move beyond foundationalism does not mean that all starting points are equally and indiscriminately good. But the postfoundationalist requires that many truth candidates be part of the conversation. With respect to the dialogue between science and religion, van Huyssteen argues that there are (1) *shared resources of rationality* between theology and the sciences (for example, logic, and the search for order and understanding), (2) *overlapping elements of rationality* (e.g., in the role of models and metaphors in theorizing), and finally (3) *distinctive forms of rationality*, which cannot easily be transferred from one discipline to another (the mathematical equations in science, for example, have no counterpart in theological rationality, whereas the search for meaning, value, and existential relevance in theology has no direct analogue in the sciences).[11]

In *Duet or Duel?* (1998), the issue of epistemology was now also approached from an evolutionary perspective. With evolutionary epistemology, van Huyssteen pointed to the common biological roots of human rationality. These roots may explain, at least in part, the "universal traits" of human reasoning:

> Evolutionary epistemology thus reveals the process of evolution as a belief-gaining process, a process that in humans, too, is shaped pre-consciously. All our beliefs, and I would argue, also our religious beliefs, thus have evolutionary origins and were established by mechanisms working reliably in the world of our ancestors. This still does not mean, however, that the theory of evolution by natural selection can offer an adequate explanation for beliefs that far transcend their biological origins. But this again underlines the fact that cognition is a general characteristic of all living beings, and that human rationality, therefore, can only be fully understood if its biological roots are understood.[12]

---

11. Van Huyssteen, *Duet or Duel?* pp. 160-166.
12. Van Huyssteen, *Duet or Duel?* pp. 151-152.

What Theology Might Learn (and Not Learn) from Evolutionary Psychology

Those who have feared that van Huyssteen during the mid-1990s went down the slope of postmodernism should be aware that, for van Huyssteen, the discourse of postmodernity remains in contact with modernity, and the discourses of modernity remain within the web of postmodern discourse.[13] And if *The Shaping of Rationality* could be interpreted as an epistemological withdrawal from the theoretical interactions between science and theology, then *Duet and Duel?* evidenced that this was far from the author's intention. Indeed, after 1999 van Huyssteen made a full return to the dialogue between science and religion, yet based on a broader concept of interdisciplinary (laid out in *The Shaping of Rationality*) and with new emphasis on the evolutionary significance of human rationality. Many of us look forward to the publication of the 2004 Gifford Lectures, *Alone in the World? Human Uniqueness in Science and Theology.* For here the question of human rationality will be discussed in close communication with the findings of human paleontology and theories of evolutionary epistemology. Whether or not van Huyssteen will deal explicitly with cognitive science and evolutionary psychology in his Gifford Lectures remains to be seen.[14] In the following sections, my aim is to assess the strengths and weaknesses of the cognitivist program of evolutionary psychology.[15]

The Embodied Mind: Ontogenetic Perspectives

Let me begin with the ontogenetic roots of human rationality. In *Philosophy in the Flesh: The Embodied Mind and Its Challenge to Western Thought*, George

---

13. Van Huyssteen, *Essays in Postfoundationalist Theology*, p. 279, with reference to Schrag, *Resources of Rationality*, p. 17. Admittedly, I myself feared an overemphasis on postmodernism in van Huyssteen's work in the early and mid-1990s. Would science and theology be taken less seriously in the wake of his pragmaticist move? When we together wrote the introduction to our coedited book, *Rethinking Theology and Science: Six Models for the Current Dialogue* (Grand Rapids: Eerdmans, 1998), we agreed to use the term "cognitive pluralism," since the term "postmodernity" has many different meanings, some of which would certainly destroy a rational project such as van Huyssteen's.

14. After the completion of this essay, van Huyssteen's Gifford Lectures were published: *Alone in the World? Human Uniqueness in Science and Theology* (Grand Rapids: Eerdmans, 2006). Indeed the issue of cognitive evolution is discussed intensively (pp. 45-109), and Pascal's Boyer's particular theory of religion is also discussed (pp. 261-267).

15. The following two sections are adapted from my lecture, "The Naturalness of Religious Imagination and the Idea of Revelation," given at the 14th Conference of the European Society for Philosophy of Religion, Clare Hall, Cambridge, August 2002, and published in *Ars Disputandi* 2 (2002): 13-25 (www.ArsDisputandi.org).

Lakoff and Mark Johnson argue that ordinary language as well as highly theoretical concepts build on primary metaphors, which are learned through sensory-motor practices from childhood and onwards: "up/down," "cold/warm," "close/distant."[16] Concepts and metaphors thus grow out of bodily experiences, which, in turn, are always accompanied by feelings and sensations. Far below the threshold of consciousness, metaphors from one source of experience (e.g., bodily location) are blended and conflated with metaphors from another source (e.g., visual sensation), and they end up forming complex networks of imageries. We can, for instance, be summoned to search for our "inner light." In addition, there is a constant flow back and forth between these spatial-bodily "source areas" and the "target areas" that one wants to address. As time goes on, metaphors and images, on the one hand, and the subject matter we want to talk about, on the other hand, are amalgamated and recombined in ever-new configurations. Consequently, we may end up understanding our inner life as a "journey" and talk about "reaching our goals" or "losing ourselves."[17] We are here already approaching the level of religious language. For networks of metaphors and images function as fundamental thought schemes that guide our very pedestrian activities (usually taken to be the "literal" ones); but they also accompany our most intimate self-reflections (often taken to build on "metaphorical imagination") and drill our theoretical concepts (often assumed to "transcend" imagination).

Not only are concepts nourished from metaphors, but because metaphors are rooted in sensory-motor experiences, they are cross-culturally associated with certain evaluative schemes: "up" is good, "down" is bad, a "warm" smile is better than a "cold" one, and a "close" friend is more important than a "distant" relative. As Lakoff and Johnson put it, "Reason is imaginative in that bodily inference forms are mapped onto abstract modes of inference by metaphor."[18]

The second-generation cognitive science that Lakoff and Johnson exemplify no longer assumes a body-free intelligence (in the mode of earlier programs of Artificial Intelligence) but an embodied mind. Accordingly the task of cognitive science is to reconstruct the emergence of mind from the natural history of evolving sensory systems.

Embodied cognitive science suggests a caveat concerning realism. Meta-

---

16. See already George Lakoff, "The Contemporary Theory of Metaphor," in *Metaphor and Thought*, ed. Andrew Ortony (Cambridge: Cambridge University Press, 1979; 2nd ed. 1993), pp. 202-251.

17. George Lakoff and Mark Johnson, *Philosophy in the Flesh: The Embodied Mind and Its Challenge to Western Thought* (New York: BasicBooks, 1999), pp. 45-73.

18. Lakoff and Johnson, *Philosophy in the Flesh*, p. 77.

phors and concepts should not be taken as representing objective realities "out there"; but neither should our cognitive capacities be seen as producing wildly "subjective" imaginations. Rather, imaginative concepts reflect ways of coping with the world, *a world with which we are already interacting as cognitive participants, who are bound to understand the world from the perspective of bodily-mental metaphors and concepts.* There is no easy dichotomy between "inner" and "outer." But note that embodied cognitive science does not commend relativism either. We could thus put the thesis of Lakoff and Johnson as follows: what bodily metaphors do "mirror" are the continuous and creative interactions between embodied minds and their environments. Information is not to be transported from the "external, objective" world into an "internal subjective world," but *information emerges out of the way in which we take up the world* in the process of learning how to receive and respond to our environments. Lakoff and Johnson call this an "embodied scientific realism,"[19] and they argue that this understanding of embodied knowledge is congenial with both the pragmatism of John Dewey and the phenomenology of Maurice Merleau-Ponty. Cognition is rooted in bodily experiences, but bodies are never "pure" bodies, but always interpreting bodies. That is, bodies are bodies for whom this or that matters.

The other point to be learnt from Lakoff and Johnson is that cognitive schemes, contrary to Immanuel Kant, are learned *a posteriori.* The distinction between the empirical and the transcendental evaporates, as the "transcendentals" are themselves the accumulated results of childhood sensory-motor learning and the subsequent learning of linguistic skills.

The Naturalness of Religion: Pascal Boyer's Evolutionary Psychology

Let us now place this view of embodied knowledge in a wider evolutionary perspective, that is, in a phylogenetic perspective. *Paleoanthropology* informs us about the fact that the anatomically modern humans *(Homo sapiens sapiens)* have existed around 100,000 years (100 kyr), but only in the "cultural explosion" between 60 and 30 kyr ago do we begin to find evidence of technological innovation, art, religion, and rituals. Among the Cro-Magnons (ca. 30

---

19. Lakoff and Johnson, *Philosophy in the Flesh,* pp. 74-117, esp. 89-91 and 97. A similar notion of a "transactional realism" can also be found in *The Shaping of Rationality,* p. 213: "The form of modest critical realism I am arguing for sees exactly our experience as a transaction or relation between the rational agent and the world."

kyr) we find elaborate burials with ochre and extensive grave goods, both of which indicate a belief in an afterlife.[20]

Now *evolutionary psychology* assumes that beneath the surface of cultural variability, human minds have developed some well-winnowed cognitive strategies that are likely to be relatively constant cross-culturally. Just as there is no dichotomy between external objective reality and inner subjective consciousness, there is no absolute distinction between nature and culture. Also, cultures have to adapt to particular problems of survival, reproduction, group cooperation, and world-orientation. Natural selection therefore applies no less to human cultures than to animal behaviors, though the means and forms of selection may be different. Unlike sociobiology, however, evolutionary psychologists do not need to assume that particular behaviors are linked to particular sets of genes. What is genetically predisposed, and what is acquired through cultural learning processes, remains an open question.[21] Neither are evolutionary psychologists concerned with behavior apart from the cognitive mechanisms implied in such behavior. Reproductive fitness as well as cultural fitness are taken to be conditioned by the operation of specialized "mental modules," which have proven themselves to be efficient in the past of our hunter-gatherer ancestors, and which, due to their hardwired neural correlates, persist from ancient agricultures up to modern cultures.

Evolutionary psychologists here follow Jerry Fodor's modular view of human cognition rather than Noam Chomsky's idea of a content-free, general-purpose brain. Thus the mind is supposed to be constituted by multiple, specialized, and content-rich mental modules that have a neural correlate in brain

---

20. Ian Tattersall, *Becoming Human: Evolution and Human Uniqueness* (San Diego: Harcourt Brace & Company, 1998), pp. 5-29.

21. On the fundamental differences between genetic and cultural transmission, see W. H. Durham, *Coevolution: Genes, Culture, and Human Diversity* (Stanford: Stanford University Press, 1991), who points out that cultural selection can enhance, oppose, or be neutral vis-à-vis natural selection. Thus there may be neither direct nor "predispositional" links ("epigenetic rules") between genes and behavior, as hypothesized by the sociobiologists E. O. Wilson and C. J. Lumsden (*Genes, Minds, and Culture* [Cambridge, MA: Harvard University Press, 1981]). An even more radical dissociation between natural selection, working on "genes," and cognitive selection concerning "memes" is expressed by Pascal Boyer, *The Naturalness of Religious Ideas: A Cognitive Theory of Religion* (Berkeley: University of California Press, 1994), ch. 9. Boyer challenges the idea that preformatted genes "express themselves" in phenotypes (pp. 278-283) as well as the assumption that memes are "copied" and transmitted as "cultural inputs" (pp. 283-288). There are no easy causal links, nor any structural similarity between genes and memes. The recurrence of cultural ideas, including religious ideas, is provided by the rich intuitive psychology and inference systems developed in human prehistory (p. 290). I will discuss Boyer's work in more detail below.

modules.²² Mental modules are operative in, for instance, spatial orientation, tool-use, face recognition, social exchange, perception and emotion, child care, friendship, face-to-face communication, and so on; learnt from childhood, these mental modules are later enhanced, restrained, or refined by social learning.²³ Accordingly, mental schemes function to a wide extent beneath the level of conscious reflection, as they become hardwired in our neural circuits.²⁴

What is characteristic for the human mind, however, is that this spontaneity is always mediated by the interaction between the different mental capacities, so that human actions cannot be understood as stimulus-response behavior. Evolutionary psychologists assume that human intelligence has eventually evolved through a combination of a general intelligence with modular intelligences, which again can be blended in higher-order cognitive processes such as artistic creativity and religious thought. In *The Prehistory of the Mind*, archaeologist Steven Mithen argues that, apart from the general intelligence characteristic of infants (phase 1), children early on develop specialized cognitive domains (phase 2). Children learn to behave differently with respect to human persons, animals, and tools, and they thus acquire a set of distinct "intuitive intelligences." Mithen mentions four such areas of intelligence: (1) social and psychological, (2) biological, (3) technical, and (4) linguistic. What is characteristic for the emergence of *Homo sapiens sapiens*, however, is the extent to which "the combining of thoughts and knowledge of the different specialized intelligences is possible" (phase 3). As soon as the specialized cognitive domains began to engage with one another — and this is what happened in the cultural explosion in the Cro Magnon Age, "the result is an almost limitless capacity for imagination." Mithen refers to this phase 3 of the typically modern human mind as having a "cognitive fluidity."²⁵

---

22. See the paradigmatic study by Leda Cosmides and John Tooby, "Cognitive Adaptations for Social Exchange," in *The Adapted Mind*, ed. J. H. Barkow, L. Cosmides, and J. Tooby (New York: Oxford University Press, 1992), pp. 163-228. See also the discussion volume, Peter Carruthers and Andrew Chamberlain, eds., *Evolution and the Human Mind: Modularity, Language and Meta-Cognition* (Cambridge: Cambridge University Press, 2000).

23. Cosmides and Tooby, "Cognitive Adaptations for Social Exchange," p. 113.

24. This of course presupposes suitable information processing in the brain. If, for instance, the *corpus callosum*, which connects the left and right hemispheres of the brain, is either not developed (agenetic *corpus callosum*) or injured by accident (well-known from the so-called "split-brain" research), the patient will not be able to form associations or have imaginations. I owe this observation to a conversation with the neuroscientist Warren Brown (Granada, Spain, August 23, 2002).

25. Steven Mithen, *The Prehistory of the Mind: The Cognitive Origins of Art, Religion and Science* (London: Thames and Hudson, 1999), pp. 70-71. The concept of "cognitive fluidity" plays a central role in van Huyssteen's more recent work on paleoanthropology.

In this perspective, religious imagination is a result of the cognitive fluidity attained at phase 3. Intelligences related to social persons and to natural history may, for example, be combined into the idea of a non-physical afterlife (having the persistence of mountains but the features of a personal mental life). These complex notions can be further combined into the generalized notion of non-physical spirits and gods. These non-physical beings are thought to be as causally effective as natural events, insofar as they can cause harm or well-being, and yet they are as communicative as human persons are.[26]

Thus, religious imagination uses the same mental modules as have developed in other human activities, such as hunting, cooking, reproducing, nurturing, and so on. Accordingly, *there exists no specialized religious module, and no distinct borderline between religious and non-religious imagination.* Rather, the emergence of religion is part and parcel of the liberation of human rationality, from the constrained nave structure of the Roman chapels to the open and fluid structures of the windows of the Gothic cathedral.

Apart from the speculative assumptions inherent in this scheme (the simplicity of which Mithen fully acknowledges), the approach of Mithen does not seem to me quite satisfying. First, what he says about the phenomenon of religion, despite the subtitle of the book, is very meager. Second, Mithen does not discuss the inner constraints on religious (or any other) imagination. If cognitive fluidity were the sufficient explanation of religion, religious imagination would just teem in all directions. But as argued by Pascal Boyer, this is not actually the case. Religious imaginations are, after all, highly constrained.[27]

In his book with the overambitious title *Religion Explained: The Evolutionary Origins of Religious Thought* (2001), Boyer offers a model for understanding how religious concepts, often amazingly counterintuitive and sometimes even baroquely exotic, have their natural place in the context of the ordinary workings of the human brain. Religious concepts are natural both in the phenomenological sense that they emerge spontaneously and develop effortlessly, and in the naturalistic sense that religious imagination belongs to the world of nature by being naturally constrained by genes, central nervous systems, and brains.[28]

26. Mithen, *The Prehistory of the Mind*, pp. 174-178.
27. See Pascal Boyer's critique of Mithen in "Evolution of the Modern Mind and the Origins of Culture: Religious Concepts as a Limiting-Case," in Carruthers and Chamberlain, eds., *Evolution and the Human Mind*, pp. 93-112, esp. 97: "cultures are not that diverse: we find recurrent templates for religious concepts, not unbounded variation."
28. See Boyer, *The Naturalness of Religious Ideas*, pp. 3-4.

Fundamental to Boyer's explanatory model is the distinction between concepts and templates.[29] *Concepts* are general ideas referring to particular beings such as a walrus or a giraffe, whereas *templates* are more general schemes. The point is that children as well as adults learn by subconsciously inferring that giraffes, even though they look very different from walruses, blackbirds, and mosquitoes, have a variety of common characteristics, because they are part of the same ontological category, the ANIMAL template. Animals have a body-plan, have a living place, eat food, reproduce, and so on. Of course, a giraffe and a walrus look different (long legs and neck versus a squat body and large tusks), have different habitats (the savannah versus the sea), eat different things (leaves versus fish), and copulate in different ways. The information about these differences will have to be provided by the concepts, derived from empirical experience. But the template ANIMAL adds the information that all animals — from mosquitoes to elephants — live, eat, and reproduce. Templates can thus be perceived as aggregates of memory. By subconsciously using templates we tacitly infer many things that we don't observe but simply take for granted. Once again, the result is an inverted Kantianism, in which the quasi *a priori* templates have accumulated through the *a posteriori* evolution of cognitive systems.

According to Boyer, there are not many cognitive templates. The exact number is a question of definition, but the following may suffice: PERSON, ANIMAL, PLANT, TOOL, ARTIFACT, NATURAL OBJECT. Human beings will have a long-term acquaintance with each of these templates. Tools and natural objects don't talk and don't eat; persons do. Persons have memory and act according to their past experiences; plants don't. And yet, since the categories can be recombined, new concepts can emerge, and the world of religion is full of such cases. Boyer mentions the examples of praying to statues, of feeding mountains for an exchange of prey, and of special (potentially dangerous) ebony trees that are able to recall the conversations of past generations. In effect, Boyer thinks that religious concepts came about by blending information coming from separate ontological categories, in particular the templates of NATURAL OBJECT and PERSON.

The hard core of Boyer's theory of religion is now that *religious concepts and imaginations are always marked by being counterintuitive* in the precise sense of counteracting expectations raised by our template categories: "[R]eligious concepts invariably include information that is counterintuitive

---

29. Pascal Boyer, *Religion Explained: The Evolutionary Origins of Religious Thought* (New York: BasicBooks, 2001), pp. 40-45. Subsequent references to this work are given parenthetically in the text.

relative to the category activated" (*Religion Explained,* p. 65). Observe that, even though the world of religions certainly does involve oddities of many sorts (at least to outsiders), the mere fact that something is unexpected is not counterintuitive in Boyer's technical sense. For example, imagining a table made out of chocolate or a giraffe with six legs certainly unsettles our ordinary knowledge but does not violate the ontological categories. The breach of expectations is here still at the level of concepts and natural-kinds. However, to say that the table felt sad when the people left the room breaks with our assumed information about what ARTIFACTS can do (pp. 80-82).

These examples, however, also show that religions are hardly satisfactorily defined by being counterintuitive (or counter-ontological, to be more precise). For so also are fairytales and science-fiction stories. Boyer does not, it seems, provide us with a very distinctive understanding of the religious ideas that he nonetheless claims to have explained. The problem is not that Boyer does not offer us a satisfying definition of what religion essentially is. Nobody can. Boyer rightly specifies religion via family resemblances rather than via identifiable essences. The problem is that Boyer has construed the family of religious ideas in a less than satisfying manner. Boyer's defining characteristic — the breaking and blending of ontological categories — is evidently too broad. Boyer is aware that religious concepts, in addition to being counterintuitive, have an existential importance. But again, fairytales and science-fiction stories may also be existentially relevant. By religious concepts he mostly seems to understand simply the idea of supernatural beings such as gods, ghosts, and zombies, or supernatural events such as miracles, "a set of ideas concerning nonobservable, extra-natural agencies and processes."[30] However, the distinction between "natural" and "supernatural" is hardly relevant to all sorts of religious understanding.[31] Religion is not confined to non-observable, supernatural entities, but redescribes the observable natural world as well. Religion is not essentially about finding traces of an absent deity in salient experiences, but more often about seeing the presence of the divine "in, with, and under" the traces themselves (to use the sacramental language of Lutherans and Anglicans).

---

30. Boyer, *The Naturalness of Religious Ideas,* p. 5.
31. As argued by the French theologian Henri de Lubac (*Surnatural: Etudes historiques* [Paris: Aubier, 1946]), the term *supernaturalis* entered theology only in the ninth century, with Carolingian translations of Pseudo-Dionysius and Scotus Eriugena; see Graham Ward, "Supernaturalism," *Encyclopedia of Science and Religion* (New York: Macmillan, 2003). One could well argue that the construal of religion as supernatural is a result of a specific rationalizing theology, which was later adopted and inverted by rationalists who wanted to confine religion to the area of the extra-ordinary, while handing over the ordinary world to secular reasoning. Boyer's own background in French rationalism may exemplify this historical trajectory.

As we will see, Boyer's "supra-rationalist" view of religion has repercussions for his approach to the concept of God. Let us start with his highly interesting point of departure. Boyer starts out from the empirical observation that there are many conceivable, yet non-viable ways of thinking about God. Not all religious concepts can be equally successfully transmitted. Boyer mentions the example of a god watching us in every detail — but instantaneously forgetting about us; this is a notion nowhere found in the history of religion. Or think of an omnipotent God existing only on Wednesdays (*Religion Explained*, pp. 51 and 56). There are barriers to the wildness of religious imagination, and cognitive fluidity does not flow everywhere; any violation of a template will need to be specific, while at the same time preserving other features of the template (p. 62).

For example, when imagining God as a person, most believers violate the category of PERSON by qualifying the template so that God is a person who is *not limited* to space and time, because God has *no body*. By contrast, it would be hard to go around with a religious message saying that God is an infinite person who has a body but *no consciousness*. The ontological category of personhood would here simply be eradicated. On the other hand, one can also enrich the concept of God by transferring specific knowledge claims gained from other source areas and applying them to God. One can, for example, use the TOOL template and praise God by saying, "You are the lamp that shines for my feet," or the NATURAL OBJECT template, and say, "The Lord is my rock."

Boyer is particularly interested in the pervasive role of PERSONHOOD templates in religious thought. Throughout evolution, humans have survived by paying attention to differences, especially to salient features that can be treated as signs standing for something, or as having a hidden meaning. *We are evolutionarily designed, as it were, to look for signs.* Boyer here stands on the shoulders of Stewart Guthrie's theory of religious anthropomorphism.[32] According to Guthrie and Boyer, we are bound to read events as signs indicating the activity of somebody. We therefore choose our perceptual bets neither randomly nor by probability, but according to their potential significance for us. What is significant for us is exactly living beings, particularly those with whom we can communicate.[33]

---

32. Stewart Guthrie, *Faces in the Clouds: A New Theory of Religion* (Oxford: Oxford University Press, 1993).

33. Stewart Guthrie, "Why Gods? A Cognitive Theory," in *Religion in the Mind: Cognitive Perspectives on Religious Belief, Ritual, and Experience*, ed. Jensine Andresen (Cambridge: Cambridge University Press, 2002), pp. 94-112, here 106: "both anthropomorphism and animism are consequences of an evolved strategy of perception: to interpret the world's ambiguities first as those possibilities that matter most — what is *alive*, what is *sociable*."

In the same vein, Boyer refers to the evolutionary psychologist Justin Barrett, who has pointed to the "hyperactive agent detection" in human cognition: "Our evolutionary heritage is that of organisms that must deal with both predators and prey. In either situation, it is far more advantageous to overdetect agency than to underdetect it. The expense of false positives (seeing agents where there are none) is minimal, if we can abandon these misguided intuitions quickly. In contrast, the cost of not detecting agents when they are actually around (either predator or prey), could be very high" (*Religion Explained*, p. 144). In this context, gods and spirits can be (and certainly have been) perceived as predators that provoked fear and anxiety. But gods and spirits can also be seen as invisible partners with whom one can seek refuge, communicate, but also possibly exchange goods (pp. 146-150). What is distinctive for religious communication is here the fact that the communication with invisible partners is *decoupled* from the ordinary social exchange, and thus offers a space for learning both social and self-reflective skills against a stable background, constituted by the relation to the Invisible Other (p. 149). In other words, the pervasiveness and persistence of notions of a personal God (despite the criticisms coming from philosophers such as Spinoza or Fichte) can partly be explained by the naturalness of the mental module of agency detection, which is operative far below the threshold of reflection. And yet, as we shall see, agency detection also elicits religious reflection.

Religious imagination thus uses the same inference systems as the human brain and mind in general. Boyer refers to empirical investigations, which show that people tend better to memorize violations of expectations than no violations, and that people recall few violations better than too many. We better remember having seen a one-armed man than a two-armed man; however, if we begin to violate a human being much further (say, a man without a perceptible face), imagination gets too strained. Similarly in the world of religious imagination. We are evolutionarily bound to pay attention to salient features and to see signs as traces of personal activity. However, as Boyer also points out, not least the elite representations of religion risk the danger of making too many violations of expectations. He mentions the Christian doctrine of Trinity, which is notable for being difficult to transmit culturally, or literate Buddhists who endorse a wholly non-anthropomorphic universe. In both cases, we find that the theological correctness maintained by scholars, priests, or monks is counteracted in popular piety by giving priority to one of the three trinitarian persons (usually Christ), or by supplementing the Trinity with more approachable figures (such as Mary). Similarly, the non-anthropomorphic universe of Buddhism is easily supplemented in public piety by a world of highly anthropomorphic ghosts and spirits.

A Critique of Boyer's Explanatory Model

So far we have examined an outline of Boyer's theory. Before we engage his theory from a theologically informed perspective, let me first say a few things about the scientific status of evolutionary psychology. Evolutionary psychology bases itself on fairly general reconstructions of the prehistoric human mind, an area in which archaeological scholarship is still guided by hunches and hypotheses, as we saw in the case of Steven Mithen.[34] In particular, Boyer's theory of religious thinking presupposes that the richness of religious semantics and communication is based on habits of inference acquired in pre-agricultural societies of gatherers and hunters. However, more reflective religious systems came about in the period of agriculture about 20 to 10 kyr ago, followed by the formation of states, cities, and alphabets as late as about 10 kyr to 1,500 years ago. As is well known, the logic of monotheism emerged in these late cultures. The vastly important shifts in religious perception within cultural evolution are, unfortunately, not reflected in Boyer's theory, a theory that mostly builds on examples from so-called primitive societies. Even though Boyer's case is strengthened by empirical work done on the learning of language in cognitive science and on the psychology of memory among present-day human beings (Julian Barrett), evolutionary psychology has yet to show how a theoretical reduction of religious thinking to the interplay between cognitive templates and empirically based concepts can be evidenced. As already mentioned, evolutionary psychology has largely given up the claims of sociobiology that one would be able to specify the genetic basis of cognitive behaviors. Boyer's work does not refer (or refers only in passing) to genes. Genes, however, are the only possible carriers, at an ultimate level, of the hardwiring of the brains, if any such hardwiring exists. Neither does Boyer point to any established causal theory about how cognitive systems and their mental modules relate to brain modules. The proximate cause of cognitive behavior would eventually have to be found in the neuronal structure of the brain, if any causal reduction of cognitive processes could at all be evidenced.

In favor of evolutionary psychology, however, it should be said that linkages between cognitive functions and brain processes are currently being investigated by the neurosciences, and by virtue of advanced neuroscanners such as SPECT (Single Photon Emission Computed Tomography) it is possible to identify the brain modules and even the trajectories of single electrons

---

34. See Ian Tattersall's critique of evolutionary psychology as a pseudo-science, "Evolution, Genes, and Behavior," *Zygon: A Journal of Religion & Science* 36, no. 4 (December 2001): 657-666.

activated under religious experience. Current studies within neuroscience are thus highly consonant with the assumptions of evolutionary psychology and may be regarded as supplementary evidence of the evolutionary approach.[35] I therefore believe that cognitive science, including the cognitive science of religious development, has to be taken seriously as a promising research program, even though Boyer and colleagues have not, as yet, offered what they claim to have offered: an "explanation" of religious thinking. Boyer himself admits that his approach does not explain the particulars of religions or the beliefs of individual persons. Evolutionary psychology can explain "the likelihood of religious 'belief'" as well as "vast trends in human groups" (*Religion Explained*, p. 319), but not the particular shape of particular religions.

The explanatory power of Boyer's theory is thus rather modest, as sometimes conceded by Boyer himself. However, there is another fundamental limit to his approach. Boyer concerns himself with cultural adaptation, with "cultural fitness," and not with the conceivability or rationality of particular religious imaginations.[36] He is thus well aware that he cannot *qua* evolutionary psychologist evaluate the internal rationality of religious belief. The self-affirmative rhetoric of "explaining religion" disguises this fact, as Boyer's many Feuerbachian side-remarks do. For a theory about the emergence of religious concepts and imaginations does not answer the philosophical question about the validity of religious beliefs, nor the issue as to whether and how religious imagination may refer to extra-linguistic realities. The *reasons* that may undergird *the unreasonable effectiveness of religious thought* (to reuse John Wheeler's famous phrase about the unreasonable effectiveness of mathematics) simply transcends the scope of evolutionary psychology. A clearer concession of this fact by Boyer would have been appropriate.

Evolutionary Psychology and the Role of Rationality

Taking evolutionary psychology seriously does not mean simply to take for granted its accounts and explanations of religious imagination. Rather, the task is to engage with its methods and findings in a critical and open inquiry.

---

35. See, for instance, Robert A. Hinde, *Why Gods Persist* (New York: Routledge, 1999), or Andrew Newberg, Eugene Daquili, and Vince Rause, *Why God Won't Go Away* (New York: Ballantine Publishing Group, 2001). See also the recent philosophical dissertation by Anne L. C. Runehov, *Sacred or Neural? Neuroscientific Explanations of Religious Experience: A Philosophical Evaluation* (Uppsala University, 2004).

36. Boyer, "Evolution of the Modern Mind," p. 104.

Let me here, for the sake of brevity, summarize some of the more general points made above:

(1) Evolutionary psychology has not yet provided any evidence of an evolutionary hardwiring of religious thinking and imagination in the human brain. Evolutionary psychology could only do so if the prevalence of particular cognitive systems were linked with specified gene functions (at the ultimate level of evolutionary explanation) *or* could be shown to be caused by particular brain modules (at the proximate level of explanation). A thoroughly naturalistic approach would require rather robust links between brain modules and mental modules. By implication, religion has in fact not been explained by Boyer's theory, neither theoretically nor empirically. Only if evolutionary psychology, genetics, and neuroscience could be theoretically linked in the future would a naturalistic explanation of religion be warranted.
(2) Explanations in terms of cognitive evolutionary science are (despite the occasional rhetoric of its practitioners) methodologically modest, insofar as cognitive science does not pretend to explain the particulars of religious development. Evolutionary psychology does not concern itself with questions such as, Why Buddhism? Why Zen? Why Christianity? Why Anglocatholicism? Why Muhammad? Why Mohammed Ali?
(3) Evolutionary psychology has indeed made a general model for explaining the psychological plausibility of religious belief as well as the ease by which religious ideas are spread socially. However, evolutionary psychology cannot explain, and cannot explain away, the rational or irrational nature of religious life, nor discuss the reality claims intrinsic to all lived religions. Accordingly, evolutionary psychology should be seen as neutral as to the validity and reality claims of religious belief. The reasons for the unreasonable effectiveness of religious beliefs simply lie beyond the scope of evolutionary theory.

However, much can also be learned from Boyer's theory. In my view, a Judeo-Christian theologian should fully acknowledge the *naturalness of religious imagination* in the twofold sense indicated by Pascal Boyer. There are, first, a spontaneity and effortlessness about religious imagination; this external observation is fully in accordance with the Judeo-Christian assumption that human beings are created in the image and likeness of God, and thus designated to engage in communication with God in the "infinitizing medium of phantasy" (Søren Kierkegaard). Second, religious imaginations are natural phenomena, because they belong to the human nature that in turn belongs to the natural order of creation.[37] There is, in this sense, nothing strange about religion. Religions are as real and as natural as atoms are. Only different!

Furthermore, what evolutionary psychology shows us is that religions consistently produce mental representations with similar contents as a result of the ordinary workings of the human mind, including its imaginative capacities. This suggests that *religious imaginations and concepts are to be treated on a par with all other sorts of human thinking.* Just as there are origins of science, so there are origins of religions; just as religious concepts are constructed by human minds, so are mathematical systems and scientific theories; and yet, in all cases we are dealing with cognitive systems that make truth-claims about realities, which are taken to exist prior to human beings, though perhaps never fully graspable. The human ability to form pictures and create metaphors is simply a fact of life that does not need justification. The philosopher or theologian is therefore freed from the burden of giving evidence of the rationality of religious concepts in general. Religious imaginations cannot be treated as a generic unity, but flow in many directions. Accordingly, their rational or irrational nature has to be evaluated on a case-by-case basis.

Where, then, is the question about the rationality of religious commitments to be asked? In my view, the question of rationality should first be asked of members of religious groups, especially to the *virtuosi* who are able to give an informed account of their traditions. For *the question of meaning logically precedes the question of validity.* We need to have an understanding of the truth candidate(s) of a given religion before we can begin to discuss the question of the validity of their putative truths. Strangers and new generations who encounter particular sets of religious imaginations will ask, first, What are their meaning and significance? Then only can they begin to ask the standard philosophy of religion type of question, What are the reasons for believing this or that to be the case? The search for truth in a trans-communal setting presupposes an internal elucidation of the available truth-candidates among current religious options. In effect this means that the philosopher of religion will need some sort of theology, professional or not, as a conversation partner.

What, then, are the truth-candidates of religious imagination? It seems that they cannot be individual images or concepts. For images and concepts are always part of wider cognitive systems, without which we could not inti-

---

37. See my article, "Mensch I: Naturwissenschaftlich und psychologisch," *Religion in Geschichte und Gegenwart*, 4th edition, vol. 5 (2003), pp. 1046-1052.

mate the meaning of such individual images and concepts. The meaning of words is determined by the context of sentences, sentences by the context of discourses, and so on. What can be learned from cognitive science is the way in which a particular concept of God, for example, cannot be treated in isolation from the more general inference systems of agency detection. What is not made clear among the cognitive scientists discussed above, however, is the extent to which the constituent concepts and imaginations are part of particular semantic networks or "traditions." What it means for "God" to be a "person," for example, is different from the perspective of a Mormon (who believes in the finite corporeality of God), a Christian (who believes in incarnation), and a Muslim (who abhors any connection between divine nature and embodiment). Thus the truth-candidates of religious imaginations must always be specified in relation to the semantic networks of particular religious communities. This salient feature of the semantic holism of religious ideas is, unfortunately, not reflected in Boyer's cognitive theory of religious concepts.[38]

But not only are terms specified in sentences, but sentences are also part of utterances, utterances are part of situations, and situations are part of socially embedded life-worlds. Therefore we have not only a "meaning holism," but also a pragmatically informed "context holism" that is of particular importance in religious life. In most religious traditions we find an *apophatic awareness* of the impenetrability of the divine. Accordingly, religious truth-claims are often not so much about depicting the reality of God as about the right manners of approaching divine reality. To Jews, God is beyond imagination, but they nonetheless argue that the Torah of God offers the right guide to the perplexed when approaching God. This pragmatic dimension of religious faith falls through the cracks in Boyer's approach. Boyer focuses programmatically on religious concepts and mental representations instead of on the pragmatic dimensions of religious communal life.[39] But meaning is never without praxis, and praxis never without meaning.

---

38. Neither is this the case in Jerry Fodor's atomistic thesis of "mental modules"; see his critique of meaning holism in Jerry Foder and Ernest Lepore, *Holism: A Shopper's Guide* (Oxford: Blackwell, [1992] 1993), pp. 1-36. The critique (borrowed from Michael Dummett) that "if holism is true, then I can't understand any of your language unless I can understand practically all of it" (p. 9) holds true only if the holist epistemologist would claim that one would need to attain a fully specified knowledge of any particular term. What happens, however, is that we tacitly make reality assumptions of a more tentative nature, as pointed out by Wilhelm Dilthey and others; see Wolfhart Pannenberg, *Wissenschaftstheorie und Theologie* (Göttingen: Vandenhoeck & Ruprecht, 1973).

39. See Boyer, *The Naturalness of Religious Ideas*, p. 276, where he defends the position

This is, I hypothesize, what the postfoundationalist philosopher-theologian Wentzel van Huyssteen could, and perhaps would, say to the evolutionary psychologist.

---

that "mental representations are the replicators, and behaviors are among the objects that make their replication possible, in other words, among their vehicles." I would argue that the behavioral patterns (say, ritual, confession, prayer, meditation) constitute the social context within which the mental ideas of individuals are transmitted. I would add, however, that the internal logic of mental representation, facilitated by cultural systems, including scriptures, can have a feedback influence on religious behaviors. The Reformation movement may count as an example.

20 Toward a Transversal Model of Interdisciplinary Thinking in Practical Theology

Richard Robert Osmer

One of J. Wentzel van Huyssteen's most important contributions to the contemporary discussion of science and theology is his development of a new approach to interdisciplinary work, a transversal model of interdisciplinarity. In this chapter, I will explore the potential contribution of this model to practical theology. I will begin with a brief overview of practical theology and then explore in some depth this field's dialogue with the social sciences, which serves as an extended example of interdisciplinary work in practical theology. I will then offer some of the reasons a transversal model is more adequate than correlational and transformational approaches. I will conclude by pointing briefly to some of the areas that need further reflection in developing this model in practical theology and, perhaps, in van Huyssteen's own thinking.

Contemporary Practical Theology

Practical theology as an academic field emerged in the context of the modern research university. It was part of the fourfold pattern of theology that structured theological education in Europe and North America, articulated by the theological encyclopedias of this era: biblical studies, church history, theology (dogmatics and ethics), and practical theology. Within this "encyclopedic" paradigm of theology, practical theology had the particular task of forming "theories of practice," which included "rules of art" (open-ended guidelines about how to carry out some form of teaching, preaching, or care).[1]

---

1. For a widely influential example of a theological encyclopedia that described practical theology in this way, see Friedrich Schleiermacher, *Brief Outline on the Study of Theology,* trans. Terrence Tice (Richmond: John Knox, 1966). Schleiermacher, however, offered a threefold, not

While I cannot pursue it here, it is worth noting in passing that the encyclopedic paradigm of theology has been called into question on many fronts in our postmodern intellectual context. One of the most important questions raised of this paradigm is the way it divides theology into relatively autonomous, specialized disciplines which work in relative isolation from one another and from other fields. In van Huyssteen's work, it is precisely this sort of isolation and hyper-specialization of the theological disciplines that is called into question by his attention to interdisciplinarity. Like many fields, practical theology has been in the midst of thinking its way beyond the encyclopedic paradigm for several decades, including the exploration of various ways of carrying out interdisciplinary work.

Beginning in the 1960s, a new understanding of practical theology began to emerge. While characterized by a high degree of pluralism, the subject matter and tasks of this approach can be summarized as follows: *Practical theology constructs action-guiding theories of Christian praxis in particular social contexts based on four interrelated forms of research and scholarship — the descriptive-empirical, the interpretive, the normative, and the pragmatic.* As noted in this definition, the primary subject matter of practical theology is some form of Christian praxis in the contemporary world. If biblical studies begins with biblical texts and church history with the artifacts of the past, practical theology begins with Christian praxis in the present. It investigates this praxis empirically, interprets it to better understand and explain its patterns, constructs a theological framework with which it can be assessed critically, and provides practical models and guidelines for its future conduct and reform. A brief description of each of these tasks may be helpful.

Descriptive-empirical research investigates what is going on in a particular field of social action using the research tools of the human sciences. Sometimes, practical theologians can draw on empirical research by social scientists. In recent decades, however, many practical theologians have come to believe that they cannot rely exclusively on the empirical findings of other fields. Sometimes, social scientists work with highly reductionistic views of religion or fail to investigate the issues of greatest importance to a religious community at a given time. For these reasons and others, many contemporary practical theologians have begun to make empirical research an important part of their work.

---

fourfold, proposal, which was not widely accepted. See also *Christian Caring: Selections from "Practical Theology,"* ed. James Duke and Howard Stone, trans. James Duke (Philadelphia: Fortress, 1988).

A second form of research and reflection in practical theology involves *interpretation* of a particular field of social action. Quite often, this follows empirical or clinical investigation. Having attended closely to what is going on in a situation or context, the goal is now to interpret what has been discovered. What is the meaning of these events or actions to those involved? What is the longer history in which they are embedded? How do social structures and cultural patterns influence these events?

The *normative* task of practical theology sets it apart from the human sciences as they often are practiced. Here, proposals are offered about what *ought* to take place in a given field of social action. Social scientists commonly are reluctant to offer this sort of normative guidance, and when they do so they draw on philosophical and ethical frameworks. In contrast, practical theologians cannot avoid offering this sort of normative guidance to the Christian community, for it is a key part of developing an action-guiding theory of Christian praxis. Such guidance, moreover, is explicitly theological and draws on the sources of Christian truth: Scripture, tradition, experience, and reason.

The *pragmatic* dimension of practical theology is the construction of models of Christian practice and rules of art, the exclusive focus of this field within the encyclopedic paradigm. Here, practical theologians seek to offer guidance to individuals and communities in how they might carry out certain activities or practices. How might a congregation cultivate the civic virtues of debate, tolerance, and respect through its educational ministry in a country which has only recently begun to practice democracy? What sort of prayers for healing are appropriate in a culture whose cosmology includes the spirit-world and in which exorcism is regularly practiced? How might premarital counseling be structured for divorced persons who were raised Catholic or Baptist and desire to be remarried in the church? Each of these examples raises issues that are context-specific; and, accordingly, practical theologians develop models of practice that are contextual in a strong sense.

To summarize, the primary subject matter of practical theology is some form of contemporary Christian praxis. It investigates this praxis empirically, interprets it to better understand and explain its patterns, constructs a theological framework with which it can be assessed critically, and provides models of practice and rules of art for its future conduct and reform. While other fields carry out some of these tasks — and thus overlap practical theology — it is the way these tasks inform one another throughout that is unique to practical theology as a field. Elsewhere, I have portrayed the interrelated character of the four tasks of practical theology in terms of a hermeneutical circle,

The Four Tasks of Practical Theology

```
        Descriptive
        Empirical
           ↑
Pragmatic ←—+—→ Interpretive
           ↓
         Normative
```

as depicted in the diagram above.[2] While the circle can be entered at any point, each of the distinctive tasks is part of a larger, interrelated whole. It is the way practical theology holds together the descriptive-empirical, interpretive, normative, and pragmatic dimensions of its work in a mutually influential fashion that distinguishes it as an academic field with its own program of research and scholarship. While other fields carry out one or another of these tasks, no other field does all of them.

Interdisciplinary Work in Practical Theology: An Extended Example

An important part of the new approach to practical theology is extensive attention to interdisciplinary work. Throughout the twentieth century, practical theologians in Europe and North America engaged the human sciences in their work. This included, for example, pastoral care's dialogue with therapeutic psychology and extensive use of the case study method in Clinical Pastoral Education, Christian education's engagement of developmental psychology, cultural anthropology, and critical social theory, and preaching's

---

2. Richard Osmer, *The Teaching Ministry of Congregations* (Louisville: Westminster/John Knox, 2005). See the Epilogue.

dialogue with rhetoric, communication theory, and congregational studies. Much of this interdisciplinary work has been influenced by the correlational approach of Paul Tillich and the revised correlational approaches of David Tracy and Don Browning. More recently, James Loder and Deborah van Deusen Hunsinger have developed a transformational approach.

I will consider these various approaches at a later point and make a case for the greater adequacy of a transversal model of interdisciplinary work. I want to build toward this claim inductively, however, beginning with a thick description of the sort of interdisciplinary issues facing practical theologians today when engaging the social sciences as a dialogue partner in their descriptive-empirical or interpretive work. Such persons face the following interdisciplinary question: *What is the nature of social science and what is practical theology's relationship to the social sciences?* Each part of this twofold question is complex in its own right and raises important interdisciplinary issues. I will explore these issues by examining two very different understandings of social science found in the writings of Bent Flyvbjerg,[3] on the one hand, and of Andrew Sayer[4] and Margaret Archer,[5] on the other.

The first part of this question asks: *What is the nature of social science?* The answer that contemporary social scientists themselves give to this question commonly involves interdisciplinary reflection, often bringing into conversation philosophy and social science (sometimes concentrating on the philosophy of science). This interdisciplinary conversation has important implications for their understanding of the nature of social science, readily apparent in the contrast between Flyvbjerg and Sayer/Archer, who draw on quite different philosophical traditions.

In *Making Social Science Matter,* Flyvbjerg retrieves Aristotle's understanding of *phronesis* to portray social science as a "phronetic discipline" taking the form of value-rationality that explores particular social problems in specific circumstances and contexts and offers value-laden judgments to the larger public discussion about how best to respond to these problems. Something like phronetic social science, Flyvbjerg argues, already is approximated in Robert Bellah's understanding of social science as public philosophy and Pierre Bourdieu's understanding of social science as fieldwork in philosophy.[6] As he puts it:

3. Bent Flyvbjerg, *Making Social Science Matter: Why Social Inquiry Fails and How It Can Succeed Again* (Cambridge: Cambridge University Press, 2001).

4. Andrew Sayer, *Realism and Social Science* (Thousand Oaks: Sage, 2000).

5. Margaret Archer, *Realist Social Theory: The Morphogenetic Approach* (Cambridge: Cambridge University Press, 1995).

6. Flyvbjerg, *Making Social Science Matter,* p. 60.

The principal objective for social science with a phronetic approach is to carry out analyses and interpretations of the status of values and interests in society aimed at social commentary and social action, i.e. praxis. The point of departure for classical phronetic research can be summarized in the following three value-rational questions: (1) Where are we going? (2) Is this desirable? (3) What should be done?[7]

Flyvbjerg, however, believes that neither Aristotle nor contemporary philosophical retrievals of an Aristotelian understanding of *phronesis* (e.g., the philosophical hermeneutics of Gadamer) provide an adequate understanding of power. Thus, he draws on the philosophy of Michel Foucault to conceptualize attentiveness to power in the social sciences. Power is to be viewed not only in terms of its outcomes (Who is in possession of what collective resources?) or centers (Who controls whom?) but also as a *process* (How is it exercised?), best viewed as a network of unequal and mobile relations and interactions that are embedded in a community's practices and discourses. Social science as value-rationality, thus, must add a fourth question to the three noted above: Who gains and who loses; by which mechanisms of power?[8] This entails reflexivity about the discourses and practices that constitute social science itself, for they too are implicated in the dynamics of power by which "experts" define "the ensemble of rules according to which the true and false are separated."[9]

Flyvbjerg's interdisciplinary dialogue with Aristotle and Foucault enables him to define the nature of social science as a phronetic discipline. While a brief summary will not do justice to the complexity of his argument, it may be helpful to provide an outline of the methodological guidelines of phronetic social scientific research developed in the ninth chapter of his book: (1) Social science focuses on values, both those discovered through research on particular groups and those of the researcher; (2) an analysis of power lies at the heart of social science; (3) researchers must get close to the group or phenomenon being studied, not only during data collection, but also during data analysis, feedback, and publication; (4) research should begin phenomenologically, asking "little" questions and developing thick descriptions of specific contexts; (5) such research should look at practices before discourse, examining the everyday practices that constitute a given field of interest; (6) phronetic research should privilege research on particular

---

7. Flyvbjerg, *Making Social Science Matter*, p. 60.
8. Flyvbjerg, *Making Social Science Matter*, pp. 60, 145.
9. Flyvbjerg, *Making Social Science Matter*, p. 125, quoting Foucault.

cases in concrete contexts, for such cases provide the kind of knowledge that informs phronetic judgment, which reasons from "critical cases" to more general judgments and to other particular cases; (7) such cases should be developed through narrative analysis which attends to processes, particular circumstances, and historical unfolding; (8) the researcher should seek to join agency and structure, focusing on both the actor level and the structural level, as well as their interrelationship; (9) the goal of phronetic research is not to offer the one, fully verified, scientific explanation of a field of study but to "produce input to the ongoing social dialogue and praxis in a society."[10] Phronetic social science that works along these lines, Flyvbjerg argues, will "matter"; it will contribute to the ongoing dialogue within society about where it is going, where it ought to be going, and how it might get there.

One enters very different waters when moving to the understandings of social science found in the writings of Andrew Sayer and Margaret Archer. They also bring social science into dialogue with philosophy, drawing on the tradition of critical realism articulated in the writings of Roy Bhaskar.[11] While it is beyond the scope of this paper to develop a detailed account of Bhaskar's philosophy, I will describe a few of his key concepts that are important to Sayer's and Archer's understandings of social science.

The defining feature of critical realism is the belief that there is a world existing independently of our knowledge of it — hence Bhaskar's reintroduction of the importance of ontology in the philosophy of science. This does not lead to a simple correspondence theory of truth or to some new form of foundationalism. Rather, the mind-independence of the world points to the fallibility of our knowledge of it. As Sayer puts it:

> Realism is therefore necessarily a fallibilist philosophy and one which must be wary of simple correspondence concepts of truth. It must acknowledge that the world can only be known under particular descriptions, in terms of available discourses, though it does not follow from this that no description or explanation is better than any other.[12]

Bhaskar's philosophy holds together ontological realism, epistemological relativism, and judgmental rationality. Scientific theories provide alternative accounts of the *same* world and if one can better explain certain fea-

---

10. Flyvbjerg, *Making Social Science Matter*, p. 139.
11. Margaret Archer, Roy Bhaskar, Andrew Collier, Tony Lawson, and Alan Norrie, *Critical Realism: Essential Readings*, Centre for Critical Realism (London: Routledge, 1998).
12. Sayer, *Realism and Social Science*, p. 2.

tures of this world, then it must be judged to be more adequate, even as it remains fallible. This view is based on a fundamental distinction found in Bhaskar's philosophy between the transitive and intransitive dimensions of knowledge. The "objects" of science — in the sense of the being of natural and social processes and phenomena — are the intransitive dimension of science. The theories that scientists form about such "objects" are the transitive dimension of science. Sayer describes the significance of this distinction as follows:

> When theories change (transitive dimension), it does not mean that what they are about (intransitive dimension) necessarily changes too: there is no reason to believe that the shift from a flat earth theory to a round earth theory was accompanied by a change in the shape of the earth itself.[13]

This distinction implies that the world should not be reduced either to human experience or to empirical accounts of it, the hallmarks of empiricism and positivism, on the one hand, and interpretive social science, on the other. Bhaskar thus goes on to make an important distinction between the real, the actual, and the empirical. The "real" refers to two things: (1) whatever exists, regardless of our capacity to give an empirical account of it; (2) the structures, powers, and capacities of particular "objects."[14] The "actual" refers to what happens when the capacities or powers of "objects" are activated and what eventuates. The "empirical" is the domain of experience, which is contingent and observable.

Bhaskar's distinction between the real, the actual, and the empirical presupposes a stratified ontology in which the knowledge-independent world in which we live is composed of genuinely different kinds of "objects," with their own distinctive properties and powers. Different strata of natural and social "objects" are accounted for in terms of the concept of emergence, the process in which preexisting elements are combined to produce qualitatively new "objects" with properties that are irreducible to their constituents. As Sayer notes, the standard example of emergence at the physical level is "the emergent properties of water which are quite different from those of its constituents, hydrogen and oxygen."[15] Similarly, emergence accounts for different strata of reality, the way social phenomena emerge from biological constituents, which emerge from chemical and physical constituents. Reductionistic

---

13. Sayer, *Realism and Social Science*, p. 11.
14. Sayer, *Realism and Social Science*, p. 11.
15. Sayer, *Realism and Social Science*, p. 12.

explanations that attempt to give an account of one stratum entirely in terms of the properties of another (often "lower") stratum are inadequate, as is sometimes seen in the attempt to explain human consciousness or social interaction in terms of the physical mechanisms of the brain.

A variety of social theorists have drawn on Bhaskar's philosophy or other versions of critical realism (e.g., Chris Smith and Michael Emerson,[16] Derek Layder,[17] and Bob Carter,[18] to name but a few). I want to focus briefly on Margaret Archer's *Realist Social Theory: The Morphogenetic Approach*, not because it exemplifies all of possibilities of realistic social theory, but rather because Archer offers a comprehensive account of the nature of social science that builds on the platform of Bhaskar's philosophy. Archer begins by distinguishing social reality from natural and transcendental reality:

> Social reality is unlike any other because of its human constitution. It is different from natural reality whose defining feature is self-subsistence.... Society is more different still from transcendental reality, where divinity is both self-subsistent and unalterable at our behest.[19]

Three unique characteristics, she goes on to argue, characterize social reality: (1) it is inseparable from its human components because the very existence of society depends in some way upon human activities; (2) society has no immutable form and is inherently transformable; (3) human agents are not immutable, for their agency takes shape in relation to the society in which they live and by their efforts to transform it.[20] The central problematic of the social sciences, as such, is providing an adequate account of the relationship and interplay of society and individuals or, more properly, of structure and agency. In developing such an account, it is the nature of social science to deal with three interrelated, but distinguishable tasks:[21]

(1) articulating a social ontology, which provides an account of the constituents of society;

---

16. Chris Smith and Michael Emerson, *Divided by Faith: Evangelical Religion and the Problem of Race in America* (Oxford: Oxford University Press, 2000).

17. Derek Layder, *Modern Social Theory: Key Debates and New Directions* (London: UCL, 1997).

18. Bob Carter, *Realism and Racism: Concepts of Race in Sociological Research* (London: Routledge, 2000).

19. Archer, *Realist Social Theory*, p. 1.

20. Archer, *Realist Social Theory*, p. 1.

21. Archer, *Realist Social Theory*, pp. 2-3, 12-13.

(2) an explanatory methodology, which provides an account of how society is properly investigated and explained;
(3) a practical social theory, which carries out research on particular social problems.

In this tripartite understanding of social science, Archer portrays social ontology as playing a regulative role; it conceptualizes social reality in certain terms, thus identifying what there is to be explained. The first part of the book develops a critique of the social ontologies of both classical and contemporary social scientists, which she believes fail to distinguish the relatively autonomous social strata of social structures, cultural systems, and human agency. She describes this in terms of conflation. Upward conflationists like symbolic interactionists and ethnomethodologists work with a social ontology in which human agents are constitutive of social reality, rendering social structures epiphenomenal. Downward conflationists like structural functionalists and certain forms of Marxism work with a social ontology in which social structures are constitutive of social reality, rendering agents epiphenomenal. Central conflationists — Archer's primary target here is the structuration theory of Anthony Giddens — fail to adequately distinguish the different strata of structure and agency in their social ontologies by conflating them into a twofold, unified process (e.g., Giddens's "duality" of structure and agency).[22]

Archer argues that the inadequacies of the social ontologies of these different forms of conflation in social science have implications at the second, *methodological* level of her tripartite schema, leading to forms of investigation and explanation that fail to take into account the relative independence and mutual influence of structure and agency. In the second part of *Realist Social Theory*, she offers an explanatory methodology that she believes is more adequate, which she calls *analytical dualism*. In so doing, she draws not only on Bhaskar's stratified social ontology to distinguish structure, culture, and agency, but also on his concept of emergence, the idea that over time new powers and properties accompany new social and cultural forms, which are brought into being through human agency and which, in turn, reshape human agency. She describes the temporality entailed by the emergent nature of social reality in terms of the three phases of the morphogenetic cycle. We will examine each in turn. (Archer's key terms are italicized.)

---

22. See Anthony Giddens, *The Constitution of Society: Outline of a Theory of Structuration* (Berkeley: University of California Press, 1984).

Structural Conditioning

Human beings are born into a world that is not of their own making but is the result of the past actions of earlier generations. They are born into different *positions* with quite different life chances, take up *social roles* defined by preexistent *institutional* configurations, and find themselves in a social environment characterized by a relative degree of social integration or tension between different institutional structures. Such preexistent structures condition (not determine) human agents by placing them in particular *situations* in which *opportunity costs* attend particular courses of action and by offering them *strategic directional guidance* in both defining and acting upon particular life *projects*.

Social Interaction

This second phase of the morphogenetic cycle focuses on the role of agents in responding to the *enablements* and *constraints* of the social situations in which they find themselves, with the capacity to reproduce or transform them and, thereby, remake themselves in the process. A stratified model of human agency posits *collective agents* or collectivities sharing the same life chances and, thus, having the same *vested interests*. *Corporate agents* self-consciously take up and advocate their interest in organized groups or movements; *primary agents* (while belonging to collectivities) remain passive and either lack the capacity or the will to organize for strategic pursuit of their interests. *Actors* are the incumbents of particular roles, which may be pursued and *personified* in quite different ways by different people. The emergence of consciousness as a constitutive property of *Homo sapiens* gives rise to the evolving construction of a personal identity at the individual level, which is not reducible to social identity and opens up a space for individual reflexivity.

Structural Elaboration

The modification of prior social and cultural forms through human interaction takes places under the conditions of group conflict and concession. It is rarely the sort of straightforward outcome described in simple cybernetic models. It includes a high degree of *unintended consequences*.

Practical Theology in Dialogue with the Social Sciences

I have chosen Flyvbjerg and Sayer/Archer because they give two very different answers to the question, What is the nature of social science? While both are philosophically informed, they draw on quite different philosophical traditions. Flyvbjerg portrays social science as a "phronetic discipline" that is qualitatively different than natural science and does not produce theories along the lines of "normal" science (in Kuhn's sense) in which research programs accumulate new knowledge and make progress over time. In contrast, Sayer and Archer portray social and natural science as sharing certain features in that they both take account of a stratified, emergent world whose "objects" and processes exist independently of our knowledge of them. The task of science in all its forms is to develop an explanatory methodology that is appropriate to the "objects" under investigation. In the case of social science, this means a methodology that acknowledges the irreducible strata of social structure, culture, and human agency which are constitutive of social reality.

Phronetic social science along the lines of Flyvbjerg or realistic social science along the lines of Sayer/Archer are only two of many proposals found among contemporary social scientists. Today, practical theologians confront the reality of pluralism in social science. In part, this is the result of interdisciplinarity within social science itself — the very different philosophical traditions engaged by particular social scientists and the explanatory methodologies which they deem consistent with their philosophical position and appropriate to empirical research. This pluralism is one of the strongest points in favor of a transversal model of interdisciplinarity, as we shall see.

In the face of this pluralism, practical theologians face the task of providing reasons for their evaluation of one approach as more adequate than others. At least in part, this obligates practical theologians to understand the issues at stake in current debates in philosophy, the philosophy of science, and social science methodology. They must also be able to give reasons for evaluating one social scientific approach as more adequate than others *on grounds internal* to philosophy and social science and to the interdisciplinary issues at stake in bringing these two fields together in a particular social scientific program.

For example, how successful is Flyvbjerg in bringing together Aristotle's concept of *phronesis* and Foucault's understanding of power? *Phronesis* presupposes a fairly strong notion of the subject engaged in practical reasoning; much of Foucault's project has involved decentering the reasoning subject and relocating it in power-laden discourses and practices. Does Flyvbjerg adequately account for the tensions between these two philosophical perspectives? This is precisely the sort of issue that practical theologians must engage on grounds internal to philosophy (and in other cases, to social science).

The second part of the question we have been exploring is: *What is practical theology's relationship to the social sciences?* Here, practical theologians are obligated to offer a *theological* account of the relationship between the sources, subject matter, and methods of theology, on the one hand, and those of social science, on the other. Broadly speaking, this is the task of articulating an explicit interdisciplinary method that regulates the relationship between theology and culture in which philosophy and social science are viewed as part of the intellectual resources of contemporary culture. Three quite different interdisciplinary approaches are currently at play in contemporary practical theology.

Models of Interdisciplinarity in Practical Theology

The *correlational* approach is found in the writings of Don Browning,[23] Johannes van der Ven,[24] and James Fowler.[25] It views theology as standing in a mutually influential relationship to the intellectual resources and/or emancipatory praxis of culture. Working within some version of this interdisciplinary approach, it is not uncommon for practical theologians to argue that the rational operations of practical theology must take their bearings from the rational operations of cognate fields. In their empirical research, for example, practical theologians must incorporate the standards and methods of contemporary social science.

From this perspective, it might be argued that a phronetic model of social science as public practical philosophy provides practical theology with important clues about its role in contemporary life. It too is a form of value-rationality that carries out empirical research and theoretical reflection in order to articulate a theological perspective in debates about important social issues. Or drawing on the quite different understanding of social science articulated by Sayer and Archer, a correlational practical theologian might find important clues about the "scientific" nature of practical theology in the conceptual framework of critical realism. This will challenge him or her to do

---

23. Don Browning, *A Fundamental Practical Theology: Descriptive and Strategic Proposals* (Minneapolis: Fortress, 2000).

24. Johannes van der Ven, *Practical Theology: An Empirical Approach* (Kampen, The Netherlands: Kok Pharos, 1993).

25. James Fowler, *Faithful Change: The Personal and Public Challenges of Postmodern Life* (Nashville: Abingdon, 1996).

more than investigate empirical regularities but to explain such regularities in terms of underlying generative mechanisms of structure and agency which are activated in particular historical, local, and institutional contexts filled with contingencies.

Yet a correlational approach to interdisciplinary work is not the only way of conceptualizing practical theology's relationship to social science. What might be called a *transformational model* is articulated in the writings of James Loder[26] and Deborah van Deusen Hunsinger.[27] Loder argues that the intellectual resources of culture enter the domain of theology only by passing across the threshold of double negation. Practical theology, as such, is not merely a sub-species of phronetic value-rationality or realistic social science but has its own distinctive subject matter and rational operations, which provide critical leverage on how the social sciences are appropriated. He typically takes quite seriously the philosophical assumptions of social science and attempts to tease out the implicit understandings of human beings, transformation, socialization, and the transcendent that are embedded in social scientific research and theory. Such anthropological assumptions are often evaluated as inadequate on grounds internal to theology and in need of negation. Only when their limitations are first exposed can they subsequently be appropriated in a practical theological framework — the negation of negation. This interdisciplinary approach is especially evident in *The Logic of the Spirit*.

Hunsinger works with a stratified model of reality quite similar to that of critical realism and argues that the forms of investigation appropriate to different strata of reality must take their bearings from the nature of the "object" under investigation. In the case of Christian theology, however, the divine "object" (or better, the divine "subject") is not properly viewed within the conceptual framework of *emergence*, for it has the form of a divine self-revelation that breaks into reality from beyond creation in the incarnation of Jesus Christ. The practical theologian must thus become bilingual (or perhaps multilingual if engaging psychology, social science, biology, neuroscience, physics, and so forth), allowing the social sciences to have their say about social reality while retaining the distinctive language and disciplinary perspective of theology, which takes its bearings from God's self-communication in Jesus Christ. Integration between theology and social science does not occur at a systematic disciplinary level; rather, it occurs in the

---

26. James Loder, *The Logic of the Spirit: Human Development in Theological Perspective* (San Francisco: Jossey-Bass, 1998).

27. Deborah van Deusen Hunsinger, *Theology and Pastoral Counseling* (Grand Rapids: Eerdmans, 1995).

person of the practical theologian as different fields are brought to bear on a particular problem or situation.

This brings me to van Huyssteen's model, a *transversal* approach to interdisciplinary work,[28] which I have drawn on in *The Teaching Ministry of Congregations*.[29] Unlike correlational models, this approach argues that interdisciplinary work must remain person- and perspective-specific in light of the pluralism found in all fields today, readily apparent in the social sciences as we have seen. It does not work at the general level of theology and culture, but rather views interdisciplinary work as the transversal intersection of particular social scientists working in very specific ways and particular practical theologians working in equally specific ways. Generalized statements about the relationship between theology and social science are avoided and in their place is a more local or concrete account of the ways particular perspectives and persons intersect one another, overlapping in some ways and diverging in others. In my view, the distinction between correlational and transversal approaches pivots on the distinction between modern and postmodern views of culture. The latter acknowledges a much higher degree of pluralization, contestation, and fluidity of boundaries in cultural communities, which is reflected in the pluralism of postmodern culture's intellectual resources.[30]

Unlike transformational models, the transversal approach argues that practical theology and social science cannot, in principle, be cordoned off from one another in advance. To the extent that practical theologians carry out empirical research or draw on the empirical research of others, they overlap the social sciences. As such, they face the task of providing an account of the ways their research is similar to social science or, perhaps better, is similar to some concrete form of social scientific research within a pluralistic field. The extent of overlap and divergence cannot be determined in advance, for it remains person- and perspective-specific.

For example, Archer explicitly acknowledges a transcendent stratum of reality in her social theory, a theme she develops more fully in her contributions to *Transcendence: Critical Realism and God*.[31] This acknowledgment of

---

28. J. Wentzel van Huyssteen, *The Shaping of Rationality: Toward Interdisciplinarity in Theology and Science* (Grand Rapids: Eerdmans, 1999); *Alone in the World? Human Uniqueness in Science and Theology*, The Gifford Lectures, University of Edinburgh 2004 (Grand Rapids: Eerdmans, 2006).

29. Osmer, *Teaching Ministry of Congregations*, Epilogue.

30. For a discussion of postmodern culture, see Katherine Tanner, *Theories of Culture: A New Agenda for Theology* (Minneapolis: Augsburg Fortress, 1997).

31. Margaret Archer, Andrew Collier, and Douglas Porpora, *Transcendence: Critical Realism and God* (London: Routledge, 2004).

the transcendent overlaps practical theology's interest in developing a normative account of the ways God is active in and responsive to the natural and social world. It is possible that a particular practical theologian might conceptualize this divine activity as including, in part, God's involvement in the emergent order of creation — thus overlapping Archer's portrait of the transcendent stratum of reality. How a particular practical theologian handles this overlap will depend on such matters as how he or she conceptualizes original and continuing creation, the activity of the Holy Spirit within continuing creation, the "lure" of God's promised future for creation, and so forth.

It is also the case, however, that this same practical theologian might engage social scientific research on some facet of the religious life that is premised on a highly reductionistic view of religion informed by neo-positivism. In such circumstances, the extent of overlap may be quite small, limited to fragments of empirical insight, while diverging sharply from the philosophical and social scientific framework in which this research is located. The important point to underscore is that a transversal approach to interdisciplinary work in practical theology cannot determine in advance the extent of overlap and divergence when engaging other fields like the social sciences. These must be determined concretely in each particular case.

In terms of my own theological stance, I believe the core theological issue at stake in the difference between transformational and transversal approaches pivots on their very different understandings of the Trinity. Transformationists like Loder and Hunsinger are so Christocentric that they allow little role for the Holy Spirit beyond bringing persons into conformity to the image of Christ, working with a subordinationist pneumatology. One might borrow Archer's term and label this a form of second-person trinitarian conflationism. In contrast, a *social* doctrine of the Trinity in which the distinct but interpenetrating powers and properties of each Person of the Trinity are maintained can underwrite ways of understanding God's immanence in the emergent strata of the natural and social world *and also* God's transcendence of the created world. I have explored the implications of this perspective for interdisciplinary work in *The Teaching Ministry of Congregations* in dialogue with the social doctrine of the Trinity developed by Jürgen Moltmann.

Further Clarification of the Transversal Model

In comparison to correlational and transformational models of interdisciplinarity, the transversal approach is relatively new. I will conclude by pointing to four areas which I believe stand in need of further reflection. First, within the approach to practical theology outlined in the initial part of this chapter, further work is needed on clarifying the distinct interdisciplinary issues involved in each of its four tasks. Empirical work, for example, involves clarifying the assumptions of research (like those explored in this chapter) and also the formulation of a specific research design with certain goals and research methods. The differences between and within quantitative and qualitative research approaches are real. Practical theologians thus face very real choices in formulating a research design. What methods will they choose to use and for what purposes?

These sorts of interdisciplinary issues are quite different from those involved in formulating a normative theological perspective in practical theology. In this task, practical theologians must evaluate the relative importance of the sources of Christian truth (Scripture, tradition, reason, and experience), which will have real bearing on the fields they engage in interdisciplinary conversation: biblical studies, dogmatic theology, Christian ethics, philosophical ethics, or social science, to name but a few. The important point is that each of the four tasks of practical theology raises its own distinct and complex interdisciplinary issues. These stand in need of further clarification.

Second, more work is needed on articulating and justifying the principle of selection in a transversal model of interdisciplinarity. By this I mean the principle(s) that justify why specific persons or perspectives are engaged as interdisciplinary dialogue partners in a particular book or research project. Under the influence of Paul Tillich, correlational models have tended to develop such principles on the basis of Christian anthropology, that is, a theological perspective on humanity is viewed as warranting a dialogue with certain intellectual resources of the contemporary world. This is the way Tillich justified his dialogue with psychoanalysis and existentialism, which were portrayed as criticizing the modern philosophy of consciousness and as analogous to the self-in-conflict and bondage-of-the-will depicted in Pauline and Reformation views of humanity.[32]

At present, no comparable principle of selectivity has been articulated in the discussion of transversal interdisciplinarity. Such principles may prove doubly difficult for this model to formulate for two reasons: (1) its rejection of a "rules" model of rationality and method, and (2) its commitment to local and contextual conversations between specific persons and perspectives that do not determine in advance what might be learned. Together, they

---

32. See particularly the essays collected in Paul Tillich, *Theology of Culture*, ed. Robert Kimball (New York: Oxford University Press, 1959).

work against formulating context-invariant "rules" that might guide the selection of interdisciplinary dialogue partners. This leaves this model vulnerable to charges that it engages only those persons or perspectives that it finds congenial and thus eliminates the real "bite" of conversations with perspectives that challenge its own. It is also vulnerable to the charge that some sort of principle of selectivity is at work but is not explicitly articulated methodologically.

Third, the transversal model needs further philosophical development. While learning from postmodernism, van Huyssteen is quite clear that he does not follow the extreme forms of intellectual postmodernism that move in the direction of a relativistic "many rationalities, many truths" perspective. Typically, he affirms what he calls a "soft" version of critical realism. While devoting an entire book to critical realism early in his career, he has not reworked his earlier thinking in light of his later "turn" toward transversality.[33]

A great deal of new work has appeared on critical realism in recent years. This includes the thinking of Bhaskar, Archer, and Sayer and many others not described in this chapter. Bhaskar explicitly affirms ontological realism, epistemological relativism, and judgmental rationality — a philosophical position that has many similarities to van Huyssteen's perspective. Further philosophical clarification is thus needed of exactly what van Huyssteen means by a "soft" version of critical realism in light of these kinds of developments.

Moreover, this further engagement of critical realism may prove to be of help in refining the status of truth claims in van Huyssteen's perspective. One of the advantages of Bhaskar's and Archer's approaches is their willingness to explore the role of explanation in truth-claims at the epistemological level without recourse to theories of scientific "laws" based on the observation of empirical regularities. They affirm the fallibilism of all truth claims, on the one hand, but make judgments about the relative adequacy of the truth of particular theories in terms of their explanatory power, on the other. Some perspectives are, in fact, more truthful than others because they better explain the generative mechanisms and contingencies in the workings of natural and social phenomena. My point is not that van Huyssteen should take over this particular perspective but that his further engagement of new developments in critical realism might prove helpful in clarifying how and why a transversal model of interdisciplinarity makes judgments about truth claims in its own proposals and those of its dialogue partners.

Fourth, further work is needed to justify the transversal model on *theological*, and not merely philosophical, grounds. Loder and Hunsinger, for ex-

---

33. J. Wentzel van Huyssteen, *The Justification of Belief* (Grand Rapids: Eerdmans, 1989).

ample, make a strong theological case for their transformational models. The revelatory and reconciling work of Christ is unique and singular in kind, they argue. Thus, one must move from the divine self-giving to human sources of truth, discovering analogies of faith. To the present, no comparable theological rationale has appeared among proponents of the transversal model.

Van Huyssteen has tended to justify this model in terms of evolutionary epistemology and contemporary philosophical pragmatism as formulated by Nicholas Rescher[34] and Calvin Schrag.[35] In my view, this raises certain issues that are in need of further theological clarification, like the adequacy of the concepts of problem-solving and adaptation as formulated in pragmatism, which are used by van Huyssteen to describe both religion and Christianity at various points. Problems have solutions; religion deals with mysteries like suffering, evil, and death that do not. Moreover, problem-solving is easily assimilated to instrumental reasoning which is so dominant in our scientific, technological era. Would not a Christian theological perspective need to offer greater clarification and critique of this concept? Similarly, the concept of adaptation inherent to evolutionary epistemology needs further clarification and critique in dialogue with the theological perspectives of Christian eschatology and church witness and mission. As a "contrast society," the church does not simply adapt to its cultural context; sometimes its witness involves actions and stances that may appear to be in real tension with "successful" adaptation but nonetheless are faithful signs of God's promised future. Moreover, does not God's promised redemption of the world take account of those creatures who have failed to adapt and have suffered, died, and been discarded in evolution's rubbish heap? Questions like these need further *theological* clarification, which is a matter of bringing the philosophical perspectives of pragmatism and evolutionary epistemology into a more robust dialogue with the perspectives of Christian eschatology, redemption, and the ecclesial mission. This is precisely the sort of commitment to interdisciplinarity to which van Huyssteen is committed, and I look forward to his future work on such issues.

---

34. Nicholas Rescher, *Rationality: A Philosophical Inquiry into the Nature and the Rationale of Reason* (Oxford: Clarendon, 1988).

35. Calvin Schrag, *The Resources of Rationality: A Response to the Postmodern Challenge* (Bloomington: Indiana University Press, 1992).

21 The Psalms and Lyric Verse

F. W. Dobbs-Allsopp

My ambition here is to begin thinking Hebrew poetry through from the lyric point of view out. The proposition I press in what follows is somewhat more specific, namely, the view that the manner of verse underlying *most* psalms may be usefully and even accurately described as lyric, a notion, in fact, already articulated during the eighteenth century by Sir Robert Lowth[1] and again at the end of the nineteenth century by S. R. Driver.[2] I operate with an (ideal) discourse continuum in mind. It is composed of narrative at one extreme and lyric at the other, with much mixing in between. This is obviously but one way to look at literature, focusing on one set of variables; it is not intended to be a comprehensive interpretive strategy. I find warrant for such an approach both in contemporary literary theory and criticism and especially in the prose/poetry dichotomy that pervades Hebrew literature and breaks down mostly along a narrative/nonnarrative divide.

Much depends on what is meant by the term "lyric," which, at least in critical vocabulary, is notoriously "elusive of definition."[3] I deploy the term

---

1. R. Lowth, *Lectures on the Sacred Poetry of the Hebrews*, trans. G. Gregory, 3rd ed. (London: Tegg & Sons, 1835), pp. 278-315.

2. S. R. Driver, *An Introduction to the Literature of the Old Testament* (1897; Cleveland: Meridian Books, 1956), pp. 359-391.

3. D. Lindley, *Lyric* (London/New York: Methuen, 1985), p. 1.

It is a distinct honor and pleasure to offer the following essay in celebration of the life, work, and thought of J. Wentzel van Huyssteen, a man whom I am most privileged to call my friend. I hope he may perceive in my own efforts here something of his commitment to a truly interdisciplinary discourse (the only way in which I believe that humanists can actually work) and a shared interest in human rationality. But above all it is Wentzel's generosity of spirit that I want most to emulate in my writing and in my person. A toast to Wentzel! *Lĕḥayyîm!*

primarily as a modal designation, what G. Genette calls a "mode of enunciation."[4] His notion is rooted in Aristotle (and ultimately Plato), who famously distinguishes between epic and drama — lyric as a nonmimetic kind of verse is apparently nowhere in view in the *Poetics* — by focusing on the "what" and the "how" and even the "in what" of imitation, with the "manner of imitation" (the "how?") being critical: epic *tells* through pure or mixed (i.e., involving dialogue between characters) narration, and drama *presents* "all [the] characters as living and moving before us" (as on stage; *Poetics* 1448a).[5] In linguistic terms, mode is chiefly a question of pragmatics, the "what" and the "how" of language use — though its literary purview extends beyond the purely linguistic. On such a construal, lyric distinguishes modally, phenomenologically, pragmatically (if you will) the various nonrepresentational, nonnarrative, nondramatic types of poetry. This is the sense of the term implicit in the (partly arbitrary) threefold distinction between lyric, epic, and drama that has been at the heart of literary criticism in the West for much of its history.[6] Such an understanding of "lyric" dates at least as far back as the Alexandrians and corresponds roughly, on the one hand, to how contemporary classicists wield the term as a catch-all phrase "covering more or less all the Greek poetry of the centuries down to 350 BC apart from epic, didactic, and other verse composed in hexameters, and drama,"[7] and, on the other hand, to the sense the term has in much contemporary theoretical and critical discussion, where it has become more or less synonymous with the term "poetry" — or, perhaps more accurately, it is taken as the prototype of a poem.[8]

"Lyric" may be construed more narrowly as well, as a more specific genre

---

4. G. Genette, *The Architext: An Introduction*, trans. J. E. Lewin (Berkeley: University of California, 1979), p. 61.

5. Genette, *Architext*, p. 11; his initial discussions of Plato and Aristotle are on pp. 8-9 and pp. 10-14 respectively.

6. Tracing and demystifying the history of this three-way distinction in Western literary criticism is the project of Genette's *Architext*.

7. M. L. West, *Greek Lyric Poetry*, World Classics (Oxford/New York: Oxford University Press, 1994), p. vii; cf. E. Bowie, "Lyric and Elegiac Poetry," in *The Oxford History of the Classical World*, ed. J. Boardman et al. (Oxford/New York: Oxford University Press, 1986), pp. 99-100; H. Fränkel, *Early Greek Poetry and Philosophy*, trans. M. Hadas and J. Willis (New York: Harcourt Brace Jovanovich, 1973), p. 133 n. 4.

8. Cf. Lindley, *Lyric*, p. 22. So, for example, J. Culler glosses "poetic" with "lyric" in his own discussion of the three overarching modes or genres (*Literary Theory: A Very Short Introduction* [Oxford: Oxford University Press, 1997], p. 69). But more to the point, lyric is simply assumed to be the prototype of poetry in most critical discussions today (a holdover from the Romantic era and from New Criticism?).

designation.[9] The features that are isolated in this usage, as D. Lindley well notes, are "profoundly affected by fluctuation in systems of classification and poetic practice through history"[10] — and, one might add, from tradition to tradition. So, in discussing early Greek lyric, for example, to accentuate the sung quality of most of this verse makes good sense in light of scholars' knowledge about the composition of these poems — to be accompanied by the lyre, *aulos,* or other instruments — and the kinds of contexts in which they were routinely performed. But when it comes to a poet like Horace, who never sang his verse, the *literal* use of music ceases to be a meaningful genre criteria.

An awareness of such historical variation has two consequences worth underscoring. First, whatever the extent of lyric verse in the Psalms, and elsewhere in the Bible, it will inevitably be shaped and marked by the particularity of its time, place, and the larger literary tradition of which it is a part. That is, I have no investment in (and see no benefit to) uncovering specific kinds of lyric verse in the Bible, whether they be Romantic, modernist, or even early Greek. Other bodies and traditions of lyric verse are, of course, crucial to the kind of study being conducted here, but principally as a means for gauging the possibilities and varieties of lyric discourse as a backdrop for a better appreciation of the kind of lyric found in the Bible. To press my point, consider the *symposium,* one of the primary contexts in which Greek monody was performed. This is an especially Greek cultural institution with nothing quite like it in ancient Israel, and thus on this basis alone one can expect both qualitative and quantitative differences in the kind of lyric verse realized in the two cultures.

Second, what ultimately is counted as lyric depends importantly on the specific criteria that are privileged. Is there any hope, then, "of defining 'lyric' as a generic label?" asks Lindley. His answer is that it "must be tentative." He elaborates:

> It must be accepted that a wide variety of determinants may properly be felt as significant in allocating a poem to a lyric category. While a "personal" poem in stanza form about the pains of love and intended to be set to music would universally be accepted as a "lyric," it is in no sense an authoritative model. For throughout literary history there has been not only a

---

9. Genette also distinguishes between lyric as a mode and as a genre, though his insistence that the former is purely a matter of linguistics and that the latter involves the addition of thematic elements does not seem to me to be quite accurate.

10. Lindley, *Lyric,* p. 5.

wide range of possible subject matter, but considerable divergence in the criteria that have been felt as paramount . . . , so that all decisions about a work's generic status must be conditioned by an awareness of that history. It is also inevitable that many poems might hover on the edges, and to pretend to a certainty that can judge infallibly between a lyrical narrative or a narrative lyric [for example] . . . , would be to misunderstand the way readers actually use (or are used by) their generic awareness and the way poets play with and upon generic expectations.[11]

Both of these senses of lyric — the modal and the generic — factor in my discussion, though keeping straight what distinguishes the two is crucial to the kinds of claims I make about psalms *as* lyric. So, for example, while there surely are psalms that were composed to be literally sung, and thus would satisfy even the narrowest definition of a lyric poem, so, too, are there psalms where such a designation seems less felicitous. My aim here is not to be reductionist or to reify classificatory schemes for their own sake; nor even is it critical that *all* psalms fit one or another of my senses of lyric. As C. Guillén rightly observes, "there are no pure forms";[12] and in any case, the lyric's "differences from other literary products are not radical," as S. Langer writes, "and there is no device characteristic of lyric composition that may not also be met in other forms."[13] The chief outcome sought in the review of the several lyric practices and tendencies that follows is finally to sharpen and extend our understanding of the inner workings of psalmic verse. That is, I pursue this particular line of inquiry pragmatically and heuristically, which is to say, in full awareness that the attrac-

---

11. Lindley, *Lyric*, p. 22.

12. C. Guillén, *The Challenge of Comparative Literature*, trans. C. Franzen (Cambridge, MA: Harvard University Press, 1993), p. 142.

13. S. Langer, *Feeling and Form: A Theory of Art* (New York: Scribner, 1953), p. 259. And similarly, D. Levertov remarks that lyric verse is constructed out of the everyday language of normal discourse — idle chat, news briefs, dinner table conversation (*The Poet in the World* [New York: New Directions, 1973], p. 87). The term "lyric" itself is not unproblematic, as demonstrated in my own attempt to disentangle at least two ways in which it might signify. Genette, too, comments on the unhappiness of this term. He notes well how "terminology" itself "reflects and aggravates the theoretical confusion. To set beside *drama* . . . and *epic* . . . we can offer [in English] . . . only the limp *lyric poem*" (*Architext*, p. 68 n. 74). That is, it is admittedly hard to hear the term "lyric" without the ghost of its ancient Greek usage coming to mind, even though the vast majority of nonnarrative, nondramatic verse before and since does not answer to such a narrow definition of lyric, and the problem is only acerbated when the term is applied to the distinctly non-Greek world of the ancient Near East. Still, as Genette observes, there is no obvious terminological alternative. So my endeavor in what follows is to illuminate the phenomenon that stands behind the term "lyric," with the hope that the term itself will not prove too distractive.

tion of my thesis lies ultimately in its usefulness for reading these poems and for making sense of their prosody. To make such judgments obviously will require a more sustained effort than can be accomplished here. For the moment, then, it will be enough to (re)introduce the notion of "lyric" (in its several senses) as a critical idiom and along the way point to some of the potential payoffs that its use holds for our criticism and interpretation of psalmic poetry.[14]

Nonnarrative and Nondramatic Poetry

One way to begin gaining a firmer fix on the lyric is, following the lead of N. Frye,[15] to say what it is not: the lyric is not a narrative; or better, it is *chiefly*, as I have already said, a nonnarrative, nondramatic, nonrepresentational kind of poetry (here accenting the modal sense of the term).[16] It is the noncentrality, and indeed frequent absence, of features and practices (plot, character, and the like) that are otherwise definitive of more discursive modes of literary discourse (e.g., narrative, drama) that so distinguishes the medium of lyric verse and shapes the basic contours of its discourse. As J. Culler succinctly states, "narrative poems recount an event; lyrics . . . strive to be an event."[17] The outstanding characteristic of biblical poetry, of course, is its fundamental *nonnarrativity*. R. Alter puts his finger on precisely this "peculiarity": "The Hebrew writers used verse for celebratory song, dirge, oracle, oratory, prophecy, reflective and didactic argument, liturgy, and often as a

---

14. The thesis that the basic medium of the psalms is of a lyric variety will not come as a surprise to most. Indeed, as noted at the outset, the notion is already very prominent early on in the work of Lowth and Driver. What I do not always perceive on the part of contemporary interpreters of the psalms is a *critical* awareness of the lyric as a distinct mode of discourse, and it is to this awareness, especially when our default reading strategies are so narratively oriented in this age of novels and Hollywood movies, that I would recall us.

15. N. Frye, "Approaching the Lyric," in *Lyric Poetry: Beyond New Criticism*, ed. C. Hošek and P. Parker (Ithaca: Cornell University Press, 1985), p. 31.

16. E.g., Langer, *Feeling and Form*, p. 259; B. Herrnstein Smith, *Poetic Closure: A Study of How Poems End* (Chicago: University of Chicago Press, 1968); W. R. Johnson, *The Idea of Lyric: Lyric Modes in Ancient and Modern Poetry*, Eidos (Berkeley: University of California Press, 1982), p. 35; M. L. Rosenthal and S. M. Gall, *The Modern Poetic Sequence: The Genius of Modern Poetry* (New York: Oxford University Press, 1983), p. 11. J. W. Johnson, "Lyric," in *The New Princeton Encyclopedia of Poetry and Poetics* (Princeton: Princeton University Press, 1993), pp. 713-714; W. H. Race, "Melic Poetry," in *The New Princeton Encyclopedia of Poetry and Poetics*, 755; Culler, *Literary Theory*, p. 70.

17. Culler, *Literary Theory*, p. 73; cf. Herrnstein Smith, *Poetic Closure*. Or, as Langer puts it, the lyric creates a "virtual history" — "the occurrence of a living thought, the sweep of an emotion, the intense experience of a mood" (*Feeling and Form*, p. 259).

heightening or summarizing inset in the prose narratives — but only marginally or minimally to tell a tale."[18] Epic verse (narrative) is well exemplified from the various surrounding cultures of the ancient Near East; but in Hebrew literature, narrative becomes predominantly the preserve of prose,[19] so much so, in fact, that the two extremes on the (ideal) discourse continuum represented by lyric and narrative are often synonymous in Hebrew with the distinction between poetry (verse) and prose. Indeed, triangulating from the various uses of verse, for example, in ancient Syria, Mesopotamia, and even Greece, on the one hand, and from the (mostly perceptible) poetry/prose divide in Hebrew literature, on the other, brings the nonnarrative, nonrepresentational nature of much Hebrew verse sharply into view. So much so, in fact, that this aspiration toward something other than narrative may well be the most tractable lyric characteristic of Hebrew verse more generally.

Alter dedicates his second chapter ("From Line to Story") in *The Art of Biblical Poetry* to illustrating the various ways in which Hebrew poems, though "fundamentally nonnarrative" in nature, do manifest at times a noticeable narrative impulse (e.g., incipient narrativity, episodic narratives). Among the poems he considers in more detail are 2 Samuel 22 (= Psalm 18), Job 16:9-14, Joel 2, Judges 5, Exodus 15, and Proverbs 7. Two aspects of his treatment are worth underscoring here: (1) the fact that modal and genre boundaries are easily (and even commonly) transgressed,[20] and (2) that in every instance the particular impulses toward narrative on display ultimately serve larger, nonnarrative ends, for example, to hymn Yahweh, to celebrate a victory, to convey moral instruction. Alter, as he himself notes, could have made many of the same points with the "historical psalms," Psalms 78, 105, and 106.[21]

In the following paragraphs I take the opposite tack from Alter. Instead of charting how Hebrew poems may move toward narrative, and as a consequence gaining a better angle from which to appreciate these poems' defining

---

18. R. Alter, *The Art of Biblical Poetry* (New York: Basic Books, 1985), p. 27; cf. Driver, *Introduction*, pp. 360-361.

19. For details regarding the transformation from poetic epic to prose narrative in Hebrew, see especially D. Damrosch, *The Narrative Covenant: Transformations of Genres in the Growth of Biblical Literature* (Ithaca: Cornell University Press, 1987); also cf. F. M. Cross, *Canaanite Myth and Hebrew Epic* (Cambridge, MA: Harvard University Press, 1973).

20. This is a point well stressed by Genette in his discussion of modes *(Architext)* and is the cornerstone of most contemporary genre theorists (e.g., A. Fowler, *Kinds of Literature* [Cambridge, MA: Harvard University Press, 1982]).

21. Accenting these psalms' fundamental nonnarrative nature, he writes: though epic-like, "they turn out to be versified summaries or catechistic rehearsals of Israelite history, with no narrative *realization* of the events invoked, their intelligibility dependent on the audience's detailed knowledge of the events" (*Art of Biblical Poetry,* p. 27).

nonnarrativity, I come at the latter by considering the swerve away from narrative in Psalm 114. Psalm 114, a somewhat unusual psalmic composition, invites the narrative comparison in two broad ways. First, it explicitly uses story — the exodus from Egypt — to frame its discourse. This is accomplished immediately in the poem's opening line: *běṣē't yiśrā'ēl mimmiṣrāyim* "When Israel went forth from Egypt" (Ps. 114:1). Psalms do not generally begin in this way, and in fact the grammar itself — "the infinitive construction with concomitant subordination of the second poetic line" — is common in narrative (esp. Exod. 13:8).[22] Second, almost every line reflects an awareness of Israel's larger narrative traditions: vv. 3 and 5 recall the events at the Red Sea (Exodus 14–15) and the crossing of the Jordan (Josh. 3:1–5:1) — though in both cases as refracted mythopoetically (e.g., Isa. 51:9-11; Ps. 74:12-17; Job 38:8-11; 40:25-32; cf. Josh. 4:23); the image of mountains and hills "skipping" *(rāqědû)* like rams and lambs (cf. esp. Ps. 29:6) in vv. 4 and 6 is taken from the old hymns recounting the march of the Divine Warrior from the southland (cf. Deut. 33:2; Judg. 5:4-5; Hab. 3:3-6; Ps. 68:8-9; also *KAjr* 15); and v. 8 draws on the wilderness traditions (Exod. 17:1-7; Num. 20:2-13).

And yet, there is no narrative here. The poem does not go on to narrate the story of the exodus, or any of these other traditions. H.-J. Kraus's observation about the narrative episodes in Psalm 106 is applicable here as well: they "are generally presumed to be familiar and therefore taken up only allusively."[23] Indeed, the poem does not appear to make good sense discursively at all. If anything it flouts good discursive logic. For example, who or what is the poem about? The topicalized entities in the first three clauses are all differently named — Israel, Jacob, Judah.[24] The clauses of the second couplet (v. 2), which

---

22. E. S. Gerstenberger, *Psalms, Part 2, and Lamentations*, Forms of the Old Testament Literature 15 (Grand Rapids: Eerdmans, 2001), p. 281. Cf. 1 Sam. 10:2; Ezek. 1:19, 21; 5:16; Jon. 2:8; Est. 1:5; 2:12, 15, 19; Dan. 10:15. It is very common with *wayhî* (e.g., Gen. 35:17, 18, 22; 38:28; Exod. 13:17; Judg. 13:20; 1 Sam. 16:6; 23:6; 1 Kings 11:15; Ezek. 10:6; Est. 2:8; Dan. 8:15). The construction without *wayhî* is fairly common in poetic texts (e.g., Judg. 5:2; Ps. 4:2; 9:4; 27:2; 68:15; 76:10; 105:12; 109:7; 142:4; Job 29:7; cf. *CTU* 1.17.V.9), evidencing something of the typical compactness of Hebrew poetry. Given the obvious creation imagery that pervades the psalm, e.g., sanctuary (v. 2), imagery drawn from the mythology of the *Chaoskampf* (vv. 3, 5; see S. A. Geller, "The Language of Imagery in Psalm 114," in *Lingering over Words*, ed. T. Abusch et al., Harvard Semitic Studies 37 [Atlanta: Scholars, 1990], pp. 179-194, esp. 182-184), it is tempting to hear the faintest echoes of a very specific kind of story, the epic of creation, e.g., *běrē'šît bārā' 'ĕlōhîm* "When God first created . . ." (Gen. 1:1), *e-nu-ma e-liš la na-bu-u ša-ma-mu* "When on high the heavens had not been created . . ." (*Enuma elish* I 1).

23. H.-J. Kraus, *Psalms 60–150: A Commentary* (Minneapolis: Augsburg, 1989), p. 316.

24. "Disturbing is the plethora of terms referring to the nation" (Geller, "Language of Imagery," p. 182).

are grammatically subordinated to those in the opening couplet, do not appear to follow any kind of story logic, or even to make literal sense: how is it that *Israel's* coming out from Egypt (literally) established *Judah* as "his sanctuary"? And who is the grammatical antecedent for the possessive suffix here and in the next line? (The poem never *explicitly* says.) And then there is the hodgepodge collection of traditions reflected in the poem. These are not sequenced or otherwise developed logically. And though the *Chaoskampf* imagery has attracted the attention of scholars (e.g., Kraus entitles his comments on the poem, "Miracles of Subduing the Sea"),[25] the poem's climax in v. 7 (*millipnê 'ādôn ḥûlî 'āreṣ* "Before [the] Lord, writhe, O land!") depends most explicitly on the old theophany traditions; the "land/earth" (*'ereṣ*) "shakes" (*rā'ăšâ*) "from before Yahweh" (*mippĕnê yhwh*) in Judges 5:4-5 and is shaken (lit. *waymōded*) by Yahweh in Habakkuk 3:6, and the whole concludes (curiously) by recalling Israel's wanderings before entering the land. Finally, the *wayyiqtol* form, the paradigm grammatical trope of Hebrew narrative, is used only once (*wayyānōs*, v. 3), and that for local effect.[26]

My point (exaggerated to be sure) is that this poem does not seem very interested in telling a story (which story?), developing characters (indeed, that which most commentators take to be the poem's chief subject, Yahweh, is never explicitly topicalized!), or even in constructing an argument. Such a presentation, as Kraus rightly notes, cannot be called "a real narration or description."[27] That is, its basic dynamics and chief practices are other than what we routinely associate with narrative; they are, I submit, expressly lyrical in orientation. To offer a fully persuasive lyric reading of this psalm would presume much of the discussion that is to follow. Still, several considerations — beyond the absence of narrative and narrativizing devices — may be offered as preliminary indicators of the psalm's lyricism.

First, there is its hymnic nature, stipulated to by most commentators (even if uneasily so).[28] The hymn is a quintessential specimen of lyric dis-

---

25. Kraus, *Psalms 60–150*, p. 370; cf. Gerstenberger, *Psalms, Part 2*, p. 283.

26. Both Langer (*Feeling and Form*, esp. pp. 260-279) and R. A. Greene (*Post-Petrarchism: Origins and Innovations of the Western Lyric Sequence* [Princeton: Princeton University Press, 1991], pp. 23-62) include interesting discussions of temporality and its linguistic manifestations (e.g., tense, deixis) in lyric verse. In this sense, the presence or absence of the *wayyiqtol* form in Hebrew psalms (especially in standard biblical Hebrew) can be a good barometer of "narrativity." There are clearly psalms (e.g., Psalms 105-106) whose narrative ambitions are announced by their liberal use of the *wayyiqtol* form.

27. Kraus, *Psalms 60–150*, p. 371.

28. At least since Hermann Gunkel (*Die Psalmen*, 5th ed. [Göttingen: Vandenhoeck, 1968], p. 493).

course (by any definition). As Lowth observes, the hymn (or "ode") is "sufficiently expressive" of its origin and abiding nature, "the offspring of the most vivid and the most agreeable passions of the mind — of love, joy, and admiration."[29] It enacts "an effusion of praise" to the deity, "accompanied with suitable energy and an exultation of voice."[30] The hymn of praise in the psalms is sometimes rendered self-reflexively and declaratively, as in Psalm 146:2 ("I will praise ['ăhalĕlâ] Yahweh as long as I live!"), but more often it is composed of a call to praise followed by a *kî* clause giving the reason for the praise (e.g., Psalm 117), with the expression of praise itself more a consequence of pragmatic implicature than conventional semantics.[31] But the main point, captured well by Lowth, is that the content of such hymns (what they are all about, what they do) is neither argument nor description but the "effusion of praise" itself, the expressed consciousness "of the goodness, majesty, and

---

29. Lowth, *Lectures*, p. 278.
30. Lowth, *Lectures*, p. 279.
31. The *kî* clause, which prototypically initiates the second movement in Israel's hymns of praise and thanksgiving (cf. P. D. Miller, *They Cried to the Lord* [Minneapolis: Fortress, 1999], p. 206), grammatically and semantically gives the reason for the praise. The underlying grammar and syntax is made clear by passages such as Judges 16:24, where the Philistines "praised their god" (*wayhalĕlû 'et-'ĕlōhêhem*) Dagan, "because they said, '. . .'" (*kî 'āmĕrû . . .*), or even Ezra 3:11, where the priests and Levites sing "with praise and with thanksgiving (*bĕhallēl ûbhôdōt*) to Yahweh because (*kî*) he is good, because (*kî*) his steadfast love endures forever over Israel" (cf. 2 Chron. 5:13). Especially since F. Crüsemann's *Studien zur Formgeschichte von Hymnes und Danklied in Israel* (Wissenschaftliche Monographien zum Alten und Neuen Testament 32 [Neukirchen-Vluyn: Neukirchener, 1969], esp. pp. 32-35), it has been customary to construe the *kî* clauses here as a direct quote (e.g., NRSV; cf. Miller, *They Cried to the Lord*, pp. 358-362).

However, this is unlikely for several reasons. First, nowhere else does *hll* "to praise" introduce direct discourse. Second, though *kî* may introduce either direct or indirect discourse in biblical Hebrew (see C. L. Miller, *The Representation of Speech in Biblical Hebrew Narrative: A Linguistic Analysis*, Harvard Semitic Monographs 55 [Atlanta: Scholars, 1996], pp. 97-116), the presence of "transparent deixis" (Miller, *Representation of Speech*, p. 65) here favors the indirect construal. And in fact one of the tendencies of late biblical Hebrew is to favor indirect discourse (see M. Eskhult, "Verbal Syntax in Late Biblical Hebrew," in *Diggers at the Well*, ed. T. Muraoka and J. F. Elwolde [Leiden: Brill, 2000], pp. 86, 90 and n. 31). Moreover, as P. D. Miller observes, "in the several [other] examples where there is a call to praise and those so called are explicitly told what to say, there is never . . . any use of the *kî* particle" (*They Cried to the Lord*, p. 359). But the discursive logic here is subordinated (pragmatically) to the poem's larger lyric ambition, which is to offer praise to Yahweh. And as such, the literal reasons given for praise (the steadfast love and faithfulness of Yahweh) are at the same time — by dint of their lyric framing, as it were — themselves expressions of praise. In other words, the poet's chief aim is not to argue a theological point (viz. the nations *should* praise Yahweh *because* his steadfast love is mighty and his faithfulness enduring) but to offer that argument as part and parcel of the poem's expression of praise.

power of God." Psalm 114, if a hymn, is a darker kind of hymn, as epitomized by the climatic call in v. 7 for the "land/earth" to "writhe [in agony]" before Yahweh.[32] The precise language used here, *ḥûlî 'āreṣ*, though surely intended to play off (and on) the more normative calls to praise (e.g., *halĕlû yāh*) that typify Israelite hymns and echo throughout the Hallel sequence in particular (e.g., Pss. 111:1; 112:1; 113:1, 9; 115:18; 116:19; 117:2; cf. 69:35; 148:7),[33] is drawn from the literary commonplace depicting the reaction to bad news (Isa. 13:8; Jer. 4:19; Hab. 3:10; cf. Isa. 21:3; Jer. 6:24; 50:43),[34] and thus evokes sensations of fear, dread, and anguish at the prospects of the warrior deity's immanent theophany — very much akin to the darkness that is hymned in Psalm 29.[35]

Second, the poem, as we have already seen, is highly fragmented, made up of bits and pieces of various traditions, and its discourse develops mostly associatively, as is typical of lyric discourse more generally (see below). The initial reference to the exodus from Egypt (v. 1) calls to mind the mythopoetic representation of that event as Yahweh's battle over the chaos power, Sea (v. 3; cf. Exodus 15). The similar personification of the Jordan (unique to this psalm) in the following line is a consequence of the tradition's explicit interpretation of the crossing of the Jordan in terms of the Re(e)d Sea events (Josh. 4:23; cf. Ps. 66:6).[36] The reaction of Sea and River then suggests the

---

32. Many would emend to *millipnê 'ădôn kol hā'āreṣ* based on the phrase's resemblances to *'ădôn kol hā'āreṣ* in Joshua 3:11 and Psalm 97:5 (e.g., *CMHE*, p. 138 n. 91; Kraus, *Psalms 60–150*, p. 371; Geller, "Language of Imagery," p. 180). However, there is no textual support for such a reading, and the Masoretic Text makes good sense, especially when the poem is read as a hymn (if the imperative is emended away, a significant basis for identifying the poem as a hymn is lost — the so-called hymnic participle in v. 8 is "hymnic" only by virtue of being in a hymn!). Besides, I suspect that the emendation is motivated by narrative assumptions about discourse continuity and logic; for example, Cross ("The hills like lambs [danced],/Before the Lord . . .") and Kraus ("Why do you [skip] . . ./O hillocks, like the lambs of the flock? — /in the presence of the Lord. . . .") make v. 7 a prepositional phrase dependent on v. 6, while Geller construes v. 7 as the explicit answer given to the question in vv. 5-6 ("Why . . . ?/It's from the Lord. . . ."). However, Geller, at least, concedes that the Masoretic Text is construable as is — a "bold apostrophe" ("Language of Imagery," p. 188 n. 25).

33. The Septuagint construes the concluding *halĕlû yāh* of Psalm 113 as belonging to Psalm 114.

34. In Jeremiah 51:29 "the land of Babylon" (*'ereṣ bābel*) is said to "writhe" (*wattāḥōl*) at the news of Yahweh's impending onslaught, and it is this deity's terrible theophany that causes "the earth to writhe" (*wattāḥēl hā'āreṣ*) in Psalm 97:4; cf. D. R. Hillers, "A Convention in Hebrew Literature: The Reaction to Bad News," *Zeitschrift für die alttestamentliche Wissenschaft* 77 (1965): 86-90.

35. Geller ("Language of Imagery," pp. 187-190) also recognizes the psalm's darker moments.

36. Esp. *CMHE*, pp. 138-139.

analogous reaction of the Mountains and Hills prevalent in the march of the Divine Warrior traditions,[37] with the latter then giving way to the poem's climatic call to "writhe!" Without plot and character the lyric, as Langer notes, "must depend most directly on pure verbal resources,"[38] and thus lyric discourse is often highly troped. Wordplay (*ḥûlî/halĕlû*, v. 7), personification (vv. 3-5, 5-6),[39] "bold apostrophe" (v. 7),[40] and the like must bear more of the meaning-making burden.[41] Continuity and coherence are built in through lineation and rhythm; the poem is constructed out of parallelistic couplets, all of which involve gapping (ellipsis), and the foreshortened second lines that result from the gapping create a rocking rhythm that mimes the writhing and skipping that the poem imagines.[42]

And finally, it is often the case in lyric discourse that as much goes on behind the scenes (or under the poem's surface), as it were, as specifically in the text. As D. Levertov observes, lyric poetry's "way of constructing" discourse depends as much on "silences" as on the selection of specific "words."[43] Kraus explains the purpose of Psalm 114 as proclaiming "the powerful appearance of the God of Israel."[44] Such an explanation is on the right track but ultimately goes astray for failing to appreciate the poem's figured "silences" — that which is left unstated, the represented absences. The presence of the deity that is hymned here is that which is otherwise not manifestly apparent, that which is literally absent. Nowhere in the poem is Yahweh specifically topicalized — the direct antithesis of the olden hymns to the Divine Warrior in which we

---

37. Gerstenberger's (and others') assertion that the "mountains and hills jumping like lambs . . . should be taken as an expression of joy" (*Psalms, Part 2*, p. 283) seems to me to ignore the significance of the biblical (and extra-biblical) literary parallels and to misread the psalm's basic tenor. Indeed, the nature of the image in Psalm 29:6 (the only other place where the image explicitly appears in the Hebrew Bible) is unmistakable: it registers "the convulsions and travail" (*CMHE*, p. 152; note also the threefold use of the root *ḥyl* in Ps. 29:8-9) that accompany the theophany of the Storm God. Similar upheavals attend the march of the Divine Warrior from the southland, too (Judg. 5:4-5; Hab. 3:3-6). In sum, the reactions of Sea and Mountains in Psalm 114 seem to me to be very much of a piece.

38. Langer, *Feeling and Form*, p. 259.

39. Or perhaps even better, a combination of apostrophe and personification not unlike that in "With how sad steps, O Moon, thou climb'st the skies," cited from Sidney's *Astrophil and Stella* (31) by T. V. F. Brogan and A. W. Halsall in "Prosopopoeia," in *The New Princeton Encyclopedia of Poetry and Poetics*, p. 994.

40. Geller, "Language of Imagery," p. 188 n. 25.

41. See Culler's discussion of what "*distinguishes* the lyric from other speech acts" (*Literary Theory*, p. 74).

42. Cf. Geller, "Language of Imagery," p. 181.

43. D. Levertov, *Light Up the Cave* (New York: New Directions, 1981), p. 60.

44. Kraus, *Psalms 60–150*, p. 375.

witness the deity march (as it were) across the surface of the poem. No antecedents for the pronominal suffixes in v. 2 are ever explicitly identified, though the referent is obvious to all. And even in the poem's "great dénouement" the deity appears only obliquely *(millipnê 'ādôn . . . millipnê 'ĕlôah)*,[45] as if we somehow just missed the appearance itself. And this figuring of Yahweh's presence amid apparent absence seems to be at the core of much of the poem. For example, the reader/hearer knows only too well that it is Yahweh whom personified Sea sees and recoils from in v. 3. But by withholding the explicit mention of the deity, Yahweh's presence is marked by literal — here linguistic — absence. And similarly in vv. 5-6. The questions put to Sea and company are not really intended to taunt or ridicule,[46] but again to linguistically figure the deity's presence amid apparent absence. With this in mind, the poem's otherwise enigmatic concluding couplet (v. 8) comes into clearer focus. It alludes to the incident at Massah and Meribah where, according to the tradition in Exodus (17:1-7, esp. v. 7), the Israelites "quarreled and tested the Lord, saying, "Is the Lord among us or not?" (NRSV). The issue there as well, then, is the presence of Yahweh whose physical manifestation was apparently in question.[47] The allusion to the episode in Psalm 114:8 would thus appear to remove Yahweh one step further from the poem's literal surface; and yet the point, nonetheless, is to (re)affirm that even at those times where the deity's absence is most palpable Yahweh is present. And thus if I were to commit the cardinal sin of New Criticism and offer a (brief) paraphrase of this psalm, it would go something like this: Writhe in anguish, O Jacob, for Yahweh is present even in the midst of the most tangible signs of his absence.

In sum, whether one agrees with every aspect of my own (abbreviated) reading of Psalm 114, I hope it is plain to see that the poem is fundamentally nonnarrative in its basic structure and orientation. Narrative, though clearly present, is subsidiary, as is common in lyric discourse. As W. R. Johnson observes, "Behind every lyric, sometimes vaguely sketched, sometimes clearly defined, is a story that explains the present moment of discourse and accounts for the singer's present moods and for his need or choice to sing. But in lyric poems . . . the story exists for the song, and what gives the poem its form, its resonance, and its texture" is a specifically lyric kind of sensibility

---

45. L. C. Allen, *Psalms 101–150*, Word Biblical Commentary (Waco: Word, 1983), p. 105.

46. So Gerstenberger, *Psalms, Part 2*, p. 282.

47. The same thing would appear to be at issue in Numbers 20:2-13, though there the point is made through the failure of Moses and Aaron to follow Yahweh's instruction literally. See the comments by E. Greenstein in *The HarperCollins' Study Bible* (San Francisco: HarperCollins, 1993), p. 111.

that is made manifest in the "selection of language, sound, and image."[48] Psalm 114 is made of the stuff of narrative — quite explicitly so — but these narrative elements are molded and deployed lyrically.[49]

The "Most Obviously Linguistic Creation"

Lyric's typical eschewal of narrative and its attendant devices, as summarily shown in the above reading of Psalm 114, entails important consequences for the kind of discourse that it enacts. The first such consequence, and in many ways the most basic as well, is that the fundamental resource of lyric proper, "its plastic medium," is, by default, language itself. Since lyric poetry (habitually) makes no recourse to plot or character, it must depend, as Langer explains, "most directly on pure verbal resources — the sound and evocative power of words, meter, alliteration, rhyme, and other rhythmic devices, associated images, repetitions, archaisms and grammatical twists. It is the most obviously linguistic creation, and therefore the readiest instance of poesy."[50] That is to say, "there is a tendency," as M. Kinzie notes, "for words [and other linguistic elements, too] in the specialized fabric of the poetic line to take on more than their usual significance."[51] This is the "babble" — those non-semantic features of language such as sound, rhythm, puns, and the like — of Frye's famed twin constituents of lyric, "babble and doodle,"[52] and it is most why the lyric, according to Frye, shows so clearly the "hypothetical core of literature, narrative and meaning in their literal aspects as word-order and word-pattern."[53] One may gain an impression of the "babbledness" of the Psalms, for example, by perusing the (sometimes mechanical) listings of figures and tropes in the late-nineteenth-century compendia of I. M. Casanowicz[54] and E. König,[55] or in the

---

48. Johnson, *Idea of Lyric*, p. 35; cf. Langer, *Feeling and Form*, p. 261.

49. Many psalms, of course, are far less interested in narrative, while some others move a long ways toward narrative. Psalms 105 and 106 are good examples of the latter. Both contain multiple narrative runs, in which a variety of devices (the *wayyiqtol* form and the like) are used to emplot action, resulting in what R. Alter aptly calls "incipient narrativity" (*The Art of Biblical Poetry*, pp. 27-61).

50. Langer, *Feeling and Form*, p. 259; cf. Johnson, *Idea of Lyric*, p. 23; R. P. Draper, *Lyric Tragedy* (New York: St. Martin's Press, 1985), pp. 4-5.

51. M. Kinzie, *A Poet's Guide to Poetry* (Chicago: University of Chicago Press, 1999), p. 142.

52. Northrop Frye, *Anatomy of Criticism: Four Essays* (Princeton: Princeton University Press, 1957), p. 275.

53. Frye, *Anatomy of Criticism*, p. 271; cf. Culler, *Literary Theory*, p. 74.

54. I. M. Casanowicz, *Paronomasia in the Old Testament* (Boston, 1894).

55. E. König, *Stilistik, Rhetorik, Poetik* (Leipzig, 1900).

richly evocative work of more recent literary scholars, such as A. Berlin, E. Greenstein, and D. Grossberg.[56] Here, however, I exemplify the foregrounding of the non-semantic features of language in the Psalms by considering, first, the (general) nature of formal structure, and second, the use of metaphor as (or in lieu of) argument. These are intended to serve as stand-ins for the other kinds of tropes (wordplay, soundplay, and the like) that typify psalmic discourse and mark it as specifically lyric in nature. These would need to be surveyed in a more thoroughgoing statement of this particular lyric quality.

One of the elemental functions of plot in narrative is to shape a story, to give it a beginning, middle, and end, and thus to provide a sense of coherence and continuity.[57] Plot is, as P. Brooks states, "the principle of interconnectedness ... which we cannot do without in moving through the discrete elements — incidents, episodes, actions — of a narrative" and "that allow us to construct a whole."[58] Without plot per se, lyric must find alternative means for organizing its discourse, for demarcating boundaries, and for guiding auditors through to a satisfying denouement. At one extreme, lyric verse routinely employs purely (or principally) formal means for articulating structure, such as with the given (conventional) forms well known from the metrical tradition of English verse (e.g., sonnet, villanelle, and the like). In Hebrew verse the most manifestly formal structuring device used is the alphabetic acrostic (e.g., Psalms 9-10; 25; 34; 37; 111; 112; 119; 145), in which the succession of letters from *aleph* to *taw* at the head of every line, couplet, or stanza articulates the poem's basic structure, builds in a sense of coherence and unity, and guides readers and hearers through to the poem's end. The acrostic, unfortunately, has not always been appreciated by biblical exegetes, many of whom routinely decry its patent artificiality. But, of course, such artificiality, or better, artifactuality, is one of the chief marks of poesy: the making out of language that is at the center of all literary discourse.[59] And, more to the point, it is in forms like the acrostic that the lyric's dependence on the double-sided

---

56. E.g., A. Berlin, "Motif and Creativity in Biblical Poetry," *Prooftexts* 3 (1983): 231-241; E. Greenstein, "Wordplay, Hebrew," in *Anchor Bible Dictionary* (New York: Doubleday, 1992), vol. 6, pp. 968-969; D. Grossberg, *Centripetal and Centrifugal Structures in Hebrew Poetry*, Society of Biblical Literature Monograph Series (Atlanta: Scholars, 1989).

57. Cf. Culler, *Literary Theory*, pp. 79-81.

58. P. Brooks, *Reading for the Plot* (Cambridge, MA: Harvard University Press, 1984), p. 5; cf. Greene, *Post-Petrarchism*, p. 49.

59. Psalm 45:2 is one of the rare instances in which a biblical writer shows some conscious awareness of craft. Here the poet prefaces his poem with a statement about how his mind is teeming with a "good word" (*dābār tôb*) and that he proclaims to/for the king "my work" (*ma'ăśay*). The latter would be the precise equivalent to the Greek notion of poesy.

(tropological) use of linguistic signs — Kinzie's notion of taking "on more than their usual significance" — is so plainly on display: the appropriate letter of the alphabet functions both at the word level (i.e., as a part of the spelling of a specific lexeme) and at the composition level (i.e., as a part of the formal conceit by which the larger whole is articulated).[60]

Other more or less formal means for articulating holistic structure in the Psalms include large-scale envelope structures, such as inclusios (e.g., *yhwh 'dnynw/mh-'dyr šmk/bkl-h'rṣ*, Ps. 8:2, 10; *bny 'dm*, Ps. 12:2, 9; *hwdw lyhwh ky-ṭwb/ky lʿwlm ḥsdw*, Ps. 118:1, 29; *halĕlû yāh*, Ps. 147:1, 20)[61] and chiasms (e.g., *'lhym lnw mḥsh wʿz//mśgb-lnw 'lhy yʿqb*, Ps. 46:2a, 12b), and the occasional use of refrains (e.g., *mh-tštwḥḥy npšy*, Pss. 42:6, 12; 43:5; *ky lʿwlm ḥsdw*, Ps. 136:1-26). And we should probably not discount the possibility that the conventional forms identified by form criticism (beginning with Gunkel) could themselves appeal "as form"[62] (though here thematic elements begin to come into play as well). For example, the bifold structure of the (imperative) hymn of praise — call to praise (with an imperative) followed by a causal clause (usually beginning with *kî*) giving the reason for praise[63] — can be used to structure whole poems (e.g., Psalms 100; 117) or sections of poems (e.g., Pss. 96:1-6; 98:1-3; 135:1-4).[64]

Far more common, however, the containing form of a Hebrew psalm is "organic," to use a term from Coleridge (though one need not retain all of the Romantic baggage that often accompanies this term); "it shapes, as it develops, itself from within," arising "out of the properties of the material."[65] That is, as

---

60. There are occasions, as well, when the tropological density on display is more than doubled, as in Psalm 9:2-3, where the opening *aleph* stanza also intentionally alliterates the guttural sound of the *aleph* in the sequence of five verbs: *'ôdâ, 'ăsappĕrâ, 'eśmĕḥâ, wĕ'e'elṣâ, 'ăzammĕrâ* (cf. *ṣôd ṣādûnî kaṣṣippôr* in the *ṣade* stanza in Lam. 3:52).

61. As elsewhere in the Psalms, it is not easy to discern whether this inclusio is compositional or editorial.

62. For this notion of conventional form, see esp. K. Burke, *Counter-Statement*, 2nd ed. (Chicago: Phoenix Books, 1953), p. 126.

63. E.g., Miller, *They Cried to the LORD*, pp. 205-206.

64. A sign of this form's conventionality (though not precisely "as form") is the frequency with which it is quoted (in part or whole) in later biblical compositions (e.g., Jer. 33:11; Ezra 3:11; Neh. 9:5; 2 Chron. 7:3, 6; 20:21). Moreover, a compelling case can be made that the Joban poet uses the model hymn of praise (though semantically inverted) to shape the opening stanza of the curse of Job's day of birth (3:3-10; an initial jussive, "let it perish," followed after much elaboration by a closing *kî* clause), which if correct shows the hymn's significance "as form."

65. The quote is taken from "Shakespeare's Judgment Equal to His Genius," in *Selected Poetry and Prose of Samuel Taylor Coleridge*, ed. D. A. Stauffer (New York: Random House, 1951), pp. 432-433, as cited in C. O. Hartman, *Free Verse: An Essay on Prosody* (Evanston: Northwestern University Press, 1980), pp. 92 and esp. 183 n. 4.

is the case more generally with non-metrical verse (or free verse poems!),[66] the patterned repetition that generates formal structure[67] — in lieu of a strong tradition of conventional stanzaic structure, rhyme schemes, and the like — will routinely involve a host of diverse linguistic elements (e.g., lineation, soundplay, parallelism, word repetition) distributed in a variety of overlapping and/or mutually informing and delimiting ways.[68] I have already noted (in passing) a simple example of such "discovered form" in the discussion of Psalm 114. There the psalm's gross structure is articulated formally by the uniform use of parallelistic couplets (eight of them), each involving gapping and comprised of slightly unbalanced lines. As B. Herrnstein Smith notes, our recognition of such formal patterning is properly "retrospective," that is, we cannot be sure of it until it is concluded (or "announced as concluded").[69] The finer points of that psalm's structure are then "figured" against this "ground" of uniform parallelism. The poem divides into three main sections (or stanzas).[70] The middle section (vv. 3-6) is the longest and is characterized above all by word- and phrase-level repetition (involving Sea, Jordan, Mountains, and Hills; only *rā'â*, *mah-lěkā*, and *kî* are not repeated). The opening (vv. 1-2) and closing (vv. 7-8) sections are distinguished by the presence of tighter intercouplet syntactic dependencies (i.e., both involve subordinating constructions — infinitival in vv. 1-2 and appositional in vv. 7-8), and thus form an enveloping structure that (formally) rounds off the poem.

The structural ground of Psalm 133 is formed (almost) in an opposite

---

66. Hrushowski's original insight that the generating principle of Hebrew prosody lies in the "free verse rhythms" of Hebrew has still not been fully developed.

67. See Herrnstein Smith, *Poetic Closure*, p. 38: "repetition is the fundamental phenomenon of poetic form." This study's relevance for an understanding of the dynamics and nature of lyric verse is much broader than the title indicates. Herrnstein Smith is an incredibly insightful and stimulating critic.

68. B. Nettl notes that "one of the best known and most widely recognized characteristics of primitive music" is "its frequently asymmetrical and irregular structure" (*Music in Primitive Culture* [Cambridge, MA: Harvard University Press, 1956], p. 62).

69. Herrnstein Smith, *Poetic Closure*, pp. 10, 12, 13.

70. As M. Oliver reminds us, though stanzaic forms in metrical verse traditions are routinely associated with rhyme schemes, metrical constraints, line counts, and the like, the term "stanza" itself designates "a group of lines in a poem" and "is used to indicate the divisions of a poem," but beyond this "there is no further *exact* definition" and "there are no absolutely right or wrong ways to divide a poem into stanzas" (*A Poetry Handbook* [New York: Harcourt Brace, 1994], pp. 60-61). She continues by suggesting — and this seems especially apt for free verse poetry — that "it may be useful, when considering the stanza to recall the paragraph in prose, which indicates the conclusion of one thought and the beginning of another, a *sensible* division" and that the "sensible paragraph" be thought of "as a kind of norm . . . from which to feel out the particular divisions that are best for a particular poem" (p. 61).

fashion. Here the interlinear dynamics are governed by enjambment (the carrying over of syntax from one line to the next)[71] instead of parallelism — this is underscored to good effect by the threefold repetition of *yōrēd* at line junctures in the psalm's central section (vv. 2, 3), escorting the reader (like the flowing oil and dew) down the page (admittedly, a very literate way of reading the trope). The poem's central part stands out mostly thematically, being composed of two similes (though they are both explicitly marked as such, *k-*, and the section is otherwise punctuated by lexical repetition and phrasal parallelism), while this is framed by an opening statement ("How good it is . . . ," v. 1) and closing rationale ("For there Yahweh commanded . . . ," v. 3), echoing the bifold structure of the hymn of praise — sound play (*gam/šām/hāʿôlām* and *nāʿîm/ʾāḥîm/ḥayyîm*) reinforcing the framing effect here. The sense of closure in this poem is more pronounced than that of Psalm 114, as here the enjambed couplets give way at the end to a lone triplet, and thus the poem's concluding movement is announced through modification of its governing pattern of repetition.[72]

A final, and more complex, example is Psalm 19. The poem divides into two main parts, vv. 2-7 and vv. 8-15.[73] Lineation is the chief formal indicator

---

71. Cf. F. W. Dobbs-Allsopp, "The Enjambing Line in Lamentations: A Taxonomy (Part I)," *Zeitschrift für die alttestamentliche Wissenschaft* 113, no. 2 (2001): 219-239; and "The Effects of Enjambment in Lamentations (Part 2)," *Zeitschrift für die alttestamentliche Wissenschaft* 113, no. 5 (2001): 370-385.

72. For a discussion of "terminal modification" as one of the most effective ways of signaling closure, see Herrnstein Smith, *Poetic Closure*, pp. 28, 43-44, 50, 56ff. Interestingly, Herrnstein Smith's discussion of closure in lyric poems is informed throughout by similar phenomena in musical composition, and this is especially true of her discussion of terminal modification (esp. pp. 56-59).

73. Whatever one makes of the compositional techniques on display in this poem — a notoriously difficult matter to discern without the evidence of explicit comment — the poem itself hangs together as a whole. Thematically, vv. 12 and 15 play key roles in unifying the two parts. Verse 12 makes explicit and implicit connections with the main foci of the poem — nature and Torah. The NRSV, for example, glosses *nizhār* as "is . . . warned," construing as a Niphal Part ms √ *zhr* II "to be warned," which given the context of the second part of the poem makes sense, as it is precisely Torah that guides the psalmist in his/her life. And yet, deriving from *zhr* I "to shine" also makes good sense, as this root is used explicitly in the Bible (e.g., Dan. 12:3) and elsewhere of the sun shining! This latter sense is especially relevant as *bāhem* comes at the end of the line, formally — though not semantically, as different antecedents are involved — pointing back to *bāhem* in v. 5c. The tone of "illumination, seeing, shining" also fits well the adoring tone of the poem as a whole. But it is not likely a matter of choosing between the two, except perhaps for translation purposes (it is hard to get both senses into English) and for determining which is primary (i.e., at the surface of the poem), since the poet would appear to have intended both senses to resonate. I would emphasize the derivation from *zhr* I "to shine" only because this has not been routinely appreciated and because there are those who still continue to insist that we

of this poem's structure, though form and content are mutually reinforcing throughout. The lines in the first section of the poem are generally longer, with several triplets thrown in amid the couplets. In the second half, the poem is characterized by couplets with short lines in which the first line tends to be longer than the second — the so-called qinah meter.[74] The only triplet in this section comes at the very end (v. 15), thus effectively signaling the poem's concluding movement. These main sections are composed of two stanzas apiece (vv. 2-5b, 5c-7; 8-11, 12-14); the theme of each stanza is topicalized in the initial word: "heavens" (v. 2), "sun" (v. 5c), "Torah" (v. 8), "your servant" (v. 12). In the first section, the "sun" stanza is further distinguished by its constituent triplets,[75] while the "Torah" stanza is differentiated in the second part by the especially tight (syntactic, grammatical, and semantic) parallelism that is manifested among its constituent couplets.

In sum, form (sometimes by itself but more frequently in tandem with thematic elements) in the lyric verse of the Psalms shoulders a great deal of the continuity and sequencing functions that in narrative more generally fall to the domain of plot, and thus does a great deal more than simply ornamenting the poem's otherwise paraphrasable meaning(s). In a similar way, instead of argument — though, of course, there is no reason why particular lyric poems should not engage in more discursive forms of discourse, for example, as in the prophetic literature or some of the didactic psalms — one finds a variety of stand-ins, including, most interestingly, metaphor.[76] Meta-

---

have two poems here instead of one. Note, too, how the notion of guarding, etc., is precisely one of the activities that is predicated of Shamash in the Mesopotamian hymn.

The closing triplet in v. 15 is well known. What may be missed is that the invocation of Yahweh as "rock and redeemer" points rather clearly — if metaphorically — to the two dominant movements in the poem — nature and Torah. Redemption, of course, is itself a legal concept. Here, what is intended (at least in part) is that it is precisely through Torah that the psalmist finds well-being, salvation.

74. Free verse compositions come most generally in long-lined and short-lined varieties (e.g., C. Beyers, *A History of Free Verse* [Fayetteville: University of Arkansas, 2001], esp. pp. 39-42).

75. Note further how the repetition of third masculine singular suffixes syntactically tracks the main actor of the stanza — the sun — but in doing so also builds (formal) coherence into the stanza. A more elaborate use of this kind of anaphora is evidenced in Lamentations. Cf. F. W. Dobbs-Allsopp, *Lamentations*, Interpretation: A Biblical Commentary for Teaching and Preaching (Louisville: Westminster John Knox, 2002), p. 49.

76. As a way of valorizing the image as a vehicle for thought, it may be helpful to recall that, according to neurobiologists like A. Damasio, "having a mind means that an organism forms neural representations which can become images" of various kinds (e.g., visual, sound, olfactory) but which only latterly become translated into language (see Damasio, *Descartes' Error* [New York: Quill, 1995], pp. 83-113, esp. 89-90). That is, image — and presumably even linguisti-

phor epitomizes the coming "to mean twice" that typifies the tropologically dense discourse of lyric verse.[77] So in Psalm 133 the poem's central invocation, "How good and how pleasant it is/that brothers dwell together" (NJV), is never argued or even exemplified (Gerstenberger: "these metaphors [in vv. 2-3] cannot very well explain the peaceful coexistence of 'brothers'").[78] Rather, it is more a matter, as Kraus says, of being "accompanied . . . by friendly sentiments."[79] That is, the exclamation is supported by two images of superabundance and refreshment — that of oil and that of dew — and we are won over to its point of view largely by the "extravagance" of these similes. In Psalm 1, simile (metaphor) is equally crucial to the poem's success. Here, too, we chiefly have to do with "a joyous exclamation,"[80] "Happy is the man . . . !", whose main appeal is secured, positively (v. 3) and negatively (v. 4), through similes. The inherent attractiveness of the tree metaphor, plus its elaboration in the poem, is one of the chief ways in which the poet presses this point. By contrast, the image of chaff that is blown by the wind is inherently negative (note that the negative particles in the poem, vv. 1, 4, 5, always characterize the activity of the wicked) and very brief — the chaff, once blown away, is no more! Such doubleness in the usage of metaphor — both as an image event in its own right and as (or in lieu of) argument — is analogous to the doubleness of form illustrated above, and both exemplify the tropological density (the taking on of "more than their usual sense") that customarily (necessarily!) attends lyric discourse.[81]

Smallness of Scale

The question of scale, though not insignificant, requires little comment. A certain smallness of scale is generally associated with the lyric. As Frye belatedly

---

cally stimulated images — is itself a most natural and congenial mode of thought for the human organism and one that should not be disparaged on account of our current love affair with all things linguistic.

77. On what "densely patterned" ways in biblical verse typically means, see Alter's comment in *Art of Biblical Poetry*, p. 113.

78. Gerstenberger, *Psalms, Part 2*, p. 372.

79. Kraus, *Psalms 60–150*, p. 485.

80. In Kraus, *Psalms 1–59*, p. 115 (citing Buber).

81. It is perhaps crucial to underscore two things here: (1) that such tropological density arises in the lyric chiefly in *compensation* for the absence of other discourse features, and (2) that such "babbledness," if typical of lyric discourse, also appears in other discourse mediums. In other words, we need not essentialize this characteristic in order to appreciate its typicality and significance for the lyric.

observes, "a lyric is anything you can reasonably get uncut into an anthology."[82] Such brevity results from the lyric's general eschewal of devices (e.g., plot, argument, temporal sequence, consistency of setting) that would enable more encompassing discourse; and it means, as a purely practical matter, that lyric poems will be limited in the scope of their subject matter. And with only language itself as the chief medium of discourse, it is difficult for lyric poems to sustain themselves over long stretches of time and space. It is this smallness of scale that so typifies biblical Hebrew poetry, and especially the Psalms, suggesting the likelihood that the lyric lies at the base of much of biblical poetry[83] — in contrast with the much longer and expansive epic verse from Ugarit (e.g., Keret, Aqhat) and Mesopotamia (e.g., Gilgamesh, Erra), for example.

Lyric verse can be written on a larger scale, and there are any number of strategies for accomplishing this. For example, form, such as that exhibited by the villanelle or the sestina well known from Western canons of lyric poetry, offers one means by which lyric poems can extend their reach. Psalm 119 masterfully exploits the alphabetic acrostic for just this purpose (cf. Psalm 37), the formal conceit of the abecedary serving to help auditors navigate the expanded discourse space. Another strategy is suggested by the epic verse traditions of the ancient Near East, namely, engaging more explicitly in narrative or utilizing the various devices of narrative, such as is in evidence, for example, in Psalms 78, 105, and 106; as noted, this is generally the topic of Alter's second chapter in *The Art of Hebrew Poetry,* entitled "From Line to Story." A third means for increasing the lyric's otherwise confining amplitude is to successively link a number of individual lyric poems and mold them into a greater, organic whole. What gets enacted in such a process, then, is a sequence of lyric poems whose nature and dynamic, holistically considered, are essentially that of a lyric poem writ large. As literary critics are discovering, this compositional strategy turns out to be quite common and knows very few chronological or geographical boundaries.[84] That the book of Psalms it-

---

82. Frye, "Approaching the Lyric," p. 31; cf. Langer, *Feeling and Form,* p. 260; Rosenthal and Gall, *Modern Poetic Sequence,* p. 3; Johnson, "Lyric," p. 714; Culler, *Literary Theory,* p. 70.

83. Driver is most emphatic: "Hebrew poetry is almost exclusively *lyric*" (*Introduction,* p. 360). He also distinguishes "gnomic" verse, but says that "the line between these two forms [i.e., lyric and gnomic] cannot always be drawn strictly" (pp. 360-361).

84. Critical research into the nature, dynamics, and extent of the lyric sequence is still very much in its infancy. Scholars have for the most part focused on the Western poetic tradition (e.g., Rosenthal and Gall, *Modern Poetic Sequence;* Greene, *Post-Petrarchism;* T. L. Roche Jr., *Petrarch and the English Sonnet Sequences* [New York: AMS, 1989]; D. Fenolaltea and D. L. Rubin, *The Ladder of High Designs: Structure and Interpretation of the French Lyric Sequence* [Charlottesville/London: University Press of Virginia, 1991]). Nevertheless, the potential for identifying other non-Western lyric sequences is good; see the comments to this effect by Rosenthal and

self may enact a more encompassing kind of fiction, on the one hand, and is comprised of various smaller and larger collections that may have had their own integrity (e.g., the "Songs of Ascent"), on the other hand, has been the focus of much research lately and would be a topic that could potentially benefit from the insights gleaned from work on other lyric sequences.[85]

Gall ("Lyric Sequence," in *The New Princeton Encyclopedia of Poetry and Poetics*, p. 729) and J. Rothenberg ("Ethnopoetics and Politics/The Politics of Ethnopoetics," in *The Politics of Poetic Form*, ed. C. Bernstein [New York: Roof, 1990], p. 13).

85. Indeed, it is likely that the Psalms as a collective whole served as a model for some of the early lyric sequences in the Western tradition, such as Dante's *Vita Nuova* (ca. 1292-1300 C.E.) and Petrarch's *Canzonierre* (1304-1374 C.E.). Beyond the current interest in the larger collective integrity of the Psalms (for bibliography and discussion, see G. H. Wilson, *The Editing of the Hebrew Psalter* [Chico, CA: Scholars, 1985]; and D. M. Howard Jr., "Recent Trends in Psalm Study," in *The Face of Old Testament Studies: A Survey of Contemporary Approaches* [Grand Rapids: Baker Books, 1999], esp. pp. 332-344) and D. Grossberg's stimulating initial forays into the larger structures of the Psalms of Ascent, Song of Songs, and Lamentations (*Centripetal and Centrifugal Structures in Biblical Poetry* [Society of Biblical Literature Monograph Series 39; Atlanta: Scholars, 1989]), I am unaware of similar attempts to investigate the potential integrity of other biblical or ancient Near Eastern collections or sequences of lyric compositions. Still, that the technological capacity for composing integrated lyric sequences was in evidence in the larger ancient Near East can at least be suggested in a preliminary way. The Mesopotamian penchant for collection and organization is well known and is exemplified by the existence of numerous literary catalogs of various kinds, including hymnic literature (for bibliography, see A. L. Oppenheim, *Ancient Mesopotamia: Portrait of a Dead Civilization*, rev. ed. [Chicago: University of Chicago Press, 1977], p. 377 n. 16; and Wilson, *Editing of the Hebrew Psalter*, pp. 25-61), as well as a multitude of scholarly collections of all kinds — laws, omens, incantations, and so on (see Oppenheim, *Ancient Mesopotamia*, pp. 206-331). And then there is the outstanding example of the collection of forty-two Sumerian temple hymns that may date as early as the late twenty-fourth or early twenty-third century B.C.E. (A. Sjöberg and E. Bergman, *The Collection of Sumerian Temple Hymns* [Locust Valley: J. J. Augustin, 1969]). Here we have an obvious collection of individual lyric compositions that have been purposefully composed and arranged as a larger whole. The first forty-one hymns share the same basic form (Sjöberg and Bergman, *Temple Hymns*, p. 5) and are ordered geographically in a general south/southeast to north/northwest orientation as one moves through the sequence (H. Zimmern, "Ein Zyklus altsumerischer Lieder auf die Haupttempel Babyloniens," *Zeitschrift für Assyriologie* 5 [1930]: 247; C. Wilke, "Der aktuelle Bezug der Sammlung der sumerischer Tempelhymnen und ein Fragment eines Klagelieds," *Zeitschrift für Assyriologie* 62 [1972]: 39, 48-49). The final hymn deviates noticeably from the formal pattern that shapes the other hymns (Sjöberg and Bergman, *Temple Hymns*, pp. 12, 149), effectively signaling the collection's impending conclusion (see the discussion of "terminal modification" above). And Enḫeduanna, En-Priestess and daughter of Sargon of Akkad, even explicitly articulates her authorial intent as she identifies herself as the "compiler of the tablet" that "no one has created [before]" (ll. 544-545). As for Egypt, one need only look as far as the multiple collections of love lyrics (conveniently, see M. Fox, *The Song of Songs and the Ancient Egyptian Love Songs* [Madison: University of Wisconsin Press, 1985], pp. 3-81) to find evidence for integrated lyric sequences or collections. From a later period, one might also note the "Psalms of

The "Utterance of a Voice"

In characterizing the lyric, Culler highlights the genre's typical vocality: it "seems to be an utterance . . . the utterance of a voice."[86] This vocality has two distinguishing properties. The first is physical. R. Pinsky gets at this physicality in his notion of lyric poetry as "a vocal, which is to say a bodily, art."[87] He continues: "The medium of poetry is the human body: the column of air inside the chest, shaped into signifying sounds in the larynx and mouth."[88] To focus as Pinsky does on the physical operation of the voice and its production of sound is to recall the lyric's debt to music (after all, lyric was synonymous with singing and song in antiquity), to stress its sonic qualities, to appreciate that it is an art form that is/was intended to be heard. Rhythm, melody, and euphony (soundplay) are all important features of Hebrew psalmody, even if our own perception of them through the preserved textual medium(s) is muffled and dim. The rhythmic cadences of Hebrew verse are the most tractable of these musical elements today. So, for example, the mostly balanced cadences of Psalms 33, 111, and 112 contrast noticeably with the unbalanced limp of Psalms 19:8-11 and 114. And though soundplay in Hebrew verse is non-systematic, its presence and even occasional scripting for larger effect (such as in the framing of Psalm 133) is beyond doubt. One of the scandals of lyric poetry, writes Culler, is precisely that these "contingent features of sound and rhythm systematically infect and affect thought."[89]

Moreover, to focus the uttered-ness of the lyric is to recall as well its re-utterability — the lyric is quintessentially that medium of discourse which is

---

Solomon" (ca. 63-30 B.C.E.), which R. B. Wright believes exhibits indicators of structural integrity, including an introduction and conclusion (*The Psalms of Solomon: A Critical Edition of the Greek Text* [JSOPSS; Sheffield: Sheffield Academic Press, forthcoming], p. 5).

86. Culler, *Literary Theory*, p. 71.

87. R. Pinsky, *The Sounds of Poetry: A Brief Guide* (New York: Farrar, Straus and Giroux, 1998), p. 8.

88. Pinsky, *Sounds of Poetry*, p. 8.

89. Culler, *Literary Theory*, p. 75. Similarly, Frye notes that what is distinctively "lyrical" is the "union of sound and sense" (*Anatomy of Criticism*, p. 272; Frye's additional notion of poetic creation as specifically "oracular," though but one way of conceptualizing the creative process, does flesh out quite vividly the lyrical fusion of "sound and sense": "an associative rhetorical process, most of it below the threshold of consciousness, a chaos of paronomasia, sound-links, ambiguous sense-links, and memory-links very like that of a dream," pp. 271-272; cf. Levertov, *Light Up the Cave*, pp. 29-45). Levertov also stresses the importance of sound to the lyric poet: "All words are to some extent onomatopoeic" (*Light Up the Cave*, p. 60), and also: "The primary impulse for me was always to make a structure out of words, words that *sounded* right. And I think that's a rather basic foundation of a poet's word" (p. 78).

intended to be re-uttered.[90] Again to quote Pinsky: "when I say myself a poem . . . the artist's medium is my breath. The reader's breath and hearing embody the poet's words. This makes the art physical, intimate, vocal, and individual."[91] And it is through its capacity to be re-uttered that lyric verse effects the superposition of "the subjectivity of the scripted speaker on the reader."[92] Or as R. Greene writes, the hearer or reader of the lyric "might be said to shed his or her all-too-specific person, and to take on the speaking self of the poem."[93] In other words, he or she entertains the statements made by the poem's speaker, tries them on, and reexperiences them from the inside, as it were.[94] It is such re-utterability that accounts for the openness of psalmic discourse and that allows for its easy appropriation. P. D. Miller, for one, captures well this aspect of psalmic verse in his comments on the identity of the enemies in the laments: "the enemies are in fact whoever the enemies are for the singers of the psalms. . . . The laments become appropriate for persons who cry out to God in all kinds of situations."[95] Such re-utterability is strikingly confirmed by the many times psalms are historicized and embedded in biblical narrative (e.g., 1 Sam. 2:1-10; Isa. 38:10-20; Jer. 11:18–12:6).

A second property of lyric vocality is its figuredness as "incantation, rather than the presentation of telling or ritual"[96] — in Culler's terms, its *seeming* to be an utterance. Here one notices most the absence of developed (fictional) characters, which more often than not appear to have mutated into disembodied or orphaned voices in the lyric (and if named are only equivocally or inferentially named).[97] Hence the well-known idea of lyric as "utterance overheard."[98] Frye provides the image of the lyric poet literally turning his or her back on the audience.[99] "It is as if each poem," writes Culler, "began with the invisible words, '[For example, I or someone could say].'"[100] Applied to the psalms: "[For example, I or someone could say]

---

90. Greene, *Post-Petrarchism*, p. 5.
91. Pinsky, *Sounds of Poetry*, p. 8.
92. Pinsky, *Sounds of Poetry*, pp. 5-6.
93. Greene, *Post-Petrarchism*, p. 6.
94. Greene, *Post-Petrarchism*, p. 9; cf. Johnson, *Idea of Lyric*, pp. 59, 74.
95. P. D. Miller, *Interpreting the Psalms* (Philadelphia: Fortress, 1986), pp. 50-51.
96. R. Pinsky, *Democracy, Culture and the Voice of Poetry* (Princeton: Princeton University Press, 2002), p. 23.
97. A. Grossman, "Summa Lyrica: A Primer in the Commonplaces in Speculative Poetics," *Western Humanities Review* 44 (1990): 7.
98. See Frye, *Anatomy of Criticism*, pp. 249-50; Culler, *Literary Theory*, p. 71.
99. Frye, *Anatomy of Criticism*, p. 271.
100. Culler, *Literary Theory*, pp. 71-72.

How good and how pleasant it is/when brothers dwell together" (Ps. 133:1), or "[For example, I or someone could say] My God, my God, why have you forsaken me?" (Ps. 22:2). And as a result of this incantatory shaping of vocality — that "it is, precisely, *invoked*"[101] — the lyric takes on what Johnson describes as its *typical*[102] pronominal form. Johnson identifies three principal patterns in which pronominal forms are deployed in lyric verse.[103] The prototypical pronominal pattern is the I-You form.[104] The speaking voice is the lyric-I who expresses feelings and ideas on all manner of things, often addressing an unidentified and frequently absent You — who in the religious lyric of the Psalms is as often as not to be identified as Yahweh.[105] What interests Johnson here is the I speaking to another, often "at a highly dramatic moment," in which the essence of the relationship, he says, reveals itself through the lyrical discourse, in the praise or blame, in the metaphors found to re-create the emotions that are thereby described.[106] The second variation is more impersonal, more meditative, as if the poet is speaking to himself or herself or to no one in particular, or even sometimes to apostrophized, inanimate objects. The last variety is more dialogic in nature. The lyric-I either recedes fully into the background, giving way to an interchange of voices, or takes part as one of the voices in a larger dialogue. That each of these kinds of discourse is prevalent in the Psalms I will simply assert, though with subjects indexed morphologically on verbs in Hebrew the presence of "literal" independent pronouns is not necessary (or so common). And perhaps as significant, in the Psalms, as elsewhere in antiquity but especially in ancient Greece, the voice heard comes in two predominant varieties: solo and choral (e.g., individual laments vs. communal laments). Both varieties, as W. R. Johnson claims, "were equally valid and equally important, each of them necessary to the total shaping of the human personality."[107]

---

101. Pinsky, *Sounds of Poetry*, p. 23.

102. Johnson himself stresses the pragmatic ("somewhat dubious even to me") nature of his categories here; they are but one grid through which to view lyric discourse and therefore should not be pressed too far or reified (*Idea of Lyric*, pp. 2-3).

103. For this assessment of the pronominal orientation of much lyric poetry, see Johnson, *Idea of Lyric*, pp. 1-23.

104. H. Vendler, *Soul Says* (Cambridge, MA: Belknap, 1995), p. 2; H. Fisch, *Poetry with a Purpose* (Bloomington: Indiana University Press, 1988), pp. 104-135.

105. Kathy Rowe of Bryn Mawr College named this for me most explicitly a number of years ago while I was working on Lamentations; cf. Fisch, *Poetry with a Purpose*, p. 108.

106. Johnson, *Idea of Lyric*, p. 3.

107. Johnson, *Idea of Lyric*, p. 177. The trick for contemporary readers is learning to appreciate the strong communal ethos that is now missing from many of our present-day Western so-

The prominence of first-person voice in Greek lyric has often been reified (especially during the Romantic period)[108] as *the* defining feature of lyric verse (see the *Oxford English Dictionary*'s definition of "lyric"). The problematic nature of such an identification is, as Lindley notes, obvious: "Though it is one of the devices that poets may employ, it is by no means self-evident that all poetry using this mode of speech is 'lyric', nor that poetry which does not should be excluded from the lyric category."[109] In fact, it is not only on conceptual grounds that such an identification fails, but on empirical grounds as well. To judge only by Johnson's own (rough) statistical sampling of the distribution of his pronominal types in various lyric poets from the Greeks forward, the lyric-I, though at times absolutely dominant (as in ancient Greece), is by no means omnipresent.[110] And in contemporary Anglo-American lyric verse it is the diversity of voice that is the norm and not a foreordained lyric-I.[111] Yet even to highlight the mode of discourse, first person or otherwise, tells us nothing in particular about the persona of that voice. Even in Greek lyric, as E. Bowie stresses, one cannot naively assume the identity of poet and the speaking I of the poem.[112] My own impression about voice in biblical poetry more generally is that it is not so overwhelmingly monopolized by first-person speech as is Greek lyric, nor perhaps as variable and multivocal as is much contemporary verse.

---

cieties but that infused ancient lyric verse without at the same time losing track of the also mostly assumed singularity of the human organism that lies behind first-person phenomena (see A. Damasio, *The Feeling of What Happens* [San Diego/New York: Harcourt, 1999], pp. 3-31, esp. 12, 19); the lyric-I in both of its ancient modalities gives compelling expression to these two lived-realities.

108. In his chapter on the Psalms ("Psalms: The Limits of Subjectivity") in *Poetry with a Purpose,* Fisch says much that is consonant with my own approach to the Psalms as lyric, including that "the one book of the Bible that . . . seems to offer itself as a model of lyrical subjectivity . . . is the book of Palms" (p. 106), though his own understanding of lyric discourse is profoundly shaped by Romantic ideology. And since the lyric subjectivity of the Psalms is not that of the Romantic poets and thinkers, he eventually prefers to characterize the Psalms as "covenantal discourse" (p. 120), which hardly clarifies the nature of psalmic discourse.

109. Lindley, *Lyric* (London/New York: Methuen, 1985), p. 3.

110. See the various rough statistics reported by Johnson himself throughout his *Idea of Lyric* (e.g., Catullus: 70 percent I-You; 14 percent meditative; 16 percent dialogic; etc.).

111. Cf. Lindley, *Lyric,* pp. 12-13.

112. Bowie, "Lyric and Elegiac Poetry," p. 99. Besides, the idea that a poet could speak through different personae was already well articulated by Plato (Lindley, *Lyric,* p. 2).

The "Rhythm of Association"

B. Herrnstein Smith identifies two principal means for generating thematic structure in poems: parataxis and sequence.[113] Of the two the latter will be well known, as sequence (of some sort) usually lies at the heart of story and plot. And while there are psalms in which the sequential order of thematic elements is generated primarily from some "extraliterary principle of succession,"[114] such as the tradition-historical rehearsal of Yahweh's "glorious deeds" in Psalm 78, more often psalm lyrics hew closer to the paratactic end of the structuring continuum. And indeed parataxis is prototypical of lyric discourse — perhaps, as Herrnstein Smith suggests, reflecting the lyric's origin in song.[115] "When repetition is the fundamental principle of thematic generation," as so often in traditional or naive song styles, "the resulting structure will tend to be paratactic"[116] and associative in nature — what Frye aptly labels "the rhythm of association."[117] In such instances, the lyric's centers of "emotionally and sensuously charged awareness," according to M. L. Rosenthal and S. M. Gall, radiate out and relate to one another associatively, through "felt relationship." The resulting play of tonal depths and shadings and shiftings is achieved through "strategic juxtaposition of separate . . . passages without a superimposed logical or fictional continuity."[118] And thus, the dislocation or omission of individual thematic units, unlike in sequentially structured discourse, will not render the whole unintelligible or make it incoherent. To the contrary, one of the hallmarks of paratactic structure is that thematic elements may be added, omitted, or exchanged quite happily. Junctures or gaps between a lyric's component elements without explicit scripting become a prominent part of the discursive fabric that is to be negotiated, and as a consequence fragmentation and disjunction — a susceptibility to disintegration[119] — become

---

113. Herrnstein Smith, *Poetic Closure*, pp. 96-150. Aristotle identified the same two organization structures in prose, which he termed *lexis eiromenē*, "strung-on or continuous" style, and *lexis katestrammenē*, "periodic or rounded" style. See R. L. Fowler, *The Nature of Early Greek Lyric: Three Preliminary Studies* (Toronto: University of Toronto Press, 1987), p. 53. Fowler helpfully goes on to make clear that parataxis need not imply a lack of logic or rationality.

114. Herrnstein Smith, *Poetic Closure*, p. 110.

115. Herrnstein Smith, *Poetic Closure*, pp. 57-59, 98-99.

116. Herrnstein Smith, *Poetic Closure*, pp. 98-99.

117. Frye, *Anatomy of Criticism*, pp. 270ff.

118. Rosenthal and Gall, "Lyric Sequence," p. 728; cf. Rosenthal and Gall, *Modern Poetic Sequence*, p. 15. Alter's discussion of "structures of intensification" in biblical poetry offers another way of articulating the generative dynamic that most distinguishes lyrical structure (*Art of Biblical Poetry*, pp. 62-84).

119. Greene, *Post-Petrarchism*, p. 18.

central to the founding fiction of the paratactically structured lyric poem. Any reading of such a lyric "must accommodate discontinuity as well as continuity, allow for the spatial dimension of lyric temporality, and offer a means of getting into and over" the junctures between elements "without brutally closing them."[120] Whatever fiction, whatever stratagem of discourse is manifested, therefore, necessarily partakes in and celebrates or otherwise gives prominence to fragmentation.

On my reading, it is the nonsequentiality of parataxis that governs the thematic structure in Psalm 114. There it is not a matter of temporal or logical sequence, but of association and juxtaposition — the events of the Red Sea calling to mind the crossing of the Jordan, nature's similar reactions to Yahweh's variously traditioned theophany attracting one another. Herrnstein Smith identifies the "list" as one of the most obvious forms manifesting paratactic structure.[121] Lists are especially prominent, for example, in Mesopotamian hymnody, but they are recognizable as well in various aspects of Israelite psalmody, such as in the typical use of the so-called "hymnic participle" or in the listing of Yahweh's various qualities.[122] But no doubt the paradigm of paratactic structure in the Psalms comes in the conventional (given) forms isolated by the form-critical study of the Psalms. Here, as H. Gunkel saw better than most, it is chiefly a matter of thematic (as opposed to strictly formal) structure that is most definitive of the various verse forms. And what is more relevant here, only rarely are these forms thematically sequenced. The psalms of lament are a case in point. These poems, communal and individual alike, have a recognizable set of family resemblances (comprised of common elements such as addresses, petitions, complaints or laments, motivational clauses, affirmations of trust). But, as is well known, "they are rarely precisely alike, though repeated formulas are not uncommon . . . ; and they may vary significantly in their length and the degree of elaboration of their component parts. Some are very succinct while others are extended in one or more of their basic elements. Some do not contain all of the elements that other [laments] do."[123] What Miller describes here is the epitome of paratactic structure!

Moreover, the play of parataxis effects a dynamic interaction among dif-

---

120. Greene, *Post-Petrarchism*, p. 20. My discussion of the fragmenting effects is dependent on Greene. His own discussion at this point has lyric sequences principally in view. But insofar as lyric sequences are essentially lyric poems writ large, his observations, as he himself would maintain, are very much applicable to the structure of individual lyric poems.

121. Herrnstein Smith, *Poetic Closure*, p. 99.

122. E.g., H. Gunkel and J. Begrich, *Introduction to the Psalms*, trans. J. D. Nogalski (Macon, GA: Mercer University Press, 1998), pp. 30-31, 34-35.

123. Miller, *They Cried to the Lord*, p. 57.

ferent (and sometimes conflicting and competing) perspectives that is not unlike the montage effect in film, which R. Alter describes in a different context.[124] Alter quotes the following description of montage offered by S. Eisenstein:

> The juxtaposition of two separate shots by splicing them together resembles not so much a simple sum of one shot plus one shot — as it does a *creation*. It resembles a creation — rather than a sum of its parts — from the circumstance that in every such juxtaposition *the result is qualitatively* distinguishable from each component element viewed separately. . . . Each particular montage piece exists no longer as something unrelated, but as a given *particular representation* of the general theme.[125]

Of course, the analogy is not exact. The seams that result from the paratactic splicing of different perspectives or images in language are much more noticeable than in photography and film, resulting in a more complex image. Not only does one have the "particular representation" created by the montage, but the component elements also signify on their own. As but one example of the montage effect of parataxis in the Psalms consider Psalm 74:12-17.[126] The passage, as J. Levenson notes, "is the *locus classicus* of the idea that the God of Israel . . . defeated the Sea and its monsters . . . and then created the familiar world." Levenson then continues:

> Surely no text would seem more imbued with [Y.] Kaufmann's "basic idea of Israelite religion," that "there is no realm above or beside YHWH to limit his absolute sovereignty." But the context of these verses [vv. 10-11, 18-20] belies the unqualified note of triumphalism in this theology. For the context of vv. 12-17 in Psalm 74 shows that the celebratory language of victory is invoked here precisely when conditions have rendered belief in God's majesty most difficult.[127]

---

124. Alter uses the analogy of film montage in his discussion of the "composite artistry" of Hebrew prose (*The Art of Biblical Narrative* [New York: Basic Books, 1981], pp. 140-141). But the analogy is equally (if not more) applicable to paratactic verse of the kind found in Lamentations.

125. Alter, *Art of Biblical Narrative*, p. 140; quoting S. Eisenstein, *The Film Scene*, ed. and trans. J. Leyda (London, 1943), p. 17; emphasis in Eisenstein's original.

126. The reading is that of J. D. Levenson, *Creation and the Persistence of Evil* (San Francisco: Harper & Row, 1988), pp. 17-20.

127. Levenson, *Creation and the Persistence of Evil*, p. 18. Levenson quotes from Y. Kaufmann, *The Religion of Israel* (New York: Schocken, 1972), p. 60.

The upshot of this (paratactic) juxtaposition, according to Levenson, is that the psalmist in Psalm 74 "acknowledges the reality of militant, triumphant, and persistent evil, but he steadfastly and resolutely refuses to accept this reality as final and absolute."[128] Such a stance is manifestly the result of the montage-like juxtaposition of two different moods, the seams of which are readily apparent; and indeed it may well be, as Levenson contends, that "the continuity between v. 11 and v. 18 strongly suggests that the hymn in vv. 12-17 has been interpolated."[129]

What is crucial to see in all of these examples is the centrality of fragmentation and discontinuity to the type of discourse enacted, and that any minimally adequate reading of them, as the quote from Greene given above makes clear, must accommodate the discontinuity that is so definitive of paratactic structure and offer ways of getting into and over the resulting gaps and junctures. Such a way of reading, of course, is in many respects the very antithesis of how we habitually read narratives.

Representative of Music

I conclude my brief inventory of lyric practices and properties by considering one of lyric's most widely acknowledged attributes, its musicality. To speak of the musical quality of lyric has often meant to foreground its manner of presentation — whether it was sung or not. This has been the predominant way in which classicists, for example, have tended to approach Greek lyric. And certainly during the effluence of Greek lyric from the seventh to the mid-fifth centuries BCE many of the solo (monody) lyrics were composed to be sung at *symposia* to the accompaniment of the *aulos* (an oboe-like wind instrument) or lyre, while choral songs were mostly performed at festivals (such as the great Panhellenic festivals) or on other special occasions. Greek lyric shares this use of music with "many other bodies of high lyric poetry" (e.g., Chinese, Provençal), among which W. R. Johnson counts Hebrew.[130] That many of the Psalms were, in fact, a specifically "sung" kind of word can be inferred (but *only* inferred) from a variety of considerations. First, although there is no extant body of criticism from ancient Israel and Judah commenting on the musicality of psalmic verse, there are nonetheless aspects of the texts themselves indicative of the presence of music. Several stand out. To begin with,

---

128. Levenson, *Creation and the Persistence of Evil*, p. 19.
129. Levenson, *Creation and the Persistence of Evil*, p. 18.
130. Johnson, *Idea of Lyric*, p. 28.

there is the terminology used for this kind of verse, which in several instances refers explicitly to "song" and "singing." The most generic term is *šîr* "song" (*šîrâ* only in Ps. 18:1).[131] As Lowth writes: "These compositions which were intended for music, whether vocal alone, or accompanied with instruments, obtained among the Hebrews the appellation of *Shir*."[132] The noun occurs approximately forty-three times in the Psalms (e.g., *ûmiššîrî 'ăhôdennû* "and I will thank him from[133] my song," Ps. 28:7), and very frequently in psalm titles (e.g., Pss. 45:1; 67:1; 68:1; 76:1; 88:1; 96:1; 98:1; 108:1; 123:1; 149:1). The verb is used another twenty-seven times (e.g., *'āšîrâ layhwh* "I will sing to Yahweh," Ps. 13:6). The other common designation for psalms, *mizmôr*, appears fifty-seven times, all in psalm titles (e.g., Pss. 13:1; 19:1; 23:1; 29:1; 48:1; 88:1; 98:1). The verb *zmr* "to sing" occurs an additional forty-one times (e.g., *zammĕrû layhwh bĕkinnôr* "sing to Yahweh with [i.e., accompanied by] the lyre," Ps. 98:5). Both designations by their semantics alone imply at least an originary concern for music for the compositions so named. Moreover, references to musical instruments are common in the Psalms (e.g., Pss. 33:1-3; 47:6; 49:1-5; 81:3, 4; 92:4; 98:6; 144:9; 147:7; 150:3-5),[134] and most scholars assume that some of the obscure technical terms in the superscriptions to individual psalms (e.g., *'al haššĕmînît*, Ps. 6:1; 12:1; cf. 1 Chron. 15:21) likely refer to instruments or to melodic or rhythmic patterns and tones.[135] Also there are textual indications of the existence of a professional group of singers and musicians (e.g., Gen. 4:21; Ps. 68:26; 1 Chron. 15:16-24; 16:4-6); "male and female musicians" are listed among the tribute sent by Hezekiah to Sennacherib in 701 BCE (according to the latter's annals), and among those deported to Babylon by Nebuchadrezzar and receiving oil rations was the "director of singers from Ashkelon."[136]

A second consideration consistent with the sung quality of Hebrew lyrics is the plethora of material remains from the Levant and surrounding areas attesting to the cultivation of music. Remains of musical instruments have been

---

131. A. Cooper, "Biblical Poetics: A Linguistic Approach" (unpublished dissertation, Yale University, 1976), p. 3.

132. Lowth, *Lectures*, p. 278.

133. The preposition *min* here is sometimes questioned (cf. Syr, Symm, Jerome), but is perhaps intelligible if a more material understanding of "song" is assumed (cf. Gen. 2:19 and comment in WOC 11.2.11d).

134. Cf. P. King and L. Stager, *Life in Biblical Israel* (Louisville: Westminster John Knox, 2001), pp. 290-298; J. Braun, *Music in Ancient Israel/Palestine*, trans. D. W. Stott (Grand Rapids: Eerdmans, 2002), pp. 8-32.

135. Cooper, "Biblical Poetics," pp. 3-4; Braun, *Music in Ancient Israel/Palestine*, pp. 37-42.

136. J. B. Pritchard, ed., *Ancient Near Eastern Texts Relating to the Old Testament*, 2nd ed. (Princeton: Princeton University Press, 1955), p. 288. See also King and Stager, *Life in Biblical Israel*, p. 286.

recovered, as well as numerous iconographic representations of instruments and musicians and singers (playing and singing), and even a complete hymn (in Hurrian) with instructions for performance.[137] Finally, from an ethnomusicological perspective, "in the earliest cultures words and music are closely associated," while solo instrumental music is clearly a secondary development.[138] That is, most "primitive" music is vocal (or partly vocal) — "music produced by the human voice."[139] In other words, where we have cultivation of music in antiquity (as we surely do in ancient Israel and Judah and the Near East more generally) we can expect most of that activity to be concerned with voice, and therefore — though we mostly lack indications of melody, tune, and the like from antiquity — the words that are preserved are in fact a most decisive indicator of ancient song; the nonnarrative poems themselves attest to the reality of ancient music and song.[140]

In sum, then, we may conclude that, as in ancient Greece,[141] many of the

---

137. See A. D. Kilmer, "Music and Dance in Ancient Western Asia," in *Civilizations of the Ancient Near East*, ed. J. Sasson, 4 vols. (New York: Scribner, 1995), vol. 4, pp. 2601-2613; King and Stager, *Life in Biblical Israel*, pp. 285-300; Braun, *Music in Ancient Israel/Palestine*, pp. 47-320. On the hymn recovered from ancient Ugarit, see A. D. Kilmer, R. L. Crocker, and R. R. Brown, *Sounds from Silence: Recent Discoveries in Ancient Near Eastern Music* (Berkeley: Bot Enki Publications, 1976). Of course, lyric forms (e.g., the hymn) commonly embed references to singing ("Sing of the goddess," *Revue d'Assyriologie et d'archéologie orientale* 22 170: I; "Let me sing of Nikkal-Ib," *The Cuneiform Alphabetic Texts from Ugarit, Ras Ibn Hani, and Other Places*, ed. M. Dietrich, O. Loretz, and J. Sanmartín [Münster, 1995], 1.24.1), and sometimes more explicit information about performance is provided as well, as in *Revue d'Assyriologie et d'archéologie orientale* 35 3 iii 14: "one of the *kalû*-singers stands up . . . and sings an e r s e m m a–song to Enlil to the accompaniment of the *ḫalḫallatu*-drum" (*The Assyrian Dictionary of the Oriental Institute of the University of Chicago* [Chicago: University of Chicago Press, 1956-], Z, 37a). For the musicality of Sumerian verse, see P. Michalowski, "Ancient Poetics," in *Mesopotamian Poetic Language: Sumerian and Akkadian*, ed. M. Vogelzang and M. Vanstiphout (Groningen: STYX, 1996), pp. 145-146.

138. M. Schneider, "Primitive Music," in *The New Oxford History of Music I, Ancient and Oriental Music* (Oxford: Oxford University Press, 1957), p. 31; Nettl, *Music in Primitive Culture*, p. 57; G. Nagy, *Pindar's Homer: The Lyric Possession of an Epic Past* (Baltimore: Johns Hopkins University Press, 1990), esp. pp. 34-35; M. L. West, *Ancient Greek Music* (Cambridge, MA: Clarendon, 1992), p. 39. Nagy points out that accompaniment by instrumental music is another way in which song is marked (and thus distinguished) from speech (*Pindar's Homer*, pp. 33-34).

139. Nettl, *Music in Primitive Culture*, p. 57.

140. As Nettl notes (*Music in Primitive Culture*, pp. 6-7), the most important role of music in "primitive" culture is "assisting in religious rituals," which, of course, is precisely the generative context for much of the lyric verse preserved from the ancient Near East, and especially in the Psalms.

141. Johnson, *Idea of Lyric*, pp. 26-29.

Psalms (and no doubt much else from the Bible as well) evolved as song and were frequently accompanied by instrumental music.

But to limit talk of a poem's musicality to its manner of presentation (whether it was literally sung) is to leave out much verse that has traditionally been described as lyric, including much Greek lyric (e.g., elegies and iambics were evidently not necessarily sung or accompanied by music), and is to risk missing what attracts most of us to lyric poetry in the first place: its language. Bowie surmises that "doubtless" many of the Greek lyrics selected for copying and transmission "were those whose words were of greater moment than music."[142] If there is a pervasive musicality to lyric verse beyond a narrowly performative aspect, it is to be found in "those elements which it shares with the musical forms"[143] — rhythm, meter, a pervasive heightening of sonority through alliteration, assonance, and the like. And though all literature may use such musical resources, it is "the frequency and importance" of such musical practices, "rather than their exclusive use," wherein lies their lyric distinctiveness.[144] And it is this kind of musicality — the thump of rhythm and the play of sound — that we surely have in the Psalms, whether or not they were ever literally sung.[145]

Conclusion

As I noted at the outset, my chief ambitions for my comments here were to (re)introduce the notion(s) of lyric as a critical idiom, to illustrate some of its

---

142. Bowie, "Lyric and Elegiac Poetry," p. 100.

143. Johnson, "Lyric," p. 714.

144. Langer, *Feeling and Form*, p. 260; cf. Lindley, *Lyric*, p. 43; Johnson, "Lyric," pp. 714-715.

145. About rhythm Nettl writes: it "is in some ways the most basic musical principle" (*Music in Primitive Culture*, p. 62). A satisfactory account of the basic rhythm(s) of Hebrew verse is still very much a desideratum, though B. Hrushovski [Harshav] with his notion of "free rhythms" has most definitely (in my opinion) pointed us in the right direction (see "Prosody, Hebrew," in *Encyclopaedia Judaica* [New York: Macmillan, 1971-72], vol. 13, pp. 1200-1203; "On Free Rhythms in Modern Poetry," in *Style in Language*, ed. T. Sebeok [Cambridge, MA: Technology Press of Massachusetts Institute of Technology, 1960], pp. 173-190). At the core of Hrushovski's thesis is the idea that the rhythmic organization of Hebrew verse is analogous to that of free verse poetries more generally. That is, it is variable and organized by other than numerical (i.e., metrical) modes and involves any number of features (e.g., lineation, stress or accent, syntax). The resulting asymmetry is precisely the "most conspicuous characteristic" of primitive musical rhythm (Nettl, *Music in Primitive Culture*, p. 63; Bruce Zuckerman put me on to the connection between the free verse-like rhythms that typify Hebrew verse and the dominant rhythmical shape of pre-classical music).

chief practices and tendencies, both modally and more narrowly, and to probe some of the possibilities that thinking psalmic verse through the lens of lyric may open up. If I happen, also, to find attractive (if mostly on a priori grounds) the stronger thesis, namely, the notion that most of the psalms are describable in differing degrees as lyric, I realize that to make such a thesis more fully persuasive would require a great deal more thoroughgoing study than I have mounted here.

Still, even from this abbreviated discussion I think the Psalms' overriding and informing lyricism is recognizable. The cluster of features just reviewed, from the ghost of music that ever so faintly haunts this poetry to its tropological density, pervasive parataxis, typical brevity, and the like, especially in cumulation, distinguishes this verse as lyric. And what is more, these features are not simply present intermittently but are themselves central to and defining of the poetic experience achieved in the Psalms, individually and collectively.

Here I need to stress, moreover, that identifying the Psalms' basic mode of discourse as lyric and foregrounding the poems' evaluative, expressive, and even aesthetic dimensions are not in any way to diminish the seriousness and intellective rigor of this poetry. The sentimentality of some contemporary lyric verse should not mislead us into thinking that lyric poetry in general is unable to accomplish serious work.[146] It can and it does. Indeed, part of the benefit of lyric poetry lies precisely in the kind of discourse that it models and enacts and what this tells us about human understanding and reflection. As S. Heaney writes, "it is obvious that poetry's answer to the world is not given only in terms of the content of its statement. It is given perhaps even more emphatically in terms of metre and syntax, of tone and musical trueness; and it is given also by its need to go emotionally and artistically 'above the brim', beyond the established norm."[147] Therefore, to (re)appreciate the Psalms' underlying lyric medium (in its various manifestations) is to be poised to think anew how these poems themselves think, to move beyond a commentary tradition that in the main has relegated its estimation of the intellective capacities of psalms to that which can be translated into conceptual paraphrase alone, to recover those parts of psalmic thinking that thrive in ambiguity and complexity, that emerge rhythmically and through the play of syntax, that are implicit in a poem's tone and get argued through the precision of an image. And as important as what psalmic thinking has to show us and teach us is

---

146. See the critique in M. Kinzie, *The Cure of Poetry in an Age of Prose* (Chicago: University of Chicago Press, 1993), esp. pp. ix-xix, 271-290.

147. S. Heaney, *Redress of Poetry* (New York: Farrar, Straus and Giroux, 1995), p. 25.

what it may engender in us as we take up and re-utter these poems. M. C. Nussbaum's comments on Greek lyric hold true for a lyrically inspired psalmic verse as well:

> The image of learning expressed in this style, like the picture of reading required by it, stresses responsiveness and an attention to complexity; it discourages the search for the simple and, above all, for the reductive. It suggests to us that the world of practical choice, like the text, is articulated but never exhausted by reading; that reading must reflect and not obscure this fact, showing that the particular (or: the text) remains there unexhausted, the final arbiter of the correctness of our vision; that the correct choice (or: good interpretation) is, first and foremost, a matter of keenest and flexibility of perception, rather than of conformity to a set of simplifying principles.[148]

That is, psalmic poetry through its very lyricism may even inspire us to new ways of seeing and imagining, even to new ways of thinking. Human rationality, after all, as J. W. van Huyssteen, our honoree, well notes, "can never be adequately housed in one specific reasoning strategy only."[149] Lyric thinking — and by extension the kind of thinking embodied by the Psalms — is most assuredly a different kind of thinking, a thinking otherwise.

---

148. M. C. Nussbaum, *The Fragility of Goodness: Luck and Ethics in Greek Tragedy and Philosophy* (Cambridge: Cambridge University Press, 1986), p. 69.

149. J. W. van Huyssteen, *Duet or Duel? Theology and Science in a Postmodern World* (Harrisburg, PA: Trinity Press, 1998), p. xiv.

22 Types of Natural Theology

David Fergusson

Disputes about the validity of natural theology often suffer from equivocal accounts of the meaning of key terms. At the outset, it may be useful to consider some of the different functions that natural theology has performed within the theological enterprise. By setting these in historical context, we may find it easier to discern the effectiveness of the standard criticisms it faces.

The Contexts of Natural Theology

In their conjoint Glasgow Gifford Lectures, John Brooke and Geoffrey Cantor patiently showed the varying motives and settings that govern works of natural theology in the modern period. Despite the onslaught of Hume and Kant, a succession of nineteenth-century writers continued to find ways of articulating the standard design argument for God's existence. While there were significant disagreements on whether, for example, human anatomy or celestial mechanics provided the most telling evidence of an intelligent designer, there emerged a discernible literary genre employed by a wide range of writers. Through standard rhetorical devices, they sought to stimulate and persuade a public audience marked by an interest in popular science.[1] This was done largely out of the desire to combat the growing threat of skepticism, deism, and atheism. Natural theology was thus pursued as a reactive if pugnacious exercise, at least until the publication of Darwin's *Origin of Species* in 1859. Other functions of the design argument are also detectable in the social conditions that obtained at that time. Natural theology could provide sup-

---

1. John Brooke and Geoffrey Cantor, *Reconstructing Nature: The Engagement of Science and Religion* (Edinburgh: T&T Clark, 1998), pp. 176-206.

port for the advancement of science through showing how it confirmed and preserved the tenets of Christian theism. This could be done without impolitely raising the more controversial and demanding features of doctrinal theology. Furthermore, much natural theology was used to protect the political status quo against reformist and revolutionary trends. In an Easter sermon in 1848 at Westminster Abbey, Dean Buckland, taking aim at the Chartists, claimed that "equality of mind or body, or of worldly condition, is as inconsistent with the order of nature as with the moral laws of God."[2]

The Darwinian appeal to natural selection as the engine of evolutionary change seriously undermined earlier versions of the design argument. The elegant matching of species to environment could be explained by natural causes, thus blocking any immediate appeal to divine providence as an explanatory mechanism. That polar bears were peculiarly well-equipped to survive the Arctic winter was not an astonishing phenomenon that required theistic explanation. An account in terms of evolutionary adaptation over long ages could render divine action redundant as a necessary hypothesis. Earlier claims for design began to look quaint and naïve with the benefit of Darwinian hindsight.

In response to this impressive high-level scientific description, theologians reworked their natural theology. Instead of becoming extinct, the design argument itself proved capable of mutation, adaptation, and survival in a more constricted intellectual niche. Several standard moves are discernible. A world that constantly changes, evolves, and displays a significant growth in complexity of life forms may be regarded as a fitting expression of a creative purpose. Divine immanence and engagement with the world could be accommodated by this scientific account of significant change, as opposed to more static and deistic accounts of a clockwork universe. Images of waste and suffering that appeared to haunt Darwin himself could be complemented and even surpassed by the sense of a kaleidoscopic beauty displayed in the ways nature enabled the birth and long prosperity of new species. Whatever the validity of such arguments, it is clear that arguments for design became more modest in their scope and intention. Rather than putting to flight the forces of skepticism and atheism, an appeal to design was more likely to assert the compatibility of theism and Darwinism. Modern science could not coerce religious belief as much writing in the first half of the nineteenth century had appeared to suggest. Yet the consistency of scientific and theological explanation was maintained. Darwin's defeater could itself be defeated. This change of tactics employed by late Victorian apologists illustrates for us today the context-dependent setting of all natural theology. Responding to the needs of

---

2. Quoted by Brooke and Cantor, *Reconstructing Nature*, p. 157.

a faith community, it is always situated within a particular intellectual and social standing.

Over a century later, the design argument shows no sign of expiring. Further mutations are apparent both in the manner in which it reacts to modern physics and biology and also in its cultural locations. Claims for cosmic fine-tuning have been rehearsed by successive Gifford lecturers, and in turn contested by recent appeals to a multiverse. Highly specified conditions during the first milli-seconds of the universe's history after the Big Bang must obtain to generate a universe of stars, planets, and conscious life-forms billions of years later. Whether this is to be reckoned as evidence of design or fluke is debated in terms that are strangely familiar to students of Hume's *Dialogues*. Issues such as the possibility of alternative explanations, the difficulties in discerning the nature and purpose of the designer, the misery besetting so much of human existence, and the problem of excluding randomness all reemerge in debate. The different ends to which arguments for cosmic fine-tuning are used today reflect the greater pluralism of the modern audience. For some, such arguments act as an apology confirming traditional Christian tenets, yet for others such arguments betoken the manner in which modern cosmology is a more reliable source of wisdom than the provincial authorities of particular faith traditions. Hence, for some cosmologists, the austere theism that emerges from reflections on cosmic origins is largely unrelated to traditional doctrines of creation.[3]

Within the less hospitable domain of modern biology, we find ambitious attempts to rehabilitate the concept of supernatural agency. Arguments for intelligent design focus on the microbiological phenomena of organisms that function through the interlocking of different component parts, none of which could have (apparently) evolved in incremental stages. This all-or-nothing observation appears to prevent explanation in terms of a variety of constituent parts gradually evolving together until such time as the whole suddenly starts to function *de novo*. Redolent of Paley's watchmaker argument, the intelligent design thesis argues against neo-Darwinian explanation as sufficient to account for the initial appearance of irreducibly complex biological systems. Some other explanatory principles require to be invoked. Here intelligent design theory becomes more elusive. It seems that one can move in either of two different directions. One is to posit divine intervention (special creation) at some point(s) in the evolutionary process to account for

---

3. Paul Davies writes, "I belong to the group of scientists who do not subscribe to a conventional religion but nevertheless deny that the universe is a purposeless accident." *The Mind of God: The Scientific Basis for a Rational World* (New York: Touchstone, 1993), p. 16.

the initial appearance of complex life-forms. The apparent difficulty with this claim is that it leaves itself vulnerable to further scientific advances that may offer a natural explanation to fill the perceived lacuna in neo-Darwinism. An alternative move is to argue that, while neo-Darwinian forces of genetic mutation and natural selection may be insufficient, additional scientific principles will indeed provide a fuller natural explanation of the phenomena. These, however, create a broader scientific worldview that places less stress on random forces. Greater scope is here afforded for the theist to argue that such a world is more likely to be the work of an intelligent designer. On the first reading of intelligent design, we have theology and science operating at the same empirical level of investigation. On the second, we have a more familiar type of design argument postulating theology and science as complementary rather than competitive types of explanation. Given the rather obvious "God of the gaps" appeal of the first approach, the second seems to be the wiser and more plausible approach to adopt. A study of the history of the nineteenth-century design argument surely has much to teach us in this respect.

Whatever its similarities to early-nineteenth-century exercises in natural theology, ID theory fulfills a different function. Like creationism,[4] it is essentially a reaction against the perceived infidelity of neo-Darwinism. Viewing this as ideologically naturalist and therefore hostile to theism, it seeks to contest its fundamental tenets. Despite the claims of some exponents to be maintaining a purely scientific outlook, it is pretty clear that there is a significant ideological hinterland to their work. Here it is assumed that a scientific worldview that is dominated by forces of randomness and chance at the biological level is one that excludes the theistic notion of purpose. A tendency to assume that evolutionary explanation is inevitably governed by the assumptions of metaphysical naturalism is evident, though this is highly problematic.[5] This reactive function of ID theory might be described as essentially apologetic rather than foundational. Its goal is the negative, though not unimportant, one of safeguarding theism from its undermining by secular ideological forces. Most of its exponents come to theism with strongly held convictions based on Scripture, creed, and church teaching. They do not begin with ID theory as a foundation upon which people can be persuaded of the rationality of the Christian gospel. It is an

---

4. Michael Ruse has dubbed ID theory as "creationism-lite" in *The Evolution-Creation Struggle* (Cambridge, MA: Harvard University Press, 2005), p. 255.

5. For an important theological criticism of the presuppositions of ID theory see Howard J. Van Till, "The Creation: Intelligently Designed or Optimally Equipped?" *Theology Today* 55 (1998/99): 344-364. Van Till's claim is that ID theorists tend with little justification to discount the possibility that the creation may have been fully endowed by God with the natural capacities that enable the evolution of conscious life-forms.

ancillary device to combat a particular threat arising in Western scientific culture.[6]

This last point illustrates the different uses to which natural theology has been put in a range of settings. Natural theology has a socio-religious context that varies strikingly across cultures. The textbook analysis of the logical structure of the classical proofs (ontological, cosmological, and design) tends to obscure this. Brooke and Cantor demonstrate this strikingly by citing the very different example of Al-Ghazali in late-eleventh-century Baghdad.[7] His exposition of the *kalam* cosmological argument is still widely discussed and used in educational contexts. Yet for Al-Ghazali this was not an abstract piece of philosophizing or an attempt to establish a foundational claim for the divine existence. It was prompted by the threat to Islamic theology posed by Aristotelian claims for the eternity of the universe. A cosmos created and governed by the personal will of God required a beginning. Hence Al-Ghazali advanced arguments that were intended to protect some of the most cherished convictions of his religious community in the face of pagan incursions.

The Functions of Natural Theology

At least five functions of natural theology in the history of the church can be discerned in different thinkers and contexts.[8]

1. A foundational role of natural theology is one that is sometimes found in modern epistemological projects. In a famous essay, Nicholas Wolterstorff detects this in Locke's arguments for the reliability of Scripture.[9] These are based upon the manner in which belief claims generally must be justified. Hence a commitment to the truths contained in Scripture must be grounded upon the justification of the credibility of the biblical writers. This is achieved, it seems, by reference to considerations about the veracity of testimony. Only as the witness of Scripture can be judged reasonable are we entitled to adhere to the distinctive truth claims of revealed theology. So the particular and essential commitments of Christian faith are grounded upon more general arguments for the

---

6. This of course does not exclude the possibility of ID theory being embraced by Muslim scholars equally, if not more, skeptical of Darwinism than their Christian counterparts.

7. Brooke and Cantor, *Reconstructing Nature*, pp. 143ff.

8. In principle, it would be possible to transpose these functions in Jewish and Islamic theology.

9. Nicholas Wolterstorff, "The Migration of the Theistic Arguments: From Natural Theology to Evidentialist Apologetics," in *Rationality, Religious Belief and Moral Commitment*, ed. Robert Audi and William J. Wainwright (Ithaca: Cornell University Press, 1986), pp. 38-81.

divine existence and the reliability of Scriptural testimony confirmed by signs and wonders.[10] Revelation can be believed as the source of knowledge not otherwise accessible, but only at the bar of natural reason. For Locke, this excluded the deplorable fanaticism and dangerous certitude of splinter groups.

2. Closely related in historical sequence, though different from Locke, is the deist commitment that perceives natural theology to be a stronger and less provincial guide to religious truth than claims based upon Scripture. This too has its distinctive historical context. At the root of much early modern conflict, claims based upon special revelation were perceived to be partial and divisive. Their epistemological status is less persuasive to an age increasingly impressed by the accessibility and universality of scientific claims. So we find a commitment to the priority of natural theology over revealed theology in writers such as Matthew Tindal. Extending Locke's reasoning, he argues for the priority and superiority of natural theology. Scripture is to be assessed for its capacity to teach and conform to what we know on independent grounds. At best, it contains a republication of the truths known to reason.[11]

3. A third type can be discerned in the work of Thomas Aquinas. Here there are some truths about God which, although presented and known through Scripture, it seems can also be attained by the use of human reason. Aspiring to such truth, the mind can comprehend in relative detachment from Scripture a knowledge of the existence and unity of God. This is a divinely ordained goal of the human intellect, even if not all human beings have the inclination, opportunity, and capacity to attain it. For Aquinas, such knowledge does not precede Scripture in any kind of epistemological priority, nor does it make Scripture redundant. In this respect, it performs a different function from the previous two types. Yet it appears to be a capacity of the human mind to reason from the world to God, at least in some rather limited ways. This function of natural theology can be found in the *Summa contra gentiles* alongside the apologetic task which is the next type:

10. The appeal to the miraculous events accompanying the writing of Scripture was long used as a supplementary mark of its divine authority. But for Locke it provides the rational warrant for believing Scripture to contain divine revelation. In this respect, revelation is epistemologically dependent upon the correct exercise of our natural reason. Cf. *An Essay Concerning Human Understanding*, Book IV, Chapter 19.

11. "I desire no more than to be allow'd, that there's a Religion of Nature & Reason written in the heart of every one of us from the first Creation, by which all Mankind must judge of the truth of any instituted Religion whatever: and if it varies from the Religion of Nature and Reason in any one particular, nay, in the minutest circumstance, that alone is an argument which makes all things else that can be said for its support totally ineffectual." Matthew Tindal, *Christianity as Old as the Creation or the Gospel a Republication of the Religion of Nature* (London, 1731), p. 52.

> Now, the human reason is related to the knowledge of the truth of faith (a truth which can be most evident only to those who see the divine substance) in such a way that it can gather certain likenesses of it, which are yet not sufficient so that the truth of faith may be comprehended as being understood demonstratively or through itself. Yet it is useful for the human reason to exercise itself in such arguments, however weak they may be, provided only that there be present no presumption to comprehend or demonstrate. For to be able to see something of the loftiest realities, however thin and weak the sight may be, is . . . a cause of the greatest joy.[12]

Nevertheless, much recent interpretation of Aquinas understands the role of philosophical reason here as neither preparatory nor semi-independent, but as set firmly within the context of faith. The limits of reason are constantly stressed by Aquinas, while even the much-discussed Five Ways may be regarded as deflationary arguments to curb human pretension or idolatry. God's existence is not self-evident, and even the hard-earned conclusions of rational argument do not take us very far. In thus accentuating the transcendence of God, the arguments caution against any hubris in the doctrine of God.[13] In this setting, natural theology has a legitimate, but clearly subordinate and circumscribed role. It is not an independent, autonomous source and norm for the knowledge of God.

For Islamic theology, this intellectual activity may itself be an obligation of faith enjoined by the Qur'an. The study of the regularity of the seasons, the motions of the planet, and the order of the universe is demanded in obedience to God. Here, according to the "sign" verses, natural theology is not merely an ancillary theological function but is itself integrated into the religious life. For Islam, there is traditionally no sharp distinction between the provinces of science and faith.[14]

---

12. Aquinas, *Summa contra gentiles*, Book One, 8.1.

13. "The point of insisting that arguments for God's existence [are] required is, then, not to convince hypothetical open-minded atheists, or even to persuade 'fools', so much as to deepen and enhance the mystery of the hidden God. From the start, the 'theistic proofs' are the first lesson in Thomas's negative theology. Far from being an exercise in rationalistic apologetics, the purpose of arguing for God's existence is to protect God's transcendence." Fergus Kerr, *After Aquinas: Versions of Thomism* (Oxford: Blackwell, 2002), p. 58.

14. "Verily in the creation of the heavens and the earth; in the alternation of night and day; in the ships that sail in the oceans, in the water that God sends down from the skies, giving life therewith to the earth after it had been lifeless; and in the beasts of all kind that he disperses on earth; and in the change of the winds and the clouds which are driven between heaven and earth — surely in these are signs for people who understand." Qur'an 2:164. I owe this reference and the above remarks to an unpublished paper by Mona Siddiqui on natural theology and Islam.

A variant of this type, which we might call 3b, claims that the natural capacity of the human mind to raise theological questions can provide a *praeparatio evangelii*, a context within which the distinctive claims of the Christian faith can be presented and more easily heard. In this respect, natural theology can serve an ancillary function as providing a "point of contact" for the communication of the church's distinctive witness. In the twentieth century, Brunner's eristics and Bultmann's appropriation of Heidegger's existentialism followed this procedure. Instead of positing an independent natural theology, they placed natural theology in the service of the faith.

4. A further function of natural theology is the more apologetic task of defeating the strongest objections leveled against some or all aspects of the Christian faith. This has already been noted as an animating impulse of much natural theology during the last two centuries, but it is also present in Aquinas.[15] In this respect, natural theology might include arguments against the eternity of the world, socio-biological explanations of morality, the claim that religion is a form of false consciousness under the oppressive conditions of capitalism, and the thesis that the freedom of the will is an incoherent notion. Although one can find arguments of natural theology in the early and medieval church performing this role, such uses of natural theology become more prominent under the conditions of modernity where belief in God is no longer a given.

5. Finally, a fifth task of natural theology might be discerned in the perceived need to display the ways in which the essential claims of revelation can coexist in positive relation to the best insights available from other disciplines and fields of knowledge. Although closely related to the apologetic function, this task of natural theology has a more positive role in showing the consistency of theology with other important forms of enquiry — for example, natural science and history. It is contained in the following remarks of Edward Farley and has been historically central to the pursuit of much systematic theology:

> [S]ome Christian communities must attest to the modern world an awareness that the Christian faith does not require rendering confessions, ancient authorities, and the denominational bearers of witness into absolutes, and some Christian communities must attest to the modern world that the Christian faith can exist in positive relation with the best knowledge of the

---

15. In his *Exposition of Boethius's "On the Trinity"* q. 2. art. 3, Aquinas argues that philosophy fulfills three functions in relation to theology: to demonstrate the preambles of the faith; to make known the things of faith by means of certain similitudes; and to resist what is said against the faith either by showing it to be false or by showing that it is not necessary. Citing 2 Corinthians 10:5, he insists that the things of faith cannot be reduced to philosophy. See Thomas Aquinas, *Selected Writings*, ed. Ralph McInerny (Harmondsworth: Penguin, 1998), p. 136.

time. Is this a strategic risk? Of course, since measured by quantity and success, all faithfulness is a risk. But here we must take our stand and say, even in these hard times, we can do no other.[16]

Given these different approaches to the function of natural theology, it is hardly surprising that its content should vary considerably also. What passes for "natural theology" may include a wide range of claims, some more modest in scope than others. Foundational (type 1) and deistic (type 2) arguments will typically make strong claims about the divine existence and nature, which either precede or exercise their validity independently of Scripture, faith, and the church. A natural theology that reflects the divinely bestowed powers of reason (type 3) will tend to be determined by estimates of the strength and virtues of the human mind outside the visible church. On one recent reading of Aquinas, noted above, natural theology may actually attain relatively little in this respect. As an attempt to persuade the neutral, detached enquirer the *Summa contra gentiles* gradually breaks down, becoming instead a description of more philosophical topics from the vantage point of faith.[17] Similarly, while Calvin attached some significance to the *sensus divinitatis* and classical arguments for God's existence, these were of minor significance compared to the theological tasks with which he was confronted. Clouded by the insidious effects of sin, our reason and judgment are unreliable without the guidance of Scripture and mother church. The apologetic agenda of theology (type 4) is largely set by secular forces and combated by negative arguments to defeat the defeaters. Hume, Darwin, Marx, and Freud presented challenges to theology that have been met in different ways but all of which were largely reactive. Similarly, the vocation of attesting that Christian faith can coexist with the best insights from other fields of knowledge (type 5) may largely be an "ad hoc" task, driven by the social and institutional context of the theologian.[18] At this point, it will

---

16. Edward W. Farley, "The Presbyterian Heritage as Modernism: Reaffirming a Forgotten Past in Hard Times," *The Presbyterian Predicament*, ed. M. J. Coalter, J. M. Mulder, and L. B. Weeks (Louisville: Westminster/John Knox, 1990), p. 66.

17. This is argued by Eugene F. Rogers, *Thomas Aquinas and Karl Barth: Sacred Doctrine and the Natural Knowledge of God* (Notre Dame: University of Notre Dame Press, 1995): "Thomas begins in the *Summa contra gentiles* with a strategic and temporary, self-consuming division of the truth into two modes. When he moves them toward coherence, however, he moves the use of the natural cognition of God away from neutrality toward the use that obtains under the conditions of faith. In so doing he mimics in the academic presentation of theology what happens in the life of a convert" (p. 158).

18. The term is borrowed of course from Hans Frei's justification of "ad hoc" apologetics and correlationism. Cf. *Types of Modern Theology* (New Haven: Yale University Press, 1992), pp. 70-91.

be apparent that the term "natural theology" has been stretched to comprehend a wide variety of theological tasks that cannot be reduced merely to a reformulation of the traditional philosophical arguments for God's existence. Yet this is what one finds in the history of the subject.[19]

The Criticism of Natural Theology

Having presented this rough typology of natural theologies, we can better assess the validity of the standard criticisms. The most sustained attack on the enterprise of natural theology is found in the work of Karl Barth, who perceived it to be antithetical to a proper expression of the Christian gospel. What distinguishes Barth's criticism is that it goes beyond any rejection of natural theology that is based on claims that it is invalid, unpersuasive, or unnecessary. Since God has chosen to reveal the divine identity in Christ, we cannot and should not look elsewhere for evidence of God's existence. As the Father of Jesus Christ, the revealed God is inescapably and irreducibly triune. Who God is and what God wills for creatures is disclosed only in this divine act. Without the knowledge that is freely imparted by the Holy Spirit, we cannot discern the essence and purpose of creation, history, and human existence. Our capacity to know God is neither controllable nor fixed; it depends always upon God's decision to become known. A natural theology that proceeds from a different starting point must inevitably compromise and distract in relation to the primary theological task. Even worse, it may threaten to subvert the true nature of the faith by the introduction of foreign and ethically dangerous materials. This last consideration was what moved Barth so vehemently to reject Brunner's limited, preparatory role for natural theology in the context of the German church struggle of the 1930s.[20] Natural theology is the ally of bourgeois complacence. By inferring the existence of a benevolent God from some aspect of the world or human nature, it is internally inclined to acquiesce in the ways things already are. The inherently redemptive character of the knowledge of God is thus threatened.

---

19. A brief survey of the history of the Gifford Lectures quickly reveals the elasticity of the concept of natural theology. According to the terms of Lord Gifford's bequest in the late nineteenth century, the lectureship is to be dedicated to the study of natural theology. Cf. Larry Witham, *The Measure of God* (San Francisco: HarperCollins, 2005).

20. The key texts of the Barth-Brunner debate are found in *Natural Theology*, ed. John Baillie (London: Bles, 1946). For further analysis of their theological differences see John W. Hart, *Karl Barth vs. Emil Brunner: The Formation and Dissolution of a Theological Alliance, 1916-1936* (New York: Peter Lang, 2001).

Barth's most sustained treatment of natural theology is found in *Church Dogmatics* II/1, where its relation to the concept of the *analogia entis* (analogy of being) is further elucidated. The project of natural theology assumes that there is an analogical relationship between specified features of created reality and God — for example, the concepts of causality or design. On the basis of our knowledge of one of the terms of the analogical relationship, we can then infer the other. This ascent of the mind from creation to creator is judged to be at the root of all natural theology, but for Barth it undermines some central claims of the Word of God. Given through the work of God, our knowledge of God is inherently redemptive. In coming to know God, our creaturely incapacity is disclosed, including any innate or autonomous ability to attain knowledge of the divine being apart from Jesus. The only proper analogy is therefore the *analogia fidei* (analogy of faith). The knowledge of God is given by divine self-revelation through faith. In proscribing natural theology, Barth is committed to the claim that this is itself an aspect of the knowledge afforded by faith in the Word of God. So Scripture has to be cited and interpreted as the reason for the rejection of natural theology. What we are offered is not a skeptical criticism but a positive theological attack on natural theology.

Against Brunner's claim that natural theology may have a preparatory role in bringing persons to faith, Barth maintains that the knowability of God is grounded only in divine self-disclosure. Any attempt to prepare persons for faith on other grounds will confuse or lead them astray; the church's mission is not well served by such strategies. Our knowledge of God is grounded in God's own knowability realized in Christ. This is confirmed by Scripture itself, even in those passages traditionally appealed to in support of natural theology. In its appeal to the starry heavens above, Psalm 19 must be seen as a testimony of Israel's faith in Yahweh. "Its starting point is the declaration of the glory of God by the Exodus, by the election of the patriarchs, by the sending of Moses, Joshua and the Judges, by the founding and upholding of the royal house of David."[21] The claims of Romans 1, often cited by exponents of natural theology, are used by Paul only negatively to illustrate the hopelessness of the human condition outside of faith. No attempt is made here to establish a bridgehead to the positive claims of Christ.

How does Barth's criticism of natural theology fare against each of the five different types outlined above? There is little question that types 1 and 2 are immediately excluded. The distinctive claims of Christian faith neither require nor proceed from any arguments of natural theology. To seek such in-

---

21. *Church Dogmatics* II/1 (Edinburgh: T&T Clark, 1957), p. 101.

dependent support is an abdication of trust in the self-authenticating truths of divine revelation. These cannot and should not be preceded by epistemologically driven arguments for their veracity. Type 3 also appears to be debarred by much of what Barth claims. Again, the pursuit of natural theology either as an intellectual exercise or as a preparatory tool for communicating the faith is misguided. At best, it is unnecessary; at worst, it will warp the content of the church's attestation of God's Word. But what about the apologetic and "ad hoc" correlationist activities noted above? Here again, some of Barth's strictures seem to apply. Where the theologian becomes obsessed with apologetics and synthesis with other disciplines, the distinctive subject matter of theology is easily neglected. Apologetic pursuits can readily supplant dogmatics within the theological syllabus on the mistaken impression that these are somehow more relevant to preaching or mission in a secular society. This is a particular temptation within the academy where, especially during a time of church decline in western Europe, respectability is sought through a positive positioning of one's discipline alongside others. John Milbank has characterized this as the pathos of modern theology.

At the same time, there is a need to pause at just this point. If valid, the criticism of the *analogia entis* will immediately outlaw the first two types of natural theology, but something of the remaining types may persist. In themselves, these need not claim an independent knowledge of God through rational procedures. The last two types can be understood as an *a posteriori* exercise proceeding from within the convictions of a faith community. These may be actions of the church looking outwards, seeking to defend and relate its faith to what is received and believed elsewhere. Against the charge that this is an unnecessary and even dangerous enterprise, one can make a strong case for the project as a necessary element of the church's pastoral and educational work. Members of faith communities are increasingly exercised by questions as to how their faith can positively relate to science, social concerns, and other religious traditions. Through their exposure to higher education and encounters in increasingly pluralist neighborhoods and workplaces with other currents of thoughts, religions, and worldviews, the issue of how Christian faith presents itself in relation to what is perceived elsewhere becomes a pressing task. An interest in Big Bang cosmology, evolutionary theory, and sociobiology is not only the result of native curiosity but also arises in relation to a widespread concern to learn how these might relate to the faith of the church. To ignore or denounce this challenge is hardly a responsible pastoral option. Here elements of types 3 and 3b present themselves, not so much as the pathway to faith, but as questions that will inevitably be pressed partly through sheer human curiosity and partly through the necessary conversations that must take place with those inhabiting different paradigms. To engage in these can hardly be dismissed as examples of infidelity or bourgeois complacency.[22]

One may also question whether the Bible as the Word of God altogether proscribes natural theology. Some of the Psalms and wisdom literature appeal to patterns of common experience and observation that are universal and provide a trans-cultural awareness of God. Comparative study has confirmed this. While such awareness of God's ways must be set within and defined by the distinctive faith of Israel, it is accorded a place in canonical reflection not far removed from type 3 above. James Barr has provocatively argued that if a Barthian had written Psalm 19 it would have come out altogether differently in stressing the revelational setting.[23]

Although deeply distrustful of all apologetic instincts, Barth appears to make a minor but important concession in his discussion of natural theology. In its proclamation of God's self-revelation, the Bible does not ignore the details of the cosmos as these are known from empirical observation and human experience. In their own way, they attest the divine truth. But this happens not as an independent or separate line of enquiry that can replace or discharge us from faith. Instead, we have within the Word of God an inclusion of and coordination with what is known and observed in the cosmos. "The voice of the Word of God . . . awakens an echo. Where the light of the Word of God falls, it causes — this is also to be understood first of all quite objectively — a light and a brightness."[24] This task of inclusion, however, does not lead us on a tangent or provide external confirmation of the truth claims of revealed theology. On the contrary, its function in Scripture is to incorporate within a single framework all that attaches to human existence in the cosmos. Rather than generating a semi-autonomous or auxiliary theological activity, the "echo" of the divine Word has the function of pointing us back always to the action of God in Israel and Jesus Christ. In this respect, the material in *Church Dogmatics* II/1 already anticipates the later discussion of the little lights of creation and their relationship of witness to the one great

---

22. It would be a mistake in my view to see natural theology in this mode as a route by which we are led to Christian faith. As Hans Frei claimed repeatedly, there are many different ways by which people come to faith, and we should not privilege or prioritize any particular one in our theological method. In this respect, I would argue that the motivation governing type 3b above is better transposed within type 4.

23. "No Barthian Psalmist would have written the 19th as it is: he or she would not have been content that this wider revelational context existed, the author would have insisted on making it explicit, on putting it expressly within the poem." James Barr, *Biblical Faith and Natural Theology* (Oxford: Oxford University Press, 1993), p. 89.

24. *Church Dogmatics* II/1, p. 110.

light.²⁵ This is not a natural theology according to any of the types outlined above, but it does come within hailing distance of type 5 and its strategy of coordination.²⁶ The difference for Barth is that this activity is a form of witness to the divine Word rather than an attempt to provide confirmation of it. Yet the distinction between witness and the task of confirmation may be a fuzzy one. One's witness to the Word of God may under some conditions include an attempt to show that it is capable of coexisting with other forms of knowledge, or at least that it is not defeated by counter-claims.

One can acknowledge many of Barth's strictures without abandoning the legitimate need for conversation with other disciplines or the recognition that their insights can enrich theology and the practice of the church.²⁷ The space that might here be created for pursuit of natural theology is akin to "the safe space" advocated by J. Wentzel van Huyssteen.²⁸ Practitioners of different disciplines and faiths can engage in dialogue that will often take place in unprogrammed, occasional, and *ad hoc* ways, yet without surrender of the integrity of their own disciplines.²⁹ Whether this merits the term "natural theology" is arguable, but the motives underlying types 3, 4, and 5 are valid *a fortiori* in pursuing theology within an increasingly diverse and pluralist public domain.

---

25. "In their own place and way, with the provisional, problematic and relative character commensurate with the nature of their theme, these lights speak and tell of creation, and laud and praise it as the work of God. . . . And as the being and existence of creation itself are glorified rather than destroyed by the events of which it is ordained to be the theatre, so its words and truths, far from being contradicted or given the lie, acquire in this context and in harmony with God's definitive Word a similar final force and value and significance." *Church Dogmatics* IV/3 (Edinburgh: T&T Clark, 1961), pp. 163-164.

26. This may in part explain why the later Barth was less troubled by the specter of the *analogia entis* and could speak of reintroducing natural theology by a christological route. Cf. Joseph Mangina, *Karl Barth: Theologian of Christian Witness* (Aldershot: Ashgate, 2004), pp. 180-181; Hart, *Karl Barth vs. Emil Brunner*, pp. 203ff.

27. This is largely the revision of Barth proposed by T. F. Torrance. See his discussion of Barth in *The Ground and Grammar of Theology* (Belfast: Christian Journals, 1980), pp. 75-109. However, Paul Molnar shows how Torrance's work at this point is animated by concerns quite different from those of Barth. See "Natural Theology Revisited: A Comparison of T. F. Torrance and Karl Barth," *Zeitschrift für Dialektische Theologie* 20 (2005): 53-83.

28. J. Wentzel van Huyssteen, *Duet or Duel? Theology and Science in a Postmodern World* (London: SCM, 1998), pp. 1-39.

29. In this respect, as van Huyssteen has consistently argued, the traditional typology of possible relations between science and theology (conflict, independence, and complementarity) needs to be deconstructed. Different approaches may be required relative to the issue in view.

23 Public Theology in Postfoundational Tradition

George Newlands

This essay explores the relevance of J. Wentzel van Huyssteen's work for public theology. It identifies three basic strands of a postfoundational public theology:

- a reasoned approach to open and engaged dialogue;
- a fresh hermeneutical retrieval of the classical Christian tradition;
- commitment to the expression of Christian commitment in rational engagement with major issues in social ethics.

Consideration of transformative engagement leads to a reconstrual of Christology as postfoundational Christology. Relating Christology to reconciliation I reflect on aspects of postfoundational Christian engagement in South Africa, where a deeply unpromising situation has been transformed into an example of engagement through justice, mutuality, and reciprocity that is the envy of many other parts of the world.

I then explore the turn towards science, which has characterized much of van Huyssteen's work, and indicate how this may be of value for the future of public theology, with special reference to the role of Christian theology in contributing to the effective enforcement of human rights.

The Postfoundational Turn

In his seminal study, *The Shaping of Rationality*, van Huyssteen asks "whether any form of interdisciplinary rationality can be credibly achieved — an interdisciplinary rationality that might finally support the claims by at least some in the theological epistemic community for a public voice in our complex, contemporary culture" (1999:3). He seeks to develop *a postfoundational notion of rationality* which will "first, fully acknowledge contextuality and the embeddedness of both theology and the sciences in the different domains of human culture; second, affirm the epistemically crucial role of interpreted experience and the way that tradition shapes the epistemic and non-epistemic values that inform our reflection about both God and our world; third, at the same time creatively point beyond the confines of the local community, group, or culture, toward plausible forms of transcommunal and interdisciplinary conversation" (1999:8).

Accepting the demise of foundationalism in explicit or implicit form — the demise of the idea that there can be one overarching theory and structure of knowledge — and the advent of nonfoundationalism, van Huyssteen wants to avoid relativism, "where incommensurability may finally stifle all meaningful cross-disciplinary dialogue" (1999:11). Knowing has experiential and hermeneutical dimensions, leading to a postfoundationalist fusion of hermeneutics and epistemology. Rationality balances "the way our beliefs are anchored in interpreted experience and the broader networks of belief in which our rationally compelling experiences are already embedded" (1999:14). These networks include the *research traditions* in which communities are embedded. These ideas are then developed systematically in dialogue with other writers in the field, notably with Calvin Schrag's notion of *transversal rationality* and Susan Haack's concept of *foundherentism.*

I have tried to re-imagine the movement beyond foundationalism and nonfoundationalism in terms of the metamodern. The metaphor of the metamodern, as I would want to use it, signals postmodernity in an *inclusive* and transformative sense, rather than as a limiting and prescriptive mode. It underlines that the postmodern is in many respects very much part of the modern, and unthinkable without the modern, not only as its origin but also as a continuing force. The metamodern acknowledges both the advantages and the disadvantages of the traditional ontological categories of the European tradition. The metamodern underlines all that Bernstein and Berlin have had to say about engaged fallibilistic pluralism and agonistic liberalism. It is then not so much a category as a *signal,* indicating inclusivity and flexibility.[1]

---

1. A valuable distinction is made by Cobb and Griffin between a postmodernism of construction, which seeks to relate the physical world to notions of Christian transformation, and a postmodernism of deconstruction, which tends to concentrate on individual self-understanding. Cf. too the excellent survey by D. P. Veldman, "Revisiting the implications of contemporary epistemological models for the understanding of religious experience," *Religion and Theology* 11/3-4:288ff.

Fundamentalism — Primary and Secondary

Van Huyssteen's recent acclaimed Edinburgh Gifford Lectures reflected on the significance of paleoanthropology for religion and for Christian theology. He unfolded the complexity of cave painting as a window into transcendence, showing how a surge in the development of cognition in *Homo sapiens* led to an appreciation of divine mystery. He did not dwell on one of the other probably significant events of the period, the genocide performed upon the Neanderthals and other humanoid species by our illustrious ancestors. Perception of difference often appears to provoke in us feelings of unease, fear, panic, and just occasionally homicidal rage — quite possibly for the very good reason it provokes very similar feelings in the other, inviting the preemptive strike and, if we are unlucky, mutually assured destruction.

Not unreasonably, we who live in the twenty-first century still feel most at home with the people of our tribe, our country, our city, people with our accents and cultural habits. We feel safe when security is in the hands of those we know, at every level. Rule Britannia. Don't mess with Texas. We are all in so many ways, even when we have not yet committed Appleby and Marty to heart, happy fundamentalists. We may be recreational fundamentalists; conceptual or cultural fundamentalists; political, religious, or even economic fundamentalists. After all, there is no good reason why the likeminded should not congregate at the same country club, the same soccer game, and worship the same basketball or other god.

Unless. Unless our light-hearted tribal rituals lead to the serious devaluing of other people, their lifestyles, their traditions, their economic welfare, the values others cherish. Exclusion rather than embrace is the *proton pseudos*. Of course we are entirely justified in seeking grounds for believing that our beliefs and practices may be better for most human beings than others. We may be justified in preventing some people from enjoying their human rights — should a mad prime minister be discouraged from exercising the right to bear arms? But on the whole many of us at least have come to think that tolerance and mutual respect, conversation and engagement, are preferable to coercion and control.

What, then, is the problem with fundamentalism, religious or secular? If it is true that absolute power (or powerlessness) tends to corrupt absolutely, then it seems to be the case that often (though not always) fundamentalism tends to slide into discrimination. Religious fundamentalism tends to promote absolute discrimination. Faith turns into fanaticism. Robustly orthodox (not to say neo- or radical orthodox) theology may slide into a gentlemanly but still deeply exclusivist fundamentalism. Liberal theology may become reductionist fundamentalism, quietly discounting God in the cultural stock market. Biblical theology (or theology based on other sacred texts) may chain the inhabitants of the present in the shackles of cultures long since past their sell-by dates.

> The danger of fundamentalism is not only that it would make the Bible's authority dependent on an extrabiblical notion of general perfection or infallibility; but also, and far worse, that the belief in the authority of the Bible is (through one absolutized scriptural conception) made into an immunization technique to ensure that the Bible will henceforth speak only in terms of that conception or model. What is speaking is no longer the Bible but merely those abusing their conception of scripture to make the Bible speak for them and their standpoint. The very soul of the Reformational heritage has rejected this from the outset. (Van Huyssteen 1989:180)

The same provisionality applies to all church confessions. Van Huyssteen's comment in *Theology and the Justification of Faith* is even more relevant in the present exponential growth of fundamentalisms.

Some religious fundamentalism is as harmless as other passions — for fast cars, tennis, or opera. Other varieties are deeply hostile to human rights and destructive of civilized community. The damage caused by extremist views is well known and well documented. Sadly, for every published study of strong fundamentalism, ten thousand new fundamentalists, usually Christian or Islamic, appear to spring up daily. What I am particularly concerned with here is the phenomenon of a kind of secondary fundamentalism, which recognizes a *particula veri* in fundamentalist positions, and lends it a measure of academic and cultural respectability. In this genre liberalism remains an essentially negative word, the extreme nature of fundamentalist claims is softened, and a strongly right-wing ideology profits from tacit acquiescence. I want to suggest that the recent sharp rise in the Christian Right in the churches and of Islamicist fundamentalism in Moslem countries should serve as a definitive wake-up call for a progressive Christian theology and spirituality. The successes as well as the failures of liberal values in church and state need to be articulated. These successes need to be built upon, not denied in self-generated embarrassment. The most likely alternative, described in graphic (perhaps slightly too graphic) terms in Philip Jenkins's *The Next Christendom* is not for many Christians a happy prospect. If it is to be avoided action needs to be taken now.

How are we to cope with this wave of secondary fundamentalism? It cannot, in my view, be dealt with by adopting a supposedly neutral stance and striking a balance beyond liberalism and fundamentalism. I do not think a post-liberal tradition will do. Sometimes a *via media* may offer a bridge for communication between different countries. But a bridge can also create one-way traffic, and can be a springboard for hegemony. It is sometimes said that liberal theology has tried to be a bridge between faith and culture, but those who have tried it have often walked across to secular culture and never returned. It may also be the case that a bridge to dialogue with fundamentalism can sometimes act as a springboard for acculturation in another direction, in this case the strengthening of fundamentalist religion.

Is there, then, no way of facilitating constructive solutions to these dilemmas? It seems to me that a postfoundational theology may well have the resources to articulate a vision of faith which is both classically Christian and authentically progressive. This will not, however, be an easy task. It may be necessary to explore further the theoretical parameters of postfoundational thought, of foundherentism and kindred concepts. Beyond this a postfoundational theology solid enough to capture the imagination of contemporary Christians and to commend itself as a support of living faith will need a grounding in spirituality, in social action, in ecclesiology, a dynamic interaction of both the mystical and the prophetic. This essay certainly falls short of any such specification. But even the theoretical equivalent of a call for papers may be worth uttering, if my reflections on the current dire state of affairs is in any way persuasive.

Do we need to be fundamentalists, or in some sense their fellow travelers, to maintain a viable and credible Christian faith in the twenty-first century? Or to use a slightly different but similar question from van Huyssteen,

> Do we still have good reasons — and if so would they be epistemological, ethical or pragmatic — to remain convinced that the Christian message does indeed provide the most adequate interpretation and explanation of one's experience of God, of the world, and of one's self? (1993:2)

Van Huyssteen's 1993 article merits closer scrutiny. Postmodern thought, he went on to reflect, rejects dominating global narratives of legitimation, and as a result embraces pluralism and diversity. But how do we distinguish between a wise celebration of diversity and a callous indifference to the welfare of any community but our own? Van Huyssteen looks to a "fallibilist, experimental epistemology" which shows itself not in flight from modernity but in the constant interrogation of foundationalist assumptions. He engaged with Nancy Murphey's notion of the practice of communal discernment. How can we have faith without fideism? We cannot claim the authority of Bible or tradition, but we can seek to develop an adequate theory of experience, which we can share with scientific paradigms. How indeed can we justify in transcommunal explanation conceptualizing conceptual experience in theistic terms in the first place? If not, fideism looms.

If reality is mostly encountered in language, then there are at least connections between theological and non-theological language. But some linguistic communications and recommendations are judged better and worse than others. Therefore there can be transcommunal, intersubjective criteria for theological language, developed through argument. When this conversation involves people outside as well as within the faith community, then theological discourse can claim to constitute knowledge that is "on a par with the epistemic status of scientific knowledge."

Here, as I understand it, faith is again firmly grounded on the traditional trajectories of the interactions of *notitia*, *fiducia* and *assensus*, while fundamentalism, even in a weak form, is avoided.

Between the Foundationalist and the Relative

The great concern which animates much foundationalist thought is the desire to avoid relativism at all costs. This is widely reflected in the writings and speeches of Pope Benedict XVI. A postfoundational approach aims to strike an intelligent balance between an essentialism which freezes all identities in what Anthony Appiah has characterized as a Medusa stare, and a value-free perspective in which there are no viable truth conditions. This research strategy has obvious implications for tackling many of the issues which haunt contemporary American politics and especially church politics — abortion, contraception, women's rights, and gay rights. It respects the realities of biology, tradition, and culture without being confined to replication of past practice. It leaves traditions open to future development. Because a postfoundational theology has a strong eschatological drive, it cannot be content to regard the conventions of the present or the past as the definitive manifestation of the divine will.

This perspective is supported by contemporary thinking in cognate philosophical research. In his excellent *Morality and Social Criticism*, Richard Amesbury sets out from Richard Rorty's proposal to replace objectivity by solidarity. He wants to replace human rights foundationalism by a human rights culture based on sentimental education. Amesbury objects that "his anti-authoritarianism — while ostensibly liberating — ironically renders Rorty incapable of seeing how it could be possible to dissent from the vast majority of one's peers without ceasing to be rational" (2005:14). Rorty dislikes the idea of obligations. But "it is difficult to see how Rorty can hope to continue to talk of 'a human rights culture' while abandoning talk of obligations that obtain irrespective of whether or not one's peers happen to hold one accountable to them" (2005:16). People have felt obliged to rescue strangers in danger, people outside their own communities. Realism without Platonist foundationalism can be reserved as a basis for social action. Amesbury's approach fits well with stress on the postfoundational.

How is critical rationality to be articulated in relation to the central structuring elements of theology? Realism without relativism characterizes van Huyssteen's approach to the Bible in his remarkable essay, *The Realism of the Text*. He speaks of "the central metaphoric concepts of the Christian tradition." The biblical text points not only to the past but to an open future:

> The text itself, as a religious text, forms the source for a long chain of continuous metaphorical reference to God and for faith in redemption in Jesus Christ. This irreversible thrust towards the future is, again, what I in an epistemological sense have called *the realism of the text*. (1987:145)

The center of divine activity is seen to be located in redemption in Jesus Christ. Our experience of redemption balances the present, which may be emancipatory, against our obligations to faithfulness to the past. The text cannot be frozen in a fundamentalist grid. "The communication of the biblical text is not complete until it has reached its final destination: The reception of the text by the reader" (1987:152). The Bible has an authorized authority.

> If the biblical texts refer to God, and if this reference ultimately refers to what we have metaphorically come to know and accept as redemption in Christ, then Jesus Christ alone authorises the Bible. (1987:154)

Central to this metaphorology is inspiration.

> And if the Spirit is in reality the creative, life-giving presence of God, then inspiration could never be attributed only to the text as a final product. (1987:159)

Rather, the community continues to be inspired in new ways in the present through the prompting of the Spirit.

Van Huyssteen's epistemology lays stress on the openness of the text. This sense of future promise is characteristic of his approach at every level. The postfoundational points to an eschatological openness in relation to word and sacrament. It preserves space for mystery at the heart of Christian experience, whether in liturgy or in the arts, as in Auden's poems or Bernstein's *Mass*.

The spirit is the spirit of freedom. But not every Spirit is the spirit of God. In Christian faith the Spirit is always the spirit of the crucified and risen Christ, the spirit of Christlikeness. God's presence is instantiated through the double helix of incarnation and inspiration.

I want in this paper to consider the impact of postfoundational theology on Christian thinking on human rights, human rights as a contextualized instantiation of redemption. In order to do this, it will be essential to reconsider the hinge of Christian engagement, the shape of a postfoundational Christology.

Tracing the Rainbow: A Christological Trajectory

Progressive Christology, contrary to some popular belief, need be in no sense a reductionist Christology. The eschatological element makes clear that all our theories are only pointers in the direction of the mystery of the divine love. The socio-historical dimension of faith, with its uncertainties and its cultural and temporal limitations, can be honestly affirmed. We do indeed participate in the life of God, but as pilgrims on the way to a mystery, a mystery which will reveal itself in all kinds of ways in the future. Christian truth is true, but it remains a suggestion, a pointer to the Christomorphic future.

Awareness of mystery is not a reason for indecisiveness. Faith remains decisively opposed to evil in all forms, to contempt for human rights and human life. Laws need to be enforceable, if rights are to be delivered. The Christomorphic shape of faith points to a *continuing invitation* to reflect on the mystery of God and of the human future in its various cultural dimensions. But the clearing away of injustice is an integral element of the Christian vision, not least where the vision has been clouded by human rights violations in the name of religion or by abusive ideological zeal. The trace of unconditional love gives a sharp refusal to the failure to respect individuals as precious to their creator. An intercultural theology will *prioritize* the most defenseless.

It is through a conception of *divine action,* for Christian faith through a sense of the *Christomorphic shape in history,* social, political, and personal, that an intercultural theology comes to speak most readily of God. In relation to human rights, in the experience of minority and marginalized peoples, issues of transcendence arise and are pointers for faith to God. We may not extrapolate from our preferred political patterns to the nature of God, to envisage a social democratic triumvirate to all eternity. Yet a God whose nature and actions are less sensitive to the human condition than the best of human thought and action can be neither respected nor worshipped by intelligent beings. For Christian faith, the Christomorphic paradigm is the icon of God's unconditional generosity. This generosity is God's nature. It is both self-subsisting and self-relating. How this is so remains the divine mystery.

Creative transcendence points to God *from within* the mystery of suffering and reconciliation in the emancipatory quest. This does not mean that all creation necessarily points to God. Clearly not, for the theodicy problem, and especially the omnipresence of luck, good and bad, and random evil, raise a question mark against all romanticism. The Christomorphic trace enables those who recognize it to cope with the created order and see it as not totally inconsistent with the divine love. Christian discernment is that faith is sometimes effective despite the appearance of things. Most of the time we can see only fragments, sometimes hardly a trace, of a Christomorphic element in the complexities of society. It is the Christian vision which "traces the rainbow through the rain," and may provide an antidote to indifference, lethargy, and despair. This is a *trace* which from a Christian perspective we may recognize in other religions and in humanist action, where we recognize the lineaments of the signature of divine love. Such lineaments are, however, more likely to be found in concrete and coordinated instances of attention to grinding poverty than in sentimental reflection.

Christology *for* Human Rights

Christology relates to confession and context.

> In the present South African situation heresy is no longer an issue governed by a theory about the unity of Christ. The far more contextual question is the visible unity of the church, and specifically the question whether apartheid, as a political system, is essentially heretical because it discredits and negates salvation through Jesus Christ and thus directly jeopardizes the truth of Christianity. (1989:191)

I want now to examine some aspects of the relationship between Christology and human rights, bearing in mind some of van Huyssteen's methodological considerations. I do not intend to offer a Christology *of* human rights. More germane, in my view, is Christology *for* human rights. Direct, one-to-one analogies with current issues as Christological molds are always in jeopardy when they attempt to fit a given mold to a society which is always changing in many directions at once. Van Huyssteen saw the difficulty of simplistic solutions.

> Because we as Christians rightly always ask the meaning of God's word for our situation, we must be very careful to avoid a type of ethical fundamentalism, which always emerges as a form of naïve Biblicism. (1983)

More helpful, perhaps, is the recognition that the relation between Christology and human rights will always be a dialectical one, in which the spirit of God is constantly active from above and from below, and our task is to try to remain alert to its prompting.

Van Huyssteen has insisted that theology has a critical task both in relation to the central confessional affirmations of the church and the social context in which the church is placed. It has to be rooted in context.

> A relational model founded on committed reflection must always lead back to involvement in the confessional and sociocritical praxis of the church. . . . A theology that defines its contextuality inter alia also as confessional can by no means separate confessional from theoretical language, nor can it depoliticize the theological task and thereby prevent the center of the Christian confession from speaking out directly on socio-political problems in our sociocultural context. (1989:169)

Christology can never be as self-contained as we often find convenient. We are always thinking of the concrete instantiation of the love of the God who is, Christians believe, the creator and sustainer of all that is. We cannot impose a God concept on rights dialogue which is genuine dialogue, as a given foundation. But we can say that Christian communities and individuals who have worked out ways of living together on the basis of gradually agreed values have drawn strength from the faith that at the root of all existence there is a power which is entirely non-coercive, and that this power is the power of unconditional love. At least in an informal sense, Christians will say with Jean-Luc Marion that before God is being, God is love. They will regard it as significant that human beings, to date the most complex entities in the cosmos, are the field in which God has become incarnate in the shape of self-dispossessing love. It is as the shape of the mystery of ultimate reality that faith in God through Jesus Christ transforms hearts and minds and societies.

This does not mean that you have to believe in God to be able to access the Christian construal of ultimate reality as love in generous relationality.

You may come from a humanist appreciation of social and ethical values without an appeal to transcendence. That distinctively Christian tradition which is centred on the self-abandonment of God does not claim a monopoly on either visions of the common good or construals of God. You may come from another religious tradition, with its own rich resources for accessing and understanding transcendence and compassion. The Christian vision is offered as a contribution, along with other contributions, to the practical tasks of delivering human rights solutions at points of greatest urgency.

The Way, the Truth, and the Life?

In a postfoundational frame, what becomes of the traditional affirmation that God is the truth, and that Christ is the way, the truth, and the life? Christians in community believe that in God's purpose for humanity Jesus Christ plays an indispensable and decisive role. This is a pointer to mystery, a Christomorphic mystery. It seems to me that all Christians can affirm gladly and doxologically their participation in the life of the triune God in faith. The eschatological element makes clear that all our theories are only pointers in the direction of the mystery of the divine love. The socio-historical dimension of faith, with its uncertainties and its cultural and temporal limitations, creates the other side of this theory of truth. We do indeed participate in the life of God, but as pilgrims on the way to a mystery, a mystery which will reveal itself in all kinds of ways in the future. Christian truth is true, but it remains a suggestion, a pointer to the Christomorphic future.

Christological Focal Points

None of the classical Christological perspectives, from the most conservative to the most radical, is likely to be as effective in coordinating human rights action as a consensus on the basic Christian norms for human rights action will be. These norms flow from the continuing experience of the presence of Christ to Christian faith in community. The apprehension of the central structuring elements of faith is affected by local theological cultures and concepts. Individual people and communities should be free to contribute in their own ways, and no *single* approach should be understood as "the" authorized way, whether from the traditionally liberal or traditionally conservative wings of the churches. That is not an easy perspective to actualize.

Engaging in reciprocity with the human rights dialogue, we may say that there is in the understanding of Christ a considerable measure of agreement on the norms of Christology, on the central strands of what constitutes the character of the love of God through Christ, without agreement on the theory of how this can be so. At the same time a Christian belief, still unfortunately widespread, that God coerces obedience to his will in ways which violate rights, individual and social, can be seen to be contrary to the central strands of the New Testament narratives and contrary to the faithful articulation of the gospel in history.

It seems clear that some Christologies have been historically entirely inadequate to support this faithful articulation, precisely because they have obscured the thrust of the gospel toward that concern for the marginalized in society which was central to the life of Jesus. Here the liberation and emancipatory theologies have performed a crucial service, and "non-absolutist" Christologies have pointed the way to a conceptually open approach. At the same time, however, the Christian faith has classically drawn strength from an understanding of Jesus Christ as effective not only through his life but also through his death, which has been seen as making a distinctive difference to the nature of the universe as God's creation, and through his resurrection as the first transformative product of that difference. This is why faith is quintessentially a trust in God against the appearance of things, often prepared to think and act *contra mundum*. It is important to recall that many Christian actions in support of the marginalized have been sustained through a faith in the efficacy of love through self-giving on the cross and a trust based on the resurrection of Christ.

God Instantiated

We are brought back to the classic but basic connection between atonement, incarnation and inspiration. A Christology for human rights pays particular attention to the many dimensions of the continuing power of reconciliation in Christ. In the events concerning Jesus we see the instantiation of the person of God in a specific human being, identified with the loss of all human rights, without remainder. This cluster of events can be envisaged through different concepts, notably of incarnation and inspiration, each of which makes its own contribution to conceiving the mystery. It is possible to speak of a bifocal or even a varifocal Christology.

Incarnation, which itself may be conceived in different and sometimes overlapping ways, points to the reality of the involvement of God with human bodies. What happens to bodies is important to God, who has shared human embodiment in every range of experience. The consequences of incarnation include the creation of visible communities of Christian faith, who continue in communion with God through word and sacrament, response to proclamation and participation in Eucharist, in the tradition of the gospel. This tradition also embodies the ambiguities of the human, yet can still act as an outlet for the divine love. Incarnation simultaneously has a wider connotation, for it is a catalyst for the reconciliation of the whole created order. Where the church is outward facing as well as inward facing, there is a constructive relationship between incarnation and response. Where the church is purely inward facing, this relationship is diminished. Incarnation is concerned with all dimensions of human life, personal and social, and with the shape of the cosmos beyond the merely human. It is not a trump card, for it is always incarnation through humiliation.

Further dimensions of the archetypal divine instantiation are expressed by inspiration. Spirit is not in conflict with but complements embodiment. The consequences of resurrection are the presence within the created order of the spirit of the risen Christ.

Within Christian community the spirit is always related to the focal areas of word and sacrament. How these are related has been the subject of endless sacramental controversy. What matters here is the intrinsic connection, and the central importance of both.

Two thousand years of Christianity has shown that the spirit of Christlikeness is not confined to Christian community. The divine love has been experienced by Christians as active in other religions and in secular spheres, in individual lives, in social and political developments, sometimes from within the church and sometimes challenging the churches from outside.

There is then a basic bond between the humiliated and exalted Christ and attention to human rights in all its dimensions. Christology is for human rights. Christian theology will understand action for human rights not as identical with, but certainly as caught up within, the much wider and more mysterious dynamic of the cosmic presence of the divine love. Because it claims this underlying ground it benefits from immersion in an inexhaustible vision, however unpromising the current outlook in any given area may become.

Where human agency produces outcomes in love and compassion, Christians may give thanks for Christomorphic traces of divine action, the spirit of Christlikeness, in the created order. This is the salvific outcome of the dynamic sequence of the life, death, and resurrection of Jesus Christ.

Inclusive Reconciliation

We are always vulnerable to forms of triumphalism. We cannot say of ourselves that because we are trying to respond in loving action to our understanding of the divine love we are automatically agents of divine action. This way madness lies. We can say only that we are hoping, in a provisional way and to the best of our ability, to follow in the way of Christian discipleship. We have seen only too plainly the disastrous consequences of Christian self-delusion and abuse of power in the past and in the present. But we may hope also to recognize in the actions of others the manifestation of the divine love and regard this as a huge encouragement for the future of God's purpose of love, peace, and justice.

For those who do not share Christian faith, Christian theology can offer the example of the life of Jesus as a significant pointer, along with other pointers, to the way toward a community of compassion and justice in society. Here is a human being whose life may be viewed as transformed and defined by constant concern for others in a less privileged position than his, a concern which has individual but also social and political dimensions. In conversation with partners who do not share a religious perspective, Jesus the man can be seen as a humane example of self-dispossession and service. For conversation partners in other religions, Jesus may be seen as a major figure among others who opens up the nature of transcendence within a particular culture, but whose significance may be appreciated within other cultures in appropriate ways.

The history of Christian action is a history which calls for humility. How could we have got so much wrong so consistently often? Yet there are still outbursts of transparent goodness produced by the Christian gospel and shared with a wider humanity. This is what faith has understood as the fruits of the Spirit. Progress here will involve a comprehensive renunciation of traditions of cultural and religious superiority. On the one hand it is important to distinguish Christian contributions from the Western or neo-colonial packaging in which they have so often been offered. At the same time it is desirable to acknowledge honestly the predominantly Western contribution of much Christian thinking. This should not be concealed. But equally, the real value of Western Christian thinking and action to the human future need not be disparaged or underplayed. Despite its serious flaws and its only partial perspective, it is also a hugely valuable legacy to build upon.

An Enduring Vision

I have constantly stressed the need for sensitivity to alternative, perhaps non-Christian perspectives in seeking to make a Christian contribution to rights issues. There will be occasions in which it will be desirable to offer an explicitly Christian approach to justice and rights enforcement. But there will be other occasions on which the approach will be entirely implicit. This is not a matter of deviousness or hesitation. Loving action in society often takes place on an anonymous basis and is all the more effective for this anonymity. Action in the public square does not always preclude silent and unobtrusive engagement.

A Christological perspective has both positive and negative value in contributing to human rights issues. Positively, reflection upon Christ has encouraged Christians to work by themselves and with others in addressing effectively many areas of human rights — individual liberty, torture, political rights such as the right to justice, and economic rights like the right to be free from hunger. It has been largely ineffective where scriptural tradition has had a strong influence in inhibiting rights — most notably in the areas of gender and sexuality. Here perhaps we have to look elsewhere for guidance. But Christianity has shown the capacity for change and development, as, for example, in relation to such issues as slavery and race.

We should not expect that today's status quo will be repeated a hundred years from now. The Christian tradition has potential, in reflecting on the dynamic of relationality and respect for others expressed in the events concerning Jesus Christ, to have universal application even in areas where it has largely failed. By facing up critically to its failures it may have a future role in encouraging other traditions, religious and secular, to confront their weaknesses and make appropriate changes of attitude and action. It may also learn from such dialogue to widen its own base of human rights commitments in the long-term future. In the present it may be important to concentrate action within the Christian tradition on human rights issues where there is a large measure of agreement, while continuing to work on areas of disagreement. It will remain open to respond to the Christological vision by working with organizations outside church structures in areas where these are more likely to be effective. In this way human rights action may be seen as part of the consequences of the form of Christ in the world.

A Framework for Persistence

It may be that for every step toward effective human rights action there is an equal step toward violation. In this case, the solution will not be to give up, but to try harder. I suggest that a Christian contribution, specifically a contribution based on reflection upon Christ, can be continued on several different levels.

First, there is the level of relationality and solidarity, with the marginalized and the not so marginalized. Jesus the Christ is who he is and does what he does through his being as being through relationality. I begin with the not so marginalized. We have to recognize that different Christians will have different views of current flashpoints. Where there are deep differences, we have to struggle to maintain mutual respect and communication. Christians who may be deeply critical of one group of marginalized people may be hugely supportive of other groups. We cannot afford to waste resources on unnecessary quarrels. There may be reason to hope that separate support of different abused groups may lead in time to awareness of common grounds for affirmation and respect.

Second, we must privilege groups whose human rights are threatened. Christ is crucified outside the gate, outside the magic circle. Everyone feels marginalized in some ways at different times. It is both possible and necessary to make the imaginative leap into trying to look at issues from this perspective. Not all marginalization amounts to denial of human rights. But this is often the next step. It is incumbent on all Christians to do what they can to indicate solidarity. Where Jews or Arabs are persecuted, it may be important in some situations to stand in solidarity as an honorary Jew or Arab, and in other circumstances, as a clear outsider who is precisely, despite huge difference, standing in total solidarity. Whether solidarity is achieved by secret diplomacy or vocal public advocacy or a combination of both will depend on what is likely to be most effective in specific cases.

Third, there is the question of inside or outside. One of the most important needs for those who are oppressed, by torture, hunger, racism, or whatever, is to retain a sense of self-respect in the face of general vilification. Here the combined efforts of Christians both inside and outside the issue are required. Only women perhaps can fully understand the devastating effect of patriarchal attitudes in church and society over the last two thousand years, not helped by a uniformly patriarchal Christology. Yet men can take the trouble to immerse themselves in the issues and take steps to remove the barriers which they have themselves created.

It is true that human rights action is a high-risk activity. It is true that Christians have supported human rights abuses with great tenacity. There is no quick fix. But as a community response Christian action has had considerable success in mitigating the effects of slavery, racism, and many other abuses over a longer time-scale. In this way human rights action may be seen as part of the consequences of the form of Christ in the world.

Postfoundational Transformation — Reconciliation and Forgiveness

Healing wounds requires reconciliation. Few countries have shown such an amazing example of the capacity for reconciliation and forgiveness as van Huyssteen's native South Africa.

Archbishop Tutu has said this:

> I can testify that our own struggle for justice, peace and equity would have floundered badly had we not been inspired by our Christian faith and assured of the ultimate victory of goodness, compassion and truth against their ghastly counterparts. (Witte 1996:xvi)

In the political realities of the contemporary world, these strands are present in different sorts of combination. We have characterized the Christ of faith as the icon of the self-giving, outward-facing love of God. In human relationships, individual and social, this translates into a catalytic capacity for reconciliation. Reconciliation recognizes damaged relationships, which are intrinsic to human rights violations, and facilitates restoration, restitution, and forgiveness. Reconciliation cannot be imposed from above. Its shape cannot be determined by one party to a complex issue. It requires patient preparation of the ground. It also requires an acknowledgement of fault. A Christian understanding of reconciliation will not necessarily always require an overtly "Christian" outcome. It will be understood as human reconciliation, worked at through faith in Christ and reflecting the divine love.

Tutu, in *No Future without Forgiveness*, gave an excellent description of the apartheid system itself:

> The highest virtue in South Africa came to be conformity, not bucking the system. The highest value was set on unquestioning loyalty to the dictates of the Broederbond. That is perhaps why people did not ask awkward questions. (1999:222)

He went on to look at the intractable problems of Rwanda.

Those who had turned against one another in this gory fashion had often lived amicably in the same villages and spoken the same language. They had frequently intermarried and most of them had espoused the same faith — most were Christian. (1999:258).

He concluded that

> Forgiving and being reconciled are not about pretending that things are other than they are. (1999:270)

Forgiveness is not in the first instance the appropriate framework for those who have been the deniers of rights. Imagined transgressions on the part of the discriminated-against have to be recognized as arising from the pressures of the situation in which they have been placed, and a new basis of partnership created. Yet here, too, there may be a significant role for forgiveness. The struggle for rights can produce victims, often unintended, on both sides. Here is an important role for forgiveness and reconciliation, as was seen in South Africa.

In *Between Vengeance and Forgiveness*, Martha Minow offered a profound reflection on the ambiguities of forgiveness, with particular reference to South Africa.

> So this book inevitably becomes a fractured meditation on the incompleteness and inescapable inadequacy of each possible response to collective atrocities. It is also a small effort to join in the resistance to forgetting. (1998:5)

> The questions will outstrip any answers. As Ruby Plenty Chiefs once said, "Great evil has been done on earth by people who think they know all the answers." (1998:8)

The language of forgiveness and reconciliation may be manipulated. Yet an awareness of forgiveness linked to compassion is a hugely valuable Christian contribution to the complex negotiation of the fruits of human rights in society. Forgiveness has often opened up the dimension of generosity, as a catalyst to move intractable issues forward.[2] The development of critical emancipatory theology provides some resources for comparative reappraisal

---

2. Cf. too James Alison, *Faith Beyond Resentment: Fragments Catholic and Gay* (New York: Crossroad, 2001).

of the history of marginal groups, and the impact of contemporary Christologies on their lives.³ It raises in acute form the problem of undoing the past and of retrospective forgiveness and reconciliation — paradigmatically in the tragedies of anti-Semitism and the Palestinian crisis.

We have to try to see beyond the failures of the churches, past and present, to the continuing vulnerable love of God. George Ellis, another South African scholar, has written of the importance of kenotic actions in conflict situations: "They are appropriate when they have the potential to transform the nature of the situation to a higher level" (Polkinghorne 2001:122-123). They should not be able to be taken for granted by opponents, for then they could not be transformative.

In the same volume Keith Ward writes:

> Jesus' life of healing the sick, forgiving the guilt-ridden, befriending social outcasts, and undermining hypocrisy, is a very good image of the compassionate and persuasive love of God. . . . In the moment of kenosis, God relates the divine being to creatures who have a proper autonomy and otherness, which it is the divine will not to infringe. (Polkinghorne 2001:166)

There is a very definite cosmic vision implicit in a Christian view of creation as a cosmic and pleromal process.

Reconciliation is not something which occurs spontaneously in complex conflicts, it requires action at various different levels, from the general to the minutely particular. It calls for a cumulative strategy which is neither distracted by detail not marooned in romantic generality. How may we try to ensure that an effective strategy is not constantly derailed by uncertainty? We shall not do this by theology alone.

---

3. Light is shed on the complexities of forgiveness in Raymond G. Helmick and Rodney L. Petersen, eds., *Forgiveness and Reconciliation: Religion, Public Policy, and Conflict Transformation* (Philadelphia: Templeton Foundation Press, 2001). In the preface, Tutu comments that "We are made to tell the world that there are no outsiders" (p. xiii). Petersen stresses relationality: "The terms of forgiveness are meant to bring us into relation with one another, not to drive us apart through self-justification or modes of insincerity" (p. 17). Miroslav Volf seeks to preserve the link with justice: "A genuine embrace, an embrace that neither play-acts acceptance nor crushes the other, cannot take place until justice is attended to" (p. 43). He comments that "The step from the narrative of what God has done for humanity on the cross of Christ to the account of what human beings ought to do in relation to one another has often been left unmade in the history of Christianity" (p. 47). Don Shriver reminds us of our own fallibility. "*We are all vulnerable to collaboration in the doing of great evil to our neighbours:* If Christians bring any gifts to politics, this truth about us all ought to be one of them" (p. 162).

Recognizing God's Love: Christology and Human Rights in a Science-Based Environment

A Christology for human rights can be articulated in a number of ways. If it is to enrich our understanding of the goals of human rights, then it should encapsulate the nature of the Christian understanding of the love of God, as we have sought to characterize this in an earlier chapter. It should illuminate the self-giving, self-dispossessing nature of divine reality as a pattern for human relationships. The relationship of Christology to human rights can, and in principle needs to be, developed in many different fields — I want to say here something about science, which shapes so many of the conditions of possibility in our time, and to which van Huyssteen has devoted much attention.

Much traditional discussion on theology and science has concentrated on the physical cosmos — still overshadowed perhaps by debates about creationism. I am going to concentrate on the dimension of the human. Christian theology argues that the fact of God has consequences for all human life. Christian theology is centred on Jesus Christ, as decisive for the welfare of humanity at every level — in individual and in social contexts. A Christomorphic vision of science and human rights is then more or less bound to argue and affirm the values of science in many forms, science as *Geisteswissenschaft* as much as *Naturwissenschaft*.

A Christomorphic vision of human rights and science will embrace human rights and the physical sciences, human rights and economics, human rights and life sciences, human rights and law, human rights and business studies, human rights and politics, human rights and culture, human rights and literature, human rights and music, human rights and medicine. human rights and life sciences, human rights and the humanities, human rights and history, human rights and engineering (including architecture and town planning), human rights and religion. It may not be desirable to build all houses in a cruciform shape, as a sub-Barthian view of Christ and culture might suggest. But it is possible to build communities in ways which enhance or diminish the humanity, and the possibility of exercising human capacities, in ways which are consonant with or inconsistent with the promise of Jesus Christ to bring life more abundant, life which is fair and just, into the world. And if the planning is not scientifically accurate, and the houses not soundly built, then none of this can happen, and the divine purpose is hindered, simply by ignorance, neglect or greed. To fail to utilize the constructive dimension of science at every level is to neglect the fruits of creation.

If we do not have a scientific approach to the events concerning Jesus, not necessarily at the beginning but somewhere along the line, then all our speculation about the relation of indirect divine action to the motion of red-green anti-quarks will be seriously compromised. This happens even in the most exalted circles.

If we are looking for a critically rational approach to Christian faith using experience in its various dimensions as an important factor, then the tradition of experience of Jesus, in his life, death and after his death, will be scientifically unavoidable. Here we have a figure who appears, in terms of reasonable probabilities rather than established empirical data, to have been committed to proclaiming and acting out a life of unconditional love, coming from and privileging the marginalized areas of society. A perspective on science and religion which does not highlight this solidarity with the marginalized can scarcely claim to be scientific.

It may be said that this is an unscientific, romantic, holistic fallacy. You need to generate the resources in the first place in order to be able to spend millions on NMR scanners, etc., to improve the health of the poor. But unless there is some effective payback directly to the marginalized, then perhaps you can forget talk of a scientific *Christian* approach to theology and science. We can speak most tellingly of science and kenosis when there is a real outcome for those in whom involuntary kenosis is most starkly apparent.

Beyond the master paradigm of a life of unconditional love there are death and resurrection. We are not God and we cannot pretend to be God. In human terms the kenosis of kenosis tends to lead to complete powerlessness. Faith believes that God brings into being new, authentic existence out of non-being through self-dispossession.

History as part of the human sciences is also decisive for the tradition of common Christian experience. Of course all history is selective and reflects the times in which it is written. But if we do not strive for the best available historical perspectives, we necessarily delude ourselves about the nature of that common experience, in its good and in its bad expressions. This is especially relevant to Christianity and human rights. Part of the tradition of the gospel, reflecting early Christian experience, is the Bible. When we cease to reflect critically on this experience, the text becomes ossified, and we have incarnation into a text rather than a person. This experience is fallible, reflecting what God said to people in the past and what people heard God to be saying. It may be revelatory and counter-revelatory by turns. The tradition of the gospel goes beyond the interpretation of the biblical texts. It includes a history of prayer, worship, and Christian social action. It includes the sacraments of baptism and eucharist, through which faith has understood God to be inviting human beings to participate in a mysterious relationship, a generous communion of hospitality. This too is part of the tradition of experience which is part of the warrant for the construction of the critical rationality of faith.

The tradition of the gospel is not simply a tradition of relationality. It is a tradition of relationality transformed. It points to reconciliation, justice, liberation. As such it suggests a critical rationality of human rights, in which the rational is not simply the intelligible but the just and fair. To be unjust and unfair is ultimately to be unscientific, if unconditional love is the ultimate ground and goal of the way things are. All else is a distortion in the sight of God.

I return to the multifaceted dimensions of a theological perspective on the human rights implications of science.

The physical sciences. Theology suggests the use of the physical sciences for the enhancement of human society rather than its destruction — the peaceful rather than the military use of nuclear power, the use of geology and seismology to warn of coming tsunamis as well as to conduct blue skies research.

The life sciences. The production and use of drugs in ethically responsible ways rather than simply to make gigantic profits.

Economics and business studies. The deployment of the resources of global market capitalism to begin to meet the needs of the billions who are locked into poverty, with all its concomitant issues of healthcare, education, and plain starvation.

Law. The focused deployment of legal resources at every level to support justice, and to combat the denial of justice.

Politics. The study of politics as a science which enables democratic participation, which does not muddy the waters of humanitarian efforts by hijacking these for political purposes, which promotes reconciliation and conflict resolution.

Culture. A scientific approach which recognizes the need for appropriate balances in different situations between pluralism, multiculturalism, identity politics, and integration.

One common characteristic of unscientific thinking is its freezing of temporality. Historical perspectives are viewed ahistorically, provisionality is ruled out, the present status quo is absolutized. Here a research tradition of imagination may allow dialogue a wider range of participants, from the voices of past civilizations to the voices, of course still contemporary but suggestive, of science fiction. But neither past nor present nor putative future is regarded as normative. We can neither be bound by the past, nor the present, nor can we hijack the future.

What is humane? We saw that human communication only became possible through the physical development of the faces of our simian ancestors. Let me go to the other end of imagination and consider the world of space fiction:

> Even as Fassin watched, another infant was thrown from one end of the giant blades, voiced a high and anguished shriek. This latest unfortunate missed the prop guards but hit a high-tension stay cable and was almost cut in half. A Dweller in a skiff dipped back into the slipstream, to draw level with the tiny, broken body. He stripped it of its welding kit and let the body go. It disappeared into the mist, falling like a torn leaf.
> Dwellers cheerfully admitted that they didn't care for their children. They didn't care for becoming female and getting pregnant, frankly, doing this only because it was expected, drew kudos, and meant one had in one sense fulfilled a duty. The idea of having to do more, of having to look after the brats afterwards *as well* was just laughable. (Banks 2004:246)

The Christian understanding of the human is a fragile, potentially transient and clearly precious contribution. If we are to defend human rights in a swiftly changing environment we shall have to take account of theology and science, not only at the level of cosmological speculation but also at the level of human rights.

Here again is where the postfoundational emphasizes the contextual as the way into the universal, the specific point of need as the clue to reconciliation undergirded by the divine love. I close with an application of postfoundationalism in a practical theological situation, the HIV/AIDS pandemic in Africa. Here Julian Müller and a team of graduate students have used van Huyssteen's work to articulate a theology of solidarity.

> It is practical theology that is "HIV positive." In other words, it is a practical theology that is local and contextual, but in such a way that it identifies with the people in the context. It is not a system of theories, which is formulated and then imposed on a certain situation, but a story of understanding, which grows from a real situation. It is a story developing out of an interaction between researchers and a context. It is postfoundationalist theology. In other words it finds its identity in a balance and dialogue between theological tradition and the context. (Müller 2004)

What could be more fitting than the application of a highly sophisticated and deeply illuminating conceptual framework to one of the most desperate problems for human rights and human salvation in Wentzel van Huyssteen's native country?

Works Cited

Amesbury, R. 2005. *Morality and Social Criticism: The Force of Reasons in Discursive Practice.* New York: Palgrave Macmillan.

Banks, I. 2004. *The Algebraist.* London: Orbit.

Minow, M. 1998. *Between Vengeance and Forgiveness: Facing History After Genocide and Mass Violence.* Boston: Beacon.

Müller, J. 2004. "HIV/AIDS, Narrative Practical Theology, and Postfoundationalism: The Emergence of a New Story." Available online at http://www.julianmuller.co.za/emergence_story.pdf.

Polkinghorne, J., ed. 2001. *The Work of Love: Creation as Kenosis.* Grand Rapids: Eerdmans.

Shults, F. L. 1999. *The Postfoundational Task of Theology.* Grand Rapids: Eerdmans.

Tutu, D. 1999. *No Future without Forgiveness.* New York: Doubleday.

Van Huyssteen, J. W. 1987. *The Realism of the Text: A Perspective on Biblical Authority.* Pretoria: UNISA.

Van Huyssteen, J. W. 1989. *Theology and the Justification of Faith: Constructing Theories in Postfoundational Theology.* Grand Rapids: Eerdmans.

Van Huyssteen, J. W. 1993. "Is the Postmodern Always a Postfoundationalist Theology?" *Theology Today* 50.

Van Huyssteen, J. W. 1997. *Essays in Postfoundational Theology.* Grand Rapids: Eerdmans.

Van Huyssteen, J. W. 1999. *The Shaping of Rationality: Toward Interdisciplinarity in Theology and Science.* Grand Rapids: Eerdmans.

Van Huyssteen, J. W., F. Swanepoel, J. Rousseau, and B. du Toit. 1983. *The Authority of the Bible.* (Church report.)

Witte, J., and J. Van der Vyver, eds. 1996. *Religious Human Rights in Global Perspective: Religious Perspectives.* Dordrecht: M. Nijhoff.

A Complete Bibliography of Works by J. Wentzel van Huyssteen

Articles and Book Chapters

"Die Geskiedenisteologie van Wolfhart Pannenberg." ["Wolfhart Pannenberg's Theology of History."] *Nederduitse Gereformeerde Teologiese Tydskrif* 10, no. 4 (1969).

"God en Werklikheid." ["God and Reality."] *Nederduitse Gereformeerde Teologiese Tydskrif* 14 (July 1973).

"Hoe waar is ons Teologiese Uitsprake?" ["How True Are Our Theological Statements?"] *Bulletin van die S.A.V.C.W.* (August 1973).

"Wat is Bybelkunde?" ["What is Biblical Studies?"] Inaugural address at the University of Port Elizabeth, 1974.

"Gesag & Vryheid in Bybelse Perspektief." ["Authority and Freedom in Biblical Perspective."] *Roeping en Riglyne* (1974).

"Bybelkunde, Teologie en die Bybel." ["Biblical Studies, Theology and the Bible."] *Nederduitse Gereformeerde Teologiese Tydskrif* 15 (1975).

"Teologie en Metode." ["Theology and Method."] *Koers* 43, no. 4 (1978).

"Antwoord aan professor Adrio König." ["Response to Professor Andrio König."] *Koers* 43, no. 4 (1978).

"Systematic Theology and the Philosophy of Science: The Need for Methodological and Theoretical Clarity in Theology." *Journal of Theology for Southern Africa* 34 (March 1981): 3-16. [English translation of "Sistematiese Teologie en Wetenskapsteorie, Die Vraag na Metodies-Teoretiese Helderheid in die Teologie." (1981). See also *Essays in Postfoundationalist Theology (EPT)*, ch. 6.]

"Opmerkinge oor Geloof en Geloofsuitsprake." ["Comments on Faith and Statements of Faith."] *Scriptura* 3 (1981): 1-8.

"Sistematiese Teologie en Wetenskapsteorie, Die Vraag na metodies-teoretiese Helderheid in die Teologie." ["Systematic Theology and the Philosophy of Science: The Need for Methodological and Theoretical Clarity in Theology."] *Tydskrif vir Christelike Wetenskap* 17, no. 1 (1981): 64-78.

"Die Sistematiese Teoloog en persoonlike Geloofsbetrokkenheid." ["The Systematic

Theologian and Personal Faith Commitments."] *Nederduitse Gereformeerde Teologiese Tydskrif* 22, no. 4 (September 1981): 291-302.

"Thomas S. Kuhn en die Vraag na die herkoms van ons teologiese Denkmodelle." ["Thomas S. Kuhn and the Origin of Theological Thought Models."] *Nederduitse Gereformeerde Teologiese Tydskrif* 24, no. 3 (June 1983).

"Rasionaliteit en Kreatiwiteit: Ontwerp vir 'n kritiese, konstruktiewe Teologie." ["Rationality and Creativity: A Design for a Critical, Constructive Theology."] *Koers* 48, no. 3 (1983).

"Fundamentalism and the Quest for Biblical Authority." (Reviews of *The Roots of Fundamentalism*, by Ernest R. Sandeen, and *The Scope and Authority of the Bible*, by James Barr.) *Scriptura* 9 (1983): 67-70.

"Bybelkunde op Universiteit as 'n vormende Wetenskap." ["Biblical Studies as a Formative Science in the University."] *Scriptura* 13 (1984): 8-20.

"Belydenis as Denkmodel — 'n Teologie Tussen Insig en Ervaring." ["Confession as Theought Model: A Theology between Understanding and Experience."] In *Teologie-Belydenis-Politiek/Theology-Confession-Politics*, ed. D. J. Smit, 7-27. Bellville: U.W.K. Publishers, 1985.

Review of *The True Church and the Poor*, by Jon Sobrino. *Missionalia* 14, no. 2 (August 1986): 113-114.

"Rationality and Creativity: A Design for a Critical, Constructive Theology." Academic Papers Series, Institute for Christian Studies, Toronto, Canada (April 1986). [English translation of "Rasionaliteit en Kreatiwiteit: Ontwerp vir 'n kritiese, konstruktiewe Teologie" (1983).]

"Understanding Religious Texts. The Role of Models in Biblical Interpretation." *Old Testament Essays* 5 (1987): 9-23.

"Scientific Realism and Theology: A New Challenge?" *South African Journal of Philosophy* 6, no. 4 (1987): 125-132.

"Evolution, Knowledge and Christian Faith: Gerd Theissen and the Credibility of Theology." *Hervormde Teologiese Studies* 44, no. 1 (1988): 6-22. [*EPT*, ch. 10.]

"Experience and Explanation: The Justification of Cognitive Claims in Theology." *Zygon* 23, no. 3 (September 1988): 247-61. [*EPT*, ch. 8.]

Review of *Natural Science and Two Themes in Human History*, by R. Maatman, *Hervormde Teologiese Studies* 44 (November 1988): 970-71. [in Afrikaans]

"Beyond Dogmatism: Rationality in Theology and Science." *Hervormde Teologiese Studies* 44, no. 2 (November 1988): 847-863.

"Paradigms and Progress: Inference to the Best Explanation? The Shaping of Rationality in Theology." In *Paradigms and Progress in Theology*, ed. J. Mouton, A. G. van Aarde and W. S. Vorster, 81-90. Pretoria: HSRC Publishers, 1988.

"Evolution, Knowledge and Faith: Gerd Theissen and the Credibility of Theology." *Modern Theology* 5, no. 2 (January 1989): 145-159. [*EPT*, ch. 10. Repeat of an earlier article.]

"Truth and Commitment in Theology and Science: An Appraisal of Wolfhart

Pannenberg's Perspective." *Hervormde Teologiese Studies* 45, no. 1 (March 1989): 99-116. [*EPT*, ch. 3.]

"Narrative Theology: An Adequate Paradigm for Theological Reflection?" *Hervormde Teologiese Studies* 45, no. 4 (1989): 767-777. [*EPT*, ch. 9.]

"The Explanatory Role of Religious Experience and Beliefs in Theology and Science." Unpublished lecture given at the Center of Theological Inquiry, Princeton, New Jersey (December 1990).

"Van Huyssteen Response to Robbins: Does the Postfoundationalist Have to Be a Pragmatist?" *Zygon* 27, no. 4 (December 1992): 455-456.

Review of *Creation and the History of Science*, by Christopher Kaiser. *Theology Today* 49, no. 1 (April 1992): 98-100.

Review of *Theology in the Age of Scientific Reasoning*, by Nancey Murphy. *Zygon* 27, no. 2 (June 1992): 231-234.

"Theology and Science: Should the Church Really Care?" *Dialog* 32, no. 3 (Summer 1993): 198-201.

"Theology and Science: The Quest for a New Apologetics." *The Princeton Seminary Bulletin*, 14, no. 2 (1993): 113-133. [Inaugural address at Princeton Theological Seminary; *EPT*, ch. 11.]

"What Epistemic Values Should We Reclaim for Religion and Science? A Response to J. Wesley Robbins." *Zygon* 28, no. 3 (September 1993): 371-376.

"Is the Postmodernist Always a Postfoundationalist?" *Theology Today* 50, no. 3 (October 1993): 373-386. [*EPT*, ch. 4.]

"Theology and Science: The Quest for a New Apologetics." *Hervormde Teologiese Studies* 49 (September 1993): 425-444. [*EPT*, ch. 11. Repeat of an earlier article.]

"Critical Realism and God: Can There Be Faith After Foundationalism?" In *Intellektueel in Konteks: Opstelle vir Hennie Rossouw*, ed. Anton van Niekerk, Willie Esterhuyse and Johan Hattingh, 253-266. Pretoria: Raad vir Geesteswetenskaplike Navorsing, 1993. [*EPT*, ch. 2.]

"Is There Still a Realist Challenge in Postmodern Theology? On Religious Experience and Explanatory Commitments in Jerome Stone's *A Minimalist Vision of Transcendence*." *American Journal of Theology and Philosophy* 15, no. 3 (September 1994): 293-304. [*EPT*, ch. 5.]

"Is There Still a Realist Challenge in Postmodern Theology? On Religious Experience and Explanatory Commitments in Jerome Stone's *A Minimalist Vision of Transcendence*." *Hervormde Teologiese Studies* 51, no. 1 (April 1995): 1-10. [*EPT*, ch. 5. Repeat of an earlier article.]

Review of "Nonfoundationalism," by John E. Thiel. *Theology Today* 52, no. 4 (January 1996): 521-523.

"The Shaping of Rationality in Science and Religion." *Hervormde Teologiese Studies* 52, no. 1 (March 1996): 105-129. [*EPT*, ch. 12.]

"Truth and Commitment in Theology and Science: An Appraisal of Wolfhart Pannenberg's Perspective." In *Beginning with the End: God, Science and Wolfhart*

Pannenberg, ed. Carol Rausch Albright and Joel Haugen, 360-377. Chicago: Open Court, 1997. [Repeat of an earlier article. See also *EPT,* ch. 3.]

"Should We Be Trying So Hard to Be Postmodern? A Response to Drees, Haught, and Yeager." *Zygon* 32, no. 4 (December 1997): 567-584.

"Why Do We Make Those Choices? Some Reflections on Faith, Pluralism and Commitment." In *Pragmatism, Neo-Pragmatism and Religion: Conversation with Richard Rorty,* ed. Charley D. Hardwick and Donald A. Crosby, 453-467. New York: Peter Lang, 1997.

"Tradition and the Task of Theology." *Theology Today* 55, no. 2 (July 1998): 213-228.

"Evolution: The Key to Knowledge of God?" In *God for the Twenty-first Century,* ed. R. Stannard, 47-50. Philadelphia: Templeton Foundation Press, 2000.

"Postfoundationalism and Interdisciplinarity: A Response to Jerome Stone." *Zygon* 35, no. 2 (June 2000): 427-439.

"Pluralism and Interdisciplinarity: In Search of Theology's Public Voice." *American Journal of Theology and Philosophy* 22, no. 1 (January 2001): 65-87.

"From Religious Experience to Interdisciplinary Reflection: The Challenge of Empirical Theology." In *The Human Image of God,* ed. Hans-George Ziebertz, Friedrich Schweitzer, Hermann Häring and Don Browning, 103-121. Leiden: Brill, 2001.

"What Are Scientists Telling Theologians About Human Uniqueness?" *Research News and Opportunities in Science and Theology* 1, no. 7 (March 2001): 20, 26.

Review of "God After Darwin: A Theology of Evolution," by John F. Haught. *Theology Today* 58, no. 1 (April 2001): 138-139.

"Fallen Angels or Rising Beasts? Theological Perspectives on Human Uniqueness." *Theology and Science* 1, no. 2 (October 2003): 161-178.

"Evolution and Human Uniqueness: A Theological Perspective on the Emergence of Human Complexity." In *The Significance of Complexity: Approaching a Complex World Through Science, Theology and the Humanities,* ed. Kees van Kooten Niekerk and Hans Buhl, 195-215. Aldershot, England: Ashgate, 2004.

"Human Origins and Religious Awareness: In Search of Human Uniqueness." *Studia Theologica* 59, no. 2 (December 2005): 104-128.

Books

Teologie van die Rede: Die Funksie van die Rasionele in die Denke van Wolfhart Pannenberg [*Theology of Reason: The Function of Rationality in the Thought of Wolfhart Pannenberg*]. Kampen: J. H. Kok, 1970.

Geloof en Skrifgesag [*Faith and the Authority of Scripture*] (with B. J. du Toit). Pretoria: N. Kerkboekhandel, 1982.

Teologie as Kritiese Geloofsverantwoording: Teorievorming in die Sistematiese Teologie. [*Theology and the Justification of Faith: The Construction of Theories in Systematic Theology.*] Pretoria: RGN, 1986.

The Realism of the Text: A Perspective on Biblical Authority. Pretoria: UNISA, 1987. [An abbreviated version can be found in *EPT,* ch. 7.]

Theology and the Justification of Faith: The Construction of Theories in Systematic Theology. Grand Rapids: Eerdmans, 1989. [English translation of *Teologie as Kritiese Geloofsverantwoording: Teorievorming in die Sistematiese Teologie* (1986).]

Essays in Postfoundationalist Theology. Grand Rapids: Eerdmans, 1997.

Rethinking Theology and Science: Six Models for the Current Dialogue (ed. with Niels Henrik Gregersen). Grand Rapids: Eerdmans, 1998.

Duet or Duel? Theology and Science in a Postmodern World. London: SCM Press, 1998. Reprint, Harrisburg, PA: Trinity Press International, 1998. [The John Albert Hall Lectures.]

The Shaping of Rationality: Toward Interdisciplinarity in Theology and Science. Grand Rapids: Eerdmans, 1999.

Duet atau Duel? Teologi dan Sains dalam Dunia Post-Modern. Jakarta, Indonesia: PT Bpk Gunugn Mulia, 2000. [Indonesian translation of *Duet or Duel? Theology and Science in a Postmodern World* (1998).]

The Encyclopedia of Science and Religion (ed. with Niels Henrik Gregersen, Nancy R. Howell and Wesley J. Wildman). New York: Macmillan, 2003.

Alone in the World? Human Uniqueness in Science and Theology. Grand Rapids: Eerdmans, 2006. [The Gifford Lectures.]

Contributors

John Hedley Brooke
Andreas Idreos Professor of Science and Religion
Oxford University
Oxford, England

Delwin Brown
Dean Emeritus
Pacific School of Religion
Berkeley, California USA

Philip Clayton
Ingraham Professor of Theology
Claremont School of Theology
Claremont, California USA

Jean Clottes
Conservateur Général du Patrimoine (honoraire)
Foix, France

F. W. Dobbs-Allsopp
Associate Professor of Old Testament
Princeton Theological Seminary
Princeton, New Jersey USA

David Fergusson
Professor of Divinity
University of Edinburgh
Edinburgh, Scotland

CONTRIBUTORS

Niels Henrik Gregersen
Professor of Theology
Copenhagen University
Copenhagen, Denmark

David Lewis-Williams
Professor Emeritus of Cognitive Archaeology
Rock Art Research Institute
University of Witwatersrand
Johannesburg, South Africa

George Newlands
Professor of Divinity
University of Glasgow
Glasgow, Scotland

Richard Robert Osmer
Thomas W. Synnott Professor of Christian Education
Princeton Theological Seminary
Princeton, New Jersey USA

Arthur Peacocke
Former Director of the Ian Ramsey Centre
Theology Faculty, Oxford University
Oxford, England

Kenneth A. Reynhout
Ph.D. Student in Philosophy and Theology
Princeton Theological Seminary
Princeton, New Jersey USA

Holmes Rolston III
University Distinguished Professor and Professor of Philosophy
Colorado State University
Fort Collins, Colorado USA

Michael Ruse
Lucyle T. Werkmeister Professor of Philosophy
Florida State University
Tallahassee, Florida USA

Contributors

Calvin O. Schrag
The George Ade Distinguished Professor of Philosophy Emeritus
Purdue University
West Lafayette, Indiana USA

F. LeRon Shults
Professor of Systematic Theology
Institute for Theology and Philosophy, Agder University
Kristiansand, Norway

Christopher Southgate
Honorary University Fellow in Theology
University of Exeter
Exeter, England

Michael L. Spezio
Postdoctoral Scholar in Affective and Social Neuroscience
California Institute of Technology
Pasadena, California USA

Mikael Stenmark
Professor of Philosophy
Uppsala University
Uppsala, Sweden

Jerome A. Stone
Professor of Philosophy Emeritus
William Rainey Harper College
Chicago, Illinois USA

Ian Tattersall
Curator, Division of Anthropology
American Museum of Natural History
New York, New York USA

Roger Trigg
Professor of Philosophy
University of Warwick
Warwick, England

CONTRIBUTORS

Keith Ward
Regius Professor of Divinity Emeritus
Oxford University
Oxford, England

Wesley J. Wildman
Associate Professor of Theology and Ethics
Boston University
Boston, Massachusetts USA

www.ingramcontent.com/pod-product-compliance
Lightning Source LLC
Chambersburg PA
CBHW032126010526
44111CB00033B/128